the structure of
American industry

EDITED BY
WALTER ADAMS
MICHIGAN STATE UNIVERSITY

the structure of American industry
FIFTH EDITION

Macmillan Publishing Co., Inc.
NEW YORK
Collier Macmillan Publishers
LONDON

Macmillan Publishing Co., Inc.
866 Third Avenue, New York, New York 10022

Collier Macmillan Canada, Ltd.

Library of Congress Cataloging in Publication Data

Adams, Walter, (date)   ed.
  The structure of American industry.

  Includes bibliographies and index.
  1. United States—Industries—Addresses, essays,
lectures. I. Title.
HC106.A34   1977   338.6'0973   76-6941
ISBN 0–02–300790–7

Printing: 4 5 6 7 8   Year: 8 9 0 1 2 3

for
Mátyás Király

preface

One of the major transformations in political economy since the first edition of this book appeared in 1950 is the renewed recognition that power concentrations are a pivotal problem in social organization. There is an inchoate, if not systematic, awareness that the power relationships in society are a matter of profound social concern and require continuing confrontation by public policy makers.

Today, in the aftermath of Watergate and related revelations, it is no longer fashionable to dismiss the Founding Fathers as anachronistic philosophers or to ridicule Lord Acton's warnings about the consequences of concentrated power. The excesses of the imperial presidency, and the abuse of executive authority to harass and oppress individual citizens, have underscored the importance of a decentralized power structure within a framework of checks and balances. As Madison put it in *The Federalist*, No. 51, "If men were angels, no government would be necessary. If angels were to govern men, neither external nor internal controls on government would be necessary. In framing a government which is to be administered by men over men, the great difficulty lies in this: You must first enable the government to control the governed; and in the next place oblige it to control itself. A dependence on the people is, no doubt, the primary control on the government; but experience has taught mankind the necessity of auxiliary precautions. . . ." And these auxiliary precautions, said Madison, require primarily a separation of power between the different branches of government, and secondarily a dispersion of power among the citizenry. The underlying purpose, he wrote, is to prevent the rulers from oppressing the ruled, and to render it improbable, if not impracticable, for one segment of society to oppress another.

This traditional, peculiarly American distrust of concentrated power is reasserting itself today—not only with respect to political, but also economic institutions. There is a growing recognition that economic power is not merely a decorative status symbol to be passively enjoyed in the counting houses and country clubs. Economic power, we are once again learning, may be used with statesmanlike forbearance and diplomatic skill. It may be used only where circumstances absolutely demand it, or when the political climate is particularly propitious. It may be accompanied by sophisticated public relations campaigns to purify its venality or sanitize the corporate image. But the fact remains that, in the long run, the possession of great power and the exercise of such power tend to coalesce. Wherever economic power exists it will eventually be used, and for ends chosen by those who control it.

Perhaps it is fitting that in 1976, as we celebrate the bicentennial of *The Wealth of Nations*, there is a growing awareness of the social role of competitive markets. Effective competition is once again being viewed not only as an instrument for achieving "the best allocation of resources, the lowest prices, the highest quality, and the greatest material progress," but also as the central nervous mechanism of a decentralized power structure. Competition is the euphemism for an economic system in which power is scattered into many hands "so that the fortunes of the people will not be dependent on the whim or caprice, the political prejudices, the emotional stability of a few self-appointed men." Competition is a device to be used by society for social purposes. It is a blueprint for limited power operating in a comprehensive framework of checks and balances. It is a network of safeguards against the use of private power to the detriment of the public interest.

Given the current concern with the control of power in a modern industrial society, the fifth edition of this book seems felicitously timed. It offers a kaleidoscopic view of American industry—a collection of case studies illustrating different types of structural organization, different behavior patterns, and different performance records. Although each industry is, of course, an "individual," the case studies offer to the student of industrial organization a "live" laboratory for clinical examination, comparative analysis, and the evaluation of public policy alternatives. For that reason the book, I hope, constitutes a useful supplement, if not a necessary antidote, to the economist's penchant for the abstractions of theoretical model building.

East Lansing, Michigan   W. A.

contributors

Walter Adams is Distinguished University Professor, Professor of Economics, and Past President, Michigan State University, and erstwhile member of the Attorney General's National Committee to Study the Antitrust Laws.

Joel B. Dirlam is Professor of Economics, University of Rhode Island, and an economic consultant to government agencies and the private sector.

Kenneth G. Elzinga is Professor of Economics, University of Virginia, and erstwhile economic advisor to the Chief of the Antitrust Division, U.S. Department of Justice.

Manley R. Irwin is Professor of Economics, University of New Hampshire, and erstwhile chief of the AT&T Taskforce of the Federal Communications Commission.

David D. Martin is Professor of Economics, Indiana University, and erstwhile chief economist of the U.S. Senate Antitrust and Monopoly Subcommittee.

Walter S. Measday is Professor of Economics, University of Maryland, and chief economist of the U.S. Senate Antitrust and Monopoly Subcommittee.

Willard F. Mueller is William F. Vilas Research Professor of Economics, Agricultural Economics, and Law, University of Wisconsin (Madison), and erstwhile director of the Bureau of Economics, Federal Trade Commission.

Roger G. Noll is Professor of Economics, California Institute of Technology, and erstwhile Senior Fellow, Brookings Institution, and Senior Economist, Council of Economic Advisors.

Elton Rayack is Professor of Economics, University of Rhode Island.

William G. Shepherd is Professor of Economics, The University of Michigan, and erstwhile economic advisor to the Chief of the Antitrust Division, U.S. Department of Justice.

Daniel B. Suits is Professor of Economics, Michigan State University.

Lawrence J. White is Associate Professor of Economics, Graduate School of Business Administration, New York University.

contents

xi

the structure of
American industry

CHAPTER 1

agriculture

DANIEL B. SUITS

I. INTRODUCTION

As supplier of most of the food we eat and of raw materials for many industrial processes, agriculture is clearly an important sector of the economy. But the importance of the industrial performance of agriculture transcends even this. For in nations where the productivity of farmers is low, most of the working population is needed to raise food and few people are available for production of investment goods or for other activities required for economic growth. Indeed, one of the factors that correlates most closely with the per capital income of a nation is the fraction of its population engaged in farming. In the poorest nations of the world, more than half of the population lives on farms. This compares with less than 10 per cent in western Europe and less than 4 per cent in the United States.

In short, the course of economic development in general depends in a fundamental way on the performance of farmers. This performance, in turn, depends on how agriculture is organized and on the economic context, or market structure, within which it functions. In the following pages the performance of American agriculture is examined. It is appropriate to commence with a consideration of its market structure.

II. MARKET STRUCTURE AND COMPETITION

Number and Size of Farms

There are about 2,700,000 farms in the United States today. This is roughly 40 per cent of the peak number reached 50 years ago, and as the number of farms has declined, the average size has risen. Farms in the United States still

1

average fewer than 400 acres, but this average can be misleading. The truth is that modern American agriculture is characterized by large-scale operations. Although only 151,000 farms—5.5 per cent of the total—are as large as 1000 acres or more, they operate more than 40 per cent of the total farm acreage. Nearly a quarter of all wheat, for example, is grown on farms of 2000 acres or more, and the top 2.6 per cent of wheat growers raise roughly 50 per cent of our wheat.

The sizes of farms vary widely by product, but even where typical acreage is small, we find production concentrated. Nearly 65 per cent of our tomato crop is grown on farms of fewer than 500 acres, but the remaining 35 per cent is marketed by the largest 9 per cent of tomato growers. Broiler chickens are raised on still smaller farms, with 55 per cent coming from farms with fewer than 100 acres. However, more than 70 per cent of all broiler chickens are raised by the largest 2 per cent of growers.

The size of the farm also varies with production technique as this is affected by region, climate, and other factors. In the southern states of the United States, 60 per cent of cotton output comes from farms of fewer than 1000 acres, whereas farms that small produce only a third of cotton grown in the more capital-intensive western states. Over all, however, the largest 3 per cent of all cotton growers produced 40 per cent of all cotton and cotton seed in the United States.

Competition in Agriculture

Despite the scale and concentration of production, however, modern agriculture remains an industry whose behavior and performance are best understood in terms of the theory of pure competition. Although production is concentrated in the hands of a relatively small percentage of growers, total numbers are so large that the 2 or 3 per cent largest growers of any given product still constitute a substantial number of independent firms. For example, although only 2 per cent of grain growers (those with annual production valued at $40,000 or more) manage to produce about 50 per cent of all grain in the United States, this 2 per cent consists of 27,000 firms. Numbers like this are a far cry from those for manufacturing. The largest number of firms of all sizes found in any one manufacturing industry are the 10,000 sawmills and planing mills engaged in the production of lumber. However, typically, manufacturing industries have many fewer firms—even industries like men's work clothing (277 firms) and cotton weaving mills (218 firms) that are widely recognized as highly competitive. Thus, even if we ignore the competitive influence exerted by the thousands of smaller farms in each line of production and look only at the very largest, we are still talking about nearly 100 times as many independent firms as are found in the most competitive manufacturing industries.

In any event, the number and size of existing firms are only partial measures of the competitiveness of market structure. An important additional consideration is the extent to which ease of entry generates potential competition beyond the firms engaged in production at any given moment. Not only do the many smaller farms produce and sell in the same market with the larger ones, but there are no special barriers to entry into agriculture. Moreover, many existing farms are adapted to the production of a variety of products and can shift output from crop to crop on the basis of the outlook for prices and costs.

As a result of this structure, even large modern farms are powerless to exert any appreciable individual influence on total output or prices through their own economic behavior. They can only plan production schedules on the basis of their own best expectations with the knowledge that the ultimate outcome will be virtually unaltered by anything they might decide. Plans for how much of which crops to grow and by which methods are arrived at on the basis of price and cost expectations. The resulting crop comes on the market and sells at prices determined by total volume in conjunction with existing demand.

Demand for Farm Products

Another important element in the structure of agriculture markets is the nature of the demand for farm products. Before exploring the nature of the demand for farm products in particular, however, it is useful to review some of the properties of demand curves in general. Potatoes are fairly typical farm products and can be used as a convenient illustration.

Demand for Potatoes

In Figure 1, the average farm price of potatoes in the United States is plotted vertically against the annual per capita consumption of potatoes, measured horizontally. Each point represents data for a recent year. The downward drift of the scatter of points from upper left to lower right confirms the everyday observation that people tend to buy more at low than at high prices. At the high price of $3.78, for example, average consumption in the United States shrank to 124 pounds per person in 1964, whereas at the low price of $1.57, consumption reached 153 pounds per person in 1971. Of course, as a glance at the chart reveals, price is not the sole influence on buying habits. Points labeled 1960, 1962, 1963, 1972, and 1973, for example, show that during these years annual consumption varied but little, yet prices ranged from more than $3.00 in 1973 to less than $2.00 in 1962 and 1963. Part of this price variation can be traced to the upward trend of income during this period. Note how the points corresponding to the three years in the early 1960s—when incomes were low—fall below those that represent the higher income years 1972 and 1973. But many other factors besides income were important. Some of the variation in potato buying can be ascribed to changes in the prices of other foods that could be substituted for potatoes in the diet, to the appearance of new ways to use potatoes—such as packaged mashed potatoes, frozen French fries, or new types of potato chips— or to changes in consumer tastes for potatoes compared to other foods.

By the use of appropriate statistical procedures it is possible to allow for the effects of many of these other influences and to estimate the effect of price alone on potato purchases. The result is shown by the curve *DD*, drawn through the

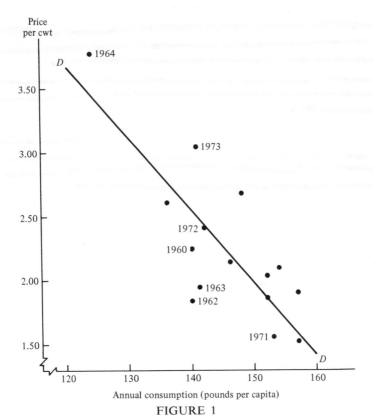

FIGURE 1
Demand for potatoes. Source: Data from the U.S. Department of Agriculture, *Agricultural Statistics*, various issues. Prices have been divided by the consumer price index to adjust for inflation.

midst of the observations.[1] Such a curve, called a *demand curve*, represents the quantity of potatoes buyers would be expected to purchase at each price, other influences being held constant.

Demand Elasticity

Elasticity Defined

The responses of buyers to changes in price are measured by the elasticity of demand. Elasticity expresses the percentage change in quantity purchased to be expected in response to a 1 per cent change in price. For example, if a 1 per cent price increase induced the buyers of a product to cut their purchases by 2 per cent, the elasticity of demand for the product would be expressed as -2. This

---

[1] The line was fitted by least-squares regression to obtain $P = 9.26 - 5.66Q + .526Y$, where P is price of potatoes, Q is per capita crop, and Y is real per capita income measured in thousands of dollars at 1958 prices. The position of the line DD in Figure 1 corresponds to demand at the average level of income during the period.

indicates that percentage changes in quantity purchased tend to be double the percentage change in price. The negative sign reminds us that quantity is altered in the opposite direction to the change in price, a rise in price being accompanied by a reduction in quantity, and vice versa. In similar fashion, the elasticity of $-.7$ would characterize the demand for a product when a reduction of only .7 per cent in purchases would occur in response to a 1 per cent price increase. An elasticity of -1 would indicate a demand when percentage changes in quantity and price tend to be equal, and so on.

The elasticity of demand for particular products is readily estimated from fitted demand curves by selecting two prices close together and reading the corresponding quantities shown by the curve. The elasticity is then calculated as the ratio of the percentage difference in the two quantities to the percentage difference in the two prices. For example, careful measurement on the demand curve DD indicates that purchasers would be ready to buy about 148 pounds per year at a price of $2.10, but if the price were lowered to $2.00, purchases would expand to about 150 pounds. The price reduction from $2.10 to $2.00 is a change of -5 per cent, whereas the increase in purchased quantity from 148 to 150 pounds is a change of only 1.4 per cent. This yields an estimated elasticity of demand for potatoes of about $1.4/-5$, or about $-.3$.

Of course, we are rarely interested in such exact measurement of elasticity, but we do need a general idea of how elastic the demand for a given product is. For this purpose it is convenient to classify demand curves into broad categories, using an elasticity of -1, called unit elasticity, as the dividing point. Demand curves with an elasticity smaller than 1 (in absolute value) are then referred to as inelastic demands. In these terms, the demand for potatoes with an elasticity of $-.3$ would be classified as *inelastic*.

Demand curves that have an elasticity greater than 1 in absolute value are termed relatively elastic. The demand for lettuce—estimated to have an elasticity of -2.8—is classified as relatively elastic.

Causes of Differences in Elasticity

Because elasticity measures buyer response to price, it varies widely among products, depending in each case on the characteristics of the product and on buyers' attitudes toward it. Products like potatoes, which generally are viewed as necessities, or food staples, have inelastic demands. Buyers feel that they need a certain amount in their diet and are reluctant to cut back on their use of the commodity as its price rises. By the same token, because they are already consuming about as much of it as they feel they need, they have use for only little more when prices fall.

In contrast, products viewed as luxuries exhibit relatively elastic demands, for their consumption can be reduced almost painlessly when prices rise, yet buyers are delighted at the chance to enjoy them when lower prices place them within reach of the budget. Among farm products, demands for fruits and fresh vegetables tend to be relatively elastic. The demand for peaches, for example, has been estimated to have an elasticity of -1.49, five times that of potatoes.

This high elasticity reflects the ease with which households can do without peaches when price rises, and the welcome accorded the fruit when it becomes cheap.

The elasticity of demand also depends on the relationship the product bears to others. In particular, products that have good substitutes to which buyers can turn as alternatives tend to have relatively elastic demands. Even small percentage changes in price lead large numbers of buyers to choose the cheaper substitute. This is probably one of the reasons that demands for fresh vegetables tend to be relatively elastic. The elasticity of demand for fresh tomatoes, for example, has been estimated at 2.2, and that of fresh peas at 2.8, largely because many other fresh vegetables can be used instead of these if the price is right.

Price elasticities of demand for a number of farm products are given in Table 1. Note that demands for basic commodities like potatoes and corn tend to be inelastic, as might be expected from their nature. On the other hand, many individual fresh fruits and vegetables have highly elastic demands, partly because of their less basic character and partly because of the availability of many close substitutes to which consumers can turn.

TABLE 1
Elasticity of Demand for Selected Farm Products

	ELASTICITY OF DEMAND	
PRODUCT	PRICE	INCOME
Cabbage	—.25	n.a.[a]
Potatoes	—.27	.15
Wool	—.33	.27
Peanuts	—.38	.44
Eggs	—.43	.57
Onions	—.44	.58
Milk	—.49	.50
Butter	—.62	.37
Oranges	—.62	.83
Corn	—.63	n.a.
Cream	—.69	1.72
Fresh cucumbers	—.7	.7
Apples	—1.27	1.32
Peaches	—1.49	1.43
Fresh tomatoes	—2.22	.24
Lettuce	—2.58	.88
Fresh peas	—2.83	1.05

[a] Not available.
Source: Potatoes, estimated from the data of Figure 1. All others estimated by the U.S. Department of Agriculture.

Elasticity of Derived Demands

A particularly important aspect of demand for farm products is that most are purchased from the farm by canners, millers, and other manufacturers who process the raw product before selling it to final consumers. Wheat is milled into flour and baked into bread before it is purchased for the table; meat is butchered and packaged before consumers buy it; and most fruit and vegetables are canned or frozen before consumers buy them—even those to be sold fresh require transportation, packaging, and other retailing costs before they can be delivered to the table.

As shown in Table 2, only 38 per cent of the retail value of food items purchased in the United States consists of their original value on the farm; 62 per cent consists of the value added by processing and marketing. Of course, these percentages vary widely among different farm products. Because of the lengthy production line required for bread and cereal products to reach the final consumer, farm value constitutes only 22 per cent of the retail price of such items. The value of the barley, rice, hops and other farm output in the retail price of a can of beer is even smaller. In contrast, the farm share is 65 per cent of the retail price of meat, poultry, and eggs that reach the table more directly.

Because of the value added by processing and marketing, the value of the farm products represents a small percentage of the retail price paid by ultimate buyers, and this tends to make the demand for raw farm products even less elastic. To make clear why this is so, let us consider a processed product with a relatively elastic demand—frozen peas, say, with a demand elasticity of about 2. This elasticity would mean that a 5 per cent reduction in the price of frozen peas would tend to increase consumption by about 10 per cent. But if frozen peas are typical of other vegetables, farm value constitutes only about 30 per cent of the final retail price, so a 5 per cent reduction in the farm price of peas would result in no more than a 1.5 per cent reduction in retail prices for frozen peas. Given

TABLE 2
Shares in Final Retail Value of Food Products

	BILLIONS OF DOLLARS	PER CENT
Final retail value	$132.2	100
Processing and marketing costs		
Labor	40.3	30
Rail and truck transportation	6.1	5
Power, containers, and other costs	31.3	24
Corporate profit (before taxes)	4.6	3
Farm value of products	49.9	38

Source: U.S. Department of Agriculture, *Agricultural Statistics, 1974* (Washington, D.C.: U.S. Government Printing Office, 1974).

the elasticity of 2, this lower price would stimulate only 3 per cent greater sales of frozen peas, and only a 3 per cent increase in the purchase of raw peas to freeze. In consequence, then, a 5 per cent price reduction on the farm level stimulates only a 3 per cent increase in the quantity of peas bought from farmers, and this gives a demand for peas an elasticity of only −.6 at the farm level, despite the highly elastic demand for frozen peas at the consumer level.

The relationship demonstrated for frozen peas holds for all derived demands. In general, the smaller the farm share in retail price, the lower the elasticity of derived demand for the product tends to be at the farm level. Because farm value is only 38 per cent of the retail value of foods and other farm products, demand at the farm level would tend to be inelastic even if retail demands for final products were relatively quite elastic. In fact, however, because retail demands for most food products are inelastic even at the consumer level, the small farm share in retail price tends to make demand at the farm level very inelastic indeed.

Commodities with Several Uses

As we have seen, the elasticity of demand for a product depends on what it is used for, but many commodities are used for more than one purpose. In such cases, demand elasticity varies among the different uses, depending on the degree to which each particular use is viewed as "necessity" or "luxury," and depending on the availability of substitutes to replace the commodity for each purpose. Wheat, for example, has two important uses. It is used not only to make bread and bakery products for the table, but also as a feed grain for poultry and livestock. As a component of bread, wheat is generally viewed as a basic necessity; moreover, because of its gluten content, wheat flour has no good substitutes in baking. Indeed, wheat is so outstanding in this regard that most recipes for "rye" bread, "corn" bread, and other "nonwheat" bakery products call for the addition of wheat flour to the other grain in order to impart cohesiveness to the dough. As a result, the demand for wheat to make into bakery products is quite inelastic. As a feed grain, however, wheat has many fine substitutes in corn, oats, sorghum grains, and other things, so the demand for wheat as feed grain is relatively elastic.

Statistical measurement by the U.S. Department of Agriculture bears out these differences in elasticity. The demand for wheat destined to be made into flour has an elasticity of only −.2, whereas the demand for wheat to be used as a feed grain has an elasticity of −3.

Taking all the uses together, the over-all elasticity of demand for a product having several uses is the weighted average of elasticities of demand in the different uses with weights proportional to the quantity consumed in each use. Because wheat is used overwhelmingly for flour, its over-all demand is highly inelastic, despite the high elasticity of demand in one of its uses.

Elasticity and Allocation of Available Crop

Differences in elasticity play an important role in the allocation of farm products among different uses. When supplies are short, the consumption of products must be cut back. Generally, there is some reduction in all uses, but the greatest reduction is in less essential uses, or uses for which the product can readily be replaced by close substitutes. These are, of course, the uses in which demand elasticity is high. Rising prices curtail consumption in these areas, leaving proportionally more for essential uses where replacement is difficult. Response to increased supply is the opposite. As price falls, more of the product is devoted to all uses, but consumption expands proportionally more in uses that are less essential, or where the cheaper product can replace substitutes.

The operation of this principle can be seen in Table 3, which shows uses of wheat during a year of high supply and a year of lower supply. During the year of low supply, wheat consumption for human food was maintained at 98 per cent of its higher level, whereas only 13 per cent as much wheat was consumed for animal feed. These proportions are about what would be expected from the difference in demand elasticity in the two uses.

Other Factors Affecting Demand

In addition to price, quantity purchased is affected by income, population, prices of substitute products, consumer tastes, and—for products like soy beans, which have important industrial uses—the state of industrial technology. The influence of change in these factors is generally represented by shifts in position of the demand curve. When, for any reason, consumers begin to buy more than formerly at given prices, this fact is represented by a bodily shift of the demand curve to the right. Reduced purchases at given prices are represented by a shift of the demand curve to the left. Curve DD in Figure 1, for example, shows the location of potato demand when real per capita income stood at the average for the period. The point representing purchases during 1973, however, lies on a curve shifted slightly to the right by the high level of income in that year, while dots corresponding to 1960, 1962, and 1963 lie on a curve shifted to the left, largely by the lower incomes characteristic of the early 1960s.

TABLE 3
Allocation of Wheat in Two Selected Years

	TONS OF WHEAT CONSUMED IN THE UNITED STATES (IN MILLIONS)	
	HUMAN FOOD	ANIMAL FEED
High supply	515.1	154.2
Low supply	503.3	20.2

Source: Adapted from data in U.S. Department of Agriculture, Agricultural Statistics, 1973 (Washington, D.C.: U.S. Government Printing Office, 1973).

Income Elasticity

Just as with prices, the effects of income on buying are expressed in terms of elasticities. The income elasticity of demand is the percentage increase in quantity bought at given prices that occurs in response to a 1 per cent increase in income. For example, calculation with the potato data indicates that a 1 per cent rise in real per capita income increases the volume of potatoes purchased by only .15 per cent, and this is expressed as an income elasticity of .15. (Unlike price elasticity, most income elasticities are positive because the demand for most commodities rises as income increases.)

An income elasticity of 1 characterizes a commodity whose consumption tends to rise in proportion to income. An income elasticity of less than 1 indicates that the quantity purchased grows less than in proportion to income. This is generally characteristic of staples and basic commodities, like potatoes, that even low-income families consume in quantity. Income elasticity greater than 1 characterizes products favored by rich people that poorer buyers cannot afford.

Income elasticity is given for most of the farm products in Table 2. As can be seen, basic staples like potatoes and onions have low income elasticities, whereas cream, fruit, and fresh vegetables are characterized by high income elasticities. These, of course, represent more expensive, preferred items whose consumption rises more than in proportion to income.

Commodities like cabbage and dried beans are characterized by negative income elasticity. That is, these are *inferior goods* that form an important part of the diet of poor people, but that are readily abandoned in favor of preferred, but more expensive, substitutes as income rises.

Because of wide differences in the income elasticities of different products, rising income does more to change the composition of demand than it does to increase the total amount of food consumed. That is, rising income increases the demand for more expensive, preferred foods, but it does so largely at the expense of reduced demand for other products. For example, families with incomes exceeding $15,000 (1973 prices) tend to eat, on the average, nearly three times as much sirloin steak as do those with incomes in the $5000 to $6000 bracket, but they eat only 20 per cent more meat of all kinds, and the difference in total food consumption is even less. Richer families merely eat steak instead of other meat, and eat meat instead of other food. In addition, rich families consume a great deal less of such inferior foods as dried beans and cabbage than poor people do, and they eat considerably more fresh and frozen vegetables.

Prices of Other Products and Cross Elasticity of Demand

The purchase of products that have good substitutes is strongly influenced by the price of the substitute. A rise in the price of beef, for example, stimulates the demand for pork, and vice versa. This influence is measured by what is called the *cross elasticity* of demand; it is calculated by the percentage change occurring in the quantity of the item purchased, given its own price, in response to a 1 per cent change in the price of its substitute. Research into the demand for meat indicates, for example, that a 1 per cent increase in the price of beef tends to increase the purchase of pork by about one quarter of 1 per cent. This response is represented by a cross elasticity of .25 between the demand for pork and the price of beef. Magnitudes of cross elasticities are a good index of how closely two products substitute for each other in the buyer's consumption pattern. Low cross elasticity indicates products that are only poor substitutes, for a change in the price of one has little effect on the quantity of the other that is purchased. The more readily products can be interchanged, the higher their cross elasticities tend to become. In the extreme case of perfect substitutes, any difference in price would lead to consumption of only the cheapest of the two products, a situation that would be represented by an infinitely large cross elasticity.

In Table 4 estimated demand elasticities are given for three kinds of meat. As would be expected, a rise in the price of any one kind of meat reduces its consumption while it increases the consumption of its substitutes. Thus, a 10 per cent increase in the price of beef tends to reduce beef consumption about 6.5 per cent (in keeping with its price elasticity of demand of −.65) while it increases the purchase of pork by 2.5 per cent and the purchase of chicken by 1.2 per cent.

Individual Commodities Versus Commodity Groups

Demands for individual commodities with close substitutes have high price and high cross elasticities, so any change in prices causes a substantial change in the proportions in which consumers purchase the several products. When we consider the entire bundle of products as a group, however, we find a much lower response to price changes when the prices of all substitutes change together. For example, the demand for beef has an elasticity of −.65, in response to changes in its own price and cross elasticities of .01 and .20 in response to changes in prices of pork and chicken, respectively. But when all meat prices change together, the buyer's response is measured not by these individual elasticities, but by their algebraic sum. Thus, in response to a 10 per cent increase in all three meat prices, consumption of beef would show an elasticity

TABLE 4

Elasticities of Demand for Beef, Pork, and Chicken

| | ELASTICITY OF DEMAND WITH RESPECT TO | | | |
PRODUCT	PRICE OF BEEF	PRICE OF PORK	PRICE OF CHICKEN	INCOME
Beef	−.65	.01	.20	$1.05
Pork	.25	−.45	.16	.14
Chicken	.12	.20	−.65	.28

Source: Calculated for the author by students in Economics 835 at Michigan State University, East Lansing, Mich., 1975.

of $-.65 + .01 + .20 = -.44$ and would decline only 4.4 per cent. Similarly, a 10 per cent rise in all meat prices would reduce pork consumption by only 4 per cent and chicken by only 3.3 per cent. In other words, when commodities are considered in groups, the demand elasticity for the group as a whole is substantially lower than the elasticities of demand for individual members of the group. The demand for feed grains as a whole is much less elastic than the demand for corn, oats, or sorghum grains taken individually, and the demand for fresh vegetables is much less elastic than the demands for tomatoes, fresh peas, or other commodities taken individually.

Demand Elasticity and Farm Incomes

The general inelasticity of the demand for farm products, especially when major commodity groups are considered as a whole, has important consequences for the behavior of farm incomes. Unlike most manufactured goods, which are priced first, with production adjusted to whatever sales materialize, farm crops are grown first and then are placed on the market for whatever price they will bring. Because these prices reflect the size of the crop, normal year-to-year variation in weather, insect pests, and other growing conditions generate year-to-year price fluctuations the magnitude of which depend on demand elasticity.

The prices of crops with inelastic demands tend to fluctuate more from year to year than output does. For example, a 10 per cent reduction in potato crops starts potato prices rising, and, to match the deficiency in output, price must increase enough to cut consumption by 10 per cent. But because potato demand has an elasticity of only $-.3$, price must rise by about 30 per cent to accomplish this. Similarly, a 10 per cent increase in the potato crop requires a 30 per cent price reduction to encourage buyers to absorb the extra potatoes.

In contrast, the prices of crops with elastic demands are more stable than output. A 10 per cent variation in the output of peaches (demand elasticity = 1.5), for example, tends to be associated with only about a 6 per cent change in price.

The continual fluctuation in output and price has important consequences for the total dollar value of crops and, hence, for the behavior of farm incomes. Because the total value of any crop is given by total quantity multiplied by price, increases in output affect crop value in two opposite ways. On the one hand, more units are sold, tending to increase the number of dollars taken in, but, on the other hand, price falls and each unit brings in fewer dollars than before. Whether the total number of dollars received by growers rises or falls, then, depends on which of these effects is larger. As we have just seen, the answer depends on demand elasticity.

When a product has a relatively elastic demand, crop fluctuations are accompanied by changes in income in the same direction. For example, a 10 per cent expansion of a crop like peaches, whose demand elasticity is 1.5, leads to only a 6.7 per cent decline in price. Because price does not fall enough to offset the increase in output, the number of dollars received by the growers expands. By the same token, a reduction in crop would lead to reduced dollar receipts.

But the prices of products with inelastic demands fall more than in proportion to increased output, and total dollar value is smaller for a larger than it is for a smaller crop. This can be tested in terms of the demand for potatoes in Figure 1. According to the demand curve DD, the production of 132 pounds per capita leads to a price of about $3 per hundred pounds, or a crop worth about $3.96 per consumer. In a nation of 200 million consumers, the total crop would be worth about $792 million. Increasing production to 150 pounds per person, however, reduces the price to about $2 per hundred pounds, making the larger crop worth only about $3 per consumer, or about $600 million all told, almost 25 per cent less than the value of the smaller crop.

Because most farm products—particularly when major commodity groups are considered as a whole—have inelastic demands, it follows that expanded production brings in fewer dollars and results in reduced farm incomes, where-as contracted production brings in more dollars and higher farm incomes. For this reason, natural year-to-year fluctuations in growing conditions make farming very much a "boom-or-bust" proposition. Poor growing conditions or crop failure in one part of the market mean severe losses to the farms affected but high incomes and prosperity for the remainder. Good growing conditions yield bumper crops but low prices and incomes to everybody.

Beyond the short-run fluctuations, however, demand exerts important long-run influences on farm incomes. Because demand is inelastic, a rising trend of farm yields means falling dollar receipts and a downward trend of farm income, unless demand is expanded by enough to absorb the additional production. There are, of course, two principal factors operating to expand farm demand. Demand tends to grow in proportion to the number of consumers and also expands as real per capita incomes rise. But growth in population raises demand only in proportion to the number of people (we might say that the "population elasticity" of farm demand is unity), whereas the income elasticity of demand for farm products is considerably less than unity. It follows directly that periods like the last 50 years, in which agricultural productivity grew much more rapidly than population, would also be periods of falling farm prices, diminishing farm incomes, and serious problems for the agricultural community.

Of course, the performance of agriculture is not exclusively a matter of demand, and before we can explore these problems further, we must turn to an analysis of agricultural supply.

III. SUPPLY AND THE PERFORMANCE OF AGRICULTURE

Just as demand represents the purchasing behavior of buyers in relation to prices, incomes, and other factors, *supply* represents the behavior of producers in response to prices and costs. Like demand, supply can be represented by a curve displaying the relationship between prices and quantities, and the response of quantity to changes in price can be expressed as an elasticity of supply. But there is an important difference between demand and supply, for although buyers tend to adapt purchasing behavior promptly to new conditions, producers often require time to revise plans and production schedules or even to acquire new facilities and equipment. For this reason, it is useful to distinguish three different supply situations according to the scope afforded producers to respond to new information about prices and costs.

Producers have the very least scope to modify output at the time the crop has already matured and is ready for harvest, but even at this point there is some possible variation. *Harvest supply* describes the relationship between price expectations and producers' behavior in harvesting and bringing to market crops already mature. Because there is so little room to affect quantity at this point, harvest supply has a very low elasticity.

Growers have somewhat greater scope to modify output at the time they are arranging their production plans and planting schedules for the coming crop season. *Short-run supply* describes the relationship between price expectations and producers' behavior in planting and cultivating acreage. Clearly, short-run supply is more elastic than harvest supply.

The greatest scope to modify output is provided when producers have sufficient time to alter their investment in productive facilities. This alteration may take the form of additional investment by existing farms or of the entrance of new producers into the market. On the negative side, it may take the form of allowing equipment to wear out without replacement, or of the outright abandonment of operations by some producers. *Long-run supply* describes the relationship between price expectations and production when time is allowed for the full adjustment of productive facilities to prices and costs. Because it encompasses the greatest scope for adapting output, long-run supply is the most elastic of the three. In this section we will consider each of the supply situations in turn.

Harvest Supply—The Very Short Run

Once crops are mature and ready for market, the total quantity available is fixed and no action on the part of farmers can generate output beyond that total. Nevertheless, the total available is rarely harvested, for it seldom pays to strip fields so carefully that every last particle is collected. Some crops mature over periods of several weeks and growers must decide when the time is best for harvest and whether it is worthwhile to return to the fields for a second harvest a week or so later. Some crops can be harvested cheaply and quickly, but with greater loss of product than would be true of a slower, more expensive harvest. Clearly, high prices at harvest time make it profitable to harvest a larger proportion of the potential crop, whereas low prices make it unprofitable to take great care with picking and often result in the outright abandonment of low-yield acreage that would be too expensive to harvest.

Although there is some flexibility in the quantity produced from a given crop, the physical limitation to what can be harvested and the relatively low cost of harvesting (roughly 20 per cent of variable cost) severely limit the extent to which output from a mature crop can be varied. Once crops are ready for market, harvest supply is extremely inelastic.

Short-run Supply and Production Costs

Since the quantity producers plan to grow depends on expected price in relation to production costs, the properties of short-run supply depend on the structure of costs.

Cost Structure

Production costs for farmers—like those of any other business firm—are of two general types. Some are fixed regardless of output, whereas others vary with the level of production. *Fixed costs* include taxes, interest on the farm mortgage, depreciation of equipment, and similar expenses that must be incurred whether production is undertaken or not and that do not vary in magnitude as production rises and falls. *Variable costs* are zero as long as nothing is produced, but they rise sharply when production is initiated. The initial increase in variable cost is associated with planning, acquisition of materials, and other general costs that would not be incurred at all if nothing were produced. An important element of this "start-up" cost consists of the labor of the farm owner and family members or of the salary of managers of corporate farms.

Once start-up costs have been incurred, output can be expanded with relatively small increases in outlays for seed, fertilizer, herbicides, labor, power, and other variable costs; in this range, cost rises slowly as more bushels are produced. There is, however, a limit to the output available from given facilities, and as this capacity limit is approached, variable cost rises more and more sharply. Additional output can be had only by extra care, additional fertilizer, or other inputs to increase yield per acre.

Costs of a Corn Grower

Variable costs per acre of corn raised on central Iowa farms are given in Table 5. In keeping with modern farming methods, labor cost is low, with chemical herbicides employed in place of labor-intensive cultivation for weed control. Extensive use is made of commercial fertilizer to maintain high yields with little or no crop rotation. All together, variable cost amounted to $41.07 per acre planted. The sources from which the data were taken gave no indication of fixed costs; however, on a national average, fixed costs for farming—largely depreciation of buildings and equipment, interest on farm debt, and taxes— amount to about a third of variable cost. On this basis, we can estimate the total cost of corn grown in central Iowa at about $62.50 per acre.

Average and Marginal Costs

Total costs are translated into average and marginal costs in Figure 2. Marginal cost (MC) is the rate at which total cost rises as production is increased. Once start-up costs have been incurred and production is under way, additional corn can be raised for little more than the cost of the seed and materials needed to cultivate additional acreage. This keeps marginal cost low until production approaches the physical limits of the farm. As this capacity is approached, greater and greater outlays are needed to extract additional output, and marginal cost rises more and more sharply.

TABLE 5
Variable Costs per Acre of Corn Production, Central Iowa Farms

COSTS	QUANTITY	COST PER ACRE (IN $)
Preharvest Costs		
Labor (including owners)	3.78 h	5.82
Seed	.23 bu	3.22
Fertilizer and lime		
nitrogen	100 lb	5.40
phosphorus	22 lb	4.58
potassium	19 lb	.99
lime	.23 ton	.91
Fuel, lubricants, repairs		3.95
Insecticides		2.18
Herbicides		2.24
Custom work		.85
Hail insurance		.30
Interest on operating expenses		1.01
Total preharvest cost		31.45
Harvest Costs		
Labor	2 h	3.08
Fuel, lubricants, repairs		1.81
Custom hired harvesting and trucking		2.85
Other harvest expenses		1.98
Total harvest cost per harvested acre		9.72
Total harvest cost per planted acre		9.62
Variable cost per planted acre		41.07

Source: U.S. Department of Agriculture, Economic Research Service, *Selected U.S. Crop Budgets, Yields, Outputs, and Variable Costs: North Central Region*, Vol. 2, (Washington D.C.: U.S. Government Printing Office, 1971).

Average variable cost (AVC) is high at low levels of production because start-up costs are spread over limited output. As production expands, start-up costs are spread over more and more bushels of corn, pulling down the average variable cost per bushel. As production approaches the capacity of the farm, however, marginal cost begins to rise more than the average start-up cost declines, and at this point average variable cost stops falling and begins to rise.

Because fixed costs are unchanged as output expands, average fixed cost is inversely proportional to output regardless of production. Average total cost is merely the sum of average variable and average fixed costs.

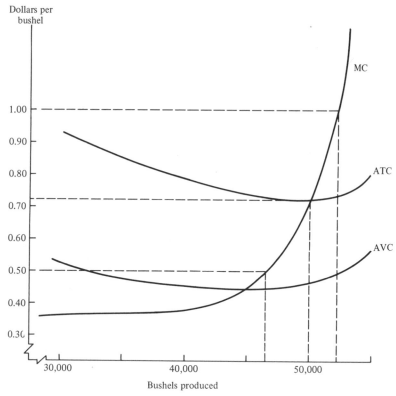

FIGURE 2
Average and marginal costs of a corn grower.

Profit Maximization and Supply Elasticity

By a familiar proposition in competitive theory, output that brings marginal cost into equality with expected price is the most profitable production plan for a competitive firm—provided only that the expected price is high enough to cover the minimum average variable cost at which the firm can operate. At an expected price of 50 cents per bushel, the farm of Figure 2 would plan to raise about 46,500 bushels. If a price of 72 cents were expected, production would be increased to 50,000 bushels, and a price of $1.00 would raise the most profitable production to 52,300 bushels.

The cost curves shown are consistent with the cost data of Table 5 and are quite typical of agricultural production. Marginal cost rises so sharply near capacity output that even wide price variations exert little influence on the output of any individual grower, at least as long as he continues in operation. In other words, if a farm operates at all, it functions very nearly at the capacity output afforded by available land and facilities. As Figure 2 shows, even a 100 per cent price increase—from 50 cents to $1.00 would induce the farmer to add only about 12.5 per cent to planned production. This degree of output response corresponds to a supply elasticity of only about .1.

But growers will continue to produce only so long as they expect prices that will cover average variable costs. Fixed costs are, of course, already sunk in the business; they will continue whether anything is planted or not, and the only way to recover them is to operate the farm. Variable costs, on the other hand, are not incurred until the farmer decides to make the outlays; if there is no prospect of getting them back, it is better to keep the money. To operate at all under these circumstances would result in losing not only fixed costs, but some part of the variable cost in addition.

This proposition can be tested in terms of Figure 2. The 52,300 bushels produced at a price of $1.00 would entail an average total cost of about 74 cents per bushel and would leave nearly $13,600 as profit above cost. But production of 46,500 bushels at a price of 50 cents would involve an average total cost of about 73 cents per bushel, so the farm would sustain a loss of about $10,700 for the year. Even so, this would be better than shutting down, for with no production at all, the farm would lose its entire $13,500 fixed cost. Because the 50-cent price is above the minimum average variable cost at which the farm can operate (about 44 cents per bushel) the farm is $2800 better off when it produces at a loss than when it shuts down.

If, however, the price of corn should fall below the 44-cent minimum average variable cost to, say, 40 cents per bushel, marginal cost would be equated to price at an output of about 43,000 bushels. At this level of production, average total cost would be about 76 cents per bushel, and the operation would generate a loss of nearly $15,500. This would be about $2000 more than the farm would lose if it simply stopped production and settled for the loss of all fixed costs.

Because farms in operation tend to operate very close to capacity regardless of price, the principal supply response to falling price occurs when farmers find it no longer profitable to produce the crop. Similarly, the principal supply response to rising prices comes when farmers find prices moving back into the profitable range and again take up production of the crop.

Variable costs differ widely among growers depending on soil type, climate, length of growing season, and skill of producer. During the same year that growers in central Iowa incurred an average variable cost of 47 cents per bushel of corn, Nebraska farmers produced corn at an average variable cost ranging from 49 cents per bushel in the lowest-cost district to 71 cents in the highest-cost area, and similar cost differences are characteristic of all other crops.

Figure 3 shows the striking variation in average costs among cotton growers in the United States. The curve shows the percentage of cotton production that was produced by growers whose average costs were lower than those indicated on the vertical axis. For example, the average variable cost line indicates that whereas practically all cotton growers had an average variable cost below 39 cents per pound, only about 75 per cent of cotton was grown by farmers with an average variable cost below 24 cents, and barely more than a third of all cotton was produced at an average variable cost below 18 cents.

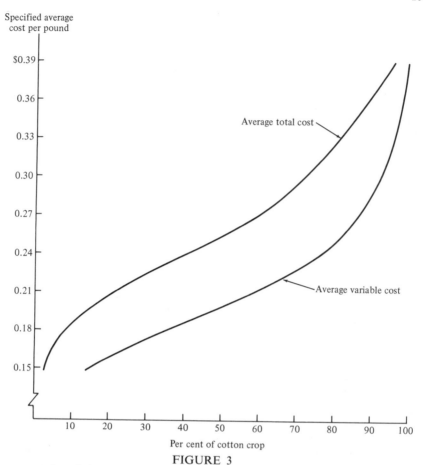

FIGURE 3

Percentage of total U.S. upland cotton crop raised by growers with average costs below those specified. Each point on the curve represents the percentage of U.S. cotton production (on the horizontal axis) raised by growers whose average costs were below the figure given on the vertical axis. *Source:* U.S. Department of Agriculture, *Costs of Producing Upland Cotton in the United States,* Economic Research Service, 1967.

Because no grower will plant cotton unless he expects price to cover at least his average variable cost, the distribution of average variable costs among growers gives a good indication of the elasticity of the short-run supply of cotton. For example, because practically all cotton grown in the United States was produced by growers with an average variable cost of 40 cents, but only about 92 per cent by growers with an average variable cost below $.30, a 25 per cent reduction of price from 40 cents to 30 cents would cause about an 8 per cent reduction in cotton output, corresponding to a supply elasticity of about .3 for the short run.

Still another source contributing to the elasticity of short-run supply is the shifting composition of the output of multiple-product farms. For several reasons, many farms produce several different crops. Hog farmers, cattle feeders, and poultry growers need grain for feed, and it is natural for them to raise some of their own requirements. Other farmers raise crops that ripen at different times in order to spread harvesting over a longer period. This avoids the high harvesting costs that would be incurred if the entire crop had to be brought in within a few days and reduces fixed cost by employing a smaller investment in harvesting equipment operated over a longer period, rather than a large investment used only briefly each year. Although it is less significant in these days of commercial fertilizer than it once was, crop rotation is another reason for multiple-product farms. Finally, producing several crops provides some degree of insurance against such natural calamities as blight, which can ruin yields for any one crop, and against the economic calamities that can result from unfavorable marketing conditions for any one particular commodity.

Regardless of reason, however, the proportions in which different crops are grown are not fixed, but vary in response to expected prices. The expectation of cheap corn and high-priced hogs, for example, leads hog raisers to increase the number of hogs, while planning to buy, rather than raise, extra feed requirements. Expectation of high prices for corn and low-priced hogs, on the other hand, induces growers to reduce hog production, while planning to sell, rather than feed, some of the high-priced corn. In similar fashion, a division of acreage between corn and soybeans, the choice between planting more tomatoes or more sweet corn, and other planting decisions depend on expectations about the relative prices of alternative crops and contributes to their supply elasticities.

Market Equilibrium and Adjustment Cycles

The interaction of short-run supply with demand for farm products governs the year-to-year behavior of production and prices. This interaction is depicted in Figure 4, where supply, SS, and demand, DD, determine a market equilibrium represented by price P^* and quantity Q^*. The P^* and Q^* values are equilibrium values in the familiar sense that no other combination of price and output could simultaneously satisfy the desire of consumers to buy—as indicated by the demand curve—and conform to the production plans of growers—as shown by the supply curve. At any price higher than P^*—at P_1, for example—farms would expand planting in keeping with the supply curve and would bring to market a total output equal to Q_1, greater than Q^*. Yet, consumers, faced by a high price like P_1, would purchase only Q_0, an amount smaller than the equilibrium quantity, and considerably less than the amount farmers would be bringing to market. Resulting unsold surpluses would, of course, make it impossible to maintain the higher price, and the market would be forced back toward equilibrium. By the same token, any price below P^*—P_2, say—would lead farmers to cut production back to Q_2, whereas the lower price would induce consumers to try to purchase a larger quantity, Q_1. The resulting inability of the market to satisfy demand would drive price and production upward toward the equilibrium values.

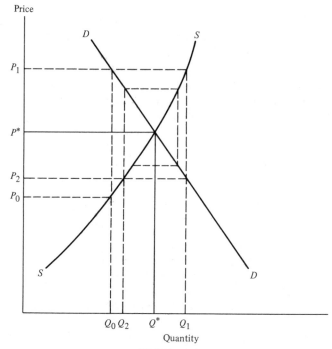

FIGURE 4
Short-run market equilibrium.

Equilibrium price and quantity compose a kind of "target" for the market, marking values toward which actual price and output are continually being pushed, but it should be understood that day-to-day price and quantity are rarely observed at their equilibrium values. For one thing, supply deals with production *plans* rather than actual outcome. The most a farmer can do is to plant and tend his crop in a manner calculated to yield the most profit under normally expected conditions. Actual output invariably depends on vagaries of weather, insect damage, blight, and other factors that affect yields.

In addition, supply relates production plans to *expected* prices, and grower's expectations are not always exact. Indeed, the fact that they must plant for next season on the basis of price expectations derived from last season's experience sometimes leads to a systematic cycling of prices and output around equilibrium. For example, suppose farmers initially expect the low price P_0 and, consequently, plant the restricted output Q_0, in keeping with short-run supply. When this limited quantity reaches market, however, price would be driven up to P_1, in keeping with demand. But on the basis of the high price P_1, growers would be induced to plant Q_1 for the next season, and price subsequently would fall to P_2. The producer response to this would be an output of Q_2, which would again force price up. Under these circumstances, as can be seen in Figure 4, price and output would be observed to perform a series of diminishing cycles as they approached equilibrium. The spiral adjustment path marked out by the dotted lines in Figure 4 reminds some people of a cob web, and for this reason the cycles of price and output observed in such markets are called cobweb cycles. Figure 4 is, of course, a highly simplified version of what actually happens. In the first place, production is not neatly divided into discrete stages, but is subject to more or less continuous adjustment. Crops once planted can be cultivated or sprayed more intensively when prices are observed to be rising, improving yields beyond what had initially been planned, or acreage can be abandoned before maturity if it appears that low prices will make it impossible to recover the additional costs that otherwise would be invested in it over the remainder of the growing season.

The process is even more complicated for products like hogs, which require a longer production time. The hog raiser's initial decision is how many sows to breed in view of prices and costs at breeding time. When pigs are born some months later, prices in relation to cost affect the number saved from the litter to be raised into mature hogs. As the pigs grow over the next 6 months to a year, prices in relation to cost determine the weight to which they are fed and the age at which they are marketed. Because of the length of time between initial breeding and marketed hogs, the quantity of hogs reaching market at any given time depends on the average of prices in relation to production cost over the preceding two years. When the short-run supply of hogs is estimated as the relationship of the number of hogs sold for slaughter each year to the average ratio of hog prices to the price of corn—the most important component of variable cost—over the two preceding years, the statistical supply curve indicates a short-run supply elasticity for hogs of about .7.

The length of time between high and low or between low and high prices in the cobweb cycle depends on the length of time between the initial planning and the marketing of the finished product. Crops, such as onions and potatoes that have annual growing seasons also tend to have prices that oscillate annually, whereas products, such as hogs, that take longer to raise have prices that oscillate more slowly. In Figure 5, the recent history of hog prices shows marked cobweb cycles. The 18-year period from the first maximum price in 1953 to the last minimum in 1971 contains 9 swings from maximum to minimum or from minimum to maximum. This works out to an average of 2 years per swing, in keeping with the hog-raising period of about 2 years.

Ironing Out Price Fluctuations

The basic cause of systematic cycles in price and production is that farmers are forced to formulate production plans on the basis of past conditions, rather than on the basis of conditions at the time the crop will be ready for harvest. When farmers have advance information about market conditions, cycles are much less severe or are eliminated entirely. One way growers can obtain such information is by contracting with buyers in advance about prices and quantities, and this is common in many lines of agriculture. For example, 98 per cent of all sugar beets, 85 per cent of vegetables grown for processing, and 95 per cent of

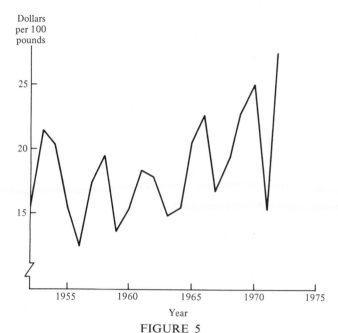

Dollars
per 100
pounds

FIGURE 5

U.S. hog prices, 1952–1973. Source: U.S. Department of Agriculture, *Statistics of Agriculture*, 1974.

all fluid-grade milk are sold to processors under contract. Contract marketing also covers 90 per cent of all broiler chickens, 55 per cent of citrus fruit, 45 per cent of potatoes, and 42 per cent of turkeys. This contrasts with barely 1 per cent of the hog production sold in advance.

A second way to iron out price fluctuations is by vertically integrating farming into the food processing industry. Integrated farms are not independent producers at all, but operate as subsidiaries of food processing firms. Vertical integration is especially common in cane sugar, where 60 per cent of all cane grown comes from acreage owned by sugar-manufacturing firms. (The other 40 per cent is grown under contract.) Similarly, 30 per cent of citrus is grown in groves operated by processors, 35 per cent of potatoes are grown on processor-owned farms, and 30 per cent of vegetables commercially grown for the fresh market are grown by subsidiaries of supermarket chains.

A third way to eliminate cycles in price and production is government action to stabilize prices by means of price-support programs. Essentially, these programs provide an advance guarantee to farmers that prices will not fall below a specified minimum, regardless of market conditions at time of harvest. The most important purpose of government agricultural price supports, however, is not to smooth out fluctuations, but, rather, as the term suggests, to maintain a level of farm prices higher than market equilibrium. We shall explore the operation of these programs at a later point.

Long-run Supply

The Role of Average Total Cost

Farms that cover variable costs but fail to recover all their fixed costs can remain in business for short periods by allowing buildings and equipment to go unrepaired and by digging into savings to meet family living costs. Sooner or later, however, a time arrives when buildings become unusable or equipment must be replaced. At this point, farmers must decide whether to continue in operation. Unless prospects are so strong that additional investment will not only be recovered, but will yield a profit, it is obviously better to shut down rather than invest more money in what is already a losing proposition. In the long run, in other words, supply depends on the ability of farmers to cover not just variable costs, but total cost of production. The long-run elasticity of supply, then, depends on the distribution of average total costs among growers. For cotton production, this distribution is shown by the average total cost curve in Figure 3, each point on which indicates the percentage of total cotton production (on the horizontal axis) grown in the United States by producers whose average total costs are less than the figure indicated on the vertical axis. For example, 92 per cent of all cotton was grown by farms with an average total cost below 39 cents, 88.2 per cent by those with an average total cost below 36 cents, and so on.

Naturally, the quantity of cotton that could be grown by farms that can cover average total cost at any given price is considerably smaller than what can be grown by those farms that could temporarily stay in production by covering average variable costs. The chart shows, for example, that whereas growers of 95 per cent of the cotton in the United States could cover average variable cost at a price of 33 cents, growers of only 81 per cent could cover average total cost at that price. If price persisted at 33 cents, output would immediately fall to 95 per cent; however, in the long run, producers of only 81 per cent could afford to stay in operation. This greater long-run responsiveness of production is reflected in supply elasticity. Whereas practically all growers had an average total cost below 40 cents per pound, growers of only 73 per cent of the cotton had an average total cost below 30 cents. Thus, the long-run effect of a 25 per cent decline in price from 40 cents to 30 cents would be accompanied by a 27 per cent decline in output, corresponding to a long-run supply elasticity of about 1.

Although supply in Figure 3 is treated only at prices below $.39 per pound, similar relationships hold for supply at higher prices. Prices above 39 cents attract higher-cost growers to production, resulting in a larger long-run response to price than that obtained in the short run.

Long-run Adjustments to Shifts in Demand

An important aspect of the performance of any industry is how effectively output is adjusted to shifts in demand. But because of the three different supply situations, adjustment of price and output to shifts in demand is not a one-and-for-all process; it is a sequence of events that may require many years for completion. Buyers whose demand has risen, for example, find themselves initially confronted by a very inelastic harvest supply. Although rising prices signal a greater demand for the product, growers have little power to satisfy it, for they are locked into the results of production plans laid many months previously and can harvest no more than has been grown. The most they can do to satisfy increased demand is to strip fields with greater care than would have been profitable at lower prices and to harvest low-yield acreage that would otherwise have been abandoned.

Although rising prices do little to elicit additional output, they, nevertheless, perform two important functions. In the first place, rising prices reallocate available supplies among alternative demands. Buyers who are in a position to do so are forced to resort to (now) cheaper substitutes, or to go without the product entirely. The reduction of purchases by these buyers, in keeping with their highly elastic demand for the crop, leaves a larger quantity available for uses in which it is essential or for which satisfactory substitutes are unavailable.

Second, higher prices for the harvest encourage growers to plan a greater output in planting for the next season and to shift some of their fields from other crops to the more profitable use. By the time of the next harvest, these efforts will have expanded output, and prices will decline somewhat from the initial peak reached just after the upsurge in demand.

In the still longer run, as higher prices persist over the next several years, production is expanded further as farmers invest in additional equipment and as new farms are attracted to the profitable crop. This long-run expansion of output is accompanied by a gradual decline in price, but so long as the price remains high enough to attract a new capacity, expansion continues. Expansion slows, however, and approaches a halt as prices approach levels that just cover average total costs of the least-efficient, highest-cost farms engaged in production.

This adjustment mechanism has profound economic significance. The production of crops requires that resources be diverted from other uses and devoted to the purpose. Consumers who want the crop signal their willingness to provide the required resources by their willingness to pay prices. But time is required to transfer resources from one employment to another. At harvest time, the most producers can do is to apply a few extra labor and machine hours and a little extra gasoline and other costs to increase recovery of the crops already in the fields and thus squeeze out as much as possible for the consumer. Even so, the resources needed to do this raise harvest costs sharply.

Given more time, growers can plan expanded production and bring prices down from the peak reached at harvest. In the longer run, resources can be shifted in a more efficient way and equilibrium price will settle to the lowest level that will permit all growers of the new equilibrium quantity to cover the average total costs of operation.

The response to a reduction in demand would be the reverse. Reduced consumer desire for the crop would be signaled by sharply falling prices, indicating that consumers would prefer fewer resources devoted to production of this crop.

But because most resources have already been irretrievably sunk in production, the most growers can do at harvest time is to divert some small amount of resources away from the harvest by the abandonment of low-yield acreage and by a less intensive harvest of the remainder. Output declines but little, and few resources are saved. In planning for the next season, however, growers who find they can no longer expect to cover acreage variable costs shift labor, fuel, and materials to other crops or release them for employment elsewhere in the economy. At this point, however, nothing can be done about the resources already sunk in farm equipment and buildings. In the long run, however, as capital equipment wears out, it is not replaced and labor and other resources that would otherwise be devoted to the production of farm machinery and buildings are freed for employment elsewhere.

III. IMPROVEMENT IN TECHNOLOGY

It is not enough for an industry merely to move resources around in response to consumer demand. It also must see that the productivity of those resources is kept as high as possible. One way to raise the productivity of resources in use is by the introduction of new, more efficient methods of production, and an important criterion of the performance of any industry is the rapidity with which it improves its technology.

In analyzing the behavior of agriculture in this regard, however, we must remember that there are two distinct aspects to the problem. One question is how fast the industry, itself, originates and developes new methods of operation. The other question is how rapidly the industry adopts and puts into use new methods as they become available, regardless of where the ideas originated.

On the first count, the record of agriculture has been rather poor. The intensively competitive structure and the relatively small scale of operation characteristic of farming simply do not lend themselves to the research and development of new ideas. The expensive laboratories and large research budgets that are commonplace in many large industrial firms could not be supported by even the largest wheat or cotton farm, hog grower, or cattle raiser. If improvements in agricultural technology had to wait until they could be developed on the farm, agricultural productivity today would be little ahead of what it was a century ago.

Fortunately, however, we have not had to depend on the farm to develop its own technical improvements, for the job has been undertaken by others. One major source of new technology has been the government-subsidized laboratores of state universities and agricultural experiment stations. To a far greater extent, however, improvements have originated in agricultural equipment firms, chemical firms, and in other industries that supply inputs to modern agriculture. For, if farmers have done little themselves to raise their own productivity, they have provided a ready market for any improvement in method, once it has been developed and demonstrated. The result has been a rate of growth in productivity that has outstripped the rest of industry.

The Profit Incentive

The strong incentive to adopt better methods derives from the profits that are available to the first growers to implement the new method. A grower who can reduce the cost of his 30,000 bushels of corn from $28,000 to $23,000 immediately adds $5000 to his annual income. His individual behavior cannot affect the price of corn, for his individual contribution to total supply is insignificant. Until others take up the new method, the entire $5000 is pure gain.

Innovation and Prices

Unfortunately for the grower, however, the new profitable situation carries within it the germ of its own destruction. For, when other growers see this demonstration of the cheaper method, their own eagerness for greater profit will lead them to imitate it. The spread of the new method produces a general increase in supply with a consequent fall in price to a new equilibrium level commensurate with the new lower cost of production.

This fall in price, which is the long-run consequence of technical innovation, has a number of important effects. In the first place, it means that exceptional profits are received only temporarily by the first growers to put the new methods into practice. As other farmers follow suit, extra gains from the lower-cost methods are wiped out as price is reduced by the rising supply of the product.

Falling prices also mean that in the long run growers have no effective choice about whether or not to adopt the new methods. As prices approach the new lower-cost levels, farmers still using the old, higher-cost methods are no longer able to cover the average total costs of production and are compelled to adopt the new methods if they are to survive. Those farmers who hold back too long are simply driven out of business.

Above all, as prices fall to the lower-cost levels, the entire gain from the new method is passed on to consumers. Growers who first adopted the method for the sake of extra profits, and those who followed along later in self-defense, have combined in an action that has not only increased the productivity of resources, but has passed the cost saving onto society at large in the form of lower prices.

Broiler Chickens—An Example of Innovations

The continual improvement of production methods is one of the most striking features of American agriculture. A good example is the revolution in the production of broiler chickens shown in Table 6. Forty years ago, broiler chickens were raised commercially on farms where they ran at large in yards, competing with one another for food, with heavy loses from accident and disease and heavy labor costs for care. In those days, it took 16 weeks and 12 pounds of feed to raise one $3\frac{1}{2}$-pound chicken, and labor cost ran as high as 8.5 hours per 100 pounds of chicken raised. It is probably difficult for modern readers to

TABLE 6
Production Cost, Output, and Price of U.S. Broiler Chicken, 1934–1970

	PRODUCTION COST PER 100 LB OF CHICKEN		PRODUCTION	RELATIVE PRICE
YEAR	FEED (LB)	WORKER-HOURS	(LB PER CAPITA)	PER POUND ($)[a]
1934	n.a.[b]	n.a.	.76	.457
1940	420	8.5	3.13	.394
1950	330	5.1	12.82	.342
1960	250	1.3	32.76	.164
1970	n.a.	.4	52.27	.135

[a] Price of chicken divided by Consumer Price Index to adjust for inflation.
[b] Not available.
Source: U.S. Department of Agriculture, Economic Research Services, and *Agricultural Statistics, 1972* (Washington, D.C.: U.S Government Printing Office).

realize that in those days chicken was too expensive for everyday use and generally was served only on holidays and other special occasions.

In about 1950, a revolution began in commercial broiler production: the chickens were raised indoors in individual cages. This eliminated wasteful competition among birds for feed, greatly reduced losses, permitted automated delivery of feed, and lowered labor costs. By 1960, a 3½-pound chicken could be raised in only 8 weeks on 7.5 pounds of feed and at labor cost of only 1.3 worker-hours per 100 pounds. By 1970, labor costs had been cut to less than 5 per cent of their level of 30 years earlier.

As a result of this great increase in supply, prices of broilers, adjusted for changes in the Consumer Price Index, declined from 46 cents per pound in 1934 to 10 cents per pound by 1970. The fall in price, partly assisted by the increased demand arising out of growing population and income, resulted in a 100-fold increase in consumption of commercial broilers. Chicken is no longer a special holiday dish, but has become the cheapest meat in the store; outside the home, chicken sold in franchise outlets has become a rival of the hamburger.

Table 7 emphasizes that the story of commercial broiler chicken is by no means unusual. The continual search for a more profitable operation has sharply reduced production costs in virtually every line of agriculture. It takes only 16 per cent as much labor per acre of corn today as it did 60 years ago, yet output per acre has almost tripled. Twice as much wheat can be raised per acre with one-sixth the labor, and a worker-hour of effort produces twice as many pounds of hogs, four times as much milk, and twenty times as many pounds of turkeys 60 years ago.

TABLE 7
Productivity of Labor and Land in U.S. Agriculture:
Selected Crops and Livestock, 1910–1969

CROP	1910–1914	1925–1929	1935–1939	1945–1949	1955–1959	1965–1969
Corn						
worker-hr per acre	35.2	30.3	28.1	19.2	9.9	6.1
bu per acre	26.0	26.3	26.1	36.1	48.7	71.1
Sorghum grain						
worker-hr per acre	n.a.ᵃ	17.5	13.1	8.8	5.9	4.3
bu per acre	n.a.	16.8	12.8	17.8	29.2	48.9
Wheat						
worker-hr per acre	15.2	10.5	8.8	5.7	3.8	2.9
bu per acre	14.4	14.1	13.2	16.9	22.3	25.9
Potatoes						
worker-hr per acre	76.0	73.1	69.7	68.5	53.1	45.9
cwt per acre	59.8	68.4	70.3	117.8	178.1	205.2
Sugar beets						
worker-hr per acre	128.0	109.0	98.0	85.0	51.0	35.0
tons per acre	10.6	10.9	11.6	13.6	17.4	17.4
Cotton						
worker-hr per acre	116.0	96.0	99.0	83.0	66.0	38.0
lb per acre	201.0	171.0	226.0	273.0	428.0	505.0
Tobacco						
worker-hr per acre	356.0	370.0	416.0	460.0	475.0	498.0
lb per acre	816.0	772.0	886.0	1176.0	1541.0	1991.0
Soybeans						
worker-hr per acre	n.a.	15.9	11.8	8.0	5.2	4.8
bu per acre	n.a.	12.6	18.5	19.6	22.7	24.2
Milk						
worker-hr per cow	146.0	145.0	148.0	129.0	109.0	84.0
lb per cow	3842.0	4437.0	4401.0	4992.0	6307.0	8260.0
Hogs						
worker-hr per cwt	3.6	3.3	3.2	3.0	2.4	1.6
Turkeys						
worker-hr per cwt	31.4	28.5	23.7	13.1	4.4	1.6

ᵃ Not available.
Source: U.S. Department of Agriculture, *Agricultural Statistics*, (Washington, D.C., U.S. Government Printing Office, issues).

Technology and Scale of Operation

Most modern technical innovations have reduced farming costs by replacing labor with mechanization or other capital-intensive methods. In a recent decade, for example, the average real value of farm productive assets per worker increased about $2\frac{1}{3}$ times from its 1964 level of \$26,000 (1958 prices) to reach \$63,000 per worker in 1974. Innovations of this kind reduce variable costs of operation at the expense of higher interest, depreciation, taxes, and other fixed costs. As a result, they generally require greater output than less capital-intensive methods if they are to realize their potential for lower average total cost.

Techniques of broiler production in general use in 1960 reached a minimum average total cost of 16.4 cents a pound at an annual output of 20,000 birds per farm. Technical improvements during the decade permitted cost to fall to 10.1 cents, but only if growers could produce and market an annual output of 95,000 birds each. If the improved methods were used to grow the same number of broilers per farm as in 1960, average total cost would be considerably higher than even the 1960 level. Thus, the same forces that press for innovation and lower cost also bring irresistible pressure for larger-scale output.

When farms get larger, what happens to the total number in operation depends on demand. Falling prices expand total output in keeping with the demand elasticity, and demand itself shifts as population grows and per capita income rises. When demand is sufficiently elastic, or shifts sufficiently rapidly, markets for output may expand enough to maintain or even to increase the number of farms in operation, despite their larger scale. But inelastic demand that shifts only slowly results in a smaller number of farms as size increases. The trend toward a smaller number of larger-scale producers in the broiler industry is evident in Table 8. During the decade 1959–1969, the average output per farm rose nearly fivefold, but total sales only doubled, reducing the number of farms by 60 per cent.

Growth in the average size of farms has been continuous throughout the agricultural history of the United States. Some idea of the development can be had from the trend in number and average acreage of farms shown in Table 9. Improvements in agriculture came slowly during the first 40 years of the period shown, and average farms were only 11 per cent larger in 1920 than they had been in 1880. Moreover, growth in demand had greatly exceeded the rate of growth in farm productivity, and there were more farms in 1920 than there had

---

TABLE 8
Number, Size, and Output of U.S. Broiler Producers

YEAR	NUMBER OF FARMS	AVERAGE OUTPUT PER FARM (NUMBER OF CHICKENS)	TOTAL PRODUCTION (MILLIONS)
1959	65,314	18,985	1,240
1964	41,778	45,193	1,888
1969	25,466	94,319	2,402

Source: U.S. Department of Commerce, *Census of Agriculture* (Washington, D.C.: U.S. Government Printing Office, appropriate issues).

TABLE 9
Number and Size of U.S. Farms, 1880–1970

YEAR	NUMBER OF FARMS	AVERAGE ACREAGE PER FARM
1880	4,008,000	133.7
1900	5,740,000	146.6
1920	6,453,000	148.5
1940	6,104,000	174.5
1960	5,388,000	215.5
1970	2,730,000	389.5

Source: U.S. Department of Commerce, Census of Agriculture (Washington D.C.: U.S. Government Printing Office, appropriate issues).

been 40 years earlier. The high point in number of farms occurred in 1920, however. In more recent decades, the tempo of technical improvement has greatly accelerated, while the rate of population growth has slowed, leading to a rapid rise in average farm size accompanied by rapidly falling numbers. In the decade 1960–1970, the average size of farms in the United States increased by 80 per cent, while total number was cut in half.

Technology and the Displacement of Farm Labor

The logic that applies to size and number of farms applies with equal force to labor cost and the number of workers engaged in agriculture. When new technology raises output per worker, whether more or fewer workers are required depends on demand. Again, unless the demand is highly elastic or expanding rapidly, rising labor productivity means fewer workers needed on farms.

The reduction of labor cost per hundred pounds of broiler chicken from 8.5 hours in 1940 to 0.4-hour in 1970 was accompanied by an expansion of sales from 414 million pounds to 10,821 million pounds. As a simple calculation shows, the expanded demand more than compensated for rising productivity, and nearly 25 per cent more worker-hours were engaged in the production of broilers in 1970 than in 1940. Yet, this was not the whole story, for the expansion of output of the broiler chicken came partly at the expense of other foods.

The overall effect of an innovation on farm employment depends on how it affects the entire pattern of production. An interesting illustration is what happened to labor engaged in growing corn and soybeans. The history of the last 40 years or so is shown in Table 10. During the period, the average labor cost per acre of soybeans declined to roughly 25 per cent of earlier levels. But, at the same time, a rapidly expanding industrial demand for soybeans for plastics and other uses increased the demand so rapidly that the total worker-hours engaged in soybean production rose steadily. Where did this extra labor come from?

TABLE 10
Labor in Production of Corn and Soybeans

YEAR	PRODUCTION (MILLIONS OF BU)		ACREAGE PLANTED (MILLIONS OF ACRES)		WORKER-HOURS PER ACRE		WORKER-HOURS EMPLOYED (MILLIONS OF HR)	
	SOYBEANS	CORN	SOYBEANS	CORN	SOYBEANS	CORN	SOYBEANS	CORN
1930	14	1753	1.1	85.5	15.9	30.3	17.5	2590
1940	78	2208	4.8	76.4	11.8	28.1	56.6	2147
1950	300	2766	13.8	72.4	8.0	19.2	110.0	1390
1960	562	3151	23.7	57.6	5.2	9.9	123.0	570
1973	1592	5649	57.3	61.8	4.6	5.3	264.0	328

Source: U.S. Department of Agriculture, *Agricultural Statistics* (Washington, D.C.: U.S. Government Printing Office, appropriate issues).

Soybeans are an especially important alternative crop for farms that would otherwise grow corn and, as can be seen in the table, the rapid expansion of acreage on which to grow soybeans came largely from transferring acreage that had previously grown corn. The slower-growing expansion of corn demand, combined with rapidly rising corn yields and rapidly falling labor costs, reduced the corn acreage to 72 per cent of earlier levels and reduced the number of worker-hours engaged in corn growing to 12 per cent of its level of 40 years ago. Despite the expanded output of both corn and soybeans, then, total labor requirements for the two crops were slashed by 80 per cent.

A similar picture emerges when agriculture is considered as a whole. Technical improvements may alter the pattern of production and may shift workers from one product to another, but the over-all effect of rising labor productivity on the farm has been reduced need for agricultural workers and the steady migration of people off the farm. In terms of our earler analysis, the demand for basic farm commodities as a whole has such a low price and income elasticity that any expansion of total consumption must derive primarily from population growth rather than lower prices. Under these circumstances, when the growth of farm productivity outstrips the growth of population, proportionately fewer workers are needed on farms to supply the consumption needs of the rest.

The force of this fact is best demonstrated by expressing the number of farm workers by a simple equation:

$$dN = rW$$

where d is the per capita consumption of farm products, N the total population to be fed, r the output per worker on the farm, and W the number of farm workers. The equation merely says that when farm workers produce, on the average, a quantity of output, r, it takes W workers to feed the population a quantity d each.

By slight manipulation, the equation can be rewritten:

$$\frac{d}{r} = \frac{W}{N}$$

showing that W/N, the fraction of the population engaged in agriculture, de-. pends on the per capita consumption, d, and the agricultural productivity, r But because the per capita consumption of farm products is little affected by technical change, d is approximately constant. It follows that the fraction of the population on farms must move inversely in proportion to r, productivity of farm labor.

This has been almost exactly the experience in the United States. For example, in 1940, when the output per hour of farm labor was represented by an index of 38 (on a basis of $1957 = 100$), 23.1 per cent of the population still lived on farms. By 1970 the output per hour of farm labor had risen to 192, five times the level of 30 years earlier,whereas the per cent of the population in the United States on farms had fallen to 4.8, almost exactly one fifth of the previous percentage.

It is, of course, the market that keeps the farm labor equation in balance. Given an inelastic demand for products, rising output per worker-hour reduces the demand for farm workers. Earnings for farm workers decline relative to those in other industries and people on farms who have skills that can be usefully applied elsewhere leave for more promising opportunities in other industries. Those without alternative employment for their skills find themselves trapped in low-paying agricultural occupations or are forced off the farm into the city where, without marketable skills, they are added to the welfare roles.

The fate of farm labor is an excellent illustration of two important aspects of the operation of competitive markets. Competition generates inexorable pressure to extract greater output from available resources and passes the gains of this greater productivity onto the consumer in the form of lower prices and higher standards of living. But, in so doing, the market operates without regard to the fate or feelings of the people involved. The supply and demand for farm labor are rigorously balanced by the competitive market, regardless of what happens to farm families caught in the adjustment.

IV. EVALUATION OF AGRICULTURAL PERFORMANCE

Left to itself, agriculture is a highly competitive industry. As such, its performance is, in many respects, almost ideal. Indeed, it is difficult to imagine a system better adapted to carry out the purely technical functions of production and allocation of products.

1. Although harvest is subject to the vagaries of random events, available supplies are rationed among competing uses in accordance with consumer priorities as expressed by demand elasticities.

2. At each stage of production, the most is extracted from available resources. In the very short run, when most costs have been already sunk into crops, relatively little can be done to adapt to consumer desires; however, given time, the investment in production closely follows up demand with matching shifts in output.

3. In addition, the industry has demonstrated a remarkable history of rapidly increasing the productivity of the resources it employs and of passing this increase onto consumers in terms of lower relative prices and increased standards of living; at the same time land, labor, and other resources have been released for the production of other products.

4. All of this has been accomplished with virtually no conscious collective planning, administrative direction, or political processes. Competitive pressure toward improvement is inexorable. It is unnecessary to debate new methods, they simply impose themselves. However, the same competitive process, when viewed in terms of the fate of many of the people who had devoted their lives to it, appears as a mindless juggernaut, for the market takes no account of the human costs of displaced people. When productivity grows more rapidly than the demand for farm products, people are driven off the farm to fend for themselves in the city as they can.

V. GOVERNMENT POLICY TOWARD AGRICULTURE

Price Supports

The severe dislocation wrought in agriculture by untrammeled technical innovation proceeding in the face of slowly increasing demand generated overwhelming pressure for governmental intervention. This intervention has largely been directed toward efforts to hold up farm prices. Price-support programs were initiated during the New Deal of the early 1930s and, although repeatedly modified as to detail, have maintained much the same general character.

Parity Prices

Any program to support prices must somehow define a target level at which to support them and then devise methods for enforcing the supports. Support levels for farm prices are defined in terms of "parity" prices. These are prices that are calculated for each commodity; they bear the same relationship to the average price of things that farmers buy (the "prices-paid" index) that the price of that same commodity did during some base period.

As originally defined, parity prices were to bear the same ratio to the average prices-paid index that they had during the base period 1910–1914. For example, if the price of cabbage had been $1.10 per hundredweight as an average during 1910–1914 when the index of prices paid by farmers averaged 100, then the parity price of cabbage would be defined for any later year by multiplying the prices-paid index during that year by .011. Many years later, when the prices-paid index reached 350, this calculation would yield a parity price for cabbage of $3.85 per hundredweight. In subsequent legislation, definitions of parity have been altered to refer to more recent base periods, and more complicated formulas are applied in the calculation of parity prices for individual commodities.

Once parity prices are defined, government policy then undertakes to support the prices of a number of key commodities at a specified fraction of their parity price. The fraction at which prices are supported varies from commodity to commodity and from time to time. Regardless of the level of support, however, one difficulty is encountered, for when prices are supported at levels higher than market equilibrium, government must somehow contend with the resulting gap between supply and demand. The problem is illustrated in Figure 6. Because the support price P exceeds the equilibrium price P^*, farmers tend to produce and bring to market a total quantity Q_s that exceeds the amount Q_d that consumers are willing to buy at that price. If market price is to be maintained at P, something must be done about this gap.

Restriction of Supply

There are three alternatives: (1) Government might induce farmers to restrict supply to $S'S'$ so that the desired support price becomes the new market equilibrium. (2) Government might purchase all output that farmers cannot sell at the support price ($Q_s - Q_d$). Or (3) the entire output might be sold on the market at whatever price it would bring (P'), while government makes up the difference between P' and P by a subsidy paid directly to growers.

Historically, government price-support programs have involved a mixture of the three techniques. Supply has been restricted, usually by paying farmers to "set aside" part of their acreage, or to divert part of their acreage into "soil-conserving" crops, or to place acreage in a "soil bank." In the early years of price supports, acreage diversion was the most important weapon of government policy. At its peak in 1966, a total of 63.3 million acres were diverted from cultivation. This amounted to nearly 6 per cent of all farm land in the United States and entitled farmers to more than $1 billion in government payments. More recently, however, outright payments to farmers for acreage diverted have been replaced increasingly by the use of acreage limitation as a criterion for receipt of other price-support payments.

The Commodity Credit Corporation

Any surpluses that remain after supply has been reduced have generally been dealth with by crop loans issued to farmers by the Commodity Credit Corporation (CCC). The CCC is a government agency that, under the direction of the Secretary of Agriculture, each year designates a loan rate on each commodity to be supported. The loan rate is the amount per unit that the CCC stands ready to lend to farmers in good standing with the price-control program who want

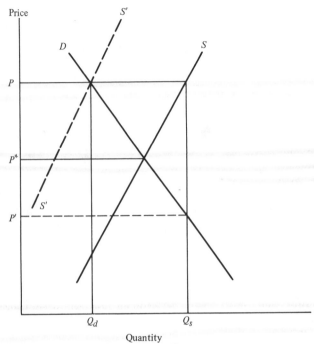

FIGURE 6
Problems of price supports.

to borrow on their crops. For example, when the loan rate for corn is $1.25, farmers are entitled to borrow $1.25 for each bushel of corn they grow, regardless of its actual market value. Now, if too much corn is grown and the market price begins to sink below the $1.25 loan rate, the farmers are privileged to default on their loans, letting the CCC take the corn. On the other hand, if the market price should rise above the $1.25 support price, the farmer can reclaim his crop, repay the loan, and sell the corn at the higher market price. Although the CCC is set up as a lending organization, its principal function is to provide a roundabout way for farmers to sell to the government any output that cannot be sold on the market at the price defined by the loan rate.

The Commodity Credit Corporation must, by law, extend loans on six "basic" commodities: corn, cotton, peanuts, rice, tobacco, and wheat and on a group of designated "nonbasic" commodities that includes, among other things, butter, honey, tung oil, rye, and wool. In addition, from time to time, as directed by the Secretary of Agriculture, the CCC extends price-support loans on an extensive and diverse list of crops ranging from staples such as dry peas, soybeans, and potatoes to such things as almonds, cotton seed, and olive oil.

The volume of crops acquired depends on loan rates in relation to production and demand levels. Huge bumper crops harvested in the face of recession-level demand can leave large, unsold surpluses in government hands. During the recession of 1958–1959, the CCC spent nearly $2 billion to acquire unsold commodities, including more than 25 per cent of the wheat crop for that year. From 1959–1963, the CCC owned an entire year's production of wheat. The growth of world population during the ensuing decade, however, sharply expanded demand, and CCC holdings have been reduced to almost nothing as a world food crisis develops.

Agricultural Subsidies

The third method of price support involves direct subsidy payments to growers of corn, wheat, cotton, sugar, wool, and a number of other commodities to make up the difference between market price and support level. In their current versions, most price-support programs integrate direct subsidies with acreage limitation and CCC loans in a rather complicated package. In general, farmers who agree to limit their acreage are offered price-support subsidies designed to bring the prices they will receive for only a designated portion of their output up to the full support level. Beyond this specified portion, production is subject to support at CCC loan rates set below the full support level. For example, in recent years, the support price of corn has been $1.35 per bushel, while the CCC loan rate has been $1.05. This has meant that farmers participating in the corn-production program were guaranteed a price of $1.35 on a specified number of bushels, whereas the remainder of their crop was supported by the CCC loan rate at a minimum price of $1.05. Similar programs have been in force for wheat, cotton, barley, and grain sorghum.

The total amount spent in recent years by the U.S. government for these acreage-diversion and farm price-support programs are shown in Table 11. As can be seen, the cost has regularly exceeded $3 billion a year. It should be noted,

TABLE 11

Government Payments to Farmers Under Price-support
Programs (in millions of dollars)

YEAR	ACREAGE DIVERSION	PRICE SUPPORT	TOTAL, ALL PROGRAMS
1968	885.2	1424.1	3055.3
1969	1014.6	1667.4	3466.3
1970	858.3	1783.2	3450.0
1971	—	2076.6	2962.3
1972	132.2	2830.5	3689.2
1973	103.1	1964.6	2442.9

Source: U.S. Department of Agriculture, Agriculture Statistics, 1974 (Washington, D.C.: U.S. Government Printing Office, 1974).

however, that the food shortage engendered by the growing world population has been exerting pressure on the demand for farm products. The resulting increase in prices reduced the cost of agricultural subsidies in the United States to less than $2.5 billion in 1973.

Not all price supports are enforced in the same manner, however. In some special cases, price supports are maintained indirectly. For example, the government sets the price that dairies must pay farmers for fluid milk destined for human consumption. Because of the elasticity of demand for fluid milk, of course, the higher this price is raised, the less milk dairies can buy, and milk that farmers cannot sell at this price is marketed as "manufacturing-grade" milk at whatever the market will bring. The price of manufacturing-grade milk is supported, however, through CCC loans on such manufactured dairy products as dry milk, butter, and cheese.

Finally, because price supports of any kind make it difficult for farm products in the United States to compete in foreign markets, the government pays special export subsidies on commodities shipped abroad. In 1973, payments under the export program included, among others, subsidies of 34 cents per bushel for exported wheat, $1.75 per hundredweight of rice, 13 cents per pound of chicken, and 14 cents per pound of butter. All told, the U.S. government spent $405 million to subsidize exports of farm products during the year.

Who Benefits from Price Supports?

Because the clear result of agricultural price-support programs has been higher prices to consumers and higher taxes to taxpayers, one might well ask who benefits. Presumably, the rationale for farm policy has been to relieve some of the suffering that resulted from rapidly rising agricultural productivity. Yet, oddly enough, practically nothing about government farm policy has benefited the people who need it the most. The history of agriculture has been a continuous story of small farmers driven out and people pushed off the farm, whereas price-support programs help only those that continue on the farm. If those who leave the farm are unable to fend for themselves, their only recourse is grudgingly given welfare.

But even among farmers who remain on the farm, most are almost completely by-passed by the benefits from farm programs. In fact, the very nature of price supports tends to concentrate the benefits among the largest, most powerful growers, rather than among the poor and weak who really need help.

In 1973, for example, the poorest 33 per cent of all farmers received only 2.5 per cent of total government payments, and nobody in this large group received more than $200 during the year. Indeed, none among the poorest 75 per cent of farms received as much as $1000 per year in payments; in total, payments to this smallest 75 per cent accounted for less than 20 per cent of all payments made that year. In contrast to the modest help provided small farms, the aid to large farms was lavish, indeed. The largest 1.5 per cent of all farms received 28 per cent of all price-support payments, giving them a whopping average of $10,000 each. The 86 largest farms among these received payments of $100,000 or more, and the very largest payment to any one farm in 1973 exceeded $1,500,000!

This highly unequal distribution of benefits is, of course, a direct consequence of programs that pay for acreage diverted, buy up surpluses, and subsidize production. When farmers are paid to divert acreage, the farms with the largest acreage receive the largest payments. When price-support subsidies are paid, those with the largest output receive the most support. In short, all price-support benefits are inevitably distributed in direct proportion to the size of the operation, which, in the very nature of things, is inversely in proportion to human need. Moreover, this is only part of the picture. For gains to farmers extend beyond what they receive directly from the government. When acreage is restricted, farmers not only receive payments for that reason, but the products that they grow on their remaining acreage sell at higher prices, providing a second benefit, but nobody knows how large this part of the benefit from government program is. It has been estimated at many times the value of the direct payments, but—whatever it is—it is distributed in proportion to the size of the operation and is concentrated in the hands of the largest producers.

Rapidly rising agricultural productivity has generated a serious problem of human displacement and has been associated with serious human suffering. Public policy toward agriculture, however, has done practically nothing about this problem. It has, instead, subsidized the largest farms.

The Declining Importance of Restrictive Policy

Regardless of their effects, however, government price supports are clearly diminishing in importance. A fast-growing world population is increasingly turned to the farms of North America as a source of desperately needed food, and, for the first time in more than half a century, the demand for agricultural products is expanding faster than supply. The resulting upward pressure on farm prices is rapidly making restrictive agricultural policy a matter of history.

SUGGESTED READINGS

Heady, Earl O. *A Primer on Food, Agriculture, and Public Policy* (New York: Random House, Inc., 1967).

Roy, Ewell P., Floyd L. Cortz, and Gene D. Sullivan. *Economics:Applications to Agriculture and Agribusiness* (Danville, Ill.: The Interstate Publishers, 1971).

Ruttan, Vernon W., Arley D. Waldo, and James P. Houck, eds. *Agricultural Policy in an Affluent Society* (New York: W. W. Norton & Company, Inc., 1969).

Schultz, Theodore W. *Transforming Traditional Agriculture* (New Haven, Conn.: Yale University Press, 1964).

CHAPTER 2

the food distribution industry

JOEL B. DIRLAM

I. INTRODUCTION

Food distribution is the most basic of the service industries. Not only is food a necessity, but food expenditures constitute the largest segment of consumption in the United States. As shown in Table 1, about 18 per cent of consumption expenditures are for food, and food store sales—which amounted to $105 billion in 1973—exceed those of any group of other retailers, including auto-

TABLE 1

Food Expenditure, 1950–1973

YEAR	TOTAL ($ BILLIONS)	PER CAPITA ($)	DISPOSABLE PERSONAL INCOME (PER CENT)	PERSONAL CONSUMPTION EXPENDITURE (PER CENT)
1950	46.0	301	22.1	24.1
1955	58.1	350	21.1	22.9
1960	70.1	389	20.0	21.6
1965	85.8	442	18.1	19.8
1968	99.7	501	16.9	18.6
1969	104.1	518	16.4	18.0
1970	112.1	549	16.2	18.2
1971	117.5	570	15.8	17.2
1972	125.0	600	15.1	17.2
1973	143.0	681	15.9	17.8

Source: *Statistical Abstract of the United States*, 1974 (Washington, D.C.: U.S. Government Printing Office, 1974). Marketing and Transportation Situation (Aug. 1974).

motive.[1] The retail food trade in 1973 employed the equivalent of 1,887,000 persons.[2] To these may be added another 550,000 employed in grocery wholesaling.[3] When food prices rise sharply, as they did in 1973 and 1974, housewives organize boycotts and congressional committees call chain store executives to Washington to justify their prices. At the Department of Agriculture, there is a constant watch on the size of the spread between the farmer and the consumer. When the farmer's share of the retail dollar declines, he protests—sometimes in dramatic fashion, by destroying animals. Conflicts for survival between chains and independents, and between wholesalers and chains, have helped to shape legislation affecting much of U.S. industry.

The food distribution industry in the United States exhibits three salient characteristics that have emerged over a period of more than a century. More than half of food sales are made by chains;[4] retail stores typically consist of five or more major departments (dry groceries, produce, meat, dairy products, and frozen foods); and self-service is almost ubiquitous.

The chain era got its start in 1859, when the Great American Tea Company decided to sell directly to the public instead of wholesaling; a few years later a line of groceries was added to tea. The name was changed to The Great Atlantic and Pacific Tea Company in 1869, and in 1912 cash and carry was introduced. Other chains whose names are household words were founded later than A&P: Grand Union dates from 1872; Kroger was organized in 1882; and Safeway was started in 1915, although it was not incorporated until 1926. For many years the chains sold only dry groceries, and if the stores carried meats and produce it was on a concession basis.

Clarence Saunders introduced self-service in Memphis, Tennessee, in 1912. In his Piggly-Wiggly grocery stores the customers selected their merchandise and carried it to a check-out counter where they paid cash. Despite achieving a spectacular dollar volume in some units and an unprecedentedly low expense rate, neither Piggly-Wiggly nor its early imitators were financially successful. The self-service feature was largely ignored by the national chains, which concentrated on acquiring and building small, clerk-operated stores.[5]

It was in Southern California that the term *supermarket* seems to have been used first to designate a large-volume food store, predominantly self-service, having at least four departments—grocery, produce, meat, and dairy. The actual marketing innovation, a unit designed to reach a large-volume target, was apparently conceived by Michael Cullen, a Kroger branch manager, in 1930. He proposed to build a 6400-square-foot food store, with ample parking space, to achieve a weekly volume of $12,500.

[1] *Statistical Abstract of the United States, 1974* (Washington, D.C.: U.S. Government Printing Office, 1974), p. 755.

[2] Ibid., p. 349.

[3] Estimated from ibid., p. 768.

[4] Defined by the U.S. Bureau of the Census as firms operating more than 10 stores. Until 1951, a chain was defined as a firm operating 4 or more stores.

[5] R. J. Martin, *The Supermarket: An Analysis of Growth, Development, and Change* (Pullman: Washington State University Press, 1963).

Compared with the supermarkets of 1975, where a selling area of less than 16,000 square feet is rare, Cullen's proposal does not appear revolutionary; but the average chain store at the time had weekly sales of only $500 to $800 and an area of 500 to 600 square feet. When Kroger turned him down, Cullen opened his first store in Jamaica, Long Island. "King Kullen the Price Wrecker" lowered gross margins to 12 to 13 per cent, compared with the chains' prevailing 18 to 19 per cent, and realized higher net profits.[6] Made particularly price-conscious by the Depression, customers flocked to Cullen and his imitators, who, using names like Big Bear, Giant Tiger, and Big Chief, occupied abandoned warehouses or garages. The merchandise was often displayed on rough pine tables or on the floor. The national food chains eventually were forced to follow suit, but as late as 1936, A&P had built only 20 supermarkets. The supermarket now symbolizes the United States' high consumption economy, and, in 1973, supermarkets accounted for more than 85 per cent of food store sales.[7] With 43 stores, the King Kullen chain operates profitably in Long Island and grossed $130 million in 1973.

Of the new supermarkets planned for 1974 by firms reporting to the Super Market Institute, 93 per cent were designed for yearly sales of more than $1.5 million, and 4 per cent for more than $5 million in annual sales volume.[8] In Chicago, Jewel is experimenting with a 66,000-square-foot hypermarket, in imitation of the European giants, called the Grand Bazaar, which, it is hoped, will have annual food sales of more than $25 million.[9]

A variant of the supermarket challenge to conventional marketing made its appearance in the early 1960s, when some food retailers attempted to attract customers by trading on the selling appeal of "discount houses" in apparel and appliances. The discount house had undercut department stores by using supermarket techniques; the food discount store attempted to convince shoppers that prices there were lower because trading stamps had been eliminated, the hours of operation were cut, and only a basic line of products was carried. Whether, in fact, after allowing for the cost reduction resulting from the elimination of stamps most food discounters actually sold at lower prices than non-discounting supermarkets is not clear. The industry has never been able to define a discount food store so as to differentiate it significantly from a large-volume supermarket. When A&P adopted "discounting" as a policy in 1972 and its stores carried the WEO (Where Economy Originates) banner, there seems to have been no associated cost reduction other than the elimination of trading stamps. By 1975, when many chains were constructing extremely large mer-

---

[6] F. J. Charvat, *Supermarketing* (New York: Macmillan, 1961), pp. 18–25.

[7] As defined by *The Progressive Grocer* and *Supermarket News*, a supermarket has annual sales of $500,000 or more. The Super Market Institute uses the term to denote departmentalized food stores with $1 million or more annual sales: *Detailed Tabulations: The Super Market Industry Speaks* (Chicago: 1974), p. iii. *Chain Store Age Super Markets* (July 1972), p. 70, has raised the minimum cutoff point to $1 million annual sales for purposes of analysis of product sales and margins.

[8] *The Super Market Industry Speaks*, op. cit., Table 35.

[9] Jewel Companies, Inc., *1973 Annual Report*, pp. 12–13.

chandise-food-store combinations, the term *discount food store* lost any precise significance it may once have had.

Independents—one-store proprietorships and small chains—have managed to survive by expanding their size and volume sufficiently to be classified as supermarkets and by affiliating with independent or cooperative wholesalers. In the 1930s, the more far-sighted wholesalers established national buying groups such as the Independent Grocers Association (IGA) and did their best to duplicate chain store purchasing methods and warehouse efficiency. Some cooperative wholesalers, such as the Certified Grocers of California, have been so well managed that they have achieved lower costs than chains.

Truly independent food retailers were responsible for only 9 per cent of grocery store sales in 1973.[10] The majority of single-store proprietorships, however, are affiliated, in one way or another, either with private wholesalers (such as S. M. Flickinger of Buffalo or Super Valu of Minnesota) or have organized their own cooperative wholesaler. "Voluntary chain" wholesalers often integrate forward by acquiring some of their customers, and yet they continue to provide wholesale service to affiliated independents. Malone and Hyde, for instance, a Memphis wholesaler, not only services 1800 independents but owns a 60,000-square-foot superstore with the not very original name of Giant Foods.[11] In the struggle for survival, the distinction between corporate chains and voluntary groups have become blurred. The promotional, buying, and private label services of the voluntary and private wholesalers closely parallel the functions of chain district managers and warehouses.

Chains, small and large, corporate and voluntary—but, nevertheless, chains —face the huge majority of consumers going about their weekly food shopping and provide the outlets on which the farmers and grocery manufacturers depend.

As the supermarkets have grown in size, and the small independents have been overtaken by oblivion, "convenience" chains have sprung up to provide strategic food items at locations close to the consumer. The small number of items stocked—typically no more than 2000—permits speedy shopping for necessities. The number of convenience stores rose from 500 in 1957 to 20,300 in 1973, and they now account for about 4 per cent of food store sales. Although their margins are higher than those of the supermarkets, they are open for business long hours and, usually, seven days a week. Their low average annual volume of $215,000 per store, a store area of 2500 square feet or less, and an average customer purchase of $1.00 or less clearly set the convenience stores apart from the bulk of food retailers.[12]

Independents and chains alike have increasingly diversified and added to the products offered for sale. In 1972, the typical supermarket carried as many as

---

[10] *Progressive Grocer, 41st Annual Report of the Grocery Industry*, Apr. 1974, p. 71.

[11] *Chain Store Age Super Markets*, July 1973, p. 58; *Progressive Grocer*, "What It Takes to Operate the Big New Store," May 1973. (Hereafter cited as *Progressive Grocer*, May 1973.)

[12] *Chain Store Age Super Markets*, July 1973, p. 60; *Progressive Grocer, 41st Annual Report of the Grocery Industry*, op. cit., p. 135; annual reports of Jewel, Grand Union, and Southland.

1000 nonfood items, including housewares, health and beauty aids, and general merchandise, bringing in about 12 per cent of its revenue.[13] The larger the selling area, the more important the nonfood items, until one reaches the level of the vast 140,000-square-foot stores where food constitutes only one of several departments.[14] Not only have some chains combined general merchandise operations (including apparel and appliances) under the same roof with food stores, but, through subsidiaries, they have entered the discount department store business. Stop and Shop's Bradlees chain and Lucky's Memco outlets are examples. Jewel Companies (originally Jewel Tea) began with home service routes, and after establishing a food store chain expanded further by acquiring a drug chain (Osco), Turn-Style self-service discount department stores, coffee and ice cream shops, and franchised convenience stores. On the other hand, after experimenting for several years with Grand Way general merchandising stores, Grand Union concentrated once more, under a new chief executive, on food retailing.[15]

Large combination food and stores are not the sole province of the corporate chains. Even small proprietorships have established superstores.

II. MARKET STRUCTURE

The analysis of market structure in food distribution will center on the full-line grocery store and its suppliers. Specialty stores selling meat, fish, produce, or dairy products provide fringe competition, to be sure, but their market share has declined to the point where their influence can be disregarded. In 1973, 93 per cent of food store sales were made by grocery stores.[16] The number of grocery stores has, however, steadily declined from a peak of about 410,000 in 1946 to an estimated 200,000 in 1972.[17]

Dominance of the Chains

Using the Bureau of the Census definition of a chain as a firm with 11 or more stores, 41,000, or approximately one fifth of all grocery stores, were owned by about 450 chains in 1973.[18] Their share of grocery store sales was close to 55 per cent, compared with about 46 per cent in 1963. If one adds the sales of multi-unit firms with 2 to 10 stores, approximately 72 per cent of grocery store sales are accounted for.[19]

Although a useful distinction among corporate chains would turn on the

[13] *Progressive Grocer*, May 1973.
[14] *Chain Store Age Super Markets*, Nov. 1974, p. 21.
[15] *Chain Store Age Super Markets*, Dec. 1974, p. 13.
[16] *Statistical Abstract of the United States, 1974*, op. cit.
[17] *Progressive Grocer*, Apr. 1974, p. 74.
[18] *Chain Store Age Super Markets*, July 1973, p. 57; *Progressive Grocer*, Apr. 1974, p. 74.
[19] Data published by *Supermarket News* in its *Distribution Study* (New York: Fairchild, 1974), p. 164, show the chains' share rising from 47.0 per cent in 1963 to 57 per cent in 1973.

extent of their dependence on middlemen as against their own manufacture or purchases directly from growers or other ultimate sources of supply, comprehensive information on vertical integration is not available. On the basis of a 1973 trade journal survey, it appears likely that the 85 chains with 36 or more stores and $100 million or more annual sales volume purchase relatively little from independent wholesalers. About 95 per cent of the corporate chain grocery chain volume was concentrated in these 85 largest chains.[20]

Not only has the share of grocery store volume generated by chains risen, but there has been an increase, also, in the share of the largest 15 chains. These chains accounted for about 36 per cent of all grocery sales in 1973 as against 27 per cent in 1967. Although the increasing proportion of all chain store sales is probably attributable to the growth of small multiestablishment firms, which add stores by acquisition or construction, the increased concentration among the top 15 has resulted from a more rapid growth by firms other than the top 4 chains. The largest 4 expanded their sales at no more than the average industry rate during these six years.[21] The fastest growing chains included Lucky, which moved from eleventh to fifth place, and Supermarkets General, which was not among the top 15 in 1967. Both these chains have diversified into general merchandise and other lines. Sales and the number of stores of the largest 15 food chains as well as the largest convenience chain, appear in Table 2.

Vertical Integration and Diversification

The large chains find it worthwhile to engage in extensive manufacturing and contracted processing. Safeway and Kroger make, or buy under specifications for private label, products that account for about one quarter of their sales. In terms of value of shipments, bread and bakery products appear to be the most important of the manufacturing activities carried on by chains, followed by milk processing and meat packing. The only comprehensive data available are for 1963, from which Table 3 is drawn. Chains have entered the bakery and dairy lines because both these products, when obtained from independent sources, are burdened with high delivery costs, which are the result of union contracts that require the payment of commissions to drivers. An alternative to entering into milk processing would be to purchase for private label from an independent dairy at a price reduction. But this concession can be challenged as a violation of the Robinson-Patman Act.

The fear of a meat shortage following World War II led many chains to establish their own packing plants, most of which had been sold to local producer cooperatives by 1963, when only 4 chains engaged in meat packing. The price control program of 1973 and the squeeze on margins forced Food Fair and National Tea to close their plants and forced some chains to integrate backward by purchasing live cattle for custom slaughter.

[20] Estimates based on *CSA*, July 1973, pp. 48–49, 57; and on the *Supermarket News Distribution Study*.

[21] See Table 2 and J. B. Dirlam, "*The Food Distribution Industry*," in *The Structure of American Industry*, 4th ed., W. Adams, ed. (New York: Macmillan, 1971) p. 33, Table 2.

TABLE 2

Sales, Number of Stores, and Sales per Store of the 16 Largest Food Chains, 1973

	SALES ($ MILLIONS)	SHARE OF GROCERY STORE SALES (PER CENT)	FOOD STORES OPERATED	CHAIN STORES (PER CENT)	SALES PER FOOD STORE ($ MILLIONS)
1. Safeway	6,774[a]	6.8	1,971	5.8	2.8
2. A&P	6,648	6.7	3,767	9.1	1.8
3. Kroger	4,205	4.2	1,285	3.1	3.3
4. American Stores	2,320[b]	2.3	791	2.0	2.6[k]
5. Lucky	2,290[c]	2.3	362	1.0	4.5
6. Jewel	2,220[d]	2.2	565[i]	1.4	2.2[i]
7. Winn-Dixie	2,110[e]	2.1	970	2.4	2.6
8. Food Fair	2,092	2.1	481	1.2	4.3
9. Grand Union	1,494[f]	1.5	531[j]	1.3	2.6[j]
10. Supermarkets Gen.	1,337	1.4	102	0.3	4.0[k]
11. National Tea	1,295	1.3	725	1.8	2.0
12. Stop & Shop	1,083[g]	1.1	155	0.4	5.1
13. Allied Supermarkets	1,036[h]	1.0	271	0.4	3.7
14. Fisher Foods	869	0.8	183	0.4	4.7
15. Albertson	852	0.8	269	0.7	3.2
16. Southland[l]	1,215	1.2	5,045	12.3	0.2
Total 15 chains[m]	36,625	36.6	12,409	31.6	—
Total all U.S. chains	55,000	55.0	40,960	100.0	—
Total grocery stores	100,000	100.0	—	—	—

[a] U.S. sales: $5,554 millions.
[b] Includes drug chain sales.
[c] Food store sales: $1,622 millions.
[d] Food store sales: $1,632 millions.
[e] $2,528 for year ended June 29, 1974.
[f] Includes revenue from general merchandise stores and stamp operations.
[g] Food stores sales: $788 millions.
[h] $1,021 millions for year ended June 30, 1974.
[i] Includes 172 covenience stores.
[j] Includes 31 convenience stores.
[k] Estimated.
[l] Convenience chain.
[m] Southland excluded.

Source: *Progressive Grocer*, Apr. 1974. p. 71; *Statistical Abstract of the United States, 1974* (Washington D.C.: U.S. Government Printing Office, 1974); and annual reports of chains.

According to the Federal Trade Commission (FTC), the average number of products manufactured by the largest 8 chains in 1967 was only slightly higher than the 1954 average of 19. The lower-ranking chains fabricated fewer than 10 five-digit products apiece.[22] Many more items are, of course, processed by

[22] FTC, *Economic Report on the Dairy Industry* (Washington, D.C.: U.S. Government Printing Office, 1973), p. 104.

TABLE 3
Food Products Manufactured by the 40 Largest Chains, 1963

PRODUCT	NUMBER OF CHAINS	VALUE OF SHIPMENTS ($ BILLIONS)
Bread products	31	417
Coffee	21	158
Ice cream	18	90
Milk	14	259
Canned fruit and vegetables	14	105
Meat	4	217

Source: FTC, *Staff Report on the Structure and Competitive Behavior of Food Retailing* (Washington, D.C.: U.S. Government Printing Office, 1966), p. 62.

manufacturers for sale under private label. Almost half the frozen fruit juices and 30 per cent of the canned fruit and vegetables were being sold under private level in 1964.[23] Although they make use of the private label, the voluntary and cooperative chains rarely engage in manufacturing. The economies of establishing milk processing or baking plants are limited because the members, being independent, cannot be required to take delivery. And, it is in reducing delivery cost that vertical integration can achieve the most substantial economies.

Many chains have attempted to diversify their images by establishing a discount food division, composed of larger stores operating on somewhat lower gross margins than the firm's more conventional units. Food Fair has its Pantry Pride; Bruno's, Food World; and Jewel Tea, the Grand Bazaar. Jewel, Grand Union, and Penn Fruit have set up convenience store chains. Ranging farther afield, Kroger, American Stores, Jewel, Grand Union, National Tea, and Albertson's own drugstore chains, and both Kroger and Grand Union are proprietors of trading stamp companies. Food Fair, Jewel, Lucky, Grand Union, Supermarkets General, and Stop & Shop have branched into the general merchandising field by buying or building discount stores. Among the largest 15 chains, only A&P, Safeway, Winn-Dixie, and Fisher's confine their operations solely to food retailing in conventional supermarkets.

A national or regional chain must inevitably be geographically diversified. Safeway, A&P, and Kroger have the broadest coverage, but each has regrouped in recent years. Safeway no longer sells in New York City, A&P has withdrawn from California, and Kroger gave up its Washington, D.C., foothold. Some smaller chains, such as Lucky, Albertson, and Fisher, on the other hand, have recently moved into new areas through building or acquisition.

---

[23] National Commission of Food Marketing, *Technical Study No. 7, Organization and Competition in Food Retailing* (Washington, D.C.: U.S. Government Printing Office, 1966), pp. 134–135. (Henceforth cited *Food Retailing*.)

Buying Power of the Chains

One indication of its buying power is a chain's national market share measured by its percentage of retail sales. According to this standard, the top four chains do not control a substantial part of the business, because a 20 per cent share is unlikely to create a strong oligopoly. This ratio, moreover, should be modified to allow for the fact that the very large chains do not centralize all of their purchasing operations. Concentration on the selling side varies among industries. Meat packing is relatively unconcentrated. In 1970, the four largest packers accounted for only 23 per cent of red meat sales, and the eight largest, 37 per cent. Poultry production is even less concentrated.[24] The adjusted average four-firm concentration ratios for milk markets was 46.9 per cent in 1970.[25] In grocery manufacturing, the chains face their most powerful and concentrated suppliers, particularly of cereals, cookies, crackers, soaps, and detergents. Spending heavily on advertising, and using cents-off deals, premiums, and allowances to retailers, these manufacturers enjoy a strong bargaining position vis-à-vis the food chains.

Purchasing organizations set up by smaller corporate chains on a cooperative basis, or by association with voluntary wholesalers, can muster a not inconsiderable buying power. Member chains of the Topco Associates buying group, for instance, had combined retail sales of $2.3 billion in 1967.[26]

Concentration in Local Markets

The most useful single index of the economic power of a food retailer is his share of a local market. The market area is determined by the distance the shopper is accustomed to travel to make major food purchases. Most supermarkets, about 85 per cent of whose customers arrive by automobile, probably have a tributary market area with a radius of more than 4 miles.[27] In congested urban areas, where lower-income customers do their shopping frequently, and usually on foot, the relevant market area may be no more than a city block, and the typical store is small. That intangible factor, convenience, sets the economic limits to the market areas within which one outlet is a practicable substitute for another.

Quantitative data on market concentration may be misleading, because the basis for calculating percentages, the Standard Metropolitan Statistical Area (SMSA), must, in many cases, undoubtedly far exceed the area within which most shoppers select their food stores. On the other hand, the same chains usually compete throughout a given SMSA.

---

[24] NCFM, *Food from Farmer to Consumer* (Washington, D.C.: U.S. Government Printing Office, 1966), Chaps. 4–9; U.S. Department of Commerce, Bureau of the Census, Annual Survey of Manufacturers, *Value of Shipment Concentration Ratios* (Washington, D.C.: U.S. Government Printing Office, 1972).

[25] A. Manchester, U.S. Department of Agriculture, *Market Structure, Institutions, and Performance in the Fluid Milk Industry*, Jan. 1974, p. 12.

[26] *United States* v. *Topco Associates, Inc.*, U.S. 596 (1972).

[27] *Progressive Grocer*, May 1973.

Grocery store sale-concentration ratios have been calculated for the years 1954, 1958, 1963, and 1967 by the Bureau of the Census. The four-firm ratio is the most important because it is unlikely that many shoppers would choose habitually among more than four supermarkets; unfamiliarity with store layout deters experimentation. In 128, or 59 per cent, of the 218 SMSAs for which market shares were available in 1967, the concentration ratio was 50 per cent or higher. The modal rate in the 12 most populous SMSAs, which together include about one quarter of the population of the United States, was below 50 per cent, perhaps reflecting the correspondingly larger geographical areas. The data for 1973 in Table 4 seem to show an increase from 1967 in concentration for most of these SMSAs. The bases for calculation of the 1973 ratios are not disclosed; they may differ from SMSA to SMSA and may not be wholly comparable with the Census percentages. It would, therefore, be rash to place much weight on the changes shown in Table 4.

In 3 of the 10 largest SMSAs for which 1973 market share information was available, a local or regional retailer was in first place. And, in Atlanta, Cleve-

TABLE 4

Concentration Ratios and Number of Stores of Four Largest Grocery
Firms in 12 Largest SMSAs: 1954, 1967, and 1973

CITIES	1972 POPULATION (MILLIONS)	FOUR-FIRM MARKET SHARE			NUMBER OF STORES 1973
		1954	1967	1973	
New York	10.0	41.1	33.0	28.7	1033
Los Angeles	7.0	29.6	28.5	33.0	292
Chicago	7.1	49.0	53.6	57.9	101
Philadelphia	4.9	52.6	59.8	58.0	463
Detroit	4.5	38.5	49.4	53.2	229
Boston	3.4	56.2	47.4	40.9	116
Washington	3.0	56.0	70.3	79.0	414
San Francisco	3.2	27.1	40.4	46.4	216
Newark	2.1	52.8	42.5	n.a.[a]	125
Dallas	2.5	53.1	41.9	64.3	165
St. Louis	2.4	34.6	39.3	n.a.[a]	171
Pittsburgh	2.4	45.0	45.0	50.6	229
Total	52.4				
Per cent U.S. population, 1972	25.2				

[a] Not available.

Source: 1954 and 1967 data, special tabulations by U.S. Department of Commerce, Bureau of the Census; 1973 data, *Super Market News' Distribution Study of Grocery Store Sales in 287 Cities* (New York: Fairchild Publications, 1974).

land, Houston, Detroit, and Los Angeles, the leading chain was not among the 15 largest national chains.

That increasing concentration of sales in chain stores has been accompanied by new entry can be deduced from information on the numbers of chain stores by size classes and from data collected by *Chain Store Age* on the expansion of specifically identified small chains. As Table 5 shows,[28] the number of chains in the 2 to 3, 4 to 9, and 10 to 25 size classes has grown substantially during the years 1964–1973. From the growth in numbers of small chains, one must conclude that the moderately high, four-firm concentration ratios should be placed against a background of increasing numbers of viable competitors.

As for specific illustrations of expansion, more than 40 new chains, each with 4 or more stores in 1973, had been established in California during the preceding decade; 29 such chains appeared in Texas, and 26 in New York. During the same period, Vescio's in Michigan grew from 9 stores to 43, Bruno's in Alabama from 14 to 42, and Fernandes's in Massachusetts from 13 to 31. These examples have been chosen at random from hundreds of expanding chains.[29]

Not only have some chains expanded and invaded new territory, but others have retreated. Large chains that have reached maturity, like A&P, Safeway and Kroger, and which are prevented by public policy from further expansion through acquisition, have been reducing the number of their stores, through the process of replacement by larger stores of older and unprofitable units. Even small food chains can operate large-volume stores. Alexander's Markets, of Dracut, Massachusetts, averages close to $8 million in annual sales in each of its three outlets—about four times the sales volume of the average A&P supermarket.[30]

Although there is evidence of new entry, of changing rank among the industry leaders, and of expansion by small chains, most local markets must be classified as oligopolies. Not only are market shares of the first four firms typically at or above the 50 per cent level, but according to a survey of the Super Market Institute, managers of newly opened stores regarded no more than three other stores as direct competitors.[31] Interdependence with identifiable, specific competing chains or independents is recognized. Whether this consciousness leads

TABLE 5
Distribution of Chains by Numbers of Stores, 1964 and 1973

	2–3	4–9	10–25	26 AND OVER
1964	2,509	648	201	115
1973	3,102	918	364	217

[28] *Chain Store Age Super Markets*, July 1973, pp. 55–56.
[29] Ibid., pp. 51–53.
[30] Ibid, p. 50.
[31] Super Market Institute, *Facts About New Super Markets Opened in 1967* (Chicago: Super Market Institute, 1967), p. 10.

to collusion, price parellelism, leadership, or other forms of avoidance of the unmitigated rigors of competition will be discussed in Section III.

Mergers

Mergers have played a significant part in forming the prevailing corporate structures of food chains. Acquisition through merger offers the possibility of increasing the asset size of the firm—and, hence, its financial power—without taking the risk of investment in untried locations where new customers have to be attracted from rivals.

At least twice in the last 50 years, chains relied heavily on the merger route to expansion. The merger movement of the 1920s saw the seven largest chains acquire more than 5800 stores by 1930, roughly a fifth of the total they operated at that date. In 1920, the four leading chains accounted for 5.7 per cent of grocery sales; by 1930, their share had risen to 23.1 per cent. Only A&P, among the top chains, was immune to the merger fever; it had merged only 300 of the 15,737 stores it operated in 1930. It continued to rely on internal growth to maintain its position as number one, until Safeway displaced it in 1973.

The second merger movement took place in the years 1949–1964, when the 20 largest chains absorbed 297 firms with total sales of $3.1 billion. Most of the retailers acquired had been growing rapidly prior to being merged, which suggests that the larger firms were looking for aggressive management as much as for new outlets. For the most part, the acquisitions were not of direct competitors.[32]

Economies of Scale: The Store

Mergers may be the proximate cause of a chain's achieving a certain absolute size in terms of volume, or number of stores. But to understand why the acquisitions took place, and, equally important, to explain the relation between the number of competing food outlets and the local markets, it is necessary to examine the evidence relevant to determining the most efficient size of store and of food chain.

According to Alfred Marshall, "an increase of capital and labor leads generally to an improved organization which increases the efficiency of work of capital and labor."[33] As his theory of increasing returns has been refined, careful distinctions are made between those economies that result from increasing the size of the plant and those economies associated with an expanded size of the firm. Reductions in real cost that often can be achieved from the use of a larger and more expensive plant and more equipment should not be confused with advantages derived from the marketing, managerial, and financial power of a large, multiunit organization.

[32] *Food Retailing*, op. cit., pp. 98–103.
[33] Alfred Marshall, *Principles of Economics*, 6th ed. (New York: Macmillan Publishing Co., Inc., 1910), Book 4, pp. xiii and 2; P. S. Florence, *The Economics and Sociology of Industry*, rev. ed. (Baltimore: John Hopkins, 1969), pp. 99–115.

In food distribution it is important to know whether significant economies of scale arise from marketing through larger stores and to arrive at a reasonable estimate of the minimum size of an efficient store. The relation between optimum, or minimum, efficient size and the market will indicate how many stores are necessary to serve a local market. Information helpful in estimating optimum size could be obtained by making a cross-sectional analysis of costs of operation in stores of different sizes, but such data are not often made public. The National Commission on Food Marketing (NCFM), however, was enabled to make just such a survey in 1966, which covered nine chains and 3000 stores. After allowing for other determinants such as wage levels, the commission found that the only variable with an important influence on the efficiency of food stores was utilization (sales per square foot). Although the lowest ratio of store operating expense to sales prevailed in the largest size class (then with 16,000 square feet of selling area), there was little tendency for larger stores to enjoy a higher volume of sales per square foot. Even a change in utilization did not appreciably affect efficiency; a 20 per cent increase in volume for store of a given size resulted in lowering cost by only 1 per cent.[34]

In spite of these findings, the average size of retail food stores has climbed without interruption. By 1973, the average new supermarket was being constructed with an area of 32,000 square feet, up 5 per cent from 1972.[35]

Weekly utilization rates reported by the Super Market Institute members for 1973 were consistently higher with larger volume, rising from $3.20 for stores with $20,000 to $29,000 in weekly sales to $7.07 for stores with $100,000 in weekly sales. These data make no allowance for the age of the store or other factors.[36] And they do not permit us to say which sales volume store class is the most profitable or has the lowest ratio of expenses to sales.

Clearly, there are certain advantages to a large store. It can carry in stock a larger number of items and, hence, appeal to more customers. A trade journal survey showed that the typical supermarket in 1972 offered 6495 items for sale, but the average superstore, with an annual gross of $5 million, stocked 24,522 items.[37] As size increases, the store can offer a variety of services, ranging from barber shops to restaurants, until, in the hypermarkets, the store will simply be a shopping plaza brought under one roof, with one owner. Customers lured into the store to buy flowers or socks may wind up buying food. But it will be difficult to apply to such an establishment the cost analysis employed by the NCFM in 1966.

There are certain offsets to the large-store advantages. Supervision becomes difficult. As departments become larger, they need additional personnel and a distinct and, therefore, more costly marketing policy. The customer may hesitate to enter the store because of the time consumed in finding the food she wants to buy and in selecting one item from many competing brands or sizes.

[34] *Food Retailing*, op. cit., Chap. 7.
[35] *Progressive Grocer*, Apr. 1974, p. 133.
[36] *The Super Market Industry Speaks*, op. cit., Table 25.
[37] *Progressive Grocer*, May 1973.

Operating savings in the large stores come with the opportunity of using fork-lift trucks to stock the shelves, where the basket, pallet, or case is never unpacked, but moves directly from the warehouse to the selling area. Price marking can be done in the warehouse; in the very newest stores it is eliminated by optical scanning. These changes offer possibilities for lowering labor cost per dollar of sales.

Because it is not easy to quantify either the advantages of the disadvantages of large-sized stores, resort must be had to the survivor test. All one can say is that, in the present conditions, and with our current technology, new stores with areas of 30,000 to 40,000 square feet, and annual sales of $3 million and more are the most popular. If an energy shortage drastically raised the cost of gasoline and curbed the use of automobiles, the hypermarket giants might be favored, because then all shopping could be done in one place, in a single visit. On the other hand, in the long run, suburban living may prove to be too expensive, and a return to public transportation and city living may favor the small store.

To the extent that the larger stores expand their volume more rapidly than the rise in household food expenditures, there will be a decline in the number of stores and a tendency for local concentration ratios to rise.

Economies of Scale: The Firm

To the extent that larger firm size permits greater economies, there should be a negative relation between the volume of sales and expenditures on purchasing, marketing, and administration per dollar of revenue. NFMC studies of relative efficiency of chains of different sizes, however, failed to uncover evidence that such a relationship exists. The commission concluded, in 1966, on the basis largely of opinion in the grocery trade, that volume need not be high for a chain to successfully process milk or operate a bakery, but that annual sales of $500 million were needed to manufacture jams, jellies, peanut butter, and mayonnaise.[38] A similar volume was necessary to operate an efficient private label program in canned goods.

According to one view, a chain large enough to set up its own field-buying staff to carry out direct purchasing activities could enjoy significant savings. Quality would be better—particularly of produce—and food brokers or suppliers' salesmen could be by-passed. A&P was alleged to have enjoyed lower costs and better quality because it was large enough to realize the economies of size in purchasing.[39]

Closer examination of the operation of giant chains shows, however, that, once discriminatory concessions obtained by the exertion of bargaining power are eliminated, the supposed purchasing advantages almost disappear. The use of brokers requires the payment of a fee, but, on the other hand, the creation and maintenance of a field-buying staff is far from being without cost. A single

[38] *Food Retailing*, op. cit., p. 152.
[39] M. A. Adelman, "The A&P Case, A Study in Applied Economic Theory," *Quarterly Journal of Economics*, **69**: 249 (May 1949).

independent store can hardly hope to supply itself at minimum cost by dealing directly with produce shippers, manufacturers of groceries, or meat packers, but this handicap can be overcome by purchasing through a voluntary group wholesaler. Small corporate chains can buy carload lots of potatoes or citrus either from shippers or brokers; the giant chain gets no consistent advantage in such purchases. The largest chains must buy a large volume of meat by a grade classification within which there may be wide differences in actual quality, but the small buyer can get his meats uniformly at the top of the scale and often competes successfully in meat prices with the chains.[40]

Newspapers are the most important medium used by food retailers to reach their customers, and newspaper advertising accounts for about 60 per cent of the chains' advertising expenditure. Yet, it is only when the retailer is so small that the local newspaper does not sufficiently confine itself to his market area that he must depend on flyers, handbills, his store windows, or in-store signs to attract customers. Economies of scale in advertising do not play much of a role in encouraging the promotion of large chains.

Without a detailed examination of other costs, including warehousing and delivery, it would be difficult to reach a conclusion about the relation between the size of the chain and efficiency. It is undeniable that, with certain methods of operation, a chain should be able to reduce management costs. The store manager's discretion can be reduced to a minimum, and his most important duties limited to overseeing deliverymen, stock boys, and check-out girls, ordering as items run out, answering customers' questions, and trying to curb stealing by deliverymen, employees, and customers. Decisions on product and brand selection, weekly and seasonal specials, promotions, and pricing can be left to divisional or chain headquarters. If a group of headquarters executives can make decisions for two stores, why not for 100? Of course, in limiting the manager's discretionary powers, the chain loses a certain amount of flexibility. The fact that single-unit or very small chains survive in competition with Safeway and A&P stores demonstrates that the uniformity of the chain's practices from store to store creates opportunities for independents to devise successful competitive strategies.

The advantages to be gained from combining several geographically dispersed divisions into a single chain are not so clear. Safeway's avowed policy is to run its 20 retail divisions as autonomous profit centers, giving full authority to the divisional managers, within the general company rules.[41] As in most such organizations, the central office retains control of investment, and, presumably, the divisional managers do not have the authority to create their own private labels, although each division has its own distribution center or warehouse. Exactly how much is gained by a Safeway division remaining attached to the company, as opposed to operating as an independent chain, one cannot say. One might inquire what benefits Fisher's Los Angeles Shopping Bag chain

[40] J. B. Dirlam and A. E. Kahn, "Integration and Dissolution of the A&P Company," *Indiana Law Journal*, **23** : 1 (Fall 1953).
[41] W. S. Mitchell, president, Safeway Co. (Apr. 23, 1974).

derives from the company's home office in Cleveland, Ohio. Shopping Bag was supplied by Certified Grocers of California, a cooperative wholesaler, in 1972, although a company-owned warehouse was being built in 1974. The function of headquarters appears to be furnishing capital and, if necessary, key management personnel. Separated by a continent from the Philadelphia headquarters, American Stores' Alpha Beta Acme Markets in Los Angeles could act as an almost self-sufficient entity.

If large chains were constantly more profitable than small ones, this could show that size and efficiency are linked. Yet, after an intensive analysis of earnings by size of chain, the National Commission on Food Marketing found that there was little difference between the medium and large-sized chains.[42] Table 6 shows the return on the equity of 16 leading chains. It will be obvious that in

TABLE 6

After-tax Earnings of Leading Food Chains 1971–1973 (in per cent)

| | RETURN ON NET WORTH | | | | | PROFIT MARGIN ON SALES | | |
| | | | | THIRD QUAR-TER 1974 | 1970–1974 | | | |
COMPANY	1971	1972	1973			1971	1972	1973
Safeway	14.7	15.7	13.1	19.6	15.8	1.5	1.5	1.3
A&P	2.2	Def.[a]	2.0	3.2	1.7	0.3	Def.	0.2
Kroger	9.2	5.4	7.6	10.5	9.5	0.9	0.5	0.7
American Stores	6.5	0.5	9.0	12.7	7.9	0.8	0.7	0.1
Lucky	22.6	19.7	18.9	20.2	24.0	1.7	1.5	1.4
Jewel Cos.	12.2	12.5	13.8	10.5	13.0	1.5	1.5	1.6
Winn-Dixie	20.3	19.7	18.9	21.4	22.2	2.1	2.1	2.0
Food-Fair	8.2	Def.	1.6	3.3	4.8	0.6	Def.	0.1
Grand Union	8.6	5.4	1.5	4.4	6.0	1.0	0.6	0.2
Supermarkets General	16.1	6.3	10.9	10.4	12.5	1.0	0.3	0.6
National Tea	6.8	Def.	Def.	Def.	Def.	0.5	Def.	Def.
Stop & Shop	5.6	9.6	12.2	8.2	10.5	0.4	0.6	0.8
Allied Supermarkets	Def.	9.9	1.7	2.5	Def.	Def.	0.1	0.4
Fisher Foods	19.0	16.8	16.8	17.2	22.1	1.4	1.2	1.1
Albertson	15.5	19.5	17.7	22.8	18.6	1.1	1.1	1.1
Southland[b]	12.6	10.5	10.9	n.a.	13.5	1.5	1.6	1.7

[a] Deficit.
[b] Convenience chain.
Source: *Moody's Industrial Manual*: *Fortune's 500 Directory* (various issues); *Forbes*, Jan. 1, 1975, Joint Economic Committee, U.S. Congress.

[42] *Food Retailing*, op. cit., p. 304.

the years 1972 and 1973 there was no tendency for profitability to rise with the size of chain. The most profitable large chains in these two difficult years were Lucky Stores and Winn-Dixie, each with a total sales volume of about a third that of Safeway or A&P.

Independents have often registered higher earnings than large chains. A large-volume, single-store operator bought out in Memphis by National Tea in 1959 earned 5 per cent on sales, compared with 2 per cent for National Tea. In a mid-western city studied in detail by Robert Holdren, local stores customarily reached profit targets twice those of the national chain units.[43]

In order to explain differences among earning rates, one would have to take into account many aspects of company policy, including selection of sites, rate of introduction and size of new stores, sensitivity to customers' needs, incentives to lower-level management, and so on. Profit sharing, for instance, may explain the consistently high earnings of Winn-Dixie. In 1973, Safeway's per store volume averaged more than 80 per cent in excess of that of A&P, which has long been plagued by overaged and inbred management.[44]

Other Barriers to Entry

With the pre-emption of space in shopping centers by existing chains and the increasing size of the new supermarkets, entry by the construction of a single store requires a greater investment, even after allowing for inflation, than it did a decade ago. To finance a 60,000-square-foot superstore in 1973 cost about $900,000 for equipment, inventory, and working capital and $840,000 for the building.[45] Another estimate gave $1,200,000 as the necessary total investment in a 25,000-square-foot store in 1974.[46] These investments mirror the pre-dominance of shopping center locations for new stores. The sums required are large, but not impossible to raise by persons with management experience in the industry.

Financing, access to private labels, membership in buying groups, and selling and promotional expertise can be obtained through adherence to a cooperative or voluntary wholesaler. From the fact that many voluntary wholesalers have absorbed and successfully operated some of their small chain clients in recent years, one can conclude that perhaps the biggest barrier to entry has been capable management. Close behind would come the availability of sites for the new and more profitable superstores.

---

[43] FTC, *National Tea Co.*, Docket no. 7453, Mar. 4, 1966, pp. 11–12; B. Holdren, *The Structure of a Retail Market and the Market Behavior of Retail Units* (Englewood Cliffs, N.J.: Prentice-Hall, 1960), p. 100, footnote 32.

[44] *Supermarket News*, Dec. 16, 1974, p. 1; *Chain Store Age Super Markets*, July 1973, p. 38: "It has been a long-standing inside joke in the industry that what many supermarket operators wanted to insure their own success was an A&P store right down the street."

[45] *Progressive Grocer*, May 1973, quoting J. R. Hyde, III, president, Malone & Hyde.

[46] Mitchell, op. cit.

III. MARKET CONDUCT

Market conduct consists of the tactics by which firms attract customers and respond to each other's competitive behavior. The most important type of conduct, pricing, determines how consumers distribute their purchases among products and retailers and, hence, in the long run, contributes to the success or failure of grocery firms and, ultimately, of their suppliers. Pricing thousands of different items sold by scores or hundreds of stores, often in scattered geographic areas, grocery chain managements can set widely varying margins that vary from item to item and place to place. To be sure, it might seem normal for food retailers in the typical local market to recognize their mutual interdependence and to refrain from the use of vigorous price competition. As everyone knows, however, oligopolistic behavior depends not on an outsider's view of what may be rational behavior, but rather on the goals of the rival firms, their financial position, their estimates of each other's strengths and weaknesses, and other characteristics such as the target rate of growth of the chain. In food retailing, for instance, a leading firm whose market share is threatened may react by unleashing and widely advertising a price-cutting campaign, although it may reap, thereby, only a temporary advantage. Even when the retailers seem to adopt a strategy of mutual forbearance, policing each other's thousands of prices presents a formidable task.

Pricing and the Retailing Service

In order to focus on the essentials of grocery store pricing, it is necessary to separate the retailing service from the product. The price of meat, milk, or mayonnaise folds the invoice cost to the retailer in with a margin for the retailing service. The retailer's pricing strategy can be regarded as relating solely to the margin, which is the price of his service, although it is never quoted separately, and, in some instances, it may be negative.

It may help to understand the nature of the margin if one by imagining a revolution in grocery marketing in which the retail service would be sold separately from the product.[47] The service would consist of the functions of storage, display, quality information, price marking, and in-store amenities. An additional charge might be made for assembling an order and carrying it to the shopper's automobile. In this scheme, the consumer would pay an admission fee for the right to enter the store and to make use of its services. An additional entrance fee could be charged for each department in the store, dependent again on the separable costs of making the items available in such a way that a choice could be effectively made. Prices for the products themselves would cover only invoice costs and costs directly attributable to the items. These direct costs might include the in-store wrapping of produce or meat, labor in stocking shelves, and interest on the investment in special equipment.

---

[47] C. S. Bell, "Macroeconomics of Unbalanced Growth: Comment," *American Economic Review*, **58**: 882 (Sept. 1968).

This outline of a mythical, unbundled price structure for food retailing should clarify the nature of the service and the actual pricing characteristics. A large part of the overhead or common store and chain headquarters costs cannot be traced to any single product or group of products. The total store margin must cover all costs, direct and indirect, variable and fixed. The food retailer is a multiproduct firm, a large part of whose costs are fixed, at least in the short or medium term. Professor Holdren concluded that as much as 90 per cent of the costs other than invoice cost "do[es] not vary with output."[48] His estimate probably exaggerates the proportion of fixed costs because many employees are part-time, and most do not have long-term contracts. According to-a more recent study, about 29 per cent of the retail food margin in 1973 consisted of direct labor costs and packaging; total labor cost, including fringe benefits, came to about 50 per cent of the margin. Indirect labor, interest expense, and profits accounted for 40 per cent of the margin; space and equipment costs accounted for 22 per cent; and advertising and promotion accounted for 9 per cent.[49]

Although the allocation principles employed in the study were inevitably arbitrary, it is interesting that the estimates of total cost by department, computed as a percentage of sales, varied from a low of 15.65 per cent for dry groceries to a high of 31.60 per cent for produce. Among different types of meats there was a wide variation in the estimated total cost in-store per pound, accounted for largely by differences in allocated labor cost, which amounted to 15.9 cents for beef compared with 6.9 cents for broilers.

How Retailers Price

In setting margins, the grocery managers must take into account demand characteristics as well as direct and allocated costs. Just as the retail store has a high proportion of common costs that must be allocated by some arbitrary rule, so the demand for retailing service is joint, or composite, as among items.

The demand for a food retailing service may be taken as equivalent to a derived demand for food. According to studies of H. S. Houthakker, the quantity of food purchased for home consumption has not been influenced by price changes, although it has increased with the rise in consumption expenditures in the years 1930–1964.[50] This conclusion does not mean that there may not be high cross elasticities among certain food stores or products. These elasticities depend on the substitutability of one product or location for another. The total level of food expenditure, however, appears to be positively related to incomes, although in a manner that has not been determined precisely. It has customarily

[48] Holdren, op. cit., p. 40.

[49] U.S. Department of Agriculture, *Marketing and Transportation Situation* (Washington, D.C., Nov. 1974), p. 26. The estimates are based on trade sources, including COSMOS, a simulation model for supermarkets using the operating experiences of members of the National Association of Food Chains.

[50] H. S. Houthakker and L. D. Taylor, *Consumer Demand in the United States: Analyses and Projections* (Cambridge, Mass.: Harvard University Press, 1970), p. 62.

been assumed that as incomes rise, a smaller and smaller percentage of the household budget is spent on food—following Adam Smith's observation that the capacity of the human stomach is limited. This conclusion seems to be confirmed by Table 1. On the other hand, the sharp inflation in 1973 and 1974 appears to have changed food buying habits in a significant proportion of even high-income customers, so that the demand for food may be more price elastic than has generally been supposed. In any event, food distributors are assured that the demand for their services will be almost unchanged in spite of an unprecedented combined coincidence of inflation and recession.

Because the demand for retailing service is a derived demand, it is less elastic than the demand for any particular food item—other things, including competitors' prices, being equal. A given percentage change in the margin will result in a much smaller percentage change in the price of the product. Consumers do, of course, substitute one product for another, in an effort to hold down total expenditures. However, among different types of food there is a very low price cross elasticity, as for instance, between beer and butter or between ice cream and potatoes. And, there is less probability of a shift in purchases from one commodity to another merely in response to a change in the margin, or implicit price of the retailing service, which averages no more than 21 per cent.

Another characteristic of consumer demand must be taken into account. Having traveled several miles to shop, once she has entered the supermarket for her weekly food supply, the typical customer is unlikely to shift any of her purchases to another food store. As a result of inflationary pressures, consumers may be more likely to spread their purchases in several stores in order to buy the specials, but the practice is far from widespread. Moreover, the vast majority of shoppers simply do not know the prices of all the items they have bought, or intend to buy, so that it is almost impossible for a shopper, once in a store, to make a mental comparison with the prices that might be charged for the same items by a competitor. During the weekly shopping expedition, therefore, the chosen retailer can exercise monopoly power.

Enjoying monopoly power, albeit temporary, the food retailer should find it advantageous to practice price discrimination. Some products will be sold at low, others at high absolute margins. Optimum discrimination would equate marginal cost with marginal revenue for each type of retailing service. Assuming, for example, that the direct in-store costs of both are the same and that the demand for canned olives is less elastic than the demand for corned beef, the price of the retailing service (or margin) associated with olives would, therefore, be higher, if profits are to be maximized.

To a limited extent, margins probably do reflect differences in elasticities, just as they may also include, as a minimum, certain product-related direct costs in the store. Any attempt to associate the level of the margin precisely with demand elasticity would, however, be doomed to failure. In the first place, the elasticity of demand for a particular product is nearly impossible to measure. Moreover, retailers may accept a low margin on an advertised or commonly purchased item in order to bring shoppers into the store on the assumption that customers will then buy a substantial amount of other items with higher margins, thus increasing sales and profits. There may be several combinations of margins that, depending on the number of additional shoppers attracted, will result in the same total store profit.

Table 7, which is based on a 1973 trade journal survey, shows representative percentage margins for major classes of items and for some specific products, such as candy, beer, and sugar. Even if the choice of margins for each item sold may seem to be irrational, or inexplicable, some general patterns emerge. Because consumers purchase them frequently, a few products have prices that are

TABLE 7

Margins, Sales, and Gross Profits Contribution, by Major Products

| | 1972 | | |
PRODUCTS	AVERAGE GROSS PERCENTAGE MARGINS	SUPER- MARKET SALES (PER CENT)	CONTRIBUTION TO GROSS OPERATING PROFIT (PER CENT)
Canned foods	16.5	8.62	7.06
Dry foods	16.5	3.01	2.46
Frozen foods	24.4	4.70	5.67
Dairy products	18.9	10.65	9.94
Soft drinks	19.2	1.89	1.80
Beer	18.8	1.40	1.29
Other beverages	8.7	2.88	1.24
Bakery	23.6	7.84	9.15
Sugar	4.1	0.85	0.17
Other bakery supplies	16.0	2.46	1.96
Desserts, garnishes, jams	19.0	3.62	3.41
Pet products	18.5	1.74	1.59
Candy	27.6	1.36	1.86
Other dry groceries	14.8	1.34	0.98
Tobacco products	8.2	4.51	1.83
Health and beauty aids	26.2	2.99	3.88
Soaps	11.4	2.23	1.26
Housewares	32.5	1.31	2.11
Laundry, general merchandise	20.2	6.20	6.20
Meat	21.2	22.14	23.20
Produce	31.3	6.91	10.69
Other	17.1	1.84	1.56
Average of all items	20.2		
Total		100.00	100.00

Source: Calculated from *Chain Store Age*, July 1973, p. 6.

fairly well known and are featured in weekly ads, in order to build up patronage. The margins on coffee, evaporated milk, detergent powders, and granulated sugar have been low or nonexistent for this reason. On the other hand, margins on delicatessen products and health and beauty aids tend to be high because competing stores specializing in these items have higher margins. Moreover, slight alterations in the average margin can have a substantial effect on profits because the percentage profit margin is so low. Retailers are admonished at conventions and in trade publications to constantly review their prices so as to push up nonfeatured items by 2 or 3 per cent and to use multiple-unit pricing (changing canned pears from 24 cents a can to two for 50 cents, for instance).

Some observers have concluded that the pricing of retail service by food distributors is often irrational. Holdren's study showed that national chains neglected local conditions in setting margins and allowed the managers little or no discretion except in close-outs. This is still the ruling practice. Most retailers literally did not know "how they arrived at their prices." Although they asserted that they attempted to realize a standard margin, including a "satisfactory profit," examination of the actual prices showed that this was not the case.[51] In another survey, Lee Preston could find no hypothesis to account for margin variations. "The individual store manager might be able to 'explain' in any particular instance how a series of historic circumstances has resulted in one 16-ounce can of pickled beets being priced at 19 cents and carrying a 30 per cent markup and another priced at 21 cents carrying a 52 per cent markup. . . . [A]n objective anslysis is tempted to conclude that this array of prices . . . reflect[s] the pyramiding of essentially random responses."[52]

Meat Margins

The price setting itself usually begins with a high-level management decision that each department should bring in a certain contribution to gross profit, based on tradition, estimates of direct cost, and anticipated sales volume. Then, the divisional or headquarters executive responsible for a particular department will set the individual item prices in such a way as to realize the target profit.

Some of the more complicated pricing procedures are involved in the pricing of meat. Because housewives plan their meals around the meat course, the price of meat will often be featured in weekly advertisements. The meat department tends, therefore, to earn a relatively low net profit. The average cost per pound of the live animal—if there is custom slaughtering—or of the side of beef—if bought from a packer—must be recouped, while minimizing the quantity of meat unsold. Variations in the price per pound of different cuts of meat reflect implicit estimates of cross elasticity among cuts, differences in direct labor expended per pound of primal cut, and the volume of demand at the prices chosen.

---

[51] Holdren, op. cit., p. 73, footnote 13.
[52] L. F. Preston, *Profits, Competition, and Rules of Thumb Pricing in Retail Food Pricing* (Berkeley, Calif.: Institute of Business and Economic Research, 1963), p. 40, footnote 54.

In late 1973 and in the first half of 1974, the sharp rise of beef and pork led to an investigation of retail meat margins. A special task force appointed by Secretary of Agriculture Earl Butz concluded that, although profit rates for meat departments of the retail store were not available, information on price spreads and marketing costs "suggests that the profits for retailing meat increased sharply during the first half of 1974. . . . [T]he recent increase in meat price spreads was caused partially by food retailers changing their *pricing policies* to increase profits in their meat departments."[53] One chain, A&P, responded with an analysis of costs and margins in its meat department. The company's average retail markup on meat, in cents, had risen from 12 cents per pound in 1968 to 21 cents in 1973, and 22 cents in the first half of 1974. On the other hand, the average meat margin expressed as a percentage of the retail selling price, had risen no more than 6 or 7 per cent, from 20.26 per cent in 1968 to 21.89 per cent in 1974. The margin had been almost as high in 1970.[54]

The analysis disclosed that the A&P headquarters did not keep itself informed on precise margins applied to different kinds of meats. Each division priced independently and the company did not have "separate expense figures for the different departments in . . . [their] stores."[55] Data were available only on direct charges that could be made solely to the meat department. Over the 7-year period, the average A&P meat margin had varied no more than slightly from 20 per cent of sales. This percentage is very close to the USDA estimated margin of 20.70 per cent, 1.18 per cent of which represented profit for all retail meat departments for 1973.[56]

Local Price Discrimination

Not only does the market power of the food retailer permit discrimination in pricing among items within the store, but diversification allows price discrimination among stores and regions. Margins have been reduced in markets where competition is keen and kept higher elsewhere. One of the practices followed by A&P in the late 1930s, as summarized by a company executive, consisted of "susbsidizing" local price cuts:

> Where stores need special attention because of unusually active competition or some other conditions beyond our control, we feel that the store in those towns should be put into a special zone and given the benefit of lower than average prices. In other towns, where the conditions may not be quite as pressing, a little better gross profit rate can be obtained.[57]

[53] Task Force Report to Earl L. Butz, *Farm Retail Price Spreads for Red Meat* (Washington, D.C., Aug. 1974).

[54] U.S. Congress, House, Agriculture Subcommittee, Nov. 19, 1974, p. 15, statement of John J. Cairns, Jr., vice-president of merchandising, The Great Atlantic & Pacific Tea Co., Inc.

[55] Ibid., p. 14.

[56] U.S. Department of Agriculture, op. cit., p. 27.

[57] C. Fulda, *Food Distribution in the United States: The Struggle Between Independents and Chains* (Association of American Law Schools, 1951), p. 172, footnote 487. The quotation is from the transcript in the A&P case, Vol. 46, p. 8983, footnote 83.

Following this policy, A&P lost money year after year in some markets; during the years 1932–1940, the Los Angeles unit had a deficit of $1.4 million. The Boston and Springfield units, attempting to meet the competition of First National Stores, failed to break even for 5 years in succession. These losses were incurred after discounts and allowances from headquarters and manufacturing profits on items made by A&P were allocated back to the store.[58]

Local price discrimination by food chains did not end with A&P's conviction by a Federal court in 1947. Safeway used the same tactic in Texas in 1954 and 1955. It sold many items below invoice cost in several zones of the Dallas division, causing losses of $2.3 million in 1954 and $3 million in 1955. The facts were summarized by an attorney in the Department of Justice, Antitrust Division: "Safeway's rate of gross profit in its highest zone, where there was no price war, was 15.62 per cent. . . . In the lowest zone, it was 1.31 per cent. . . . [T]he defendent Warren [president of Safeway] has said . . . it takes 11 per cent just to meet the cost of running the store."[59]

Other chains have incurred losses in areas where they had to meet especially severe competition. When National Tea expanded into the Memphis region by acquisition and building new stores, 22 per cent of its stores in that division failed to cover their overhead in 1955; by 1959, 58 per cent failed to do so. During those years, National Tea was realizing sizable profits in its Chicago division.[60]

In metropolitan Washington in the spring of 1967, Safeway and Giant, which controlled more than 70 per cent of the food business, introduced special reduced pricing zones, confined to the immediate vicinity of two stores that Shop Rite, a New Jersey chain, planned to open. Giant met all of Shop Rite's lower prices and Safeway carried 177 items in four contiguous stores at prices 25 to 30 per cent below the price in 70 other Safeway Stores in the same district.[61]

Additional evidence of price discrimination can be found in data made available to the Joint Economic Committee in 1974 showing that Safeway's divisional net income before taxes in the first 9 months of 1974 ranged from 4.53 per cent in Little Rock and 4.56 per cent in Salt Lake City, down to 1.61 per cent in San Francisco and 0.41 per cent in Southern California.

Nonprice Competition

Nonprice competition in service is a segment of a continuum of management strategy in food distribution, along with pricing and product line policies. Shifts in emphasis from one aspect of competition to the other seem to be a function

---

[58] If retailing costs and returns are to be determined properly, the stores should be allocated only that part of manufacturing profits attributable to the combined operations of manufacturing and retailing. Dirlam and Kahn, op. cit., p. 18.

[59] *Food Retailing*, op. cit., p. 407.

[60] Ibid, p. 385.

[61] FTC, *Economic Report on Food Chain Selling Practices in the District of Columbia and San Francisco* (Washington, D.C.: U.S. Government Printing Office, 1969), p. 23.

of market structure, changing consumer incomes, and the business cycle. The adoption and rejection of particular forms of nonprice competition manifest a kind of periodicity.

Differentiation of the retailing service can play an important role in the food distribution industry, because the products offered for sale tend to be standardized from one store to another. National manufacturers, by and large, determine the characteristics for dry groceries. Meats and fresh fruits and vegetables are produced by commercial farmers, satisfy basic Department of Agriculture grades and classifications and cannot be differentiated easily. In an effort to lure the consumer away from his rival's store, the supermarket operator can rely on a bizarre name or promotions not directly related to selling food, such as games and trading stamps. These moves, however, can be countered quickly by rivals.[62]

Some food store characteristics are designed to improve the environment in which shoppers make their choices. Accessible parking lots, automatic door openers, air conditioning, check cashing, and assisted package carry-outs have now become so common that customers probably assume they are to be found in all stores. Only their nonavailability would tend to identify a store to a potential customer. More esoteric amenities, such as hostesses, flower shops, snack bars, and opticians, can be found in the larger stores. Yet, many of these features can be imitated, at least in time, by building new stores or remodeling old ones.

Some types of nonprice competition are effective in attaching customers to a particular store because they cannot be duplicated exactly. Encyclopedias, dictionaries, silverware, and china offered piece by piece or part by part for a long period of time keep the customer returning to the store until the set is complete. These lures may not be economically priced, but the customer may think they are or finds it easier to buy an expensive item on a weekly basis. A cookbook in 13 parts, at the rate of 89 cents for the first, and $1.49 for each of the others, is not cheap.

Trading stamps, now at a trough of their cycle of adoption, are similar to the installment sales of household articles in that they create customer loyalty. When they were a comparative novelty, in 1950, they drew customers with ease. At the peak of their popularity, almost 80 per cent of the supermarkets felt obliged to use them, including giant chains like A&P and Safeway, which at first were hostile. Under most plans, retailers paid $2.00 to $3.00 per thousand for stamps that were distributed to customers at the rate of one stamp for each 10 cents in purchases. In order to make the stamps attractive to retailers, the stamp companies limit the number of franchises in each market and try to prevent organized stamp exchanges. When almost all chains used stamps, none could reap the benefit of added volume.[63]

Food stores have frequently resorted to extravagant promotions to call

[62] The use of premiums is almost as ancient as grocery retailing. They were indispensable to route salesmen. Jewel Companies, Inc., *Sharing*, Fall 1974, p. 8; S. Hollander, "Entrepreneurs Test the Environment: A Long-run View of Grocery Pricing," Mimeo., Sept. 3, 1966.
[63] *Food Retailing*, op. cit., Chap. 21.

attention to the name of the chain or draw a customer into the store in an irregular or sporadic fashion. Customers holding winning numbers have been given cash prizes, and drawings have been held for new cars. After a 2-year study, the FTC found that the games used by grocery stores and service stations had been deceptively advertised in many cases. Chances of winning were overstated, and the prizes offered were not fairly distributed. Leading chains in Washington, D.C., "systematically allocated their major winners to certain stores."[64] Although games conceivably give some persons enjoyment, they disappoint customers who do not win, and add to the cost of food.

Brand Strategy

Private label (also called distributor's label or house brand) products are packaged to specifications either by a manufacturer or by the distributor itself for sale under a trademark, brand name owned by the distributor. Private label policies differ among chains. A few, such as Winn-Dixie, rely heavily on national brands. Most push private labels. Thus, Safeway has developed a demand for its Lucerne milk, which it processes at its own plants or packages under the Lucerne label where volume does not justify setting up its own plant. The development and quality control of the national brand, on the other hand, are the responsibility of the manufacturer, who must also move the product through the distribution system by advertising and promotion and by maintaining contact with the food stores to coordinate sales campaigns. For the private label product, the chain or voluntary buying group checks quality and takes over the marketing functions.

Food retailers use private labels for three interrelated reasons.

1. Private label products can be sold at prices averaging about 20 per cent below nationally advertised brands and, thus, help to establish a low-price image for the store.

2. If the customer is satisfied, private label items build loyalty to the retailer, because they are available only in his stores.

3. Private label products may be more profitable. Their gross margins may be higher than those of national brands. A 1966 survey of a dozen items frequently sold under private label found the margin on the private label products was 24.8 per cent compared with 22.4 per cent for the national brand.[65] From the gross margin, however, the retailer had to pay for certain functions that are normally covered in the invoice cost of the national brand. If the private label products do not sell as rapidly as the nationally advertised brands, they may return a lower gross profit on investment; moreover, if the store has to stock more than one brand of the same product, costs of handling and administration go up. Comparative rates of sale vary from product to product, and it is impossible to say a priori which produces a higher profit.[66]

[64] FTC, *Economic Report on Food Chain Selling Practices in the District of Columbia and San Francisco*, op. cit., p. 5.

[65] *Food Retailing*, op. cit., p. 133.

[66] Ibid., p. 136.

Chains have been accused of assigning their private label products better facings—at eye level—or more shelf footage than national brands. Dairy or soft drink deliverymen, who are paid on commission, often take care of stocking shelves, thus relieving the store manager of a time-consuming task. But they will give their own product as much space as they can get away with. For this reason, some chains will not let any manufacturer's or processor's deliverymen in their stores. Kellog's takes charge of cereal stocking for many chains, and some manufacturers—Clorox, for liquid bleach, and Frito-Lay for snacks— even introduce their own shelving and identification of products, with the inevitable freezing of facings and, hence, perpetuation of market shares.

If retailers were fully informed, and rational, they would purchase so as to carry just those brands and quantities that will maximize store profits. When the "battle for shelf space" is presented as though the retailer were auctioning his facings off to the highest bidder, this overlooks the fact that by providing services, such as stocking and removing overaged perishables, or by giving discounts, the manufacturer is in effect cutting his price and, so, making it more profitable for the retailer to carry his product. That a manufacturer may have to make do with less shelf space than he would like and, hence, the possibility of a lower sales volume does not necessarily demonstrate that the retailer is exercising monopoly power. Shelf space is not a free good; the variable cost of allotting it to one brand is the profit the retailer might make by using the same shelves for his private label or another competing brand.

Competition and Collusion Among Retail Chains

In December 1974, the U.S. Joint Economic Committee distributed a questionnaire to 17 national food chains. Among the questions asked were the following:

1. What relation does the cost of the product have to the prices that are finally charged at retail?
2. How do identical prices show up so often among the major food chains in the market when presumably their costs vary?
3. Has mutuality of interest in this industry reached the point where it has led to a lack of price competition?[67]

The preceding discussion should help to provide qualified answers to these probing questions.

The relation between invoice cost and price, as pointed out earlier, varies from item to item. Because a large proportion of store costs are fixed and common costs, allocation among products must be determined by a variety of factors, including differing elasticities of demand, which in turn depend on consumers' awareness of prices of comparable products in other stores. It is

---

[67] Press release, Dec. 4, 1974.

impossible to arrive at a typical, much less an optimum, difference between cost and price, except on an aggregate basis.

To the extent that it exists, identity of prices among competitors can be explained in a number of ways. Some chains employ comparison shoppers. The larger the number of items priced identically in competing stores, however, the more one can suspect that the identity results from collusion. It is unlikely that price matching could take place by chance for thousands of items. Although the nature of the market and consumer ignorance of prices make price competition among stores on every item improbable, duplication of price could be arranged by setting up a mechanism for exchanging information, for the purpose of confining competition to nonprice methods. Whether such mutuality of interest is present can be determined only on a market to market basis.

Normally, chains to not duplicate a competitor's price list in its entirety; in some instances, in the 1950s, when independents or competing chains managed to get A&P's price lists, they copied only those low prices that they believed would be most instrumental in holding customers. In a 1966 survey, the National Commission on Food Marketing found that competition was characterized by only a limited use of price leadership and followership. Instead, rivalry centered about the use of features, or "specials." Specials appear to have been introduced in the 1930s. Prices listed in the Thursday newspaper advertisements by the independents attracted customers from the older chains such as A&P, which had stressed its "everyday low-price policy." According to the NCFM,

> [The independent supermarket operator] met the chain store image yet sold enough of the higher priced items to cover his costs which might be higher than the chains'. This orchestration of prices, which is so important in supermarket merchandising, creates what is referred to as the "sales mix." . . . [I]t is possible to identify the store with the "lower price" only in the most simple, clear-cut cases.[68]

Surveys of the composite cost of 105 items prominent in consumers' budgets, more than half of which were featured frequently in weekly ads, revealed roughly similar totals for chains in the same markets. This did not mean that the price of each product was the same in all stores. The advertised items are not priced uniformly among retailers. In many cases, the price, in spite of the prominence given to it in the advertisement, is not below the customary level. For food discounters, specials have been replaced, in the ads, by everyday supposedly low prices. Nevertheless, the Joint Economic Committee disclosed that in Kansas City, Missouri, in 1974, Safeway and A&P had priced more than 2000 items identically, showing that price lists must have been exchanged.[69] Except for such rare cases of deliberate duplication of a price list, however, adjacent food stores do not have identical prices. At the same time, there is a close similarity among average margins for departments, which tend to equal those shown in Table 7.

---

[68] *Food Retailing*, op. cit., p. 169.
[69] *New York Times*, Dec. 16, 1974, p. 1.

Have the major chains reached a kind of tacit agreement to adopt the same margin percentages to limit price cutting? Just this kind of behavior with respect to meat department margins was alleged in a West Coast suit against A&P, in 1974, which resulted in an award of $32 million in damages. According to the mayor of San Francisco, "the National Association of Food Chains [NAFC] is the instrumentality and the vehicle by which the chief executives of the chief chain stores of this country have an opportunity to meet with each other on a regular basis." He cited a meeting of the NAFC meat committee in October 1969, at which supermarket executives, packers, cattlemen, and government officials discussed such topics as "the net profit against gross profit aspects" and "pricing of primal cuts at retail."[70] The price conspiracy, according to Mayor Alioto, was reinforced by use of the "Yellow Sheet" by the chains to signal to each other their buying prices on meat. The "Yellow Sheet" is a private meat price report, prepared in a ramshackle old house on Chicago's near North Side by nine elderly reporters who work under a publisher who began his career in 1923. Through telephone calls to packers, brokers, and buyers, the "Yellow Sheet" reporters manage to cover no more than 25 per cent of the open market sales of meat, and the proportion is probably closer to 10 per cent. Yet, 90 per cent of all wholesale meat sales are tied to the "Yellow Sheet" quotations. In making their purchases from the packers, the "chains keep prices geared to the upper end of the spectrum" quoted.[71] The mechanism by which Safeway and A&P were supposed to reach the same buying price still remains unclear.

If collusion among the leading chains were continuous and widespread, A&P would surely never have attempted to expand its local market shares by its discounting attack. Actually, as a result of A&P's tactics, price cutting approached the "suicidal" in 1972, according to one trade journal;[72] there was "price competition like nothing that had been seen since the Thirties" according to another.[73] It was, of course, the margins that were being shaved rather than the ultimate price to the consumer. As Table 7 shows, the average food chain net operating profit (before imputed interest and cash discounts) fell from 0.59 per cent of sales in 1969–1970 to a deficit of −0.46 per cent in 1972–1973. True, some firms responded to the A&P WEO campaign by emphasizing nonprice tactics, such as 24-hour operation. The nonprice response could not increase the total volume of food sales. Instead, it increased operating costs, putting further pressure on profits.

Because its competitors countered its price reductions, A&P was unable to raise its volume sufficiently to break even. The kink in the retail food demand curve appears to be located where gross margins yield a profit rate on sales of around 1 per cent. By calling off its price warfare in 1974, A&P recognized market realities. But one would misread the experience to deduce that the recovery of margins in late 1973 and 1974 constituted collusion.

[70] *Supermarket News*, Dec. 16, 1974, p. 1.
[71] *Wall Street Journal*, Dec. 6, 1974, p. 1.
[72] *Progressive Grocer*, Apr. 1974, p. 78.
[73] *Chain Store Age Super Markets*, July 1973, p. 38.

IV. MARKET PERFORMANCE

The performance of the food distribution industry can be tested by applying several criteria. Have the firms earned monopolistic, supernormal profits? Are stores and firms of optimum size and are they operated efficiently? Has the industry been backward in adopting new, cost-saving technology? Has the organization of food distribution imposed social costs on the community?

Profits

Using as a measure of profitability the rate of return on equity, or net worth, a comparison with both the food manufacturing industry and all manufacturing fails to disclose the existence of a monopolistic differential for food distribution. In 1972 and 1973, food chain earnings were far below the level realized by the other two groups. The comparison has its shortcomings, of course. Some of the firms included in the food and in the all-manufacturing sample may themselves be earning more than a competitive rate of return. Moreover, food retailing has outperformed meat packing, except for the years 1972 and 1973. However, meat-packing profits have usually been regarded as subnormal.

Some chains have done better than the average, but one hesitates to attribute their high earnings to the exercise of monopoly power. Winn-Dixie, Lucky, Fisher, and Albertson all earned more than 16 per cent on their stockholders' investments in 1972 and 1973, years when the industry average was well below 10 per cent. Yet, Lucky is credited by the FTC with introducing vigorous price competition into the Washington, D.C., area in 1970.[74] By 1974, the chain had built five discount stores; it had 2 per cent of the food sales in the D.C. market. In Los Angeles, Lucky's home territory, it has a market share of only 7.5 per cent and ranks fourth.[75] Although all of the other three highly profitable chains have leading shares in a few market areas, they also face competition throughout most of their sales territories. All three are regarded as being exceptionally aggressive and efficient; in December 1974, the vice-president of Albertson was induced to assume the presidency of A&P, the first outsider to do so in the company's history.

In contrast, A&P used its remnants of market power to *lower* prices and wipe out profits in 1972 and 1973. Even if it had refrained from systemwide price cutting, the company would have earned less than the manufacturing average, judging from its record. Its management moved only belatedly to close "outmoded, small, inefficient supermarkets."[76] In the 5 years ending in February 1973, it had closed 1306 stores, or 28 per cent of those operating in February 1968. Yet, average sales per A&P store in 1973 were only $1.8 million, compared with $2.8 for Safeway, or one third less.

[74] FTC, *Discount Food Pricing in Washington, D.C.* (Washington, D.C.: U.S. Government Printing Office, 1971), p. 21.
[75] *Supermarket News' Distribution Study of Grocery Store Sales in 287 Cities* (New York: Fairchild, 1974), p. 7.
[76] *Chain Store Age Super Markets*, July, 1973, p. 38.

If the companywide profit records do not indicate the exertion of excessive market power, what can be learned from more restricted data? Information on divisional or other territorial earnings has only rarely been made available to the public, usually as part of the record in an antitrust case. In December 1974, however, the Joint Economic Committee persuaded Safeway to submit divisional pretax earnings and sales, which can be compared with rough estimates of Safeway's and the leading four chains' concentration ratios. There appears to be a tendency for higher profits to be associated with larger market shares and higher four-firm concentration ratios. In the Kansas City division, however, Safeway's profits were relatively high, although its market share was quite low. It was in Kansas City that Safeway maintained price identity with A&P, the second-ranking chain.

If local profit rates are not disclosed, retail food price levels might be tested for monopolistic influences by correlating them with four-firm concentration ratios and with other variables capable of affecting supply and demand, including number of families, family incomes, and checkers' wage rates. An ordinary least-squares regression analysis employing these independent variables failed, however, to explain a significant amount of the variance among retail food price indices in 30 SMSAs.[77]

Efficiency, Margins, and Spreads

Trends in retailing efficiency can be traced through changes in the proportion of retailing costs to sales, assuming that the functions of retailing remain much the same during the period analyzed. Long-run, cyclical variations in margins, derived from several sources, appear in Figure 1. Absolute gross margin levels are not the same for each series, but the tendencies are clear. We are slightly below the peak of a cost cycle, where food retailing is appropriating about 35 per cent more of the consumer's dollar than in the late 1940s.

On the basis of past performance, therefore, the industry can be charged with inefficiency. Unfortunately, the absence of a consistent series running through three decades makes it impossible to assign the precise degree of responsibility to be borne by any particular expense category. Making a broad value judgment, the NCFM attributed most of the post-World War II upward trend in margins to wage rates outdistancing improvement in labor productivity, to a higher level of promotional expenditures, and to the construction of more expensive stores.[78]

Turning to more recent trends in margins, Table 8 shows that there was a modest decline from 1968–1969 to 1973–1974. A fall in profits and a lower promotional expense rate (perhaps reflecting the abandonment of trading stamps) together account for most of the decrease in margins.

Prospects for further compression to the margin are not good, unless the industry's recent mediocre record in store operations can be improved. Sales

[77] Study by R. Frank, Economics Department, University of Rhode Island, Jan. 1975.
[78] *Food Retailing*, op. cit., pp. 266–268.

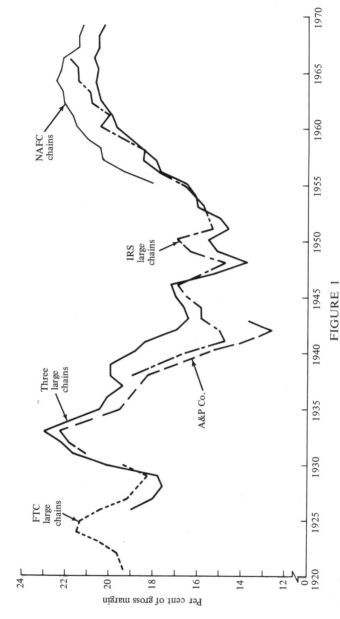

FIGURE 1

Retail gross margins of large food chains, 1921–1969. Source: Appendix Tables 43 through 48 as updated, "Economic Report on the Structure and Competitive Behavior of Food Retailing," Staff Report of the FTC, 1966.

71

TABLE 8

Food Chain Gross Margins, Expenses, and Earnings (in per cent of sales)

	1968–1969	1972–1973	1973–1974
Gross margin	21.48	20.93	20.90
Expenses			
Payroll	10.53	11.57	11.59
Supplies	0.90	0.93	0.97
Utilities	0.73	0.79	0.82
Services purchased	1.22	1.36	1.25
Promotional activities	1.49	1.07	0.71
Insurance	0.51	0.68	0.72
Taxes (except income)	0.92	0.91	0.98
Rentals	1.68	1.55	1.53
Depreciation	0.84	0.81	0.81
Credits and allowances	—	(−0.63)	(−0.51)
Other: repairs, travel, etc.	1.37	1.70	1.62
Total expenses (before interest)	20.19	20.74	20.47
Interest	0.70	0.65	0.60
Total expenses (including interest)	20.89	21.39	21.08
Net operating profit	0.59	(−0.46)	(−0.18)
Other income			
Cash discounts, credits	0.62	0.61	0.62
Other	0.82	0.80	0.67
Net income before taxes	2.03	0.94	1.10
Income taxes	1.01	0.44	0.54
Net earnings	1.02	0.49	0.56

Source: Cornell University, "Operating Results of Food Chains, 1973–1974" (Ithaca, N.Y., 1974).

per man-hour rose from $24.84 to $42.63, or 72 per cent, from 1960–1973; however, if an allowance is made for the 61 per cent increase in the retail food price index during the same period, productivity improvement appears to be negligible.[79] After deflating for changes in the price level, sales per man-hour actually fell in 1971–1973.[80] A turnover rate no better in 1973 than in 1966 is another indication of the inability of retail management to find a method of raising real output.[81] And, although average sales per square foot increased by 25.6 per cent from 1968–1973 for firms reporting to the Super Market Institute, it must be noted that retail food prices went up 37.8 per cent in the same period.[82]

    The retail cost of the annual average quantity of purchased farm food per

[79] G. F. Bloom, Productivity in the Food Industry: Problems and Potential (Cambridge, Mass.: MIT Press, 1972), p. 214 and Supermarket Institute, op. cit., Table 19.

[80] G. F. Bloom, "The Future of Productivity in the Food Industry" (Paper delivered at the Fifteenth Annual Meeting of the Food Distribution Research Society, Oct. 7, 1974), p. 2.

[81] Progressive Grocer, Apr. 1974, p. 181.

[82] Supermarket Institute, op. cit., Table 19.

household, the "market basket," appreciated 4.8 per cent in 1972, 17.3 per cent in 1973, and 7 per cent in the first 9 months of 1974. The farmer's share, although fluctuating slightly from year to year, was the same, 41 per cent, in September 1974, as the average for 1966. Only during the postwar years 1947–1949, did the farmer realize as much as 50 per cent of what the consumer paid for food.[83] Although the share of retailing in the total marketing spread from farmer to consumer cannot, by itself, show whether that function is being exercised efficiently, an analysis of spreads can provide some insight into the relative responsibility of retailing for what the consumer pays for different food items.

The retailing share of the total spread varies widely from product to product, as shown for selected items in Table 9.[84] For some products—orange juice, canned tomatoes, and salad oil—processing cost was the largest element in the spread. Retailing, like any other activity, has been affected by inflation. Invoice and store operation costs have gone up because of increases in the prices of packaging materials and containers, which jumped 30 per cent in 1974. The retailers' total labor cost was about 20 per cent higher in 1974 than in 1973, although the number of employees remained about the same.[85] Figure 2 shows the percentage share of the various components of the marketing spread for farm food products in 1973.

The farmer could obtain a larger share of the food dollar if through intensified price compeitition, or by an alteration in the nature of consumer demand for retailing services, the spectrum of food retailing services could be substantially simplified. But this would not necessarily bring about a higher price at the farm.

According to the cogent summary of an ex-food chain executive, "The

TABLE 9
Retail Marketing Spreads for Selected Items

PRODUCT	RETAIL SHARE OF MARKETING SPREAD (PER CENT)
Choice beef	62.5
Broilers	47.4
Milk	15.8
Lettuce	49.4
Frozen orange juice	33.0
Canned tomatoes	20.6
Salad oil	12.5
Bread	23.0

Source: Calculated from U.S. Department of Agriculture, Marketing and Transportation Situation, Washington, D.C., Nov. 1974.

[83] U.S Department of Agriculture, op. cit., p. 7.

[84] U.S. Department of Agriculture, Marketing and Transportation Situation, Washington, D.C., Nov. 1974, pp. 24–28.

[85] Ibid., p. 13.

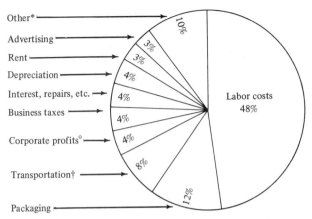

Other*
Advertising
Rent
Depreciation
Interest, repairs, etc.
Business taxes
Corporate profits°
Transportation†
Packaging

10%
3%
3%
4%
4%
4%
4%
8%
12%

Labor costs
48%

*Residual includes such costs as utilities, fuel, promotion, local for-hire transportation, insurance.
°Before taxes
†Intercity rail and truck.
ΔPreliminary data.

FIGURE 2

Components of bill for marketing farm foods, 1973. Source: Economic Research Service, Department of Agriculture.

supermarket in America is suffering from a bad case of marketing schizophrenia. It does not know whether it is in fact a small warehouse intended to distribute food to customers at the lowest possible cost, or a merchandising establishment in which the most sophisticated techniques of display, departmentalization, decor, and equipment utilization are combined to induce consumers to buy what the operator wants to sell."[86]

Innovations

The outstanding innovations in food distribution in the last 70 years have been self-service retailing and the multidepartment, large-volume store, which resulted in the supermarket. Neither should be classified as an "invention" in the conventional sense of the term because they were not characterized by the application of any novel engineering or physical principle, nor could they be said to have introduced a new product. Self-service merely shifted to the customer many of the selection chores formerly done by the employees, while the increased volume of business used space more intensively. In order to speed up check-out, retailers induced manufacturers, and eventually produce shippers, to package a much larger part of their output, again shifting to others activities that had been carried on in the store or by the customer. Whether these changes resulted in real savings in resources in distribution is debatable,[87] although one-stop, once-a-week, large-volume food shopping economized clerk time.

[86] Bloom, *Productivity in the Food Industry*, op. cit., p. 212.

[87] V. R. Fuchs, *The Service Economy* (New York: National Bureau of Economic Research, 1968), pp. 100–104. Fuchs is uncertain whether the unit by which productivity should be measured is the transaction itself or the food and associated services purchased in the transaction. By the first standard, productivity has been diminished by once-a-week shopping; by the latter, it has increased.

Larger sales volume per store has undoubtedly contributed to more efficient delivery and to the adoption of computerized inventory control. These improvements, to which must be added the use of forklift trucks and pallets in one-story warehouses, permitted substantial savings in labor and capital inputs in the 1950s and early 1960s.

Two innovations were on the threshold of widespread adoption in 1975. One, at the warehouse, involves the installation of a nearly completely automated system, except for shipping. The operations of receiving, stacking, and item selection for shipping will be directed by computer, and the more labor-intensive forklift truck will be largely replaced for storage by stacker cranes. In the selection process, cases and cartons will be automatically released to conveyors and will arrive in the proper order for loading onto the delivery truck.

This change should reduce warehouse labor costs, or at least check its upward climb, by raising the tons handled per man-hour. In recent years, physical productivity in warehouses has been dropping because of the increase in the number of items stocked, with widely varying turnover rates. Because roughly 85 per cent of warehouse costs consist of wages and salaries, and incentive pay is regarded unfavorably by the union, greater capital intensitivity is attractive to management.[88]

The second innovation is embodied in electronic point-of-sales systems, focused around the Universal Product Code (UPC). Although use of the UPC will impose costs on manufacturers, produce shippers, and warehouses, which will obligate them to make sure that every item is marked with its identifying symbol, food retailing will be able to improve labor efficiency. Optical scanning at the check-out counter eliminates the need for price marking each item in the store and speeds up the check-out process. The electronic terminal substitutes for the cash register and is tied to a computer. Information will be available at all times to control inventory levels, detect the amount of pilferage, and monitor cash. The new system will probably intensify pressure for delivery in cases or cartons that can be directly shelved or remain on the pallets, which will be conducive to the construction of still larger-volume stores.

Social Cost and Food Retailing

Families living at the poverty level spend about 40 per cent or more of their budgets on food. A Bureau of Labor Statistics study has shown that food prices are substantially higher in ghetto neighborhoods. The higher prices do not, however, appear to be the result of deliberate discrimination by chain stores. According to the FTC, the primary reason low-income, inner-city residents pay more for food is that there are too few supermarkets in these areas. Unaffiliated independent stores are concentrated in low-income neighborhoods. They have a low annual sales volume and high unit-operating costs. Their customers, therefore, pay more for food. Chains are relatively uninterested in opening new supermarkets in inner cities because land costs are high, population is shrinking, and

---

[88] See the discussion in Bloom, *Productivity in the Food Industry*, op. cit., Chap. 4.

transactions per customer are low. Those chain supermarkets selling at lower-than-average markups tend to be found in the suburbs, where other grocery chains are active. There is less competition from this source in the ghettos. Differences among chains in the number of stores they operate in poverty areas, and in their pricing policies, make generalizations difficult, but it appears that average chain prices are slightly higher in these areas.[89]

Food retailing investment policy may waste resources and give rise to social costs. Following their policy of planned obsolescence of stores, the chains contribute to the deterioration of older stores and their neighborhoods and aggravate the shortage of open space near cities. A market test shows that, lured to a bigger, brighter store with a delicatessen and an on-the-premises bakery, customers will generate enough revenue to make the new, but not necessarily more efficient, supermarket profitable. However, the income statements will register neither the social costs of creating excess capacity nor the alternative social benefits that might be obtained if the same resources were used for slum clearance, mass transit, or creating parks.

There is evidence that some markets are "overstored," as the industry says—that is, there are not enough customers within normal driving distance to permit all of the stores in the market area to operate at optimum levels of sales.[90]

In addition, food retailing inevitably suffers from under-utilized capacity during the first four days of the week and in the morning hours. Most shoppers visit the supermarket on the last three days of the week. If consumers spread their shopping evenly over the hours of the day and days of the week, fewer stores would be needed, and the number of check-outs per store could be reduced. Nevertheless, habits cannot be easily changed, and as long as they cannot, the number of stores, and their facilities, must be geared to serve the peak. If price discrimination could encourage a shift in the hour or day of the week by a sufficient number of shoppers to make it pay, one can assume the industry would already have adopted it.

Conclusion

That the introduction of the supermarket reduced the inputs of clerical service per unit of food purchased is obvious. As processors and wholesalers have taken over and added packaging functions, these types of inputs into retailing similarly have tended to decline at the retailing level. The character of the retailing service has changed by throwing on the consumer and the supplier costs that used to be retailer's or were avoided altogether. Unquestionably, the display service and the greater array of items (up to the point where choice becomes fatiguing) represents improvements, except for confirmed addicts of

[89] *Food Retailing*, op. cit., pp. 336–338; FTC, *Economic Report on Food Chain Selling Prices in the District of Columbia and San Francisco*, op. cit.

[90] *Progressive Grocer*, Apr. 1965, p. 61; Apr. 1974, p. 133. In 1974, 49 per cent of the chains interviewed had thought that the "oversaturation of stores" was "very important" in reducing their projected growth rate.

Americana, on the environment of the homey, old-fashioned grocery store, where prices varied from customer to customer and the cat slept in the cracker barrel.

Nevertheless, considering the arbitrary and irrational patterns of much of food pricing and consumption, we are far from having reached an economic optimum in food retailing. There is much to show that excessive quantities of resources are devoted to this sector and that the prevailing discrimination in margins does not induce the most desirable mixture of purchases by consumers. Unable to make reliable price comparisons—a November 1974, survey discovered that "only one shopper in ten can name the exact price of even one out of a broad range of common food store items"[91]—and unequipped to calculate the maximum nutritional benefit for the minimum outlay, the ill-prepared housewife sallies forth on her weekly expedition.[92]

V. PUBLIC POLICY

Antitrust Control of Mergers and Acquisitions

The Supreme Court, in 1966, held that Section 7 of the Clayton Act forbids the merger of direct competitors in food retailing when their merger creates a firm ranking relatively high in a local market.[93] Before their merger in 1960, Von's and Shopping Bag were the third and sixth largest chains in the Los Angeles market, respectively. After the merger the combination became the second largest. Even so, their postmerger share was only 7.5 per cent. However, the Court took into account also the trend toward disappearance (not necessarily by merger) of thousands of independent small stores, the number of mergers occurring in Los Angeles, and acquisitions of local Los Angeles retailers by national chains.

The *Von's* decision has drawn criticism because the parties to the merger were not national chains, and because the divestiture could be interpreted as trying to "roll back the supermarket revolution." It is true that the combined sales of the two chains—$172 million at the time of the merger—did not come close to the $500 million limit that the Federal Trade Commission had established as the maximum beyond which further economies were not likely to be realized in manufacturing operations, private label programs, and field buying of perishables. Both chains were, however, independently viable and, had other similar acquisitions taken place, the Los Angeles area could very shortly have become dominated by a few large sellers.

[91] W. H. Heller, "What Shoppers Know—And Don't Know About Prices," *Progressive Grocer*, Nov. 1974, pp. 39–41.

[92] V. E. Smith, "A Diet Model with Quality Protein Variable," *Management Science*, **20**: 971 (1974) and Jim Hightower, *Eat Your Heart Out* (New York: Crown Publishers, 1975), Chap. IV.

[93] *United States* v. *Von's Grocery*, 384 U.S. 270 (1966).

At about the time the Justice Department attacked Von's acquisition of a direct competitor, the FTC moved against "market extension" mergers in food retailing—that is, entry into new territory by acquisition. Complaints were filed against National Tea, Grand Union, Winn-Dixie, and Kroger. In 1966, National Tea was ordered to refrain from further acquisitions without prior commission approval,[94] and substantially similar consent agreements were obtained from Grand Union and Winn-Dixie. Kroger's purchase of the Market Basket chain in Los Angeles went by default, the case being dismissed 15 years later because the commission had never reached a decision. In 1967, the FTC generalized the National Tea decision in a policy statement, tied to its analysis of economies of scale. An acquisition raising the annual food store sales of a corporate chain, or cooperative or voluntary group, above $500 million would be suspect, warranting the commission's "attention and consideration." Acquisitions by chains with annual sales between $100 million and $500 million would call for "investigation," but the FTC did not, as in the case of the larger sales volume state that there would be "questions regarding their legal status." When smaller chains merged with direct competitors that were leaders, the commission saw the possibility of a threat to competition. Mergers of not more than four stores, or including sales of food products not in excess of $5 million annually, or no more than 5 per cent of the food store sales in a local market, were given what amounted to a safe conduct pass.[95]

According to the FTC, its antimerger policy has been effective not only in checking further acquisitions by leading food chains, but also in stimulating price competition by encouraging new entry. "Prior to the case victories and this strong statement of policy, some 70 per cent of foodstore acquisitions were made by the largest national chains; afterward [fewer] than 1 per cent were."[96]

That FTC guidelines must now be taken into account by prospective merging chains goes without saying. Exactly how the commission's policy has shaped structure is far from clear, however, and to evaluate its economic consequences is not easy. In the first place, the four largest chains have shown almost no interest in expanding by merger for at least 15 years. Kroger withdrew of its own volition from Chicago; Milwaukee, and Washington, D.C. Safeway found it advantageous to sell its New York division to First National Stores. A&P abandoned Los Angeles and Seattle, Washington, and its new president has announced a policy that will result in further geographic concentration. American Stores has remained inactive in terms of territorial expansion. As for National Tea, its share has drastically diminished in the Chicago, Indianapolis, and Denver markets, where the FTC had said it held a "strong market position" that "may be maintained for years without either an erosion of profit or market

[94] FTC, *Opinion and Order*, Docket no. 7453, Mar. 4, 1966.
[95] FTC, *Enforcement Policy with Respect to Mergers in the Food Distribution Industry* (Washington, D.C.: U.S. Government Printing Office, Jan. 3, 1967).
[96] FTC, *Economic Report on Discount Food Pricing* (Washington, D.C.: U.S. Government Printing Office, 1971), p. 14.

position."[97] The chain is suffering losses that it has been unable to staunch. Meanwhile, it has sold off several divisions.

Some recent market extensions, carried out presumably with the FTC's blessing, appear to have nurtured a new crop of geographically conglomerate firms. Through an ironic twist, Fisher, based in Cleveland and ranking seventeenth nationally, with annual sales of $650 million, acquired Shopping Bag in 1972, several years after its divestiture by Von's. Von's operates only in Southern California, and ranks twenty-sixth nationally. Fry's a California chain, was purchased by Dillon, ranking twenty-first nationally and headquartered in Kansas, and with sales, after the merger, of $513 million. Should the FTC permit the formation by merger of chains of this magnitude, even though they are still not as large as the big four? The prosperous persistence of regional chains much smaller than Fisher and Dillon demonstrates that growth beyond $100 million in annual sales has not been accompanied by significant declines in costs. If the FTC's policy has led, as it asserts, to entry by new construction by the very large chains, it may, paradoxically, have fostered the excess capacity and nonprice competition that partially accounts for the high level of retail margins.

For these reasons we cannot be sure that antimerger policy has been responsible for reshaping food distribution in such a way as to bring substantial benefits to the consumer. At the same time, the FTC has injected itself into the minutiae of the decision-making process, being called on to review the purchases of one or a few food stores.[98]

Purchasing Tactics

The 1936 amendment to Section 2 of the Clayton Act, called the Robinson-Patman Act after its legislative sponsors, was drafted by the counsel for the United States Wholesaler Grocers Association, Harold Teegarden. It was intended, among other things, to prevent large food chains from extracting discounts from manufacturers not available to independents and their wholesale suppliers and to outlaw the payment of brokerage as another type of discriminatory concession to these large buyers. The Robinson-Patman Act was, therefore, supported by grocery wholesalers, independent retailers, and food brokers. The atmosphere in which the act was passed can be illustrated by Senator Huey Long's ringing challenge, "I would rather have thieves and gangsters in Louisiana than chain stores."[99] In 1935, the director of the National Association of Retail Grocers told the Judiciary Committee of the House of Representatives, "The present condition of affairs in the food industry has put thousands of salesmen out of work. It has driven many brokers out of business. It has closed the doors of many wholesaler grocers and has shut up thousands of retail grocers. . . . And this was done, not to bring goods to the consumers any cheaper

---

[97] *Food Retailing*, op. cit., p. 368.
[98] See *Supermarket News*, Jan. 6, 1975.
[99] Quoted in F. C. Beckman and H. Nolen, *The Chain Store Problem* (New York: McGraw-Hill, 1938), pp. 228–229.

but in order to fatten the income of a few chosen people who invested their money in chain stores."[100]

The text of the Robinson-Patman Act outlawed price discrimination that made more than due allowance for differences in cost of manufacture sale, or delivery, where competition might be lessened or disadvantaged competitors or customers injured. Meeting competition, however, excused otherwise illegal discrimination. Brokerage payments to buyers and promotional allowances not available to customers on a proportionate bases to all customers were unqualifiedly outlawed under Sections 2(c) and (d).

Although not sympathetic with the arcane intricacies of the Robinson-Patman Act, which can, if rigidly applied, inhibit price competition, the Antitrust Division succeeded in convicting A&P in 1946 under the Sherman Act on grounds of exerting monopolistic buying power to obtain discriminatory discounts. Some observers defended the policy condemned by the courts on the grounds that only A&P's exertion of buying power could crack the tightly oligopolized markets for meat, canned goods, and produce. According to the theory, the discriminatory discounts allowed to A&P were transformed into reduced retail prices, thus obliging A&P's competitors to obtain similar concessions. Professor J. K. Galbraith, of Harvard University, built his theory of "countervailing power" on the explicit example of A&P as a big buyer who performed a public service by wringing concessions from suppliers.[101] Although the giant dimensions of A&P were supposed to be crucial in obtaining the discounts, critics of the Sherman Act proceeding maintained that economies of scale were so unimportant in food retailing that there was no danger of oligopolistic pricing at the retail level.[102]

Whatever the theoretical possibility of a big buyer cracking a cartel of oligopolistic suppliers, there was, in fact, little to show that the discriminatory concessions actually given to A&P made competition more workable. Few discriminatory allowances were obtained from powerful sellers. "It was precisely the highly differentiated products which were the most rarely affected by discrimination."[103] Important discriminatory discounts were obtained mainly from small canners and vegetable shippers.

Following the conviction of A&P, and numerous investigations by the FTC, the large chains took warning, so that most discounts to big purchasers today are on a sporadic basis only, offered in connection with special deals. Nevertheless, from time to time the FTC has moved against discriminatory concessions, prevalent in the marketing of fluid milk, ice cream, and bakery products. There is reason to believe that the inability to get such discounts has led to the chains' vertical integration into fluid milk processing and bakery operation.[104]

---

[100] Quoted in Fulda, op, cit., p. 1.
[101] *American Capitalism* (Boston: Houghton, 1952), Chaps. 9, 10, and passim.
[102] M. A. Adelman, "The Great A&P Muddle," *Fortune*, **40**: 122 (Dec. 1949).
[103] J. B. Dirlam and A. E. Kahn, *Fair Competition: The Law and Economics of Antitrust Policy* (Ithaca, N. Y.: Cornell University Press, 1954), p. 238.
[104] FTC, *Economic Report on the Dairy Industry*, op. cit., pp. 106–107.

The brokerage provision of the Robinson-Patman Act has turned out to be a boomerang. Many voluntary and cooperative wholesalers and buying groups had been accustomed to receiving brokerage payments from suppliers. They relied on these allowances to finance the advertising and to provide the marketing assistance that helped their members compete with corporate chain stores. Enforcement of Section 2(c) hurt not only A&P, which was forced to give up its captive brokerage subsidiary, but the very wholesalers who had supported the Robinson-Patman Act. In the *Central Retail-Owned Grocers* case, Commissioner Elman pointed out that Section 2(c) was being perverted when it was applied against a cooperative or voluntary wholesaler. "For what [the majority] holds is that any price concession to a cooperative buying organization—which of necessity performs functions which buyers' brokers would perform—will be deemed in lieu of brokerage in per se violation of Section 2(c)."[105]

A cooperative buying group came under attack by the antitrust division when it attempted to enforce territorial exclusivity on its members. Topco Associates united some 23 retail chains with total sales of $2.3 billion for the purpose of buying under a private label; the Topco products accounted for about 10 per cent of their annual sales. With the exception of Allied Stores, none of the members were among the 15 largest chains. Fourteen had annual sales of less than $250 million each, and very few had contiguous territories.[106] The Supreme Court refused to entertain the defense that only by marketing a strong private label could the members compete with large corporate chains. The Court said that they could not restrain competition among themselves in the process.[107] Topco still exists and has not been damaged, it seems, by the decision.

One can scarcely marshall much enthusiasm for the governmental policing of buying concessions and brokerage and various promotional allowances. On the other hand, it is extremely unlikely that the FTC proceedings have impeded the functioning of grocery competition. The chains can still use private labels and compete with manufacturers by vertically integrating. Nevertheless, governmental interference with price policy at any level is fraught with danger for a system relying on the independence of enterprise decision making. The maintenance of numerous viable competitors, as long as it does not involve the continuous supervision of chain policies, is an available and preferable substitute for the close surveillance of buying practices.

Predatory local price discrimination by both A&P[108] and Safeway[109] was attacked by the Department of Justice. And, in the course of the evidence supporting its decision to restrict further mergers by National Tea, the FTC cited the company's policy of sustaining "large" losses for several years in its Mem-

---

[105] FTC, *Dissenting Opinion*, Docket no. 7121, May 14, 1962, pp. 10–11.

[106] *United States* v. *Topco Associates, Inc.*, 1970 TRR Par. 73, 388.

[107] *United States* v. *Topco Associates, Inc.*, 405 U.S. 596 (1972).

[108] *United States* v. *A&P*, 173 F.2d 79, 82 (1949). Safeway and Kroger had pleaded *nolo contendere* to similar indictments. *United States* v. *Safeway Stores*, No. 7196 Criminal, Jan. 20, 1943, *United States* v. *The Kroger Grocery and Baking Co.*, Criminal 7197, Jan. 20, 1943, Dist. Ct. for the Dist. of Kansas, 1st Dist.

[109] *United States* v. *Safeway Stores*, Criminal Action No. 9584, 1955.

phis, Detroit, and Davenport markets.[110] It is likely that these three cases have discouraged national chains that might be tempted to subsidize losses or below-average profit in certain cities by hither than average profits elsewhere. Nevertheless, the wide variations in Safeway's pretax divisional profit margins, disclosed by the Joint Economic Committee, raise questions about the fairness of competition between Safeway and local chains in Los Angeles, where the divisional profit margin was only 0.41 per cent in the first three quarters of 1974, compared with 5.27 per cent in Seattle.[111]

The proper path for public policy in cases of local price discrimination is far from clearly marked. In the long run, the consumer was not likely to benefit from A&P's ability, as the largest chain in the United States, to selectively lower its margins and accept losses in order to repel the invasion of a single independent in Richmond, Virginia, or to combat the severe price competition of a regional chain in New England. The giant chain drew on its geographically conglomerate financial strength to eliminate or discipline smaller and perhaps equally efficient competitors. On the other hand, National Tea's policy can be read as an endeavor to secure a foothold in new territory, where it faced entrenched, larger rivals, including A&P and Kroger. Market invasion and the price competition that usually accompanies it help to keep local oligopolies from choosing a quiet life and competing exclusively through expensive, nonprice tactics.

Size and diversity give management the freedom to manipulate margins and pose problems for public policy. Chains that, through subsidiaries, engage in nonfood retailing may be able to sustain losses or below-average returns on their food sales by drawing on their earnings in other lines. Food sales in large discount stores may be assigned a relatively small proportion of overhead, with the exception that low food prices will draw customers into the store, where they will buy high-margin clothes, appliances, or cameras.

The Robinson-Patman Act has not been invoked to challenge local price discrimination in food retailing; the practice can probably be successfully defended on the grounds that margins were lowered to meet competition. As for the conglomerate use of subsidization, to determine whether or not it is in the public interest, one would have to rely on comparisons between the efficiency of single- and multiple-line firms and stores. Apart from setting a ceiling on the creation of extremely large firms by merger and forbidding predatory sharp-shooting, it would seem desirable to let the market decide, in the long run, which types of organization of food distribution should survive. To prevent all forms of price or margin discrimination would entail an enormously costly bureaucratic surveillance. In any event, such control would be futile, for there are no immutable economic laws that can be applied to the allocation of overhead costs. Limits to discrimination are set, in principle, by state statutes forbidding below-cost sales. Cost is usually defined to include a minimum markup over

[110] FTC, *Opinion*, Docket No. 7453, Mar. 4, 1966.
[111] Press release, Dec. 1974, Joint Economic Committee.

invoice cost. Proof of violation is difficult, and the remedy, usually an injunction, is of little value because it may be June before a complainant can obtain a finding that a special price on Thanksgiving turkeys was illegal.

Insofar as chains, on the basis of information widely disseminated by trade journals and trade associations on rates of turnover and prevailing margins, adopt closely similar departmental targets for their stores, the consumer may in the end pay more for his food. But the antitrust laws cannot be used to enforce aggressive price rivalry or to enjoin firms against concentrating their competitive efforts on differentiation of the retail service. And, the power of the Federal government under the antitrust laws to restrict the dissemination of market information is limited, as it should be. If, however, as Mayor Joseph Alioto has alleged, the major food chains indeed exchange data on margins in order to set prices and avoid competition, then, under the *Container Corporation* doctrine,[112] not to mention the *Hardwood* case,[113] they may have violated Section 1 of the Sherman Act. Whether deliberate margin fixing has actually taken place is far from sure; if one large chain merely matches the margins, or prices, of its principal rival, enforcement agencies are presented with the perennial antitrust dilemma: How can they move against an oligopolistic structure that has fostered noncompetitive behavior, yet without overt collusion or agreement? And, although a reduction in market concentration may change behavior, the differences in goals and strategies among the dozens of chains are so pronounced that it would be rash, on an a priori basis, to equate a given market structure with any particular form of behavior.

Consumer Protection

Thanks to a combination of state and Federal legislation and to voluntary action by chains and grocery manufacturers, following prodding by Senator Philip Hart, the housewife is less likely to be confused or misled in grocery shopping than she was 10 years ago. In many states, some form of unit pricing is now required so that the costs of purchases of different sizes of packages and brands can now be compared in a meaningful way, even though quantities or weights may differ. Administered by the Department of Health, Education and Welfare (HEW) and the FTC, the Fair Packaging and Labeling Act has promoted the standardization of sizes and weights and requires that information for nonstandard containers be especially clearly marked. The secretary of commerce, as provided in the act, has persuaded some manufacturers to reduce the number of sizes of containers of products sold in food stores, thus improving efficiency as well as simplifying consumers' decisions. Under the same act, the FTC and HEW have set bounds to the "cents-off" and "economy-size" package techniques that had been used deceptively. A manufacturer can employ a cents-off label only when the product is invoiced at a reduction to the retailer

---

[112] *United States* v. *Container Corporation*, 393 U.S. 333 (1969).
[113] *United States* v. *American Column and Lumber Co.*, 257 U.S. 377 (191).

from the ordinary price at least equal to the amount allowed off. Economy-size labels have been disallowed unless another size is available, and the economy size must sell at a unit price substantially reduced below the actual prices of other sizes.

To enforce these regulations may require more policing staff than either of the enforcing agencies can muster.

Under Section 5 of the Federal Trade Commission Act, the FTC has set bounds for the promoting of "specials." The products advertised must be available for sale, and conspicuously visible, at the advertised price. If the item is out of stock, the consumer must be given a rain check. The necessity for the issuance of the rule had been shown by an investigation that revealed the widespread unavailability of advertised items and high overpricing rates.[114]

The use of trading stamps not only increases retailing cost, but, by adding an additional dimension to value, intensifies the consumer's handicaps in making comparisons among stores. Moreover, according to the NCFM, the effective price paid by customers redeeming stamps in goods was higher than they would have paid in a department store for the same items.[115] Ideally, customers should be given the option of a cash rebate equal to the cost of the stamps to the retailer. Because the exclusive franchise feature prevented small chains and independents from access to the most desirable brands, the use of stamps was thought to injure competition. Their use, however, so diminished that it would scarcely seem worthwhile for the FTC or state legislature to take additional steps to control stamps.

Conclusion

In food retailing, entry into local markets is relatively easy even for small chains. As long as ambition and other incentives spur entrepreneurs on to expand, and predatory tactics by large firms are suppressed, domination of such markets by one or the same few chains will be unlikely to persist for long. On a national level, however, although newcomers have displaced some of the lower-ranking chains, they have yet to threaten any of the top four. Nevertheless, the very largest chains have modified their structures so as to concentrate geographically.

Although these tendencies have moderate structural rigidities, they have not offset, and may even have encouraged, reliance on nonprice competition. Moreover, capital-intensive innovations will reinforce the propensity to use more elaborate and complicated forms of merchandising.

One is obliged, reluctantly, to conclude that, as long as the minimum efficient store size is so large in relation to the local market that the number of competitors is severely limited, there is little that public policy can do to reverse the tendency to "trade up" retail food service. In the absence of collusion, neither

[114] FTC, *Trade and Regulation Rule, Retail Food Store Advertising and Marketing Practices* (Washington, D.C.: U.S. Government Printing Office, July 12, 1971).
[115] *Food Retailing*, op. cit., p. 459.

the Antitrust Division nor the FTC can sue to require food retailers to cut either their hours of service or the number of items offered; and there are few, if any, local markets where it could justify further disintegration of sellers. Only if there were a major reversal in the character of demand would some oligopolist find it profitable to offer simpler and less costly retailing service.

SUGGESTED READINGS

BOOKS AND PAMPHLETS

Bloom, Gordon F. *Productivity in the Food Industry* (Cambridge, Mass.: MIT Press 1972).

Hightower, Jim. *Eat Your Heart Out* (New York: Crown Publishers, 1975).

Holdren, Bob. *The Structure of a Retail Market and the Market Behavior of Retail Units* (Englewood Cliffs, N.J.: Prentice-Hall, Inc., 1960).

GOVERNMENT PUBLICATIONS

Federal Trade Commission. Staff Report. *On Food Chain Profits* (Washington, D.C., 1975).

Manchester, Alden C. *Market Structure, Institutions, and Performance in the Fluid Milk Industry.* Agricultural Economic Report, no. 248 (Washington, D.C.: U.S. Department of Agriculture, U.S. Government Printing Office, Jan. 1974).

National Commission on Food Marketing. *Food from Farmer to Consumer.* Report. (Washington, D.C.: U.S. Government Printing Office, 1966).

National Commission on Food Marketing. Technical Study, no. 7, *Organization and Competition in Food Retailing.* (Washington, D.C.: U.S. Government Printing Office, 1966).

Parker, Russel C. *Discount Food Pricing in Washington, D.C.* FTC Staff Report (Washington, D.C.: U.S. Government Printing Office, 1971).

CHAPTER 3

the steel industry

WALTER ADAMS

I. INTRODUCTION

At the end of World War II in 1945, America's steel industry was the most powerful in the world. Its plant capacity was almost double that of all "iron curtain" countries combined, and there was no apparent chance that the devastated facilities in Germany and Japan would ever again rise to challenge American mastery. Today, the situation is radically different. The United States accounts for less than 20 per cent of the world's steel output (approximately the same as the Soviet Union), while the European Economic Community (EEC) has become the largest, and Japan the fourth largest, producer. Most significantly, the steel industry in the United States has lost its erstwhile dominance over domestic markets, which are subject to progressive erosion by burgeoning steel imports.

History

Before 1898, the steel industry was the scene of active and, at times, destructive competition. In this early period, various gentlemen's agreements and pools were organized in an effort to control the production of steel rails, billets, wire, nails, and other products, but the outstanding characteristic of these agreements was the "frequency with which they collapsed."[1] Their weakness was that inherent in any pool or gentlemen's agreement, "60 per cent of the agreers are gentlemen, 30 per cent just act like gentlemen, and 10 per cent neither are nor act like gentlemen." If production and prices were to be controlled, these loosely knit agreements had to be superseded by more stable forms of organization.

---

[1] H. R. Seager and C. A. Gulick, *Trust and Corporation Problems* (New York: Harper, 1929), p. 216. This book is an excellent source on the early history of U.S. Steel.

The latter came upon the industry with the suddenness and intensity seldom paralleled in American industrial history.

From 1898–1900, a vast concentration movement took place in the steel industry. Large companies such as Federal Steel, National Steel, National Tube, American Bridge, and American Sheet Steel were organized. Dominated by three financial interest groups—Carnegie, Morgan, and Moore—these consolidations did not succeed in bringing "stability" to the industry. In fact, a fight between the newly formed giants seemed unavoidable.

Because each of the major interest groups was peculiarly vulnerable in case a "battle between the giants" materialized, and because cooperation promised to be more profitable than competition, stubbornness yielded to reason. In 1901, with the help of J. P. Morgan, the interested parties agreed to form the "combination of combinations"—the U.S. Steel Corporation, which, at the time of its formation, controlled approximately 65 per cent of the nation's steel capacity.

Considerable disagreement has attended discussions of the motives behind the organization of the U.S. Steel Corporation. The announced motives were to form a completely integrated steel company; to secure the advantages of the most advanced technical organization; and to develop an extensive export trade. Judge Elbert H. Gary testified that the latter was the "dominating factor" favoring the creation of the corporation.[2] Most disinterested observers, however, agree that the "intent to monopolize" played a significant, and perhaps dominant, role. The policies of the corporation, subsequent to its organization in 1901, seem to bear out this opinion; for the corporation proceeded to acquire properties that would put it in a position to dominate the steel industry. Especially significant was the acquisition of essential raw material assets, particularly coking coal and iron ore mines.

By 1907, however, the corporation became concerned with more immediate problems than the long-run elimination of *potential* competition through a monopolization of some raw material supplies. It had to face a spasm of *active* price competition that had been brought on by the business panic of that year. To meet this challenge and to restore price stability under its own leadership, it innovated the famous Gary dinners. The purpose of these dinners—in the words of the host, the president of U.S. Steel—was "to maintain to a reasonable extent the equilibrium of business, to prevent utter demoralization of business and destructive competition."[3] Judge Gary *achieved* this objective by urging "his guests, who represented fully 90 per cent of the industry, that they cooperate in holding prices where they were."[4] He exhorted them like a Methodist preacher at a camp meeting to follow the price leadership of U.S. Steel. There was no need for any formal agreements, no need to force a group of reluctant competitors into a cooperative arrangement. U.S. Steel merely assumed the lead

---

[2] U.S. Congress, House, *Hearings Before the Committee on Investigation of the U.S. Steel Corporation*, 62d Cong., 2d sess., 1911, Vol. 1, p. 104. (Hereafter referred to as *Stanley Hearings*.)

[3] *Stanley Hearings*, op. cit., p. 264.

[4] Ida M. Tarbell, *The Life of Elbert H. Gary* (New York: Appleton, 1930), p. 205.

incumbent on a firm its size; its rivals followed, fully realizing the security and profitability of cooperation. Under these circumstances, the Gary dinners were a singular success and presented but another vivid illustration of Adam Smith's observation that "people of the same trade seldom meet together, even for merriment and diversion, but the conversation ends in a conspiracy against the public or in some contrivance to raise prices."

Available evidence indicates that the dinners were held at irregular intervals until 1911. However, when the government became increasingly suspicious of their price-fixing function and when it finally filed suit for the dissolution of U.S. Steel, the dinners were abruptly abandoned. But the damage had been done. The corporation stood accused in the Federal courts as a monopoly, and the government demanded the extreme penalty—dissolution.

Due to the outbreak of World War I, the case was not decided until 1920, when the fervor of earlier trust-busting campaigns had died down. By a vote of 4 to 3, the Supreme Court decided against dissolution.[5] Without considering the effects of price quotation under the Pittsburgh-Plus system, the Court declared that mere size was no offense. While conceding that U.S. Steel was guilty of an attempt to monopolize the steel industry, the court maintained that such a monopoly had never actually been achieved. However, if any one factor responsible for the Court's rejection of the government plea were singled out, it would undoubtedly be the friendly attitude that U.S. Steel evidenced toward its competitors. This fact more than anything else probably explains why U.S. Steel was allowed to survive while the Standard Oil Company and the American Tobacco Company were unceremoniously dissolved. This was a vindication of a policy very close to Judge Gary's heart, a policy over which there was considerable dispute with the corporation's board of directors; for Gary's "directors, worthy men but of a cruder age, were honestly puzzled. It was bewildering to hear their chairman preach the community of interests of all steelmakers, to see him consistently refusing to use the corporation's size as a club over the rest of the industry. Destructive competition, they pointed out, had made hundreds of millions for Rockefeller's oil trust. But the day came when Gary could point out that the oil trust was busted and that the steel trust survived, and that its survival was largely due to his policy of 'friendly competition.'"[6]

After 1920, U.S. Steel continued to dominate the industry, although its percentage control over total industry sales declined steadily. The corporation remained sufficiently big, however, to keep its competitors "in line" without threats and without displays of force. The friendly competition, which had paid such handsome dividends in the past, endured as the basic characteristic of the industry.

Then, in 1929, came the big Depression. For the steel industry, it was a traumatic experience, causing widespread unemployment and a terrific drop in production. In 1932, plants were operated at 19.5 per cent of capacity. Under the pressure of a rapidly falling demand, individual firms began to grant unofficial

[5] *United States* v. *United States Steel Corporation*, 251 U.S. 417 (1920).

[6] "U.S. Steel: I," reprinted from *Fortune*, **13**:157 (Mar. 1936), by special permission of the Editors. Copyright Time, Inc.

and secret price concessions in order to increase plant utilization and, thereby, spread fixed costs over a larger volume of output. Even the formerly effective basing point system seemed powerless to check the activity of panicky price cutters and "chiselers" with the result that the stable structure of uniform delivered prices broke down.

When anarchy seemed certain to gain control of the industry's price determination process, the National Industrial Recovery Act (NRA) of 1934 was passed. Under the NRA code of fair competition—drafted by steel leaders and approved by the president—the steel industry was almost totally immune against antitrust attack. It could, for the first time in its history, fix prices legally —or quasi-legally at any rate. So enthusiastic were steel executives over this government sanctioned price-maintenance scheme that Charles M. Schwab, former president of the Bethlehem Steel Corporation, claimed that never before in his 50 years' experience in the trade had he seen a year "when the business of the industry could be conducted on a commonsense basis." Little wonder can be expressed at this enthusiasm when it is considered that all price concessions under the NRA had to be approved by the Code Authority for the Steel Industry. This code authority consisted of none other than the board of directors of the American Iron and Steel Institute, the official trade association of the industry, in which the nine largest companies exercised majority (52 per cent) control.

Even government sanctioned price fixing, however, could not provide more than a palliative for the Depression ills of the steel industry. The fact remained that, given a low level of demand for producer goods, price rigidity alone could not solve the basic problem of the steel industry in the 1930s. The one sure way of getting steel out of the doldrums was by restoring full employment in the economy as a whole. This occurred only when production was stimulated by the outbreak of World War II and by the eventual entry of the United States into that conflict.

During the war, the industry made great forward strides in production and employment and, by 1943, was operating at 98.1 per cent of capacity. Prices, of course, were carefully regulated by the Office of Price Administration (OPA) and intricate priority and allocation systems were worked out to govern the distribution of steel among essential users. After V-J day, the industry returned to its "normal" pattern of rigid, administered pricing. It behaved as if the world would never change until, in the 1960s, it was confronted by a rising tide of steel imports. The industry responded not by mobilizing its economic weapons in the market place, but by launching a political campaign to obtain government protection against this novel source of competition. It used its political power— in collaboration with that of the United Steel Workers—to maintain its accustomed hegemony of power and market control.

II. MARKET STRUCTURE

The iron and steel industry is divided into four principal branches—iron ore mining, pig-iron production, steel making, and steel rolling. Depending on the function performed, the individual companies composing the industry are classified as integrated, semi-integrated, and nonintegrated. Integrated companies are those that operate in all four of the industry's branches. Semi-integrated concerns do not make their own pig iron, but purchase it to make steel and rolled products. Nonintegrated producers either make pig iron exclusively (these are the so-called merchant blast furnaces) or buy ingots or semifinished steel for rolling and further processing.

The steel industry today is—structurally speaking—an oligopoly and is dominated by a relatively few, large, integrated producers. These, taken together, own or control about three quarters of the nation's ore reserves,[7] blast furnace capacity, ingot and "steel for casting" capacity, and finished hot-rolled capacity. Both horizontally and vertically, therefore, steel is a highly concentrated industry.

Today, there are some 90 companies in the United States engaged in basic steelmaking. As Table 1 shows, the 4 largest produce 53 per cent of the nations' steel tonnage, the 8 largest 74 per cent, and the 12 largest about 81 per cent. These percentages, however, understate the degree of concentration in particular product lines and particular market areas because not every steel company produces every steel product or sells in every section of the country. Thus, the four largest producers account for 53 per cent of the raw-steel output, but in some product lines—like skelp, tube rounds, steel piling, electrical sheets and strip, axles, joint bars, and so on—they contribute close to 90 per cent of the domestic production. Regional concentration in some cases is also higher than Table 1 might suggest.

Historically, the share of the largest firms has decreased over the last 50 years, but there have been few dramatic changes in the concentration pattern during the post-World War II period. Because steel typically has been a capital-intensive industry in which the capital cost of an efficient-sized plant is large, entry into the industry has been rare indeed. However, deconcentration trends recently have begun to appear that tend to attenuate the oligopoly control exercised by the integrated majors. Let us examine these trends, as well as the factors that have worked in the direction of solidifying the oligopolistic control of the industry.

Concentration Factors

The Disposal of World War II Steel Plants

At the end of World War II—as of October 8, 1945—the War Assets Administration (WAA) held the following steel and related facilities: (1) 29 plants, valued at more than $5 million each, that were technically capable of disposal

---

[7] "Management and operation of iron-mining properties is concentrated in a few large companies which are either partly or wholly owned by the large iron and steel producers or otherwise closely affiliated with them." U.S. Tariff Commission, *Iron and Steel, War Changes in Industry Series*, no. 15, (1946), p. 88. See also U.S. Congress, Temporary National Economic Committee (TNEC), *Hearings*, Pt. 18, p. 10,426; Lake Superior Iron Ore Association, *Lake Superior Iron Ores*; also the *Mining Directory of Minnesota* (Minneapolis: Mine Experiment Station, University of Minnesota). Data on iron ore holdings in Michigan can be obtained from the Department of Conservation, Lansing, Mich.

TABLE 1

U.S. Steel Industry

COMPANY	RAW STEEL CAPACITY, 1974		RAW STEEL PRODUCTION, 1974		NET PROFIT AS PER CENT OF STOCKHOLDER EQUITY		
	MILLIONS OF TONS	PER CENT OF TOTAL	MILLIONS OF TONS	PER CENT OF TOTAL	1972	1973	1974
U.S. Steel	38.0	23.4	33.9	23.3	4.1	8.4	15.3
Bethlehem	25.2	15.5	22.3	15.3	6.3	9.2	14.4
National	11.3	6.9	10.8	7.4	6.9	9.2	15.3
Republic	11.3	6.9	10.6	7.3	4.1	7.9	14.3
Top 4	85.8	52.7	77.6	53.3	—	—	—
Armco	9.4	5.8	8.9	6.1	6.8	9.2	16.7
Jones & Laughlin	8.3	5.1	8.0	5.5			
Inland	8.2	5.0	8.0	5.5	7.7	10.0	16.3
Youngstown	6.1	3.7	6.0	4.1			
Top 8	117.8	72.3	108.5	74.5	—	—	—
Wheeling-Pittsburgh	4.4	2.7	4.2	2.9			
Kaiser	3.2	2.0	2.9	1.9			
McLouth	2.4	1.5	2.0	1.4			
Sharon	1.3	0.8	1.2	0.8			
Top 12	129.1	79.3	118.8	81.5	—	—	—
Industry total	162.7	100	145.7	100	6.0	9.5	16.7

Source: Staff report, U.S. Council on Wage and Price Stability, *A Study of Steel Prices* (Washington, D.C.: U.S. Government Printing Office, July 1975).

as independent operating units; (2) 20 plants, valued at more than $5 million each, that were classified as "scrambled with privately owned facilities"; and (3) plants, costing less than $5 million each, that were classified as partly "scrambled." The lion's share of the government's investment in steel facilities was in the first category. It amounted to $770 million and represented 59 per cent of the government's total investment in this area.[8]

Of the 29 larger plants capable of independent operation, four were integrated steel plants: the Geneva plant (erected at a cost of $202 million) whose wartime operator was U.S. Steel; a Chicago plant operated by Republic Steel during the war (costing $92 million); a plant at Houston, Texas, operated by Armco (valued at $37 million); and the Homestead, Pennsylvania, plant operated by U.S. Steel (valued at $124 million). These important plants, with the exception of Geneva, carried a purchase option by their wartime operators, and two of of the four might have been difficult to run by anybody else. Whatever the considerations that influenced the government's decision, however, the fact remains that these plants were sold to their wartime managers—that is, to the large integrated producers of the industry. The effect of this action, whatever the justification for it, was to strengthen the hand of oligopoly in the steel industry and to encourage perpetuation of the status quo in the industry's economic structure. Especially significant is the fact that, in some areas—especially in the far West —the disposition of these plants allowed the major producers to increase considerably their percentage control of output in the local market. This is made clear when we consider that acquisition of the Geneva plant (built at a cost of $202 million to the government and sold to U.S. Steel for approximately $47 million) enabled U.S. Steel to increase its total capacity in the Pacific Coast and mountain states from 17.3 to 39 per cent, and to bring its total of steel-ingot capacity in the area up to 51 per cent.

The oligopolistic structure of the steel industry was further strengthened by the Supreme Court decision in the Columbia Steel case.[9] This decision sanctioned the acquisition of a relatively small—small on a national scale—Pacific Coast plant by U.S. Steel. The company in question (Consolidated Steel) accounted for 11 per cent of the total fabricated structural products made in the West. Together with U.S. Steel, it would account for 25 to 30 per cent of the total fabricated structural products produced in the 11-state Pacific Coast and mountain states region. The merger of Consolidated with U.S. Steel constituted —in the minority opinion of the Supreme Court—a "purchase for control, a purchase for control of a market for which U.S. Steel has in the past had to compete but which it no longer wants left to the uncertainties that competition in the West may engender." The effect of the merger was not only to encourage concentration in the newly developing markets of the West, but to permit the growth of a major company that, according to Justice William O. Douglas, was "big enough."

---

[8] U.S. Tariff Commission, op. cit., p. 71.
[9] See *United States* v. *Columbia Steel Company et al.*, 334 U.S. 495 (1948).

The Concentration on Iron-ore Reserves

The concentrated ownership of iron-ore reserves also has tended to fortify the oligopoly control of the integrated producers. Today, the nine largest integrated steel producers and the four major iron-ore merchants account for over 95 per cent of the "measured" reserves in the nation's richest iron ore area—the Lake Superior District.[10] In the other iron ore districts—the northeastern, southeastern, and western—the integrated companies also exercise substantial control, at least with respect to high-grade ores. Of the nine major steel companies, only U.S. Steel has more than enough ore to support its steel-making operations. Its competitors—including such companies as Bethlehem, Republic, Armco, and Inland—lack adequate iron-ore reserves and depend on the corporation for a portion of their supplies.

The four major ore merchants offer the small ore users and semi-integrated steel companies little hope of an assured iron-ore supply. Nor are they likely to provide an open market in competition with the integrated majors. The fact is that, by 1948, the ore merchants had virtually become satellites of the major steel companies to whom they were tied by partnership arrangements, long-term supply contracts, and joint ownership. Approximately half of the ore handled by these houses went to the nine big steel companies under existing partnership arrangements. Almost all of the remaining ore was tied up under long-term contracts with the same nine companies. As a result, the spot market for iron ore, so far as sales by the ore merchants was concerned, had practically disappeared.[11]

In the control of foreign ore deposits—in Labrador, Liberia, and Venezuela (which recently nationalized its ore mines)—the major integrated companies seem to enjoy a commanding lead. Only Kaiser's control over some Australian ores represents a breach in the oligopoly's dominance of foreign ore holdings.

In summary, the concentration of iron-ore reserves helps explain the oligopolistic structure of the steel industry and the commanding role of its leader, the U.S. Steel Corporation. Whether technological innovations, or the substitutability of scrap for pig iron, or the availability of low-grade (that is, high-cost) ores will change this picture remains to be seen. It is noteworthy, however that a newcomer among the world's steel powers like Japan does not seem to have been hampered by its lack of control over iron-ore reserves.

Forward Integration by the Majors

The forward integration by the major producers also has been a factor in the strengthening of the steel oligopoly. In the past, a good part of steel fabrication was left to the smaller independents—the semi-integrated and nonintegrated finishers. The dominance of the integrated companies in this branch of the

[10] FTC, *Report on the Control of Iron Ore* (Washington D.C.: U.S. Government Printing Office, 1952), p. 87, hereafter cited as *FTC Iron Ore Report*. For the entry implications of this concentration pattern, see Joe S. Bain, *Barriers to New Competition* (Cambridge, Mass.: Harvard University Press, 1956), pp. 153–154.

[11] *FTC Iron Ore Report*, op. cit., p. 82.

industry was always much less than in the production of pig iron, ingots, and semifinished steel. Since 1939, however, the situation has changed. Large steel producers have integrated forward; large steel consumers have integrated backward; and independents have been subjected to a periodic vertical price squeeze. In periods of steel shortage, independent fabricators also have complained of a supply squeeze.

This forward integration—achieved largely through mergers and acquisitions—has, in some cases, resulted in the virtual disappearance of entire "small business" industries. Thus, steel-drum fabrication was almost completely absorbed by the basic steel producers, a process that *Iron Age* described as follows:

> Long, long ago, in 1939, before the words postwar and planning were wedded, the manufacture of heavy steel barrels and drums was a rather volatile business firmly in the hands of a large number of highly individualistic entrepreneurs. Most of these fabricators had started on a precarious shoestring and were justifiably vocal in their pride of success in the classical Horatio Alger Pluck and Luck Tradition.
>
> A few weeks ago, the purchase of Bennett Mfg. Co., Chicago, by the U.S. Steel Corporation pretty well completed the capture of the entire barrel and drum business by the major steel producers. Some 87 per cent of the business, representing about 435,000 tons of steel consumption yearly has been corralled by the mills, and the remaining 64,500 tons of independent capacity will probably remain so for a variety of reasons.[12]

The significance of such forward integration is twofold: It tends, on the one hand, to extend the oligopoly of steel making into steel fabrication; and, on the other, to tie up an increasing portion of the semifinished steel that formerly was available on the open market. As a result, nonintegrated steel users, dependent on the open market for their supplies, may be deprived of essential raw materials and find it increasingly difficult to stay in business.[13]

One other aspect of the vertical-integration movement is noteworthy—namely, the price squeeze. When forward integration by the majors is combined with a vertical price squeeze against the independents, there are likely to be fatalities. For, the nonintegrated fabricator—caught by the denial of supplies, on the one hand, and manipulation of his profit margin, on the other—may find survival unduly expensive, if not altogether impossible.

An example of how the vertical squeeze works is afforded by the price changes instituted in the spring of 1948. In February of that year, U.S. Steel raised *semifinished* steel prices by an average of $5 per ton, and other companies promptly

---

[12] *The Iron Age*, **154**: 103 (Sept. 21, 1944); quoted in FTC, *The Merger Movement: A Summary Report* Washington, D.C.: U.S. Government Printing Office, (1948), p. 46.

[13] This is especially true in times of steel shortage, when the independents complain about the alleged increase in steel shipments to the steel companies' own fabricating subsidiaries; the alleged increase in steel shipments to the steel companies' own warehouses; and the alleged increase in the proportion of steel sold in the more expensive cold-rolled and other highly finished types at the expense of the less costly hot-rolled types. See FTC, *The Distribution of Steel Consumption, 1949–1950* (Washington, D.C.: U.S. Government Printing Office, 1952). On this point, see also Simon N. Whitney, *Antitrust Policies* (New York: Twentieth Century Fund, 1958), Vol. 1, pp. 319–321.

followed. Three months later, in May, U.S. Steel led the industry to a price reduction on *finished* steel, concentrating primarily on products made by semi-integrated and nonintegrated mills. This move, which *The Iron Age* characterized as "one of the most unusual in steel history,"[14] elicited the following conclusion from the FTC:

It is apparent that by raising the prices of semifinished steel in February and by cutting the prices on the products made therefrom in May, U.S. Steel Corporation applied a double squeeze on the smaller semi-integrated and nonintegrated mills. The leadership of U.S. Steel was followed by the other large integrated companies in both instances, though apparently somewhat more reluctantly on the second occasion. These companies were themselves caught in the squeeze when the prices of finished-steel products were cut. However, their loss of revenue at the finished-steel level was partially offset by larger receipts for semifinished steel, whereas the nonintegrated companies, as a result of the double action, were squeezed at both the semi-finished and finished levels.[15]

More recently, the independent, nonintegrated fabricators accused their integrated supplier-competitors of raising the price of raw materials (wire rods) at a faster rate than the prices of finished products (wire fence, nails, barbed wire, and so on). One of the independents testified to the nature of the squeeze in a 1963 proceeding before the U.S. Tariff Commission:

Mr. Reagan: . . . I have here in front of me a quotation on wire rod from Bethlehem Steel Company to Florida Wire Products Corporation, and one from U.S. Steel Corporation to Florida Wire Products Corporation, which roughly amount to a price of $156 per ton for the raw material f.o.b. Miami, Florida.
The sales price for our finished product f.o.b. Miami and the sales price of U.S. Steel for their finished product f.o.b. Miami is $150 a ton.
Mr. Graubard: Just to get this straight, you are saying that U.S. Steel Corporation is selling the finished product at less than it offers to sell you wire rod?
Mr. Reagan: Yes, sir.
Mr. Graubard: These are delivered prices?
Mr. Reagan: Yes, sir.[16]

Such vertical price maneuvers are but one manifestation of the vertical-integration movement and the entry of the major producers into steel fabrication. The effect is to impose a serious handicap on the independent, whose predica-

---

[14] *The Iron Age*, **161**:125B (May 6, 1948). That this was a price squeeze seems clearly to have been recognized by the late Senator Robert A. Taft who was then chairman of the Joint Committee on the Economic Report. See the interesting colloquy between Senator Taft and Benjamin Fairless, then president of U.S. Steel, in *Hearings Before the Joint Committee on the Economic Report*, 80th Cong., 2d sess., 1948, pp. 14–15. Some time after this hearing, Senator Taft is reported to have said that the power of the steel companies over prices seems to be such as perhaps to require some supervision in the public interest.
[15] FTC, *Monopolistic Practices and Small Business* (Washington, D.C.: U.S. Government Printing Office, 1952), pp. 53–54.
[16] W. Adams, "Vertical Power, Dual Distribution, and the Squeeze: A Case Study in Steel," *Antitrust Bulletin*, **9**:503 (1964). See also W. Adams and J. B. Dirlam, "Steel Imports and Vertical Oligopoly Power," *American Economic Review* (Sept. 1964).

ment arises from the fact that he is dependent on the integrated producers for his supply of raw materials while competing with them in the sale of finished products.

Deconcentration Factors

The Decline of U.S. Steel

The relative position of U.S. Steel in the industry has been declining ever since its formation in 1901. Several factors are responsible for this development. First, U.S. Steel did not want to become too big for fear of prosecution under the anti-trust laws. Judge Gary was impressed with the William Jennings Bryan rule that no business should be allowed to control more than 50 per cent of an industry. Gary felt that if U.S. Steel confined itself "voluntarily to a size approved by the most popular and trusted of radicals, [it] surely [could] not be attacked for monopoly."[17]

Second, starting in the 1920s, the "independents" in the industry took part in an aggressive consolidation movement. In 1922, Bethlehem acquired all the properties of the large Lackawanna Steel Company near Buffalo, New York; it erected extensive modern facilities at Sparrows Point, Maryland; it acquired the large Cambria Steel Company (1923); and, in 1930, it bought the assets of the Pacific Coast Steel Company and the Southern California Iron and Steel Company. (Its attempt to merge with Youngstown Sheet and Tube, the nation's sixth-largest steel producer, was blocked by judicial decree in 1958.) In 1930, another powerful independent arose when a merger between the Re-public Iron and Steel Company, the Central Alloy Steel Corporation, the Donner Steel Company, and the Bourne Fuller Company was consummated. A third important merger during this period resulted in the formation of the National Steel Corporation (1929), which united steel plants in the West Virginia and Detroit areas and the blast furnace properties of the M. A. Hanna Company of Cleveland.[18]

A third factor contributing to the relative decline of the U.S. Steel Corporation was the gradual transformation in the demand for steel from heavy products (such as rails, plates, and structural shapes) to lighter products (such as sheets and strip). This shift in demand had important repercussions on the position of U.S. Steel, which was deeply committed, as far as plant capacity was con-cerned, to the production of heavy products. What made this shift in demand even more painful for the corporation was the geographic source of the new demand—especially that of the growing auto industry—which often was located at a considerable distance from the corporation's main plants. To the extent that the smaller companies were more flexible, they could, of course, accommodate themselves more readily to these changing patterns of steel consumption and, thus, improve their position relative to U.S. Steel.

[17] Tarbell, op. cit., pp. 257–258.
[18] For a history of the merger movement in the steel industry, see U.S. Congress, House, *Hearings Before the Committee on Small Business, Steel—Aquisitions, Mergers, and Expansion of 12 Major Companies, 1900–1950*, 81st Cong., 2d sess., 1950.

A fourth factor affecting the position of the industry's giant was the impact of changing technology. Here U.S. Steel lagged significantly behind its integrated rivals. In 1926, the American Rolling Mill Company bought the patents on the continuous rolling mill process, which was the major American advance in steel technology during the interwar period. Republic Steel became the leader in the growing alloy-steel field. Finally, technological innovations that permitted an increasingly large use of scrap in the production of steel tended to shift the most advantageous location pattern for the industry away from coal-producing regions and toward consumption areas, which were rich sources of scrap.

New Technology and the Minimill

Recent technological changes have substantially reduced the barriers to entry and deprived the integrated producers of their dominant position vis-à-vis the potential newcomer. As long as the open hearth was the workhorse of raw steel production, companies that owned extensive ore reserves, coke ovens, efficient blast furnaces (to make pig iron), and large open hearths (to make steel) had a decisive advantage deriving from size and vertical integration. The capital investment required by new facilities made entry by small producers virtually impossible.

In the last 20 years, however, the introduction of the basic oxygen furnace and the adaptation of the electric furnace to the production of carbon steel has substantially reduced the cost of entry.[19] The electric furnace, especially, has made it possible to construct minimills—without the necessity of integrating backward into iron ore, coke ovens, and blast furnaces.

The electric furnace, originally used primarily for producing specialty steels, now enjoys considerable popularity as a low-cost, high-tonnage steel producer. First, it is an efficient and versatile producer of both specialty (alloy and stainless) and carbon steels. Second, it operates efficiently on a 100 per cent scrap charge, thus obviating the need for facilities making pig iron and molten metal. Third, it can be built in small sizes and can produce steel in small batches, without the same cost penalty for smallness as other steelmaking methods. Fourth, an associated technical development—the continuous and other direct

---

[19] The dramatic shift in the relative popularity of different raw-steel production techniques in the last 20 years is indicated by the following percentages:

YEAR	OPEN HEARTH	BASIC OXYGEN	ELECTRIC
1950	89.1	—	6.2
1955	90.0	0.3	6.9
1960	87.0	3.4	8.4
1965	71.6	17.4	10.5
1968	50.4	37.1	12.5
1970	36.5	48.2	15.3
1975	19.0	61.5	19.5

methods of casting steel as it comes from the furnace—makes it possible to transform molten steel directly into semifinished shapes. By displacing the intermediate steps formerly necessary, it reduces capital costs, operating costs, and space requirements.[20]

William Haller, Jr., an expert on the electric furnace, summarizes its impact on competition as follows:

> Yet for actual or potential steel producers without their own supplies of hot metal, and for those with limited or obsolescent facilities for producing it, the cost advantage of the scrap-charged electric furnace seems almost conclusive. The cost penalty for small-scale production is moderate: The Battelle study finds that a 200,000-ton electric furnace plant can produce a ton of steel at a cost of only $3.08 greater than a 1,500,000-ton plant. Therefore, a moderate widening of the gap between scrap and hot metal prices, or a limited or geographically isolated market may offer opportunities for moderate- or small-size plants.
>
> The cost penalty of small-scale production becomes even less if continuous casting is used. The Battelle study estimates that a 500,000-ton plant with continuous casting can produce 8- × 8-inch blooms for $14 a ton less than can a 1,500,000-ton plant using conventional casting methods, and for only 10 cents a ton more than a 1,500,000-ton plant also using continuous casting. The advantage for small billets is apparently at least as great. The president of Roblin Steel Corporation claims that his electric furnace and continuous casting plant will produce about 120,000 tons of billets a year for a "safe $20 a ton less than the $115 per ton that is the market price for billets."[21]

Given low-cost scrap, a reasonable power rate, and proximity to local markets, combined with ultrahigh power on the electric furnace and continuous casting, the minimill seems to be cost competitive with respect to the giant producers. Thus, Georgetown Steel Corporation in South Carolina, a $20 million venture with a 300,000-ton capacity of bar and wire products, is a minimill that faces the future unafraid. By using electric furnaces and continuous casting, it claims to be producing at a cost of 5 to 10 per cent lower than the big steel companies. It counts on its lower overhead and greater flexibility in meeting changing market conditions as distinct advantages in battling its stodgy domestic competitors and the aggressive challenge of imports.[22]

Other technological advances—such as the SL-RN method for direct reduction of iron ore—also point toward lowering the high capital costs, which, in the

---

[20] U.S. Congress, Senate, Subcommittee on Antitrust and Monopoly, *Hearings on Economic Concentration*, 90th Cong., 1st sess., pt. 6, 1967, pp. 2692–2694; 3163–3197. Hereafter cited as *Economic Concentration Hearings*. See also "On Come the Electrics," *Steelways* (Nov.–Dec. 1969).

[21] *Economic Concentration Hearings*, op. cit., p. 3169.

[22] Willy Korf, the German entrepreneur who controls Georgetown Steel, has little doubt about the competitive viability of the company. He recalls that when he first entered the German steel industry, his large competitors reacted by slashing the price of reinforced bar by 25 per cent. The reaction of Mr. Korf, who accounts for 20 per cent of Germany's output, was typical. "This price will still give us a profit. But the big mills will lose money on it. Next year we will supply 30 per cent of the market," he said. *New York Times*, Jan. 26, 1969, p. F1.

past, have been a formidable entry barrier.[23] However, it would be premature to predict that the new technology will be more than a peripheral check on oligopolistic giantism in steel. Its procompetitive impact is clear, but, so far, at least, the impact is only at the margin.

Steel Imports

During the 1960s, steel imports began to play a major role in modifying the oligopolistic structure of the domestic industry. Prior to 1958, annual steel imports into the United States remained below the 2-million-ton level (except in 1951, a Korean War year, when 2.18 million tons were brought in). The 1959 steel strike, it seems, opened the floodgates and witnessed the importation of 4.4 million tons. From then on, imports steadily increased, reaching a total of 6.4 million tons in 1964, 10.8 million tons in 1966, and a high of slightly less than 18 million tons in 1968. Only with the imposition of "voluntary" quotas in 1969 was the trend partially reversed.

The structural impact of imports on the steel oligopoly had rather pronounced implications for the industry's competitive strategy, as we will see in the following sections. However, the industry's success in obtaining a "voluntary" quota system in 1969 has signaled at least a partial return to the *status quo ante*—an oligopolistic structure substantially insulated from the Schumpeterian gales of creative destruction.

Other Factors

Three other factors that have some bearing on the structure of the steel industry deserve some mention *en passant*. First, some large steel consumers like the Ford Motor Company and International Harvester Company have integrated backward and become raw-steel producers. Other firms in that category —primarily the automobile and agricultural equipment makers—represent potential entrants into the steel industry. Second, substitute materials like aluminium, plastics, cement, and glass pose some threat to the steel oligopoly— at least at the margin. Although it is difficult to predict technological change, it would appear that substitute materials can contend effectively for about 5 per cent of the market now held by steel. Third, the steel industry, like American industry generally, has been immersed in the conglomerate merger movement of the 1960s. Major companies have either merged with, or been acquired by,

---

[23] Usually, iron ore and iron-ore pellets go directly into a blast furnace where they are converted into pig iron. Then the pig iron goes into an open-hearth or basic-oxygen furnace where it is converted to steel.

The new process substitutes a rotary kiln, basically a 250-foot-long oven, for the blast furnace. The kiln bakes iron ore concentrate at 1100°F, producing pellets that can be converted directly into steel in an electric arc furnace.

With the kiln, it is claimed, a producer could build a 200,000-ton-a-year steel mill that is economically competitive with the industry giants. It would cost at least 40 per cent less than a convention steel mill. "Will Kilns Give Steel a New Cast?" *Business Week*, no. 2049:149 (Dec. 7, 1968).

firms outside the steel industry—namely, Jones & Laughlin (LTV), Youngstown·
Sheet & Tube (Lykes), Colorado Fuel & Iron (Crane), Sharon (NVF), Crucible
(Colt), and so on. Also, many steel companies have announced their intention
to diversify into other industries in order to obtain better returns on investment
than they think is available in steel. The effect of these conglomerate trends in
the structure of the steel industry cannot yet be assessed with scientific assurance.

Summarizing our discussion of market structure, we may conclude that, due
to a variety of competitive forces, a single firm no longer dominates the steel
industry; that this dominance is now shared by a dozen large, integrated producers who operate in an oligopolistic framework; and that this oligopoly is
subject to peripheral checks primarily from some entry by small producers and
from import competition.[24] The implications of this oligopolistic structure for
market conduct becomes apparent in an analysis of the industry's price policy.

III. MARKET CONDUCT

Price policy, especially in a basic industry like steel, is of crucial importance.
It influences the amount of steel consumed in a given year and the extent to
which capacity is utilized. It stimulates or retards steel-using industries. It sets a
pattern for other basic industries and, thus, plays a central role in the economy.
Without too much exaggeration, one can say that "as steel goes, so goes the
nation." Hence, it is important to understand the industry's price policy and its
underpinnings—namely, basing points, price leadership, and price stability.

The Mechanics of Basing Point Pricing

Although it was officially abandoned in 1948, the basing point system is deeply
imbedded in the philosophy of the steel industry and may still be used, at least
in modified form, especially in times of recession. The mechanics are simple.
Under the single basing point (Pittsburgh-Plus) system, steel prices at any given
delivery point were uniform—regardless of where the steel was shipped from.
To achieve this uniformity, sellers did not have to meet in a smoke-filled room
or preview each others' bids. They simply had to adhere to the basing point
formula of (1) uniform base prices, (2) uniform delivery charges, and (3) uniform
prices for "extras" and "deductions."

1. The base price was the charge for a ton of steel applicable at designated
basing points and measuring up to standard specifications (gauge, thickness,
length, chemical composition, and tolerance). Until 1924, Pittsburgh was the

---

[24] This conclusion is corroborated by Professor Haller's observation that "(c)learly the big
eight hold a powerful and secure position in the industry's competitive structure. There is little
indication that any of them will be forced to a lower rank, or that the medium or small firms
individually will match them in size. But the slight decline in their group share, the more marked
decline in the individual share of the largest firm, and the indications of growth and new entry
among the medium and small firms are symptoms of potential competition emerging at some
points into actuality." *Hearings on Economic Concentration*, op. cit., p. 2690.

only basing point and all steel prices were quoted in terms of the Pittsburgh base plus the cost of transportation to the point of delivery. As a rule, base prices were set by U.S. Steel and widely publicized in the trade press, so that other companies would have no difficulty in following the leader.

2. Transportation charges, the second element in the formula, had to be uniform in order to make delivered prices identical at any one destination. Obviously, the delivered price in Detroit would not be identical if one company charged an all-rail rate while its competitors charged a part-rail, part-water rate. Moreover, if one company charged the actual transportation costs and another collected "fictitious" freight charges, it would be impossible to maintain uniform delivered prices. For many years, therefore, the American Iron & Steel Institute published a book of freight rates showing the rail cost for transporting a ton of steel from Pittsburgh to every delivery point in the United States.

3. Extras and deductions, the third element in the formula, were merely additions to, or deductions from, the basic price—in order to make allowance for special variations from standard specifications. Here, again, the objective was to assure uniform delivered prices; U.S. Steel, often after consultation with other companies, set up and publicized its schedule of extras, which its rivals chose to follow with amazing regularity.

Here is a concrete example of how the Pittsburgh-Plus system operated: In 1920, the Pittsburgh price for steel was $40 per ton, and the freight charge from Pittsburgh to Chicago (then not a basing point) was $7.60. The delivered price in Chicago, therefore, was $47.60—regardless of where the steel was shipped from and regardless of which company happened to make the sale. In an extreme case, where steel was wheeled through a party wall opening from a Chicago producer to a Chicago consumer, the latter still had to pay $7.60 for transportation, even though no transportation cost had been incurred. Such "phantom freight" came into being whenever steel was shipped from a mill nearer than the basing point to the place of delivery. The amount of phantom freight was measured by the excess of the "official" over the actual transportation cost.[25]

To carry our example a step farther: If the Chicago producer shipped to a customer in Pittsburgh, he would get a delivered price of $40 (base price plus cost of transportation from the *basing* point to the point of delivery). He would be unable to collect any freight charges, even though it cost him $7.60 to transport the steel to Pittsburgh. He would have to "absorb freight"—the exact amount being the excess of the actual over the "official" freight charges. On this transaction, therefore, he would receive a mill net price of $32.40—in contrast to the mill net of $47.60 on his sale to the Chicago customer.[26] He would discriminate against the nearby (well-located) consumer and in favor of the distant (poorly located) consumer.

[25] Phantom freight also arose when a producer charged his customer an all-rail rate while actually using cheaper transport means, such as water or truck.

[26] Mill net is defined as the price received at the mill after the payment or allowance for the actual transportation from mill to destination has been deducted from the invoiced, delivered price.

In 1924, this Pittsburgh-Plus system was superseded by a multiple basing point system. The principle of quoting uniform delivered prices, however, remained intact. The only modification was to create new basing points like Chicago, Birmingham, and Sparrows Point, and to quote prices in terms of the *nearest* basing point (called the governing basing point) plus the transportation cost to the point of delivery. In Des Moines, therefore, the delivered price would be computed on a Chicago, instead of a Pittsburgh, base, but all mills shipping into Des Moines would still quote identical prices at the point of delivery.

The Case for Basing Point Pricing

Steel-industry executives have defended the basing point system with uncompromising consistency.[27] They supported the efforts to legalize the system even after the Supreme Court declared it to be a violation of the antitrust laws. Their arguments are as follows:

1. The basing point system is the quintessence of perfect competition because it results in one price in one place at one time: "Competition is at its perfection of expression when all of the sellers are on the same level."[28]

2. The system cannot be harmful because it does not work. Thus, the president of U.S. Steel told a congressional committee that "[i]f base prices as announced were followed in every transaction, and . . . the nearest basing point to the consumer governed, and . . . rail freight was added from that point, and the delivered price actually arrived at in that manner, there wouldn't be any competition in the steel industry. It would be a one-price industry, pure and simple."[29] Industry spokesmen point out, however, that basing point prices are "fictitious"; they are prices "we want to get"—"prices that we feel fair." "We don't succeed in getting those prices because competition won't permit it,"[30] the spokesmen contend. In times of slack demand, there is some truth in this argument. The deeper the recession, the greater is the pressure on steel firms to shade the list prices computed under the basing point formula.

3. The basing point system, some say, is necessary—not to promote competition but to prevent its excesses. In the steel industry, overhead costs are a significant portion of total costs, and profits depend largely on the extent to which capacity is utilized. As steel output goes up, average costs decline and profits

[27] In this, they have had the support of some distinguished economists. See, among others, J. M. Clark, "Imperfect Competition Theory and Basing Point Problems," *American Economic Review*, 33:283 (June 1943), and "Law and Economics of Basing Points," ibid., 39:430 (Mar. 1949); A. Smithies, "Aspects of the Basing Point System," ibid., 32:705 (Dec. 1942); H. G. Lewis and T. O. Yntema in *TNEC Papers* (New York: United States Steel Corporation, 1940).

[28] TNEC, *Hearings*, pt. 5, p. 1882. To this argument, TNEC members replied that, under perfect competition, a single price in a given market at a given time is the result of an interplay of many buyers and sellers, whereas under the basing point system—by contrast—there prevails a single *bid* price at a point of delivery, a price quoted *outside* the market and then imposed *on* the market. It is further contended that this basing point price in fact results in variable mill net prices; that it is, therefore, in effect, a discriminatory price based on a predetermined formula collusively derived. Compare ibid., pp. 1862–1863, 1873, 1882, 1911–1913.

[29] TNEC, *Hearings*, op. cit., pt. 27, p. 14172.

[30] Ibid., pt. 19, pp. 10,511–10,512.

increase. The converse is also true. It is imperative, therefore, that steel companies operate as close to full capacity as possible in order to maximize profits, and here is the rub. Given high overhead costs, and in the face of a slack demand, steel companies will be tempted to secure additional sales by offering price concessions. They will tend to accept additional orders at any price in excess of variable cost (out-of-pocket expenses). If one company does this, there are no adverse effects; but if all resort to the same solution of their overhead cost problem, the inevitable result is a devastating price war—waged without regard to average costs.[31] Such a war may cause prices on *all* sales to be cut below average total costs and may eventually result in a victory for the financially most powerful producers (those who can sustain short-run losses because of their financial staying power) rather than in the survival of the industry's most efficient firms. Such a war would only lead to cut-throat competition, the extinction of some producers, and a further tendency toward concentration in the industry.

At this point the clincher is applied to the overhead-cost argument. Steel producers, it is said, are under constant pressure to spread their overhead costs over as large an output as possible. Because they dare not cut prices and, thus, invite certain retaliation and perhaps a disastrous price war, they have only one alternative—to discriminate.[32] By following the basing point system—by absorbing freight in their invasion of distant markets—steel producers can solicit additional sales without incurring the dangers of price competition. In order to stimulate volume, they can accept a lower mill net price on sales outside their "natural" market areas in the hope of solving their overhead cost problem. The only difficulty with this solution is that freight absorption has to be paid out of the producer's pocketbook. Moreover, it may prove self-defeating if other producers resort to the same solution, as they inevitably will and must.

4. The basing point system, steel leaders point out, is a necessary instrument of price stability because the demand for steel is highly inelastic—that is, price cuts will not bring about a proportionate increase in steel consumption. To be sure, the individual producer faces an elastic demand schedule; if he cuts prices, he can increase sales. But, if all producers do the same thing, they cannot increase their sales sufficiently to overcome the inelastic demand for the industry as a whole. Therefore, it is argued, it is desirable to prevent price competition through some stabilizing mechanism like the basing point system.

Steel spokesmen cite the following evidence for the inelasticity of steel demand. First, they point to the fact that steel is a raw material, the demand for which is

---

[31] This argument is based on the assumption of an inelastic and cyclically derived demand.

[32] J. M. Clark describes the paradox of price confronting a firm burdened by high overhead costs as follows: "If any business that would pay its own particular costs is refused because it will not pay its share of overhead, there is a loss. Yet, prices must be charged, which will cover overhead, so long as industry depends on private enterprise. There is only one answer to this dilemma—discrimination. The overhead costs must be levied on such parts of the business as will stand the burden, while other parts of the business, which cannot otherwise be had at all, are charged whatever they can pay, regardless of overhead costs. However," Clark significantly concludes, "this is only a partial answer to the question, and creates more problems than it solves." *The Economics of Overhead Costs* (Chicago: University of Chicago Press, 1923), p. 23.

derived from the demand for other products. Hence, if the aggregate demand for such items as automobiles and washing machines is depressed (because of a recession), cutting the price of steel is futile as a demand stimulant.

Second, they argue that the "substitution of steel for other materials, or a reverse substitution, is not an important factor in the cyclical fluctuations in the demand for steel."[33] Because the substitution factor is not very important in the demand for steel, "price reduction would result in very little additional steel being sold as substitutes for other products, and a price advance, unless abnormal, probably would not result in additional competition from substitute products."[34]

Third, so runs the argument, the demand for steel is inelastic because steel generally constitutes a very small portion of the total cost of the products in which it is contained as a raw material. It is pointed out, for example, that, under 1948 conditions, "a $5 per ton change in the price of all steel products going into a $1500 automobile would affect the cost of producing the automobile about $8; a $20 electric toaster would be affected by less than 1 cent; a $285 electric refrigerator by 61 cents; a $184 gas range by 49 cents; and a $130 washing machine by 25 cents, while the cost of building a 35-story steel-frame office building would be affected by six tenths of 1 per cent."[35]

It is for these reasons that industry leaders hold the demand for steel to be inelastic, and consider the price stabilizing functions of the basing point system to be vital to the preservation of a healthy price structure for steel products.

5. Another favorite argument in defense of the basing point system alludes to the dangers of local monopoly in case the system were abandoned and replaced by f.o.b. mill pricing. The f.o.b. mill prices, it is charged, "would put [the consumer] generally at the mercy of the nearest mill," because the latter could make the shipment of steel into its "natural" delivery area unprofitable to rivals. The nearest mill could eliminate competition in its immediate vicinity by setting a price so low that no competitor could meet it.[36]

[33] Study by the United States Steel Corporation, Exhibit no. 1410. TNEC, *Hearings*, op. cit., pt. 26 (Washington, D.C.: U.S. Government Printing Office); reprinted in the TNEC Monograph, no. 42, *The Basing Point Problem*, 1941, p. 15.

[34] TNEC Monograph, no. 42, op. cit., p. 16. This argument is, of course, at loggerheads with the industry's contention that steel is subject to intense interindustry competition.

[35] Statement by Arthur B. Homer, president of the Bethlehem Steel Corporation, U.S. Congress, *Joint Committee on the Economic Report*, 80th Cong., 2d sess., Mar. 2, 1948. Cf. also T. Yntema, "A Statistical Analysis of the Demand for Steel, 1919–1938" in the United States Steel Corporation, *TNEC Papers* (New York: United States Steel Corporation, 1939); General Motors Corporation, *The Dynamics of Automobile Demand* (New York: General Motors Corporation, 1939).

[36] If it were the inevitable result of f.o.b. mill pricing, however, the consumer can certainly be no worse off than under the basing point system; for, if the local mill ever attempted to exploit its regional monopoly by charging exorbitant prices at a given point "A," producers located in nearby areas would again find it profitable to make deliveries at "A," thus destroying the potentially evil effects of local monopoly. A local monopoly in steel, therefore, would be no more serious than the monopoly enjoyed by the neighborhood grocer due to his strategic location in respect to the market. Under these conditions, "The mercy of the nearest mill might be preferable to the mercy of a whole industry united on one price." Compare: "U.S. Steel II: Prices," reprinted from *Fortune*, **13**:136 (Apr. 1936), by special permission of the Editors. Copyright Time Inc.

The Case Against Basing Point Pricing

In its legal skirmishes against the basing point system, which lasted some 30 years, the FTC relied on the following major arguments:

1. The system, according to the commission, promotes collusion and results in the elimination of price competition. The system worked so well that companies located at widely separated points, and in ostensible competition with one another, would submit sealed bids to the Federal government that were identical to the fourth decimal place.[37] At any given destination, there would be no price competition—regardless of which company made the sale or where the steel was actually shipped from.

The basing point formula, according to the FTC, is a more effective instrument of collusion than old-fashioned price agreements. It is the eye that discovers the chiseler and the hand that wields the punishing whip. Under its rules, price cutting does not pay and, in its enforcement, price cutting is not "necessary." Price cutting does not pay because the chiseler's reduced price immediately becomes the base price in his area and is "matched" by all his competitors. This means that "all delivered prices are identical again and the fellow hasn't gained anything by cutting his price except a headache."[38] Moreover, price cutting is not necessary because the steel industry's "live-and-let-live" tradition makes for a protective umbrella that is high and wide enough for everyone—including the inefficient producers.

2. The system, according to the FTC, is artificial and discriminatory. The customer located nearest to the production site from which the steel is actually shipped does not always get the lowest price and often "would be as cheaply supplied if the nearby mill did not exist."[39] Moreover, he suffers discrimination even if he is located right at the basing point. This is so because base prices must be high enough to permit mills to absorb freight on sales to less fortunately located customers. Such discrimination would persist, even if all production points were to become basing points. Although phantom freight would disappear, the system of uniform delivered prices would still result in freight absorption and, hence, differential (discriminatory) mill nets.

3. The system, the FTC charges, results in wasteful cross hauling—that is, the reciprocal invasion of the "natural" market areas of steel mills producing identical products.[40] As Charles Schwab, former president of Bethlehem Steel

[37] See TNEC, *Hearings,* op. cit., pt. 5, p. 1897. While the commission does not consider the basing point formula illegal per se (that is, when used by *one* or a *few* producers independently), the formula is held to become unlawful when it serves to implement collusion and price fixing among *all* the producers in an industry. *Notice to Staff* (Oct. 12, 1948). As such, it is deemed illegal under Section 5 of the Federal Trade Commission Act because the commission believes it to be "an obvious fact that the economic effect of identical prices achieved through conscious parallel action is the same as that of similar prices achieved through overt collusion." Ibid., p. 3.

[38] TNEC, *Hearings,* op. cit., pt. 5, p. 1868.

[39] TNEC Monograph, no. 42, op. cit., p. 2.

[40] In this connection, it is interesting to note the attempt of Professor Smithies of Harvard to show that a rational monopolist would certainly have eliminated the wasteful practice of cross hauling. Smithies regards preservation of cross hauling under the basing point system as one item of evidence that the basing point system is not necessarily an instrument of collusion. A. Smithies, "Aspects of the Basing Point System," *American Economic Review,* **32**:423 (Dec. 1942).

Corporation, candidly observed, it "is manifestly uneconomic for a steel manufacturer in Chicago to ship 100,000 tons of steel to Pittsburgh at a time when a Pittsburgh manufacturer is shipping a like quantity of like material from Pittsburgh to Chicago."[41] Not only is such cross hauling self-defeating, it also dissipates part of the producer's revenue on unnecessary transportation and imposes an additional burden on the consumer, who ultimately has to pay for this wasteful extravagance. Competition is diverted from base price reductions that would benefit *all* consumers to increased freight absorption, which entails no price advantage to *any* consumer.

4. The basing point system is also said to result in an uneconomic location of both steel producers and consumers. The latter may locate at an unfavorable site just to be close to a basing point, whereas under a different pricing system they might have chosen a better location near a steel mill that was *not* a basing point. Similarly, steel producers can afford to maintain their investment in anachronistic locations because "under the umbrella of a controlled price system the test of profitable plant location ceases to be essentially a matter of cost of production and distribution. . . . Plants thereby may be established at uneconomic points in terms of production costs."[42]

Why, some critics ask, should Detroit have only 5 per cent of the nation's steel capacity when Detroit industries consume nearly three times as much? Why should Pittsburgh produce almost twice as much steel as is needed in its market area? Can the present location of steel plants be explained purely in terms of proximity to raw materials and markets? Obviously not. The basing point system bears part of the blame for whatever distortion exists because it allows "every steel mill to compete on a substantially equal footing for any piece of business anywhere in the country," thus tending to neutralize the advantages of location.

Price Leadership

Although most of these arguments against the basing point system are valid, it would be a mistake to carry them too far. In an industry like steel, geographic price discrimination and restraints on price competition can be explained not so much in terms of the basing point system but by the dearth of sellers, the homogeneity of steel products, the importance of overhead costs, the difficulty of entry, the substantial concentration on the buyer's side of the market, and the danger of cut-throat competition (especially when firms are hungry)—in short, by the structure of the industry. It is a fundamental fact that steel is an oligopoly and that its prices will, therefore, be "administered." This can be done "in many different ways. There may be no other technique of price administration

[41] Quoted in C. D. Edwards, "Basing Point Decisions and Business Practices," *American Economic Review*, 38:840 (Dec. 1948).
[42] Reprinted from David Lynch, *The Concentration of Economic Power*, p. 191. Copyright 1946 by Columbia University Press, New York.

that is so elegantly simple to operate as the basing point system, but there may be many others that will yield socially equivalent results."[43]

With or without a basing point system, price leadership is a pervasive characteristic of the steel industry. Typically, U.S. Steel sets the pace and the other companies follow in lockstep—both in their sales to private customers and in their secret bids on government contracts. Often, steel producers shipping from different locations will quote delivered prices identical to the thousandths of a cent per pound. Roger Blough, former president of U.S. Steel, explained this phenomenon by citing a Naval Gun Factory contract as an example: "United States Steel offered a delivered price to meet the lowest delivered price it anticipated would be bid on this item. From its prior knowledge of dealings with the Naval Gun Factory and of the market, U.S. Steel could and did expect that Bethlehem would offer a bid on this invitation. Upon evaluation of these competitive circumstances, U.S. Steel found that if Bethlehem bid its announced price for the item at its producing mill at Sparrows Point, Maryland, from which it could be expected to offer to ship, plus freight from that mill to the Naval Gun Factory, its delivery price would be $0.07205 per pound. U.S. Steel accordingly reduced its own delivered price for shipment from its Fairless Works to the Naval Gun Factory by an amount which would enable it to meet the equally low price of its competitor."[44]

"Meeting competition" is the industry's euphemism to explain this price uniformity. On the downside this is understandable. Given the high degree of standardization of steel products and the negligible differences in quality, price cuts by one producer must quickly be matched by his competitors. "There isn't certainly any steel company in the first ten or in the first twenty," the president of U.S. Steel told a congressional committee, "that couldn't require us to change our prices overnight simply by taking action which is different than the action that we take."[45]

But what about "meeting competition" on the up side? Why do powerful companies like Bethlehem or National seldom challenge U.S. Steel's decision to increase prices? Such price followership seems anomalous, especially in those lines and those areas where these companies surpass U.S. Steel in production volume. In 1957, for example, Bethlehem held 72.2 per cent of the capacity for rolled-steel piling (compared to U.S. Steel's 26.6 per cent); yet, it dutifully followed U.S. Steel's price leadership. In the northeastern states, National ranked first (18.9 per cent) and U.S. Steel sixth (7.2 per cent) in cold-rolled sheets capacity; yet, National was not inclined to challenge the price leader.[46] This price followership is also anomalous because different steel companies have different costs and earn different profits.

[43] J. K. Galbraith, "Light on a Hot Subject," reprinted from *Fortune*, 39:211 (Apr. 1949) by special permission of the Editors. Copyright Time, Inc.

[44] U.S. Congress, Senate, Subcommittee on Antitrust and Monopoly, *Administered Prices in Steel*, S. Rept. no. 1387, 85th Cong., 2d sess., 1958, p. 122. (Hereafter cited as *Kefauver Committee Report*.)

[45] Ibid., p. 78.

[46] Ibid., pp. 90–94.

Meeting the price *increases* of a computer is what the steel executives call competition. They liken it to the Gimbels-Macy's rivalry. But the late Senator Kefauver rejected the Gimbels-Macy's analogy: "Would New Yorkers," he asked, "have the benefit of greater competition, of greater freedom of choice, if the prices of Macy's and Gimbels were invariably identical? Would . . . competition . . . be greater if every price increase by Macy's was immediately matched by Gimbels? If Macy's and Gimbels turned to what we have heard here about the steel industry, then a new Macy's slogan might wave over Herald Square, 'Our prices are always exactly as high as Gimbels.'"[47] Price uniformity in a competitive industry is one thing. In an oligopoly, it is quite another.

This lockstep price uniformity is maintained by punishing any major mill that shows deviationist tendencies. "In 1968, for example," the Council on Wage and Price Stability reports, "Bethlehem Steel cut the price of cold-rolled sheet steel from $113.50 a ton to $88.50, in order to discipline efforts by other steel firms to sell cheaper and take business; shortly afterward, the price was raised to $125 and respected by all."[48] This exercise does not have to be repeated too often to convey to the players of the administered price game what is expected of them.

Price Rigidity

This tendency toward price uniformity is reinforced by a tendency toward price rigidity. In comparison to other industries, where prices are more responsive to automatic, competitive market forces, steel prices appear remarkably stable and inflexible. Contrast steel with textile and agricultural products, for example. In these industries, a cyclical change in demand tends to result in relatively drastic price changes without a similar effect on output and employment. In steel, the process is reversed. Production and demand are equated by an administered price that results in relatively wide output and employment fluctuations and proportionately smaller price fluctuations. In other words, price stability is obtained at the expense of instability in output (see Figure 1).

Such stability, of course, is not natural or inevitable, but the result of conscious administrative direction. In the past, U.S. Steel has tended to resist substantial price increases in times of high demand and opposed any marked reductions in times of slack demand. It has tried to hold prices constant—often for months and years. In the case of Bessember steel rails—to take an extreme example—annual average prices fluctuated from $67.52 to $17.62 per ton between 1880 and 1901—that is, during the competitive era preceding the organization of U.S. Steel. From May 1901, however, less than 60 days after the founding of the corporation, a price of $28 per ton was in effect until April 1916 (a period of 180 months). After some fluctuations, a price of $43 per ton was announced in October 1922, which remained in effect until October 1932 (a period of 121

[47] Ibid., p. 100.
[48] *Staff Report*, *A Study of Steel Prices* (Washington, D.C.: U.S. Government Printing Office, July 1975), p. 1.

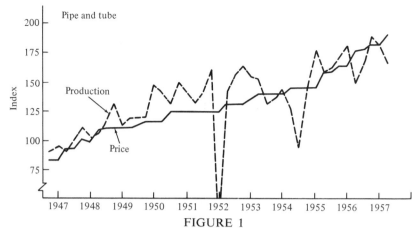

FIGURE 1

Trends in the price and production of pipe and tube, 1947–1957 (1947–1957 = 100).
Source: U.S. Congress, Senate, Subcommittee on Antitrust and Monopoly, "Administered Prices: Steel," *Senate Report no. 1387*, 85th Cong., 2d sess., 1958, p. 21.

months).[49] Other steel products have experienced similar, though less pronounced, price stabilization. "Unless impelled by sharp increases in direct costs or dangerous sniping by rivals," say Kaplan, Dirlam, and Lanzillotti, U.S. Steel has generally preferred to resist "either price increases or decreases," and to sacrifice stability "only when the decision [was] unavoidable."[50]

In recent years, however, this policy seems to have undergone some change. According to the Kefauver committee, steel prices have tended to become more flexible—but flexible in an upward direction only. Since 1947, the committee reports, there has emerged a fairly consistent pattern of "stair-step" price increases at regular intervals—with base prices usually going up in midsummer and extra prices rising in midwinter. Moreover, this upward flexibility has at times been achieved in the face of declining demand. Thus, between December 1955 and August 1957, the price index on cold-rolled sheets rose 20 points, while the production index declined 80 points; on cold-rolled strip, the price index advanced 23.8 points, while the production index slumped 45.6 points; on hot-rolled sheets, the price index rose 30.4 points, while the production index fell 58.6 points. Similar trends were observed in hot-rolled bars, pipe and tube, rails, plates, and other steel products.[51]

[49] See A. R. Burns, *The Decline of Competition* (New York: McGraw-Hill, 1936), pp. 205 ff.
[50] A. D. H. Kaplan, J. B. Dirlam, and R. F. Lanzillotti, *Pricing in Big Business* (Washington, D.C.: Brookings, 1958), p. 175.
[51] *Kefauver Committee Report*, op. cit., pp. 17–26. Prices of different steel products are, of course, adjusted to varying market elasticities. In general, prices and profit margins are highest on items facing less intense (domestic or import) competition, like steel rails and cable. "Stainless steel, galvanized sheets, and tin plate, on the other hand, which are in direct or potential competition with substitutes from aluminum to lumber, had narrower profit margins." The same holds true for products like cold-rolled sheets, which are sold to buyers (for example, automobile and farm equipment manufacturers) "who are able to exert strong pressures because of size and ability to threaten, at least, to make their own." See Kaplan, Dirlam, and Lanzillotti, op. cit., p. 172.

Since World War II, it seems, steel prices have not only shown a remarkable insensitivity to market conditions, but have risen with virtually unbroken regularity. They have increased even when demand and production declined (as in 1949, 1954, and 1957). They continued their climb even when unit labor costs declined (as in 1950 and 1955). According to the Kefauver committee, "no matter what the change in cost or in demand, steel prices since 1947 have moved steadily and regularly in only one direction, upward." The fact that prices were raised again in 1957, and that this increase was "made to stick" in the face of a general recession, was further "tribute to the perfection with which price leadership in the steel industry maintains price rigidity."[52] With few exceptions, events during the 1960s and 1970s only served to buttress this generalization.

One final comment on price rigidity. Some economists, typically followers of the Chicago school, argue that price rigidity in oligopolized industries is deceptive because "transaction" prices tend to be far more flexible than "quoted" prices. Whatever the validity of this contention in other industries, however, it is not true in steel. As G. J. Stigler and J. K. Kindahl found in their comprehensive study, the quoted and transaction "prices of steel products move together so closely that a description of one is a description of the other. . . . This finding, it must be confessed, comes as a surprise to us. The steel industry is now unconcentrated as compared with the first decade of the century, or indeed as compared with many other industries in our sample. Import competition was growing fairly steadily during the period. With the exception of three steel products, however, we were not able to learn of any important and continuous departures from quoted prices. The exceptions were reinforcing bars (where we saw, but could not obtain, records of extensive short-run price fluctuations), pipe, and stainless steel products. One encounters minor incidents of price cutting such as quantity discounts granted on small orders and the supply of qualities somewhat better than minimum specifications. Nevertheless, the general picture was one of close adherence to quoted prices even for very large buyers of steel."[53]

IV. MARKET PERFORMANCE

Price Escalation and Loss of Competitiveness

The persistent price escalation of steel prices during the 1950s was the primary cause of the industry's lackluster performance during the 1960s—resulting in the erosion of domestic markets by substitute materials and imports, the loss of export markets not tied to Agency for International Development (AID) control, and the decline in return on investment.

The facts on steel pricing are beyond question. According to the Council of Economic Advisers, "Steel prices played an important role in the general price

---

[52] *Kefauver Committee Report*, op. cit., p. 129. Again, it should be noted that those prices subject to more intense competition or buyer pressures have increased less than others, but the composite index for *all* steel products has clearly risen.

[53] G. J. Stigler and J. K. Kindahl, *The Behavior of Industrial Prices* (New York: National Bureau of Economic Research, 1970), pp. 72–74.

increases of the 1950s. Between 1947 and 1951, the average increase in the price of basic steel products was 9 per cent per year, twice the average increase of all wholesale prices. The unique behavior of steel prices was most pronounced in the mid-1950s. While the wholesale price index was falling an average of 0.9 per cent annually from 1951 to 1955, the price index for steel was rising an average of 4.8 per cent per year. From 1955 to 1958, steel prices were increasing 7.1 per cent annually, or almost three times as fast as wholesale prices generally. No other major sector shows a similar record."[54]

During the 1960s, steel prices entered a relatively quiescent stage. The major factor in dampening the industry's enthusiasm for marching in lockstep toward constantly higher price levels was the burgeoning of import competition. Thus, between January 1960 and December 1968, a period of 9 years, the composite steel price index increased 4.1 points—or 0.45-points per year. Starting in January 1969, however, after the State Department had successfully persuaded the Europeans and Japanese to accept "voluntary" quotas on their sales to the United States (that is, to enter into an informal international steel cartel), imports were cut back drastically and the domestic steel prices resumed their pre-1960 climb. In the four years between January 1969 and December 1972, the steel price index rose 26.7 points—or 6.67 points per year. Put differently, steel prices increased at an annual rate fourteen times greater since the import quotas went into effect than in the nine years prior thereto. Through most of this period, the policy of price escalation was pursued in the face of recession, low volume, and the idleness of roughly 25 per cent of the nation's steel capacity.

The Nixon Administration's price controls, in effect from August 1971 through April 1974, temporarily attenuated the steady climb of steel prices. But, in 1974, spurred by a worldwide steel shortage, they resumed their long-run trend upward—rising 30 per cent, compared with 17 per cent for all industrial commodities. The industry, it seemed, had once again returned to its traditional behavior model. The leaders again set prices "at full costs—fixed costs plus marginal costs—plus target rate of return, subject to certain limits."[55] The followers again did what was expected of them. Inevitably, prices were characterized by uniformity and upward rigidity.

The industry justifies this policy by arguing that its competitive position can be improved only by increasing profits that it claims are indispensable in order to attract the necessary capital for investment in more efficient and modern plants.[56] Whatever the merits of this argument, a cost-plus, target-rate-of-

[54] Council of Economic Advisors, *Report to the President on Steel Prices* (Washington, D.C.: U.S. Government Printing Office, Apr. 1965), pp. 8–9. Hereafter cited as *CEA Steel Report.*

[55] Staff Report, Council on Wage and Price Stability, op. cit., p. 1.

[56] Roger Blough, in defending the industry's 1962 abortive price increase, clearly articulated this philosophy: "While the price rise might have appeared to intensify our competitive difficulties with cheaper foreign steel, that steel is usually priced in relation to ours anyway, and in the long run, the increase would have improved our competitive strength. By using the added profits produced by the price increase to help obtain the most modern and efficient tools of production, we could hope eventually to narrow the gap between American and foreign steel prices." *Look* (Jan. 29, 1963), **27**:23. Thus, Mr. Blough proposed to meet the competition of cheaper foreign steel by *raising* prices.

return policy tends to be workable in periods of rising prices and in the absence of foreign competition. But, as events during the 1960s demonstrated, such a policy also makes the industry vulnerable to both substitute competition and imports—with deleterious effects on output growth, capacity utilization, and profit levels.

Substitute Competition

Part of steel's woes can be traced to the deterioration of its price competitiveness vis-à-vis substitutes. "On a comparative basis," reports the CEA, "the price of basic steel products rose substantially relative to the prices of competing materials. Relative to plastics, the price of basic steel products was more than twice as high in 1963 as it was in 1974. The prices of cement, glass, plastic materials, and aluminum all rose substantially less than steel. With this sharp deterioration in the relative price position of steel products vis-à-vis other materials, failure of iron and steel production to keep pace with the growth of the economy is not surprising."[57]

It is not surprising, therefore, that between 1947 and 1967, the aluminum industry increased sixfold, the plastics industry twentyfold, and the glass, cement, and brick industries about doubled in size—whereas iron and steel output rose only 35 per cent. In the 3 years from 1964 to 1967, while the level of steel production remained unchanged, total industrial production increased 19 per cent, the production of glass 10 per cent, cement 4 per cent, aluminum 28 per cent, and plastics 33 per cent. Although other than price factors undoubtedly played a role, steel's deteriorating relative position is partly attributable to its upward, rigid price policy.

Loss of Export Markets

In the mid-1950s, the United States exported about four times as much steel as it imported. By 1960, the United States had become a net importer of steel and, by 1968, imports exceeded exports by a margin of 8 to 1. Even so, the lion's share of our exports represented "tied" sales under the AID program. Here, again, the noncompetitive price policy of the steel industry was the primary factor explaining this performance record.

Typically, American steel exports were priced at U.S. list prices (f.o.b. producing mill or service centers) plus freight costs to the point of delivery. As the Senate Finance Committee concedes, "generally no attempt is made to align export pricing on the substantially lower prices quoted in third markets by the European or Japanese steel producers."[58] This means, of course, that American steel exports carry the albatross of high prices and rigid prices into the arena of international competition.

The rigidity of American steel export prices stands in remarkable contrast to

---

[57] *CEA Steel Report*, op. cit., p. 28.
[58] U.S. Congress, Senate, Finance Committee, *Steel Imports*, 90th Cong., 1st sess., 1967, p. 126.

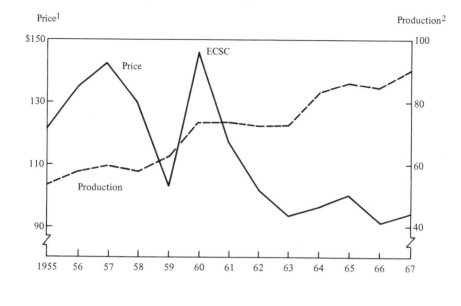

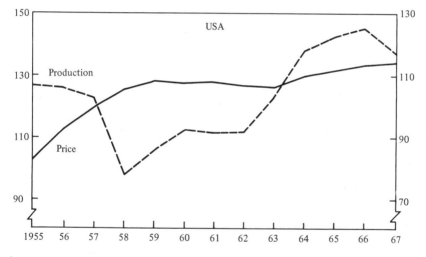

[1]Average export prices, open-hearth grade, beginning of year, per metric ten.
[2]Millions of metric tens.

FIGURE 2

Steel export prices and production, European Coal and Steel Community and the United States, 1955–1967. Source: Economic Concentration Hearings, pt. 7, p. 3445.

that of Common Market prices. Between 1955 and 1967, according to Egon Sohmen, "steel prices were almost completely rigid in the United States (for all practical purposes, they were adjusted only in an upward direction) while they were remarkably flexible in Europe. . . . Largely as a consequence of this rigidity in price, the level of production suffered major setbacks in the United States

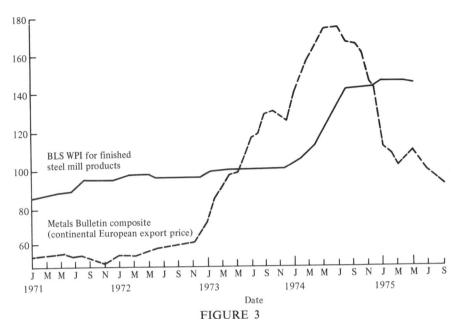

FIGURE 3

European export price index compared to BLS price index for finished steel mill products (May 1973 = 100). Source: Council on Wage and Price Stability, Staff Report, *A Study of Steel Prices*, July 1975 (updated).

whenever business activity receded so that steel works operated at less than two thirds of capacity for many years. Steelmakers in Europe, on the other hand, were able to operate near capacity more or less continuously until [the late 1960s]."[59] Figures 2 and 3 underscore this point. It is also noteworthy that the United States turned from a net exporter to a net importer of steel precisely during a period—the late 1950s and early 1960s—when its own steel-producing capacity was seriously underutilized.

The magnitude of the damage inflicted by the industry's noncompetitive behavior on the U.S. balance of trade has been estimated by Sohmen: "Had the industry worked at capacity during the early sixties, and had it exported the additional steel at world market prices, the additional export revenue (taking into account the fact that steel prices on the world market would have been somewhat lower as a consequence) would have eliminated the U.S. balance-of-

[59] *Hearings on Economic Concentration*, pt. 7, 1968, p. 3444. The Organization for Economic Cooperation and Development (OECD) Iron and Steel Committee observed in its 1960 report, "[there seems to be] a fundamental difference in the export price policy pursued by producers in the various exporting areas . . . the producers in the E[uropean] C[oal] and S[teel] C[ommunity] and Japan, seem to adopt a much more flexible policy . . . to try to expand their share of the export market by making sacrifices . . . . This policy is in marked contrast to that followed in the United States and, it would seem, in the United Kingdom where the steel industries seem less disposed to offer heavy cuts in prices to overseas consumers." *The Iron and Steel Industry in Europe* (Paris: OECD 1960), p. 97. Nor, one can add, are they inclined to readily reduce prices to domestic consumers to meet foreign competition.

payments deficit during these years. One need hardly go into details of what the United States would have been spared in this event. . . . This comparison is, if anything, likely to understate the contribution of high steel prices to the U.S. balance-of-payments troubles. If steel prices in the United States had uniformly been at the lower world market levels, many important American industries using steel (the automobile or the machinery industries, to name only a few) could have reduced their prices. This would have entailed a rise of exports of these industries and a fall of competing imports, further improving the U.S. trade balance.'[60]

Erosion of Domestic Markets by Imports

The dramatic rise in steel imports during the 1960s, and the increasing share of the domestic market captured by imports, is further evidence of the industry's counterproductive (and even, suicidal) price policy.[61] Given the industry's re-fusal to meet such price competition in the market place (except under the rarest circumstances), the erosive impact of steel imports was an almost foregone con-clusion. It explains the industry's persistent and unrelenting pressure on the government for protection—whether through "antidumping" measures, "tem-porary" tariffs, mandatory or "voluntary" quotas, "buy American" policies, and so on.

This demand for government protection centers on the claim that the domestic steel industry cannot be expected to compete against foreign producers enjoying substantially lower labor costs. The claim, although plausible, is not substan-tiated; like most protectionist arguments, it borders on the disingenuous. Thus,

---

[60] *Economic Concentration Hearings*, op. cit., pt. 7, p. 3446. This contrast between the flexibility of European steel prices and the upward rigidity of U.S. steel prices characterized not only the 1960s, but the 1970s as well, as the following table indicates.

Steel Price Changes
European Export Price Index and BLS WPI (in per cent)

	EEC EXPORTS	BLS
Jan. 1970–Nov. 1971	− 26	+ 17
Nov. 1971–Dec. 1973	+ 143	+ 6
Dec. 1973–June 1974	+ 39	+ 25
June 1974–Feb. 1975	− 62	+ 16

Source: Staff Report, U.S. Council on Wage and Price Stability, *A Study of Steel Prices* (Washington, D.C. : U.S. Government Printing Office, July 1975).

---

[61] *Fortune*, for example, finds it curious that, "while complaining about the low costs and the low prices of foreign steel, leading steel companies have chosen this particular time, of all times, to *raise* their own domestic prices when their mills are still working at well under full capacity. Put all this together and one is reminded of that old British march to which Cornwallis surrendered at Yorktown called *The World Turned Upside Down*." *Fortune*, **76**:116 (Oct. 1967).

Richard Thorn, although conceding the wage-cost differential between U.S. and foreign producers, found that this differential is more than offset by the lower material costs, capital costs, transportation costs, and prevailing tariff rates— both vis-à-vis the European and Japanese producers. The explanation for the lower price of steel imports must be sought in directions other than in the lower costs of foreign producers, Thorn concludes. "For most steel products, American steel products are already 'cost competitive' in U.S. markets. For most of those foreign steel products that have a present cost advantage, the American industry has it in its power to eliminate this advantage in most products through a higher rate of new investment and greater research and development expenditure. 'Cost competitiveness,' however, cannot be equated with price competitiveness. What is lacking is an aggressive price competitiveness to match the high cost competitiveness of the American industry."[62] In short, like most observers, Thorn views the rise in steel imports as a dramatic and highly visible index of the American steel industry's aversion to price competition.

Thorn's analysis, using 1960s data, is even more relevant today. The differentially more severe impact of the energy crisis and the relatively greater cost inflation in Europe and Japan, as well as the effect of two successive devaluations of the U.S. dollar in the early 1970s, have made American steel plants the world's lowest-cost producers.[63] This means that if the industry could overcome its congenital aversion to price competition, it could stem the erosion of its domestic markets by imports and substitutes, become once again a net exporter of steel, and move toward a reversal of its deplorable industrial performance record.

Technological Progressiveness

Historically, according to the American Iron & Steel Institute (AISI), American steel has been able to compete in world markets because of its technological superiority. Steel spokesmen assure us that they have done "everything in the book to make this industry as efficient and as competitive as it is possible for any industry to be." U.S. Steel calls itself the company "where the big idea is *innovation*," and its general counsel claims that the "distinguishing characteristic of the American steel industry is its tremendous productiveness, a quality which other countries have been unable to emulate so far"—that U.S. Steel, in particular, "is fully aware of, and has continuously studied and tried out, new processes developed both in this country and abroad."[64]

[62] "Steel Imports, Labor Productivity, and Cost Competitiveness," *Western Economic Journal*, 6:383 (Dec. 1968). Thorn found that the total cost advantage of American steel producers ranges from $1.64 to $6.25 per metric ton over Japan, and from —$0.28 to $15.24 over the Common Market. These figures take into account a unit-wage cost differential of —$17.63 and —$18.62 to —$10.72, respectively (ibid., p. 380).

[63] Industry observers with divergent viewpoints, such as U.S. Steel chairman Edgar B. Speer and German industrialist Willy Korf, are in agreement on this score. See *Industry Week*, 185:28 (May 12, 1975).

[64] W. Adams and J. B. Dirlam, "Big Steel, Invention, and Innovation," *Quarterly Journal of Economics*, 80:175 (May 1966).

TABLE 2

An International Comparison of Performance: The Steel Industries of the United States, Japan, Belgium-Luxembourg, and Germany

(1)	(2) RAW STEEL PRODUCTION INDEX (1967 = 100)				(3) UTILIZATION OF CAPACITY (IN PER CENT)				(4) FINISHED STEEL PRICE INDEX (1967 = 100)			(5) IMPORTS AS PER CENT OF DOMESTIC CONSUMPTION				(6) EXPORTS AS PER CENT OF PRODUCTION			
YEAR	U.S.	JAPAN	BEL-LUX	GERMANY	U.S.	JAPAN	BEL-LUX	GERMANY	U.S.	JAPAN	EEC[a]	U.S.	JAPAN	BEL-LUX	GERMANY	U.S.	JAPAN	BEL-LUX	GERMANY
1960	77.8	35.6	79.4	92.8	66.6	88.4	92.2	96.5	96.3	124.2	137	4.7	<1.0	0.2	13.7	3.2	—	67.2	23.0
1961	77.0	45.5	78.3	91.1	65.6	91.3	89.1	90.7	95.9	117.9	117	4.7	<1.0	0.2	12.6	2.3	—	63.3	24.6
1962	77.3	44.3	80.0	88.6	65.1	85.9	89.8	85.6	95.7	101.1	106	5.6	<1.0	—	15.3	2.3	—	66.1	24.8
1963	85.9	50.7	81.4	86.0	69.0	82.9	86.9	79.5	96.2	102.3	100	6.9	<1.0	—	—	2.3	—	—	—
1964	99.6	64.0	93.6	101.6	77.6	85.9	90.5	91.2	97.0	107.7	114	7.3	<1.0	30.8	16.3	2.9	16.5	64.7	22.3
1965	103.3	66.2	96.9	100.2	79.5	80.1	89.4	80.9	97.5	103.8	103	10.3	<1.0	34.9	17.7	2.2	23.4	69.2	25.9
1966	105.4	76.9	93.7	96.1	81.0	82.4	81.6	74.2	98.8	94.5	101	10.9	<1.0	39.4	19.3	1.5	19.9	68.1	27.4
1967	100.0	100.0	100.0	100.0	76.1	91.9	78.7	76.9	100.0	100.0	100	12.2	<1.0	41.5	19.2	1.5	14.1	67.9	32.7
1968	103.1	107.6	115.6	112.0	77.6	87.7	84.0	86.0	102.5	92.5	100	16.7	<1.0	40.3	23.0	1.9	19.1	68.1	31.1
1969	111.0	132.2	129.3	123.3	83.6	91.1	90.7	89.6	107.4	123.5	140	13.7	<1.0	43.1	22.4	4.0	18.9	68.6	28.2
1970	103.4	150.2	127.3	126.6	77.7	90.6	86.6	84.8	114.3	142.6	147	13.8	<1.0	47.6	22.2	5.7	18.8	69.4	26.8
1971	94.7	142.5	124.6	109.7	73.6	74.3	81.2	69.7	123.0	119.4	131	17.9	<1.0	46.3	27.2	2.6	26.2	68.4	32.6
1972	104.5	155.9	140.8	118.9	81.3	78.1	83.2	74.0	130.4	143.3	144	16.6	<1.0	53.5	28.1	2.4	21.6	71.9	31.8
1973	118.5	192.0	151.1	134.8	90.0	92.1	—	—	134.1	199.1	257	12.4	<1.0	60.9	26.3	3.0	20.8	73.8	34.9
1974	114.5	188.4	159.8	150.3	—	—	—	—	170.0	—	377	13.4	<1.0	—	—	4.5	27.5	73.1	41.7
1975	91.8	164.4	114.2	110.0	—	—	—	—	196.6	—	244	13.5	<1.0	—	—	2.6	28.3	77.8	40.3

[a] European Economic Community.

Source: Calculated from data of American Iron and Steel Institute, Economic Commission for Europe, European Economic Community, Japanese Steel Federation, United Nations, and Wirtschaftsvereinigung Eisen und Stahl.

Unfortunately, the facts do not support this *hubris*:

1. A 1966 report of the National Science Foundation (NSF) shows that the steel industry ranks shockingly low in its research and development expenditures. In 1964, it spent only 60 cents of every $100 in sales revenue on research and development compared to a $1.90 average for all manufacturing industry. Moreover, all the industries producing steel substitutes—aluminum, cement, plastics, and glass—invested more in research and development than did the steel industry, sometimes five or six times as much.

2. The major steel inventions in recent years—including the basic oxygen furnace, continuous casting, and vacuum degassing—came from abroad. They were not made by the American steel giants.

3. In innovation, as in invention, the American steel giants seem to lag, not lead. The oxygen furnace, for example, the only major technological breakthrough in basic steel making since the turn of the century, was invented and innovated by the miniscule Austrian steel industry in 1950. It was first installed in the United States in 1954 by a small company (McLouth) and not adopted by the steel giants until more than a decade later: U.S. Steel in December 1963, Bethlehem in 1964, and Republic in 1965. (See Table 3, which shows that, as of September 1963, the largest steel companies, operating more than 50 per cent of basic steel capacity, had not installed a single LD furnace, whereas smaller companies, operating only 7 per cent of the nation's steel capacity, accounted for almost half of the LD installations in the United States.)

Indeed, despite the fact that the new oxygen process entailed operating cost savings of roughly $5.00 per ton, as well as capital cost savings of $20 to $25 per ton of installed capacity, the U.S. steel industry during the 1950s "bought

---

TABLE 3

Distribution of L-D Oxygen Capacity Among United States Steel Producers, September 1963

U.S. STEEL COMPANY'S RANK IN THE INDUSTRY[a]	OXYGEN STEEL CAPACITY (TONS)	U.S. OXYGEN STEEL CAPACITY (PER CENT)	TOTAL U.S. STEEL CAPACITY[a] (PER CENT)
1st, 2nd, 3rd	0	0	52.27
4th, 5th, 6th	6,550,000	50.62	14.76
9th, 10th, 12th, 15th, 19th	6,390,000	49.38	7.06
All companies	12,940,000	100	100

[a] Based on company ingot capacity as of Jan. 1, 1960.
Source: American Iron and Steel Institute, *Iron and Steel Works Directory of the United States and Canada*, New York (1960); Kaiser Engineers, *L–D Process Newsletter* (Sept. 27, 1963).

40 million tons of the wrong kind of capacity—the open-hearth furnace."[65] As *Fortune* observed, much of this capacity "was obsolete when it was built," and the industry, by installing it, "prepared itself for dying."[66] Or, as *Forbes* put it more mildly, "In the fifties, the steel industry poured hundreds of millions of dollars into equipment that was already obsolete technologically—open-hearth furnaces."[67] The technological blunder may have cost close to $1 billion in "white elephant" facilities.

4. The belated adoption of continuous casting by the steel giants is a further illustration of their technological lethargy. Again, it was a small company (Roanoke Electric), with an annual capacity of 100,000 tons, that pioneered in introducing this European invention in the United States in 1962. Other small steel companies followed, so that by 1968, firms with roughly 3 per cent of the nation's steel capacity accounted for 90 per cent of continuous casting production in the United States.[68] The record was embarrassing to the giant firms. Said William P. Hill, engineering executive of National Steel: "There were eight companies operating continuous casting machines before 1965 handling small tonnage. The outstanding thing was all of these companies were small, independent companies. They are competing by continuous casting their entire tonnage. These companies are demanding the low cost, low operating, and first cost in order to produce small tonnage. It is a little embarrassing to some of us when we see this." As for the continuous casting of slabs, Hill warned his colleagues in big steel: "This means that we have to be a little more progressive. The larger companies will have to help develop these large slab casting machines and not depend on the small independent companies to carry the load."[69]

5. Even defenders of the American steel giants concede that it was the cold winds of competition rather than the sheltered atmosphere of protectionism that ultimately forced the domestic majors (belatedly) to follow the path of technological progress. Thus, Alan McAdams admits that by "1962 it appears that the costs to United States producers for *not* innovating were significantly raised by actual and threatened competition from both domestic and foreign oxygen steelmakers."[70] Competition, not protection, broke down the industry's habitual lethargy and resistance to change.

Summing up the industry's performance with respect to technological progressiveness, it is fair to conclude that the giant companies lagged, not led, both in invention and innovation—both vis-à-vis their smaller domestic rivals and their foreign competitors.

[65] *Business Week* (Nov. 16, 1963), p. 144.

[66] *Fortune*, **74**:135 (Oct. 1966).

[67] *Forbes*, **99**:23 (Mar. 1, 1967).

[68] "Continuous Casting," *Iron and Steel Engineer*, **33**:52 (May 1968).

[69] Quoted in R. Easton and J. W. Donaldson, "Continuous Casting," *Iron and Steel Engineer*, **43**:80 (Oct. 1966). See also D. Ault, "The Continued Deterioration of the Competitive Ability of the U.S. Steel Industry: The Development of Continuous Casting," *Western Economic Journal*, **11**: 89–97 (Mar. 1973).

[70] Alan McAdams, "Big Steel, Invention, and Innovation: Rejoinder," *Quarterly Journal of Economics*, **81**:473 (Aug. 1967).

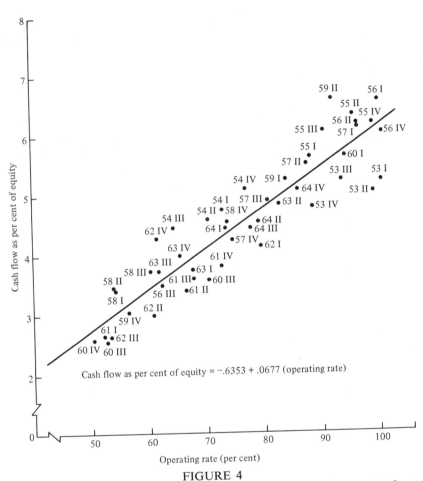

FIGURE 4

Relationship between cash flow as per cent of equity and operating rate in the steel industry. Source: American Iron and Steel Institute and Council of Economic Advisers.

Profits

Reported profit rates, as the CEA warns, provide a very limited basis for comparison of the real profitability of an industry over a period of years or for comparison with other industries. Changing accounting practices and different rates of capacity utilization tend to distort meaningful comparisons. Cash flow—that is, the sum of profits after tax plus depreciation and depletion allowances—is a better, although far from perfect, measure of profitability.

Whether we examine steel's reported profits or cash flow, however, the industry's record is far from impressive. On both counts, steel ranks below the average for all manufacturing—primarily because of its technological lethargy and the inadequate capacity utilization, attributable to a noncompetitive price policy. As Figure 4 shows, there is a very strong positive relationship between capacity utilization and cash flow. According to the CEA, a "four-point improvement in operating rate leads to over a one-point improvement in cash flow as a percentage of equity. Thus, if the steel industry were back to the operating rates of the mid-1950s, both the ratio of cash flow to equity and the relative

TABLE 4
Steel Industry: Production, Price, and Return on Equity, 1950—1975

(1) YEAR	(2) FINISHED STEEL PRODUCTS PRICE INDEX $(1967 = 100)$	(3) RETURN ON EQUITY (PER CENT)	(4) TOTAL PRODUCTION RAW STEEL (MILLIONS OF TONS)	(5) CAPACITY UTILIZATION (PER CENT)[a]
1950	63.2	14.3	97	97
1951	64.5	12.3	105.2	101
1952	67.5	8.5	93	86
1953	73.0	10.7	111.6	95
1954	74.7	8.1	88.3	71
1955	79.9	13.5	117.0	93
1956	87.2	12.7	115.2	90
1957	93.9	11.4	112.7	85
1958	96.5	7.2	85.3	61
1959	96.5	8.0	93.4	63
1960	96.1	7.2	99.3	67
1961	95.8	6.1	98.0	71
1962	95.6	5.4	98.3	70
1963	97.3	7.0	109.3	76
1964	96.8	8.8	127.1	88
1965	98.0	9.8	131.5	88
1966	99.4	10.2	134.1	88
1967	100.8	7.7	127.2	82
1968	103.1	7.6	131.5	85
1969	110.0	7.6	141.3	91
1970	116.6	4.3	131.5	86
1971	128.0	4.5	120.4	81
1972	130.2	6.0	133.2	85
1973	135.4	9.5	150.8	96
1974	192.0	16.7	145.7	94

[a]Note the difference between these estimates of capacity utilization and the (probably more reliable) estimates reported in Table 2.
Source: Staff Report. U.S. Council on Wage and Price Stability, A Study of Steel Prices (Washington, D.C.: U.S. Government Printing Office, July 1975).

position of the industry compared with others would be much more favorable than at the present time [1965]."[71]

The recent study by the Council on Wage and Price Stability underscores this point. It finds that profit rates from the end of World War II through 1957 were good because of rapidly increasing prices and a high rate of capacity utilization. Between 1958 and 1972, the council says, profits were poor because foreign competition prevented the industry from raising prices substantially and because the industry's market strategy (that is, its refusal to cut prices to meet import competition) resulted in suboptimal levels of production. Only with the restriction of imports after 1969, the termination of government price controls in 1973, and an abnormally strong worldwide demand for steel in 1974 was the industry able to operate at near full capacity and, hence, earn higher profits (see Table 4).[72]

Generalizing, then, we can say that the industry's profitability is intimately linked with its ability to maintain high-capacity levels of operation and to post price increases that outpace cost increases.

Summary

Summarizing, then, steel is a concentrated industry. Its behavior conforms closely to the oligopolistic pattern. Price uniformity is assured through price leadership (with or without resort to the basing point system). Price stability is attained, often at the expense of extreme fluctuations in production and employment. Price levels are geared to a break-even point of around 50 per cent of capacity and are only remotely influenced by natural market forces. The industry leader sets prices like a public utility, aiming for a predetermined profit target (after taxes), and the other firms usually follow in lockstep. In short, the industry's performance hardly measures up to the standards of workable competition. As George Stocking correctly concludes, the industry's "structure contribute[s] to conduct incompatible with an effective interplay of market forces, and its structure and conduct [result] in unacceptable performance."[73]

V. PUBLIC POLICY

What should be the public policy toward the steel industry? Is the performance of the industry sufficiently good to justify a policy of noninterference? Could performance be improved by a change in structure, or is it enough to press for a rehabilitation of behavior? Above all, is effective competition in the steel industry possible, and/or desirable? If so, how can it be promoted?

Ever since the Supreme Court's refusal to break up U.S. Steel in 1920, the

[71] CEA, *Steel Report*, op. cit., p. 56.
[72] Staff Report, Council on Wage and Price Stability, op. cit., pp. 17 ff.
[73] "The Rule of Reason, Workable Competition, and Monopoly," *Yale Law Journal*, **64**: 1136 (July 1955).

government has confined itself mainly to combating collusive, discriminatory, and exorbitant prices. For more than 50 years, the Justice Department and the FTC have battled in the courts—first to eliminate the single- and then the multiple-basing-point system. These battles were eventually won. The Pittsburgh Plus system was proscribed in 1924, and the multiple-basing-point system and systematic freight absorption were banned in 1948. These rulings have not caused havoc in the industry. Nor have they assured the competitive pricing of steel products. Now, as before, price leadership and collusion in the economic sense are hallmarks of this industry.

It is unrealistic, of course, to suppose that mere abstention from the basing point system will achieve either price competition or price flexibility—a fact illustrated by the recurrent official inquiries into steel prices and profits. Congress has investigated, exposed, and condemned. Presidents have pleaded, admonished, and warned. Steel labor and steel management have been exhorted to exercise restraint and to forego desired wage and price increases in order to combat inflation and thus preserve the American way of life. "The response," as Ben Lewis observes, "has been not only less than spectacular; it has been imperceptible." Voluntary restraint, creeping admonitionism, and economizing by conscience have simply not worked. They have become, as Lewis says, "a symptom of, and not a cure for, organic disabilities which are beginning to be plainly discernible in our economic body."[74]

From society's point of view, the objective is not to keep steel prices low in prosperity and high in depression. The function of steel prices, as of all prices, should be to promote a proper allocation of society's resources—to channel resources into those uses where the consuming public most wants to have them. Thus, given a high demand for steel, an uncompetitively low administered price brings in its wake gray markets and allocation problems. Such a price is, in effect, a subsidization by the steel industry of steel-consuming industries. It distorts the allocation of resources in accordance with the dictates of the market. It strikes at the central nervous system of a free enterprise economy. The same is true in times of slack demand. At such times, the effort by the steel industry to stabilize prices and to maintain prices at higher levels than the market justifies again results in distortions of the allocation process. It represents an unwarranted tax on steel-using industries imposed by steel producers. It is an attempt to cure recessions by cartel-like restraints on the free market. Not only are such attempts futile, as history amply demonstrates, but they represent a crucial deviation from the fundamentals of free enterprise.

No! Creeping admonitionism, voluntary restraint, and the corporate soul are not likely to solve the basic problem. Nor will a conscientious adherence to f.o.b. pricing make the steel industry a paragon of competition. The problem goes deeper. It is inherent in the structure of the industry. It is the problem of "size," and any attack on oligopolistic pricing without an attack on oligopolistic

[74] "Economics by Admonition," *American Economic Review Proceedings*, **49**:384 (May 1959).

structure will be no more effective than the treatment of a symptom instead of the disease itself. In other words, public policy toward this industry must concern itself with the basic problem of structure and how it can be changed. This, in turn, raises questions about the relation between the size of firms and technological efficiency—in short, the feasibility of increasing the number of competitors. If it is possible to increase the number of firms and, thus, create a more competitive industry structure, this would enhance the prospects for more competitive behavior and the likelihood of nonconformity in pricing and other aspects of business policy. Whether this can be done is the problem to which we now turn.

The Problem of Size

On the basis of available information it seems reasonable that iron and steel making require firms of considerable size—firms that are not only significant horizontally (that is, within any one branch of the industry) but that are also integrated vertically. Vertical integration seems economically justifiable because of the "geographic concentration of the industry, the magnitude of individual operations necessary for efficiency in mining and manufacture, and the economies obtained by continuous operation, which makes possible the immediate use of the end product of one stage of production as the material in the next stage."[75] Thus, there are definite economies to be obtained from a combination of the operations of blast furnaces and steelworks. These economies are obtained (1) by transforming pig iron into steel by a continuous process without permitting the iron to cool, thus using it in a molten state; (2) by recovering the valuable by-product gasses from blast furnaces and coke ovens; and (3) by avoiding the cost of transporting pig iron, a cost that is high in comparison to its value.

On the other hand, there is little evidence to indicate that firms must be of Brobdignagian size to be efficient. Various studies indicate that (1) operational efficiency, (2) technological progressiveness, and (3) profitability might best be promoted not by preserving, but by reducing, the size of some steel giants.[76]

First, with respect to operational efficiency, it is interesting that the capacity of the giant steel companies is not concentrated in a handful of large plants. Thus, when 51 steel making plants belonging to the eight largest companies were classified according to size, it was found that only five had annual capacities of more than 3 million ingot tons; 24 had ingot capacities from 1 to 3 million tons; and the remaining 20 plants had capacities of fewer than 1 million tons.[77] These, remember, were plants owned by the eight largest steel companies.

Moreover, it is doubtful if the combination of spatially and functionally

---

[75] U.S. Tariff Commission, op. cit., p. 42.

[76] See, for example, Bain, op. cit., p. 236. On this point, see also U.S. Congress, House, Subcommittee on the Study of Monopoly Power, The *Iron and Steel Industry*, Report, 81st Cong., 2d sess., 1950, pp. 69 ff., which corroborates Bain's estimate.

[77] Bain, op. cit., pp. 236–237. The data are for 1952.

separate plant units yields any significant economies. To be sure, there are advantages in integrated steel production at Pittsburgh, or Gary, or Birmingham; but is there any technological justification for combining these three functionally independent plant units under the administration of one firm? Consider for a moment that U.S. Steel's Gary plant alone is bigger than the total operations of Jones & Laughlin or Inland. One plant of the nation's largest steel producer is bigger than all the plants of the sixth largest producer. This inevitably raises the question of whether Jones & Laughlin and other companies of similarly substantial size are big enough to be efficient. If they are, then certainly U.S. Steel's Gary plant—standing on its own feet and divorced from the industrial family of U.S. Steel—should also be capable of efficient operation. The same goes for the corporation's integrated units at Pittsburgh and Birmingham. Divorcing these plants from the home office should hardly result in a loss of efficiency.[78]

In fact, such an action might result in more, not less, operational efficiency—at least, if the evidence in the hitherto unpublished Ford, Bacon & Davis report is reliable. This report was prepared by Ford, Bacon & Davis (a private management consulting firm) at the request of U.S. Steel itself, and was of course undertaken at the corporation's expense. Its findings, as summarized by George Stocking before the Celler committee, pictured the corporation as

> a big sprawling inert giant, whose production operations were inadequately coordinated; suffering from a lack of a long-run planning agency; relying on an antiquated system of cost accounting; with an inadequate knowledge of the costs or of the relative profitability of the many thousands of items it sold; with production and cost standards generally below those considered everyday practice in other industries; with inadequate knowledge of its domestic markets and no clear appreciation of its opportunities in foreign markets; with less efficient production facilities than its rivals had; slow in introducing new processes and new products.
>
> Specifically, according to the engineers, it was slow in introducing the continuous rolling mill; slow in getting into production of cold-rolled steel products; slow in recognizing the potentials of the wire business; slow to adopt the heat-treating process for the production of sheets; slow in getting into stainless steel products; slow in producing cold-rolled sheets; slow in tin-plate developments; slow in utilizing waste gases; slow in utilizing low-cost water transportation because of its consideration for the railroads; in short, slow to grasp the remarkable business opportunities that a dynamic America offered it. The corporation was apparently a follower, not a leader, in industrial efficiency.[79]

---

[78] See the very interesting testimony of Benjamin Fairless on this question in U.S. Congress, House, *Hearings Before the Subcommittee on Study of Monopoly Power*: 81st Cong., 2d sess., 1950, pt. 4A, pp. 498–505. Also interesting in this connection is the testimony by Professor George Stigler that "all the largest steel firms, and most of the oligopolies in other industries are the product of mergers. Not one steel company has been able to add to its relative size as much as 4 per cent of the ingot capacity of the industry in 50 years by attracting customers. Every firm that has gained 4 or more per cent of the industry's capacity in this half century has done so by merger." *Ibid.*, p. 996.
[79] *Ibid.*, p. 967.

On the basis of the powerful indictment in this engineering report (as well as other evidence), Stocking concluded that "the Steel Corporation has lagged, not led"; that "it was neither big because it was efficient, nor efficient because it was big."[80] This conclusion was supported by the testimony of other leading economists who maintained that the dissolution of U.S. Steel into at least three separate integrated units was technologically quite feasible. They assured the Congress that "one can be opposed to economic bigness and in favor of technological bigness in most basic industries without inconsistency."[81]

Second, with respect to technological progressiveness, it is noteworthy that the small- and medium-sized steel companies compare quite favorably with U.S. Steel. Moreover, it was Europe that taught us how to make stainless steels and how to save millions with by product coke ovens. European inventors, not the American steel giants, developed the revolutionary basic oxygen process and continuous casting.

Third, with respect to profitability, it is significant that some of the medium-sized companies have fared better over the years than the giant U.S. Steel Corporation.[82] To the extent that profit figures are valid as measures of efficiency, the record would not show a balance in favor of the giant firms. Moreover, multiplant companies seem to have performed no better than single-plant organizations. Thus, Professor Bain found that between 1936–1940 and 1947–1951 there was "apparently no significant relation of profit rate on equity to size of firm among the 15 largest steel firms in the United States, although these firms ranged in size from U.S. Steel, with about 19 mills, down to single-plant firms. Although these profit-rate data are not conclusive," says Bain, "they are consistent with the hypothesis that economies did not result from expansion beyond a single integrated plant with from one to 2.5 million ingot tons capacity."[83]

On the basis of the little authoritative information available, we can say that although large firms may be necessary for efficient steel production, and al-

[80] Ibid., p. 969. See also W. S. Bowman, "Toward Less Monopoly," *University of Pennsylvania Law Review*, 101:590 (Mar. 1953). In fairness, it should be said that the corporation has done much to correct the situation described in the Ford, Bacon & Davis report. Today it is a far more efficient organization than it was 30 years ago.

[81] U.S. Congress, House, *Hearings Before the Subcommittee on Study of Monopoly Power*, op. cit., p. 996. This was the statement of Professor Stigler, who argued that Bethlehem, and possibly Republic, might also be subjected to dissolution proceedings.

[82] Care must be exercised in making profit comparisons the measure of relative efficiency in corporations of different sizes. Profit rates often do not measure relative efficiency because "the rate of profit is affected by bargaining advantages and various other factors as well as efficiency of operation. Because bargaining advantage tends to grow with size, a corresponding increase of profits might be attributable to corporate power, whereas a failure of profits to increase, too, might be a persuasive indication that the level of efficient operation had been passed." From *Maintaining Competition* by C. D. Edwards, p. 119. Copyright 1949. Reprinted by courtesy of the McGraw-Hill Book Company, New York. For a general discussion on the relation between size and efficiency in multiple-plant enterprises, see ibid., pp. 113–120.

[83] Bain, op. cit., p. 255. Even though the optimum size of steel plants has increased since the 1950s, Bain's generalization about the potential economies resulting from multiplant operations is still valid.

though a considerable degree of vertical integration may be imperative for maximum efficiency, the optimum size of a firm is substantially smaller than that of the largest companies today. Although there can never be enough firms in the steel industry—from the point of view of the technological and economic optimum—to assure even an approximation to perfect competition, there can, nevertheless, be enough firms to assure more intense competition than prevails today. There can be enough decentralization of power to assure a basic minimum of freedom for individual action "so that new ideas, new men, and new organizations will have the bona fide chance to introduce themselves."[84]

One more point is relevant here. Even if we hesitate to achieve greater decentralization through antitrust surgery, some structural reform is, nevertheless, easily attained. Foreign competition, as our experience with steel imports has demonstrated during the 1960s, can provide some moderating influence on oligopolistic excesses and be a valuable yardstick for improving industry performance. Such competition should be encouraged, not stifled. Thus, there is no justification for steel tariffs, quotas, or similar government restraints on competition. Let public policy not be misused as a protector and promoter of monopoly![85]

What makes the achievement of more effective competition in the steel industry so compelling is a consideration of the alternatives. Once we grant the unworkability of competition, the only alternatives seem to be: (1) a supervision of steel prices by a government commission (along the Interstate Commerce Commission pattern);[86] (2) a government counterspeculation agency;[87] (3) direct government participation in the steel industry; (4) industry self-government along NIRA lines; and (5) outright socialization. A perusal of the choices available should convince us that experimenting with the workability of competition is worthwhile, Only after fair trial and definite failure should we consider abandoning a competitive plan for the steel industry.

[84] D. McC. Wright, "What's Best for the Competitive Enterprise System" in U.S. Chamber of Commerce (Washington, D.C.?), p. 205.

[85] George C. Eads, acting director of the Council on Wage and Price Stability, underscores this point in the letter transmitting the council's study of steel in prices in July 1975: "Throughout this report, the crucial role that import competition plays in moderating domestic steel price increases has been continually stressed. We are disturbed, therefore, by reports in the press that, if flat rolled-sheet steel begins to flow into this country in increasing amounts as a result of any price increase that does take hold after Oct. 1, the steel industry plans to request that the Treasury initiate an antidumping investigation. While we must protect ourselves against unfair foreign competition, there is a tendency on the part of many industries to consider *all* foreign competition 'unfair.' Domestic firms cannot be allowed to take advantage of their market power to raise prices during periods of weak demand and then expect the government to protect them from the consequences. Consequently, I have instructed the council staff to monitor steel imports closely, and, if such a dumping complant is filed, to be prepared to present evidence in whatever forum is appropriate concerning the extent to which any alleged 'injury' due to imports can be directly traced to recent pricing moves by U.S. producers." Staff Report, Council on Wage and Price Stability, op. cit., p. ii.

[86] This proposal was advocated by Judge Gary, former president of United States Steel, before the Stanley committee in 1911.

[87] See A. P. Lerner, *The Economics of Control* (New York: Macmillan, 1944).

Conclusion

In conclusion, let us note that the steel industry today stands at an important crossroads. It is on the horns of the proverbial dilemma. If it concedes that effective price competition is feasible, it must go out and play the capitalistic game according to its naked and shameless, yet vitalizing and invigorating, rules. If, on the other hand, it follows Judge Gary's lead and insists that competition in steel is impossible, that competition must somehow give way to co-operation, the industry must then accept some form of government regulation to protect the public interest. In any event, the industry can hardly continue with a structural organization under which every price change becomes the subject of a congressional investigation, every labor dispute the cause of a national emergency, every hint of foreign competition a pretext for protectionist campaigns or moves toward an international cartel. The brutal choice before the steel industry seems to lie between the painful rigors of competition and the anguished frustrations of bureaucratic regulation.

SUGGESTED READINGS

Clark, J. M. *The Economics of Overhead Costs*. Chicago: University of Chicago Press, 1923.

Cockerill, A. *The Steel Industry: International Comparisons of Industrial Structure and Performance*. New York: Cambridge University Press, 1974.

Daugherty, C. R., M. G. de Chazeau, and S. S. Stratton. *Economics of the Iron and Steel Industry*. 2 vols. New York: McGraw-Hill Book Company, 1937.

Fetter, F. A. *The Masquerade of Monopoly*. New York: Harcourt Brace Jovanovich Inc., 1931.

Hogan, W. T. *Economic History of the Iron and Steel Industry in the United States*. 5 vols. Lexington, Mass.: D. C. Heath & Company, 1971.

————. *The 1970s: Critical Years for Steel*. Lexington, Mass.: D. C. Heath & Company 1972.

Machlup, F. *The Basing Point System*. New York: McGraw-Hill Book Company, 1949.

GOVERNMENT PUBLICATIONS

Council of Economic Advisers. *Report to the President on Steel Prices*. Washington, D.C.: U.S. Government Printing Office, Apr. 1965.

Council on Wage and Price Stability. Staff Report. *A Study of Steel Prices*. Washington, D.C.: U.S. Government Printing Office, July 1975.

FTC. *Report on the Control of Iron Ore*. Washington, D.C.: U.S. Government Printing Office, 1952.

Temporary National Economic Committee. *Price Discrimination in Steel*. Monograph, no. 41. Washington, D.C.: U.S. Government Printing Office, 1941.

————. *The Basing Point Problem*. Monograph, no. 42. Washington, D.C.: U.S. Government Printing Office, 1941.

U.S. Congress, *Hearings Before the Temporary National Economic Committee. Iron and Steel Industry*, pts. 19, 20, 26, and 27, 1940.

U.S. Congress, House, Judiciary Committee, Subcommittee on the Study of Monopoly Power, *The Iron and Steel Industry*, 1950.

U.S. Congress, House, Judiciary Committee, *Hearings Before the Subcommittee on the Study of Monopoly Power, Steel:* ser. 14, pts. 4-A and 4-B, 1950.

U.S. Congress, Senate, Judiciary Committee, *Hearings Before the Subcommittee on Antitrust and Monopoly, Administered Prices: Steel*, pts. 2, 3, and 4, 1957.

———. *Economic Concentration*, pts. 6 and 7, 1967.

U.S. Congress, Senate, Finance Committee, *Steel Imports*, 1967.

U.S. Congress, Senate, Judiciary Committee, Subcommittee on Antitrust and Monopoly, *Administered Prices: Steel*, 1958.

United States v. *Bethlehem Steel Corp., et. al.*, 168 F. Supp. 576 (1958).

JOURNAL AND MAGAZINE ARTICLES

Adams, W., and J. B. Dirlam. "Steel Imports and Vertical Oligopoly Power." *American Economic Review*, **54**:626 (Sept. 1964).

———., and J. B. Dirlam. "Big Steel, Invention, and Innovation." *Quarterly Journal of Economics*, **80**:167 (May 1966).

Ault, D. "The Continued Deterioration of the Competitive Ability of the U.S. Steel Industry: The Development of Continuous Casting." *Western Economic Journal*, **11**: 89–97 (Mar. 1973).

Bava, G. "The Concentrated Control of Iron Ore by Major Steel Companies as an Unfair Method of Competition." *Southern California Law Review*, **46**: 1116 (Summer 1973).

The Iron Age. New York, various numbers.

CHAPTER 4

the petroleum industry

WALTER S. MEASDAY

I. INTRODUCTION

As the American Petroleum Institute told us, "A Country That Runs on Oil Can't Afford to Run Short." The self-evident truth of this statement was not brought home to the American people until the winter of 1973–1974. The Arab embargo, which was only partially effective, brought the country close to panic, from motorists waiting by the hour in gasoline lines to the highest levels of government.

The nation became aware of the extent to which its economy depends on energy and for energy on the petroleum industry. In 1920, primary energy consumption in the United States amounted to 20 quadrillion Btus. It took 35 years, until 1955, for consumption to double. The next doubling took only 20 years; except for a deep recession, consumption in 1975 would have passed 80 quadrillion Btus. And the best estimates are that, unless checked by strong conservation measures or resource shortages, energy consumption could again double, to 160 quadrillion Btus by the early 1990s.

The petroleum industry has made a unique contribution to fueling this energy growth. In 1920, some 78 per cent of primary energy consumption was supplied by coal, 18 per cent by oil and natural gas from the petroleum industry, and the remaining 4 per cent from hydropower. In 1973, with consumption nearly four times what it had been a half century earlier, the relative contributions of coal and gas were reversed. Coal's share of energy had dropped to 18 per cent, while petroleum (42 per cent) and natural gas (35 per cent, including natural gas liquids) had a combined share of 77 per cent. Hydropower held the same 4 per cent share as in 1920, while nuclear fuel provided the remaining 1 per cent.

Since 1970, oil and gas have provided more than three quarters of the basic energy needs of the United States. Despite current efforts to increase coal utilization and to develop alternative fuel sources, something close to this ratio

130

will persist at least into the 1980s. In short, if one were forced to pick a single key industry in the economy, it would be petroleum.

The economic importance of the industry needs little elaboration. In 1974, the refining companies had sales within the United States in excess of $117 billion and accounted for 25 per cent of the net income of all manufacturing companies in the United States; 15 per cent of all manufacturing assets were in the petroleum industry.[1]

Exxon, passing General Motors in sales for the first time in 40 years, gained the undisputed title in sales, assets, and net income as the largest industrial corporation in the United States in 1974.[2] Compared to the leading firms in other industries, Exxon's worldwide sales of $42 billion were equal to the *combined* sales of General Electric, IBM, U.S. Steel, and du Pont. Five of the ten largest companies and 16 of the top 50 were oil companies. Although there were only 34 oil companies among the select 500 industrials, they accounted for 24 per cent of the entire group's sales, 25 per cent of the assets, and 34 per cent of the profits.

These companies and thousands of others constitute an elaborate chain of production and distribution facilities, stretching from the oil fields to retail service stations. They provide employment to more than a million workers. In February 1975, the identifiable total from the Bureau of Labor Statistics (BLS) was 1.1 million: 307,000 workers in oil and gas extraction, 146,000 in petroleum refining, 16,000 in pipeline operations, and 630,000 retail service station employees.[3] But these figures do not include the tens of thousands of other employees in wholesale product distribution, in water and highway transportation, or in the provision of specialized equipment and supplies ranging from oil field equipment to service station pumps.

It is customary and convenient to recognize that the "petroleum industry" really encompasses four separate industries: crude oil production, refining, marketing, and transportation. Producing firms are engaged in the location and extraction of oil and natural gas from underground reservoir formations, which may be so close to the surface that their presence is indicated by oil seeps or so deep that they are reached only after drilling 4 or 5 miles. The refining industry manufactures a wide range of finished products—from gasoline to petroleum coke—from crude oil. Wholesale and retail marketers distribute these products to consumers. An essential link tying these three sectors together is a specialized transportation industry—pipelines, tank ships and barges, and trucking operations—that move crude oil from the fields to refineries and finished products from refineries to the marketers.

The majority of companies in the petroleum industry tend to specialize in one or another of these subindustries. Thus, Louisiana Land and Exploration,

---

[1] FTC, *Quarterly Financial Report*, Fourth Quarter (Washington, D.C.: U.S. Government Printing Office, 1974).

[2] "The 500 Largest Industrial Corporations," *Fortune*, May 1975.

[3] U.S. Department of Labor, Bureau of Labor Statistics, *Employment and Earnings* (Washington, D.C.: U.S. Government Printing Office, Apr. 1975).

Superior Oil, and General Crude Oil are substantial crude oil and gas producers that have confined their activities to this area. Ashland Oil is the thirteenth largest refiner in the country and has some pipeline interests; but it has little domestic crude production relative to its refining capacity and sells most of its gasoline to independent distributors. Martin Oil Service, an Illinois firm, typifies the larger independent wholesale and retail marketers, dependent on the other segments of the industry for their supplies. Finally, there are some independent pipeline companies, such as Williams Brothers and Kaneb, and a number of tanker and barge operators and trucking companies that transport large volumes of petroleum products but do not engage in production, refining, or marketing.

The industry is dominated, however, by the integrated major companies. Heading the list is Exxon, the largest producer of crude oil and natural gas, the largest refiner, second to Texaco in gasoline sales but still the largest marketer of all petroleum products, and one of the largest operators of petroleum transportation facilities of all types. Five of the United States firms are among the group of seven international oil companies, often referred to as "The Seven Sisters" (Exxon, Texaco, Mobil, Gulf, Standard Oil of California, British Petroleum, and the Royal Dutch-Shell group) that controlled the world oil market from the 1920s until at least 1973.

Following Exxon, in the United States, in order of their refining capacity, are Shell Oil (controlled by the Royal Dutch-Shell Group), Standard Oil of Indiana, Standard Oil of California, Gulf Oil, and Atlantic-Richfield.

To the 8 industry leaders, a second group of 8 lesser majors can be added: Union Oil of California, Sun Oil, Standard Oil of Ohio (Sohio), Phillips Petroleum, Continental Oil, Marathon Oil, Cities Service, and Getty Oil (including its subsidiary, Skelly Oil). Purely as a historical footnote, half of the 16 majors (Exxon, Mobil, Standard Oil of California, Standard Oil of Indiana, Standard Oil of Ohio, Continental, Marathon, and Atlantic Richfield) are lineal descendants of companies divested by the Standard Oil Trust in 1911.

It should be noted that anyone's list of "major oil companies" is a matter of subjective judgment. For example, the inclusion of Marathon (which is less integrated into marketing than others on the list) or Standard Oil of Ohio (with little domestic crude production) could be questioned.[4] Similarly, many observers other than this writer now include Amerada Hess in the ranks of majors, on the basis of the company's crude production and its 700,000-barrels-a-day refinery in the Virgin Islands.[5] In short, the reader is entitled to make up his own list,

---

[4] Sohio's crude position will change radically when Alaskan North Slope oil starts to flow. Through its merger agreement with British Petroleum (BP), under which BP's initial 25 per cent voting interest in Sohio will grow to a 54 per cent controlling interest, BP-Sohio holds approximately half of the North Slope's total proved reserves.

[5] The author feels that Amerada Hess has not yet developed major brand product identification and that the offshore refinery, established by government favor in the mid-1960s and maintained through the 1974–1975 crisis by the Federal entitlements program is exceptionally vulnerable to changes in the nation's oil import policy.

TABLE 1
Major Oil Companies (ranked by U.S. refining capacity)

	REFINING CAPACITY (THOUSANDS OF BARRELS)	COMPANY SIZE, 1974	
		SALES	ASSETS
		($ MILLIONS)	
Exxon	1,243.0	42,061.3	31,332.4
Shell Oil (U.S.)	1,156.0	7,633.4	6,128.9
Standard Oil (Indiana)	1,115.0	9,085.4	8,915.2
Texaco	1,098.0	23,255.4	17,176.1
Standard Oil of California	983.5	17,191.2	11,640.0
Mobil Oil	944.3	18,929.0	14,074.3
Gulf Oil	866.3	16,458.0	12,503.0
Atlantic-Richfield	809.8	6,739.7	6,151.6
Union Oil of California	496.0	4,419.0	3,458.7
Sun Oil	484.0	3,799.6	4,063.3
Standard Oil (Ohio)	432.3	2,116.2	2,621.4
Phillips Petroleum	408.0	4,980.7	4,028.1
Continental Oil	362.0	7,041.4	4,673.4
Marathon Oil	324.0	2,882.2	1,799.9
Cities Service	268.0	2,806.3	2,897.9
Getty Oil	218.7	2,742.3	3,003.6

[a] Daily crude oil input capacity, U.S. refineries, Jan. 1, 1975.
Source: *Oil & Gas Journal*, Apr. 7, 1975; *Fortune*, May 1975.

but the term *majors* in the remainder of this chapter will refer to the 16 companies named in the preceding paragraphs.

II. MARKET STRUCTURE

The structure of the petroleum industry can be viewed through the structures of its four functional subindustries. Each of these—production, refining, marketing, and transportation—has its own structural characteristics, yet they are inextricably intertwined through the vertical relationship that exists among them and the presence of the same dominant firms in each of them. Structure per se cannot be examined meaningfully without recognition of this relationship.

Crude Oil Production

The supply of domestic crude oil in the United States amounted to more than 3.3 billion barrels (9.2 million barrels a day) in 1973. This total was produced by some 8000 to 9000 individual firms engaged in the exploration for, development of, and production from oil and gas reservoirs. Producers vary in size from individuals with outputs of a few hundred barrels a year to Exxon, whose wells in the United States produced 10.3 per cent of the nation's oil and 10.8 per cent of its natural gas in 1973.[6]

Entry into the industry, at least in onshore production, is relatively easy because the minimum efficient scale is one well that produces more than enough oil or gas to cover its operating costs. At 1975 prices of $12 to $13 a barrel for oil, even a few stripper wells (wells producing fewer than 10 barrels a day) provide a generous income to the owner. The typical small entrepreneur also finds exit easy if, as is frequently the case, he exhausts his investors' funds with a succession of dry holes.

Entry is far more limited by financial requirements in areas where deep drilling is required or the environment is hostile, as on the Outer Continental Shelf or the North Slope. Thus, in 1972 the average oil well in the under-1250-foot-depth class was 860 feet deep and cost $10,120 ($11.72 a foot) to drill and equip. The average well 10 times as deep (8736 feet in the 7500 to 9999-foot bracket) cost 18 times as much to complete, $181,000, or $20.72 a foot. The one ultradeep oil well completed in 1972 to a depth of 23,287 feet cost $1.7 million, or $73.74 a foot.

On the Outer Continental Shelf, under Federal control, development of a 5760-acre block appears to cost today from $20 million on up, to cover the costs of exploratory drilling to delineate any reservoirs under the block and to place one or two permanent production platforms from which up to three-dozen wells can be directionally drilled. The development cost is frequently dwarfed by tens of millions of dollars paid in lease bonuses to the Federal government simply for the right to look for oil in the first place—the record so far is a $213 million bonus for a single block!

Production from the North Slope also combines the investment in lease bonuses and enormously expensive development costs. In addition, at least the major firms had to commit themselves to arrange financing, originally estimated at $950 million and currently at $6 billion, for the Alaskan pipeline.

The number of producers and the ease of entry into the less costly areas lead many observers to accept the industry's view of itself as exceedingly competitive. In fact, given the number of firms involved, concentration seems to be rather high. The first Annual Survey of Oil and Gas conducted by the Bureau of the Census shows that, in 1973, the 8 largest majors produced 54 per cent of the nation's crude oil and 51 per cent of its natural gas. The 16 major companies accounted for 72 per cent of total crude production and 67 per cent of total natural gas.[7]

---

[6] U.S. Congress, Senate, Subcommittee on Antitrust and Monopoly, *Hearings on S. 1167, The Industrial Reorganization Act*, pt. 9, 1975, p. 464.

[7] The first 16 producers in the census tabulation had 72.3 per cent of total production. The first eight companies are the eight largest majors. Based on other company reports, it appears that the second eight census companies would include Amerada Hess. Substituting Sohio (the twenty-first largest producer) for Amerada Hess (sixteenth) would give a concentration ratio of 71.7 per cent for the traditional majors.

TABLE 2
Concentration in Crude Oil Production (in per cent)

	1955	1965	1973
4 largest	21.2	27.9	33.8
8 largest	35.9	44.6	53.8
20 largest	55.7	63.0	76.3

Note: Company gross production.
Source: FTC and Bureau of the Census company reports.

Furthermore, it is evident from Table 2 that concentration in crude oil production has been increasing steadily since the mid-1950s, with a tilt toward the largest companies. The market share of the four largest companies increased from 21 per cent to nearly 34 per cent. The share occupied by the second four firms rose from 15 per cent to 20 per cent, whereas the share of companies ranked 9 to 20 increased only from 20 to 22½ per cent of the market.

Rising concentration can be explained only partially by the increasing cost of finding new oil. A much more significant explanation is the wave of acquisitions made by the major companies, probably triggered by import controls that limited their ability to meet domestic refining needs from their own foreign crude sources. Today's 16 majors were the 20 majors of 1955. Within the group, Union merged with Pure Oil, Sun with Sunray DX, and Atlantic Refining acquired both Richfield and Sinclair. For 15 of the majors (excluding Sohio) the Federal Trade Commission (FTC) staff has identified more than 130 full or partial acquisitions of independent producers' reserves between 1955 and 1970.[8]

As a further point, published concentration ratios tend to understate effective concentration because of institutional arrangements within the industry. One of the most important is the farm-out. The majors have the financial resources to maintain huge inventories of leases and options to undeveloped, but potential, oil and gas acreage.[9] Most independents cannot afford adequate lease blocks. A major, however, frequently will "farm out" acreage to an independent producer—providing the independent with a drilling site and the major with valuable exploratory information on which the major can base its own decisions as to the development of contiguous acreage.

The usual farm-out agreement gives the original leaseholder an overriding interest (ranging from an eighth to a half, depending on the prospect and whether the major helps to finance drilling) in any oil or gas found. More important, the leaseholder generally retains a perpetual call on all of the production from the farm-out—that is, he can purchase as much as he wants at any time,

[8] FTC, Staff Report, *Concentration Levels and Trends in the Energy Sector of the U.S. Economy* (Washington, D.C.: U.S. Government Printing Office, Mar. 1974), pp. 45–52.

[9] At the end of 1973, six of the largest majors (not including Exxon and Texaco) reported more than 69 million acres under lease—an area larger than 43 of the 50 states.

provided he meets the competitive price.[10] This provision can be a strong deterrent to other potential buyers of oil from the farm-out.

Next, concentration in reserve ownership is even more important, particularly for the future, than concentration in current production. And the largest companies control most of the proved reserves. The FTC staff found that, in 1970, our 16 major companies controlled 77 per cent of the net proved oil reserves in the United States and Canada. The producer has effective control, however, over all of the oil he lifts, including the shares for royalty owners and other non-working interest holders. In terms of gross reserves, the 16 majors may control more than 90 per cent of existing proved reserves.

Finally, as will be discussed at a later point, the major oil companies dominate the transportation system by which crude oil moves from the oil field to the refinery. Even the independent crude producer operating on his own lease will find most of the time that he must sell his oil to a major in order to get it moved from the well.

The structure of the crude oil industry can be summarized briefly. The major oil companies account for a large share of the production from, and a much larger share of the reserves held by, the thousands of firms in the industry. The independent sector accounts for a significant share of production, but many (and perhaps most) of the firms in this sector exist in a type of symbiotic relationship with the majors, which keeps control of the crude oil market firmly in the hands of the major companies.

Refining

Refining refers to the complex of processes by which usable products—ranging from liquefied petroleum gases and gasoline to residual fuel oil and petroleum coke "at the bottom of the barrel"—are extracted from crude oil. Refining was originally a relatively simple distillation process in which, for example, gasoline was boiled out of crude at a relatively low temperature range, kerosene in a somewhat higher range, followed by distillate fuel oil, leaving residual oil as the undistilled portion of the original input. The economic incentives to maximize the lighter, more valuable fractions have stimulated technological development of a wide variety of additional processes in such areas as cracking (breaking down heavier molecules into lighter ones) and reforming (restructuring molecules) to provide an improved utilization of crude. The fruits of this development even in the last two decades can be seen in a reduction of the residual oil yield from an average in the United States of more than 20 per cent of crude inputs in 1950 to 6.5 per cent in 1970; indeed, Midcontinent refiners in Oklahoma and Kansas have average residual yields in the neighborhood of 2 per cent.

---

[10] Very little domestic crude oil is sold on long-term contracts. The normal sales agreement is a 30-day "evergreen" contract that can be renewed automatically each month for years but that can be canceled by either party at the end of any 30-day period. Thus, exercise of the leaseholder's call forces the farm-out operator to cancel any other sales agreement.

On January 1, 1975, there were 259 individual refineries owned by 136 companies in operation in the United States, exclusive of 3 in Puerto Rico and 1 each in the Virgin Islands and Guam.[11] Their combined crude oil input capacity was more than 14.8 million barrels a day. Roughly three quarters of these refineries reported gasoline production capability. The remainder, with only 3 per cent of the industry's total capacity, were, for the most part, asphalt or lubricant plants that might produce small amounts of gasoline as a by-product of their principal activity.

The refineries that reportedly produce gasoline vary in size from "tea kettles," with as little as a 500-barrels-a-day capacity, to Exxon's 445,000-barrels-a-day complex at Baton Rouge, Louisiana; not included in our list is Amerada Hess's 640,000-barrels-a-day plant in the Virgin Islands.

Concentration in refining is as marked as it is in crude production. One characteristic of the structure, however, is that there is no clearly dominant firm standing head and shoulders above the others, such as one finds in the automobile, steel, or computer industry. All 4 of the largest companies have capacities in the 1.1 to 1.2 million-barrels-a-day range, and even the smallest member of the "big eight" has two thirds the capacity of the largest. As a group, the 8 operate 66 refineries with 55 per cent of the total refining capacity within the 50 states. There is a clear break between these companies and the second 8 majors, whose capacities are in the 200,000 to 500,000-barrels-a-day range. Nevertheless, the 99 refineries operated by the 16 traditional majors account for more than 75 per cent of the industry's capacity.

Ten independent refiners with at least 100,000 barrels a day of crude capacity —from Crown Central at the bottom of the range to Ashland Oil, the thirteenth-largest refiner—have 11 per cent of the total capacity. The remaining share of the market, less than 14 per cent, is split among 110 companies with individual capacities ranging downward from the Oil Shale Corporation's 87,000 barrels a day to Oriental Refining's miniscule 150 barrels a day.[12]

Economies of scale are cited frequently as an important barrier to entry into the refining industry. The minimum efficient scale for a full-range refinery, designed to maximize gasoline and distillate fuel output, is generally considered to be one with a crude input capacity of 150,000 barrels a day, representing an investment of $300 million, at 1974 prices. Unit costs do not appear to rise very sharply until plant scale drops well below the 100,000-barrel-a-day level; that is, a 100,000-barrels-a-day refinery is not at any significant economic disadvantage with respect to much larger plants.

If scale economies are truly a significant barrier, we are hard put to explain the apparent ability to survive of so many plants that are far below the minimum efficient scale for refining. Even the majors operate a number of theoretically inefficient plants. Thus, of the 66 refineries operated by the eight largest companies in early 1975, only 20 had capacities above 150,000 barrels a day with

[11] "Annual Refining Survey," *Oil & Gas Journal,* **73**: 98 (Apr. 7, 1975).
[12] "Miniscule" is a relative term here; at today's prices the annual output of a 150-barrels-a-day refinery could be worth about $800,000.

another half dozen above 100,000 barrels a day; at the other end of the range, they operated 26 refineries with capacities of fewer than 50,000 barrels a day.[13]

Two factors may be involved here. First, if the capital costs of an older small refinery have been substantially written off through depreciation, its operating costs may well be below the combined capital and operating costs of a newer, more efficient large refinery. Next, in serving a given limited market area, the higher costs of a local small refinery may be more than offset by the transportation expense in moving the product from a large refinery located at some distance from the market.

In short, scale economies are probably not an insuperable barrier to entry by small firms into refining. The principal barrier that does exist is access to crude oil. Basically, construction of a new refinery requires, first of all, some reasonable assurance of a 15- to 20-year supply of crude. For example, in one case that may be typical, a banking group's agreement to finance a new refinery is contingent on the company's ability to provide evidence of a long-term supply equal to at least 75 per cent of the planned capacity. Thus, any influence that restricts access to the crude oil market for potential entrants limits entry at the refining level.

Pipelines

The transportation system is a key element in the entire petroleum industry. Some 13 million barrels (more than half a billion gallons) of domestic and imported crude oil must flow into the nation's refineries each day of the year. On the average, some 17 million barrels of domestic and imported refined products must be moved every day from refineries, ports, and natural gas plants to ultimate markets. Under supply-and-demand conditions normal in the past, these volumes would be growing substantially from year to year.

Furthermore, transportation must be a continuous process in order to avoid an incredibly large investment in storage capacity. A 100,000-barrels-a-day refinery would require in excess of 3 million barrels of crude oil storage if its crude were delivered only once a month. As it is, the average refinery maintains sufficient storage capacity to blend its "crude slate," or the mixture of different types of crude best suited to its refining process, and to provide a few days' margin against delays in deliveries. At the other end of the delivery chain, the typical retail station has very limited storage relative to its sales volume. Unless its tanks are filled every few days, the station runs dry, as thousands of motorists learned from the "No Gas—Mechanic on Duty" signs seen everywhere in early 1974.

Petroleum can be shipped in several ways—by truck, rail, water, or pipelines. Truck transportation is generally used where small deliveries are involved, such as moving gasoline from a terminal or bulk plant to retail stations, although

---

[13] Individual companies vary considerably. All five of Atlantic-Richfield's refineries are in the 100,000 to 200,000-barrels-a-day range. But only two of Texaco's 11 refineries and three of California Standard's 11 have capacities of at least 100,000 barrels a day.

some crude oil fields too small to justify pipeline construction are also served by trucks. A substantial amount of products and some crude are transported by rail. Both truck and rail transportation are too expensive, however, to be basic forms of transportation. Water transportation is far cheaper where it can be used—that is, in ocean shipping or barge traffic on the coastal and inland waterways. It would cost about as much, for example, to move a barrel of crude oil by truck from West Virginia to Philadelphia as it would to ship the same barrel from the Persian Gulf.

Pipelines are the most important mode of oil transportation within the United States, where large volumes must be moved overland.[14] According to the Association of Oil Pipe Lines, the industry supports some 220,000 miles of lines, of which more than 170,000 miles in 1973 were operated by 100 interstate carriers subject to Interstate Commerce Commission (ICC) regulation. Much of this mileage (42,000 miles reported by the interstate lines and most of the intrastate mileage) consists of small-diameter gathering lines, which collect crude oil from the individual wells in an oil field and move the field's output to a trunk line for shipment to refinery centers.

The separate trunk systems supplying crude to refineries and delivering finished products from refineries to marketing areas present a classic case of scale economies. A 36-inch diameter pipeline has a capacity equivalent to seventeen 12-inch lines or a hundred 6-inch lines.[15] Because the expenses of construction and operation go up far less than proportionately to capacity, cost per barrel-mile drops sharply as diameter increases. A 40-inch line, for example, moves oil at one fourth the cost of a 12-inch line.[16]

From the standpoint of market structure, there are three significant organizational forms by which pipelines can be financed and operated. A single company, usually an integrated oil company, can build its own pipeline. Alternatively, where a project is very large, a group of oil companies can combine in a joint venture. The joint-venture line is separately incorporated, and the owning companies are entitled to ship in proportion to their equity shares. The third form is a hybrid, the "undivided interest" pipeline. Here, a group of oil companies join to construct a pipeline, with one of their number designated as the operator. Unlike the joint-venture line, the undivided-interest line has no corporate existence; during its operating cycle, each owner is entitled to exclusive time on the line (its undivided interest) in proportion to the owner's capital contribution. The ICC would view, say, a four-company undivided-interest line as four separate pipelines.

The distinction is important to an understanding of the industry. One of the myths involved is that all interstate pipelines are common carriers, regulated in

[14] In 1974, refineries received 87 per cent of their domestic crude oil by pipeline, 11 per cent by water, and 2 per cent by rail and truck.
[15] U.S. Congress, Senate, Special Subcommittee on Integrated Oil Operations, *Hearings on Market Performance and Competition in the Petroleum Industry*, 93rd Cong., 1st sess., Dec. 12, 1973, p. 978. Statement of Mr. Jack Vickery, Association of Oil Pipe Lines.
[16] U.S. Congress, Senate, Subcommittee on Antitrust and Monopoly, *Hearings on S.11.67, The Industrial Reorganization Act*, pt. 9, 1975, p. 491.

the public interest by the Interstate Commerce Commission (ICC). This is largely true of joint-venture lines. The chairman of the ICC has explained, however, that single company-owned pipelines that carry their own products are common carriers only in a limited legal sense.[17] They are subject to ICC reporting and rate-of-return regulation; but they are not obligated to post their tariffs or to accept any other company's commodities for transportation.

The dominance of the major oil companies over pipeline transportation is shown in Table 3. During 1973, more than 92 per cent of the crude oil pipeline shipments reported to the ICC originated in lines owned, or almost completely controlled, by the 16 integrated majors.[18] Much of the remaining percentage would be accounted for, if statistics were available, by the limited participation allowed to independent refiners in the undivided-interest lines dominated by the majors. Apart from an insignificant amount (0.2 per cent of the total) moved by Buckeye Pipe Line Co., all of the crude oil shipments reported to the ICC were moved in refiner-owned lines.

Nearly 76 per cent of the product shipments originated by refineries (as distinct from those received from connecting carriers) went into major-owned

TABLE 3
Shipments Originated in Major Oil Company Pipelines, 1973[a]

	MILLIONS OF BARRELS	BARRELS (PER CENT)
Crude oil lines		
8 largest majors	1897.4	64.3
8 other majors	442.5	15.0
Joint ventures[b]	385.3	13.1
Total, 16 majors	2725.2	92.4
U.S. total	2949.9	100.0
Refined product lines		
8 largest majors	919.1	29.2
8 other majors	369.7	11.7
Joint ventures[b]	1095.9	34.8
Total, 16 majors	2384.8	75.8
U.S. total	3147.3	100.0

[a] ICC reporting lines, except Lakehead, Trans-Mountain, and Portland pipeline companies, volumes exclude shipments received from connecting carriers.
[b] Lines owned or controlled by groups of two or more major companies.
Source: U.S. Department of Commerce, ICC.

[17] Market Performance and Competition in the Petroleum Industry, op. cit., p. 897.
[18] Three pipelines reporting to the ICC are excluded. Trans-Mountain and Lakehead move Canadian oil to Northern Tier refineries, and Portland transports foreign oil in bond from Portland, Me., to Montreal refiners.

lines. A few lines owned by independent refiners exist primarily to deliver a product to major pipeline connections. In contrast to crude transportation, a significant share of the market, 22 per cent in 1973, is held by a dozen lines that are not owned by refiners. Two of these "outside" owners are natural gas pipeline companies, Texas Eastern Transmission and Northern Natural Gas, with subsidiaries engaged in the transportation of propane and butane. Three systems are operated by railroads: Buckeye (Penn Central), Southern Pacific, and Santa Fe. Among the rest, Williams Brothers and Kaneb should be singled out as important nonintegrated product pipelines.

Marketing

Descriptions of marketing structure generally focus on the 40 per cent of the total product market represented by motor gasoline. The reason is not relative importance, but the lack of data regarding the other 60 per cent. About all one can say is that there are various channels of distribution for these other products from the refiner to the customer. Residual fuel oil, for example, may go to large industrial and utility customers directly from the refinery or through a few terminal operators and large dealers equipped to handle the product. Petrochemical feedstocks and commercial jet fuel are generally sold through contracts between the refiners and their customers. Highway diesel fuel is sold through a number of specialized truck stops and a few retail gasoline stations. The same is true for other products.

For more than half a century, gasoline has been the most familiar petroleum product to consumers and the most profitable one to refiners. Most gasoline reaches the consumer through an estimated 193,000 retail service stations (in 1975), down some 15 per cent from a peak of 226,000 stations in 1972. These figures do not include an indeterminate number (more than 100,000) of other outlets, such as motels, car washes, grocery stores, and so on, that also retail gasoline as a secondary activity.

Retail stations can be divided conveniently into three groups: those affiliated with major oil companies selling major brand gasoline; a much smaller number affiliated with independent refiners; and, finally, a substantial number of stations operated by nonintegrated independent marketing companies. Price competition in the industry has been provided chiefly by the latter two groups.

The larger private brand marketers tend to own and operate their retail stations directly with salaried managers. Several refiner-dealer relationships are employed by the major brand companies. Some are operated directly with salaried managers; at the other end of the spectrum, some dealers own their stations but operate them under major brand franchises. The vast majority of major brand stations, however, are owned by the refiners and are leased to "independent" dealers. The independence of the lessee dealers is ephemeral. Because most leases are on an annual basis and are subject to cancellation even within the lease period for a variety of reasons, the dealer is as subject to the dictates of his supplier as would be any formal employee. In effect, the major controls the outlet, but the dealer bears most of the operating risks.

Two thirds of the gasoline sold is delivered to retail stations at "dealer tank wagon" prices through refiner-owned bulk plants and terminals. The remainder is delivered through intermediate wholesalers, known as jobbers, who buy from refiners at a discount (about four cents a gallon) from the tank-wagon price. All of the majors employ both forms of wholesale distribution. The type used in a particular marketing area depends on whether the refiner believes his own costs of distribution would be less than the jobber discount. Where he has good station representation in a densely populated area, the refiner will usually choose direct distribution; he will employ jobbers in territories where his stations are few and scattered.

Concentration in the national gasoline market as shown in Table 4 is impressive but not startling. The leading marketer, Texaco, had just over 8 per cent of the market. The 8 largest majors had 52 per cent of the market in 1974, while the 16 majors together held slightly more than 71 per cent. Twenty-three other integrated refiner-marketers had 13 per cent, while other marketers accounted for 16 per cent of gasoline sales. There is, in other words, a substantial fringe of independent competition at the retail marketing level.

Furthermore, as F. C. Allvine and J. M. Patterson have pointed out, there has been a significant decline in gasoline marketing concentrations since the late 1960s.[19] The 10 leading marketers (the 8 largest majors plus Phillips and Sun) had 66.1 per cent of national gasoline sales in 1968, 63.0 per cent in 1970, and 59.5 per cent in 1972. From this, it is clear that the market share of the 16 majors

TABLE 4
Concentration in Gasoline Sales, 1974

	VOLUME (MILLIONS OF GALLONS)	VOLUME (PER CENT)
Majors		
4 largest	30,056	29.8
Next 4	22,172	22.0
Next 8	19,708	19.6
16 companies	71,936	71.4
Other refiner-marketers		
23 companies	12,785	12.7
Other marketers	16,053	15.9
U.S. total	100,774	100.0

Source: *National Petroleum News*, Factbook Issue, Vol, 67, no. 5A, 1975, p. 99.

[19] F. C. Allvine and J. M. Patterson, *Highway Robbery* (Bloomington: Indiana University Press, 1974), p. 77.

as a group has declined from something over 80 per cent in 1968 to the 71 per cent reported in 1974. There is, of course, a real question as to whether this trend toward competitive deconcentration can be maintained in a period of shortages, without active government intervention to preserve it.

Another aspect of marketing structure is its apparent regionalization. Only Texaco markets gasoline in all 50 states and the District of Columbia.[20] Standard of Indiana (Amoco) and Mobil miss the mark by two states each. Half a dozen other majors have at least some branded outlets in 40 states or more, but other companies can best be described as regional marketers. Even the large majors tend to exhibit regional strength rather than national dominance. Thus, Exxon's strongest market appears to lie on the East Coast, from the Carolinas to New Jersey; the company is not among the four leading marketers in more than half of the 46 states in which it operates. Standard of California (including Chevron and Kyso) concentrates on the eastern and far western markets, with some representation along the Gulf Coast.

Increasing regionalism appears to be the wave of the future. Phillips' famous "March to the Sea" in the early 1960s, climaxed by its acquisition of Getty's Tidewater West Coast refinery and marketing outlets in 1966, gave the company national distribution. Since 1972 Phillips has been withdrawing from several of these markets, and in June 1975, pursuant to a court-ordered divestiture, the company agreed to sell the Tidewater properties. Exxon was rumored to be pulling out of several midwestern states in 1973. Gulf announced late in 1972 that the company would withdraw from 14 midwestern and 6 northwestern states. Other large companies were making similar announcements. Marketing realignments were checked by the Emergency Petroleum Allocation Act of 1973, which forced refiners to supply their 1972 customers, but they will undoubtedly reappear when controls are relaxed.

III. CONDUCT AND PERFORMANCE

Market conduct and performance in the oil industry have been inextricably intertwined with government policy to the main point where it is impossible to understand one without reference to the other. In recent years, a number of scholars have viewed government as an exogenous influence imposing its will on the industry. Thus, one author speaks of pricing as determined by government policy rather than market forces; of resource allocation as the result of government decisions rather than competition; and, in general, of "government intervention with anticompetitive consequences."[21]

The statement of the effects of government intervention is perfectly accurate. What appears to be overlooked is that for half a century or more public policy has been precisely what the most influential segments of the petroleum industry

---

[20] Cf. *National Petroleum News*, Factbook Issue, **67**, no. 5A: 100–105 (1975).

[21] T. Duchesneau, *Competition in the U.S. Energy Industry* (Ford Foundation Energy Policy Project, 1975), Chap. 3, p. 150.

have wanted it to be. Given the economic ease of entry into crude oil production and refining, the task of maintaining "orderly" markets is beyond the resources of even the major integrated companies. The support of government had to be secured in order to effectively create a cartel for the industry.

Control of Supply: Prorationing

An important influence on the development of the crude oil producing industry was the extension by state courts of the ancient "rule of capture" from wild game to subsurface mineral resources. In the United States, oil belongs to the person who brings it from the ground. To understand this, imagine that a rich oil reservoir lies beneath your property and that of your next-door neighbor. If he drills a well, he can drain all of the oil in the pool. Your only chance to share in the wealth is to drill a well on your own property. Your neighbor can then drill additional wells in order to hold on to the lion's share of the oil, and your defense must be to match his efforts well for well. You will both waste money overdrilling the field; you may also damage the reservoir itself by excessive initial production.

This was the pattern in nearly every oil field in the nation throughout the early 1930s. Once oil had been discovered in an area, there would be a mad rush to acquire leases and to drill as many wells as possible. Clark and Halbouty mention one East Texas tract the size of a small suburban lot (60 by 150 feet) on which 12 wells were drilled. One result was enormous waste. Associated natural gas, which had a limited market, was flared or burned off. Crude produced faster than transportation became available was stored in open pits where much of it was lost.

More important to the industry, the rapid development of production at a time when oil was easy to find steadily depressed prices. The average wellhead value drifted downward from $3.07 a barrel in 1920 to $1.27 by 1929. Then, in October 1930, "Dad" Joiner brought in his East Texas discovery well. Within a year, oil from the East Texas field was selling for as little as 10 cents a barrel. Higher-cost fields elsewhere were shut in, and the average price of crude dropped to 65 cents a barrel in 1931.

The principal oil-producing states had been trying to develop production controls to avoid physical waste, over the strong objections of most of the industry. The approach developed into the "MER" concept—a maximum efficient rate, defined as the highest rate of sustainable production from a field that can be achieved without damaging the reservoir or impairing maximum ultimate recovery.

From the avoidance of physical waste, it is only a short step to the avoidance of "economic waste," the industry's euphemism for a production level that would depress the market price. And, as crude prices collapsed, the industry, which had opposed government intervention for physical conservation, now embraced the concept of "market demand" prorationing as a means of restricting supply. This means simply the further limitation of production below physical allowables through a market demand factor (expressed today as a percentage of the physical allowables) sufficient to maintain any given price level.

State prorationing efforts became effective only after they were buttressed by Federal power early in the New Deal, first under the National Industrial Recovery Act (NIRA) and, in 1935, with two other pieces of legislation. The Connally Hot Oil Act prohibits the interstate shipment of crude oil, or products refined from crude oil, produced in excess of state quotas. The Interstate Oil Compact Commission Act, while forbidding price fixing, provides a forum within which the state regulatory agencies can coordinate their conservation efforts.

The major oil companies played the key role in the operation of market demand prorationing at least until 1972, when the shortage of domestic crude made prorationing an academic question. Each month they appear before the prorationing authorities as buyers of their own and independent crude, to present their "nominations"—the amounts of crude they expect to purchase within each state during the following month.

Clearly, major buyers' nominations have been the principal influence in establishing the state market demand factors each month and, hence, the level of domestic crude production. To a large extent, the prorationing agencies simply translate a market consensus of the major oil companies into limits on the competitive behavior of independent crude producers. It was this union of the oil industry and government that provided the control essential to creating domestic cartels.

Import Controls

From the 1930s into the 1950s, state prorationing, reinforced by the Connally "Hot Oil" Act, was able to prevent suppliers' price competition in the domestic crude market. This was possible so long as there was no external competition from foreign oil sources, and for years there was none. The United States was the major exporter to the world market. More important, the Seven Sisters adhered to a basing point system in which crude and product prices throughout the world were quoted on the basis of U.S. Gulf Coast prices plus transportation. This meant that any crude price increases in the United States were matched throughout the world.

Several developments strained, and ultimately destroyed, this comfortable state of affairs. During World War II, the British admiralty protested the cost of fuel for its Indian Ocean naval operations. And, indeed, there was no reason why fuel oil produced at BP's Abadan (Iran) refinery and shipped to Aden (at the end of the Arabian Peninsula) should have been priced as if it had been refined in Texas and shipped halfway around the world. The cartel responded to this to the extent of establishing the Persian Gulf as a second basing point, but with prices identical to those at the U.S. Gulf Coast.

In the immediate postwar period, prices at both basing points rose sharply at a time when the U.S. Economic Cooperation Administration (ECA) was footing most of the oil bill for rebuilding Europe. ECA was able to exert successful pressure for further price adjustments. By 1949, Persian Gulf crude prices had dropped to approximately two thirds of the comparable level in the United States, and modest amounts of Mideast oil began to reach East Coast refineries.

Perhaps the most significant factor was the decline of British influence in the area and the consequent emergence of governments in the Mideast able to control their own affairs. The exclusivity of the Seven Sisters was threatened by the granting of concessions to "outsiders," and nationalistic pressures to expand Mideast production could not be ignored. The seven majors were still able to control the growth in world production, but only to the extent necessary to prevent a gradual, orderly decline in prices from turning into a price collapse. The transactions price of the Mideast "reference" crude, 34-degree light Arabian f.o.b. Ras Tanura, drifted generally downward from $1.93 a barrel in 1953 to $1.80 by the end of 1960 and into the $1.30 to $1.40 range during the mid-1960s.

The impact on crude production in the United States was enormous. Crude oil imports rose from 272,000 barrels a day (5.8 per cent of refinery runs) in 1947 to more than 900,000 (12.5 per cent of runs) in 1956. By 1958, Texas wells subject to market demand control were limited to 122 days of production.

The handwriting on the wall was unmistakable. With increasing imports of low-priced foreign oil, state production controls could not be counted on much longer to preserve a high domestic price level. World prices were no longer hinged to U.S. prices. Indeed, we were speedily approaching a condition in which domestic prices would be determined by the world price.

A politically powerful coalition of domestic crude producers and coal operators, organized to fight the import threat, persuaded President Eisenhower to announce a Voluntary Oil Import Control Program in 1957. The title was a misnomer. Existing importers "voluntarily" agreed to accept quotas established by the Oil Import Administration (under the threat of mandatory controls), while newcomers were required to apply for permission to import at least 6 months before bringing in any foreign oil. The voluntary program soon foundered and the president issued Proclamation 3279, establishing a Mandatory Oil Import Control Program, effective March 11, 1959.

Under the mandatory program, two import ceilings for crude and unfinished oils and finished products were established in the five "Petroleum Administration for Defense" (PAD) districts into which the country was divided. In PAD District V (the West Coast, Arizona, Nevada, Alaska, and Hawaii), the ceiling was set annually, or in some years semiannually, as the difference between demand forecast by the Bureau of Mines, and domestic supply, including the Canadian crude imported by Texaco, Shell, and Mobil for their Washington refineries.

For districts I through IV (east of the Rockies), ceilings were set first at 9 per cent of the forecast demand and, from 1963 on, at 12.2 per cent of the forecast domestic production of crude oil and natural gas liquids.

The program was reasonably straightforward in its early years. Imports from Canada were permitted without license, in theory at any rate, for refiners who had access to them.[22] Finished-product quotas were limited through 1967 to the 1957 level (76,634 b/d) and were licensed only to the small number of firms that actually had imported such products in 1957. An "estimate" of Canadian imports and the finished-product quota was subtracted from the over-all ceiling to provide a subceiling for offshore foreign crude and unfinished oils.

Licenses, commonly known as "tickets," for this oil were distributed to all refiners on the basis of their refinery inputs. Although the tickets technically could not be sold or transferred, imports could be exchanged for domestic oil in a manner that amounted to the same thing as a sale of tickets. Something close to an organized market developed in which, for most of the program, tickets had a value of $1.25 a barrel in districts I through IV and 75 cents in District V.

The program offered economic benefits for everyone, except the consumers who had to pay for it. Producers enjoyed high crude prices. The large East Coast refiners could enjoy the maximum advantage of cheap foreign oil only within their own quotas, but they could acquire additional tickets from other refiners at a cost that was 40 to 50 cents a barrel less than the differential between the costs of foreign and domestic oil delivered to their refineries. The ticket "sellers" got something for the right to import oil, which they could not have used economically in any case. Thus, with the 1968 quota, a 10,000-barrel-a-day inland refiner got an economic benefit of roughly $1 million for his tickets; Shell, which did not run foreign oil at the time, got more than $12 million.

Pipeline Control

Control over pipeline transportation may well be the real key to the major refiners' domination of the industry. At the crude level, the popularity of single-company and undivided-interest lines, which may not really provide common carriage, is highly significant.[23] The crude producer does not sell his oil on an open market. Almost always he sells it to a major-owned pipeline company at the price posted for his field by the major buyer; his alternative in most fields is to have his oil trucked out at considerably greater cost than the pipeline gathering charge.

Large fields are often served by two or more gathering systems and trunk lines. Some students view the possibility of "switching connections" from one buyer to another in such fields as an important competitive force in the crude market. Now, it is true that connections can be and have been switched, but this is an infrequent occurrence. In the first place, the pipeline that purchases crude

---

[22] In practice, the United States made a secret deal with Canada to placate Venezuela for limitations placed on U.S. imports. The Canadian Energy Board prohibited the shipment of western Canadian crude beyond Toronto, reserving the eastern Canadian market for crude imported primarily from Venezuela. In return, the United States and Canada annually negotiated the "estimated" volume of Canadian crude that could be imported into the United States.

[23] Why, for example, are large, multicompany crude lines such as Capline (Gulf Coast-Midwest) or TransAlaska organized as undivided-interest lines, while comparable product lines, such as Colonial (Gulf Coast-East Coast) and Explorer (Gulf Coast-Midwest) are usually organized as incorporated joint ventures?

from a lease is required to distribute the proceeds among the holders of working
and royalty interests in the lease on the basis of a "division order." Another
pipeline that "jumps" the lease must execute a new division order, signed by
every holder of an interest. This process takes days or weeks, during which no
oil flows from the lease. Second, according to an executive of a large gathering
system, "There's honor among thieves—we don't usually jump other lines'
leases, and they don't jump ours."

The position of the independent producer with respect to the majors is
illustrated by a comment in Kewanee Oil Company's 1974 Annual Report to
its stockholders:

> As an independent oil and gas producer, crude oil and natural gas produc-
> tion is sold at the wellhead to major oil pipeline companies and [Kewanee]
> has very little control of the price it receives for its products.

This company is a small producer (21,000 barrels a day in 1973) compared to
Exxon, Shell, or Texaco, but it is still among the 30 largest crude producers in
the industry. What is true for Kewanee must be equally true for the thousands
of other even smaller producers.

Thus, the crude pipeline operations of the majors give them control over most
of the oil produced by independents, in addition to their own 70-plus per cent
of total production. In that way, they not only assure themselves of crude
supplies for their own refineries, but also determine the availability of crude to
nonintegrated independent refiners. A few large independents, such as Ashland
Oil and Clark Refining, have integrated backward into crude transportation,
generally through participation with majors in undivided-interest lines, in order
to secure some portion of their crude requirements. Even these companies depend in large part—and the majority of independent refiners depend almost
wholly—on their major competitors for access to crude.

The lines that carry finished products from refineries to marketing areas
appear to differ from crude lines both in the existence of a substantial nonintegrated sector and in some preference for joint ventures as distinct from single-
company lines. The eight largest majors' lines originated only 29 per cent of total
product shipments, compared to 64 per cent of pipeline crude oil in 1973; conversely, major joint ventures accounted for 35 per cent of the product receipts
from refineries, compared to 13 per cent of the crude delivered into the pipeline
system.

The nonintegrated pipeline companies provide a valuable contrast between
independent and shipper-owned transportation facilities. The former provide a
public transportation service for unrelated refining or marketing customers; the
latter exist primarily to provide economic access to markets for their owners.
The independent lines normally seek new business aggressively from refiners
and marketers, providing storage tanks and pumping facilities at origin and
destination points on reasonable terms. The shipper-owned "common carriers"
generally act in a way that discourages shipments by nonowners.

Colonial Pipeline, owned by 10 majors and by far the largest product line in
the country, offers an example. For the first few years of operation, Colonial

had no nonowner shippers, except for those who could arrange with an owner to ship on the owner's account. This policy was relaxed only when a Department of Justice antitrust suit appeared imminent. Today a nonowner can ship on his own account if he can meet the requirements of the line: a minimum tender of 75,000 barrels of any one product repeated at frequent intervals over an undisclosed contract term, a sizable capital investment in storage and pumping facilities at the origin and delivery locations, and, if necessary, construction of a spur from the source of supply to the trunk line. Thus, Murphy Oil and Tenneco constructed the $12 million Collins Pipe Line from their refineries in southern Louisiana to Collins, Mississippi, in order to get their products on Colonial.

Finally, the utilization of a joint-venture products line supplies owners with invaluable information about their competitors' marketing policies. The discussions that are essential to planning the initial capacity of a pipeline and any subsequent extensions, the location and sizes of stub lines or spurs off the main line, and terminal connections all involve disclosure by each owner of his long-range marketing plans to the others. Pipeline financing normally hinges on owners' throughput commitments, pledges by each owner of the minimum volume he will ship through a projected line over a period of as many as 40 years.

More detailed information is available in the short run because scheduling requires that each shipper submit his intentions by type and quantity of product well in advance of actual shipment. In a typical case, a pipeline will require that each shipper place his tenders for a full month (showing when and how much of each product he wants to put on the line and what quantities of each product he will take off the line at various discharge points) by no later than the tenth day of the preceding month. This information, as a practical matter, is available to every owner almost immediately.

Control of product pipelines through joint ventures, in short, offers a mechanism to reduce the uncertainty about competitors' marketing behavior that plagues most firms in other oligopolistic markets. It is a valuable complement to the influence over competitors' inputs provided by control of crude oil lines.

Company Interties

Industrial organization theory suggests to us that concentration ratios are an important indicator of market structure and a clue to competitive behavior. By this test, the oil industry should be far more competitive than it appears to be. One of the reasons it may not be comes from arrangements that tie each of the majors to its competitors in a variety of activities.

Crude oil and product exchange agreements are particularly significant. In the case of a crude exchange, an integrated refiner, X, may have plenty of crude at location A, whereas its refinery is some distance away at location B. If it can locate another refiner, Y, who needs crude at A and has a surplus at B, X will agree to sell oil to Y at location A and buy an equal volume from Y at location

B. During 1974, for example, Exxon had a net domestic crude production of 701,000 barrels a day, purchased 868,000 barrels a day (including royalty oil from its own leases), and sold 780,000 barrels a day.[24] Apart from its royalty oil, it is probable that most of Exxon's purchases and sales were pursuant to exchange agreements.

Product exchanges occur for a similar reason, when a refiner supplies a market area distant from his refinery by product received from a competitor's refinery, in exchange delivering the product to his competitor in an area more accessible to his refinery than to his competitor's. Product exchanges, in contrast to crude exchanges, are normally direct barrel-for-barrel swaps rather than simultaneous purchases and sales.

There are real economic benefits from exchanges, as the industry points out. Wasteful cross hauling is eliminated, and transportation charges are minimized. Many economists, however, are concerned about exchange agreements. For one thing, they foster close working relationships among competitors in production and supply. For another, it would seem that the economic benefits of exchanges could be achieved as efficiently through open market transactions. The exchange system replaces open markets, accessible to all potential buyers and sellers, with a web of bilateral or multilateral barter agreements among the exchange partners. The result may well be to minimize or eliminate prices as the resource-allocating mechanism within the industry.

Joint ventures represent another important form of intercorporate relationship. Every major oil company is tied in with its competitors—other majors and large independents—in a network of joint ventures that number in the hundreds throughout the world.

Joint ventures within the United States have been limited primarily to transportation and lease acquisitions as a result of the antitrust laws. Pipeline joint ventures, discussed earlier, involve a large degree of advance commitment to production and marketing strategies. A company that takes 30 per cent of a million-barrels-a-day product pipeline, for example, is notifying its competitor-partners that it intends to supply 300,000 barrels a day for the next 30 or 40 years in the pipeline delivery territory. The partners, in turn, are revealing their long-range future plans.

Joint bidding for offshore leases has long been a common practice as a means of risk spreading. Basically, a partnership can bid on more blocks than a single firm, increasing the probability of finding oil or gas for each member. What is often overlooked is that the partnership carries over into production and development if oil or gas is found. A study of Federal offshore producing leases, as of 1972, found that only four of the majors (Exxon, Shell, Gulf, and Standard of California) solely owned more than half of their producing leases.[25] At the other extreme, Continental owned 1 lease itself and had partners in 118 leases, Atlantic-Richfield owned 3 out of 94, Getty owned 2 out of 100, and Cities

---

[24] U.S. Congress, Senate, Subcommittee on Antitrust and Monopoly, *Hearings on S.1167, The Industrial Reorganization Act,* pt. 9, 1975, p. 529.
[25] *Market Performance and Competition in the Petroleum Industry,* op. cit., pp. 1164–1165.

Service was sole owner of 1 lease out of 101 in which it had interests. These companies shared most of their leases with each other as members of the CAGC group, one of the oldest and most durable of the offshore bidding combinations.

Foreign joint ventures of U.S. companies with each other and with foreign competitors extend from production through refining and, in some cases, even marketing. From the well-known Iranian Consortium and Aramco to the Irish Refining Company (Shell, Exxon, Texaco, and British Petroleum), one finds a pattern of joint activity linking most of the petroleum companies of the world.

As with exchange agreements, there are economic benefits to be derived from joint ventures. As one witness before the Haskell subcommittee expressed it:

> The purpose of a joint venture is encased in goodness. It increases the ability to raise capital, to make use of complementary or overlapping techniques and research, to achieve potential economies of vertical integration, and to spread risk over two or more companies. . . . Joint ventures are advantageous to society when they result in lowering of costs, with a consequent reduction in price.[26]

Questions may be raised, however, as to how many of the joint ventures in existence are necessary on economic grounds and whether the advantages of any single joint venture may not be offset if an accumulation of similar ventures among competitors should dull the sharp edge of competition. These questions cannot be answered with any certainty, but the absence of answers does not eliminate the questions.

As a concrete example, Standard of California and Texaco have shared most of their foreign operations for the last 40 years through the Cal-Tex group of companies. They also held 60 per cent of Aramco (prior to Saudi government participation beginning in 1973), with the balance being held by Exxon and Mobil. The dividends each received in 1973 from the Cal-Tex companies and from Aramco were of about the same magnitude as Standard Oil of California's entire reported net income and two thirds of Texaco's. And, here, of course, is the problem. Given the long-standing duration of their relationship and the importance of it to the financial welfare of each company, can we expect either to embark on a course of independent competitive action that might strain the relationship or impair its financial performance? Even in other areas remote from Cal-Tex affairs, will Socal and Texaco act as strong competitors against each other or as old friends?

Petroleum Pricing

Once upon a time there was a crude oil market, complete with exchanges on which crude certificates were bought and sold and that effectively provided a competitive price. In 1895, the Rockefeller purchasing agent, Joseph Seep, announced that, henceforth, Mr. Rockefeller would pay fair and reasonable prices in the field, but not necessarily the exchange prices. Such was Standard

---

[26] Ibid., p. 928. (For the record, the witness, J. M. Calhoon, then proceeded to rebut the arguments advanced for joint ventures.)

Oil's power both as a buyer and over transportation that, within a year, the last exchange was closed. From that time to this, crude oil prices have been those "posted" in each field by the principal buyer or buyers; indeed, small buyers in a field will generally specify a major buyer's posting as their contract price.

Under this system in the past, prices tended to be rigid for considerable periods of time. The monthly Midcontinent crude price (Oklahoma 36-degree oil), for example, was stable at $2.97 a barrel from March 1959 through July 1964. It fell 5 cents, staying at $2.92 from August 1964 through August 1966. It then moved up in two steps, 6 months apart, to $3.07, where it remained from August 1967 through February 1969, rising then to $3.35 for the balance of the year. Since 1970, as crude supplies tightened, prices have shown more flexibility in an upward direction to the extent that increases have not been constrained by price controls.

The major refiners had a clear interest, through 1974, in maintaining posted prices. First, as they were also the major crude oil producers, it paid them to take their profits primarily at the crude level. The depletion allowance was a source of tax-free income—$27\frac{1}{2}$ per cent of gross crude revenues through 1968 and 22 per cent from 1969 through 1974. Because the allowance was limited to 50 per cent of net income before depletion, enjoyment of the full tax benefit required a highly profitable crude production operation.

Next, to the fully integrated firm, the cost of producing its crude oil is the real input cost of its refining operations. To the nonintegrated refiner, however, it is the price of crude oil that determines the refiner's input costs. The higher the price of crude oil relative to the prices of refined products, the narrower is the margin within which the independent refiner can compete with the majors.

It should be recognized that, except for Getty, none of the majors is fully integrated in the sense that its domestic crude production equals its refinery runs. A price increase raises the cost of oil they must purchase to supplement their own production, and an increase that could be attractive to Exxon (75 per cent self-sufficient in 1972) might not be acceptable to Shell (56 per cent self-sufficient). Thus, the industry engages in a balancing act where crude prices are concerned, weighing the benefits of higher crude profits against potential increases in refining costs and the extent to which these costs can be passed through into product prices. Note, however, that any increase in crude prices will raise the costs of a nonintegrated refiner by a much greater amount than the costs of a refiner that produces any substantial amount of its own crude.

The crude oil pricing picture changed markedly after 1970. Domestic production peaked in that year at 9.6 million barrels a day and declined, thereafter, to no more than 8.6 million barrels a day by 1975. At the same time, domestic refinery runs were rising with the demand for products.

The Organization of Petroleum Exporting Countries (OPEC) emerged as a viable cartel when the Teheran Agreement of February 1971 marked the first increases in posted prices for Mideast crude in 14 years. This success was followed by others, and by 1974 foreign crude oil was delivered to U.S. refineries at a cost of nearly $13 a barrel. Roughly 65 per cent of domestic crude in early 1975 was subject to ceiling prices that averaged $5.25 a barrel. Prices for the remainder, exempt from price controls, have risen with import costs and the temporary tariff imposed by President Ford. In short, the landed cost of imported crude oil has become, in 1975, the key to domestic prices.

Competition appears to play a more active role in refined products pricing, at least within the limits of refining and marketing margins. Because adequate quality specifications exist for all petroleum products, industrial and commercial buyers are able to negotiate on the basis of price alone. To a lesser extent, this is true of household heating oil customers, who may be held to a dealer by credit terms and service but never by brand loyalty.

Product differentiation has been an important factor only in the retail gasoline market. Here, the major companies, at least until 1974, engaged in heavy advertising to develop consumer brand preferences on the basis of "secret" additive packages and "proved" performance tests.

They succeeded within limits, to the extent that most customers would pay 2 or 3 cents a gallon more for major brand gasoline than for a private brand product. Whenever the difference in a marketing territory reached 4 or 5 cents a gallon, the majors lost substantial volumes of sales to independents and were forced to reduce prices or precipitate a true price in order to hold their market shares.

Thus, the stability of prices within any marketing territory has depended on the presence or absence of aggressive independent price marketers. In the Washington, D.C., area, dominated by majors with little independent competition, a "price war" has meant for years that a few stations shave 1 or 2 cents a gallon off the area price. Where independent competition has been strong, as in Kansas City or Detroit, price wars in the late 1960s and early 1970s drove prices down as much as 10 or 12 cents on frequent occasions.

The majors do not appear to have been unduly concerned about price competition at the retail level. They rarely compete against each other, but they will meet or beat the competition of price-cutting independents. Their primary concern has been to maintain retail volume, profitably if possible but unprofitably if necessary, in order to preserve the crude oil market in which most of their profits are earned.[27]

In 1975, however, nothing appears more certain than future changes in major oil company marketing and pricing policies. The direction of these changes defies prediction. On the one hand, the early 1974 gasoline shortage and subsequent unprecedented price increases have convinced most consumers that "gasoline is gasoline," to be bought on the basis of price rather than brand. This, in itself, will tend to increase competition.

On the other hand, faced with declining domestic crude supplies and the apparent loss of most of their foreign oil, the majors have made it clear that they intend to increase the profitability of their "downstream" refining and

---

[27] A Gulf Oil Company executive has remarked that his marketing department used to be considered the "disposal division." *Oil Daily*, no. 5, 902, May 29, 1975, p. 1.

marketing operations. This involves a drive toward greater efficiency through closing down unprofitable outlets, realigning their marketing territories, and so forth. But it could also mean that independent competitors may find it more difficult to obtain supplies.

Financial Performance

Despite the apparent degree of market control in the industry, reported financial profits of the oil companies have not been exceptional. Refining and integrated companies in the First National City Bank series earned an average annual rate of return on net worth of 12.8 per cent during the 25-year period 1950–1974, compared to 12.6 per cent for other manufacturing companies. Significantly, nonintegrated crude oil producing companies earned 15.4 per cent.

Data for the last 5 years, 1970–1974, are shown in Table 5. The improvement in earnings in 1973 and 1974 pulled the refining companies' average noticeably above that for all manufacturing. In the Citibank series, 1973 was the first year since 1941 during which crude production was less profitable than refining and integrated operations—crude prices rose more slowly in the first 5 months than product prices and were frozen more rigidly by the Cost of Living Council through November. Nevertheless, during the 5-year period, crude oil production maintained its historic high profitability.

Census data for 1973 confirm the profitability of oil and gas production.[28] Total expenditures for production, exploration, and development may be

TABLE 5

Rates of Return on Net Worth: Petroleum Industry and Other Manufacturing (in per cent)

	OIL AND GAS PRODUCING COMPANIES	REFINING AND INTEGRATED COMPANIES	OTHER MANUFACTURING COMPANIES
1950–1954, average	17.2	14.8	13.4
1955–1959, average	14.5	12.4	12.7
1960–1964, average	13.9	10.7	11.2
1965–1969, average	15.9	12.3	13.6
1970	13.3	10.9	9.8
1971	13.6	11.1	10.7
1972	14.0	10.6	12.5
1973	15.2	15.7	14.7
1974	21.0	19.9	14.0
1950–1974, average	15.4	12.8	12.6

Source: Petroleum Department, First National City Bank, New York, N.Y. Apr. 1975.

[28] U.S. Department of Commerce, Bureau of the Census, *Annual Survey of Oil and Gas, 1973* (Washington, D.C.: U.S. Government Printing Office, 1973), Tables 1 and 2.

allocated between operators' net production of oil and gas on the basis of the respective lease revenues. Lease bonuses are not included in the calculation because they are based on expected profits and contribute nothing to the actual development of new reserves.

On this basis, the average cost of finding, developing, and producing the domestic output in 1973 came to $2.49 a barrel for crude oil and 14.1 cents per thousand cubic feet (Mcf) of natural gas. Average prices received by producers were $3.90 a barrel for oil and 22.7 cents per Mcf for gas. Furthermore, the eight largest producers had costs substantially below the average—$2.03 a barrel for oil and 11.5 cents per Mcf of gas.

Pipeline operations are another area of great profitability. Under a 1941 consent decree applicable to most of the companies involved, pipeline earnings and dividends are limited relative to their rate base—the earnings limits are 8 per cent on crude lines and 10 per cent on product lines, whereas dividends are limited to 7 per cent of the rate base. The rate base is the ICC valuation of the property, normally in excess of total assets because reproduction costs are considered in the determination.

Pipelines, however, appear to be considered virtually risk-free by the financial community. Thus, they can be financed largely by debt, frequently in the ratio of 10 per cent equity to 90 per cent debt. This leverage can raise a reasonable rate of return on the total valuation to an extraordinary rate on the equity investment.

The average rate of return on equity for pipelines reporting to the ICC in 1973 was 17.4 per cent.[29] A few large lines that have been financed primarily by equity capital do have returns well below the average—for example, Gulf's pipeline company with 7.2 per cent and Texaco's with 8.0 per cent in 1973. The more highly leveraged lines did much better in 1973—that is, Shell (18.2 per cent), Exxon (31.7 per cent), and Standard of California's Chevron Pipe Line Company (61.6 per cent).

Colonial Pipeline Company, the largest products line in the nation, is a classic case with a 1973 rate of return on a net worth of 65.3 per cent. The nine major oil company owners provided 10 per cent of the original capital, or $36 million, and borrowed the rest. In eight and one-half years of operation, from mid-1965 through 1973, Colonial earned $273 million for its owners; the average annual dividend has been 86.1 per cent of the owners' investment.

The fact that crude oil production and pipeline operations yield above-average profits reinforces the view that the refining and marketing operations of the majors have earned below-average returns in the past. The ability of nonintegrated independent refiners to survive in these circumstances, without the support of crude oil profits, suggests that they are at least as efficient as the majors. The ability of independent marketers not only to survive but to increase their share of the market by price competition suggests that they are far more efficient marketers than the major oil companies.

[29] U.S. Department of Commerce, ICC, *Transport Statistics in the United States*, pt. 6, "Pipe Lines" (Washington, D.C.: U.S. Government Printing Office, 1973).

IV. PUBLIC POLICY

Antitrust Policy

In 1911, the Supreme Court upheld a finding that the Standard Oil Company, the giant of the industry, had violated the Sherman Act in achieving monopoly power in the refining, marketing, and transportation of petroleum. This had been accomplished through a variety of predatory practices—that is, through unlawful conduct. A structural remedy was imposed when the parent holding company was ordered to divest itself of the controlling stock interests in 33 subsidiaries. Although dozens of other antitrust actions have been brought against oil companies, this was the last successful "big case" involving the industry.

Not until 1940 was another major structural attack launched, this time with so broad a scope as to become known as the "Mother Hubbard Case."[30] Twenty-two major oil companies and 344 subsidiary and secondary corporations, with the American Petroleum Institute as a policy-coordinating agency, were charged in a Justice Department civil suit with violating both the Sherman and Clayton acts. The original complaint sought both pipeline and marketing divestiture as relief. The case was postponed with the onset of World War II and, thereafter, languished until it was dismissed, without prosecution, at the department's request in 1951.

A third effort is now being made, this time by the FTC.[31] The eight largest oil companies have been charged with, among other things; individually and collectively maintaining a noncompetitive market structure in the refining industry in Districts I and III (the eastern and Gulf Coast states); restricting the supply of crude oil to independent refiners and potential entrants through their control over pipelines and their crude oil exchanges with one another; pursuing a common course of action to keep profits at the crude oil level artificially high and refining profits artificially low in order to prevent new entry into refining; and pursuing a common course of action in refusing to sell refined products to independent marketers and to avoid price competition among themselves. The question of relief is left open in the complaint, although it is presumed that some form of divestiture will be sought in the courts. The case is still in the prehearing discovery stage; a determined optimist might predict a final settlement in fewer than 10 years, if the commission were to pursue the case that far.

It is true that a number of antitrust cases relating to conduct have been brought successfully. "Successfully" means here that the cases were won by the government and legal principles were firmly established, not that they made any real changes in industry conduct.

The California stations case (1949) established the principle that a refiner may not require his dealers to carry his brand of gasoline exclusively.[32] The Supreme

---

[30] *United States* v. *American Petroleum Institute et al.*, Civil no. 8524 (D.D.C., Oct. 1940).
[31] FTC, *In re Exxon*, Docket no. 8934, July 17, 1973.
[32] *Standard Oil of California and Standard Stations* v. *United States*, 337 U.S. 293 (1949).

Court said, in effect, that any Chevron dealer, for example, is legally entitled to add an Exxon, a Texaco, or a Terrible Herbst pump to give his customers some brand choice. The number of "split-pump" operations in the nation can be counted on one's fingers. Any major brand dealer knows that his supplier can find some other grounds to cancel his lease if he sells someone else's brand of gasoline.

Similarly, a series of cases makes it clear that a refiner may not pressure his dealers to carry particular lines of tires, batteries, and accessories.[33] Yet, dealer after dealer complains that this pressure is still being exerted by his refiner's representatives.

Again, in the *Sun-Jacksonville* case, the Supreme Court found illegal price discrimination when the supplier granted a discount to one dealer not available to other Sun dealers in the marketing area.[34] The major refiners responded with zone pricing, in which a city is divided into a large number of zones, many containing only a single station, each defined as a separate marketing territory. Zone pricing has not been attacked since by the FTC, and the discrimination continues.

Some of the cases that have not been brought are interesting. The Justice Department did block a merger of Pennzoil and Kendall Refining, with combined assets of $150 million, in the mid-1960s; but this was sandwiched in between clearances granted for the Atlantic-Richfield and Union-Pure Oil mergers, each involving about $1.5 billion in assets. Justice began an investigation of Colonial Pipeline in 1963, later broadened to include several other joint-venture lines. In 1975, the matter was still "under review"; no complaints have been issued. Indeed, Justice has shown a marked reluctance since the late 1950s to undertake any major structural case involving the petroleum industry. It did establish an oil industry task force, with some fanfare, early in 1974. A few months later, however, key personnel were assigned to work instead on two cases that ranked higher on the agency's scale of priorities: One involved an international mink pelt cartel, the other a price-fixing conspiracy in the toilet seat industry.

In short, there has been a great deal of antitrust sound and fury since the 1911 Standard Oil case, but very little has happened to alter either the structure or the conduct of the industry. At best, it can be said that antitrust policy has prevented things from getting much worse than they are.

Federal Tax Policy

Among the most important benefits bestowed on the petroleum industry by the Federal government has been the special tax treatment accorded to oil and gas producers. (Note that nonintegrated refiners and marketers are treated like any other business operations.) The effect of this treatment is to create a wide

---

[33] See, for example, *Atlantic Refining Co.* v. *Federal Trade Commission*, 381 U.S. 357 (1965) or *Shell Oil* v. *Federal Trade Commission*, 360 F.2d 470 (1966).
[34] *Federal Trade Commission* v. *Sun Oil Co.*, 371 U.S. 358 (1963).

gap between taxable income and the income reported to stockholders. In 1963 and 1964, for example, the taxable income of petroleum companies, dominated by the integrated majors, was only 35 per cent of accounting income, compared to an average 89 per cent ratio for other industries.[35]

One tax benefit is the right to expense so-called intangible drilling costs for productive wells.[36] The average businessman who acquires a capital asset must recover his outlay through depreciation during the useful life of the asset. In contrast, from 75 to 80 per cent of the cost of a successful oil well (site preparation, drilling, casing, cementing, anything not readily salvageable) can be charged off against the first year's income from the well. The oil company recovers most of its well investment, tax-free, immediately, instead of over a long period of years.

The percentage-depletion allowance was the most publicized benefit available to the industry until it was eliminated for all but small producers in 1975. The producer could (and still can) claim cost depletion to recover his actual investment during the producing life of his wells. Alternatively, he could subtract from pretax profits 22 per cent of the gross revenue from oil and gas production, up to 50 per cent of net income before taxes and depletion. Furthermore, percentage depletion was not limited to original costs, but continued throughout the producing life of a property. The investment in the average successful lease could be recouped, free of income tax, many times over before the lease was abandoned.

The third important benefit is the foreign tax credit. A U.S. company doing business abroad is subject to U.S. income taxation on its foreign earnings; it may also be liable for income taxes levied by the countries in which the foreign income is earned. Tax policy has long permitted foreign income taxes to be credited, dollar for dollar, against the U.S. tax liability on foreign income, in order to avoid double taxation. To be considered for credit, a foreign tax must be levied on net income and be generally applicable to all firms doing business within the taxing country.

The principle of the foreign tax credit is perfectly sound. The issue is the extraordinary elasticity with which the principle has been applied to international oil operations.

After World War II, foreign producing governments began to press the oil companies for higher royalty payments. The customary rate throughout the Middle East, for example, was still the four shillings gold a ton (about 13 cents a barrel) established in the earliest pre-World War I concession agreements. A royalty payment is a deductible business expense—that is, at a 48 per cent tax rate, an extra $100 in royalties would reduce a corporation's income tax by $48, but it would reduce its own net income by $52. The oil companies and the U.S. government collaborated, therefore, to persuade foreign producing nations

---

[35] U.S. Congress, Senate, Subcommittee on Antitrust and Monopoly, *Hearings on Governmental Intervention in the Market Mechanism, Petroleum Industry*, pt. 2, 91st Cong., 1st sess., 1969, p. 819.

[36] Dry holes can be written off whenever they are abandoned.

to utilize income taxes rather than higher royalties, offsetting U.S. taxes up to the U.S. rate instead of corporate aftertax income. Because the statutes were designed to tax foreign oil companies rather than all business firms, they did not meet Internal Revenue Service (IRS) standards for tax creditability, yet IRS accepted them for that purpose.

Moreover, from 1960 on, the OPEC nations used tax reference prices (well above market prices) as the basis for computing hypothetical profits, to establish a fixed "government take" per barrel of oil. By no stretch of imagination could this be called a tax on realized income. Still, the IRS continued to allow tax credits. In the words of an industry executive, "The artificiality of the system is obvious and well known, but it has not been challenged by the IRS."[37]

The result has been that the burden of meeting host government demands has been shifted from the oil companies to the U.S. Treasury. The companies completely escape taxation in the United States on their foreign earnings.

The importance of these tax benefits to the large companies is evident. In 1974, percentage depletion was worth a $251 million tax saving to Exxon. On the company's foreign earnings of $1.8 billion after all foreign taxes, no U.S. income tax was paid. Because most of the foreign taxes were, in fact, royalties to producing countries, tax credit treatment may have saved Exxon roughly $800 million. Continental Oil, with one quarter the earnings of Exxon, saved $52 million through percentage depletion and $205 million through the foreign tax credit.

Tax legislation passed in March 1975 withdrew the percentage-depletion option except for small producers (2000 barrels a day of oil or 12 million cubic feet a day of gas, phasing downward to a 15 per cent allowance for 1000 barrels a day or 6 million cubic feet a day in 1985). In essence, Congress concluded that the arguments used to preserve the depletion allowance when oil was worth $3.00 a barrel could not be heeded when the average value of domestic crude is $9.00 a barrel. Although use of the foreign tax credit was substantially tightened, the economic impact of the changes on the international companies will be minor. This will still provide a more substantial tax break for the international oil companies than it does for other business operations.

Public Policy for the Future

Shortages of crude oil and refined products climaxed by the Arab embargo during the winter of 1973–1974 have plunged the United States into a serious debate on national energy policy. Whatever decisions are made will have an enormous impact on the domestic petroleum industry. At this point, however, we can only indicate some of the alternatives before us.

The one clear fact, as of early 1975, is that the regulatory system developed by the Federal Energy Administration (FEA) during 1974 (under the Energy

---

[37] U.S. Congress, Senate, Subcommittee on Multinational Corporations, *Hearings on Multinational Corporations and United States Foreign Policy*, 93d Cong., 2d sess., pt. 4, 1974, p. 109. Mobil Oil Co. cable traffic.

Emergency Act of 1973) does not provide a satisfactory long-run solution. FEA regulations govern supply and price relationships throughout the industry.

Crude oil is priced on a two-tier basis. Maximum price ceilings averaging $5.25 a barrel were placed on so-called old oil volumes equal to production from leases during comparable months in 1972. Three classes of oil are exempt from price ceilings: "new oil" produced in excess of the 1972 base or from new leases, some old oil released from controls as a stimulus to increasing production, and stripper production from leases averaging fewer than 10 barrels daily per well. Prices for exempt oil, about 35 per cent of total production, were in excess of $12.00 a barrel by May 1975.

Independent refiners have been protected from the loss of domestic crude supplies by a freeze on producer-refiner supply relationships to those in effect on December 1, 1973. A cumbersome "entitlements" program was instituted in late 1974 to equalize crude oil input costs among refiners. Entitlements equal to the estimated volume of old oil available each month are shared among all refiners in proportion to their refinery inputs. Refiners blessed with a higher-than-average input percentage of old oil are required to buy entitlements from those refiners who are forced to rely more heavily on expensive exempt and imported crude. The entitlements price is fixed by the FEA at a figure equal to the difference between the old oil ceiling and the average cost of exempt and imported crude.

Independent wholesale distributors and retail marketers are protected against cutoffs by suppliers through regulations that maintain the supply relationships in effect during 1972 and that require any shortages to be allocated fairly among all customers by refiners. Finally, retail customers are minimally protected from price pyramids by provisions that limit refiners to passing through cost increases into product prices; the margins of jobbers and retailers over product costs are also fixed.

The entire program has developed into a system of enormous complexity, one that has created in Washington a new generation of lawyers and consultants versed in the intricacies of FEA rules and procedures. The program has tended to lock all units of the industry into an economic straitjacket in which survival is determined by FEA allocation and pricing rules rather than by market forces. Although it may have been an essential response to a crisis, it should not be perpetuated any longer than necessary.

Yet, one of the alternatives under serious consideration would do just this. The petroleum industry would be recognized as a public utility and subjected to permanent FEA-type regulation, at least through the refining level. The number of firms in the industry and the complexity of its processes would make such regulation exceedingly difficult over the long run. Regulation of the well-head price of natural gas over the last two decades has been beset with problems, despite the fact that we are dealing with a single, simple product. Beyond this, the track records of such agencies as the Federal Power Commission (FPC) and the ICC offer little hope that a public utility approach for the petroleum industry would respond adequately to the public interest.

The opposite alternative, advanced by a number of economists, is the complete removal of controls. Prices for crude and products would rise to market-clearing levels during periods of shortage and decline as supplies eased. The industry nominally, but only nominally, favors this approach. Crude producers urge the removal of price ceilings so that their old oil prices can rise to the "competitive" level established by OPEC; at the same time, they demand guarantees in the form of quotas or flexible tariffs so that they will not have to meet the competition of OPEC prices should these decline in the future. Refiners and marketers would like to be free to raise prices, but demand that their crude and product supplies be preserved on some "equitable" basis by government fiat.

The principal difficulty with the free market alternative is that it depends on the existence of free markets. Given the present structure of the industry and the prospect of a long-run shortage of energy supplies, the result would be a steady increase in the economic rents enjoyed by the major oil companies and independent crude producers. With the majors controlling most of the crude supplies and transportation facilities, many competitive independent refining and marketing firms in the industry would either disappear or be converted fully into concubines of the majors.

There is, however, an option available under which a free market policy could work with some hope for satisfactory performance. Concentration ratios in production, refining, and marketing are not so high as to preclude workable competition in each sector of the industry. The principal obstacles to competition arise from the vertical integration of the major companies and the intercorporate relationships that facilitate tacit collusion among them. If these obstacles can be removed, there is no reason why competitive markets will not develop.

As a simple, easily accomplished first step, the exemption granted to oil companies from the commodities clause of the 1906 Hepburn Act should be repealed. No company engaged in the production, refining, or marketing of petroleum should be permitted to hold any financial interest in a pipeline that carries its products. All pipelines, including crude gathering systems, should be required to operate as true common carriers, independent of the oil companies for which they provide transportation services. Independent refiners, crude oil producers, and marketers could then negotiate oil and product sales in the knowledge that they had access to transportation facilities.

The next and more difficult step could be to require the separation of crude oil production from refining and marketing. Integration through either ownership or long-term supply contracts would be prohibited. In other words, crude producers would have no alternative to offering their oil on a market equally accessible to large and small refiners, including new entrants. All refiners would face the same market prices for their inputs, so that survival and growth in the refining industry would depend on efficiency in this industry and not on the subsidization through crude oil profits now available to integrated companies. This step, in itself, would ensure competition at the marketing level.

Divestiture of this magnitude sounds like an impossible task. An interesting "laboratory experiment," however, might demonstrate its practicality. Gulf Oil is reorganizing its corporate structure in 1975 into a group of worldwide functional subsidiaries, among them an extractive industries company (including oil and gas production), a refining and marketing company, a transportation company, and a science and technology company to provide and market Gulf research and technical services.

In theory, at least, the separate companies will be autonomous investment centers dealing with each other as they would with outside firms. Should the Gulf experiment be successful, it will go a long way toward demonstrating the feasibility, if not the wisdom, of vertical divestiture.

A major problem is that large imports of crude oil will be essential into the foreseeable future. Thus, with any phase-out of price controls, domestic prices will rise to the levels set by the landed costs of OPEC oil. Now, this would happen with or without any divestiture program, but it is conceivable that divestiture could help to restrain future OPEC increases.

For more than 40 years the private cartel of the Seven Sisters controlled the output and prices of most of the free world's oil outside the United States. Since 1973 ownership of crude oil production and reserves has passed rapidly into the hands of the OPEC cartel of governments. Any cartel, however, can maintain a given level of prices only so long as it can control the aggregate output of its members. The OPEC is no exception.

Just as individual states in the United States were unwilling to yield control over oil production within their borders to bureaucrats in Washington, so individual OPEC members are unwilling to permit prorationing decisions to be made by bureaucrats at OPEC headquarters. Within the United States the major companies preserved their own system of posted prices by balancing their offtake among the prorationing states. The system would have come apart had a situation developed in which, say, Louisiana wells were allowed to operate at 80 per cent of capacity while Texas authorities restricted production to 30 per cent in order to maintain prices. Similarly, most OPEC nations have continued to sell their oil primarily through the international majors, in the belief that the companies' self-interest in marketing OPEC oil will persuade them to allocate their liftings equitably among the member nations. The major companies, therefore, will continue to control the disposition of most OPEC oil even though they no longer own it.

If the vertically integrated majors can control the marketing of OPEC oil, the absolute level of OPEC prices is a matter of indifference to them. They can pass any crude oil price increases through their own integrated operations, secure in the knowledge that refining competitors whom they supply with OPEC oil must meet the same increases. Indeed, OPEC price increases confer a positive benefit on the integrated companies by raising the value of their crude oil reserves elsewhere in the world. In the Prudhoe Bay, Alaska, field alone, for example, a one-dollar rise in the value of reserves is worth nearly $10 billion to Exxon, Atlantic Richfield, and Sohio/BP.

The major firms have no incentive to aggressively oppose, and considerable incentive to tolerate, OPEC pricing policies. Suppose, on the other hand, that all major companies desiring to do business in the United States were required to separate their worldwide production interests from refining and marketing activities. The OPEC producers would then be faced by the largest refiners in the world, each actively bargaining to ensure that its crude oil costs were as low as its competitors' costs. The resulting market discipline might not bring immediate reductions in the price of crude oil, but it would certainly provide a restraining force on future price increases. Prices 5 years or 10 years from now would be lower with divestiture than they will be if the present industry structure is maintained.

To conclude, the one public policy option not available is a return to the conditions under which the petroleum industry operated prior to 1973. One alternative is legislative restructuring of the industry in a manner that would create a true intermediate crude oil market in which producers and refiners meet as arms-length bargainers. Were this accomplished, competition would be sufficiently workable to permit the market to operate without government interference. A second alternative is acceptance of permanent FEA-type regulation, with all of the problems attendant upon bureaucratic attempts to usurp market functions. Finally, short of complete nationalization, there is the possibility of direct government participation in one or more phases of the industry—embracing options ranging from government equity participation in enterprises to the establishment of government corporations that compete with private firms. Examples of this approach can be found in West Germany, France, Italy, the United Kingdom, and Canada; and it is under Congressional consideration in the United States.

Regardless of which option or combination of options may be chosen, national policy decisions will be made in the near future that will determine the structure of the petroleum industry for years to come.

SUGGESTED READINGS

BOOKS AND PAMPHLETS

Adelman, M. A. *The World Petroleum Market*. Baltimore: The Johns Hopkins Press, 1972.

Allvine, Fred C., and James M. Patterson. *Competition, Ltd.: The Marketing of Gasoline*. Bloomington: Indiana University Press, 1972.

Clark, James., A., and Michel T. Halbouty. *The Last Boom*. New York: Random House, Inc., 1972.

DeChazeau, Melvin, G., and Alfred E. Kahn. *Integration and Competition in the Petroleum Industry*. New Haven: Yale University Press, 1959.

Duchesneau, Thomas D. *Competition in the U.S. Energy Industry*. Cambridge, Mass.: Ballinger Publishing Co., 1975.

Engler, Robert. *The Politics of Oil*. Chicago: University of Chicago Press, 1961.

Jacoby, Neil H. *Multinational Oil*. New York: Macmillan Publishing Co., Inc., 1974.

Lovejoy, W. F., and Paul T. Homan. *Economic Aspects of Oil Conservation Regulation.* Baltimore: The Johns Hopkins Press, 1967.

McLean, John C., and Robert W. Haigh. *The Growth of Integrated Oil Companies.* Boston: Graduate School of Business Administration, Harvard University, 1954.

GOVERNMENT PUBLICATIONS

FTC. Staff Report. *Concentration Levels and Trends in the Energy Sector of the U.S. Economy.* Washington: D.C.: U.S. Government Printing Office, 1974.

U.S. Congress, House, Select Committee on Small Business, *Anticompetitive Impact of Oil Company Ownership of Petroleum Product Pipelines,* 92d Cong., 2d sess, H. Rept., 1972.

U.S. Congress, Senate, Committee on Foreign Relations, Subcommittee on Multinational Corporations, *Multinational Oil Corporations and U.S. Foreign Policy,* 93d Cong., 2d sess., H. Rept., 1975.

U.S. Congress, Senate, Committee on Government Operations, Permanent Subcommittee on Investigations, *Investigation of the Petroleum Industry,* 93d Cong., 1st sess., S. Rept., 1973. (FTC Report.)

U.S. Congress, Senate, Committee on the Judiciary, Subcommittee on Antitrust and Monopoly, *Hearings on Governmental Intervention in the Market Mechanism: Petroleum,* pts. 1–5, 91st Cong., 1st and 2d sess., 1969, 1970.

———. *The Industrial Reorganization Act: Hearing on.* pt. 8: 93d Cong., 2d sess., 1974.

U.S. Congress, Senate, Select Committee on Small Business, *The International Petroleum Cartel,* 82d Cong., 2d sess., 1952 (FTC Report).

CHAPTER 5

the automobile industry

LAWRENCE J. WHITE

I. INTRODUCTION

Despite continuing predictions of its imminent demise, the automobile remains an important part of American society and the American economy. As of the end of 1973, there were 101 million automobiles on the roads in the United States.[1] There were 11.4 million new cars sold in the United States in the same year, at a total retail value of well over $40 billion. Approximately one job in six is estimated to be directly or indirectly involved in the manufacture, distribution, repair, or use of automobiles.[2]

The automobile is a tremendously important device, offering personal transportation convenience, speed, and flexibility that would have been unthinkable a century ago. It has been an important influence on the shape and structure of modern metropolitan areas. It is an important personal asset for many families, a source of pride, pleasure, and prestige. It is also the most frequent subject of consumer complaints about malfunctioning and unsatisfactory repair. More than 55,000 people were killed in accidents involving automobiles in 1973, and automobile operation contributes significantly to air pollution in many metropolitan areas.

The industry that produces these cars is, thus, an important part of the American economy. The employment decisions of the automobile companies—hiring or laying-off—are front page news in most newspapers. Pricing decisions by the companies are similarly front page news. Four large companies—General Motors Corporation, Ford Motor Company, Chrysler Corporation, and American Motors Corporation—produce virtually all of the domestically built automobiles sold in the United States. They are, respectively, the first,

---

[1] *Automotive News*, 1974 Almanac Issue, Apr. 24, 1974, p. 2.
[2] *1973–1974 Automobile Facts and Figures* (Detroit, Mich.: Motor Vehicle Manufacturers Association, 1974), p. 51.

third, fifth, and ninety-eighth largest manufacturing companies in the country.[3] Their absolute sizes make them important participants in the American economy. A past president of General Motors, Charles E. Wilson, once remarked, "I always thought what was good for our country was good for GM, and vice versa."

The fact that there are so few automobile companies in the United States also provides us with excellent case study material about the workings of an oligopolistic industry. Although the representatives of the automobile companies frequently proclaim their industry to be the most competitive in the world, it is a far cry from the situation that most economists would describe as a competitive industry. With only four domestic producers—and with the first three accounting for 97 per cent of the domestic total—they are acutely aware of each other's presence in the market and are constantly concerned with the likely impact of their own actions on their rivals and with the likely reactions of their rivals. *Conjectural interdependence* is clearly an operative concept in the automobile industry. The "competitive" nature of the automobile industry should not be confused with that of wheat farming or of the gray cotton goods industry.

In this chapter an overview of the important aspects of the American automobile industry—its strengths and weaknesses, efficiencies and deficiencies, and commissions and omissions—is offered.[4] Section I provides background information with a review of the important historical landmarks of this industry, from its early experimental days to the present. Section II follows with a discussion of the important structural characteristics of the industry and of the product. Section III then examines the behavior of the industry and tries to relate it to the structural characteristics discussed in Section II. Section IV assesses the performance of the automobile industry. Section V offers a review of public policy as it has related to the American automobile industry, plus a discussion of possible improvements in policy.

History

It is impossible to identify one man as "the inventor" of the automobile (although, as we will see, a smart patent lawyer had an early patent on the automobile), nor can we identify a specific time or place.[5] Instead, the idea and the actuality of the automobile drew on many sources; a number of men, virtually

[3] "500 Largest Manufacturing Corporations," *Fortune*, **89** (May 1974).

[4] Interested readers desiring more details on the automobile industry might look at Lawrence J. White, *The Automobile Industry Since 1945* (Cambridge, Mass.: Harvard University Press, 1971); John B. Rae, *The American Automobile: A Brief History* (Chicago: Chicago University Press, 1965); FTC, *Report on the Motor Vehicle Industry* (Washington, D.C.: U.S. Government Printing Office, 1939); and other sources listed in the bibliography at the end of this chapter.

[5] A large number of sources have been drawn on here, including White, op. cit.; FTC, op. cit.; Allan Nevins, *Ford: The Times, the Man, the Company* (New York: Scribner's, 1954); Alfred P. Sloan, Jr., *My Years with General Motors* (Garden City, N.Y.: Doubleday, 1964); Automobile Manufacturers Association, *Automobiles of America* (Detroit, Mich.: Wayne State University Press, 1968); and chapters by Donald A. Moore and Robert F. Lanzillotti in previous editions of this book.

simultaneously, were formulating and developing vehicles that were forerunners of today's automobiles.

The first means of land transportation that did not rely on animal (or human) motive power was the steam locomotive. The steam engine was first developed in England as a pumping device in the late seventeenth century and then was vastly improved a century later by James Watt as a general source of motive power for operating machinery. By the early 1800s, the steam engine had been applied to vehicles as a means of locomotion, but primary emphasis was given to wheeled vehicles on a fixed track—the railroad. British inventors in the first half of the nineteenth century had also developed and received patents on steam-powered vehicles for normal roads, omnibuses, and private carriages. A number were even manufactured and put into use, but the British parliament (encouraged by railroad and horse-coach companies) progressively limited the use of these vehicles until, in 1865, they were effectively doomed by an act that severely limited their speed and required any such vehicle using the highways to be preceded by a man with a red flag.

In the United States, there were no such prohibitions, but population densities and road conditions did not encourage the development of these vehicles, even though there were working models by the 1870s and 1880s. Steam tractors and road rollers had been developed, however, and Henry Ford, at the age of thirteen, in 1876, apparently was deeply impressed by the sight of a steam engine (used for threshing and sawing wood) connected by a chain to the rear wheels of a wagon and, hence, propelling itself from job site to job site.[6]

The technology that did develop during the nineteenth century for wheeled vehicles (railroads and horse-drawn coaches and wagons) was nevertheless, influential in the eventual development of the automobile. The development of improved axles, springs, brakes, and coaches provided an important technological base. Coach and wagon builders, like Studebaker and the Fisher brothers, were later to become important in the automobile industry. Improvements in manufacturing techniques and the development of large numbers of machine shops, which could provide machinery and components in areas like Detroit, were equally important.

The form of motive power eventually used on automobiles, the internal combustion engine, was also developed in the nineteenth century. First conceived at the end of the eighteenth century, it did not receive extensive development until the 1850s and 1860s. By the mid-1870s the engine had achieved limited commercial success as a source of stationary power. The Otto engine, developed by Nikolaus A. Otto in Germany, and the Brayton, developed by George B. Brayton in the United States, were among the leading engines at the time. All such engines were two-cycle engines, having an explosion, or burning, of the fuel just before each down-stroke of the piston in the engine's cylinder. In the late 1870s, however, Otto developed and patented a four-cycle engine in which the explosion occurred on every other stroke, with a flywheel to provide

---

[6] Nevins, op. cit., p. 54.

the inertia to carry the engine through its nonpower stroke. This allowed more complete exhaustion of the burned fuel and improved the intake of fresh fuel. The engine was quiet and compact and, hence, earned the name "silent Otto." The four-cycle engine soon dominated the field and became the eventual source of power for the automobile.

With all of the pieces available, it remained for someone to put them together. In the 1860s, Joseph E. Lenoir, in Paris, had designed and built a vehicle, powered by a two-cycle engine, that completed a distance of 24 kilometers in 3 hours. But he failed to continue its development. Siegfried Marcus, a German working in Vienna, apparently had a sophisticated working vehicle powered by a four-stroke engine (predating Otto's) in 1875. But he saw little prospect of commercial success and did not pursue its development. In the United States, a Rochester patent attorney named George Selden was interested in such vehicles and designed a "mechanical road carriage" to be propelled by a two-cycle engine.[7] He applied for a patent in 1879, describing the vehicle in broad terms to try to include almost anything on wheels that was powered by an internal combustion engine. He then cleverly delayed the granting of the patent for 16 years, through leisurely amendments to his original claim. The patent was finally granted in 1895.

In the interim, the bicycle industry had matured, both in America and in Europe, and this provided further impetus to the development of the automobile. It encouraged thoughts about horseless means of road travel, it spurred improvements in metallurgy, and it brought improvements in manufacturing techniques.

Gottlieb Daimler, in Germany, in 1886, developed a tricycle with a four-stroke engine. Karl Benz, a year earlier, had received a patent on a motorcycle and, in 1886, received a patent on a four-wheeled motor carriage. By 1892, the French firm of Panhard & Levassor had pushed their development and production of four-wheeled, four-cycle motor vehicles to the point of issuing illustrated catalogues of its vehicles.

In America, Charles and Frank Duryea developed and operated a motorized vehicle in 1893, and Elwood Haynes developed another the following year. Ransom E. Olds, who had developed a steam automobile in 1887, developed a vehicle relying on the internal combustion engine in 1895. By the middle of the decade, a large number of inventors were at work on automobiles, many in ignorance of the work of the others. The announcement of races of motorized vehicles, however, helped spread knowledge and quickened interest in the vehicles. The American Motor League, founded at the end of 1895, helped this process. Nevertheless, motor vehicles were still exotic devices. The prevailing sentiment of the day was that steam was for rails and horses for roads. In rebuttal, Olds, as early as 1892, claimed the following advantages for his steam carriage: "It never kicks or bites, never tires on long runs, and never sweats in

---

[7] For a complete description of Selden and the patent case that he eventually provoked, see William Greenleaf, *Monopoly on Wheels* (Detroit, Mich.: Wayne State University Press, 1961).

hot weather. It does not require care in the stable and only eats while on the road."[8]

As the decade wore on, more vehicles were developed. For a while, it appeared that electric vehicles might be the superior form of transportation. By 1898, there was a fleet of 100 electric cabs on the streets of New York. But the electric vehicles were limited in range, heavy, and required slow and expensive recharging of their batteries. As Greenleaf has noted, "the reputation of the electric vehicle lived off the imperfections of the gasoline engine."[9] But new and better gasoline-powered vehicles were being brought forward by inventors like Henry Ford, Alexander Winton, Edgar and Elmer Apperson, Charles B. King, and Hiram Percey Maxim. Steam vehicles—including the famous Stanley Steamer—also were being developed. Automotive races and reported feats of speed and endurance continued to fuel the public interest in these vehicles. By the turn of the century, other names like the Locomobile, the Packard, and the Peerless had appeared on the scene. The nation's first automobile show was held in New York in 1900. In that year, more than 4000 cars were sold.

During the next decade, production expanded rapidly, so that annual sales by 1910 were 187,000. Entry into the industry was comparatively easy. The manufacturer of automobiles was largely an assembler of parts. The new entrepreneur needed to design a vehicle, announce its imminent appearance to the public, and contract with machine shops and carriage makers for the engines, wheels, bodies, and other components, often obtaining these parts on 30- to 90-days' credit. The assembled autos could be sold for cash to dealers or directly to customers. The capital requirements for a new company were not steep. The Ford Motor Company, incorporated in 1903, was capitalized at $150,000, but had actually only $28,000 in cash at its beginning.[10] More than 1100 companies are reported to have "entered" the industry between 1895 and 1926, although many of them never actually got into production.[11] It appears that only 181 companies actually lasted beyond the manufacture of one or two cars. Table 1 shows the pattern of entry—and exit—in the industry during the first two decades of the twentieth century.

As of 1903, the leading manufacturer was Ransom E. Olds; the Oldsmobile held a quarter of the market. Other familiar names in the market at the time included the Ford, the Cadillac, the Buick, the Packard, the Rambler, the Pierce, the Auburn, the Autocar, the Franklin, and the Marmon. Prices varied widely, from $650 up.

During this decade the technology of the automobile developed rapidly, providing improved reliability, speed, and comfort. The increased sales, noted here, reflected this. By the end of the decade, there was little doubt that automobiles would be the vehicles of the future, although there was considerable

---

[8] Nevins, op. cit., p. 138.
[9] Greenleaf, op. cit., p. 56.
[10] Nevins, op. cit., p. 238.
[11] R. G. Cleveland and S. T. Williamson, *The Road Is Yours* (New York: Hawthorn Books, 1951), pp. 270–291.

TABLE 1

Early Entry into and Exit from the Automobile Industry

YEAR	NUMBER OF ENTRANTS	NUMBER OF EXITS	NUMBER OF FIRMS REMAINING
1902	—	—	12
1903	13	1	24
1904	12	1	35
1905	5	2	38
1906	6	1	43
1907	1	0	44
1908	10	2	52
1909	18	1	69
1910	1	18	52
1911	3	2	53
1912	12	8	57
1913	20	7	70
1914	8	7	71
1915	10	6	75
1916	6	7	74
1917	8	6	76
1918	1	6	71
1919	10	4	77
1920	12	5	84
1921	5	1	88
1922	4	9	83

Source: From *The Automobile Industry*, p. 176, by Ralph Epstein. Copyright 1928, A. W. Shaw Co. Used with permission of McGraw-Hill Book Company.

doubt as to which companies would actually survive. As Table 1 indicates, both entry and exit were high.

Also during this decade, the Selden patent came up for challenge. Selden had assigned his patent to the Electric Vehicle Company, in 1900. The company promptly began suing manufacturers of gasoline engine automobiles for infringement of the Selden patent. As an alternative, the company proposed a trade association of manufacturers, based around the patent, with the company receiving a 5 per cent royalty on the sale of cars. The price proved too steep, but, in 1903, the company agreed to a $1\frac{1}{4}$ per cent royalty rate, and a number of companies joined with the Electric Vehicle Company to form the Association of Licensed Automobile Manufacturers (ALAM). The leading manufacturer, Olds, was among them. The ALAM's goal appears to have been at least a partial cartelization of the industry, discouraging new entry. It advertised its warnings of infringement lawsuits to nonroyalty paying manufacturers, dealers, and their customers. The Ford Motor Company tried to join but was rejected, partly because of the desire of Detroit auto manufacturers within ALAM to reduce competition by making things more difficult for Ford.[12] Ford then decided to fight the ALAM and contest the validity of the patent.

In October 1903, as expected, Ford was sued by the ALAM for infringement on the Selden patent. The case dragged on in Federal court for 6 years. In the interim, Ford and most of the other nonlicensed companies formed the American Motor Car Manufacturers Association (AMCMA), as a rival trade group to the ALAM. Most of the ALAM companies were committed to producing expensive automobiles ($3000 to $6000), whereas most of the AMCMA were selling less expensive vehicles aimed at a larger market. Thus, the legal battle between the ALAM and Ford (and AMCMA) took on, somewhat, the character of a battle between those who wanted to cater only to the rich, versus those who were interested in the welfare of the poor man (or at least the middle class). It was also portrayed as a battle of free enterprise against the monopoly trusts, a popular theme during "trust-buster" Theodore Roosevelt's presidential term of office. Shrewd advertising by the Ford Motor Company played on both these themes.

Finally, in September 1909, Judge Charles M. Hough, much to most people's surprise, ruled in favor of the ALAM and supported the validity of the Selden patent. This buoyed the fortunes of the ALAM, causing most of the members of the rival AMCMA to defect and apply for licenses. Ford, however, resisted and appealed. The circuit court of appeals heard the appeal and, in January 1911, ruled in favor of Ford and against the ALAM. The Selden patent was held to be valid, but only for the very limited combination of wheeled vehicle and two-cycle engine that Selden had actually chosen, despite his efforts to have the patent cover "any form of liquid hydrocarbon engine of the compression type." Thus, the producers of the day, most of whom used four-cycle engines and a few of whom used improved two-cycle engines, were not infringing on the patent. The ALAM folded, to be succeeded eventually by the Automobile Manufacturers Association (today, the Motor Vehicle Manufacturers Association). The automatic cross licensing of patents at nominal royalties among members, a practice started by the ALAM, was adopted by its successor organization. And the standardization of components, another practice encouraged by the ALAM, eventually became a primary function of the Society of Automotive Engineers.

At the time of Ford's victory, the Selden patent had only a year of life remaining. By 1911, the Ford Motor Co. was strong enough so that it could easily have afforded the back payment of royalties, had it lost the case. Thus, the victory at this point was relatively unimportant, although it did bring greater fame to Henry Ford and help create the image of Ford as the champion of the common man. The importance of the case was in the effect that the patent and the ALAM might have had on the industry.[13] If Ford had abandoned the industry in 1903

---

[12] Greenleaf, op. cit., p. 107.
[13] Ibid., pp. 237–238.

after he was denied a license by the ALAM, the advent of the mass-produced inexpensive automobile might have been delayed.

As it was, Henry Ford did persist. His goal was to provide an inexpensive car that would reach a large market. Standardized production, with specialization of manufacturing processes and of labor effort, was the way he envisaged lowering manufacturing costs enough so that the necessary combination of quality, reliability, and technological progressiveness would be feasible at the price at which he was aiming. The product of these efforts was the Model T. Brought out in the fall of 1908, the Model T remained largely unchanged for 19 years. Table 2 records the progress made by the Model T during these years, in both quantity and price. It vaulted the Ford Motor Company from a position as simply one of the principal companies in a still small industry to the largest company in a major American industry. By 1921, Ford's Model T alone had more than 50 per cent of the market.

The standardizing of the product—motor and chassis were largely unchanged for those 18 years—allowed Henry Ford and his engineers to focus their attention on improved manufacturing processes, with emphasis on dividing jobs into individual operations that each would be done by only one worker; the item to be assembled moved from worker to worker, by means of a continuously moving assembly line, and each worker did his particular operation as the piece moved by. The concepts of mass production, standardization, division of labor, and the moving assembly line were known and practiced at the time in other industries. But Ford and his associates combined them in a way that left an indelible mark on the automobile industry and on manufacturing in general.

In the first decade of the twentieth century, a number of other patterns in the industry were established that have persisted to the present. The companies chose to sell their cars through systems of retail dealers. The dealers provided the capital for their own facilities and had to pay cash for their cars; they sometimes even had to put up deposits in advance of the receipt of their cars. They received from Ford, for example, a 25 per cent discount off of the list price as their margin. As of 1906, the industry had enlisted at least 1545 dealers, of which Ford had about 450; 7 years later, Ford alone had almost 7000 dealers.[14]

In 1909, Ford realized that it was too expensive to ship large numbers of fully assembled automobiles in boxcars over long distances. A branch assembly plant was built in Kansas City, Missouri, and other branch assembly plants followed. This allowed many more autos, in the form of stacked parts, to be shipped per boxcar and, thus, greatly reduced freight charges per auto.[15]

The demand for automobiles, of course, was not restricted to the United States. The American companies initially exported their vehicles to sell in competition with foreign manufacturers, but some also established subsidiary com-

---

[14] Nevins, op. cit., pp. 264–265 and 403.

[15] Only in the 1960s, with the development of the bilevel and trilevel rack railroad cars, which allowed the economical rail shipment of assembled cars, was the economic advantage of branch assembly plants substantially reduced.

TABLE 2
Prices and Sales of the Model T Ford

YEAR	PRICE OF MODEL T TOURING CAR($)	TOTAL FORD CAR SALES	TOTAL INDUSTRY CAR SALES	FORD SALES (PER CENT OF TOTAL)
1909	950	12,000	124,000	9.7
1911	690	40,000	199,000	20.1
1913	550	182,000	462,000	39.4
1915	440	342,000	896,000	38.2
1917	450	741,000	1,746,000	42.4
1919	525	664,000	1,658,000	40.0
1921	355	845,000	1,518,000	55.7
1923	295	1,669,000	3,625,000	46.0
1925	290	1,495,000	3,735,000	40.0

Source: FTC, *Report on the Motor Vehicle Industry* (Washington, D.C.: U.S. Government Printing Office, 1939), pp. 29 and 632; the industry total for 1909 comes from *Automotive News*, 1974 Almanac Issue, Apr. 24, 1974, p. 2.

panies to assemble vehicles. Canadian subsidiaries were established early, and Ford established an assembly plant in England in 1911.

The final important event of that first decade was the formation of General Motors. William Crapo Durant, a shrewd and colorful financier, envisaged a group of companies combined under one corporate roof that would be strong enough to weather the pitfalls and uncertainties of the automobile market. In 1904, he entered and revived the Buick Motor Company. In 1908, General Motors was formed, and, by the end of 1909, he controlled about 25 auto and parts companies, including Cadillac, Oakland, and Oldsmobile. He had tried to buy the Ford Motor Company twice, once in 1908 and again in 1909, but each time the demanded price required more cash than he could raise. By 1910, Durant's General Motors had 20 per cent of the United States automobile market. But Durant had swallowed a bit more than he could digest. Some of the car lines that he had bought—the Ewing, the Elmore, the Marquette, the Carter-car, the Welch, and the Ranier—were not successful, and the company found itself in a cash squeeze. A group of New York and Boston bankers bailed out the company with a large loan but insisted that Durant end his active role in the company. More conservative leadership controlled General Motors for the next 5 years, with Charles W. Nash (later to head the Nash Motors Company) as president and Walter P. Chrysler as head of Buick.

Durant, however, was down but not completely out. He allied himself with Louis Chevrolet, a manufacturer of a car that could compete with the Ford. In 1911, he formed the Chevrolet Motor Company and then gradually traded Chevrolet stock for General Motors stock. By 1916, he controlled enough

General Motors stock to regain control of the corporation and install himself as president. Chevrolet Motor Company was then absorbed as part of General Motors. Durant began again to acquire other companies, this time mostly parts companies. Some of the acquisitions also brought valuable personnel. The purchase of the Hyatt Roller Bearing Company brought with it Alfred P. Sloan, Jr.; the Dayton Engineering Laboratories Company (Delco) acquisition brought Charles F. Kettering. A 60 per cent interest in the Fisher Body Corporation was purchased in 1919. A year earlier, in June 1918, Durant purchased the Guardian Frigerator Company, as a way of providing his car dealers with something to sell in case the continuation of World War I meant an end to car production. This later became the Frigidaire division of General Motors. Also, the du Pont Company acquired over a quarter of the stock of General Motors during this period.

But Durant had again overextended himself. The postwar depression (1919–1920) brought another financial crisis to General Motors, and this time, when the banks (and du Pont) rescued the company, Durant was out for good.

The decade that ended in 1920 saw continued improvement in auto technology. The electrical starter motor, the V-8 engine, the closed passenger compartment, and improvements on tires, lights, and electrical systems were introduced on more expensive cars and then gradually filtered down to the less expensive models. A major effort was also launched to improve the roads of the nation; in 1916, the Federal Aid Road Act provided the first Federal subsidies to the states for road building. The automotive industry gained respectability with the listing of automotive company stocks on the New York Stock Exchange in 1911. And, in 1914, John and Horace Dodge decided to end their role solely as a supplier of engines and parts for other manufacturers and to bring out their own automobile.

The 1920s opened with the continued success of Henry Ford's Model T and his vision of mass production that lay behind it. But equally important were the changes within General Motors after Durant's departure. A new management system was developed, largely by Alfred P. Sloan, Jr., that stressed a divisional structure for the companies. The managers of the operating divisions—for example, Chevrolet, Oakland (later to become Pontiac), Buick, Oldsmobile, Cadillac, A. C. Sparkplug, Delco, and so on—were to have a maximum of independence and autonomy. The central management of the corporation would serve as over-all coordinators and as financial managers, but primary initiative would remain in the divisions. The concept was new, but it worked extremely well and has since formed the bases for many other corporate management structures.

The second important decision within General Motors was on its strategy for selling in the auto market, which, in turn, had two parts. First, contrary to Ford's emphasis on a single model, General Motors decided on a broad range of products that would blanket the market. "A car for every purse and purpose" was its motto. This made good sense for the corporation because it had a number of separate car lines, with separate dealer organizations and separate identities in the minds of consumers. It also made good sense in the market. There clearly were demands for more than one type of vehicle. There were many demands for Ford's utilitarian Model T, but there were also demands for more luxurious vehicles. By blanketing the market, General Motors could catch more of these customers. And, because replacement demand was becoming an increasingly important part of the automobile market (that is, there were now many buyers who were replacing their previous cars rather than buying for the first time), a broad range of cars might encourage the replacement customer to "trade up" within the corporate family of cars.

A second marketing strategy was aimed directly at this replacement demand. Again, contrary to Ford's Model T, General Motors decided to modify its cars each year, with a combination of engineering advances, convenience improvements, and interior and exterior styling changes. This annual model change, even though it might sacrifice some cost savings, would induce owners to replace their cars sooner and, thus, increase sales by enough to compensate for the higher costs.

On the basis of these strategies, General Motors rose from a poor second place in the industry, with sales equal to only a third of Ford's for the 1920–1922 period, to first place temporarily in 1927 and 1928 and then permanently in 1931.

A General Motors "graduate," Walter P. Chrysler, also recognized the advantages of these marketing strategies. Leaving General Motors in 1920, he quickly revived the ailing Willys-Overland Company and then turned his attention to the Maxwell-Chalmers Corporation, which was also in trouble. He soon turned that company around and became president in 1923. The following year the company introduced the Chrysler 6, featuring a "high-compression" engine (4.5-to-1), four-wheel brakes, a seven-bearing crankshaft, and a replaceable cartridge oil filter. The car sold well, and the next year Walter Chrysler took full control of the company and changed the name to his own. In 1928, he purchased the Dodge brothers' estate from the group of bankers that had been running the company; he introduced the Plymouth and DeSoto makes in the same year. Chrysler was now in third place, behind General Motors and Ford.

Ford persisted with the Model T until 1927. By then it was apparent even to Henry Ford, an increasingly cantankerous man in his mid-sixties, that the market for the car had declined severely. A new model, the Model A, was produced at the end of 1927 and proved successful enough to vault Ford back into first place in 1929 and 1930. But the car embodied the same philosophy: a basic single model that would remain largely unchanged for a number of years. Earlier, however, Ford did expand its product line, by buying the Lincoln Motor Company at a receiver's sale in early 1922. The purchase was almost more a favor to the head of Lincoln, Henry M. Leland, a popular "elder statesman" in the industry (and the man who, 20 years earlier, had brought out another high-quality car, the Cadillac), than it was a conscious effort to diversify.

The 1920s saw major expansionary moves abroad by the two leading firms. Ford expanded its operations in England and established assembly plants in other European countries, with the German and French plants eventually dominating the others on the Continent. All turned out the Model T. General Motors initially also assembled American cars abroad, but then decided that local conditions (especially the European horsepower taxes) favored locally designed and produced vehicles; the purchase of going concerns was General Motors' strategy of entry. The company first became interested in Citroen of France, but serious negotiations never developed. It next tried to buy the Austin Company, in England, in 1925, but the deal fell through. Instead, it bought a smaller firm, Vauxhall Motors Limited, in the same year. Four years later it bought the German firm of Adam Opel A.G.[16]

A second trend in the 1920s was the increased vertical integration of the large companies. Ten years earlier they had ceased being pure assemblers and had begun manufacturing their own major components, such as motors, transmissions, and bodies. Now they extended further back into the manufacturing process. General Motors, largely on the basis of its acquisitions, stressed electrical components, carburetors, radiators, and the like. Ford manufactured somewhat fewer components but extended further into raw materials. It built a steel mill and a glass plant; acquired ore fields, coal mines, timber lands, a railroad, and a shipping fleet; and even developed rubber plantations in Brazil. (Both companies also entered the then infant aircraft manufacturing industry, as a way of hedging their bets on a new industry that conceivably could replace autos. The Ford trimotor airplane was by the late 1920s a leading model in the industry. Both companies later extricated themselves from the aviation industry, except for wartime building.)

By the end of the 1920s, then, the automobile industry had taken on a shape that has persisted to the present. Three large firms dominated the automobile market, accounting for 72 per cent of total sales of 4.6 million units in 1929. The smaller firms still appeared to be successful, but they no longer posed a serious threat to the position of the Big Three. Walter Chrysler's success at mid-decade marked the last time that a significant rearrangement of the leading companies would occur. Entry into the industry, still relatively easy at the beginning of the decade, had become much more difficult by its end. Walter Chrysler calculated that building the necessary facilities to bring out a new car (as an alternative to buying Dodge) would have cost $75 million.[17] As it was, he paid $70 million in Chrysler stock for the Dodge facilities. These were large sums to risk for an industry in which the rate of failure was high. The industry had had 84 active firms at the beginning of the decade; by 1929 it had less than half that number.

The depressed 1930s continued the structural trends of the previous decade. New-car sales fell from their 1929 peak to a 1932 level that was only a quarter as large. Although sales subsequently improved, they failed during that decade to regain the 1929 level. The smaller companies were hurt the worst, and many

[16] Chrysler's expansion overseas occurred much later. In 1958, it bought into Simca of France; in 1964, it acquired shares of Rootes Motors of England. It now fully controls both.
[17] Allan Nevins and Frank E. Hill, *Ford: Expansion and Challenge, 1915–1932* (New York: Scribner's, 1957), p. 473.

folded. By 1941, there were only eight firms left in the industry: The Big Three, Studebaker, Hudson, Nash, Packard, and Willys.[18] The smaller companies tried to diversify and expand their product lines during the decade: Studebaker introduced the Rockne; Hudson tried the Terraplane; Nash introduced the Lafayette; and Packard tried the Clipper. But the 1930s were not a propitious time for introducing new makes, and none of the new names survived. The smaller companies came to be known as Independents, which was an implicit recognition of the dominance of the Big Three.[19] At the end of the decade, as Henry Ford's son Edsel gained greater control of the company, the Ford Motor Company embraced the marketing strategies that its two large rivals had already grasped. The Mercury was introduced in 1938, and annual model changes became standard. Chrysler, however, had passed Ford and achieved second place in 1937.

Technological improvements continued. Cars became larger, heavier, and more powerful. Six- and eight-cylinder engines were standard. Ford brought out a new model car, the V-8, to replace the Model A, in 1932. Bodies were all enclosed (except for convertibles) and entirely of steel. "Aerodynamic," streamlined designs replaced the square, boxy designs of the 1920s. And attention turned to automatic transmissions, which would eliminate gear shifting. In 1938, Chrysler introduced a semiautomatic transmission, Fluid Drive, and in the following year General Motors introduced a fully automatic transmission, Hydra-Matic.

World War II meant the cessation of all automobile production and the conversion to munitions production. At the end of the war, as the industry retooled for automobile production, the prospects for entry by new producers appeared to be bright again, for the first time in 20 years. The stock of automobiles on the road was smaller and $3\frac{1}{2}$ years older than it otherwise would have been. Consumer demand was predicted to be high. At the same time, the Federal government was selling or leasing wartime factories and machinery at bargain prices. And, potential dealers were willing to pay advance deposits for the privilege of receiving a franchise. At least 32 firms were contemplating entry in the late 1940s.[20] But only two firms actually entered production: Kaiser-Frazer and Crosley Motors. Kaiser-Frazer produced standard sized cars. In 1948, it succeeded in selling 166,000 units for 5 per cent of the market and was the leading independent producer that year. But the firm had failed to raise enough capital, and it had an insufficient financial cushion when sales fell sharply in 1949.[21] The company struggled through red ink for another 5 years and then

---

[18] Graham-Paige, Bantam, and Hupmobile were also technically in the industry, but their combined sales in 1941 were less than a thousand units. None of the three bothered to tool up for the short-lived 1942 model year.

[19] The term *Independents* appears to have originated from efforts to distinguish the makes of the smaller one-make companies from those of the Big Three, the latter makes being under some higher coordinating corporate control.

[20] Paul H. Banner, "Competition in the Automobile Industry" (Ph.D. diss., Harvard University, 1953), p. 38.

[21] See "Kaiser-Frazer—The Roughest Thing We Ever Tackled," *Fortune*, **44** (July 1951).

ended United States passenger car production in 1955.[22] Crosley Motors was even less successful. It chose to produce a small, light car, but could only sell 25,000 units in 1948, its best year. Production ended in 1952.

The Ford Motor Company, badly managed since the 1920s, suffered a serious loss when Edsel Ford died in 1943. By the end of World War II, the company was in an advanced state of disarray. Organization, responsibility, coordination, and control had all disintegrated. In 1945, Edsel's son, Henry Ford II, assumed the leadership of the company and hired Ernest R. Breech away from Bendix Aviation to take over the presidency of Ford. Breech brought General Motors men and methods with him and began to reorganize the company. A major effort was launched to bring out a successful postwar car. That car, the 1949 Ford, appeared on the market in June 1948. It was a success, and it propelled the company permanently back into second place in the industry, ahead of Chrysler. Had the car failed, it is quite possible that the Ford Motor Company would have gone under.

The industry struggled with materials shortages and "gray markets" in the immediate postwar years, a recession in 1949, and production and price controls during the Korean War. With the lifting of controls in 1953, however, production expanded rapidly. The Independents quickly found themselves in difficulties. With higher manufacturing costs than the Big Three, lacking the powerful V-8 engines and automatic transmissions that had become popular, and generally stuck with the image of "off-brands," the Independents saw their sales decline while those of the Big Three expanded.[23] By the end of 1953, among the Independents only Studebaker was still profitable. Mergers seemed to offer the only hope. Willys and Kaiser-Frazer merged in 1953. A year later, Nash and Hudson merged to form American Motors, quickly followed by a merger between Studebaker and Packard. In good times, these mergers would have offered the diversification and stability that the multiple makes of the Big Three offered. But the Independents were in such poor sales and financial shape that they could not benefit. Kaiser-Willys folded in 1955. Studebaker-Packard struggled on until 1966, when it finally ceased automobile production. American Motors quickly dropped the Hudson line and, thus, again became a one-make company, concentrating its efforts on its small car, the Rambler, which finally attracted consumer support.

The year 1955 was a boom year for the Big Three. Retail sales were 7.2 million units, of which the Big Three captured more than 95 per cent. Big cars sold well that year, especially General Motors' middle-level cars: Buick, Oldsmobile, and Pontiac. Ford, feeling weak in this area, planned a new car that would provide it with a greater degree of diversification in the auto market. The car, the Edsel, appeared in the fall of 1957. But, by then, consumer tastes had changed. Small cars were in greater demand, and the Edsel flopped.

In the 1960s and 1970s, small cars appeared (prompted by imports), sporty

[22] The company merged with Willys in 1953 and continued to produce the Jeep until 1969, when it sold its Jeep operations to American Motors.
[23] See White, op. cit., pp. 14–15, 271–272.

cars grabbed a large part of the market, and safety and air pollution became important issues. These areas will receive more attention in the following discussion.

II. MARKET STRUCTURE

With this overview of the industry's history completed, we can turn our attention to the structural characteristics of the industry. An understanding of these structural elements should provide us with some insights into the behavior and performance that are likely to follow. We will focus on three key structural elements: (1) the nature of the product, (2) the size distribution of firms, and (3) the barriers to entry (including economies of scale).

The Nature of the Product

Product and buyer characteristics are clearly an important determinant of industry behavior. We would expect the selling behavior for paper napkins to households to be different from that of sheet steel to industrial users, and both to be different from the sale of luxury yachts to millionaires. Product characteristics matter.

The automobile is a large, expensive, technically complex, durable good. It provides transportation services. It also provides, for many, prestige and status. It is the most expensive item that many families buy and the second most expensive, after a house, for most others. The demand for new automobiles does appear to be moderately sensitive to prices and fairly sensitive to incomes. Estimates of the price elasticity of demand range in the -0.5 to -1.5 range; income elasticities are in the 1.0 to 4.0 range.[24] The demand for new automobiles comes from three kinds of buyers: the first-time buyer, the buyer who is adding a second or third car to his family's stock of vehicles, and the buyer who is replacing his present car. The last kind of buyer is the dominant element in the market place, and, as we shall see, this importance of the replacement demand for cars has been an influential determinant of the auto industry's behavior.

The automobile is a technically complex product, and most consumers do not have the time or the inclination to become experts on its technical aspects. Considerations of styling, comfort, previous experience, reputation, and price are the important considerations in comparative choices among cars. Most car owners do not repair their own cars and expect repair services and repair parts to be available from dealers, gasoline stations, and repair shops; because cars can be taken on long trips, they expect these parts and services to be available nationwide.

Fleet buyers (for example, rental agencies, leasing companies, business firms providing cars to their salesmen and other personnel, and local, state, and

---

[24] For a summary of recent econometric estimates of these elasticities, see ibid., pp. 94–95. For an argument that these price elasticities are probably biased downward, see pp. 120–121.

Federal governments) are an important group of buyers (accounting for 10 per cent of sales) for whom technical and price considerations are more important than for most. They have the time and the resources to gain expertise and to shop around and the buying clout to be able to bargain with the auto companies. As we shall see, the companies' behavior toward this group has been different from their behavior toward the rest of the market.

Over all, the demand for automobiles is highly variable. Demand is cyclical, as befits an income-sensitive commodity. Year-to-year swings of 15 per cent in over-all demand are not uncommon. Individual producers face these swings, plus the vagaries of consumer tastes with respect to particular styles and models. Brand loyalty helps existing producers (and makes it difficult for new ones), but it is not sufficient to damp out the major fluctuations that the producers must face. If these demand fluctuations could be predicted accurately in advance, or if styles and models could be altered instantly (and production processes and schedules similarly changed), the fluctuations would be of little concern. As it is, they are not predictable, the manufacturing processes require long lead times, and, hence, automobile manufacturing is potentially a risky business. We will return to this question of risk throughout the remainder of this chapter.

TABLE 3
New Car Market Shares, 1913–1973 (in per cent)

YEAR	GENERAL MOTORS	FORD	CHRYSLER	OTHER DOMESTIC MANUFAC- TURERS	IMPORTS
1913	12.2	39.5	n.a.	48.3	n.a.
1923	20.2	46.0	1.9	31.9	n.a.
1929	32.3	31.3	8.2	28.2	n.a.
1933	41.4	20.7	25.4	12.5	n.a.
1937	41.8	21.4	25.4	11.4	n.a.
1946–1950	41.8	21.4	21.6	15.1	0.2
1951–1955	46.2	25.7	18.6	8.9	0.6
1956–1960	45.5	28.0	14.6	5.7	6.2
1961–1965	49.7	26.2	12.2	6.0	6.1
1966–1970	46.2	24.5	15.8	2.8	10.6
1971–1973	44.9	23.9	13.8	3.0	14.3
Average, 1946–1973	45.8	25.0	16.3	6.9	5.8

[a] Not available.
Source: FTC, Report on the Motor Vehicle Industry (Washington, D.C.: U.S. Government Printing Office, 1939), pp. 29 and 549; Automotive News, Almanac Issue, various years; Automotive Industries, Annual Statistical Issue, various years.

Size Distribution

The size distribution of firms in the industry tells us something about the likelihood of oligopolistic interdependence and implicit or explicit coordination of behavior. The fewer the firms, the more concentrated is the market structure, and the greater is the likelihood of coordinated behavior.

As was noted in the introduction, the U.S. automobile industry has a tight market structure. Tables 3 and 4 provide a summary of current and past market structure. There are currently only four domestic manufacturers, and they account for 85 to 90 per cent of new car sales; imports make up the rest.[25] General Motors is the leading firm and has been since 1931; its market share has been in the 40 to 50 per cent range. Ford is the second largest company and has been in that position since 1949; its market share has hovered at around 25 per

TABLE 4
New Car Sales, 1973

	REGISTRATIONS	PER CENT
General Motors		
Buick	696,000	6.1
Cadillac	286,000	2.5
Chevrolet	2,455,000	21.6
Oldsmobile	809,000	7.1
Pontiac	808,000	7.1
Total	5,054,000	44.5
Ford Motor Company		
Ford	2,137,000	18.8
Lincoln	116,000	1.0
Mercury	414,000	3.6
Total	2,667,000	23.5
Chrysler Corporation		
Chrysler-Imperial	176,000	1.6
Dodge	588,000	5.2
Plymouth	749,000	6.6
Total	1,513,000	13.3
American Motors	392,000	3.5
Miscellaneous	12,000	0.1
Imports	1,720,000	15.2
Grand total	11,351,000	

Source: *Automotive News*, 1974 Almanac Issue, Apr. 24, 1974, p. 4. R. L. Polk & Co. Further reproduction prohibited.

[25] Checker Motors, a small manufacturer of primarily taxicabs, sold only 5691 cars in 1973.

cent. Chrysler is in third place, with market shares of 10 to 20 per cent. American Motors is in fourth, with a market share of 2 to 4 per cent. Imports have made up the balance of sales, ranging from virtually zero in the prewar and immediate postwar period to 14 per cent in the 1970s.

This tight market structure would lead us to predict a high degree of oligopolistic interdependence. It is not a monopoly; there are, after all, three large producers and one small producer, rather than just a single seller. And, imports have provided effective competition for some segments of the market. Still, the domestic producers are a very small number of firms, and it would be impossible for them not to recognize the existence and likely reactions of their rivals.

Barriers to Entry

The conditions of entry into an industry are a second important structural feature. Easy entry can place severe limits on the behavior of monopolists or oligopolists; if entry is difficult, that behavior will be much less hindered.

Joe S. Bain has argued that there are three major kinds of entry barriers: (1) economies of scale; (2) absolute capital requirements; and (3) special resources, licenses, and legal restrictions.[26] We will deal with each in turn.

Economies of Scale

For every product, at a given state of technology and a given set of factor prices, there is likely to be some range of output over which long-run total costs do not rise proportionately with volume—that is, long-run average costs (unit costs) fall with greater volume.[27] The crucial questions are (1) whether this process ceases at some point (that is, is there a point at which the economies of scale are effectively exhausted?), and if so, (2) what is this point of minimum efficient size (MES) and how large is it in relation to the over-all size of the market? If the MES is large relative to the relevant market, there will be room for only a few efficient producers; they have more room to raise prices without fearing that they have left too great a potential market for a potential entrant; and the entrant cannot slip in "un-noticed," but will likely face the full brunt of retaliatory efforts by current producers.

To measure economies of scale and MES is an extremely difficult and imprecise art. Estimates are usually based on a combination of engineering data, econometric (statistical) estimations, observations on new construction and old failures, and conversations with managers who are close to the scene.

To try to estimate the MES for automobile manufacturing, we have to decide what production processes we consider to be the essential parts of automobile manufacturing. Since the 1920s, the successful manufacturers have almost uniformly included the following processes: design, engineering, and testing; stamping of major sheet metal body parts; casting of items like engines and trans-

---

[26] Joe S. Bain, *Barriers to New Competition* (Cambridge, Mass.: Harvard University Press, 1956).
[27] This should be expressed as volume per time period—for example, cars per year.

missions; machining of the cast items; and final assembly of all the components into a finished car.[28] Although the manufacturers do many things—for example, some manufacture their own radios or vinyl upholstery or window glass—these production processes also are contracted out frequently and do not appear to be essential to the car manufacturing processes per se.

Before the 1920s, the car manufacturers were largely designers and assemblers, buying almost all of their components. At that time, with cheap labor and relatively little mechanization, the MES was probably quite low; 20,000 units a year is probably a good guess. There were coordination advantages, however, to integrating the stamping, casting, and machining processes with the design and assembly and, by the 1930s, with the general use of the all-steel body, the MES had increased substantially. Paul Hoffman, president of Studebaker, testified that this point was about 100,000 units.[29]

In the postwar period, with higher wage rates and greater mechanization, the MES appears to have risen substantially. Joe S. Bain's research in the early 1950s indicated that the MES was 600,000 units; George Romney, president of American Motors, testified in 1958 that the MES was 400,000 units.[30]

These estimates still appear to be valid for the 1970s because the technology has not changed appreciably. The minimum efficient size for one make is probably around 500,000 units, with a possible small extra-cost savings (less than 1 per cent of unit cost) beyond that point.[31] But a one-make company would have a difficult time surviving in the automobile industry (and the historical record bears this out). Demand is highly variable and unpredictable. A single-make company could easily guess wrong on styling or engineering and find itself with an unpopular model. It takes, at best, two years to design and make preparations for manufacturing a new model. In the interim, the company would be losing money and experiencing low management morale. If the company were to guess wrong a second consecutive time, it could easily go into a tailspin from which it could not recover. By contrast, a company with two makes, even if it guessed wrong with one, would have the other to continue to provide it with money and

---

[28] For a further description of these processes, see White, op. cit., Chap. 3.

[29] U.S. Congress, Temporary National Economic Committee, 76th Cong., 2d sess., 1940, pt. 21, pp. 11,215–11,218.

[30] Bain, op. cit., p. 245; U.S. Congress, Senate, Committee on the Judiciary, Subcommittee on Antitrust and Monopoly, *Hearings on Administered Prices, Automobiles*, 85th Cong., 2d sess., 1958, pt. 6, p. 2851. (Hereafter cited as *Administered Prices, Automobiles*.)

[31] Efficient scale in assembly is 200,000 to 250,000 units. It is somewhat higher in casting and machining. The largest economies are in sheet-metal stamping. Heavy presses can turn out two million stampings or more a year, and, as John S. McGee has pointed out, the best metal-shaping dies can last considerably longer than that. (This writer previously estimated die life incorrectly at 400,000 units. See White, op. cit., p. 21.) But, as McGee's figures show, the cost advantages for rates beyond 500,000 a year are relatively minor, amounting to less than 1 per cent of the unit costs of a $3500 car. See John S. McGee, "Economies of Size in Auto Body Manufacture," *Journal of Law and Economics*, **16** (Oct. 1973). McGee has argued that the economies of scale in automobile manufacturing extend beyond even the current scale of production. See also *Hearings on the Industrial Reorganization Act*, U.S. Congress, Senate, Committee on the Judiciary, Subcommittee on Antitrust and Monopoly, 93rd Cong., 2d sess., 1974, pt. 4, pp. 2652–2658. Statement of John S. McGee. (Hereafter cited as *The Industrial Reorganization Act*.)

management morale. It could hedge its bets and would be much less likely to go under.[32]

The MES, then, for the automobile industry, would appear to be around one million units annually. This would be a firm with two makes of around 500,000 units each—that is, two kinds of cars that enjoy separate identifications in the eyes of consumers. It would be virtually exhausting the manufacturing economies for each make.[33] It would have enough volume to support adequately a nationwide system of dealers and to achieve the advantages of large-scale advertising. With sales revenues of more than $3 billion a year, it would have the resources to support a more-than-adequate design, testing, and research-and-development capability. At that size, it would rank among the 40 largest manufacturing companies in the United States.

An MES of one million units represents about 10 per cent of the new car market. This is a significant fraction of the market. It is unlikely that a new firm of this size could enter unnoticed by the existing manufacturers. Entry at a smaller scale might be perceived as a lesser threat by the existing companies, but the entrant would then face increasing unit-cost penalties and/or greater risks.

This comparatively large MES, then, represents a significant barrier to entry.

Absolute Capital Costs

The financial capital required for a MES firm can also constitute a barrier to entry. If the amount required is large in absolute amount and the endeavour carries appreciable risks of failure, banks and other financial institutions are unlikely to be interested or may require very high interest rates. Potential entrants may find it difficult to obtain the necessary capital.

How much would it cost to establish a MES firm of one million units? In the late 1960s, the land, buildings, machinery, design and engineering investment, and the working capital for a firm of 800,000 units would have required a total of $1 billion.[34] For a firm of one-million units, at the inflated prices of the mid-1970s, the required sum would likely be close to $2 billion.

Even at 1970s prices, $2 billion is a large sum of money, much larger than the capital markets would normally be willing to advance to a new enterprise. This, then, also constitutes a significant barrier to entry.

---

[32] Even though the logic of this proposition would argue that three or more makes in a company's stable would be better still, the postwar experience has indicated that two makes would be sufficient. See White, op. cit., pp. 47–48.

[33] With 1 million units spread over two makes, the company could achieve some further small economies by using some common parts or using the same basic dies, but modifying them with special inserts. It is interesting to note that the views of General Motors officials on the gains to be had from large-scale production have changed over the years. In 1955, they were emphatic in asserting that scale of operations had nothing to do with General Motors' profitability; in 1973, they were equally emphatic in asserting the opposite. See U.S. Congress, Senate, Committee on the Judiciary, Subcommittee on Antitrust and Monopoly, *A Study of the Antitrust Laws, Hearings*, 84th Cong., 1st sess., 1955, pt. 7, pp. 3544–3545, and pt. 8, p. 4044; and *The Industrial Reorganization Act*, op. cit., pp. 2463 and 2467.

[34] See White, op. cit., pp. 56–61.

Special Resources

If there were restrictive government licenses, crucial patents, or specialized resources controlled exclusively by existing firms, a new firm would find entry difficult. These could constitute barriers to entry.

A potential entrant into the automobile industry would not find these kinds of barriers. There are no serious government restrictions on entry, controlling patents on automotive technology are absent, and there are no crucial natural resources or location sites that would not be available to a new entrant.

There is, however, another kind of barrier that a new entrant would face. The automobile is not a standardized item (as compared to, say, wheat); existing manufacturers take great efforts to differentiate their products from those of their rivals, mostly through design differences. They also advertise their products heavily. They have, thus, succeeded in building up strong brand loyalties. Repeat buying from the same company is an important part of the car market. Furthermore, the existing makes have reputations for reliability, and a new make would be an unknown commodity. Because most consumers are technically unsophisticated concerning the product and a car purchase represents a large monetary outlay, most buyers would be reluctant to take a chance on an unknown newcomer (although there is a small minority that appears eager to experiment). This kind of brand loyalty and hesitancy toward new brands would constitute a significant barrier that a new entrant would confront. Massive advertising and/or lower prices for otherwise comparable products would be the strategies that a new entrant would likely adopt. Both would be costly.

Finally, a new entrant would have to establish a distribution system. An entrant would likely use a dealer system comparable to that used by present manufacturers (and importers). Finding the dealers and assisting them in getting established would require money and effort on the part of the new manufacturer, even though the dealers would bear the major financial burden. This would constitute an additional impediment to entry, although not an extremely difficult one, as some foreign manufacturers have discovered.

A Review of Structure

We can now offer a review of the salient structural features of the automobile industry. First, the industry is highly concentrated. Second, the barriers to entry are quite high, particularly the capital requirements barrier. Third, even though the economies of scale in the industry are substantial, with a MES at 10 per cent of the market, these economies do not fully explain the current size distribution of firms. General Motors is four to five times larger than a MES firm; Ford is two to three times larger; Chrysler is one and one-half times larger; and American Motors is less than half the MES size. We need a better explanation.

This explanation can be found by combining the structural features we have discussed with the history of the previous section. In a market for a "big-ticket" item that requires a large investment and a long lead time and that has a variable and uncertain demand, a successful manufacturer needs at least two separately identified makes or a string of very good luck. William Durant discovered the former principle for General Motors early; Walter Chrysler successfully exploited the same principle in the 1920s. Henry Ford relied on the latter principle, and he eventually lost the leadership of the industry in doing so. Only in the late 1930s did Ford diversify also. Other manufacturers either failed to recognize the importance of diversifying or chose to do so at inopportune times. Burdened with small volumes (frequently below MES) and sometimes with bad management, the Independents usually had manufacturing costs that were above those of the Big Three, and their prices for roughly comparable models were above those of the Big Three. When the inevitable string of bad luck or bad judgment came, they had no successful second makes to sustain them, and they gradually folded.

The disappearance of the Independents would not have been serious for the structure of the automobile industry if the barriers to entry had been low. But, as we have seen, they have been high. Even as early as the late 1920s, it took $75 million to enter at a scale that Walter Chrysler considered appropriate. It is striking to note that all four of the present firms have their origins in the years before 1915—that is, in the last 60 years there has not been a single successful entrant into the automobile manufacturing industry. The last successful introduction of a new make, with a separate identity and dealer organization, was Chrysler's Plymouth, in 1928. Even Ford, with an investment of $250 million in the 1950s, could not successfully "enter" the medium-price market with the Edsel. Only foreign manufacturers, with established manufacturing operations and reputations abroad, have been able to enter the American market, but only at the marketing end. In September 1973, the Swedish manufacturer Volvo announced the construction of an assembly plant in Chesapeake, Virginia, that will begin assembling Volvos in 1976; still, however, this is a car that is designed primarily for the European market.[35] There has yet to be successful new entry of an automobile designed specifically for the American market.

III. CONDUCT

Current theories of oligopoly, unfortunately, do not offer precise predictions as to behavior. Rather, they offer general statements about probabilities: Oligopolists are most likely to recognize their interdependence and achieve a result approximating that of a monopoly when producers are few, barriers to entry are high, buyers are numerous and unconcentrated, and producers are similar in their outlook and cost structures. Oligopolists recognizing their interdependence will find it easiest to coordinate their actions on prices. The ease with which price-cuts away from the joint monopoly level can be matched will be apparent to all, and, hence, each producer will realize that he is unlikely to

[35] Less than 25 per cent of Volvo's sales are in the United States.

gain by cutting his price. This is less likely to be true for nonprice aspects of the product—for example, quality, styling, advertising—because these are less easily matched by rivals. Hence, we are likely to see the potential rivalry among firms channeled into these areas, though even here some recognized interdependence may prevail.

The oligopolistic industry that is hoping to avoid competing on price will need some sort of coordinating device when cost or demand conditions change and a new price or set of prices is required. The antitrust laws forbid explicit communication to set new prices, so an implicit method is required. A system of price leadership, in which all firms implicitly agree to follow and adhere to the price changes of one particular firm, is a convenient device for coordinating these price changes. The industry, thus, avoids the unsettling conditions that might occur as each firm groped its way toward a new price that might be different from that which its rivals chose.

Furthermore, we would expect to see efforts at price discrimination. A monopoly will try to set different prices (relative to marginal costs) in different markets: relatively high prices where demand is inelastic (and substitutes are not easily available) and lower prices where demand is more elastic. A successfully coordinated oligopoly will likely try the same. By contrast, a competitive industry would have prices equal to long-run marginal costs (inclusive of normal profits) in all markets, and this kind of discrimination could not take place.

Thus, we do have a number of predictions concerning oligopolies. And, as we will see, they are largely borne out by the automobile industry. We first will examine pricing behavior and then turn our attention to nonprice aspects of behavior.

Pricing Behavior

Price Leadership

Each fall, the automobile companies have to decide on the prices for a wide range of cars, models, and options. When the dust has settled, the prices for roughly comparable models (for example, top-of-the-line full-sized Chevrolets, Fords, and Plymouths) will be in close proximity to each other. This is exactly what we would expect in any market, regardless of its structure. Similar products will inevitably sell for similar prices (or else the high-priced product will be driven from the market), and this by itself is no evidence of oligopolistic collusion or coordination.

The method by which these prices are determined and changed, however, does provide more interesting evidence of oligopolistic behavior. Price leadership has been a prevalent behavioral phenomenon in the automobile industry for the last 50 years. During the 1920s and 1930s, Ford was the price leader, largely because of the dominance of the Ford automobile and the decision by Henry Ford to be the low-price producer in the market. The manufacturers of similar cars had to keep their prices not too far above Ford's or see their sales decline. This situation was summed up by a vice president of General Motors in 1932:

Mr. Ford, who won't play, is pretty much the price setter in this industry. I'll bet if Mr. Ford's cars were $50 higher ours would be $50 higher. We care about Ford. We have been struggling with him for years.[36]

Since World War II, General Motors has been the price leader in the auto market. Testimony before congressional committees indicates clearly that General Motors has set its prices on the basis of its own rate-of-return goals, with due consideration for what its rivals might do; Ford and Chrysler, by contrast, largely see themselves as price followers.[37] In practice, too, it is General Motors' prices to which the others will adjust their prices. Even if Ford or Chrysler announce their prices first, they will then adjust their prices to correspond to those that General Motors subsequently announces for roughly comparable models—either up or down. In a now famous incident, Ford, in the fall of 1956, announced its prices first. General Motors followed two weeks later with prices for Chevrolets that were 3 per cent higher. Ford promptly raised its prices to Chevrolet's level; a firm less inclined to be a price follower might have waited for Chevrolet to drop its prices. In the late 1960s, Ford and Chrysler tended to announce first with higher prices and then subsequently drop their prices closer to General Motors' levels.

New list prices are determined each September or October for the new model cars. In the 1950s and 1960s, these list prices tended to remain unchanged throughout the model year; during the inflationary first half of the 1970s, list prices tended to rise during the model years, as sharp increases in raw materials costs were passed on by the automobile manufacturers. But actual retail transactions prices have tended to be below the list prices, with the list prices providing a benchmark, a general guide from which actual prices vary as the state of demand fluctuates during the year. When the new models first come out, there are some new car buyers who are eager to own the new model while it is still relatively uncommon. Their demand is relatively inelastic—both the manufacturers and dealers recognize this—and these buyers are likely to pay a price that is close to list price. As the model year wears on, buyers with more elastic demands come into the market. Dealers are apt to accept smaller margins, and the manufacturers will cut their wholesale prices to the dealers, through special rebates and sales-incentive schemes.[38] The rebates are typically in the $30 to $100 range, although they can go as high as $500 for slow-moving models. That they do get passed on to the consumers can be seen in the actual pattern of retail prices, as reflected in the consumer price index for new cars. Table 5 shows the pattern for the 1966, 1967, and 1968 model years. In each year, there is a drop of roughly 3 per cent between the high in November and the low in the following September.

Why do the companies continue to maintain the fiction of an unchanged list

---

[36] FTC, op. cit., p. 33.

[37] For a summary, see White, op. cit., pp. 112–114.

[38] If car sales fall appreciably below levels that had been expected, rebates will be larger and sooner than usual. In early 1975, a new element was added, when the rebates were offered directly to consumers.

TABLE 5

Consumer Price Index for New Cars (1957–1959 = 100)

1966 MODEL YEAR		1967 MODEL YEAR		1968 MODEL YEAR	
1965 Oct.	97.7	1966 Oct.	98.4	1967 Oct.	101.1
Nov.	98.7	Nov.	99.3	Nov.	101.4
Dec.	98.7	Dec.	98.6	Dec.	101.3
1966 Jan.	97.4	1967 Jan.	97.6	1968 Jan.	100.1
Feb.	97.2	Feb.	97.3	Feb.	100.8
Mar.	97.1	Mar.	97.2	Mar.	100.6
Apr.	97.4	Apr.	97.0	Apr.	100.3
May	97.0	May	96.9	May	100.3
June	96.8	June	96.8	June	100.1
July	96.7	July	97.0	July	99.8
Aug.	95.8	Aug.	96.9	Aug.	99.1
Sept.	94.4	Sept.	96.1	Sept.	98.4

Source: U.S. Department of Labor, Bureau of Labor Statistics, *The Consumer Price Index: U.S. City Average and Selected Areas* (Washington, D.C.: U.S. Government Printing Office, 1965–1968), monthly.

price through the model year, even though actual prices are falling progressively below it? It does provide a convenient benchmark against which oligopolists can measure the extent of price cutting that is occurring, and, thus, it may help prevent price cutting from getting out of hand. It provides a convenient point of reference for determining the next year's set of prices. The rebate system allows greater flexibility in providing or withdrawing price cuts without calling the attention of the press and of Washington to these actions. At new model announcement time, the increase in list prices from the old list prices will be much less than from the actual transaction prices in effect at the end of the previous model year; this has obvious public relations advantages. And, changes in the list price inevitably would mean that the same cars in a dealer's inventory would carry different list prices on their stickers, which could be confusing and frustrating to customers. In all, a relatively fixed list price with wholesale rebates to the dealer when necessary makes life considerably easier for the companies, and if the inflationary surge of the early 1970s subsides, we are likely to see this pattern re-emerge.

Pricing in the Fleet Market

As we noted in the Section II, the fleet market does constitute an important separate market for automobiles. The important distinguishing characteristics of this market are the fewness and size of the buyers. They provide a strong temptation for the manufacturer that might be willing to shade prices a bit to gain a large chunk of sales, and the fleet buyers have the time and expertise to shop around and to try to induce this kind of price cutting. We would predict that the automobile companies would have a more difficult time maintaining price discipline and price leadership in this market.

This prediction has, in fact, been borne out. The industry has wobbled back and forth between periods in which fleet buyers were offered no special incentives (and had to negotiate the best deal they could with dealers) and other periods when they were offered substantial price-cuts so that they were getting their cars effectively at prices below the dealers' wholesale cost. In 1948, General Motors announced an end to a 3 per cent rebate plan on fleet sales, and the others followed. By the mid-1950s, however, price cutting on sales to fleet buyers had become fierce, with rebates of $500 or more being offered. Then, in 1958, General Motors announced an end to rebates, and again the others followed. The early 1960s, however, saw a renewal of price cutting. Chrysler, in particular, became aggressive in 1962, forming a leasing company that would allow it to lease cars directly to large fleet customers. Ford followed, but General Motors held back. Finally, in the fall of 1965, General Motors, too, began offering special price-cutting deals to fleet buyers, and during the next few years the price-cuts escalated. Then, in the spring of 1970, General Motors and Ford, in a sequence of actions, announced an end to most of the price-cuts, and Chrysler subsequently reduced its price rebates, so that pricing in the fleet market had again tightened up.[39] It is unclear how long this new discipline will last.

Price Discrimination

The automobile companies have jointly practiced price discrimination in different markets. The fleet pricing experience described provides one example. At times, fleet buyers have been able to buy virtually identical cars for prices that are hundreds of dollars below those that individual consumers were paying.

The companies also have charged higher prices in Canadian markets than in U.S. markets for virtually identical cars. Prior to 1965, this had a cost basis, because Canadian models had shorter production runs. But since the United States-Canadian Automotive Agreement of 1965, the companies have been able to ship cars duty-free both ways across the United States-Canada border and, hence, have been able to rationalize their North American production. In effect, the United States and Canada have become a unified production area, with uniform costs to both areas. Yet, Canadian prices have remained higher than U.S. prices.[40] The causes of this difference probably lie in the higher import duty that Canada levies on imports from Europe and Japan and in a perceived smaller price elasticity of demand for cars in Canada.[41]

---

[39] The Department of Justice charged General Motors and Ford with price fixing on the basis of their actions in 1970 and brought both criminal and civil suits. Both suits were decided in favor of the companies in 1973 and 1974. See *United States* v. *General Motors Corp. and Ford Motor Co.*, 1974-2 Trade Cases, no. 75,253.

[40] See Carl E. Beige, *The Canada–U.S. Automotive Agreement: An Evaluation* (Washington, D.C.: National Planning Association, 1970), pp. 115–116; *Financial Post*, Jan. 27, 1973, p. 1.

[41] The price discrimination is possible because the companies can ship cars across the border duty-free, but individual buyers cannot.

A third area has been in the companies' pricing of subcompact and full-sized cars and in the relative changes in these prices that took place in the early 1970s. The subcompacts, Pinto and Vega, were introduced in 1970 to compete with the low-priced foreign makes and were priced accordingly. Between 1971 and 1974, the materials and labor costs of producing automobiles rose substantially, and prices rose. In the absence of any special demand or cost considerations for particular models, we would expect to see roughly equal percentage changes across the board. But there were special demand considerations for small cars. Because of inflation abroad and the devaluation of the dollar in 1971 and again in 1973, the prices of imported cars rose substantially. As a consequence, the percentage rise in the prices of the domestic subcompacts was much higher than the percentage rise in the prices of full-sized cars. With an eased constraint from foreign competition, General Motors and Ford could raise the prices of their subcompacts to more profitable levels than would otherwise have been the case. The magnitude of these prices changes, between the spring of 1971 and the winter of 1974, is illustrated by typical price changes in Table 6. Prices for imports rose by 52 per cent; they rose by 34 per cent and 45 per cent for the subcompacts and by only 18 per cent and 21 per cent for the full-sized cars. We have here, then, a case of a change in price-cost margins for one set of cars relative to another set, as demand conditions (competition from imports) changed. This would definitely qualify as an example of price discrimination.[42]

TABLE 6
Prices and Price Changes, 1971–1974

	1971 MODEL LIST PRICE, MARCH 1971 ($)	1975 MODEL LIST PRICE, DECEMBER 1974 ($)	ABSOLUTE DIFFERENCE ($)	DIFFERENCE (PER CENT)
Vega, 2-door	2090	2799	709	34
Pinto, 2-door	1919	2769	850	45
Volkswagen "Beetle"	1899	2895	996	52
Toyota Corolla 1200, 2-door	1798	2711	913	51
Chevrolet Impala, 4-door sedan[a]	3759	4561	802	21
Ford LTD, 4-door sedan[a]	3915	4615	700	18

[a] Includes V-8 engine, automatic transmission, power steering, and power brakes.
Source: Automotive News, various issues.

[42] In January 1975, it appeared that this attempt at price discrimination had not succeeded. Very soft demand for the subcompacts led both General Motors and Ford to offer $200 rebates to buyers of the basic subcompacts. Also, the 1975 Pinto price that appears in the table was originally $2919, but Ford dropped the list price by $150 in late November ($66 was the "real" price cut and $84 was the elimination of radial tires as standard). It will be interesting to follow the future prices of the subcompacts compared to imports and to large cars.

Styling and Model Changes

With price competition muted, the companies have tended to focus their attention on nonprice areas for their rivalry for sales. As noted in an earlier section, General Motors, in the 1920s, realized that replacement was becoming a dominant element in the purchase of new cars and chose a strategy of annual model changes as a way of encouraging faster replacement and, hence, higher sales. Other companies, sooner or later, adopted similar strategies, and now styling, annual model changes, and the introduction of new models have become the dominant areas of rivalry.

TABLE 7

Number of Models Offered and Average Output per Model, 1949–1973

YEAR	NUMBER OF MODELS AT END OF MODEL YEAR	MODEL YEAR PRODUCTION DIVIDED BY NUMBER OF MODELS OFFERED
1949	205	21,400
1950	243	26,700
1951	243	24,700
1952	224	17,000
1953	210	29,000
1954	240	20,200
1955	216	33,500
1956	232	27,100
1957	245	25,300
1958	263	16,100
1959	239	23,300
1960	244	24,600
1961	260	20,800
1962	296	22,600
1963	336	21,900
1964	336	23,500
1965	348	25,400
1966	368	23,400
1967	370	20,700
1968	368	22,800
1969	365	23,100
1970	375	20,300
1971	341	21,200
1972	297	28.900
1973	304	32,600

Source: *Automotive News*, 1974 Almanac Issue, Apr. 29, 1974, pp. 23, 54; 1971 Almanac Issue, Apr. 26, 1971, pp. 55, 60.

This is not the only strategy to induce faster replacement that could have been chosen. An alternative would have been a strategy that relied more heavily on technological and engineering changes in the product to induce faster replacement. This alternative would have had two problems to face, however. First, most consumers are not very sophisticated with respect to automotive technology and have a difficult time judging the merits of new engineering advances; but they know what they like in an automotive style. Second, this would be a riskier strategy because research and development are always uncertain processes, and a firm could not be sure that it would always have a ready stream of engineering advances for each year's new cars. By contrast, the firm always knows it can produce a new style (even though it cannot know how consumers will react to it). In this sense, then, a styling strategy is somewhat safer.

The normal pattern has been for cars to get a major model change every 2 or 3 years, with "face-lifting" minor changes in exterior sheet metal, front grills, and chrome adornments in the interim years. Prior to the 1960s, the major changes occurred every 3 years; this cycle was keyed to the lead times required for engineering and the production of new tooling. Reductions in lead times allowed a 2-year cycle in the 1960s. But, with rising costs of tooling (and increased attention to safety and air pollution matters) in the 1970s, the companies appear to have slowed down the cycle to 3 and, in some cases, 4 years.

Model proliferation—the production of a wider range of models—has been a supplementary strategy for inducing faster replacement and greater sales. Table 7 shows the increase in the number of models that have been offered since 1949. The increase is all the more striking when one remembers that between 1952 and 1964 six Independents had dropped out of the market. This proliferation has not meant a serious erosion of scale economies. Increased sales volumes have meant that average sales per model have not decreased, as shown in Table 7, and technological advances in increased assembly-line flexibility and in improved inventory practices have also eased the impact of this proliferation. In the early 1970s, the companies appeared to have consolidated their offerings somewhat.

Small Cars

The behavior of the automobile industry with respect to the production and sale of small cars in the postwar period deserves separate attention.[43] The Big Three have traditionally been unenthusiastic about small cars.[44] Only American Motors has enthusiastically embraced them. The Big Three have seen them as less profitable items, that would only steal sales and profits from the large, full-sized cars that Detroit considered standard. Furthermore, the attitudes of the Big Three toward small cars may well have included recognition of their mutual interdependence. The production of a small car by a single producer might well

---

[43] For more details, see White, op. cit., Chap. 11.
[44] See William S. Rukeyser, "Detroit's Reluctant Ride into Smallsville," *Fortune,* **79** (Mar. 1969).

have been worthwhile for that producer because it would mostly take sales from the others. But production of small cars by all three would mean that they would jointly be depriving themselves of sales. In the absence of external pressures, it is unlikely that the Big Three would have produced small cars.

The external pressures have come from foreign manufacturers—imports. In the late 1950s, consumer tastes had turned toward smaller cars, and foreign manufacturers were ready and eager to meet this demand. Imports grew from 0.5 per cent of the market in 1954 to 10.2 per cent in 1959. After protesting that in building a small car "you take out value much faster than you can take out cost" and that "anyone who wants cheap transportation can always buy a used car," the Big Three finally offered their own small cars in the fall of 1959. They were larger than the imports, but they served to win sales back from the imports. By 1962, imports had declined to only 4.9 per cent of the market. In that same year, Ford at the last minute dropped plans to introduce a still smaller car. The company evidently estimated that consumer tastes were changing and that the threat from the imports was over. It guessed wrong.

During the 1960s, the Big Three's compacts grew in size, luxury, and price. Their antipathy toward small cars was clearly revealing itself. But imports grew again. From their low point in 1962, they grew to more than 10 per cent of the market in 1968. Once again the Big Three were slow to respond, hoping that the demand for small cars would disappear. Finally, again deciding that low-profit customers were better than lost customers, General Motors, Ford, and American Motors brought out a new set of small cars, subcompacts, in 1969 and 1970. This time, Chrysler could not make up its corporate mind on the issue and repeatedly delayed introducing a compact. The latest plans are for Chrysler to introduce one in 1977.

The subcompacts were close to the imports in size and spirit, and, with the assistance of two dollar devaluations and faster rates of inflation abroad, they successfully met the import challenge. Imports stabilized at 15 per cent of the market in the early 1970s.

Technological Change

Vast changes have occurred in automobiles over the last 75 years. Cars have clearly become more comfortable, more reliable, easier to drive, faster, and more powerful. These changes have tended to occur gradually, rather than in large leaps. It is difficult to quantify or make precise statements about this kind of progress. Furthermore, there frequently are significant lags between the introduction of improvements and their general adoption. Nevertheless, if one were to characterize the general pace of technological change, the fastest pace would seem to have occurred before the 1920s. The automobile was still a new and highly fascinating object, the industry was young and exciting, entry was easy, and new men with new ideas could come forward and put their ideas (the bad along with the good) into practice.

After the 1920s, the pace of technological change clearly slackened. An important reason was surely the changed emphasis by the large companies on styling and model changes. Also, the barriers to entry were much higher, so it was harder for new ideas from outside the industry to be put into practice. Perhaps, also, the inherent possibilities for new progress had narrowed, although this is always a difficult judgment to make. It is worth noting that the Independents accounted for a disproportionately large number of the major innovations prior to 1941, far out of line with their market shares.[45] Market dominance by the Big Three did not mean (or rest on) an equal dominance of innovation.

The period since World War II has also been a period of slow improvements rather than fundamental change. The major changes in postwar cars—the introduction of automatic transmissions, power steering, power brakes, and high compression engines—were refinements in prewar technology (which had largely been developed for trucks) rather than fundamental breakthroughs.[46] A good 1946 mechanic would have had little difficulty in understanding a 1968 automobile. In the 1970s, new developments in engines, ignition systems, and exhaust systems were encouraged by the pressure of air pollution control requirements. Some developments, such as transistorized ignition (replacing the breaker points), exhaust recycling, exhaust catalysts, and interest in the Wankel (rotary combustion) engine, were genuinely new. Others, such as renewed interest in the stratified charge engine, represented new refinements on basically old technology. Even in the 1970s, however, progress on really different sources of motive power (like electric cars or turbine engines) has been very slow, and success has seemed as far away as it did in the 1960s. It is noteworthy that the firms that were first interested in pursuing different kinds of engines, notably the Diesel, the Wankel, and the stratified charge engine, were not the U.S. firms but the European and Japanese manufacturers.

With fewer Independents, it is not surprising that most of the innovations in the postwar period were introduced by the Big Three. But the companies have tended to rely a great deal on their suppliers for advances in technology. The parts suppliers—for example, Bendix, Budd, Kelsey-Hayes, Wagner Electric, Borg-Warner, Dana, Thompson Products (now TRW), Motorola, and Electric Auto-Lite—did much of the pioneering development work on new items like power steering, power brakes, ball joints, alternators, transistorized ignition, and others. Also, many of these items were used on European cars before the American companies decided to adopt them. Similarly, the materials suppliers —steel, aluminum, glass, plastics, and paint companies—have provided much of the development work on new uses of materials. Effectively, the auto companies have allowed their suppliers to take the risks and absorb the initial costs of developing new technology. This pattern of behavior reinforces the impression that the auto industry's main attention has been directed elsewhere—notably at styling.[47]

[45] See *Administered Prices, Automobiles,* op. cit., pt. 7, pp. 3812–3813.

[46] Other, less striking improvements included 12-volt electrical systems, alternators, transistorized ignition, ball-joint front suspension, and disc brakes.

[47] By contrast, the truck industry, with more technologically sophisticated customers and with more Independent producers willing to take risks, has produced a faster rate of technological change.

There is a second kind of technological change that is also of interest—namely, improvements in manufacturing techniques. Here progress during 75 years has been substantial, although gradual; except for Henry Ford's early innovation with the moving assembly line, it would be hard to find large leaps. Improvements in dies, presses, machinery, equipment, and assembly techniques have been brought about partly through the efforts of the auto companies themselves and partly through the efforts of their suppliers, who supply improved materials and equipment. When there have been fundamental changes in manufacturing processes, these have usually been pioneered in other industries. The automobile industry has usually been fairly prompt in adopting and adapting these processes, but, again, as in automotive technology, the industry has let others take the risks of initial development.

Automotive Air Pollution

Automotive air pollution represents a classic case of negative externalities. Potentially deleterious gases—hydrocarbons, carbon monoxide, and nitrogen oxides—are spewed out of the tailpipes of cars and account for a significant fraction of the total tonnage of pollutants discharged into the atmosphere from all sources. Drivers are inflicting uncompensated costs on others. It is difficult to identify the specific sources of the automotive pollution and the specific injuries caused by it. Those who are injured have no way of fixing specific responsibility on those who pollute or of collecting damages. Thus, it is clear that, in the absence of some kind of government action, drivers have no incentive to stop polluting, and the automobile companies have no incentive to provide cars that pollute less (if less pollution means a more costly car).

In fact, this is the way that the automobile companies have behaved. When government officials from Southern California first approached the companies about the smog problem in the early 1950s, the companies formed an industry-wide committee to investigate the problem. They delayed, stalled, and claimed that more research and data was needed. This went on for 10 years.[48] Finally, in the early 1960s the state of California wisely provided some direct incentives for the auto companies to provide pollution control equipment (the state licensed four parts companies to provide control devices), and the companies quickly discovered that they could provide the equipment sooner than they previously had said they could.

At the national level, Federal emission standards were first set for the 1968 model year. They were progressively tightened for subsequent years. The Clean Air Act of 1970 set fairly tight standards, mandating a 90 per cent reduction in hydrocarbon and carbon monoxide emissions by 1975 and a 90 per cent reduction in nitrogen oxides emissions by 1976. The companies complained bitterly.

---

[48] In Jan. 1969 the Justice Department charged that this behavior, including a cross-licensing agreement, was a collusive restraint of trade and constituted a violation of the antitrust laws. The case was settled by a consent decree, with no admission of guilt by the companies, in Sept. 1969. See *United States* v. *Automobile Mfrs. Assn., Inc.*, 1969 Trade Cases, no. 72907.

Their research approaches consisted of divising ways of modifying current engines and adding catalysts so as to achieve the standards. Little attention was paid to new engines or other new approaches. Foreign manufacturers were able to develop alternative engines—Diesels, Wankels, and stratified charge—that could meet the standards.

In the spring of 1973, the companies appealed to the Environmental Protection Agency (EPA) to delay the standards for one year. The EPA agreed, setting new interim standards for 1975. A main reason for the EPA's decision was its belief that Chrysler would not be able to meet the original standards for 1975. There was some question as to whether Chrysler, by changing catalyst suppliers at a relatively late date, had deliberately delayed its emissions control research. The only alternative that the EPA had was to forbid Chrysler to sell its 1975 cars if it could not meet the standards. The EPA was unwilling to do this, and so it granted the delay. Congress has since granted further delays, and it appears unlikely that the original 1975 standards will ever be achieved.

Automotive Safety

There are two aspects to automotive safety: preventing accidents that cause damage and injuries to other parties and to a car's occupants; and reducing damage and injuries to the car's occupants in the event of an accident. The damage to others may constitute an externality, if liability insurance does not fully cover the costs or is uncertain or delayed.

Prior to the mid-1960s, the automobile companies stressed technological advances that reduced accidents—better brakes, better headlights, and improved steering. They largely avoided items that would reduce injury in the event of an accident (except safety glass and improved door locks). They seemed to be afraid that the mere mention of injuries from accidents would scare customers away. The exception was the 1956 Ford, which stressed safety and injury reducing features such as seatbelts, padded dashboards, and recessed steering wheels. The 1956 Ford sold poorly. Whether this was because it was poorly designed (compared to Chevrolet) or because it stressed safety can never be known. In any event, the effort was not repeated.

In the mid-1960s the Federal government became actively concerned about automotive safety. It first mandated safety specifications on government cars and then on all cars. These included such items as seatbelts, padded dashboards and other interior surfaces, and impact-absorbing steering wheels. In time, new specifications were added, including antitheft ignition locks and damage-reducing bumpers. One major specification that sparked controversy was the requirement in 1974 cars of an ignition interlock that would prevent a car from starting unless the front seatbelts were fastened. New car owners were very unhappy about this, and Congress rescinded the requirement.

The companies' behavior was largely passive, meeting the standards, occasionally objecting (as they have to the proposed airbags), and only occasionally pushing ahead of the standards with safety equipment that was not required.

Dealers and Distribution

The companies have chosen to sell their cars at retail through independent franchised dealers. The companies franchise only a limited number of dealers; they do not allow any retailer who walks in off the street to sell their cars. The companies consider the dealer to be an important part of the over-all sales effort. They spend a great deal of time and effort supervising the dealers activities, training his mechanics, and urging him to sell more cars. They set standards and sales goals and will rescind a franchise if they find that the dealer is not doing a satisfactory job.

The dealer system has its origins in the early days of the industry, when fledgling companies were short of cash and eagerly welcomed a set of retailers who would help finance finished inventories. Today, the dealer system can be seen as one in which the companies are able to benefit from the selling efforts of independent entrepreneurs, while they avoid the extra management problems of supervising the individual sales personnel. Through the companies' ability to be able to set sales standards as a condition for the retention of the franchise, they are still able to exert a fair level of over-all control over the dealer.

This last point has been a continuing source of friction between the companies and the dealers. The latter almost always see too many cars being forced on them by the companies; the companies are always afraid that the dealer would otherwise sell fewer cars, to the detriment of the company. This is a source of conflict that will persist as long as the franchised dealer system persists.

Prior to World War II, the companies usually insisted on exclusive dealing clauses in the franchise agreements; dealers could handle only the make or makes of the company granting the franchise.[49] Exclusive dealing has clear advantages for the companies. It gives the dealer less bargaining power in any negotiations with the manufacturing company; it is easier for the company to force cars on the dealer. Also, it encourages product differentiation and discourages comparison shopping by customers because they can look at only one make at a time. Furthermore, particularly in the prewar period, it probably served as an additional barrier to entry to new firms and a hindrance to the smaller firms because they could not rely on the existing dealer network of the large firms to sell their cars.

Following a set of antitrust decisions in 1941 and 1949, the companies dropped the exclusive dealing clauses from their franchises.[50] But the companies' preferences for exclusive dealing remain, and it is likely that they continue to discourage dual franchises across companies. One indication of this is that, of the 25,000 dealers selling U.S. makes in 1974, fewer than 3 per cent handled the makes of two or more U.S. companies.

---

[49] See FTC, op. cit., Chap. 7.
[50] *General Motors Corp.*, Docket no. 3152, 34 FTC 58 (1941); and *Standard Oil of California and Standard Stations, Inc.* v. *United States*, 337 U.S. 293 (1949).

Warranties

Automobiles are extremely complicated mechanisms. Inevitably, some cars will malfunction. The likelihood of this happening will be a compound of the design of the product, the length of time it has been in production (it takes time to get the "bugs" out), the quality control of the manufacturer and of the dealer, and the maintenance and care given by the owner. Who should bear the financial responsibility for repairing the car? This has been a continuing and major source of controversy for consumers, dealers, and manufacturers alike.

Prior to 1960, the manufacturers offered warranties for the first three months or 4000 miles, whichever came first—that is, they would repair, free of charge, factory-caused faults in the automobile during that period. In 1960, the warranty was extended to 12 months or 12,000 miles.

A major improvement in warranties occurred in the fall of 1962, when Chrysler extended the warranty on the drive-train components (engine, transmission, and rear axle) to 5 years or 50,000 miles. It is interesting to note that this was not an isolated move by Chrysler. It had suffered poor sales and poor financial results for the previous year and a half. It chose to try to expand its sales in a number of ways. It offered a substantial quality improvement—the 5/50,000 warranty—to retail buyers. It became more aggressive in the fleet market, as we have described. And, it also became more aggressive in offering low-pollution vehicles to Southern California local governments, breaking away from the go-slow policies that the auto companies had maintained until then. This 1962 experience is an interesting one, for it shows the kind of aggressive behavior, ultimately for the benefit of the consumer, that can arise when even a major company finds itself hard-pressed.

The other companies gradually followed and improved on the warranty until, by the fall of 1966, the 5/50,000 warranty covered most components, and a warranty for 24 months or 24,000 miles covered the rest. But that marked the high point of warranty protection. The companies must have found it too expensive. Beginning in the fall of 1967, the terms of the warranties were gradually reduced until, by the early 1970s, they were back at 12 months or 12,000 miles.[51]

It is worth noting that, even though the companies offer the warranty, it is the dealer that actually does the repair work. Warranties have been a headache for dealers. They claim that many consumers do not understand the warranties or try to get free repairs for work that is not covered by the warranty and that the manufacturers' reimbursement for warranty work is slow and inadequate.

It is likely that automobile defects and warranties will continue to be a source of irritation for all concerned. The costs of producing automobiles that are 100 per cent defect-free would be truly prohibitive—if it could be done at all. Alter-

---

[51] American Motors, however, offered extra features with its warranty plan, and, for the 1975 model year, Chrysler extended its warranty to unlimited mileage in the first 12 months. Perhaps another warranty war will flare up.

native arrangements for repairs may arise. There have been independent auto repair insurance plans that have developed in some areas. But even these are likely to run into the problems of trying to encourage owner maintenance that would avoid repairs (the problem of "moral hazard") and of dealing with the occasional car that simply runs poorly (the "lemon").

Advertising

Advertising is a powerful method for providing consumers with information about products they are interested in buying. It can also be a powerful method for building up brand familiarity and brand loyalties and, hence, raising the barriers to potential entrants. It is clear that both effects are at work in the automobile industry.

The automobile companies are among the largest advertisers in the American economy. In 1973, the Big Three producers ranked fourth, eighth, and eleventh among the country's advertisers. In that year, all four domestic manufacturers spent a total of $406 million on automobile advertising. This averaged $42 per car. The higher-volume makes have usually spent less than the industry average per car, with the lower-volume makes spending more. The dividing line is roughly between 300,000 and 500,000 units.[52] At volumes above that level, the amount spent per car seems to be relatively constant (or, at least, unrelated to production volume). This tends to reinforce the view, expressed in the section on structure, that a production volume of one million units would be quite adequate to capture economies of scale in advertising.

Much advertising is clearly informative. New models come out, new styling, new features, new prices, and the manufacturers need to inform potential buyers of their wares. Other advertising seems to have much less information content. Advertising slogans like "Come home to Ford" and "See the USA in your Chevrolet" have little information content and probably only serve to strengthen brand recognition and brand loyalty. Distinguishing between the two kinds of advertising, however, is extremely difficult, if not impossible.

IV. PERFORMANCE

Our simple model argues that industry structure, operating through behavior, should be an important determinant of performance. To the extent that an oligopoly can effectively coordinate its behavior, its performance is more likely to resemble that of a monopoly than that of a competitive industry. We will examine a number of areas of performance: allocative efficiency, technological progress, responsiveness to consumer demands, rate of price increase, and externalities.

[52] See White, op. cit., pp. 222–227.

Allocative Efficiency

The major test that economists use to judge performance in an industry is the test of allocative efficiency: Are prices equal to long-run social marginal costs? And here the monopoly-competition model provides a precise prediction: Monopolies facing sloping demand curves for their products set prices greater than long-run marginal costs, which, in the absence of externalities, means allocative inefficiency (too little is produced); an industry behaving competitively sets prices equal to long-run marginal costs (including a normal profit or return on capital), which implies allocative efficiency.

Attempts actually to ascertain whether prices are at or above long-run marginal costs usually founder on the extreme difficulty in measuring long-run costs. Usually, the appropriate data are not available. As a consequence, economists usually look at profit rates as a proxy for the price-cost relationship. To the extent that profits in some industries are persistently higher than in others, this is a likely indication of a wider spread between price and long-run marginal costs and, hence, a likely indication of allocative inefficiency. Our model predicts that monopolies or oligopolies that can successfully coordinate their behavior are more likely to be earning high profits, especially if they are protected by high barriers to entry; a competitive industry will compete away any excess profits and earn only "normal" profits—that is, profits equal to the alternative opportunities open in other easily entered industries or fields.

The proper profit rate to look at is after tax profits divided by the stockholders investment, or the rate of return on equity. Because it is the stockholders for whom the company is being run (and for whom profits are supposed to be maximized), and it is their capital that, in principle, might be shifted to seek an alternative return in another industry, this is the proper measure. The profit-rate figures that one can obtain from balance sheets and profit-and-loss statements are by no means perfect—the vagaries of corporate accounting being what they are—but they are likely to offer us a good indication of allocative efficiencies or inefficiencies.

We have seen thus far that the structural characteristics of the industry should encourage coordinated behavior and that the actual behavior of the industry has largely borne out this prediction. We would expect this behavior to yield above-normal profits, which would be indicative of allocative inefficiency. This prediction, too, is borne out. Table 8 provides the average postwar rates of return on equity for the Big Three, for the industry as a whole, and for the industry less General Motors. For the years 1946–1969, data for comparisons are available for all corporations and for all manufacturing corporations. As can be seen, average profits for the automobile industry have been appreciably higher than the average for all corporations in the economy, or even for all manufacturing corporations, even though the latter are particularly likely to include firms in other industries that are earning above-normal profits based on market power. This postwar data reinforces prewar data by the FTC, which showed that the major automobile producers (except for the mismanaged Ford Motor Company)

TABLE 8
Average Rates of Return: Net Profits After Taxes
Divided by Net Worth (in per cent)

	1946–1973[a]	1946–1969[a]
General Motors	19.7	20.4
Ford	12.3	12.3
Chrysler	10.7	11.8
American Motors[b]	7.3	7.9
Total auto industry[c]	16.00	16.46
Total auto industry, excluding GM[c]	11.11	11.25
All corporations	n.a.[d]	7.7
All manufacturing corporations	n.a.	9.0

[a] Arithmetic averages.
[b] Includes Nash before 1954.
[c] Weighted average.
[d] Not available.
Source: *Moody's Manual of Investments*, various years; U.S. Department of the Treasury, IRS, *Statistics of Income* (Washington, D.C.: U.S. Government Printing Office), various years; and corporation returns, various years.

earned very healthy profits during the 11 years 1927–1937. General Motors earned 35.5 per cent; Chrysler earned 27.3 per cent; Packard earned 21.2 per cent; and Nash earned 18.9 per cent.[53] This was during the deepest years of the Great Depression, when profits were generally low and bankruptcies frequent.[54] There is a fairly strong presumption, then, that resources have been misallocated in the automobile industry: prices have been too high, and output has been too low.

These conclusions should be qualified in a number of ways. First, we have argued previously that automobile production is a risky business. Because most investors are probably risk-averse, more risky businesses will have to earn somewhat higher profits than less risky businesses to be able to attract investors. Can this account for the higher profits of the automobile industry? Probably not. It would be hard to argue that an investment in Ford or General Motors has been a risky proposition. Through dominant market positions, multiple makes, and the other behavior described, they have been able to overcome or avoid the risks of the industry. Their profits in each year have been above the average for all manufacturing corporations, except for years of major strikes and 1958

[53] FTC, op. cit., pp. 1061–1062.
[54] Stigler's data indicate that all manufacturing corporations averaged 3.6 per cent on total assets for 1927–1937. This would be equivalent to roughly 5 per cent on equity. See George J. Stigler, *Capital and Rates of Return in Manufacturing Industries* (Princeton, N.J.: Princeton University Press, 1963), p. 203.

(for Ford, the year of the Edsel). Furthermore, a systematic measure of risk, the correlation (or, really, covariance) of a company's yearly profit rates with those of a "portfolio" of all corporations in the economy, shows that only a small risk premium would be required for the profitability patterns of the Big Three.[55] Risk cannot explain the high profit rates of the automobile industry.

Second, the profit figures may underestimate the true potential profitability of the auto industry because costs have been higher than they would be under more efficient management. For example, poor management decisions on labor relations by Ford, Chrysler, and the Independents have led to higher labor costs than General Motors has incurred.[56] Chrysler, in particular, has had a reputation for being a poorly managed firm that has sustained costs higher than they otherwise should have been. The evidence from profit rates alone, then, may be an understatement of the true inefficiencies in the automobile industry.

Finally, to make a statement concerning allocative efficiency, we have to ascertain that there are no significant externalities—no social costs or benefits that are not being captured within the automobile market. On the manufacturing side, there are no obvious externalities that need to be included. Automobile manufacture is not a particularly "dirty" or polluting process—no more so, at any rate, than most manufacturing processes. And, as long as the automobile manufacturers are paying approximately true social costs for the resources they buy, we need not worry about the resource usage of automobile manufacture.[57] On the consumption side, there are externalities associated with automobiles: air pollution, noise, uncompensated accidents caused to others, and traffic congestion. Note, however, that these externalities are caused by automobile *use* rather than ownership. Even though autos are bought to be used, there are large differences in the intensity with which they are used. The first-best way of dealing with these externalities is to limit automobile use by raising the private costs of automobile use until they equal the social costs. A limit on use would inevitably imply fewer purchases. But purchases have been limited, by a Federal excise tax from 1932–1971 and by state sales taxes. Even if further use restriction is desired, limiting auto sales through high prices charged by auto companies is a second-best way of dealing with the externality problem (limiting use is first-best), and it means a substantial income redistribution because the proceeds of the "tax" on auto purchases are going into private hands (the companies) rather than public hands (government treasuries).

Many critics of the automobile and the automobile industry feel that too many resources are being devoted to automobiles, even with the taxes and the high prices charged to buyers. To the extent that this view rests on the externali-

---

[55] This measure of risk has emerged from the capital asset pricing model of portfolio theory. See Michael C. Jensen, "Capital Markets: Theory and Evidence," *Bell Journal of Economics and Management Science*, 3 (Autumn 1972).

[56] Robert M. MacDonald, *Collective Bargaining in the Automobile Industry* (New Haven, Conn.: Yale University Press, 1963), Chap. 7. See also James Jones, "The Key to Chrysler's Return to Prosperity," *Ward's Quarterly*, 1 (Winter 1965).

[57] A thorough investigation of the markets in which the automobile manufacturers buy their materials is beyond the scope of this chapter.

ties mentioned here, the proper way to deal with the problem is to deal with the externalities themselves: tax pollution so as to discourage it, higher user fees for congested facilities at peak times, and so on. (We shall return to these prescriptions in Section V.) But often this view rests on judgments about what other people's tastes ought to be. People ought to prefer bicycles to cars; they ought to use mass transit instead of private automobiles; and they have somehow been induced to buy and use more automobiles by persuasive advertising and the mass media than would otherwise be the case.

The economist has little that is useful to say with respect to these latter criticisms. Our judgments about the workings and welfare implications of markets are based on the assumption that consumers largely know their own best interests and behave accordingly. Within this framework, A's criticism of B's tastes has very little standing, unless A is directly affected (that is, externalities). If we leave this framework, we are implicitly saying that A knows more about B's welfare than B himself does. This may well be true—and, in fact, we put this kind of belief into practice when our governments license doctors, forbid gambling, and limit or forbid the sale of dangerous drugs, toys, *and cars*—but there is no way of logically or empirically proving this proposition, or the original one. We can only say that the proposition that each individual knows his own interest best is more consistent with another important ideal in our society—personal liberty.

Technological Progress

In addition to questions of static efficiency, we are interested in improvements over time. How rapidly are new products and processes introduced? How fast are productivity increases occurring? Here we have two conflicting hypotheses linking industry structure with performance on this measure. The Schumpeterian hypothesis argues that large firms and firms with market power are necessary for a rapid rate of technological progress, the former because there are substantial economies of scale to research and development (R&D) and the latter because there are risks to R&D and because one needs a strong market position to capture the returns to R&D (which could otherwise be appropriated and competed away in a competitive industry, thus dulling the incentive to engage in R&D). The contrary argument is that large firms and firms with market power become lazy and complacent and do not have strong incentives to innovate because they are sheltered from competition; a competitive environment is necessary to provide an important incentive: the fear that a competitor will innovate first.

There is a further problem in judging performance in this area. We lack a good standard for comparison. There is no normal or expected rate of technological progress against which we can compare progress in a particular industry. Accordingly, our judgments in this area have to be somewhat more tentative than they were for allocative efficiency.

The automobile industry's performance in promoting technological change has been mixed. In the area of manufacturing processes, the industry has not been outstanding in its development of new technology since the basic application of the moving assembly line 60 years ago. However, it has been reasonably rapid in assimilating new technology and improving on it after it has been pioneered elsewhere. Output per manhour has increased by roughly 4 per cent per year during the postwar period in the automobile industry. The increase has been only 3 per cent in all of manufacturing and about 3 per cent also in the over-all economy. Although one might want to ask what the *potential* for progress was for automobile manufacturing compared to that of the rest of the economy, there are no ready answers. Over all, it is hard to complain about the automobile industry's performance in this area.

Performance with respect to automotive technology offers a different picture. Since the 1920s, the industry's main attention has been on styling, not on engineering innovation. Progress has occurred. Cars in 1975 are clearly superior to those of 1925. But progress has been slow, the sources of innovations have frequently been supplier firms or foreign automobile manufacturers, and American manufacturers have often been slow to adopt improvements. The major changes have been in power brakes and steering, automatic transmission, and air conditioning, and even in these areas the pioneering work was frequently done elsewhere. Until the 1970s, there had been no fundamental changes in the basic engine, carburation, ignition, and suspension systems. Some manufacturers abroad have been more innovative in this area, offering diesel engines, Wankel engines, stratified charge engines, fuel injection, and pneumatic suspension systems. Other entrepreneurs have proposed fundamental alternatives to the internal combustion engine, such as steam and electric vehicles. Turbines frequently appeared to be a potential alternative. Yet, until pollution control requirements tightened in the 1970s, the auto companies showed at most only sporadic interest in fundamental changes and alternatives.

If the large size and tight concentration of the automobile companies had any special value for technological progress, it should have been in these risky areas of fundamental change. Yet, the record of the industry, particularly in the postwar period, is woefully lacking.

Responsiveness to Consumer Demands

The automobile companies have generally been quite responsive to consumer demands. They responded rapidly to consumer desires for large cars, bigger engines, and power equipment in the 1950s. They provided sporty cars and lots of optional equipment when consumers demanded them in the 1960s. It would have been surprising for a group of profit-seeking firms to have done otherwise.

They have been slower in providing small cars to meet consumer demands. The Big Three saw small cars as less profitable for the industry as a whole, and recognition of their interdependence seems to have helped delay their response. In the absence of pressure from imports, it is possible that the Big Three might never have offered small cars to the American public. It is clear that their performance in this area has been reluctant.

Is the variety of cars—including models, colors, and options—too large? Would costs and prices be lower if each company were to standardize on a very few basic models, with little variety? The answer to this last question is yes, but costs would probably not fall by very much. Modern assembly-line flexibility has permitted a large variety of models to be built on the same line, with very little cost penalty. Many makes and models are at large-enough volumes so that the basic economies of scale are virtually exhausted, and added variety at the assembly-line stage adds only small extra costs. The purchasers of low-volume cars (e.g., Cadillac, Imperial, Lincoln, or the specialty cars of other makes) may pay a premium because of the cost penalties of low volume, but they always have the alternative of buying a high-volume standard model for which the economies of scale have been exhausted. A drastic standardization of models might offer some modest cost and price savings, but the consumer satisfaction sacrifice for most buyers would be substantial. It is this satisfaction to which the companies have catered by offering more varieties. Given the modest cost, it would be hard to argue that they should have done otherwise.

Have model changes been excessive and added more to costs than consumers if given a choice, would have been willing to pay? The net costs of model changes in the 1960s were about $130 to $140 per car.[58] Would consumers have been happier with cars that had fewer wrinkles and curves and changed shapes less frequently but that cost $130 to $140 less? A few might have been. Most probably would not. Again, it is hard to blame the companies in this area.

Finally, particularly in the energy-conscious 1970s, there has been considerable criticism of the "gas-guzzling monsters" that Detroit has produced; many people think that the auto companies should not produce large cars whose engines get poor gasoline mileage. Again, this production is in response to consumer tastes. Ironically, in mid-1974, at the same time that this criticism was mounting, Detroit was having the most difficulties in selling its smaller cars, which were much more economical in their use of gasoline. After the shortages and the long waiting lines of the beginning of the year subsided, buyers went back to buying larger cars. When consumers have a choice and choose to consume the gas-guzzling monsters, it is hard to blame the companies for providing them.

Rate of Price Increase

In the inflationary late 1960s and 1970s, the rate of price increase in an industry became an important public concern. Here, our monopoly-competition model offers no guidance. The monopoly model says that monopolies will *maintain* prices that are higher than those of a competitive industry, but it says nothing about price increases or rates of price increase. If costs go up, prices will rise for both kinds of industries. We cannot differentiate by industry structure.

[58] See White, op. cit., pp. 263–226, and U.S. Congress, Senate, Committee on Small Business, Subcommittee on Monopoly and Subcommittee on Retailing Distribution and Marketing Practices, *Hearings on Planning, Regulation, and Competition: Automobile Industry—1968*, 90th Cong., 2d sess., 1968, p. 6, "Response by General Motors."

Nevertheless, it is worth noting the performance of the automobile industry in this area. The industry's performance has been quite good. Table 9 shows the consumer price index for new cars and for the entire index for the postwar period. The new car price index rose by only 34 per cent between 1949 and 1973, whereas the over-all index rose by 86 per cent. The actual list prices of cars has risen by considerably more. In 1949, the cheapest four-door Ford listed for $1474. In the fall of 1974, the cheapest 1975 four-door Ford (Maverick) listed for $3016, or more than double the 1949 price; the cheapest 1975 full-sized four-door Ford listed for $4615; and a car with roughly the same dimensions of that 1949 Ford, a 1975 Chevrolet Chevelle, listed for $3415. The difference between the changes in the new car price index and the list prices of new cars has been partly due to the fact that cars sold largely at list price in 1949 but now frequently sell at $300 to $400 below list and partly due to quality adjustments in the price index. Since 1959, the Bureau of Labor Statistics (BLS) has been adjusting the new car price index for changes in the quality of automobiles. Thus, when higher prices are announced but extra features are also included as part of the car (for example, a better engine, better brakes, and pollution control or safety equipment), the BLS subtracts its estimate of the value of the extra equipment from the price increase and records the net increase (or decrease) as the change in the price index for new cars. Although observers may quibble with the BLS's exact procedures, it is clear that 1975 cars are superior to 1949 cars: they have better engines, better brakes, better tires, and improved ignition systems; they require less frequent maintenance for some items; and they include or have the option of including power equipment, air conditioning, and automatic transmissions; they also have roughly $420 worth of safety and pollution control equipment. Unfortunately, the BLS does not uniformly correct all components of the over-all consumer price index for quality adjustments, so it is difficult to tell how valid is the comparison between the new car component and the over-all index.

This price record is impressive but, given the productivity increases that have

TABLE 9
Consumer Price Index

YEAR	ENTIRE CONSUMER PRICE INDEX	NEW CAR COMPONENT
1949	71.4	82.8
1959	87.3	105.9
1969	109.8	104.4
1973	133.1	111.1
Difference, 1949–1973	86.4%	34.2%

Source: *Monthly Labor Review*, various issues.

occurred in the industry, not surprising. The 1 per cent edge in annual productivity increases that the automobile industry has had over the rest of the economy explains half of the difference in the postwar price changes, and the incomplete quality adjustments in the over-all index probably explain the rest.

Auto Safety and Pollution

The auto companies' performance in the auto safety and pollution areas has been mixed. Under the pressure of government regulations, progress has been made in these areas; however, particularly in the case of air pollution control, the progress has been slow and uninspiring. In the absence of governmental pressures, it is clear that progress would have been much slower. Even in the face of government pressure on air pollution, the industry may well have colluded in the 1950s and early 1960s to delay the development of control devices, as the Justice Department charged in 1969. Chrysler may well have deliberately slowed down its efforts in 1972 and 1973 so as to force a delay in the 1975 standards.

It is important to see this performance, not as a consequence of an effort by a small group of men to "do in" the public, but rather as the natural consequence of a group of managers interested in maximizing profits for their stockholders and recognizing their interdependence and their importance in the economy. Pollution is an externality; providing control equipment adds to the cost of the car but does not add directly to utility for the buyer; and, thus, firms naturally resist a program to require pollution control equipment. Safety is an area that seems to exercise legislators much more than it does most car buyers; again, firms would naturally be reluctant to add costly equipment that they thought buyers did not want.

These profit-maximizing drives are unlikely to disappear from the automobile industry, or from the American economy. These drives can be extremely powerful forces for improving social welfare, as Adam Smith recognized 200 years ago with his description of "the invisible hand of competition." But, to gain these benefits, we do need a reasonably competitive framework and we need to force consumers and producers to take account of externalities. The major task of public policy should be to try to ensure the harmonization of these profit-maximizing drives by firms (and individuals) with overall social welfare. It is to that task that we now turn.

V. PUBLIC POLICY

Public policy has affected the automobile industry in a number of areas. Our discussion will try to review past policy measures and propose changes for the future, where appropriate. We will discuss a number of areas: taxation, complements, prices and dealers, safety and pollution, and antitrust.

Taxation

Two kinds of taxation, aside from the general corporation income tax, have affected the automobile industry: import duties and excise taxes. The infant automobile industry was protected by an infant industry tariff of 45 per cent, which gave it plenty of protection. As the industry grew and matured, the tariff was lowered until, in 1930, it stood at 10 per cent. It remained at that level for 20 years and then gradually fell to $6\frac{1}{2}$ per cent in the mid-1960s. It fell farther as a consequence of the Kennedy round of negotiations on tariffs with America's trading partners. As of 1975, it stood at 3 per cent. (It has been zero since 1965 for auto company shipments of cars to and from Canada, due to the United States–Canadian Automotive Agreement of that year.)

There seem to be no pressing revenue or balance-of-payment reasons for keeping the tariff. Imports have provided exceedingly healthy competition for the U.S. industry; without them, American consumers would have been considerably worse off. Imports ought not to be subject to any needless penalties.[59] It is to the credit of the automobile industry that the company executives have never asked for special protection or quotas against imported cars.

The Federal excise tax on automobiles was first imposed in 1932 (as a means of helping balance the budget). The rate was 3 per cent, which persisted through the 1930s. In the immediate postwar period, the rate was 5 per cent; it was raised to 10 per cent in 1951, during the Korean War. It fell to 7 per cent in 1965, and then was abolished in August 1971, as part of President Nixon's New Economic Program. There seems to be no good reason to revive it.

Complements

There are two important complements to automobiles: roads and gasoline. Government policy has been active with respect to both.[60]

Prior to the development of the automobile, roads were almost entirely a state and local government responsibility. For the first two decades of the automobile this pattern continued. Significant Federal activity began with the Federal Aid Road Act of 1916, which provided Federal subsidies for state highway departments. The Federal Highway Act of 1921 provided for Federal funds to match state funds for "such projects as will expedite the completion of an adequate and connected system of highways, interstate in character." Federal interest and involvement with a national highway system continued to grow over the next three decades, culminating in the Federal Aid Highway Act of 1956. The act, and its subsequent amendments, provided for 90 per cent Federal funding of a 41,000-mile system of limited access highways, the interstate highway system.

Funding for the road system has come largely from road users themselves.

---

[59] Exchange-rate adjustments are usually the proper way to deal with balance-of-payment problems, and monitary and fiscal policies, supplemented by special adjustment allowances, are the proper way to deal with the employment adjustments that imports might create.

[60] The historical parts of this section have been drawn from John B. Rae, *The Road and the Car in American Life* (Cambridge, Mass.: MIT Press, 1971).

Fees for registrations and drivers' licenses were charged as early as 1900, and state gasoline taxes were first levied in 1919. The Federal excise tax on autos, mentioned here, began in 1932, and a Federal excise tax on gasoline was begun in the same year. The link between highway financing and user taxes at the Federal level was formalized in 1956, when a Highway Trust Fund was established into which the Federal user taxes would be paid and out of which the interstate highway system would be financed. In addition, during the 1940s and 1950s a number of states east of the Mississippi built high-speed toll highways. Because many drivers were from out of state (and, hence, would not be contributing to that state's road financing through state and local user charges), the toll roads made good sense.

Over all, automobile drivers and other road users have fully paid for the roads they use, largely through gasoline taxes.[61] But rush-hour motorists on urban freeways are underpaying; their gasoline taxes do not cover the costs of the extra lanes that are required to handle the extra traffic at those times.[62] And motorists in congested areas generally are not paying their true marginal costs because their extra presence on a congested road or freeway creates costs for others, in terms of slowing down the speed of traffic. This is another example of the familiar externalities problem.

This underpayment by rush hour and congested area motorists tends to encourage excessive use of automobiles for commuting and for urban trips generally. This has been compounded by government policies that have tended to *raise* the costs of alternative forms of urban transportation. Taxicab systems are usually local monopolies or oligopolies that are protected from new entry by local government franchises. Jitneys, "gypsy" cabs, and other forms of small-scale, somewhat informal transportation that could offer lower cost urban transportation services have been discouraged or forbidden, ostensibly because of safety, but really because they offer a serious challenge to established taxi and transit systems in many areas.[63] At the same time, the latter forms of transport have become increasingly costly to operate and have raised their prices accordingly. Only in the 1960s did transit systems begin to receive substantial subsidies, and even these have not been sufficient to fend off sizeable fare hikes.

A more sensible public policy in this area would be two-pronged. First, rush hour and congested area motorists should be required to pay the full social costs of their travel. This would involve charging differential rates on existing toll roads, bridges and tunnels—higher for peak travel. This would also involve extending the differential toll concept to other highways and facilities, at least for peak periods. With some electronic ingenuity, cars might be equipped with a toll plate that could be automatically and quickly read by machine, ending the

---

[61] J. R. Meyer, J. F. Kain, and M. Wohl, *The Urban Transportation Problem* (Cambridge, Mass.: Harvard University Press, 1965), pp. 61–62.

[62] Ibid., pp. 69–74.

[63] See the statement of George W. Hilton, *The Industrial Reorganization Act*, pt. 4, pp. 2234–2235; and Ross D. Eckert and George W. Hilton, "The Jitneys," *Journal of Law and Economics*, 15 (Oct. 1972).

need for congestion-creating tollbooths; billing could be done by mail at the end of each month. Or, a sealed meter in each car could be sensitive to electronic signals along the roads, and the signals could be adjusted automatically according to congestion conditions.[64] Second, jitneys and other informal forms of transportation should be permitted. The currently protected monopolies of taxicab companies should be ended.

Thus, by raising the private cost of peak time car travel to something closer to its true social costs, and by allowing competition to lower the costs of alternative forms of urban transportation, a better pattern of automobile use will be encouraged. In the end, it would probably mean a small decrease in the number of automobiles purchased.

Prices and Dealers

There have been two major areas in which public policy has affected automobile prices. During periods of Federal price controls—1946, 1950–1953, and 1971–1974—automobile prices have been controlled. Requests by the auto companies for price increases during these periods received wide publicity and frequently were pictured as a confrontation between the industry and its regulators. These confrontations usually were settled by compromise. In addition, in the late 1960s, even though there were no legal price controls, the automobile industry was subject to informal "jaw boning" from Washington concerning its price increases for new models. These formal and informal price controls have had little long-run effect on the industry, and they may even have had little short-run effect because, in a confrontation situation, the companies' initial price increase requests were probably above those that they expected to achieve. In all, price regulation has not been a very successful means of dealing with the automobile industry.

There is also a Federal requirement that the list price of each car be attached to the car. This law was passed in 1958. Prior to this, dealers were in the habit of giving some customers an excessive allowance for their used car trade-in but then "packing" the price of the new car with hidden charges and extras to make up the difference. Some customers found it difficult to find out what the actual list price of the car was supposed to be. It is not clear that significant numbers of consumers were really hurt by this practice, but the dealers were unhappy enough to ask and convince Congress to put an end to this practice by requiring the list price to be attached to every car. This does provide a clear point from which dealers and buyers can bargain about the final price and avoids whatever confusion used to exist over list prices.

Dealers have been unhappy over their relatively weak position vis-à-vis the manufacturers since the beginning of the industry. The manufacturers' practices of pressuring dealers to sell large numbers of cars and canceling the franchises of

---

[64] See William S. Vickery, "Pricing in Urban and Suburban Transport," *American Economic Review*, **53** (May 1963).

those who failed to meet the manufacturers' expectations have naturally rankled many dealers. In the late 1930s, the dealers prevailed on Congress to direct the FTC to investigate distribution policies. The result, *Report on the Motor Vehicle Industry*, duly chronicled the dealer complaints, but nothing was done about them. Dealer dissatisfaction peaked again in the mid-1950s, and the dealers, in 1956, succeeded in getting Congress to pass the Automobile Dealers' Day in Court Act. They hoped that this act would provide the dealers with a stronger position in suing the companies for lack of good faith in the event of a franchise cancellation. In practice, the act has not provided much support for the dealers, although it may have served to limit some of the more arbitrary actions of the companies. Most dealers appear to have resigned themselves to living with the companies' pressure, but proposals to limit the companies' power over the dealers occasionally surface in Congress.

The franchise system poses a tough dilemma for public policy. Unhindered entry is usually a desirable goal for public policy. The automobile companies' policy of restricting who can sell their cars runs counter to that goal. But, by limiting their franchises, they also gain the power to force cars on dealers and, thereby, keep actual retail prices at low levels (for any given wholesale price). This last is clearly in the interests of consumers. But the companies also gain the power to discourage their dealers from also selling another company's cars. This power was formally exercised through exclusive-dealing clauses in franchise agreements before the 1940s, which had the unfortunate effects of making entry for manufacturers more difficult (at a time when other barriers were much lower than they are today) and of making survival more difficult for the more numerous small manufacturers then in existence. Today, the clauses are gone, but the persuasive power of the companies remain. This makes it more difficult for foreign manufacturers to enter the U.S. market (only 7 per cent of dealers selling U.S. cars also sell imports), and it makes comparison shopping that much more difficult.

In all, the present distribution system has both pluses and minuses for public welfare. This writer believes that, despite its faults, it is probably better than the alternatives that have been proposed, which range from giving the dealers more power to resist manufacturers' pressures to ending the restrictive franchise system altogether. Greater public scrutiny, however, should be given to the pressures for exclusive dealing that still remain.

Air Pollution and Safety

As we have already noted, public policy has been quite active in these areas. Air pollution control legislation began in California in the early 1960s; Federal legislation began in 1965; and standards have become progressively tighter since. Safety efforts by the states extend back to the 1920s and 1930s, but they have focused largely on such areas as highway conditions and discouraging drunk driving. Effective legislation concerning safety equipment came at the Federal level in the mid-1960s and has been extended progressively since then.

In both the air pollution and safety areas there are elements of externalities and, hence, legitimate grounds for government action. But there are possible questions as to whether past and current policies have achieved the correct balance between the costs and benefits of corrective action and whether the policies are structured to achieve the best performance from the companies and from motorists.

Let us take pollution first. The 1975 interim Federal exhaust standards, for example, reduced hydrocarbon and carbon monoxide emissions by more than 80 per cent and nitrogen oxide emissions by 24 per cent, compared to an un-controlled car.[65] But the achievement of these standards is not free. The 1975 model cars cost roughly $120 more because of the extra equipment involved.[66] They will require $100 more maintenance over their lives and will burn $76 worth of more costly fuel over their lives. New car buyers (plus subsequent used car buyers) will spend $296 extra over the life of each new car. For annual sales of 10 million cars, this means an extra $3 billion. Is it worth it? Should yet stricter standards, which will reduce emissions further but also be more costly, be imposed? Or should less strict standards be imposed? A judgment requires weighing the benefits of emissions controls against these costs. The benefits from air pollution reduction, although easy to list—improved health, reduced cleaning and maintenance to buildings and materials, reduced agricultural crop loss due to pollution, and increased aesthetic pleasure in clean air— are difficult to quantify and difficult to assign dollar values to. The best current effort to estimate the benefits and compare them to the costs of present and proposed (stricter) programs indicates that the benefit-cost ratio is probably favorable and would certainly be so if (1) stricter controls were applied only to hydrocarbons and carbon monoxide but not to nitrogen oxides or (2) only cars in high-pollution areas (roughly one third of all cars) were required to have stricter controls than the 1975 standards.[67]

The programs, then, do seem to be worthwhile, even though the precise levels of control that would maximize the difference between benefits and costs cannot be determined. But are the present policies the best way to achieve pollution abatement? Economists normally favor dealing with negative externalities through a policy of marginal financial incentives. A tax on automotive air pollution would be a straightforward example. The tax should be set equal to the marginal damage caused by extra pollution and it should apply to all emitters—that is, new and old cars alike (as well as other sources of air pollution). It would require periodic vehicle inspections. But it would provide a strong incentive for new car buyers to choose models that have low emissions.

[65] Emissions from two other sources, crankcase blowby and evaporation from gas tanks and carburetors, have been remedied at relatively low cost.

[66] *Report by the Committee on Motor Vehicle Emissions* (Washington, D.C.: National Academy of Sciences, Nov. 1974), p. 85.

[67] National Academy of Sciences and National Academy of Engineering, *Air Quality and Automobile Emission Control*, Vol. 4, "The Costs and Benefits of Automobile Emission Control," prepared for the Senate, Committee on Public Works (Washington, D.C.: U.S. Government Printing Office, Sept. 1974).

And, this, in turn, would provide a strong incentive for the manufacturers to develop and provide low-pollution vehicles. If emission reduction were too costly, motorists would have the alternative of paying the tax, and the public treasury would have extra revenues available to compensate those who are injured by pollution.

By contrast, the current policies have focused almost exclusively on setting standards for new cars and then setting deadlines for the manufacturers to meet them—"holding their feet to the fire." The only enforcement sanction is a fine of $10,000 per vehicle that is not properly equipped; this is equivalent to shutting down any manufacturer who fails to meet the deadline. Is this sanction credible? Would the Congress really allow General Motors, Ford, or Chrysler to be shut down completely if it failed to meet a deadline? And, if not, can we be sure that present programs really are keeping the manufacturers' feet to the fire? There is no doubt that the manufacturers have made a substantial effort to meet the air pollution requirements. Still, the original (stricter) Federal standards for 1975 had to be suspended in 1973 when Chrysler appeared unable to meet them; Chrysler may have deliberately delayed its efforts by changing catalyst suppliers at a late date. The present policies, at best, provide a mix of incentives. A pollution tax program would provide an undiluted incentive for rapid and cost-minimizing pollution control. Even a second-best alternative— a pollution tax on new cars only—would provide a superior set of alternatives to the present programs. Had pollution taxes been legislated—in the mid-1950s in California and in the mid-1960s at the Federal level—it is likely that we would now be seeing faster, more effective, and lower-cost automotive emissions control than has in fact taken place.

In early 1975, the Federal government appeared to be ready to strike a "bargain" with the automobile manufacturers: No stricter pollution control requirements would be imposed for 5 years (that is, the interim 1975 standards would be made permanent for 5 years), in return for a promise of a 40 per cent improvement in gasoline mileage in new cars. We should first ask why the government needs to worry about gasoline mileage. Why are not consumers' choices, in light of the price of gasoline and the price of cars, the right ones, and why would not these choices lead manufacturers to the right decisions concerning engines and gasoline mileage? Still, if we accept that there is some legitimate reason for government intervention here, the logic of the previous paragraphs indicates that the "bargain" represents misguided public policy. A pollution tax, combined with a new car tax on gasoline mileage, would provide an incentive for the manufacturers to improve gasoline mileage *and* continue their efforts to reduce emissions.

Safety policies can be subjected to the same kind of scrutiny. The safety components on a 1975 car cost roughly $300. Are they worth it? The benefits are reduced accidents and, hence, reduced property damage, medical costs, and deaths to car occupants and to other parties. Costs to other parties are reduced by items that eliminate accidents: dual braking systems, side- and rear-view mirrors, back-up lights, better windshield wipers, and so on. Costs to occupants are reduced by these devices and by better "packaging" in the event of an accident: seatbelts or other restraints, padded dashboards, better door locks, impact-absorbing steering wheels, and so on. The benefits are probably worth the costs for most of these items.[68] But should they be required? Should new car buyers be forced to buy equipment that they do not want?

Damage to others does constitute an externality, but liability insurance can internalize it, and differential insurance rates on cars with different safety characteristics provide the right incentives to drivers and car buyers; high insurance rates seem to have been responsible for the decrease in the sale of high-power "muscle" cars in the early 1970s. But, to the extent that insurance payments are incomplete, uncertain, or slow, or to the extent that deaths are involved (for which proper compensation may be impossible), the externality remains, and there are good grounds for governmental intervention. But what about the better packaging devices? What if drivers refuse to wear seatbelts? Only 20 to 30 per cent of drivers actually wear them. Should they still be required to pay for them? This issue came to a head in 1974, over the seatbelt and ignition interlock system. New car buyers grew increasingly unhappy with the system, and Congress finally passed a law eliminating it. Perhaps the absence of driver revolts over other requirements indicates much less dissatisfaction. Still, the issue is one of government paternalism and of who knows best concerning the welfare of the car buyer. This writer would prefer to see more information and fewer requirements. Modern, flexible assembly lines could easily handle the resulting diversity of demands, providing cars with lots of safety equipment for those who want it and cars with less for those who want less.

The design of Federal safety policies has been similar to pollution-control policies: requirements with deadlines. Again, a taxation system would be a superior form of policy. This is most readily seen in the area of passive restraints. The airbag—a large balloon that would inflate on impact and, thus, provide an automatic cushion for passengers—has been proposed, developed, and tested for a number of years. Opinion inside and outside the automobile industry has been devided on the merits of the airbag, and some manufacturers have opposed it. Originally suggested deadlines have been delayed. (The seatbelt and ignition interlock system were supposed to be a partial substitute for it.) A taxation scheme related to passive restraints would have provided a strong and undivided incentive for the companies to develop a workable and low-cost airbag or a suitable substitute.

Antitrust

Antitrust has been an important tool of American policy for improving the structure and behavior of industries and, hence, of improving their performance. But antitrust has had only a minor impact on the automobile industry.

[68] U.S. Office of Science and Technology, *Cumulative Regulatory Effects on the Cost of Automotive Transportation* (*RECAT*) (Washington, D.C.: U.S. Government Printing Office, 1972). But Peltzman has argued that the safety standards have had no effect. See Sam Peltzman, "The Effects of Automobile Safety Regulation," *Journal of Political Economy*, **83** (Aug. 1975).

Structural antitrust actions have been aimed at the periphery of the industry. A government suit eventually forced Ford, in 1972, to divest itself of Electric Auto-Lite (a spark plug and electrical components firm that Ford had bought in 1961).[69] General Motors signed a consent decree, in 1968, to divest itself of the Euclid Road Machine Company (a producer of heavy, off-the-road trucks that General Motors had bought in 1953).[70] A government antitrust suit, in 1964, deterred a proposed merger between Chrysler and Mack Truck. In 1957, du Pont was forced to divest itself of its holdings of General Motors stock because General Motors was a major customer of du Pont.[71] Earlier, the government had won a criminal suit, in 1939, charging that General Motors had forced its dealers to use its wholly owned subsidiary, GMAC, for financing.[72] Efforts to split GMAC away from the parent company failed, however, and the government settled for a consent decree, in 1952, in which General Motors agreed that its dealers should be free to deal with independent finance companies.[73] On the side of acquiescence, the Justice Department approved the mergers of Kaiser-Willys, in 1953, and of Nash-Hudson and Studebaker-Packard, in 1954. Mergers offered the only hope for survival for these companies.

Behavioral antitrust efforts recently have aimed closer to the center of the industry. In January 1969, the government charged that the automobile companies' cross-licensing agreement on pollution-control devices in the early 1950s and subsequent behavior by the companies constituted an illegal restraint of trade in the development of pollution-control equipment. The case was settled in September 1969, with a consent decree, in which the companies agreed not to coordinate their future pollution-control efforts.[74] In 1972, the government charged Ford and General Motors with price fixing in the fleet market, particularly with respect to a series of price increases in the spring of 1970. The criminal suit was decided in favor of the companies in December 1973; the civil suit was decided in their favor in September 1974.[75]

As this brief review of automotive antitrust case indicates, there has been no antitrust attack on the heart of market power in the industry: the high level of concentration. Yet, if performance is to be improved where it is weak—pricing and the allocation of resources, automotive technological change, and response to consumer tastes in some areas—it can only be done by fundamental structural change: increasing the number of producers in the market. With more independent centers of initiative, there would be a greater likelihood of more competitive behavior in all aspects of the industry. More competitive behavior in pricing would likely to occur. There would be an increased probability that one of the firms in the industry might decide on a strategy of technological change as its

[69] *Ford Motor Co.* v. *United States*, 405 U.S. 562 (1972).
[70] *United States* v. *General Motors Corp.*, 1968 Trade Cases, no. 72,356.
[71] *United States* v. *E. I. du Pont de Nemours & Co.*, 353 U.S. 586 (1957).
[72] *United States* v. *General Motors Corp.*, 121 F. 2d 376 (1941).
[73] *United States* v. *General Motors Corp.*, 1952–1953 Trade Cases, no. 67,323.
[74] *United States* v. *Automobile Mfrs. Assn., Inc.*, 1969 Trade Cases, no. 72,907.
[75] *United States* v. *General Motors Corp. and Ford Motor Co.*, 1974-2 Trade Cases, no. 75,253.

way of winning customers. And firms would be less likely to think of new items (like small cars) from an industry point of view. If an item were profitable for the firm, then it would be pursued, even if it were unprofitable from the standpoint of the whole industry. Because the barriers to entry in this industry are extremely high, increased numbers of domestic producers can only be achieved by breaking up the present producers.

It was argued in Section II that a firm with two makes and total sales of one million units per year would be at minimum efficient size. Again, this means that a firm of this size would virtually exhaust the economies of scale in the industry. It would be large enough to engage in full-scale research and development, advertising, and distribution.[76] A firm of this size should not be confused with a "Mom and Pop" grocery store. With sales of more than \$3 billion a year, it would rank among the top 40 manufacturing companies in the country.

Production by the four companies in the United States and Canada combined averaged 9.5 million units in 1970–1973.[77] Thus, if one could somehow "start over," there would be room for 9 or 10 efficient firms instead of the present 4. Starting over is probably not feasible.[78] But it would be feasible to split the existing Big Three into 8 viable firms.[79] With American Motors, this would make 9 firms in the industry, plus imports. This would not be the textbook picture of "perfect competition," but there would be an increased likelihood of more competitive behavior.

Could this be done under the present antitrust laws? Section 2 of the Sherman Act, which would be the operative clause here, forbids attempts to "monopolize" an industry. Past interpretations of this section have imposed a "market power plus" standard; market power unjustified by economies of scale, plus some forms of exclusionary or predatory behavior by the firms in the industry in question. By this standard, an antitrust action would fail. Even though current market concentration in the automobile industry is not justified by economies of scale, the behavior of the present producers have largely been exemplary. With the possible exception of the exclusive dealing clauses in franchise agreements before the 1940s, the companies' behavior has not been exclusionary or predatory.

Judicial interpretations may change, or new antitrust legislation embodying

[76] It appears that a company does not have to be large to be technologically progressive. The two firms that were able to develop new engines to meet the 1975 pollution standards are far smaller than the Big Three: Toyo Kogyo, manufacturer of the Mazda rotary (Wankel) engine, produced 466,000 cars in 1973; and Honda, manufacturer of the Honda stratified charge engine, produced 257,000 cars in 1973.

[77] Since the 1965 United States-Canadian Automotive Agreement allows the companies to consolidate their North American production, it seems sensible to think about restructuring the industry in North American terms.

[78] But see the testimony of Stanley E. Boyle, *The Industrial Reorganization Act*, op. cit., pt. 3, pp. 2107 ff., and U.S. Congress, Senate, Committee on the Judiciary, Subcommittee on Antitrust and Monopoly, *A Reorganization of the U.S. Automobile Industry*, Feb. 1974, for a proposal that would radically decompose the automobile industry into individually owned assembly plants, engine plants, stamping plants, and so on.

[79] For the details of this proposal, see Lawrence J. White, "A Proposal for Restructuring the Automobile Industry," *The Industrial Reorganization Act*, op. cit., pt. 3, pp. 1950–1967.

a market structure standard may be passed. In that event, it may be possible to restructure the industry to increase the number of producers and improve performance.

Are there alternative ways of improving performance? Public utility regulation, full nationalization or partial nationalization (that is, the government buying the assets of one firm or one make) are sometimes mentioned as alternatives. The performance record of government regulation in other industries is not bright; this remedy would likely be worse than the disease. Full nationalization would eliminate private excess profits, but it might also lead to greater over-all inefficiency in the use of resources. Replacing four centers of initiative with only one center does not seem to be a very good way to encourage new ideas in the automobile industry. Finally, partial nationalization has some precedents in the United States—notably the Tennessee Valley Authority (TVA)[80]—and abroad, but the performance record of these cases is unclear. The concept of a government-controlled firm setting the socially right prices and, thus, by its actions forcing its rivals to do the same sounds attractive. Whether it would actually work out that way in practice is another question.

This writer believes that a more competitive structure for the automobile industry plus the proper pricing of externalities provide the best hope for improved performance in this industry.

Conclusion

In this chapter the history, structure, behavior, performance, and public policy of the automobile industry have been summarized. There are strengths and weaknesses in that performance and in the public policies that have dealt with the industry. Clearly, there is room for improvement in both.

SUGGESTED READINGS

BOOKS AND PAMPHLETS

Automotive News, Annual Almanac Issue.
Automobile Manufacturers Association. *Automobiles of America*. Detroit, Mich.: Wayne State University, 1968.
Bain, Joe S. *Barriers to New Competition*. Cambridge, Mass.: Harvard University Press, 1956.
Beige, Carl E. *The Canada–U.S. Automotive Agreement: An Evaluation*. Washington, D.C.: National Planning Association, 1970.
Boyle, Stanley E. *A Reorganization of the U.S. Automobile Industry*. Prepared for the U.S. Senate, Committee on the Judiciary, Subcommittee on Antitrust and Monopoly, 93d Cong., 2d sess., Feb. 1974.

---

[80] The TVA has been one of the major exceptions, with partial nationalization designed to provide social benefits and provide a "yardstick" for private company electrical rates. It is an experiment that has not been repeated.

Brooks, John. *The Fate of the Edsel and Other Business Adventures.* New York: Harper & Row, Publishers, 1963.

Cleveland, R. G., and S. T. Williamson. *The Road Is Yours.* New York: Hawthorn Books, 1951.

Edwards, Charles E. *Dynamics of the Automobile Industry.* Columbia: University of South Carolina Press, 1965.

Greenleaf, William. *Monopoly on Wheels.* Detroit, Mich.: Wayne State University Press, 1961.

MacDonald, Robert M. *Collective Bargaining in the Automobile Industry.* New Haven, Conn.: Yale University Press, 1963.

Meyer, J. R., J. F. Kain, and M. Wohl. *The Urban Transportation Problem.* Cambridge, Mass.: Harvard University Press, 1965.

Motor Vehicle Manufacturers Association, *Automobile Facts and Figures.* Detroit, Mich.: annual.

Nevins, Allan. *Ford: The Times, The Man, The Company.* New York: Charles Scribner's Sons, 1954.

Nevins, Allan and Frank E. Hill. *Ford: Expansion and Challenge, 1915–1932.* New York: Charles Scribner's Sons, 1957.

———. *Ford: Decline and Rebirth, 1933–1962.* New York: Charles Scribner's Sons, 1962.

Pachigian, Bedros Peter. *The Distribution of Automobiles, An Economic Analysis of the Franchise System.* Englewood Cliffs, N.J.: Prentice-Hall, Inc., 1961.

Rae, John B. *The American Automobile: A Brief History.* Chicago: Chicago University Press, 1965.

———. *The Road and the Car in American Life.* Cambridge, Mass.: M.I.T. Press, 1971.

Sloan, Alfred P., Jr. *My Years with General Motors.* Garden City, N.Y.: Doubleday & Company, Inc., 1965.

White, Lawrence J. *The Automobile Industry Since 1945.* Cambridge, Mass.: Harvard University Press, 1971.

ARTICLES

Burck, Charles G. "Detroit Turns Against the Gas Guzzlers." *Fortune,* **89** (Jan. 1974).

Cordtz, Dan. "The Face in the Mirror at General Motors." *Fortune,* **74** (Aug. 1966).

Eckert, Ross D., and George W. Hilton, "The Jitneys." *Journal of Law and Economics,* **15** (Oct. 1972).

Jones, James. "The Key to Chrysler's Return to Prosperity." *Ward's Quarterly,* **1** (Winter 1965).

Louis, Arthur M. "Chrysler's Private Hard Times. "*Fortune,* **81** (Apr. 1970).

Loving, Rush, Jr. "The Automobile Industry Has Lost Its Masculinity." *Fortune,* **88** (Sept. 1973).

McGee, John S. "Economies of Size in Auto Body Manufacture." *Journal of Law and Economics,* **16** (Oct. 1973).

Menge, John A. "Style Change Costs as a Market Weapon." *Quarterly Journal of Economics,* **76** (Nov. 1962).

Peltzman, Sam, "The Effects of Automobile Safety Regulation." *Journal of Political Economy,* **83** (Aug. 1975).

Rukeyser, William S. "Detroit's Reluctant Ride into Smallsville." *Fortune,* **79** (Mar. 1969).

Vatter, Harold G. "The Closure of Entry in the American Automobile Industry." *Oxford Economic Papers*, *4* (Oct. 1972).

Vickerey, William S. "Pricing in Urban and Suburban Transit." *American Economic Review*, **53** (May 1963).

White, Lawrence J. "The Auto Pollution Muddle." *The Public Interest* (Summer 1973).

GOVERNMENT PUBLICATIONS

FTC. *Report on the Motor Vehicle Industry*. Washington, D.C.: U.S. Government Printing Office, 1939.

National Academy of Sciences. *Report by the Committee on Motor Vehicle Emissions*. Washington, D.C.: National Academy of Sciences, Nov. 1974.

National Academy of Sciences and National Academy of Engineering. *Air Quality and Automobile Emission Control*. Vol. 4. "The Costs and Benefits of Automobile Emissions Control." Prepared for the U.S. Senate, Committee on Public Works, Sept. 1974.

U.S. Congress, Senate, Committee on Commerce, Special Subcommittee on Automobile Market Practices, *Hearings on Unfair Competition and Discriminatory Automobile Marketing Practices*, 90th Cong., 2d sess., 1968.

U.S. Congess, Senate, Committee on the Judiciary, Subcommittee on Antitrust and Monopoly, *Hearings on Administered Prices*, *Automobiles*, 85th Cong., 2d sess., 1958.

———, *Hearings on Franchise Legislation*, 90th Cong., 1st sess., 1967.

———, *Hearings on The Industrial Reorganization Act*, 93rd Cong., 2d sess., 1974.

———, *Hearings on A Study of the Antitrust Laws*, 84th Cong., 1st sess., 1955.

———, Select Committee on Small Business, Subcommittee on Monopoly and Subcommittee on Retailing, Distribution, and Marketing Practices. *Hearings on Planning, Regulation, and Competition: Automobile Industry—1968*, 90th Cong., 2d sess., 1968.

CHAPTER 6

the beer industry

KENNETH G. ELZINGA

I. INTRODUCTION

In 1620, as every youngster knows, the Pilgrims landed at Plymouth Rock. What is less commonly known is that the Pilgrims had originally planned to end their voyage in Virginia not in Massachusetts. What led them to change their minds? One of the voyagers recorded the following entry in his diary: "Our victuals are being much spente, especially our beere." One can only speculate about the changes wrought on the course of American history by the gastronomic inventory problem of the Pilgrims. Speculation is not required, however, in ascertaining the structure and level of competition in the beer industry today. Here economic analysis eliminates the need for conjecture.

Definition of the Industry

Beer is a potable product with four main ingredients.

1. Malt, which is simply barley (or some grain) that has been allowed to germinate in water and is then dried.
2. Flavoring adjuncts, usually hops and corn or rice, to give beer its lightness and provide the starch that the enzymes in the malt convert to sugar.
3. Cultured yeast, which ferments the beverage and feeds on the sugar content of the malt to produce alcohol and carbonic acid.
4. Water, which acts as a solvent for the other ingredients.

Because the process of *brewing* (or boiling) is so intrinsic to the making of beer, the industry is often called the brewing industry.

The brewing process does not produce a perfectly homogeneous product. The white beverage (spiced with a little raspberry syrup) that is favored in Berlin, the warm, dark-colored drink served by the English publican, and the near-freezing amber liquid kept in the cooler of the American convenience store all are beer. Generically, the term *beer* means any beverage brewed from a starchy (or farinaceous) grain. Because the grain is made into a malt that becomes the main substance of the beverage, another term for beer is malt liquor, or malt beverage. In this study, the terms *beer*, *malt liquor*, and *malt beverage* will be used broadly and interchangeably to include all such products as beer, ale, porter, stout, and malt liquor. Because the terms *beer* and *malt liquor* are also known as specific products that are distinct from each other and from other malt beverages, to avoid confusion these terms in the narrow sense will be preceded by the word *product*—for example, the product beer, the product malt liquor.[1]

For this study, then, beer includes a variety of products. It includes those products that are branded as beer; it also includes products branded as ale and malt liquor. The factor common to the beverages of this industry, and that which differentiates them from all other alcoholic and nonalcoholic beverages, is that all are brewed by a process of fermentation applied to a basic grain ingredient.

Note, however, that a unique production process is not the key to defining an industry. The concept of an industry implies a group of firms (or conceivably one firm) supplying a set of products that consumers, voting in the market place, find to be close substitutes for each other. To be sure, some avid drinkers of the product beer may not prefer to substitute, say, the product ale; but these people would prefer to substitute milk even less. The cross elasticity of demand is high between malt beverages. And the cross elasticity of demand between beer and other alcoholic beverages, for most consumers, is low.[2] It is this fungibility characteristic that enables the distinction of malt beverages as a separate industry to be made.

The delineation is supported, moreover, by the high cross elasticity of supply between the separate products of this industry. If a firm is producing some brand of beer and notices that ale production is very profitable, its management can shift to ale production with only moderate difficulty. A brewer would be much more hard-pressed to shift into a nonmalt beverage such as milk. For that matter, to shift to another alcoholic beverage such as wine or distilled spirits would be expensive. The cross elasticity of supply between malt beverages and other alcoholic beverages is very low.

Early History

Beer was a very common beverage in England in the 1600s and the early settlers in America had not only a taste for beer but also a supply of it on the ships that brought them. In 1625, in New Amsterdam, the first recorded public brewery was established. Other commercial brewing followed, although con-

---

[1] The product beer is the most commonly consumed malt beverage in the United States. In fact, the product beer commands such an overwhelming share of all malt beverage consumption that, for many purposes, the study of the beer industry is the study of the product beer.

[2] For certain individuals this figure may be relatively high. Some Germans claim the reason Dinkelager is such good beer is because it must compete with the fine wines also produced in the Stuttgart area.

siderable brewing was done also in homes in seventeenth-century America. All that was needed in the way of equipment at the time were a few vats, one for mashing, one for cooling, and one for fermenting. The resulting product would be scarcely recognizable (or consumed) as beer today. The process was very crude, the end result uncertain. Small wonder brewing was referred to as "an art and mystery."

Brewing was often publicly encouraged in early America. For example, the General Court of Massachusetts passed an act in 1789 to support the brewing of beer "as an important means of preserving the health of the citizens . . . and of preventing the pernicious effects of spiritous liquors." James Oglethorpe, trustee of the colony of Georgia, was even blunter: "Cheap beer is the only means to keep rum out."

Lager Beer: The Jumping Off Point

The 1840s and 1850s were important decades in the brewing industry. The product beer, in the basic form consumed today, was introduced in the 1840s with the brewing of lager beer.[3] Prior to lager beer's introduction, malt beverage consumption in America resembled English tastes—heavily oriented toward ale, porter, and stout. Lager beer represented the influence of German tastes and brewing skills. The influx of German immigrants provided not only skillful brewers, but also eager customers for this type of beer.

In 1851, a man named Valentin Blatz took over a small brewery in Milwaukee. Four years later, in the same city, another German, Frederick Miller, acquired a brewing establishment. And, one year afterward, a fellow named Joseph Schlitz decided to buy a brewery and go into the beer business for himself. The following year, in St. Louis, a soap manufacturer named Eberhard Anheuser joined with his son-in-law Adolphus Busch to begin what has become a not unsuccessful brewery. These are names now familiar to all beer drinkers. At the start of the decade in 1850, there were 431 brewers in the United States producing 750,000 barrels of beer.[4] By the end of that decade, 1269 brewers produced more than a million barrels of beer, dramatic evidence of the high expectations held by many of this industry's future.

The latter half of the nineteenth century saw not only the successful innovation of lager beer in America, but also the prospering of the industry through the adoption of several important technological advances that affected the production and marketing of malt beverages. Mechanical refrigeration greatly aided the production process as well as the storage of beer. Prior to this development, beer production was partly dependent on the amount of ice that could be cut from lakes and rivers in the winter. Cities such as St. Louis, which had

---

[3] Lager beer is bottom fermented—that is, the yeast settles to the bottom during fermentation. Also, lager beer is aged (or "lagered") to mellow. The result is a lighter, more effervescent potation.

[4] A barrel of beer contains 31 gallons or 446 eight-ounce glasses (allowing for spillage), or almost 14 cases of 24 twelve-ounce bottles.

underground caves where beer could be kept cool while aging, lost this (truly natural) advantage with the advent of mechanical refrigeration. Pasteurization, a process originally devised to preserve wine and beer, was adopted during this period. This meant that beer did not have to be kept cold, could be shipped into hot areas, and could be stored for a longer period of time without refermenting. Once the stability of beer was secured through pasteurization, the way was opened for wide-scale bottling and off-premise consumption of beer. In addition, developments in transportation technology enabled brewers to expand production beyond their local markets. The twentieth century saw the rise of the national brewer.

Prohibition

The twentieth century also saw the legal banning of beer sales. The temperance movement, which began as the promotion of voluntary moderation and abstention from hard liquors, slowly moved toward a goal of universal compulsory abstention from all alcoholic beverages. The beer industry seemed blissfully ignorant of the movement. Many brewers thought (or hoped) the movement would lead to a ban only on liquor.

In 1919, 36 states ratified the Eighteenth Amendment to enact the national prohibition of alcoholic beverages. This led many brewers simply to close up shop; some produced other products. Schlitz sold candy; Blatz produced industrial alcohol. Pabst made cheese, soft drinks, and even machinery. Anheuser-Busch and others built a profitable business selling malt syrup, which was used to make "home brew." Because a firm could not state the ultimate purpose of malt syrup, the product was marketed as an ingredient for making baked goods, such as cookies.

Prohibition lasted until April 1933. The rapidity with which brewers reopened after repeal was amazing. By June 1933, 31 brewers were in operation; in another year, the number was 756.

The Demand for Beer in the Post-World War II Period

The total market demand for beer exhibits seasonal fluctuations due to greater thirsts during hot weather. On an annual basis, the over-all demand began a slow decline in 1948 from a 1947 record sale of 87.2 million barrels. The 1947 figure was never surpassed until 1959, with sales of 87.6 million barrels. During this period, per capita consumption fell from 18.5 to 15.0 gallons in 1958. In the 1960s, total demand began to grow again at an average rate of better than 3 per cent per year. The year 1965 marked the first year with more than 100 million barrels sold, and the figure for 1974 was 145.5 million barrels. Per capita consumption has increased from 1958's level of 15 gallons to 1974's level of 21.1 gallons. The rightward shift in the demand curve for beer has been due to the increasing number of young people in the United States (the result of the post-World War II baby boom) and the lowering of age requirements in many populous states. In 1970–1973, 20 states lowered their legal drinking age. Moreover, the amount of geography in the United States that is "dry" has shrunk considerably. In addition, the increasing ease with which beer can be purchased and taken out has enhanced the increase in demand.

The demand for beer in the United States is not only seasonal, but also varies from region to region. The east north central and mountain states show the highest per capita consumption; the east south central and south Atlantic states show the lowest. By states, the demand for beer differs considerably. Alabama and Utah had per capita consumptions of 13.9 and 14.2 gallons in 1974, respectively. Needless to say, with a national per capita consumption in 1974 of 21.1 gallons, some states register a heavy demand to compensate for the more moderate states. In fact, 11 states have per capita figures of more than 24 gallons; of these, New Hampshire and Nevada outdistance all others with a per capita consumption of over 33 gallons. Parenthetically, the increasing demand for beer is not a phenomenon unique to the United States. The demand shift is the most stark in countries like Japan, where beer is now more popular than sake; in France and Italy, where beer sales have cut into wine consumption; in Russia, where beer drinkers queue up to purchase the drink, which the Communist party urges on citizens as a substitute for vodka; and in some African countries where beer is becoming a major industry and its consumption a sign of economic status. Worldwide consumption of malt beverages has doubled in the last 10 years.

Although economists are not able to measure price elasticity infallibly, statistical estimations indicate the market demand for beer to be inelastic, in the range of 0.7 to 0.9. However, brand attachment for most beer drinkers is not so strong as to make the demand for any particular malt beverage inelastic. Indeed, the demand for individual brands of beer appears to be quite elastic.[5] This elasticity places an important limitation on the market power of domestic brewers.

One indication of how responsive consumers have been to price changes can be seen in the records of a price discrimination case to be discussed later. Table 1 shows the percentage of the St. Louis market recorded on various dates by Anheuser-Busch, three important rival brewers, and the combined total of the other brewers. At the close of 1953, Anheuser-Busch's Budweiser beer was selling for 58 cents per case more than the three rivals and had 12.5 per cent of the market. Early in 1954, the price of Budweiser was cut 25 cents; but, because this was a wholesale price, it had only a small impact on the retail price. Still, the Anheuser-Busch market share increased.

In June 1954, Anheuser-Busch cut its price to $2.35 per case, the same as its rivals. By early in 1955, Budweiser was the largest beer seller in St. Louis. At that time, prices were increased by all the sellers in such a manner that Bud-

---

[5] Thomas F. Hogarty and Kenneth G. Elzinga, "The Demand for Beer," *Review of Economics and Statistics*, **54**:197 (May 1972). Income elasticity is approximately 0.4.

TABLE 1

Percentage of the St. Louis Market Recorded by Anheuser-Busch

	DEC. 1953	JUNE 1954	MAR. 1955	JULY 1955
Anheuser-Busch	12.5	16.6	39.3	21.0
Griesedieck Bros.	14.4	12.6	4.8	7.4
Falstaff	29.4	32.0	29.1	36.6
Griesedieck Western	38.9	33.0	23.1	27.8
Others	4.8	5.8	3.9	7.2

Source: Taken from *Federal Trade Commission* v. *Anheuser-Busch*, 363 U.S. 536 at 541. Subsequent evidence indicated that factors in addition to price accounted for the Griesedieck Bros.'s drop in market share.

weiser again sold at a differential of 30 cents per case. Note that the Anheuser-Busch market share then dropped, evidence that consumers will shift brands in response to price incentives.

II. MARKET STRUCTURE

One general conclusion of economic analysis is that consumers are more apt to be able to buy the exact product they want at the lowest price when they face a large number of independent rivals. When facing a monopolist (or tightly knit oligopoly), choice is reduced and the price is likely to be elevated. Because of this, the question of the *structure* of the beer industry—the total number and size distribution of firms arrayed before beer consumers—is of economic importance. Is the beer industry unconcentrated, with its customers courted by many firms, or concentrated, leaving beer drinkers with little choice?

In the post-World War II period, there have been two contrary trends at work in the industry, one leading to increased concentration, the other in the opposite direction. On the one hand, there has been a marked decline in the number of brewers in the United States. At the same time, there has been an increase in the size of the market area potentially served by existing brewers. We shall examine each of these trends in turn.

The Decline in Numbers

The decline in the number of individual plants and independent companies in the brewing industry has been dramatic. In 1935, shortly after repeal, there were 750 brewing plants operating in the United States. Since that time the number has declined, dropping in every single year with the exception of three, to a total of 108 in 1974. Table 2 shows the decline in the number of companies and plants. Note that, in the period shown, the number of breweries was more

TABLE 2

YEAR	INDEPENDENT COMPANIES	SEPARATE PLANTS
1947	404	465
1954	263	310
1958	211	252
1963	150	211
1967	93	176
1973	62	110
1974	58	108

Source: Adapted from *Breweries Authorized to Operate*, Department of the Treasury, Bureau of Alcohol, Tobacco, and Firearms (Washington, D.C.: U.S. Government Printing Office), various years; and *Modern Brewery Age, Blue Book* (Stamford, Conn.: Modern Brewery Age Publishing Co., various years).

than quartered (although beer sales increased by more than 50 million barrels). Few other American industries have undergone a similar structural shake-up.

Concomitant with the decline in the number of companies has been the increasing share of national business done by the largest brewers. As shown in Table 3, in 1947, the top five companies accounted for 19 per cent of the industry's sales; in 1974 their share was almost 64 per cent.

TABLE 3
Percentage of Sales by Top Brewers

YEAR	5 LARGEST	10 LARGEST
1947	19.0	28.2
1954	24.9	38.3
1958	28.5	45.2
1964	39.0	58.2
1968	47.6	63.2
1973	59.4	77.0
1974	64.0	80.8

Source: Adapted from A. Horowitz and I. Horowitz, "The Beer Industry," *Business Horizons*, **10**:14 (1967), and various trade publications.

The Widening of Markets

To understand the offsetting structural factor to this decline in brewing companies, one must realize that, in the days of hundreds of brewing companies, most beer drinkers faced an actual choice of only a few brewers. This was because the majority of brewers were small and the geographic market area they served was severely limited. Beer is an expensive product to ship, relative to its value, and few brewers could afford to compete in the "home markets" of distant brewers.

Thus, at one time it was very meaningful to speak of local, regional, and national brewers. Of these, the local brewer who brewed for a small market, perhaps smaller than a single state, often only a single metropolitan area, was the most common. The regional brewer was multistate, but usually encompassed no more than two or three states. The national brewers, those selling in all, or almost all, the states, were very few in number. In addition, it was very uncommon for a firm to operate more than one plant.

Today, to talk of local, regional, and national brewers is still common parlance in the industry, but the terms are less meaningful than in the past. The average geographic market served by one brewer from one plant has widened because of the economies of large-scale production and, to some extent, marketing. With the average-size brewing plant much larger today, the brewing company may extend itself geographically to maintain capacity operations.

For example, the Stroh Brewing Company operates out of one plant in Detroit, Michigan. In 1957, it sold beer in 7 states; by 1974, it sold in 15 states and considers it possible to ship to most states east of the Mississippi on a profitable basis, an example of the exploding scope of the market served by regional brewers.

Supporting the ability to serve new geographic regions is the propensity on the part of large brewers now to operate more than one plant. In 1955, the top ten brewers operated 10 breweries, only one apiece. In 1961, the top ten operated 40 plants and, by 1973, 46 plants.

Size of the Market

The problem of determining the degree of concentration in brewing is inextricably tied up with delineating just how wide the markets are for beer. If there is one market, a national one, then concentration statistics for the entire nation are relevant. But if brewing, like cement or milk, has regional markets, then delineating their boundaries is necessary before the industry's structure can be ascertained.

The Federal courts have to solve this problem when deciding antimerger cases in the brewing industry.[6] A couple of examples taken from their attempts will indicate that, to understand the supply and demand forces in this industry, one must look to a wide geographic market, but probably not so wide as to include the entire country.

---

[6] In order to determine the possible effect of a merger on competition, the relevant geographic market has to be determined.

In evaluating the merger of Schlitz with a California brewer and its stock control over another western brewer, a California district court, noting that freight rates were important in beer marketing, singled out an eight-western-state area as a separate geographic market.[7] The judge was impressed by the fact that, in 1963, 80 per cent of the beer sold in this area was also produced there and 94 per cent of the beer produced in the area that year was sold there. The Continental Divide was seen as a transportation barrier of sorts from outside the area, as evidenced by those brewers who, having plants both in the eight-state area and outside, generally supplied the eight-state area from their western plants only.

Given these figures, many economists would agree that, if one wants to see what determines the supply and demand for beer in this eight-state area, one need be concerned only slightly, if at all, by supply-and-demand conditions in the regions east of the Continental Divide. Even here, however, the geographic area is not perfectly clear-cut. Adolph Coors Company, located in Colorado, outside the eight-state area, was the leading seller of beer in the eight-state area in 1963, with 13.6 per cent of the total sales; some economists might well argue that any market area that overlooks this important seller overlooks an important force on the supply side. The market, in its economic sense, should include all the buyers and sellers that are important in explaining the supply-and-demand conditions in any one place.

In another case involving the merger of two brewers located in Wisconsin, the Antitrust Division asked an eminent economist at nearby Northwestern University to testify in support of the view that Wisconsin is a separate market for beer. The economics professor told the government lawyers this position was economically untenable. Nevertheless, the lawyers persisted and eventually persuaded the Supreme Court that Wisconsin, by itself, is "a distinguishable and economically significant market for the sale of beer."[8]

Although Wisconsin may be a separate market for legal purposes, to single it out as a meaningful market in the economic sense is to draw the market boundaries too narrowly. In 1974, brewers in the state of Wisconsin sold 18.5 million barrels of beer; that year, consumers in Wisconsin bought 4.4 million barrels of beer.

Because beer is also "imported" into Wisconsin from brewers in other states, obviously more than three fourths of Wisconsin beer is "exported" for sale outside the state. To say, then, that Wisconsin is a separate geographic market is to overlook the impact of over three fourths of the production in that state, not to mention the impact on the supply of beer coming into Wisconsin and competing with the "home" brewers. In 1961, the time of the antitrust contest, roughly 25 per cent of the beer consumed in Wisconsin was not produced there.[9]

Consequently, one cannot explain the price of beer in Wisconsin without

---

[7] See *United States* v. *Jos. Schlitz*, 253 F. Supp. 129 (1966); aff'd. 385 U.S. 37 (1966). The states were California, Oregon, Washington, Nevada, Idaho, Montana, Utah, and Arizona.

[8] *United States* v. *Pabst*, 384 U.S. 546 (1966) at 559.

[9] Ibid. Trial transcripts: testimony of M. A. Adelman, p. 2007.

looking at the supply-and-demand conditions in other states that buy the bulk of Wisconsin's beer production. In this case, the court erred by singling out the state of Wisconsin as an economically meaningful market.

Despite the difficulties of ascertaining with numerical exactness the geographic scope of the brewing industry, brewing *is* a concentrated industry. Consider the case of a beer consumer in Wisconsin. In 1955, there were 43 breweries operating in Wisconsin; by 1973, this figure had fallen to nine, a drop of 80 per cent. In 1973, seven "out-state" brewing companies exported beer into Wisconsin, so clearly the Wisconsin beer drinker is now courted by fewer suitors. It is probable that the forces that work to widen markets are more than offset by the forces that increase concentration.

Reasons for the Decline in the Number of Brewers

What are the reasons for the precipitous drop in the number of rival brewers? In a sense, each brewer's demise is unique. But many have common characteristics. In this section, two factors leading to the decline in brewers will be considered: mergers and economies of scale. In a later section, the effect of entry conditions and product differentiation on the industry's structure will be assessed.

Mergers

The conventional (and often accurate) explanation for an industry's oligopolization is a merger-acquisition trend among the industry's firms. In the period 1958–1973, the 30 leading brewers made approximately 55 acquisitions. Because some of the acquiring firms are well-known brewers, it might seem, at first glance, that mergers are the primary cause of the rising concentration in the industry. Actually, mergers explain practically none of the increase.

Leonard Weiss developed a means of delineating the impact of mergers on an industry's structure and found that, in the period 1947–1958, only a small part of the increase in concentration in brewing was due to mergers.[10] Doing the same calculations for the period 1959–1972, when the share of the top four almost doubled, indicates that, once again, mergers accounted for practically none of the increase. The top four firms have, in recent years, refrained from growth by merger and have expanded entirely by internal growth. Even with the merger route closed off, their market shares have increased. Nevertheless, it is instructive to examine more closely the role of mergers in this industry because the antimerger law has left an important stamp on this industry's present structure. Moreover, some important antitrust doctrine has been established through cases brought in this industry.

Mergers have one of three effects on competition:

1. They strengthen it, by forming a viable rival where one previously did not exist.

[10] "An Evaluation of Mergers in Six Industries," *Review of Economics and Statistics*, **42**:172 (May 1965).

2. They lessen it, by removing from the scene an important established or potential rival.
3. There is no recognizable effect.

Mergers in brewing have been of all three types.

In some cases, brewers have been strengthened through their acquisition programs. G. Heileman Brewing Company, by way of example, acquired four moderately sized breweries in the period 1967–1974. Through a program of selectively scrapping some and modernizing and expanding others, Heileman has become one of the more vigorous brewers of less than national scope.

Most of the mergers in the beer industry did not involve financially successful firms. Generally, they represented the demise of an inefficient firm, salvaging some remainder of its worth by selling out to another brewer. The acquiring brewer gained no market power but might have benefited by securing the barrelage to bring one plant to full capacity or gain access to an improved distribution network or new territory. Mergers such as these are not the *cause* of structural change; rather, they are the effect, as firms exit through the merger route. This type of merger should be allowed—even encouraged—for, in a roundabout way, easing the exit process facilitates entry. If exit is difficult, potential aspirants will be unlikely to enter any industry. The owner of a small Wisconsin brewery has complained that the antimerger law is now so stringent that " We couldn't sell out now. . . . We would have to just quit."[11]

But not all of the mergers in brewing can be dismissed as having salutary or *de minimus* effects on competition. The first antimerger action by the Antitrust Division in the beer industry was taken in 1958 against the industry's leader, Anheuser-Busch. Anheuser-Busch had purchased the Miami brewery of American Brewing Company. Florida, because of its unique geography, faces potential competition from out-state brewers from only one direction. The government argued that this merger would eliminate American Brewing as an independent brewer and remove its rivalry with Anheuser-Busch in Florida. The final judgment called for Anheuser-Busch to sell this brewery and refrain from buying any others without court approval for a period of 5 years.[12] Due to this action, Anheuser-Busch has foregone any policy of acquiring rival brewers and has since undertaken an extensive program of building new plants in Florida and other locations.

The Schlitz Brewing Company, the second-largest brewer in the country, also has been found in violation of the antimerger law. In 1961, Schlitz acquired Burgermeister Brewing Corporation, a brewer of popular price beer located in San Francisco. In 1964, it purchased controlling interest in John Labatt, a Canadian brewery that in turn controlled, through stock interest, General Brewing Corporation, a U.S. firm. Schlitz, therefore, gained control of General Brewing.

---

[11] "A Small Brewery's Fight for Survival," *Journal Courier*, Oct. 28, 1973, p. 24. (The newspaper is published in Jacksonville, Ill.)

[12] *United States* v. *Anheuser-Busch*, 1960 CCH Trade Cases, para. 69,599.

Both Burgermeister and General Brewing (brewer of Lucky Lager beer) were prominent regional brewers in the west. In addition, Labatt was attempting to introduce its own premium price Canadian beer into the United States through the General Brewing sales organization. Through the merger route, Schlitz could have quickly become the dominant seller of popular price beer in the west, eliminated two rival sellers of popular price beer in the process, and been able to stop the further introduction of Labatt premium price beer in competition with its own premium brand.

A district court correctly found that both acquisitions would likely lessen competition in the beer industry. The Supreme Court, on an appeal by Schlitz, affirmed the lower court, and Schlitz was ordered to sell the Burgermeister assets and divest itself of the Labatt stock. Since this time Schlitz has foregone the merger route and has expanded through internal growth.

In 1958, the Pabst Brewing Company acquired the Blatz Brewing Company. In 1957, Pabst was the tenth largest brewer in the country; Blatz was the eighteenth. The acquisition catapulted Pabst to number five in the industry and eliminated both the Pabst–Blatz rivalry in the 40 states in which Blatz sold and the potential rivalry of Blatz in the remaining states. By 1961, the combined Pabst–Blatz amalgamation was the third largest seller of beer in the nation. In 1959, the Antitrust Division challenged this merger. The wheels of justice revolved sluggishly, but, after more than a decade, during which three court decisions were made, Pabst was finally required to sell Blatz. Essentially, the Blatz brewery had already been closed down, so only the brand could be sold, and this was done in 1969 to the G. Heileman Brewing Company.

The fifth-largest brewer in the country, the Adolph Coors Company, has never made an acquisition. Its stated policy is to brew its beer only in one location: the town of Golden, Colorado. There are no other breweries in town to acquire, even if the antimerger law would permit such a purchase (which it would not). The fourth-largest brewer in the country, the Miller Brewing Company, was itself the subject of an acquisition, a purely conglomerate one, when it was acquired in 1969 by Philip Morris.

While the *Pabst* case established important legal doctrine regarding mergers between *actual* rivals, Falstaff's acquisition of the Narragansett Brewing Company, in 1965, led to the Supreme Court's expounding on the law as it applied to mergers among *potential* rivals.[13] In this instance, Falstaff had not been a seller in the New England area; Narragansett was the largest seller there. At the time of the suit's filing, Falstaff was the fourth-largest brewer in the country and had stated its intentions to become nationwide. Thus, the merger would have removed whatever competitive force was exerted "in the wings" by Falstaff as well as eliminated the possibility that Falstaff would enter the New England market de novo. The Antitrust Division would have preferred Falstaff's building a new plant in the area or acquiring a small New England brewer. Because Falstaff denied ever intending to enter New England other than by

[13] *United States* v. *Falstaff Brewing Corp.*, 410 U.S. 526 (1973).

major acquisition, the prominent issue in the case was whether Falstaff could manifest a significant force of potential competition in New England and what sort of evidence would be supportive of such a contention. The Supreme Court, in a split decision, reversed the district court's dismissal of the case and remanded it for further factual consideration of the potential competition issue. In the fall of 1974, almost a decade after the merger's consummation, the district court held that this corporate union did not violate the law.

The antimerger law has made an imprint on the structure of this industry. Its enforcement has been partly responsible for the emphasis on internal growth by the leading brewers. However, its application now can do little to stem the rising concentration or the demise of independent brewers. The vast majority of mergers consummated in this industry involve less than optimum-sized plants or firms with declining sales.

Economies of Scale

Economies of scale pertain to the size of the plant needed to attain the lowest unit costs. Economies of scale exist if "big plants" produce at lower unit costs than small ones. When discussing economies of scale, economists generally plot a smooth, continuous average cost curve that is the envelope of a host of similarly curvaceous short-run average cost curves, each one representing a different size. What is seldom mentioned in the discussion of these curves, however, is that great confidence cannot be attached to the location of any point on these cost curves, in spite of their appearance of a precision rendering.

With this caveat firmly in mind, Figure 1 is a representation of economies of scale in the brewing industry. Note first the fairly sharp decline in long-run unit costs until a plant size of 1.25 million barrels per year of capacity is reached. This size brewery is approximately the minimum efficient size (MES) plant. Beyond this, costs continue to decline, but less sharply, until a capacity of 4.5 million barrels (an enormous brewery) is attained. Here economies of large scale seem to be fully exploited.[14]

Table 4 shows one method used by economists to estimate the extent of economies of scale: the survivor test. This test, like all techniques for estimating economies of scale, is not without its difficulties.[15] But, as its name implies, it distinguishes those size plants that have been surviving over time. In brewing, there has been a steady decline (dramatic in some cases) for every brewery size under a 1-million-barrel capacity. Moreover, the truly large brewing operations are not only surviving but growing in number, *prima facie* evidence of their lower unit costs. Corroborating the data in Figure 1 and Table 4 is the size of the new plants built since 1958. Breweries built since then have averaged almost 2 million barrels in capacity, and the most recent of these have averaged almost 2.5 million. One can understand much better the concentration statistics in

[14] See Kenneth G. Elzinga, "The Restructuring of the U.S. Brewing Industry," *Industrial Organization Review*, **1**:105–109 (1973) and the sources cited therein.
[15] See William G. Shepherd, "What Does the Survivor Technique Show About Economies of Scale?" *Southern Economic Journal*, **34**:113 (July 1967).

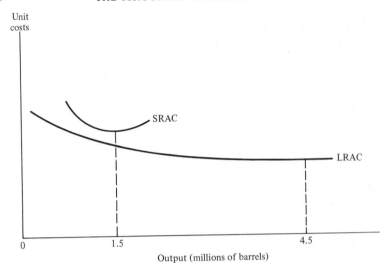

FIGURE 1
Economies of scale in brewing.

TABLE 4
Surviving Breweries by Capacity: 1959–1973

LISTED CAPACITY BARRELS (000)	1959	1961	1963	1965	1967	1969	1971	1973
0–25	11	9	8	7	3	3	2	2
26–100	57	51	46	44	33	23	19	11
101–250	51	44	39	30	26	23	19	11
251–500	40	37	33	24	18	14	14	10
501–750	14	15	13	12	13	15	12	5
751–1000	16	19	20	20	22	20	20	15
1001–1500	14	14	12	13	15	13	13	13
1501–2000	4	5	5	3	3	8	8	7
2001–3000	5	6	6	7	5	6	9	9
3001–4000	3	3	4	5	5	3	3	3
4001+	2	2	3	3	4	7	7	11

Source: Compiled from plant capacity figures listed in the *Modern Brewery Age Blue Book* (Stamford, Conn.: Modern Brewery Age Publishing Co., various years), and industry trade sources. These figures do not include plants listed only on a company-consolidated basis (in the case of multiplant firms) or single-plant firms not reporting capacity in the *Blue Book*. Most plants list their capacity.

brewing after learning that the average plant size of the top four brewers is about 2.8-million barrels in capacity.

Figure 1 also has drawn on it a single short-run average cost curve above the long-run average cost curve. A long-run cost curve itself represents the envelope of different-sized plants, each of which uses the latest in capital equipment and production techniques. The curve standing by itself better portrays the situation of many breweries that have met (or will meet) their demise. They are not only too small to exploit all the scale economies, but their capital equipment is of such an outmoded vintage that their costs are elevated even more.

Some of the economies from larger operations come in the packaging of the beer. The bottling lines at the new Schlitz plants in Winston-Salem and Memphis and the Pabst plant in Georgia have line speeds of 750 to 800 bottles per minute. The canning lines are even faster: 1200 to 2400 cans per minute. It would take a brewery of substantial brewing capacity just to keep such equipment fully utilized. There are other savings in labor for large brewing tanks as well as economies in the mechanization of warehousing and shipping. The vintage capital effect can be seen in the statistics, which show Schlitz producing more than 9000 barrels of beer per worker in its North Carolina and Tennessee plants, while the comparable figure for the not insubstantial (but less modern) Rheingold and Falstaff breweries is 2300 and 3000, respectively. Indeed, Schlitz recently found it less costly to serve its New England customers from Winston-Salem than from its (now closed) Brooklyn plant; the transportation-cost disadvantage (relative to Brooklyn) was more than offset by the cost-savings in production enjoyed by the Tarheel establishment.

In a broad sense, economies of scale relate not only to some finite productive capacity, but also to management's ability to use the capacity efficiently. Shortly after repeal in 1933, there was a flood of new entrants into the brewing industry, all expecting to be faced with thirsty customers. However, the demand for beer was unexpectedly low after repeal. From a high of 750 brewers operating in 1935, almost 100 were quickly eliminated in but 5 years. Quite a few of these enterprises had operated before prohibition, but many were under new management. Some were family-owned firms, and heredity had been cruel to the second or third generations, not endowing them with the brewing and/or managerial capabilities of their fathers or grandfathers. Competitive pressures, with no respect for nepotism, eliminated such breweries.[16]

The more recent closures, however, include soundly managed firms that produced salable beer.[17] However, the plants were either too old or too small (or both) to competitively brew and market beer. A detailed study was made of the closures during the period July 1, 1958, through the end of 1972. During this period, 138 brewing plants discontinued operations. At the start of this period,

---

[16] Alfred Marshall saw this phenomenon as one of the important factors limiting the growth and size of firms and an important determinant in the preservation of competition. See his *Principles of Economics*, C. W. Guillebaud, ed. (New York: Macmillan, 1961), pp. 315–317.

[17] This is evidenced by the fact that the brand names and trademarks of many of these firms are being continued by other breweries.

the average plant capacity in the whole industry was about 560,000 barrels. By the end of the period, as brewers (generally the largest ones) exploited the economies of large, capital-intensive plants, the average brewery produced about 1.3 million barrels. But the 138 plants that exited from the industry had an average capacity of fewer than 350,000 barrels, well under the MES of Figure 1. Moreover, at the time of their demise, these breweries were operating at only 39 per cent of their capacity; so they were not even at the least cost combination of what were probably inefficient plants.

Conceivably, a small brewer in a metropolitan area, by serving only that area and keeping transportation costs at a minimum, could survive in today's industry by finding a special niche for itself. This seems to be the status of San Francisco's tiny Anchor Steam Brewery. However, such cases will be exceptions that prove rules. In brewing, unlike many manufacturing industries where optimum sized plants seem to be getting smaller, large, capital-intensive brewing plants are necessary to exploit scale economies and survive in the industry. In markets where vigorous competitive pressures exist, firms that do not exploit scale economies or operate with internal efficiency will not survive. This has been the fate of many brewers; they have exited from the industry because of inefficient plants, poor management, or both.

The Condition of Entry

The ease with which outsiders can enter an industry is a structural characteristic of great importance in ensuring competitive performance. If entry is easy, if potential rivals are lurking in the wings, so to speak, existing firms will be reluctant to use what market power they may have to raise prices—lest they encourage an outbreak of fresh competition. On the other hand, if entry is barred, perhaps by a patent or government license, existing firms will find the potential for garnering monopoly gains greatly enhanced.

Entry into the beer industry is not hindered by the traditional barriers of patents and exclusive government grants. Nor is the monopolization of key resources or economies of scale so important that an efficient entrant would have to supply an enormous share of industry output. However, the sheer expense of entering the beer industry is considerable (although it would be less if profits were higher, thereby making credit easier to acquire). With the expiration of the small brewery has come the demise of the inexpensive brewery. The price of a modern 2-million-barrel brewery is $70 million. And, once the brewery is built, the cost of introducing the new brew will also be high because entrants will have to overcome the entrenched product differentiation of the established brewers.

A look at the record indicates the low probability of any potential threat facing existing producers of beer from outside aspirants. Since World War II only five new firms have constructed breweries in this country. Four failed. In the past, this paucity of entry was explained by the relatively low profitability of the industry, the slow increase in demand, and the ominous fate of so many existing firms.

The beer industry has been classed as one with moderate, although increasing, barriers to entry.[18] Presently, the most promising source of new competition is that of an established brewer moving into a new geographic market, or the importation of foreign beer. Beer imports to the United States, most of which come from the Netherlands and Germany, have increased about 60 per cent in the period 1967–1974. However, imports represent less than 1 per cent of domestic consumption, and most imports are expensive brands that sell in the super-premium category.[19]

Product Differentiation

To the extent customers are persuaded that the product of one firm is superior to that of others, the favored firm can raise its price somewhat without losing these customers. This phenomenon is called product differentiation. Interestingly, studies have shown that under test conditions beer drinkers cannot distinguish between brands of beer.[20] And, there is little persuasive evidence that the more expensive brands cost proportionately more to produce. Yet, considerable talent and resources are devoted to publicizing real or imagined differences in beers, with the hope being to produce product differentiation.

One indicator of the relative amount of advertising done by industries is the ratio of advertising expenditures to sales. One economist had called any percentage of 5 per cent a "significantly . . . substantial level."[21] For some companies in the soap, cosmetic, and drug industries, this ratio is greater than 10 per cent. For the malt beverage industry, this ratio is notable but has been falling. In the years 1961–1965 it was close to 7 per cent; in 1969, it approached 5 per cent, and by 1971 it was 4.3 per cent.[22]

The amount spent on advertising beer is large, and this is not surprising. There are millions of actual and potential beer drinkers a brewer wants to inform of the quality and availability of his product. New customers come of age and producers seek to inform them; old customers may forget and producers seek to remind them. Nevertheless, at some stage, massive advertising offers only inframarginal information and may have the effect of entrenching the industry leaders. Unfortunately, economic analysis does not provide a tool for determining at what stage advertising becomes redundant and wasteful.

---

[18] H. Michael Mann, "Seller Concentration, Barriers to Entry, and Rates of Return in Thirty Industries, 1950–1960," *Review of Economics and Statistics*, 48:299 (Aug. 1966).

[19] The United States exports much less beer than it imports. Most U.S. beer exports go to Caribbean countries and Australia.

[20] For examples, see J. Douglas McConnell, "An Experimental Examination of the Price-Quantity Relationship," *Journal of Business*, 41:439 (Oct. 1968); F. B. Meeker and R. D. Bettencourt, "Perceptual Learning of Discrimination in Beertasting: Effects of Ss' Belief in Their Ability to Discriminate," (Paper delivered at the Western Psychological Association Meeting, Apr. 1973); and Ralph I. Ellison and Kenneth P. Uhl, "Influence of Beer Brand Identification on Taste Perception," *Journal of Marketing Research* 1:36 (Aug. 1964).

[21] Joe S. Bain, *Industrial Organization* (New York: Wiley, 1969), pp. 390–391.

[22] As calculated from U.S. Department of the Treasury, *Corporation Source Book of Statistics of Income* (Washington, D.C.: U.S. Government Printing Office), various years. The Treasury data include figures for the malt industry as well. Because the product malt is not as extensively advertised as beer, this understates somewhat the actual ratio for brewing.

The most absorbing aspect of product differentiation in this industry is that attached to "premium beer." The phenomenon of the premium beer began years ago when a few brewers decided to attempt to sell their beer nationally and added a price premium to offset incremental transportation costs encountered in shipping greater distances. To secure the higher price, the beer was promoted as superior in taste and quality, allegedly because of the brewing expertise found in their locations. Although, at one time, the premium price was absorbed by higher shipping costs, the construction of efficient, regionally dispersed breweries by most of the large shippers now eliminates the transportation disadvantage. But the premium image remains. Thus, with transportation costs equalized, and with production costs generally being lower, these firms are now able to afford vigorous advertising (and price-cutting) campaigns in areas where regional and local brewers were once the largest sellers.

The national brewers also have two other advertising advantages: (1) None of their advertising is "wasted," whereas regional brewers do not always find media markets (especially in television) that coincide with their selling territories; and (2) their advertising investment is less likely to be lost when a customer moves to another part of the country.[23] Still, advertising presents no inevitable relationship between firm growth and promotion expenditures. It is well known that the rapid growth of Coors has occurred with relatively low advertising expenditures; and even though the advertising-sales ratio for this industry is declining, the concentration trend continues.

III. CONDUCT

Pricing

Judging from the early records of the preprohibition beer industry, life in the industry was very competitive. Entry was easy and producers were many. Economic theory would predict a competitive industry given these two characteristics, and the evidence bears this out. Some brewers made a fortune and perhaps held some market power; they were also the ones that pioneered new techniques for producing and marketing quality malt beverages.

In fact, the early beer industry offers a classic example of the predictions of price theory. Given the inelastic demand, brewers saw the obvious advantages to monopolizing the industry, raising prices, and gleaning monopoly profits. Various types of loosely and tightly knit cartels were seen as advantageous, but the difficulty of coordinating so many brewers and the lack of any barriers to entry prevented any of these efforts from being successful, at least for long. The degree of competition is evidenced by reading this plea from Adolphus Busch to Captain Pabst:

[23] Yoram Peles, "Economies of Scale in Advertising Beer and Cigarettes, *Journal of Business*, **44**:32 (Jan. 1971).

I hope also to be able to demonstrate to you that by the present way competition is running we are only hurting each other in a real foolish way. The traveling agents . . . always endeavor to reduce prices and send such reports to their respective home offices as are generally not correct and only tend to bring forth competition that helps to ruin the profits . . . all large manufacturing interests are now working in harmony . . . and only the brewers are behind as usual; instead of combining their efforts and securing their own interest, they are fighting each other and running the profits down, so that the pleasures of managing a brewery have been diminished a good deal.[24]

This is the sort of letter a competitive market structure should elicit. A year earlier, the Western Shipping Brewers' Association had been formed to divide markets and maintain prices in the Midwest. There is no evidence that it was successful—except in abolishing the trade practice of giving away expensive novelties such as knives and ash trays to retail dealers.

The beer industry also escaped the horizontal mergers that transformed the structure of so many industries—such as steel, whiskey, petroleum, tobacco, and farm equipment—during the first great merger movement. There were attempts, mostly by British businessmen, to combine the large brewers during this time. One attempt called for the amalgamation of Pabst, Schlitz, Miller, Anheuser-Busch, and Lemp into one company, a feat that, had it been successful, would have greatly altered the structure and degree of competition in the industry. But the attempt failed and brewing entered prohibition with a competitive structure that responded with competitive prices.

The Pricing Pattern

Basing point pricing systems, which had been common in industries like steel and cement, have never been representative of pricing in the beer industry. Instead, beer is generally sold f.o.b. the brewery; and prices vary according to differences in transportation costs, taxes, and competitive conditions.

The present pattern of prices dates back to the turn of the century with the introduction of premium beers, an aspect of the industry discussed earlier. These brands will generally be priced just above the price level of "popular" price beers that themselves will be a shade above "local" (or "price" or "shelf") beer. For example, in California, Schlitz and Labatt are premium price beers, Lucky Lager is at popular prices, and Fisher is in the third category. A more contemporary category is the superpremium, a beer selling at a price above premium. A number of major brewers market their own brand of superpremiums, and most imported beers fall in this price category.

This is not to say that the differential is an exact and predictable paradigm, for some beers do not seem to fit into this tripartite pattern. In California, Coors and Olympia have sold at a price between the premium and popular price beers. On the other hand Coors beer, which was "bootlegged" out of that brewer's western marketing area, sold (rather rapidly) in Washington, D.C., at the

[24] Thomas C. Cochran, *The Pabst Brewing Company* (New York: New York University Press, 1948), p. 151. (Letter of Jan. 3, 1889.)

super-superpremium price of $3.30 per six-pack, more than twice the market price of premium brands. Moreover, at times, the premium beers will be selling at a price that matches those of regional brewers. In fact, this differential has narrowed over the years. Pabst, one of the initiators of the premium price beer, is now sold at popular prices, as is Blatz. Pabst's jump in rank after going popular attests to the high cross elasticity of demand among beer brands.

In spite of these situations, it is still common to talk of a three-part price pattern. Anheuser-Busch once conducted a survey involving 113,305 price comparisons in 78 areas. In more than 100,000 comparisons, a differential of 5 cents per can, or per 12-ounce bottle, existed between Budweiser and the popular priced beers. In more than 90 per cent of the comparisons, a 10-cent differential existed over local beers.

Note again that the pattern for beer prices is different from the price differentials that exist between various grades of lumber, steel, or aluminum. In these latter cases, the differential is attributable to some identifiable physical characteristic of the product. In the case of malt beverages, price differences are in part due to customers' tastes and are, thus, subjective. Beer drinkers have not distinguished themselves by their ability to discern taste differences or brand identities when a beer's corporate genus is kept secret.

The wholesale price index suggests something about the competitive nature of the pricing process in brewing. During the decade 1963–1973, wholesale prices of beer rose at an annual average rate of less than 1.5 per cent. Even in the 2 years between 1971–1973, when the prices of almost all food and beverage products began to escalate, the wholesale price index for malt beverages went from a 1971 average of 110.2 to a 1973 average of only 111.6. Indeed, in 1973, when the industry had permission from the Cost of Living Council to raise prices (because of cost increases), competitive pressures prevented this price adjustment. In 1974, the substantial increase in costs, especially for containers and grain, finally did manifest itself in significant price increases for the industry: about 8 per cent. The pricing of beer remains a competitive process. But inflation has kicked up the nominal price and the day will never return when the beer drinker in, say, Cincinnati can go to "Glossner's or Billiod's where the bartender put a mug on a scale and then added beer until it weighed a pound more —at a cost of 3 cents."[25]

Price Discrimination

In 1955, the Federal Trade Commission (FTC) issued a complaint against Anheuser-Busch, charging it with unlawful price discrimination. Anheuser-Busch had dropped the price of its premium brand to all buyers in the St. Louis area; but it did not make this reduction in any other areas. The FTC maintained that this was price discrimination and the result would be to impair the intensity of competition by diverting beer sales from the Anheuser-Busch regional rivals in St. Louis to Anheuser-Busch.

---

[25] William L. Downard, *The Cincinnati Brewing Industry* (Athens: Ohio University Press, 1973), p. 6.

The charge against Anheuser-Busch was brought under Section 2(a) of the Robinson-Patman Act. Proof of such a violation involves answering three questions:

1. Is there price discrimination?
2. If so, does the respondent have a defense?
3. If not, might the discrimination lessen competition?

Reasonable individuals disagreed strongly on the answer to each of these questions in this matter.

There was no doubt that, after the price cut, Anheuser-Busch's Budweiser brand beer was selling for less money per case in St. Louis than anywhere in the country, and that this differential could not be explained fully by the lower transportation costs from the Anheuser-Busch brewery in St. Louis. Query: Is this automatically price discrimination?

The circuit court of appeals said no. It argued that price discrimination, as construed in antitrust, could not exist unless different prices were charged to competing purchasers. The circuit court put it this way:

> Anheuser-Busch did not thereby discriminate among its local competitors in the St. Louis area. By its cuts, Anheuser-Busch employed the same means of competition against all of them. Moreover, it did not discriminate among those who bought its beer in the St. Louis area; all could buy at the same price.[26]

This court argued that a mere price differential is not price discrimination unless some competitive relationship exists between the customers paying different prices, so that the ones paying the lower price have a competitive advantage.

The FTC and, ultimately, the Supreme Court disagreed with this interpretation. The Court said price discrimination is "selling the same kind of goods cheaper to one purchaser than to another" and, thereby, overruled the circuit court.[27]

Ever since the "Detroit case,"[28] a defense to a charge of price discrimination has been to show that one's lower price was offered to meet the equally low price of a rival. Prior to the FTC complaint, Budweiser was selling at $2.93 per case in St. Louis; its rivals were three regional brewers selling at $2.35 per case. In two successive cuts, Anheuser-Busch dropped to $2.35. Query: Could not Anheuser-Busch argue that it was only meeting the equally low price of its rivals?

Anheuser-Busch tried, but, interestingly, the FTC rejected this defense. Note what this implies: Anheuser-Busch went on record, so to speak, that its premium beer, Budweiser, is the same product as popular price beer—that is, "beer is beer." The FTC, however, argued that, at $2.35 a case, Anheuser-Busch "was selling *more value* than its competitors were . . . the consumer has proved . . .

---

[26] *Anheuser-Busch, Inc. v. Federal Trade Commission*, 265 F.2d 677 (7th Cir. 1959) at 681.
[27] *Federal Trade Commission v. Anheuser-Busch, Inc.*, 363 U.S. 536 (1960) at 549.
[28] *Federal Trade Commission v. Standard Oil*, 355 U.S. 396 (1958).

that [he] will pay more for Budweiser than . . . for many other beers."[29] Note that this statement comes very close to saying that Budweiser, because of its "superior public acceptance," should, and must, be priced at a differential over regional and local beers.

After the Supreme Court ruled that Anheuser-Busch had priced in a discriminatory fashion, the circuit court had to decide whether competition might be lessened by Anheuser-Busch's St. Louis pricing practice. The FTC, arguing from the figures given earlier on the changing market shares in St. Louis, said yes, that this practice would give Anheuser-Busch market power in St. Louis by increasing its market share.

. The circuit court disagreed, ruling that the simple diversion of business was not an indication that competition in St. Louis was being lessened. The court's decision pointed out that Anheuser-Busch was not subsidizing St. Louis with revenues from other markets, and that none of the Anheuser-Busch rivals in St. Louis had felt so "pushed" as to lower its prices in response to the Anheuser Busch cut. The only result was that consumers of beer in St. Louis could buy Budweiser for less money, which, the court felt, is what market competition is all about.

Consider another important issue here: What if the FTC had won its case and Anheuser-Busch had been barred from making this price cut in St. Louis? One might argue that competition would be increased, for companies would be prevented from making selective price cuts to eliminate smaller rivals or to enforce price leadership. But there is another possible implication of this per se approach to selective price cutting in the beer industry. Barring selective price cuts may come dangerously close to barring price competition. How is Anheuser-Busch to respond to the loss of sales in its own backyard? True, it could cut prices across the board all over the country. But, as one observer put it, "If a seller by law must lower all his prices or none, he will hesitate long to lower any."[30]

Charges of anticompetitive price cutting have been leveled against most of the national brewers, and several private antitrust suits brought by local and regional brewers are presently (or were recently) being litigated. Unfortunately, the evidence that might verify or rebut these charges is at present mostly confidential. It may be that the major brewers are attempting to pick off certain market areas with below-cost sales. However, the data available thus far indicate that these suits, if successful, will thwart legitimate price competition, stabilize and raise prices, and work to protect regional brewers who are the victims not of predatory pricing, but of high-cost brewing operations. One probably unfortunate response to the price competition of the national brewers is the legislative efforts in a number of states to have price posting laws. Under these laws, any price change must be maintained for some period of time, such as 180 days. Although such legislation has the façade of protecting consumers of beer against

---

[29] *In the matter of Anheuser-Busch*, FTC, Docket no. 6331, p. 19. Italics supplied.
[30] F. M. Rowe, "Price Discrimination, Competition, and Confusion: Another Look at Robinson–Patman," *Yale Law Journal*, **60**: 959 (1951).

quick price increases, its impetus actually comes from smaller brewers who see such laws as protecting them against competition from periodic price cuts, week end specials, and promotional price campaigns by the national brewers. New York has a 180-day price-posting requirement that then Governor Nelson Rockefeller signed into law in June 1973. On the other hand, when the Kentucky Alcoholic Beverage Control tried to institute a similar measure in its state, a court held that the agency had no authority to do so.

Marketing

Although all industries are subject to various Federal and state laws that affect the marketing of the industry's product, the brewing industry faces an especially variegated pattern of laws and regulations concerning labeling, advertising, credit, container sizes, alcoholic content, tax rates, and even, in some states, container deposit requirements.

For example, Michigan does not permit a beer label to show alcoholic content; Minnesota requires an accurate statement of alcoholic content; in Indiana, advertising is strictly regulated; and Louisiana has no advertising restrictions. Some states require sales from the brewer to wholesaler to retailer to be only on a cash basis; others allow credit. The size of containers, both maximum and minimum, is stipulated in some states. Alabama permits no package beer containers larger than 16 ounces; Colorado permits a giant 128-ounce container. States have varying requirements on the permissible alcoholic content, ranging from no limit to 3.2 per cent by weight. In some states, alcoholic content may be different for different types of outlets.

The governmental involvement in the beer industry also includes taxation. The Federal tax alone on a barrel of beer is $9.00, and, in 1974, the Treasury Department coffers gathered over $1.3 billion in beer taxes. The state taxes on beer vary substantially but average about $4.63 per barrel. In addition, brewers, wholesalers, and retail outlets pay Federal, state, and sometimes local occupational taxes. Taxes represent the largest single-cost item in a glass of beer, about 35 per cent of its price.

There is little forward integration by brewing firms into the marketing of beer. The possibilities here would include owning distributors and retail outlets. In England, the brewing industry has extensive holdings in the retailing of beer, owning more than half of all retail outlets, including about 80 per cent of the public houses and hotels.[31] But, in the United States, brewers are prohibited by law from owning any retail outlets whatsoever, which leaves the wholesale distribution of the product as the only legitimate forward vertical integration route. The retailing of beer is done through two general types of independent

[31] The British Monopolies Commission has investigated this vertical relationship in England and concluded that such integration retards the efficient distribution of beer, raises the entry barriers in brewing, hinders price competition, and protects inefficient producers. But, for a defense of the "tied house," see Kevin Hawkins and Rosemary Radcliffe, "Competition in the Brewing Industry," *Journal of Industrial Economics*, **20** : 20 (Nov. 1971).

outlets: those allowing on-premise consumption and those allowing only off-premise consumption.

Most brewers rely on independent distributors to channel their product to these retail outlets. In 1972, there were more than 6600 wholesalers of beer, the vast majority being independent merchant wholesalers. Some brewers own a portion of their wholesale channel. For example, Anheuser-Busch distributes about 75 per cent of its beer through independent wholesalers; the remainder is marketed through branch offices in large metropolitan areas.

An important policy issue in the marketing of beer is the amount of discretion the independent wholesaler should have in deciding how much to charge and choosing where to try and market the brand(s) of beer for which the wholesaler is franchised. These and other characteristics of the franchise agreement between the wholesaler and the brewer have been a matter of some litigation in brewing, as well as in other industries. The FTC also has taken a keen interest in this issue, one that led to a lawsuit against Coors.[32] Coors had contractual relationships by which it restricted the territories and the customers of its wholesalers. Allegedly, Coors also threatened to terminate distributors who were price cutters or who, themselves, sold beer to retail outlets known as price cutters. The FTC charged that such practices violate the antitrust laws. The original decision in this matter by the FTC held that Coors' marketing practices were both reasonable and pro-competitive. Parts of this decision read like an advertisement, so complimentary are they to the company. However, the opinion was reversed by the full commission and, early in 1975, the Supreme Court rejected Coors' appeal and let stand the commission's order. Just as was the case with the beer industry and antimerger doctrine, this decision in the *Coors* case could well have implications for all wholesaling. Coors has indicated that if it cannot maintain this type of control over the marketing of its product, the company will be forced to "distribute beer ourselves, which gives us the unalterable right to determine where and to whom Coors beer is to be sold."[33]

The beer wholesaler at one time distributed mainly kegs of beer for on-premise draught consumption. In 1935, only 30 per cent of beer sales were packaged—that is, in bottles or cans suitable for on- or off-premise consumption. Since that time, there has been a steady increase in the percentage of beer sold packaged, relative to draught; by 1974, almost 88 per cent of beer sales were packaged. The popularity of the can and one-way bottle, the changing consumption habits of the male, the apparent loss of the "saloon habit" during prohibition, and the preferences of the female mean that the beer distributor, today, will make more delivery trips to the grocery store than the tavern.

This trend in beer marketing works to the disadvantage of the small brewer. When beer sales were primarily by the keg for on-premise consumption, the small brewer could survive by selling to taverns in his immediate area. But packaged beer sales are primarily for off-premise consumption, and the distri-

---

[32] See *In the Matter of Adolph Coors Company*, FTC, Docket no. 8845.
[33] Statement of Adolph Coors Company, reprinted as "Why Coors Will Appeal FTC Decision," *Modern Brewery Age*, Oct. 21, 1974, p. 22.

bution of packaged beer increases the importance of product differentiation and brand emphasis.

Moreover, the increasing emphasis in the industry on product differentiation via package "innovations" is to the disadvantage of the small brewer. The rapidity with which new openers, new shapes, and new materials are introduced into beer bottling and canning, and the advertising flourish with which they are promoted, cannot be matched by the resources of the small brewer.

Whether these changes in cans and bottles are meaningful in the sense of making the beer customer better off is an open question. But there is no doubt that these marketing changes have been to the detriment of the small brewer, who, even if efficiently brewing relatively small batches of beer, might no longer survive in the race to market it.

PERFORMANCE

Profits

If an industry is effectively monopolized, we might expect to see this reflected in its profits. This is not, of course, necessarily so. (1) Demand may not be sufficiently high to yield profits in spite of monopoly; (2) the monopolists may be inefficient; (3) or the accounting records may not show the monopoly gains because accounting records often are imperfect measures of economic costs and profits. In spite of all these difficulties, economists regularly look at profit data for some insight into an industry's performance.

Brewing firms earned rather modest returns in the post-World War II period until recent years. Their rate of return, after taxes, on owner's equity was usually below 8 per cent, until 1967, when it went to 9.1 per cent. The figure reached 10.1 per cent in 1969 and then dropped to 8.8 per cent in 1971.[34] The comparable rate of return for all manufacturing in 1967, 1969, and 1971 was 11.7, 11.5, and 9.7 per cent, respectively.[35]

As one might expect from the earlier discussion on economies of scale, the largest brewers have done better than the industry average. Beginning in 1964, the top four companies began to outperform the rest of industry in terms of profits. Prior to that time the top four's profit record was not all that much better than that of the rest of the industry and was usually inferior to the firms ranked five through eight.[36]

[34] Compiled from U.S. Department of the Treasury, *Corporation Source Book of Statistics of Income* (Washington, D.C.: U.S. Government Printing Office, various years).

[35] Calculated from FTC, *Quarterly Financial Reports for Manufacturing Corps.* (Washington, D.C.: U.S. Government Printing Office, various years).

[36] See FTC, *Report of the Federal Trade Commission on Rates of Return in Selected Manufacturing Industries, 1960–1969* (Washington, D.C.: U.S. Government Printing Office); *Quarterly Financial Reports for Manufacturing Corps.*, op. cit., for 1961–1970.

Externalities

Externalities, or spillover effects, occur when transactions between parties (such as the simple sale of a product) have economic consequences on others not party to the transaction. These spillover effects can be positive or negative in value and, to the extent an industry manifests externalities—either in the production process or in the consumption of its product—the social performance of that industry is likely to be affected.

The beer industry is remarkably free of the negative externalities in production commonly associated with manufacturing enterprises: air and noise pollution. Brewing is a very "clean" industry (breweries must be more sanitary than hospitals, in fact), and brewing firms are often courted by areas seeking industry partly for this reason. The brewing industry performs well on this count.

The externality problems in brewing occur in the consumption of the product. True, there would be positive externalities for members of the Beer Can Collectors of America in finding along the roadside an empty can of Monticello beer (with its emblem of Mr. Jefferson's home) or Olde Frothingslosh (with its rather rotund female bathing beauty trademark). However, most citizens are able to restrain their enthusiasm for that proportion of the billions of beer cans and bottles that end up as litter—that is, that are negative externalities imposed on them even though they neither sold nor bought the beer.

Although legislation banning or restricting the sale of beer containers is commonly proposed, only a few states (Oregon, Vermont, and North Dakota, thus far) have actually passed such laws. The most well-known is the 1971 Oregon "bottle bill," which bans all cans with detachable pull tabs and places a compulsory 5 cents deposit on all beer and soft drink containers. Because retail stores particularly do not want to handle returned cans, this has drastically reduced the sale of beverages in this container[37] and, of course, offers an inducement to the use of returnable containers. In Oregon and Vermont, the legislation apparently led to reductions of 60 and 80 per cent, respectively, in roadside beverage container litter. However, the statewide (or local) approach cannot solve the problem (say, in Vermont) of customers going "over the line" (to New Hampshire) to avoid the Vermont deposit requirement and higher prices.

The United States Brewers Association (with the exception of Coors) opposes all taxes and bans on containers, stressing instead voluntary action and other litter-recovery programs. The latter, if generously financed, could solve the litter problem, but partially at the expense of nonproducers and nonconsumers.

The economic question of where the liability for any externality should be placed depends on which party—the consumer, the producer, or a third party (or some combination of the three)—would be the most efficient at removing the externality. And, on this complicated question, the evidence is not yet in.

---

[37] Coors is testing a "reverse vending machine" into which empty beer cans could be placed, the cans would then be crushed, and a receipt given to the shopper for receiving a deposit. This device could induce stores to stock canned beverages under a deposit law. See "Coors Tests New Can Crusher," *Modern Brewery Age*, Aug. 26, 1974, p. 1.

Moreover, although data are being gathered on the expense of various remedial proposals, due to estimation difficulties, little is known of the monetary value of the damages from such litter. This makes cost-benefit calculations more than recondite. Efficiency questions aside, an equity standard would suggest that the costs for removing the externality should be borne by the consumers and the industry itself. A full discussion of the externality problem in brewing would require many pages. And it should include what is also a significant externality: the economic costs imposed by behavior influenced by alcohol. To distinguish this negative externality in the consumption of beer from the concomitant ones associated with distilled spirits—where the problem is undoubtedly of much greater magnitude—would also be a difficult task. This whole area is one still in need of much research.

Competition

Increasing concentration at the national level and the unlikely entrance of new rivals pose a threat to the future level of competition in the beer industry. Thus far there is no evidence of collusion in the industry. But, as the industry becomes populated by fewer and fewer companies, the possibility and likelihood will be enhanced of their engaging in tacit or direct collusion—given the inelastic nature of demand—to establish a joint profit-maximizing price and output. Similarly, the chances will become slimmer that individual firms in the industry will follow a truly independent price and production strategy, vigorously striving to take sales away from rival brewers. With only a few sellers will come the increasing awareness that parallel business behavior might be feasible. A danger is that misguided legislation or unfortunate antitrust action will end up facilitating such action by penalizing the rather high degree of price competition and flexibility in the industry now. Currently, the FTC is undertaking an extensive study of the competitive performance of this industry.

If the weapon of price cutting is sheathed, a seller may select nonprice methods of gaining sales, such as advertising. An industry's emphasis on advertising as its form of rivalry has public policy implications. Advertising rivalry, if seen as a substitute for product and price rivalry by brewers, will provide beer customers with a narrower range of genuine choices. As was mentioned earlier, some economists are persuaded that in highly concentrated markets where rivalry takes the form of advertising and slogan emulation, the costs of such endeavors are excessive and provide no meaningful benefit to the consumer of the product who ultimately pays for them.

Rivalry from foreign producers has never been a strong force in the beer industry. However, the amount of beer imported into the United States has been increasing and provides a modest source of rivalry to high-priced brands. Presently, imported beer faces a tariff of approximately $3.85 per barrel. To preserve the present degree of competition, it is important that the threat of foreign rivalry remain. Consequently, the tariff on beer should not be increased —but, preferably, removed.

All this is not to overlook the present degree of competition in the industry. The statistics on the structure of the beer industry, the pricing and marketing conduct of its members, and the profits it has received do not mark it as a monopolized industry. The extent of exits from brewing in the last decade indicate that this is hardly an industry in which the inefficient producer is protected from the chilling winds of competition.

SUGGESTED READINGS

BOOKS AND PAMPHLETS

Arnold, John P., and Frank Penman. *History of the Brewing Industry and Brewing Science in America.* Chicago: privately printed, 1933.

Baron, Stanley Wade. *Brewed in America.* Boston: Little, Brown and Company, 1962.

Brewers Almanac. Washington, D.C.: United States Brewers Association, an annual.

Cockerill, Anthony. *Economies of Scale in the Brewing Industry: A Comparative Study.* Department of Economics, Cambridge University, England, private circulation.

Downard, William L. *The Cincinnati Brewing Industry.* Athens: Ohio University Press, 1973.

Modern Brewery Age: Blue Book. Stamford, Conn.: Modern Brewery Age Publishing Co., an annual.

Shih, K. C., and C. Y. Shih. *American Brewing Industry and the Beer Market.* Brookfield, Wis.: W. A. Krueger, 1958.

Thomann, Gallus. *American Beer.* New York: United States Brewers Foundation, 1949.

GOVERNMENT PUBLICATIONS

Anheuser Busch v. *Federal Trade Commission,* 265 F.2d 677 (1959); 363 U.S. 536 (1960); 289 F.2d 835 (1961).

In the Matter of Adolph Coors, FTC, Docket no. 8845.

United States v. *Anheuser-Busch,* 1960 C.C.H. Trade Cases, para. 69, 599.

United States v. *Falstaff,* 410 U.S. 526 (1973).

United States v. *Jos. Schlitz,* 253 F. Supp. 129 (1966); 385 U.S. 37 (1966).

United States v. *Pabst,* 233 F. Supp. 475 (1964); 384 U.S. 546 (1966).

ARTICLES

Branch, Ben. "Nonreturnable Containers and the Environment." *Atlanta Economic Review,* 49–52 (Sept.–Oct. 1973).

Elzinga, Kenneth G. "The Restructuring of the U.S. Brewing Industry." *Industrial Organization Review,* 1 : 101–114 (1973).

Greer, Douglas F. "Product Differentiation and Concentration in the Brewing Industry." *Journal of Industrial Economics,* 19 : 201–219 (July 1971).

Hawkins, Kevin, and Rosemary Radcliffe. "Competition in the Brewing Industry." *Journal of Industrial Economics,* 20 : 20–41 (Nov. 1971).

Hogarty, Thomas F., and Kenneth G. Elzinga. "The Demand for Beer." *Review of Economics and Statistics,* 54 : 195–198 (May 1972).

Horowitz, Ira, and Ann Horowitz, "Firms in a Declining Market: The Brewing Case." *Journal of Industrial Economics,* 13 : 129–153 (March 1965).

————. "The Beer Industry." *Business Horizons*, **10** : 5–19 (Spring 1967).

Jones, J. C. H. "Mergers and Competition: The Brewing Case." *Canadian Journal of Economics and Political Science*, **33** : 551–568 (Nov. 1967).

McConnell, J. Douglas. "An Experimental Examination of the Price-Quality Relationship." *Journal of Business*, **41** : 439–444 (Oct. 1968).

Modern Brewery Age. Stamford, Conn.: Modern Brewery Age Publishing Co., tabloid edition, 40 times a year.

Peles, Yoram. "Economies of Scale in Advertising Beer and Cigarettes." *Journal of Business*, **44**:32–37 (Jan. 1971).

Scherer, F. M. "The Determinants of Industrial Plant Sizes in Six Nations." *Review of Economics and Statistics*, **55** : 135–145 (May 1973).

Weiss, Leonard W. "An Evaluation of Mergers in Six Industries." *Review of Economics and Statistics*, **42**:172–181 (May 1965).

CHAPTER 7

the pharmaceutical industry

WALTER S. MEASDAY

DEVELOPMENT OF THE INDUSTRY

One of the more widely quoted remarks attributed to the late Sir William Osler is that the desire to take medicine is perhaps the greatest feature distinguishing man from the animals. Any practicing physician will confirm that there is at least a strong ring of truth to Osler's exaggeration. Some of the more cynical writers of advertising copy for over-the-counter remedies for acid indigestion, headaches, constipation, or tired blood would question whether Osler exaggerated at all.

Given man's awareness of the problems of illness and his propensity to seek cures, it is not surprising that the story of pharmaceutical remedies is as old as recorded history. Macbeth's witches, to say nothing of a modern physician, might shrink in horror from some of the concoctions served up to patients in the past. Most of these remedies were useless; their efficacy rested upon the psychological satisfaction that a large segment of humanity derives from taking medicine. Lest we think too harshly of our ancestors, it can be noted that more than a few drugs on the market today have been shown to have no greater therapeutic effects than placebos (pills manufactured from inert ingredients known to generate no physiological response). A number of the ancient remedies are still in use, albeit in purified form. Quinine, digitalis, strychnine, colchicine, reserpine, and the opiates, among others, have genealogies that can be measured in centuries, or even millenia.

To speak of the ancient history of drugs, however, is a far cry from describing the pharmaceutical industry, which is a comparatively recent development. Well into the nineteenth century, botanical drugs as well as the few early chemical remedies were collected and compounded by the physicians and apothecaries who dispensed them. It is no accident that the first *United States Pharmacopoeia*, published in 1820 (with texts in both English and Latin) described more than

200 drugs in terms useful to the doctor or druggist who, so to speak, "rolled his own."

As medicine itself became more scientific, its practitioners found a need for standardized drugs. It was to meet such needs that the ethical drug industry was founded during the nineteenth century. One of the earliest "industrialists" was a German apothecary, H. E. Merck, who began production for the wholesale distribution of morphine, quinine, strychnine, and a growing list of other drugs in 1827; the U.S. branch of the firm was established some 65 years later. In the United States, in 1854, Edward R. Squibb developed a process for distilling ether of uniform purity and strength and gave up the practice of medicine shortly thereafter to concentrate on supplying the drug requirements of his colleagues. By the end of the nineteenth century, factory production had supplanted the art of the individual apothecary in the preparation of ethical drugs.

This is not to say that the modern pharmaceutical industry was created fullblown in the nineteenth century; a more appropriate designation for this purpose would be World War II. Through the 1930s, botanical products remained an important part of the manufacturer's business. The work of Louis Pasteur and others had provided an impetus to the production of biologicals (serums, antitoxins, and vaccines). Paul Ehrlich can lay the greatest claim to the foundation of modern chemical pharmacology. His discovery of arsphenamine, or Ehrlich 606, the first successful treatment for syphilis, is most widely known to the laymen. Of greater importance was his development of the earliest systematic theory of selective drug action, which provided a logical basis for the search for new chemical drugs. The search proceeded slowly, however, for many years.

There were differences other than the pace of development between the pre-World War II industry and that of the postwar period. Today more than 97 per cent of all prescription drug items reach the retailer in finished form. Before World War II, however, the production of finished medications was largely confined to the proprietary field. The typical ethical drug manufacturer then purchased his basic chemicals from a "fine" chemical firm, such as Merck, Pfizer, or Mallinckrodt. From these, he prepared the active drug ingredients, which he sold in bulk form, almost exclusively through wholesalers, to the retail trade.

The pre-World War II pharmacist was not so far removed from the apothecary of earlier centuries, in that he still had to compound most of the prescriptions he sold. Using the bulk powders and crystals obtained from the drug manufacturers, the pharmacist added excipients and binders, rolled his own pills, filled capsules, and prepared liquid suspensions and tinctures. For most products, because the skill of the local pharmacist contributed as much to the finished item as did that of the manufacturer, brand names (as distinct from a general reputation for reliability) played a much smaller role than they do today.

The industry underwent a veritable revolution in the 1940s, generated in part by an upsurge in new drug discoveries and in part by the production requirements of World War II. Sulfanilamide, the first of the modern "wonder drugs," appeared on the market in 1936. Possessing remarkable antibacterial properties in comparison to other drugs then available, it came into wide use and was the principal antiinfective drug used by the military through 1943. Sulfanilamide's usefulness, despite its toxicity, encouraged research for other safer, and even more effective, drugs. Success came with the production of penicillin, the first of the antibiotics that have contributed so much to modern drug therapy. The story of penicillin provides an excellent illustration of the factors that revolutionized the drug industry during and after World War II.

Penicillin was first observed by Alexander Fleming in 1928, when bread mold spores accidentally contaminated a staphylococcus culture, destroying staph germs in the vicinity of the spores. Investigation continued on a small scale, but not until 1940 did E. B. Chain and H. W. Florey, at Oxford University, succeed in preparing enough pure penicillin to try it on human patients and establish its invaluable pharmaceutical efficacy. With Britain fully mobilized, Florey came to the United States in the hope of persuading American drug companies and the government to develop commercial production. His hope was realized through the cooperation of industry and government on a large scale, which provided sufficient penicillin capacity to meet military requirements by early 1944. The War Production Board's target was 3600 billion units of penicillin, a level that it was feared would create a serious postwar problem of idle capacity. (Today, despite the competition of a number of other antibiotics, annual penicillin production is nearly four hundred times the wartime target.)

Considerable research effort, both publicly and privately supported, was directed to the discovery of other antibiotics. The effort, which involved the mass screening of thousands upon thousands of different molds, paid off handsomely. Selman Waksman and Albert Schatz, at Rutgers University, found streptomycin, which was being produced commercially by the end of the war. Merck, which had financed Waksman, later developed dihydrostreptomycin. Bacitracin was isolated at Columbia University and chloramphenicol by a research team at Yale.

The most important of the postpenicillin discoveries, however, have been the tetracyclines. These are broad-spectrum antibiotics—that is, they are active against a much wider range of organisms than is penicillin. The first, chlortetracycline (Aureomycin), was marketed by American Cyanamid's Lederle Laboratories in 1948. It was followed by a variant, oxytetracycline (Terramycin), introduced by Pfizer in 1950. By 1954, tetracycline itself had been prepared by several firms, including American Cyanamid, Heyden (whose antibiotic facility was acquired by Cyanamid), Pfizer, and Bristol Laboratories. A number of other antibiotics, some of considerable use and others of only minor importance, were discovered in the 1950s; by 1960, the impetus given to antibiotic research by World War II and the later commercial success of antibiotics appeared to have run its course, and few new products have appeared since.

World War II not only stimulated the research and production of antibiotics and other drugs, but it changed the industry in other ways as well. The exigencies of military medical practice left no room for the local compounding of prescriptions from bulk drugs. To meet military needs, the drug manufacturers had to invest in the mixing, tableting, and encapsulating equipment necessary to provide finished drugs, ready for administration to the patient. By the end of the war, the compounding function of the retail pharmacist was irrevocably passing into history. More important, once the original manufacturer had come to provide drugs in the form in which they reached the ultimate consumer, the value of brand names was immeasurably enhanced; ethical drug advertising and promotion to the medical and allied professions surged upward toward the levels that now prevail.

World War II and a quarter of a century of postwar prosperity for the industry also attracted a number of newcomers. Entry in many cases has been accomplished through the acquisition of existing drug firms, to secure both a sales force familiar with the unique problems of pharmaceutical merchandising and the entree of a name with which the medical profession is acquainted. Several distinct groups of entrants can be identified.

First, some of the fine chemical companies secured wartime contracts under which they had supplied drug products in finished form. Thus, at the end of the war, they had become drug manufacturers rather than simply suppliers of chemicals to the industry. Merck & Company and Chas. Pfizer & Company provide excellent examples. Each had been a manufacturer of drug-grade chemicals for the pharmaceutical industry before World War II, and each came out of the war as a leading producer of drugs, particularly in the antibiotic field. Each solved the problem of entry into the civilian market by acquisition of an established firm. Pfizer, which had only a dozen chemical salesmen, purchased J. B. Roerig, a well-known drug firm with a large pharmaceutical sales force. Merck sold its products to other firms for distribution until it acquired Sharp and Dohme, one of the largest drug manufacturers and distributors, with a reputation dating from the Civil War. Today, the two companies rank first and second, respectively, in industry sales of ethical pharmaceuticals.

Next, a number of companies known primarily as proprietary firms expanded their activities in the ethical field to take advantage of the rapid growth in the latter area. In 1939, shipments of proprietary drugs exceeded shipments of ethical products; since the mid-1950s, shipments of ethical drugs have been nearly triple the volume of proprietaries. The proprietary companies had the advantages of familiarity with production techniques and retail drug distribution; their major problem has been to overcome the longstanding distrust of the medical profession toward patent medicine hucksters.

To solve this problem, they have utilized what had been minor pre-World War II ethical subsidiaries, the establishment of new divisions and, to a lesser degree, acquisitions. Thus, American Home Products has employed Wyeth Laboratories (acquired in 1931) and Ayerst (purchased shortly after World War II), to promote ethical products in a manner that minimizes physician identification of these products with the corporate producer of such items as Anacin, Bi-So-Dol mints, and Kolynos toothpaste. Bristol-Myers (Sal Hepatica, Bufferin, Ipana, Mum, Ban, and so on) established Bristol Laboratories, which has prospered on the basis of tetracycline and semisynthetic penicillins. In a similar manner, Norwich Pharmacal Company created Eaton Laboratories to overcome any reluctance of physicians to prescribe drugs supplied by the manufacturer of Pepto-Bismol. The Vick Chemical Company, which had coated the chests of untold millions of Americans with Va-Po-Rub, has even changed its corporate name to Richardson-Merrell, in order to develop a new image as an ethical, rather than a proprietary, manufacturer.

Finally, mention should be made of the entry of companies with little or no primary relationship to the pharmaceutical field. In such cases, a customary route of entry has been the acquisition of existing ethical drug firms. Johnson & Johnson, the largest manufacturer of surgical dressings and similar textile products, acquired McNeil Laboratories in 1959 and has since become a major factor in the oral contraceptive market. Phillips Electronics Co., controlled by Phillips Incandescent Lamp (of the Netherlands) became Phillips Electronics and Pharmaceutical Industries (now PEPI, Inc.) through the purchase of Columbus Pharmacal Co. When Dart Industries, formerly Rexall, decided to leave the ethical drug industry in 1970, Minnesota Mining and Manufacturing Company was the eager buyer of Dart's Riker Laboratories. Since the mid-1960s, such cosmetic manufacturers as Revlon Inc. have been moving into pharmaceuticals, presumably because this is the only other industry offering a comparable rate of return on investment. Given the profitability of drug manufacturing, it is not surprising that plants within this industry are operated by companies that themselves are classified primarily in such other diverse industries as animal feeds, women's and children's underwear, soaps and detergents, plastics products, household appliances, or photographic equipment.[1]

It should be noted that the invasion of the ethical drug field by outsiders has been paralleled in recent years by a growing diversification movement among the traditional ethical drug houses. Not surprisingly, a major area of diversification has been into the proprietary market. An obvious factor here is, of course, the profitability of proprietary drugs. Related to this is the fact that an ethical drug company that develops a product safe enough for over-the-counter (non-prescription) sale is faced with a choice: it can keep its ethical image by promoting the drug to physicians and pharmacists, relying on them to recommend it, or it can advertise directly to the consuming public. In most cases, the latter alternative is chosen.

Some companies, such as Upjohn and Squibb, market proprietary items under their own names, on the theory that the consumer can be more easily persuaded of a drug's quality if it is advertised by the same firm whose products are prescribed by his own doctor. Other companies fear that any broad promotion of over-the-counter remedies will contaminate their carefully nurtured ethical images in the eyes of the medical profession. Using the same strategy as proprietary manufacturers entering the ethical sector, but moving in the opposite direction, these ethical companies have either formed or acquired subsidiaries

---

[1] Cf. U.S. Department of Commerce, Bureau of the Census, *1963 Enterprise Statistics*, (Washington, D.C.: U.S. Government Printing Office, 1968), pt. 1, Table 6.

to market proprietaries in a manner that will minimize any physician identification of their proprietary activities.

The combination of pharmacological advance, marketing changes, and new entrants has markedly changed the character of the pharmaceutical industry. Before World War II, ethical drug manufacturing was dominated by a handful of "old-line" companies, usually family-controlled, such as Lilly, Abbott, Squibb, Upjohn, and Parke, Davis. Very little effort was expended on research, and advertising, even in reputable professional journals, was considered dangerously akin to the promotional activities of the proprietary segment of the industry. In the words of one author: "Conservative and steeped in tradition, they put great emphasis on public responsibility, product quality, and close association with physicians. These segments of the industry, in fact, give the industry many of the aspects of an exclusive gentlemen's club."[2] Developments since World War II have drastically altered the gentlemen's club image of the industry. It has become highly competitive, although this competition among the major companies is seldom on the basis of price. Research and product development, as a marketing strategy rather than for their own sake, have become an accepted form of competition. The other is advertising and promotion directed to the medical profession on a scale that rivals that of any other industry in the economy.

II. MARKET STRUCTURE

It is difficult to define the drug industry with any degree of precision. Although the concern of this chapter is principally with the ethical sector of the industry, the available statistics include both ethical and proprietary output; indeed, this is unavoidable because today the same companies often operate in both areas. The Bureau of the Census includes both in the "pharmaceutical preparations" industry.

The growth of the market for human use alone since before World War II is shown in Table 1. For a period of 30 years, the industry expanded its shipments from $301 million to $4.5 billion. It may be a commentary on our society that shipments of tranquilizers alone today exceed the entire output of the industry in 1939 by a wide margin. What is especially notable, as suggested earlier, is the rapid growth of the ethical drug sector, at a rate three times that of the proprietary sector. Not included in Table 1 are veterinary products (ethical and proprietary), which have accounted for a relatively constant 3 to 4 per cent of the total market. Although they will not be discussed further, it is worth noting that the current level of sales ($252 million in 1974) has become large enough to attract the participation of most of the leading manufacturers of drugs for human use.

[2] David M. Kiefer, "Prognosis for the Drug Houses," pt. I, *Chemical and Engineering News*, **42**:73 (Aug. 10, 1964).

TABLE 1

Pharmaceutical Preparations for Human Use[a] and Value of
Shipments, Selected Years 1939–1973 (in millions of dollars)

| YEAR | DOMESTIC SHIPMENTS | | EXPORT SHIPMENTS[b] | TOTAL |
	ETHICAL	PROPRIETARY		
1939	148.5	152.4	—[c]	301.0
1947	520.7	317.6	—[c]	838.3
1954	1088.9	368.3	—[c]	1457.2
1958	—[c]	—[c]	—[c]	2256.9
1963	2001.6	787.1	99.3	2888.1
1967	2885.8	999.5	112.7	3998.0
1968	3223.0	1123.4	103.5	4450.0
1969	3455.8	1262.2	137.7	4855.8
1970	3682.0	1271.6	144.3	5097.8
1971	4015.2	1355.8	134.4	5505.4
1972	4286.6	1427.7	124.9	5839.3
1973	4628.5	1487.9	141.3	6257.7
1974	5032.9	1589.6	218.7	6841.2

[a] Except biological products.
[b] Includes shipments to foreign subsidiaries.
[c] Not separately reported.
Source: U.S. Department of Commerce, Bureau of the Census, Census of Manufacturers, (Washington, D.C.: U.S. Government Printing Office, various years); and Current Industrial Reports, series no. MA-28G.

Within the ethical sector of the market, several groupings of companies can be distinguished. Leading the list are perhaps 25 to 30 large companies that promote their products to physicians on a national scale; their emphasis is almost always on brand names rather than price, and they tend to dominate the private prescription market. Next, there is a great number of smaller manufacturers that cannot afford the cost of heavy promotion. Although they occasionally have some local or regional brand reputation, their products normally are sold by generic name either to the retail trade through wholesalers or to governmental and nongovernmental institutions on the basis of competitive bidding. Finally, there is a fringe of about 100 "repackaging houses" often controlled by physicians. The repackaging house buys generic drugs from the lowest-cost source and resells them under its own brand names at much higher prices (frequently above the prices charged by the leading firms in the industry). By prescribing these brands, the stockholding physicians assure a market for the firm and dividends on their own investments at the same time.

Entry into the industry is not inherently difficult. The technical expertise and ability to maintain the high quality necessary for drug manufacturing are well within the reach of small enterprises. Nor are capital requirements for production any barrier. Of the drug companies filing income tax returns in 1968, 32 per cent had no more than $50,000 in assets and 95 per cent were below the $5 million mark.[3] The problem lies not in becoming a drug manufacturer, but in becoming a drug marketer. It is only in this context that questions of industry structure and patterns of competitive conduct can be understood.

Demand for Drugs

It is desirable to preface the analysis of market structure in the pharmaceutical industry with some mention of the nature of market demand. Little needs to be said about proprietary drugs because these are not markedly different from such other consumer nondurables as soft drinks, breakfast foods, cosmetics, toiletries, and so forth. The demand for proprietaries depends largely on the extent to which consumers suffer, or can be persuaded that they suffer, from headaches, indigestion, insomnia, nervous tension, acne, vitamin deficiency, nasal congestion, or a host of other real or imagined ailments. The consumer diagnoses his own need and then shops around for a product that hopefully will meet this need.

The nature of demand for individual ethical drugs, however, is very nearly unique, at least where private buyers are concerned. With most consumer products, the consumer himself makes the buying decision. For ethical drugs, in the words of the late Senator Kefauver, "He who orders does not buy; he who buys does not order." The decision is made for the consumer by his physician when the latter writes out a prescription, generally by brand name. The pharmacist is usually obligated to fill the prescription exactly as it is written.[4] If, for example, the physician has specified Achromycin, the druggist must supply American Cyanamid's brand of tetracycline and not the identical product offered by Pfizer, Bristol, Squibb, or Upjohn. The average patient may not even know what he has purchased, apart from the fact that it is a bottle of small pink pills, or large white ones, or yellow capsules; in the majority of cases, neither the physician nor the pharmacist tells him clearly what has been prescribed.

The customer's ignorance of the product is matched by his ignorance of prices. The most prevalent retail markup on ethical drugs is 40 per cent of the retail price (that is, $66\frac{2}{3}$ per cent above the cost to the druggist). In any major metropolitan area, however, a given prescription may be filled over a wide range of prices. Some druggists may accept much lower margins, offering substantial savings to customers. Others, especially in the case of less expensive prescriptions, may employ a minimum "professional fee," which results in a higher markup. A quantity of pills that costs the druggist $1.50 would be retailed at

---

[3] Pharmaceutical Manufacturers Association, *Prescription Drug Industry Fact Book, 1973* (Washington, D.C.: Pharmaceutical Manufacturers Association, 1973), p. 9.

[4] Although it has always been unethical for a pharmacist to substitute a different drug for the one prescribed, the protection of individual brands of the same drug is of recent origin. As late as 1953, only 4 states had laws prohibiting brand substitution. The National Pharmaceutical Council, representing the major companies, managed to secure such laws or pharmacy regulations in all 50 states and the District of Columbia by 1965. The tide may have turned in 1974. Laws permitting limited substitution were enacted in Florida and Michigan and narrowly missed passage in at least 10 other states.

$2.50, but might be available in some outlets for $2.00, or in others for as much as $3.50, depending on the pricing policy of the retailer.

Comparatively few customers will shop around to have a prescription filled at the lowest price. Until recently, this would have been difficult in any case because only one state, Ohio, permitted prescription drug advertising. In 1972, for example, the Michigan Board of Pharmacy sought to revoke the licenses of pharmacists employed by a chain that advertised nothing more than a 10 per cent discount on prescriptions for senior citizens. Since 1972, however, a number of states (20 by the end of 1974) have enacted legislation either permitting advertising or requiring in-store posting of prescription drug prices.

Next, consider the physician, who is frequently described as the purchasing agent for his patient's drug requirements. In contrast to other purchasing agents, most physicians have little knowledge of price or price alternatives. This stems from what is probably a distortion of an ancient and excellent principle: The physician's prescription of a drug should be based solely on his judgment of the best therapy for his patient. Thus, in the flood of advertising and promotional literature with which the major drug companies inundate the medical practitioner, there is never any mention of price, nominally on the ground that such commercialism might be interpreted as an attempt to taint professional judgment. The physician who is concerned about drug prices must find them out in the same way as anyone else; and, with the best will in the world, he simply has no time to engage in economic research.

Finally, remember that the patient has visited his doctor in the first place because he is experiencing certain symptoms that worry him even if they do not incapacitate him; the doctor's prescription offers him the hope that these symptoms can be cured. The patient will have the prescription filled, unless he has absolutely no resources (either of his own or through public aid) to pay the cost. When this underlying reason for seeking medical advice is viewed in juxtaposition to the inability of either the physician or the patient to include price as a factor in the buying decision, we can see that the demand for prescription drugs, either in the aggregate or as individual products, approaches closer to complete inelasticity with respect to price than the demand for any other commodity that readily comes to mind.

In the institutional sector of the market (hospitals and governmental agencies), the demand for ethical drugs in the aggregate is probably as inelastic as it is in the private prescription sector. Total demand will depend on such factors as hospital patient loads or the number of people eligible to receive drugs through governmental channels, rather than on drug prices. Within the aggregate framework, however, the demands for many individual drugs and particularly for different brands of the same drug may exhibit considerable elasticity.

A majority of the nation's hospitals have adopted formularies from which staff physicians are expected to prescribe as a means of holding down hospital costs. The purpose of a formulary can be understood from the foreword to the one issued by the Baltimore City Health Department: "The principal criteria for admission of substances to this formulary are therapeutic efficacy, simplicity, and economy." Therapeutic efficacy is clear enough. Simplicity is achieved by limiting the number of drugs in the formulary. If, say, 40 or 50 drugs on the market are available to treat the same illness, the formulary committee will choose four or five for inclusion. In this connection, it may be noted that there are upwards of 7000 ethical drug products (single drugs and combinations of two or more active ingredients) offered to the medical profession by the industry. The director of one of the leading hospitals in the country has stated that a formulary containing only 400 of these products covers more than 99 per cent of patients' drug requirements.[5] Economy is achieved both through simplicity and through a common provision that the hospital pharmacy may fill any prescription on a generic basis—that is, if a staff physician prescribes Meticorten, the pharmacy may dispense equally reliable, but much less expensive, generic prednisone.

In the institutional market, as distinct from the private prescription market, therefore, price becomes an important influence in the choices made by purchasing authorities. The degree of this influence may vary considerably according to the ability and objectivity of the decision makers, and drug manufacturers woo these decision makers even more assiduously than they do individual practicing physicians. Some hospitals and agencies have done an excellent job; at the other extreme, the state of New Mexico, in the mid-1960s, used the *Physicians' Desk Reference* as its official "formulary."[6] This is a commercial advertising compendium, distributed free to physicians and utilized almost exclusively by the major drug companies. Despite such variations in standards, it is clear that price elasticity of demand can be a significant factor in the institutional market. It is becoming even more significant as both hospital costs and public expenditures for out-of-hospital prescription drugs for the needy and elderly continue to rise.

To summarize, two submarkets for ethical drugs can be distinguished. The private prescription market accounts for between two thirds and three fourths of total demand, and the institutional market for one quarter to one third. In the former, demand—whether considered in the aggregate for different drugs within the same therapeutic class, or for individual brands of the same drug—is extraordinarily inelastic. In the latter, because price is a factor in decisions involving choices among different drugs for the same therapeutic purpose and in choices among alternative brands of a given drug, an important element of price elasticity may be introduced into the demand functions for individual products and brands.

Market Concentration

Company concentration ratios, developed by the Bureau of the Census and the Senate Subcommittee on Antitrust and Monopoly are shown for the phar-

[5] U.S. Congress, Senate, Select Committee on Small Business, *Hearings on Competitive Problems in the Drug Industry* (90th Cong., 1st sess., pt. 2, 1967), p. 676.
[6] Task Force on Prescription Drugs, "The Drug Prescribers," *Background Papers* (Washington, D.C.; U.S. Government Printing Office, 1968), p. 46.

TABLE 2

Pharmaceutical Preparations Industry Concentration Ratios, 1947–1970

YEAR	NO. OF COMPANIES	VALUE OF SHIPMENTS ($ MILLIONS)	PERCENTAGE ACCOUNTED FOR BY THE LARGEST			
			4	8	20	50
1972	680	7149.5	26	44	75	91
1970	n.a.ᵃ	6027.8	26	43	n.a.	n.a.
1967	791	4696.4	24	40	73	90
1963	944	3314.3	22	38	72	89
1958	1064	2533.4	27	45	73	87
1954	1128	1643.1	25	44	68	n.a.
1947	1123	941.3	28	44	64	n.a.

ᵃ Not available.
Source: U.S. Department of Commerce, Bureau of the Census, *1972 Census of Manufactures*, *Concentration Ratios in Manufacturing* Series, no. MC72(SR)-2 (Washington, D.C.: U.S. Government Printing Office, 1975).

maceutical industry in Table 2. It should be noted that the shipments portrayed are those of plants classified within the industry—that is, they include both ethical and proprietary products for human or veterinary use, as well as any other products (biologicals, chemicals, flavorings, cosmetics, and so on) manufactured in pharmaceutical plants.

There are approximately 700 firms in the industry. The majority are small enterprises; other data suggest that at least 80 per cent have fewer than 20 employees.[7] No more than 50 companies today would account for 91 per cent of the industry's output. Nevertheless, on the surface, the industry's structure is not inconsistent with a reasonable expectation of competition. The four largest firms have less than a quarter of the market, and the eight largest have 44 per cent. Furthermore, it is obvious that, in the years for which 20-firm ratios are available, the medium-sized firms grew far more rapidly than the industry leaders. Companies in the 9 to 20 size group increased their market share of total shipments from 20 per cent in 1947 to 33 per cent in 1972, whereas the share of the four largest declined and the next four remained reasonably constant.

Although some drug companies are much larger than others, there do not appear to be any industrywide dominant firms such as those one finds in automobiles, steel, or a number of other industries. Instead, the bulk of the market is shared among 20 to 30 leading firms, with a substantial fringe of competitors.

This is the view of the industry emphasized by the Pharmaceutical Manufacturers Association and not a few outside observers. To accept such a view uncritically, however, is to ignore the fact that the over-all drug market is frag-

[7] U.S. Department of Commerce, Bureau of the Census, *1963 Enterprise Statistics* (Washington, D.C., U.S. Government Printing Office, 1968), pt. 1, Table 9.

mented into a number of separate, noncompeting therapeutic markets: Antibiotics are not substitutes for antidiabetic drugs, and tranquilizers are not substitutes for vitamins. Manufacturers do not compete on an industrywide basis, and, hence, concentration must be evaluated within the various therapeutic groups of drugs in which competition does occur.

When this is done, even on the basis of the fragmentary data available, it is clear that high levels of concentration within important therapeutic classes are a more meaningful element of structure than the relatively moderate level for the industry as a whole. Examples can be found from the overly broad therapeutic classes used by the Bureau of the Census. The four largest producers of central nervous system drugs (including a wide variety of products from aspirin and other analgesics through tranquilizers to anesthetics) accounted for 43 per cent of the market in 1972, whereas the eight largest had 63 per cent. In the anti-infective drug class (including antiparasitic products, antibiotics, antimalarials, and even simple antiseptics), the four largest firms held 45 per cent and the eight largest 67 per cent of the market. For preparations affecting neoplasms, the endocrine system, and metabolic diseases (lumping together drugs for the treatment of cancer, arthritis, and diabetes with the oral contraceptives, anti-obesity drugs, and others) the four and eight company concentration ratios were, respectively, 48 and 70 per cent. These are high, not low, concentration ratios, and they would be much higher still were the bureau census to compute them on the basis of realistic therapeutic divisions rather than agglomerating widely diverse products into broad categories.[8]

Another aspect of the pharmaceutical industry, concentration of bulk drug production, is an important consideration even when there may be an impressive number of suppliers of any given finished product on the market. The Tariff Commission identifies the manufacturers of roughly 650 bulk medicinal chemicals. In 1972, only six of these were produced by more than four manufacturers, while nearly 500 were available from a single domestic source.[9]

The nature of this type of concentration can be readily illustrated. Ascorbic acid (vitamin C) in dosage form is offered by more than 100 companies; the entire output of the vitamin itself, however is produced by Merck, Pfizer, and Hoffman-LaRoche. Finished reserpine products are offered by at least 60 suppliers; S. B. Penick is the sole manufacturer of the active drug. Meprobamate (Miltown) tablets are available from nearly 50 suppliers; the actual drug is manufactured by Abbott and Millmaster Onyx. It is obvious, in such cases, that the bulk producers may have considerable power to control the effectiveness of competition by their selling policies.

In the first two instances, ascorbic acid and reserpine, the bulk manufacturers are selling under conditions that appear to permit remarkably effective price

---

[8] Shepherd has estimated an average four-firm concentration ratio of 90 for the pharmaceutical industry, adjusted for noncompeting submarkets. See W. G. Shepherd, *Market Power and Economic Welfare* (New York: Random House, Inc., 1970), Appendix Tables 8 and 9.

[9] U.S. Tariff Commission, *Synthetic Organic Chemicals, 1972* (Washington, D.C.: U.S. Government Printing Office, 1974).

competition at the dosage-form level. In the case of meprobamate, there was a very real limit to price competition while the Carter-Wallace patent was effective. With the unfortunate blessing of the Justice Department, the licenses of the bulk meprobamate manufacturers required that they sell all of their output to Carter; they did so, in 1966, at an average price of $2.54 a pound. All compounders of meprobamate products, in turn, had to purchase the meprobamate from Carter at a price of $20 or more a pound, or eight times the price that Carter paid the actual manufacturers. In other words, the meprobamate for, say, a thousand 400-milligram tablets cost Carter about $2.35 (including a wastage allowance), and Carter's competitors $18.75, not an inconsiderable advantage to the firm that controls the bulk supply.

In short, concentration ratios for the pharmaceutical industry as a whole convey a somewhat misleading impression of the industry, although they are useful in the broad sense of supplying information on the number and approximate size distribution of drug firms. From a standpoint of the influence of industry structure on competitive behavior, however, it is necessary to go beyond the industrywide ratios and examine concentration in therapeutically significant categories and in bulk drug production. On this basis, it appears that high concentration in these separate categories, rather than the moderate concentration of the entire industry, is the dominant structural characteristic.

Government Barriers to Competition

Underlying the types of nonprice competition developed by the major drug companies are a variety of governmental policies that facilitate monopolistic practices in the industry. Especially important are policies with respect to patents, trademarks, and new-drug approval. The first two have nothing at all to do with the protection of consumers' health, whereas the third is sometimes administered in such a manner as to go beyond its primary essential purpose.

Patents were not an important factor in the drug industry prior to World War II. Only in part can this be explained by the slow pace of innovation and the relative scarcity of novel drugs at that time. More important, a long tradition in the medical profession and the industry considered that patenting an essential drug was a questionable practice. The United States Pharmacopoeial Convention, for example, held to this position for the first 120 years of its existence; not until 1940 was a patented drug admitted to the *United States Pharmacopoeia*. The reversal of this tradition and the subsequent proliferation of drug patents have created a significant new element in the structural characteristics of the industry during the last quarter century.

A patent monopoly may be exploited in several different ways. The patent holder can, and often does, if he is an established manufacturer, preserve his monopoly to himself. Frequently, however, the patent is licensed to one or a few other manufacturers. Although such arrangements may provide alternative sellers in the market, they rarely lead to price competition. Finally, licenses are occasionally granted to a number of competitive sellers for reasons not necessarily related to a spirit of benevolence. Thus, Ciba granted an unrestricted license to S. B. Penick to make reserpine, which Penick sells in bulk to a large number of other firms; it is possible that this was motivated, to some degree, by the desire to avoid legal challenge to a patent on the active ingredient of a botanical product in use for at least 2000 years. Again, in recent years, Carter-Wallace freely licensed competitors to market meprobamate products (compounded from bulk meprobamate purchased through the company), but only in settlement of an antitrust case brought by the Department of Justice.

Even a dubious patent held by a major company can be a source of great profit because the mills of justice grind slowly. There is no clearer example of this than the patent on tetracycline, the leading broad-spectrum antibiotic. The basic tetracycline patent was awarded to Pfizer in 1955, following the settlement of complex claims and counterclaims by American Cyanamid and Bristol. Pfizer licensed Cyanamid and Bristol to manufacture and sell tetracycline products; Bristol received the additional right to sublicense Squibb and Upjohn to market finished products made from Bristol's bulk tetracycline. Under this happy arrangement, the five companies marketed the drug at identical high prices for a number of years.

In 1958, 3 years after the patent was issued, the Federal Trade Commission challenged the methods used to obtain the patent and the subsequent licensing arrangement. Ten years later, in September 1968, the Sixth Circuit Court of Appeals affirmed a final order of the commission directing that any qualified manufacturer desirous of producing tetracycline be licensed to do so at a royalty rate not exceeding 5 per cent. The compulsory licensing order became effective when the Supreme Court declined to review the case on April 2, 1969; the patent on tetracycline expired on January 10, 1972. Despite a unanimous FTC decision that the patent was obtained, in the words of Commissioner Jones, "by fraud . . . and by deliberate misrepresentation and withholding of essential and relevant data relating to the patentability of tetracycline" it served its purpose as well as any more valid patent for nearly all of the 17 years it could possibly run. There is one solid bit of evidence for a bare minimum indication of the profits involved. In an attempt to settle a collateral price conspiracy case brought by the Department of Justice, early in 1969, the five companies voluntarily offered to establish a $120 million fund to reimburse tetracycline buyers for overcharges.

Although there are thousands of unpatented drugs on the market, the patented products occupy a strategic position. A good indication of this is provided by the so-called Master Drug List assembled by the Task Force on Prescription Drugs. The list contains 366 drugs most frequently prescribed in 1966 for persons aged sixty-five years and over, and accounts for nearly 90 per cent of both the number and cost of prescriptions filled by retail pharmacies for the elderly.[10] Of this number, 293 products (80 per cent of the total) were "still under patent,

---

[10] Task Force on Prescription Drugs, "The Drug Users," *Background Papers* (Washington, D.C.: U.S. Government Printing Office, 1968), p. 31 ff. As published, the Master Drug List contains 409 items, but with extensive duplication of brand names for identical products (for example, Miltown, Equanil, and meprobamate are separately entered).

available only under brand name from a single supplier."[11] In addition, despite an erroneous conclusion of the task force to the contrary, many of the drugs available from more than one supplier were also covered by patents, under licensing arrangements not conducive to price competition. Although such a list for the entire population would be somewhat different from that for the elderly, there is no reason to believe that the relative significance of patented products would be any less.

In 1974, the 200 most frequently prescribed drugs accounted for more than two thirds of private prescription costs. No more than 15 to 20 of these were available from more than one supplier. At least 90 per cent were single-source products covered by patents, and, of course, many less popular drugs are also protected by patents. Clearly, the patent system severely limits entry into the largest part of the prescription drug market and confines meaningful competition to what is quantitatively a small segment of that market.

The use of trademark brand names, as distinct from the generic, or "official" names of drugs, introduces another governmentally sanctioned interference with the competitive process. Even though virtually all patented drugs are sold under brand names, the trademark can be particularly valuable to a manufacturer in marketing a drug that either cannot be patented or, if patented, has been so freely licensed as to minimize the competitive barrier of the patent itself. The Master Drug List for the elderly offers numerous examples of each situation.[12] Thus, chloral hydrate is unpatentable because it has been used medicinally as a hypnotic, or sedative, for a full century. It is available from a number of suppliers; nevertheless, Squibb's Noctec brand of chloral hydrate had more than half of the market in the task force survey—and, at wholesale prices, from 3 to 4 times the cost of the generic product offered by reliable small firms. Meprobamate has been mentioned as a patented drug freely licensed. Despite this, American Home Products (Equanil) and Carter-Wallace (Miltown and Meprospan) appear to retain 80 per cent of the market, at prices to the druggist that are more than double the prices charged by generic suppliers. Ciba's brand of reserpine (Serpasil) outsells generic reserpine by a wide margin at wholesale prices that are up to 30 times those charged by some of its competitors.

It can be argued that brand names are a pervasive characteristic of the American economy; hence, one should not be surprised to see them used in the pharmaceutical industry. This ignores the very basic distinctions between the marketing of prescription drugs and, say, detergents or gasoline. In the first place, official standards for drugs establish the identity of products from different suppliers to a degree not found in most other consumer goods. Confirmed cases in which branded and generic versions of the same drug have not been chemically and biologically equivalent are exceedingly rare.

More important, we return to the basic fact that the physician makes the buying decision for the patient. Exxon Corporation undoubtedly would be happy

[11] Ibid., p. 36.
[12] Ibid., Appendices B and N.

to get twice as much per gallon for gasoline as independent dealers get for their products, but the company knows that is impossible. No matter how heavily it is promoted, the value of the Exxon trademark in the minds of consumers is at most 2 or 3 cents a gallon over the price of "generic" gasoline; if the differential widens in any market, the company is forced to cut prices to hold its market position. Because physicians are, to a large degree, insulated from price considerations, however, the major pharmaceutical companies can achieve and hold dominant positions in ethical drug markets, solely through promotion of their brand names; furthermore, a firm that has established itself as a leading seller of a drug can enjoy average revenues per unit of output that are 2, 3, 10, or more times those that can be realized by its generic competitors. There is no other industry in the economy in which a trademark can be exploited so successfully to the benefit of the seller.

A third influence of government on market structure and conduct is the New Drug Application (NDA) procedure of the Food and Drug Administration (FDA). Unlike patents and trademarks, this procedure is essential to the protection of the public, and thus, to a large extent, its impact on the industry is unavoidable. Old drugs (or, in good bureaucratese, "not-new" drugs) may be marketed by any registered manufacturer so long as they meet established standards of purity, strength, and quality. It is unlawful, however, for any manufacturer to offer for sale a new drug unless he holds an effective NDA for the product—that is, one approved by the FDA.

The proof of safety and efficacy required for FDA approval of an application necessarily requires an elaborate program of animal and clinical (human) testing at a cost that is beyond the reach of most smaller companies. Thus, the introduction of new drugs and the marketing advantages accruing from them tend to be confined to the major companies. In an industry so marked by the rapid introduction of new products as drug manufacturing has been, this gives an inevitable competitive edge to size.

So long as a drug is on new-drug status, each marketer other than the innovator must also hold an effective NDA. For years this required each subsequent marketer to repeat the costly clinical tests of the innovator. This was particularly valuable when the new drug was unpatentable or after an innovator's patent had expired or been declared invalid. The FDA's policy here has been to protect the "property rights" of the innovator, rather than the public's safety. A, the original NDA holder, could authorize a subsequent marketer, B, to incorporate A's clinical tests in his own NDA precisely as if B himself had carried them out. This was done frequently in patent licensing and product exchange agreements among major firms.

The FDA modified this policy after some years of congressional criticism to permit "abbreviated" NDAs (ANDAs) for a great many new drugs. Approval of an ANDA generally requires only that the subsequent marketer demonstrate that his product meets the *United States Pharmacopoeia* (USP) quality standards (based on the innovator's product) and that he adheres to "current good manufacturing practice" standards. Late in 1974, the FDA announced that even the

ANDA requirement would be phased out by transferring drugs from new-drug to old-drug status as rapidly as possible. Thus, competition has been broadened immensely as patents have expired on products introduced in the 1950s.

There is still a problem with some important drugs for which essential information relating to manufacturing practice, safety, and efficacy has not been revealed, even to the *United States Pharmacopoeia*, by either the original manufacturer or the FDA. In such cases, the FDA can deny approval to a "me-too" drug that meets all published standards on the ground that "the standards are inadequate." Even the latest FDA disclosure regulations, required by the Freedom of Information Act, specifically exempt safety and efficacy data, manufacturing- and quality-control procedures, and formulations unless publicly disclosed by the original NDA holder.[13] Some NDAs will still qualify for the appellation, *superpatents.*

The nature of demand for drugs would tend to produce high levels of concentration in meaningful therapeutic markets. This tendency is reinforced to a significant degree by a variety of governmental policies. What remains to be explored are the patterns of market conduct that both flow from and maintain these levels of concentration.

III. CONDUCT AND PERFORMANCE

The major ethical drug manufacturers, like their compatriots in other industries, are convinced that they operate an intensely competitive environment. From a businessman's viewpoint, they are certainly correct. The number of persons suffering from a given illness represents the ultimate market for drugs used to treat that illness. A new product can gain a place in the market only by winning a share away from other products with similar therapeutic uses. Any product, no matter how well established, may find its market position eroded almost to the vanishing point by the successful introduction of a new product. This rivalry among the major firms seldom expresses itself in the price competition of classical economics, at least so far as the private prescription market is concerned; the fields of combat are product development and product promotion.

Research and Development

The stimulus to research and new-drug development provided during World War II carried over into the postwar era, although, by 1950, there had occurred a very real change in its focus. There were no product patents on the original penicillin G, and the basic process patents were held by the government, which freely licensed all interested manufacturers. Two of the largest producers, Merck and Pfizer, were still fine chemical manufacturers who sold bulk penicillin and finished dosage forms to other drug companies rather than market them under

---

[13] Cf. "Freedom of Information—HEW-FDA Rules on Disclosure: Effective 1-23-75," *Federal Register*, Dec. 24, 1974, pt. 2.

their own brand names. As a result, the penicillin market was highly competitive. When the drug was released by the War Production Board for sale through normal channels in 1945, Merck's bulk price was $6000 per billion units. By December 1948, the bulk price had dropped below $1000 per billion units, and, in another 4 years, the $100 level was reached. In 1965, the average sale value of the principal medicinal salts (procaine and potassium) of penicillin G was below $15 per billion units.[14] Competition and the absence of patent restrictions ensured that the benefits of technological progress in the manufacture of penicillin G reached the market, through price reductions of nearly 99.8 per cent.

Any check provided to research incentives by the price erosion of competition in the case of penicillin was soon offset by American Cyanamid's success with chlortetracycline (Achromycin), followed by Parke, Davis's chloramphenicol (Chloromycetin) and Pfizer's oxytetracycline (Terramycin), in 1949 and 1950. Here the combination of private-patent monopoly and heavy promotional campaigns demonstrated the amazing capacity of new drugs to make profits for their innovators. It was at this point that the major pharmaceutical firms discovered the importance of research and development, not so much for its own sake, but as a basic element in competitive strategy.

The dimensions of the research revolution can be seen in the annual research activity surveys conducted by the Pharmaceutical Manufacturers Association (PMA) since 1951.[15] In that year, firms that conducted nearly all of the industry's research reported expenditures (excluding government contracts) of $50 million. Ten years later, company-financed research outlays for human-use drugs were more than $200 million, whereas by 1973 they had risen to nearly $740 million.

Company-financed research-and-development expenses, like sales, tend to be highly concentrated within the larger firms. Within the PMA group in 1972, more than 86 per cent of the total outlay was accounted for by 23 companies with budgets of $10 million and more. Forty-two companies with research-and-development budgets of at least $1 million a year reported 97 per cent of the total. The use of research as a competitive strategy is primarily the prerogative of the major companies. This should not be surprising in view of the nature and the cost of drug research and development.

Even at the basic research stage, costs are high. The principal starting point is one of "mass screening"—that is, the investigation of hundreds or thousands of substances on the random chance that a few might have some desirable therapeutic effect. In large part, this reflects the fact that pharmacology is still in its infancy, better equipped to describe effects than to explain causes. We know a great deal about what a large number of drugs will do in the treatment of illness and very little about how these drugs accomplish their results. With a weak theoretical foundation on which to build, there can be little alternative to mass screenings as a means of developing new products.

[14] U.S. Tariff Commission, *Synthetic Organic Chemicals 1965* (Washington, D.C.: U.S. Government Printing Office, 1967).

[15] *Prescription Drug Industry Fact Book* (Washington, D.C.: PMA, 1973), p. 41, and "PMA Survey of Ethical Drug Industry Operations, 1972–1973" (Washington, D.C.: PMA, 1974).

An appreciation of this research approach may be gained from the PMA detailed survey for 1970. In that year, the companies who replied to the PMA questionnaire indicated that they had investigated 126,000 chemical substances for possible therapeutic use. A total of 1013 showed sufficient promise to be advanced to a stage of clinical trials. Of this number, it may be predicted that 20 will reach the market, where, with a little bit of luck and a lot of promotion, perhaps 10 or 12 will achieve some commercial success. This is an extraordinarily expensive way to develop new models for the marketing department to sell.

The new-model analogy is hardly farfetched. Few of the new chemical entities marketed in any year are truly original. The majority are congeners (new salts or other minor molecular variations) of existing drugs. These may, but more often do not, represent a real improvement over the drugs on which they are modeled. What the molecular variants do offer is the basis for additional patents, through which rivals can enter a field from which they would otherwise be foreclosed, and the opportunity for promotion as "significant therapeutic advances." The benzothiazide diuretics can provide an illustration. Chlorothiazide (Diuril), introduced by Merck in 1957, secured a major share of the diuretic market almost overnight. Within 3 years, eight other closely related compounds were on the market, with two more added in 1961 and 1963. Merck itself marketed two of the variants, for in the pharmaceutical industry the developer of a successful original drug cannot rest on his laurels; knowing what his competitors' reactions will be, he must exert every effort to produce his own new models.

There are two sides to any evaluation of the research performance of the industry. On the one hand, the industry can rightly claim that its research effort is impressive (with a higher ratio of privately financed research to sales than can be found anywhere else) and that the result has been a flow of products that have revolutionized the practice of medicine. Even the oft-maligned molecular manipulation can be defended in numerous instances where the goal of experimentation has been to produce a drug that has a broader range of therapy or less toxity than one already in use. On the other hand, the proliferation of me-too drugs arising from molecular manipulation aimed solely at product marketing involves an unfortunate waste of scarce resources and talents. This view is not confined to extramural critics of the industry. Nowhere has it been better expressed than by the research director of one of the finest firms in the industry:

We cannot ignore the criticism that we have created an abundance of new drugs, related structurally and therapeutically, which in the minds of many serious-minded clinicians contribute little but confusion. . . .

In viewing the congener-drug developments of recent years, I have often wondered why medicinal chemists in so many laboratories had chosen to direct their efforts into molecular modification of new drugs discovered by others. Although this massive surge has created new knowledge for the medicinal chemists at an almost explosive rate, its productiveness in the field of medicine can be questioned.[16]

---

[16] Task Force on Prescription Drugs, "The Drug Makers and the Drug Distributors," *Background Papers* (Washington, D.C.: U.S. Government Printing Office, 1968), p. 22.

Advertising and Promotion

The layman often assumes that because ethical drugs are not advertised to the general public, they are not advertised at all. Nothing could be further from the truth. No other products on the market are promoted as intensively as ethical drugs. Like so many other aspects of the industry, this has been a post-World War II development. Prior to the war the promotional efforts of the old-line drug companies were limited to a small amount of restrained advertising in professional journals with occasional visits to physicians by company sales representatives, stressing the quality of the companies' product lines.

The change came in 1948, when American Cyanamid's Lederle Laboratories first used the blitz technique to introduce Aureomycin to the medical profession. The 142,000 physicians then in active practice were inundated with journal advertisements, direct mail, and ten freight-car loads of samples that alone were said to have cost $2 million.[17] The blitz approach was adopted by Merck and Pfizer, both of whom were then making the difficult transition from fine chemical manufacturing to ethical drug marketing. During the following decade, aggressive sales promotion became the principal characteristic of market conduct. The newer entrants found it an effective way of penetrating the market, and the old-line companies followed defensively.

"Educational effort" (as the industry prefers to call drug promotion) is directed almost entirely to the select group of about 250,000 practicing physicians who are in a position to decide what drugs and which brands will be purchased by the ultimate consumers. The effort begins when the physician is still a medical student and continues throughout his active career. For the leading companies, drug promotion has been successful in developing brand and company loyalties within the profession, which can be far more effective in maintaining sales than the therapeutic value of the particular drugs promoted. Furthermore, it is a mode of competition requiring enormous resources beyond the reach of all but the major firms in the industry.

The funds devoted to drug promotion can only be guessed. In the course of the Kefauver investigation, 22 companies reported that advertising and promotional expenses for their drug operations alone amounted to $580 million in 1958; the subcommittee staff estimated that the industry total was $750 million.[18] Allowing for increases in salesmen's salaries and expenses, advertising rates and mailing costs, as well as the growth in manufacturer's shipments, a conservative estimate for 1974 would be well over $1 billion. The magnitude of this sum can be appreciated best in terms of the small audience courted by the drug companies —the expenditure averages at least $5000 per physician.[19]

[17] Charles E. Silberman, "Drugs: The Pace Is Getting Furious," *Fortune*, **61**:140 (May 1960).

[18] U.S. Congress, Senate, Subcommittee on Antitrust and Monopoly, *Administered Prices— Drugs*, Rept. no. 448, 87th Cong., 1st sess., 1961, p. 157.

[19] A slightly more modest estimate, $4500 per physician, was provided to the Task Force on Prescription Drugs by Dr. James Goddard, former FDA commissioner. See Task Force on Prescription Drugs, "The Drug Makers and the Drug Distributors," op. cit., p. 28.

Perhaps half of the total expenditure is used for advertising, as such. This includes advertising in the Journal of the American Medical Association (AMA) and other AMA publications. Such advertising, together with the rental of membership lists to drug companies for direct-mail campaigns, provides a third of the AMA's income. Nearly 200 other professional journals are published by medical specialty groups and by regional, state, and even county medical societies, as well as pharmacy and dental associations. In addition, there are a number of "controlled-circulation" publications, distributed free to physicians and supported entirely by advertising. These periodicals contain articles ranging from laudatory reviews of particular drugs to helpful hints for the tired physician as to the best European golf courses for his vacation.

Heavy as it is, journal advertising is dwarfed in dollar volume by direct-mail promotion, particularly in the introduction of new products. For example, in promoting Achromycin, its brand of tetracycline, Lederle Laboratories spent nearly $900,000 (at 1954 prices) in direct-mail advertising during the first year that the product was on the market; this included an average of two mailings a week to every physician in the country.[20] An advertising executive estimated that, by 1962, the average doctor was receiving 4000 promotional pieces a year.[21]

The very magnitude of journal and direct-mail advertising causes it to lose much of its impact. The average physician is too busy to do more than glance at the mass of material that comes into his office, and much of it is thrown away unopened. For this reason, the key element in any major company's promotional effort is the sales representative, or "detail man." Most people have seen a detail man without realizing it—he is a conservatively dressed gentleman, with an attaché case, sitting quietly in the doctor's waiting room until the physician can spare him 5 or 10 minutes between patients. His function in that brief period is to persuade the doctor to prescribe his company's drugs, especially any new products that are being marketed.

This persuasion function may be considered either education or brainwashing, depending on how one views the industry. There is some evidence for the latter point of view. The detail man has neither enough of the doctor's time nor the qualifications to present a balanced scientific report on the product he is pushing. At best, he will give a one-sided, but reasonable, presentation of the benefits of the drug. At worst, his approach raises serious ethical questions.

In 1968, the Nelson subcommittee reprinted a series of bulletins from a regional sales manager to his detail men, regarding promotion of an anti-rheumatic drug, indomethacin.[22] The scientific level of these documents is illustrated by his description of elderly patients as "the real crocks and cruds of everyday practice." At one point, he informed his superior: "Our guys are using a real

[20] U.S. Congress, Senate, Subcommittee on Antitrust and Monopoly, *Hearings on the Drug Industry Antitrust Act*, 87th Cong., 1st sess., pt. 2, 1961, p. 783.

[21] Pierre S. Gerai, "Advertising and Promotion of Drugs," *Drugs in Our Society* (Baltimore: Johns Hopkins, 1964), p. 192.

[22] U.S. Congress, Senate, Subcommittee on Monopoly, *Hearings on Competitive Problems in the Drug Industry*, 90th Cong., 2d sess., pt. 8, 1968.

expanded claim"—translated, this means that his salesmen were making therapeutic claims to physicians that went far beyond any clinical evidence submitted by the company to the FDA. Coupled with this was a slanderous attack on the leading competitive product, including the implication that any physician using the rival drug "is a gambling sole" [sic] willing to risk a malpractice suit. The "educational" theme of the campaign is best expressed in the conclusion of one bulletin: "Tell 'Em Again and Again and Again—Tell 'Em Until They're Sold and Stay Sold."

Nevertheless, the detail man does provide an educational service in the present state of pharmacological communication. Few physicians have the time to keep up with professional literature in the drug field, and not many more are influenced solely by company advertising. A number of surveys of drug information sources are in agreement that the majority of doctors get their first knowledge of new drugs from detail men. It is for this reason that the industry devotes so much of its promotional outlays to the support of detailing. The cost of this promotion is high. The Kefauver subcommittee learned that, in 1958, there were some 15,000 detail men in the industry. The cost of keeping a single detail man in the field—salary, expenses, training, and so on—was about $16,000. By 1974, the number of detail men had grown to more than 20,000 at a cost of $25,000 to $30,000 per detail man. The total annual detailing outlay by the industry was between $500 million and $600 million a year at this time.

From the standpoint of market performance, the issue of drug advertising and promotion has a significance that transcends its economic cost. Almost any drug good enough to be useful has some potential for toxicity. A number of distinguished pharmacologists are in agreement that drug company promotional efforts have led to overprescribing on a large scale, which has created an increasingly serious problem of illness, hospitalization, and deaths caused by the drugs themselves. It is in the area of product promotion that the basic conflict between the goal of the drug company as a profit-seeking organization and its function of meeting a vital human need is most evident.

Pricing Policies

Drug companies, like other firms, are in business to make profits; this means, simply enough, that any firm's over-all price structure must be sufficient to provide revenue that more than covers costs. The nature of these costs can be illustrated by two surveys of leading firms made some 8 years apart and covering different but overlapping groups.[23]

The two surveys are in substantial agreement. Both sets of figures shows that production costs absorb a minor portion, roughly one third, of total revenue for the leading firms. The costs of nonprice competition (research and brand promotion) are of the same order of magnitude as manufacturing costs. Within

---

[23] The subcommittee's 1958 survey was based on detailed financial reports, covering drug operations only, from 22 companies. The task force's survey, including 13 of the companies in the subcommittee's sample, was derived from published information for 17 companies.

this area, advertising and selling expenses account for a far larger share of the corporate budget than research into new or improved drugs. This has led observers to suggest that, for the major pharmaceutical companies, prices determine costs rather than the other way around—that is, a company tries to establish a price structure high enough to finance the degree of nonprice competitition required to maintain its market position.

Table 4 provides some illustrations, from the HEW task force study, of differences between the costs to druggists of brand-name prescription quantities and the identical drugs from generic suppliers. Because the generic drugs on the list are regularly offered at the prices shown, we can assume that these prices are sufficient to cover costs and to provide a reasonable profit margin to the supplier. The table, thus, provides an illustration of the influence of brand name promotion on manufacturer's pricing policies, despite the existence of competitive suppliers. It can be noted that for half the drugs shown, the generic version was not prescribed often enough to gain a place on the task force's list of those most frequently prescribed, and, in most other instances, brand-name products held the lion's share of the market.

Differences between prices of major brand and generic drugs within the United States are hardly more dramatic than the differences often found between domestic and foreign prices for identical products. The Senate Antitrust Subcommittee collected prices for a dozen drugs in a number of foreign markets in the spring of 1959. In more than a few instances the U.S. manufacturer was selling his own product abroad at substantially lower prices than at home. In other cases, a foreign producer related to the U.S. company as the licensee or licensor of a patent was the low-price seller. The principal exception was tetracycline, for which prices in 11 of 16 foreign countries were above the U.S. price.

TABLE 3

Breakdown of Sales Dollar, Leading Drug Companies (in per cent)

	1958 22 COMPANIES	1966 17 COMPANIES
Net profit	13.0	13.5
Income taxes	12.8	10.0
General and administrative expense	10.9	35.0[a]
Advertising and selling expense	24.8	
Research and development	6.3	6.5
Cost of goods sold	32.1	35.0

[a] This figure covers both "General and administrative expenses" and "Advertising and selling expense."

Source: U.S. Senate, Subcommittee on Antitrust and Monopoly, *Report on Administered Prices: Drugs* (Washington, D.C.: U.S. Government Printing Office, 1961), p. 31; Task Force on Prescription Drugs, "The Drug Manufacturers and the Drug Distributors," *Background Papers* (Washington, D.C.: U.S. Government Printing Office, 1969), p. 14.

TABLE 4
Brand Names Versus Lowest Price Generic Drugs: Cost to Druggist
of Typical Prescription, 1966

BRAND NAME; GENERIC NAME	COST TO DRUGGIST ($)	
	BRAND	GENERIC
Achromycin; tetracycline hydrochloride	2.04	.66
Chlor-Trimeton; chlorpheniramine maleate	.71	.15
Decadron; dexamethasone	3.10	1.36
Dexedrine; dextroamphetamine sulfate	2.71	.19
Miltown; meprobamate	2.75	1.01
Nembutal; sodium pentobarbital	.46	.12
Noctec; chloral hydrate	1.08	.29
Pentids; penicillin G potassium	1.99	.23
Peritrate; pentaerythritol tetranitrate	2.42	.10
Prolixin; fluphenazine	1.91	.09
Seconal Sodium; secobarbital sodium	.49	.12
Serpasil; reserpine	2.04	.05

Source: Task Force on Prescription Drugs, "The Drug Users," *Background Papers* (Washington, D.C.: U.S. Government Printing Office, 1969), Appendix N.

The Social Security Administration made a similar survey in January 1971.[24] Prices to druggists for 20 major products (per 100 tablets or capsules of uniform strength) were collected from eight foreign countries. The results paralleled those of the earlier study.

Eli Lilly, for example, sold Darvon (propoxyphene HC1) to druggists in the United States for $7.02 per 100. Lilly's prices to druggists in Sweden, the United Kingdom, and Ireland were, respectively, $3.33, $1.92, and $1.66.

Upjohn's price for Orinase (tolbutamide, 500 milligrams), sold under an exclusive U.S. license from Hoechst of West Germany, was $8.33 to the American druggist. Hoechst's own price in the foreign markets ranged from $6.34 in Canada to $2.22 in Ireland.

Merck's price for Elavil (amitriptyline HCl, 25 milligrams) in the United States was $8.55 at the same time that Merck was selling the same product, under the tradenames of Tryptizol and Tryptanol, for $3.33 in Australia, $2.28 in England, and for $2.26 in both Ireland and Brazil.

In all, 157 out of a possible 160 foreign prices were reported. Roughly 10 per cent of these were higher than the price in the United States. As in 1959, tetracycline was the one product for which the price in the United States was below those in a majority of the countries surveyed. Foreign prices for tetracycline, in 1971, were well below what they had been in 1959. The price in the United States,

[24] E. M. Jacoby and D. L. Hefner, "Domestic and Foreign Prescription Drug Prices," *Social Security Bulletin*, May 1971.

however. had dropped by more than 80 per cent as a result of antitrust actions brought by both the FTC and the Department of Justice.

At the other end of the spectrum, more than half (82) of the foreign prices were less than 50 per cent of the corresponding U.S. prices. This reflects a variety of institutional restraints on drug prices in the eight countries surveyed as well as in a number of other nations. Six of the eight countries have national health-insurance programs that cover all, or a substantial part of, prescription expenditures. Canada does not have a national system, but many of her provinces have provincial insurance programs. The eighth country, Brazil, fixes the price of each newly introduced drug and seldom permits any increase, despite galloping inflation. In short, each of these countries has either a direct or indirect interest in keeping drug prices at reasonable levels and exercises its power to do so.

Given lower foreign drug prices, it is surprising that companies in the United States have gone to great lengths to expand their foreign sales. Perhaps the British Monopolies Commission provided a clue in its 1973 investigation of Hoffman-LaRoche's prices for Librium (chlordiazepoxide) and Valium (diazepam).[25] Prices for these products were less than two fifths of the U.S. level in 1972. Still, the commission found, Roche product's pretax profits on Librium and Valium sold in the United Kingdom were an astounding 58.8 per cent of net sales, after all costs including contributions for the Swiss parent's research and overhead were met. In 1974, the commission told the company to reduce its prices by 60 per cent!

In sales to institutional buyers, much depends on the nature of competition and the desire of a company to move its products into these channels. The influence of competition was explored by the Kefauver subcommittee in respect to sales to the Military Medical Supply Agency, then the drug procurement agency for the Armed Forces.[26] A significant inverse relationship was found between the number of bidders and prices offered. Thus, Upjohn's bids on hydrocortisone (five bidders) and cortisone acetate tablets (ten bidders) were, respectively, 25 per cent and 28 per cent of the company's prices to direct-buying retailers; in the case of the oral antidiabetic drug tolbutamide (Orinase), for which Upjohn was the only supplier, the company's price to the government was 90 per cent of the price to the druggist. More recently, the city of New York was purchasing 50-milligram Benadryl capsules from Parke, Davis at a price of $15.63 per 1000; as soon as the city adopted the generic specification (diphenhydramine capsules), it was able to buy the same item for $3.00—from Parke, Davis.[27]

Meeting competitive prices in the institutional market has a significance beyond the immediate sale. Prescribing habits acquired by military physicians, medical students and interns in teaching hospitals, and staff physicians in com-

[25] The Monopolies Commission, *Chlordiazepoxide and Diazepam* (London: H.M. Stationery Office, 1973), p. 77.

[26] U.S. Congress, Senate, Subcommittee on Antitrust and Monopoly, *Report on Administered Prices: Drugs,"* op. cit., pp. 88–97 and 262.

[27] U.S. Congress, Senate, Subcommittee on Monopoly, *Hearings on Competitive Problems in the Drug Industry*, 90th Cong., 1st sess., pt. 1, 1967, p. 389.

munity hospitals are carried over into private practice. George Squibb, a former marketing director himself, has stated:

> We know that if a certain product is used in a teaching hospital, where a large proportion of the physicians of a community practice, that the use of this product outside the hospital on private practice prescriptions will be larger . . . this is a real factor in the success of a product.[28]

Hoffman-LaRoche gives its detail men a 20-page pamphlet outlining the type of campaign necessary to get Roche products accepted by hospital formulary committees. The pamphlet concludes by emphasizing the beneficial spillover into out-of-hospital prescribing patterns:

> When we can say in our office presentations to the attending staff physician of a particular hospital, "Doctor, this product is on your hospital formulary," we have gone a long way toward convincing him that it is the most efficaceous product available in this category of drugs.[29]

Most companies view entry into important segments of the institutional market as a logical extension of their over-all promotional programs. Discriminatory pricing in this area (Robinson-Patman Act restrictions exempt sales to governmental and nonprofit agencies) may be one of the less-expensive methods to develop a market for a product.

Given the nature of demand and the limitations of price competition in the pharmaceutical industry, pricing policy appears to be the weakest area of performance. Monopolistic competition has created a situation in which a large part of the private consumer's outlay goes for prices that are higher than they need be by any standards, such as the costs of production or product improvement, prices to institutional buyers, or the prices at which competitive products are available.

Drug Company Profits

Table 5 shows the average rates of return on stockholders' investment from 1958 to 1975 for 12 large companies, the drug industry as a whole, and all manufacturing. During the entire period, the annual rates of return for all manufacturing averaged 11.0 per cent, compared to 18.1 per cent for the drug industry and 19.7 per cent for the 12 large companies.[30] Furthermore, as Table 5 suggests, there has been relatively less variation in drug industry profits than in all manufacturing. The industry's profits after taxes rose in every year from 1958 ($343

---

[28] Ibid., pt. 5, p. 1566.

[29] Hoffman–LaRoche, "Getting on Formulary," reproduced in U.S. Congress, Senate, Committee on Labor and Public Welfare, *Hearings on S.3441 and S.996*, 93d Cong., 2d sess., pt. 3, 1974, pp. 1109–1126.

[30] The companies include Abbott Laboratories; American Home Products; Eli Lilly; Merck & Co.; Chas. Pfizer; Richardson-Merrell; Smith, Kline & French Laboratories; Sterling Drug; Upjohn Co.; and Warner Lambert Pharmaceutical Co. Two other firms in the FTC series for 1958–1968, Rexall (drug manufacturing business sold) and Parke, Davis (merged with Warner Lambert), were replaced by Schering Corp. and G. D. Searle from 1969–1975.

TABLE 5
Rates of Return on Average Stockholders' Investment,[a]
Pharmaceutical Industry and All Manufacturing, 1958–1975 (in per cent)

| YEAR | 12 LARGE COMPANIES | | DRUG INDUSTRY | ALL MANU-FACTURING |
	AVERAGE	RANGE		
1975	20.5	13.2–29.5	17.8	11.6
1974	21.3	14.8–29.9	18.8	14.9
1973	21.8	14.8–30.3	19.0	12.8
1972	20.6	14.1–28.4	18.6	10.6
1971	19.9	8.9–31.0	17.9	9.7
1970	19.6	14.5–29.2	17.6	9.3
1969	20.8	14.2–28.5	18.4	11.5
1968	18.8	9.0–26.1	18.3	12.1
1967	19.0	10.4–28.1	18.7	11.7
1966	21.1	14.4–29.8	20.3	13.4
1965	21.0	14.3–32.7	20.3	13.0
1964	18.9	13.6–33.0	18.2	11.6
1963	17.8	11.2–32.7	16.8	10.3
1962	17.1	6.3–33.0	16.8	9.8
1961	17.6	10.3–32.7	16.7	8.8
1960	18.4	10.3–31.6	16.8	9.2
1959	20.3	11.5–37.5	17.8	10.4
1958	20.3	13.3–35.4	17.7	8.6

[a] Net profit as a per cent of the average of net worth at the beginning and end of each year.
Source: FTC, *Rates of Return for Identical Companies in Selected Manufacturing Industries* (Washington, D.C.: U.S. Government Printing Office, annual); FTC "Quarterly Financial Reports" (Washington, D.C.: U.S. Government Printing Office); company annual reports.

million) to 1975 ($1.6 billion), including those years in which net manufacturing income as a whole declined. Few, if any, other industries in the economy can match this record.

A coterie of distinguished economists retained by the PMA explained to the Nelson subcommittee, in 1968, that the rate of return in this industry reflects a substantial risk factor. If this were so, during a reasonable period of time, losses would presumably offset extreme profits so that something approaching the average return in the economy would result. There is no evidence that this has occurred. In the most recent 5-year period, 1971–1975, the average rate of return in manufacturing was below 12 per cent. Abbott Laboratories and Richardson–Merrell were the poorest performers among the large companies; yet their returns during the period averaged 14 per cent or more, substantially above that for manufacturing generally. At the other extreme, Merck, Schering, and American Home Products each averaged 26 per cent or better.

Thus, although variation in profits from company to company does exist, the "risk" appears to lie between earning a normal rate of return and some significant multiple of a normal rate. This would seem to support what has been said earlier concerning the barriers to effective price competition in the industry.

Conclusion

Many aspects of the pharmaceutical industry's economic performance can be criticized. Market-oriented research has been wasteful of scarce technical and professional talents, promotional methods leave much to be desired, and price and profit levels are difficult to defend on any rational basis. Yet, no evaluation of performance can be complete without recognition of what may truly be called the facts of life. A baby born in 1920 had a life expectancy of 54 years; one born today can reasonably hope for a life span of more than 70 years. Medical advances, better nutrition, higher educational levels, and a host of other factors have been of great importance, but the drug industry is entitled to no small share of the credit for this improvement.

A number of the dreaded diseases of the past are much less serious problems today. In the early 1930s, for example, pneumonia was treated in a manner that was more sophisticated (leeches and emetics had been discarded), but hardly less rudimentary, than had been the practice for centuries. Basically, the infection ran its course, with physician and relatives gathering around the bedside for the "crisis" to learn whether the patient would live or die. Since then, penicillin and the broad-spectrum antibiotics have reduced the mortality rate of pneumonia by more than 60 per cent. Between 1950 and 1972, the death rate from diseases of early infancy were cut by 60 per cent, from hypertensive heart disease by 89 per cent, from tuberculosis by 90 per cent, and from syphilis and its complications by 96 per cent.

The development of preventive serums and vaccines has been of incalculable value, especially in the protection of children. Diphtheria antitoxin has reduced the incidence of this often fatal disease from 85,000 cases in 1929 to 152 in 1972. The Salk and Sabin vaccines have virtually eliminated the horror of poliomyelitis; more than 33,000 cases were reported during the polio epidemic of 1950, and only 31 cases in 1972. The sharp reduction in measles cases since 1960 offers the hope that this disease, too, may join the ranks of those that the medical student must learn about from a textbook because they are so rarely seen in clinical practice.

Tranquilizers and other psychotherapeutic drugs have shown excellent results in the treatment of mental illness. Persons who formerly would have been hospitalized for extensive periods are now treated in out-patient clinics while retaining their status as self-supporting members of society; the period of confinement has been dramatically reduced for many of those who still require hospital treatment. Despite an increase in the number of persons treated for mental illness, the patient population of mental institutions has fallen steadily from its 1955 peak to the point where many of these facilities are being converted to general hospitals.

The examples suggested, and many others, can be judged best in terms of the prevention of disease, the mitigation of physical and mental suffering, and the extension of life itself. In these terms, the ethical pharmaceutical industry has made a magnificent contribution to human welfare. The function of the economist is to analyze what exists, in the hope that improvement in the allocation and management of resources may lead to even greater progress in the future, but not to deny the very real accomplishments of the industry to the present.

IV. PUBLIC POLICY

Public policy has been concerned primarily with the safety and efficacy of drug products. Safety is a less simple matter than it might appear to be. Any drug, from aspirin through the spectrum of pharmaceutical remedies, has some potential for toxicity, so that safety is a relative term, and the determination of safety standards is an extraordinarily complex problem. Efficacy refers to the probability that a drug will have the therapeutic results for which it is prescribed. More is involved here than the waste of money in buying safe, but useless, drugs; treatment with such drugs can lead to serious or fatal delays in the institution of effective therapy.

The Pure Food and Drugs Act of 1906 was the first significant piece of Federal drug legislation. Passage of the act required years of work by its supporters (who included most ethical drug companies), the crusading efforts of Dr. Harvey W. Wiley, and, ultimately, a catalyst for public opinion in the form of Upton Sinclair's novel *The Jungle*. This book described conditions in the meatpacking industry so graphically that public consumption of meat dropped sharply, and the press entered the fray. President Theodore Roosevelt called for reform, and Congress was moved to speedy action, passing first a meat inspection bill in 1905 and then the omnibus food and drug bill a year later.

The 1906 act established the *United States Pharmacopoeia, The National Formulary*, and the *Homeopathic Pharmacopoeia* (seldom used today) as official compendia, establishing enforceable standards for the purity, strength, and quality of drugs. All drug products had to be clearly labeled as to identity and composition, and no drug could be described as USP, NF, or HP unless it could be demonstrated by tests and assay that it was identical to the official drug included in the appropriate compendium. For the first time, physicians could have some confidence that the patient would receive the drug prescribed by his doctor.

From a modern point of view, the 1906 act was woefully inadequate, lacking either safety or efficacy provisions. Any drug, no matter how dangerous or worthless it might be, could be freely marketed. The government could not move against a toxic product—and then only by a lengthy process—until the product had actually caused injuries or deaths in use. In this respect, it is interesting to note that the Biological Serums and Antitoxins Act of 1913 required manufacturers of these products for veterinary use to demonstrate both the safety and the efficacy of the items they proposed to market. It took Congress another half century to extend the same protection to human consumers.

In 1933, President Franklin D. Roosevelt proposed new legislation that would require food processors and cosmetic manufacturers (not covered by the existing law) to prove the safety of any chemical additives or cosmetic mixtures used; for drug products the proposed requirements included both safety and efficacy. Although leading ethical drug producers supported the safety provisions, they balked at the efficacy proposal, and this was quietly dropped. There was strong opposition to any change in the law from the proprietary drug, the food, and the cosmetics industries. The bill languished for several years, until once again an event occurred to arouse public opinion and galvanize the Congress into action. This time the catalyst was the "Elixir Sulfanilamide" disaster.

Sulfanilamide, the first of the "wonder drugs," appeared in 1935. With any such drug there is a great demand for a liquid suspension for children and adults who find it difficult to swallow tablets or capsules. Unfortunately, sulfanilamide proved to be insoluble in water, alcohol, or any other known drug solvent. A chemist employed by S. E. Massengill Company found that the drug would dissolve in diethylene glycol, a sweet, syrupy liquid used primarily as a dye solvent. The elixir, which was rushed to the market without safety tests, claimed 107 known victims, nearly all of whom were children.

In the wake of this tragedy, Congress passed the Food, Drug, and Cosmetics Act of 1938, which, as amended, is still the basic law of the land. The act greatly expanded the powers of the FDA to protect the public against unsafe products. In broad terms, this was accomplished by defining foods, drugs, or cosmetics as adulterated, if they contained any substances found by the FDA not to be demonstrably safe for human use. So far as drugs are concerned, since 1938, any manufacturer who wants to market a new drug must first secure an Effective New Drug Application. Note that "effective" does not mean "efficacious" in this context.

Under the 1938 act, the NDA had to include (1) reports of animal tests and clinical investigations made to determine the safety of the drug; (2) a list of substances used as components of the drug; (3) a full statement of the composition of the finished product; (4) a description of manufacturing methods, facilities, and quality controls used in producing the drug; (5) samples required by the FDA for testing; and (6) specimens of all proposed labeling for the drug. If the application was not disapproved by the FDA, it automatically became effective at the end of 60 days, unless the agency exercised an option to extend its review for up to another 120 days. In any event, the power of the FDA was essentially a negative one of rejection, rather than a positive approach of approval. Should the application be rejected, of course, the applicant was entitled to judicial review.

The act had a number of shortcomings in addition to its failure to require any proof of efficacy. Because the FDA jurisdiction began with the marketing stage, dangerous drugs could be distributed widely to unqualified investigators for clinical testing; such drugs might even reach the market from some companies that included only favorable clinical reports in their applications. Medical advertising was unregulated and tended to be both inaccurate and misleading.[31] Although the act provided the first statutory basis for factory inspection, enforcement required a lengthy criminal prosecution, which was seldom employed. These shortcomings were intensified by an FDA leadership that, in the case of the ethical drug industry, failed to enforce vigorously the powers that it did possess.

Once again, any reform needed both a crusader and a catalyst. The crusade was provided by Senator Estes Kefauver, whose hearings on the ethical drug industry, beginning in December 1959, attracted wide public attention. The senator's legislative proposals, however, appeared to be a lost cause until another near disaster occurred.

Thalidomide was a sedative-type drug developed by Chemie Grunenthal of West Germany and widely marketed throughout Europe. Richardson-Merrell secured a U.S. license, distributed clinical testing quantities to nearly 1300 physicians, and filed a NDA for marketing in this country. Fortunately, the FDA scientist, Dr. Kelsey, responsible for this application delayed action as long as she could, in light of foreign reports that pregnant women treated with thalidomide delivered horribly deformed infants with disturbing frequency. The entire case, including the pressure on Dr. Kelsey from her superiors to approve the application, made newspaper headlines before the drug was released. As a result, a compromise bill, the Kefauver-Harris Amendments to the act of 1938, was passed by Congress and signed by the president in October 1962.

Under the amendments, positive approval of a NDA is required before a drug can be offered for sale. Approval cannot be granted unless the applicant offers "substantial evidence" of therapeutic efficacy in addition to proof of safety. Furthermore, the secretary of HEW may withdraw approval of any drug marketed between 1938 and 1962 if the manufacturer is unable to furnish satisfactory evidence of its efficacy. The impact of this provision became evident in 1969, when the FDA began to remove from the market hundreds of drugs, including 90 popular and profitable antibiotic combinations, following an authoritative review of the therapeutic evidence.[32]

The FDA has received the power to regulate clinical testing to ensure maximum safety and quality. Before beginning such tests now, a manufacturer must have carried out thorough animal toxicity tests and must hold an approved Investigational New Drug (IND) application. The IND describes the nature of the tests, as well as the names and qualifications of investigators. Careful records

---

[31] The FDA held that responsibility for medical advertising, as distinct from labeling, rested with the FTC; the FTC, in turn, could not, or would not, regulate advertising directed solely to an audience professionally qualified to evaluate its merits.

[32] Some 5600 "ineffective drug products" (ethical and proprietary) were ordered off the market through 1973. U.S., Congress, Senate Small Business Committee, Subcommittee on Monopoly, Hearings on Competitive Problems in the Drug Industry, 93d Cong., 2d sess., pt. 24, 1974, p. 9958.

must be kept, with unfavorable, as well as favorable, results made available to the FDA.

Governmental control over drug quality has been vastly improved. The FDA is empowered to issue and enforce good manufacturing practices regulations covering both production methods and quality-control procedures. Every manufacturer or packager is required to register his plants annually, and these establishments must be inspected at least every 2 years. Federal courts are now authorized to issue injunctions against refusals to permit inspection. In the special case of antibiotics, the FDA must sample and certify every batch produced before it can be used in finished products; this is an extension of earlier amendments covering penicillin and four other antibiotics.

Finally, the Kefauver-Harris Amendments, as implemented by FDA regulations, have raised the standards of prescription drug advertising. Advertisements of brand names must also feature prominently the generic names of drugs. They must contain summaries of side effects and contraindications (that is, conditions such as pregnancy, heart trouble, or diabetes, in which a given drug should not be administered). Advertising claims must not go beyond the therapeutic evidence submitted to the FDA for a drug's efficacy. Any drug that is improperly advertised is considered to be misbranded, subject to seizure and removal from the market.

Present legislation, if properly enforced, can ensure the quality and the utility of drugs reaching the consumer. Little attention was paid until the 1970s, however, to the economic conditions under which drugs are distributed. The changing climate at this time reflects the growth of public programs and, to a lesser extent, private insurance plans, which cover drug costs. In all of these programs, the "third party," who reimburses either the consumer or the pharmacist, develops a vested interest in retail drug prices.

Federal outlays for prescription cost reimbursement (for Medicare, Medicaid, and several smaller programs) passed $1.3 billion in 1973, a 66 per cent increase over the 1969 level. Together with half a billion dollars in state outlays, and nearly the same amount by private insurance carriers (Blue Cross, Aetna, Metropolitan, and so on), somewhere between 40 and 50 per cent of consumer prescription costs are now reimbursed by third parties. The extension of public insurance programs beyond the elderly and the poor to the general population would provide coverage of nearly all prescription expenditures.

The magnitude of the sums involved in present and potential drug cost coverage must inevitably lead to efforts to influence drug prices. In 1974, some 35 states limited prescription reimbursement under their state-administered Medicaid programs to the wholesale cost of the drug plus a dispensing fee averaging about $2.00. Late in 1974, the secretary of HEW moved to implement this approach nationally for all programs financed in whole or in part by the Federal government.[33]

A Pharmaceutical Reimbursement Board was to be established early in 1975.

---

[33] *Federal Register*, Nov. 27, 1974, pt. 2.

The board would set a national schedule of dispensing fees—in effect, the retail pharmacist's margin. Beyond this, for multiple-source drugs, the board would establish maximum allowable costs (MAC) for the reimbursable acquisition of these drugs by the pharmacist. Testimony by HEW officials before congressional committees during 1974 made it clear that the department's intention is to set MACs at something close to competitive generic drug levels wherever possible.

It would be a mistake to expect too much from this program initially. The estimate of HEW is that savings of 22 to 36 per cent (at retail) are possible for drugs available from competitive suppliers, but that this will save only 5 to 8 per cent of total Federal outlays because three quarters of prescription expendi-.tures are for patented, single-source drugs.[34] At least three more steps are necessary to secure a substantial reduction in drug expenditures.

The first is reform of the patent system so far as drugs are concerned. For example, Eli Lilly's 17-year monopoly on propoxyphene HCl (Darvon) expired in 1972, and there were identical competitive products available at a fraction of the Darvon price. Limitation of reimbursable costs to the competitive level will bring down even the Darvon price. But, a year or two before this patent ran out, Lilly introduced a newly patented minor congener, propoxyphene napsylate. The company is now making a massive effort to persuade physicians to switch to the new, improved version—Darvon-N—which would be fully reimbursable at Lilly's price. If Lilly is successful, Darvon-N, like Darvon before it, may become the most widely prescribed analgesic drug in the industry (despite the weight of evidence from controlled tests that indicates that propoxyphene is less effective than plain aspirin).

There is no reason for the Patent Office to encourage the proliferation of pharmaceutical monopoly in this manner, where the modifications are hardly innovative advances. Indeed, consideration should be given to legislation that provides for the compulsory licensing of patents at fair royalties after some limited period of time, such as 3 to 5 years, if it appears that the patent holder is unfairly exploiting consumers. This approach has been used in England and several other countries with good results in holding down drug prices.

Second, the average physician needs better information about drugs than he gets from the industry's marketing departments. This need could be filled by an authoritative compendium covering the availability, uses, and prices of products on the market. The AMA promised such a work in 1961, in order to head off legislation that would have established an FDA compendium. After years of delay, the AMA turned the task over to its prestigious (and independent!) Council on Drugs.

The council issued the first edition of *AMA Drug Evaluations* in 1971, with flat "not recommended" conclusions for a number of products widely advertised in AMA publications. In the face of industry protests, the reaction of the AMA's board of trustees was swift and sure. The 65-year old Council on Drugs was abolished, and the association's own staff rushed into print with a watered-down second edition inoffensive to advertisers.

[34] *Federal Register*, Nov. 15, 1974, p. 40,303.

Finally, under congressional pressure, the FDA has agreed to develop a compendium. The agency hopes to have a pilot volume ready by the end of 1976, some 15 years after it was first suggested as an FDA responsibility by Senator Estes Kefauver.

The third step toward controlling consumer drug costs involves the avoidance of waste through physician education. The classic example is the widespread prescribing of antibiotics for the common cold, a self-limiting viral infection that is unresponsive to antibiotic therapy. Waste also can occur when the correct drug is given for an illness in too small a dose or for too short a period to be effective, or in excessive dosages that expose patients to the hazards of toxicity as well as unnecessary expenditures.

An adequate compendium and postgraduate short courses are valuable in this respect. A more direct approach, however, is peer review of drug utilization. Here a doctor's prescribing habits are reviewed by a panel of physicians and pharmacists; he is quietly informed if deviations from good practice are found.

Despite an AMA opposition to "second-guessing" any physician's decisions, this is not a revolutionary concept. Staff pharmacy and therapeutics committees in the better hospitals have been performing such a function for years. Local professional standards review organizations (PSRO) are now required by HEW regulations to monitor the quality of medical care provided under Federally sponsored programs. The department has assured Congress that PSRO review will be extended to cover drug utilization.

There is little question that improvement in the quality of information available to physicians and peer review of drug utilization patterns will do much to reduce the waste and the avoidable dangers of irrational prescribing. The strict enforcement of drug-quality standards coupled with an effective MAC program where government reimbursement is involved should reduce drug prices by improving the climate for price, rather than brand, competition. Finally, legislation introduced in the 94th Congress, with far better chances of passage than ever before, may restrict easy access to patent monopolies.

It is no accident that nearly all of the major drug manufacturers have begun to promote generic lines of drugs to retail pharmacies with as much emphasis on price as on the "reliability" of the supplier. The 1970s may yet be the decade in which the pharmaceutical industry becomes workably competitive.

SUGGESTED READINGS

BOOKS AND PAMPHLETS

Dowling, Harry F. *Medicines for Man*. New York: Alfred A. Knopf, Inc., 1970.
Garb, Solomon, and Betty Jean Crim. *Pharmacology and Patient Care*. New York: Springer Publishing Company, Inc., 1962.
Harris, Richard. *The Real Voice*. New York: Macmillan Publishing Co., Inc., 1964.
Harris, Seymour E. *The Economics of American Medicine*. New York: Macmillan Publishing Co., Inc., 1964.
Mintz, Morton. *By Prescription Only*. Boston: Houghton Mifflin Company, 1967.
Talalay, Paul, ed. *Drugs in Our Society*. Baltimore: The Johns Hopkins Press, 1964.

GOVERNMENT PUBLICATIONS

Task Force on Prescription Drugs. *Background Papers* (Washington, D.C.: U.S. Government Printing Office, 1968, 1969): "Approaches to Drug Insurance Design," "Current American and Foreign Programs," "The Drug Manufacturers and the Drug Distributors," "The Drug Prescribers," and "The Drug Users."

————. *Final Report.* Washington, D.C.: U.S. Government Printing Office, 1969.

U.S. Congress, Senate, Subcommittee on Antitrust and Monopoly, *Hearings on Administered Prices*, pts. 13–24, 1960–1962.

————. *Hearings on the Drug Industry Antitrust Act*, pts. 1–7, 1962.

————. *Report on Administered Prices: Drugs*, 1962.

U.S. Congress, Senate, Subcommittee on Health, *Examination of the Pharmaceutical Industry*. pts. 1–6, 1974.

U.S. Congress, Senate, Subcommittee on Monopoly, *Hearings on Competitive Problems in the Drug Industry*, pts. 1–24, 1967–1974.

ARTICLES

Kiefer, David M. "Prognosis for the Drug Houses." *Chemical and Engineering News*, **42**:68 (Aug. 10, 1964).

————. "The Challenge of Change in the U.S. Drug Industry." *Chemical and Engineering News*, **42**:114 (Aug. 17, 1964).

May, Charles D. "Selling Drugs by 'Educating' Physicians." *Journal of Medical Education*, **36**:1 (Jan. 1961).

Reese, K. M. "Drug Prices." *Chemical and Engineering News*, **46**:66 (Jan. 29, 1968).

Silberman, Charles E. "Drugs: The Pace Is Getting Furious." *Fortune*, **61**:138 (May 1960).

Steele, Henry. "Patent Restrictions and Price Competition in the Ethical Drug Industry." *Journal of Industrial Economics*, **12**:198 (July 1964).

CHAPTER 8

the computer industry

DAVID DALE MARTIN

I. INTRODUCTION

The computer industry comprises a large and growing sector of America's economic activity. The products of the industry are rapidly becoming essential, or basic, goods and services used in all other sectors of the economy. Any definition of this industry is somewhat arbitrary. In this chapter the term *computer industry* should be construed to mean the portion of American industry directly involved in the design, production, and distribution of electronic equipment used for data processing and other equipment and services closely related in production or use to electronic data-processing equipment.[1]

The industry as thus defined includes all the activities of a large number of firms and a portion of the activities of many other firms. One corporation—International Business Machines (IBM)—plays so great a role, however, that one might be justified in viewing the American computer industry as that part of the American economy managed by IBM and its competitors.[2]

History

The computer industry is both very new and changing very rapidly, compared with most other industrial sectors. For that reason, the structure of the computer

[1] Because other segments of the communications industry are discussed elsewhere in this book, this chapter will deal only incidentally with the design, production, and distribution of electronic data-processing equipment specifically designed for, and used in, activities normally considered communications. It should be kept in mind, however, that technological developments in electronics during the last quarter century have resulted in the electronic processing of communications data in much the same manner as the processing of data generally. Furthermore, recent developments in electronic computing equipment have made possible networks of computing equipment with components that are interconnected by means of electronic communications equipment.

[2] IBM manages much more than its portion of the American computer industry because it is also a major factor in the computer industries in the rest of the world.

industry will be described in historical terms in the hope that the reader will be able to foresee, or at least better understand, the many changes in structure that may make an essay such as this obsolete soon after it is written.[3] The evolution of the industry structure is described in terms of changes in both the technological characteristics of the products and the role of the major corporations involved. That evolution can be expected to continue at a rapid pace at least in the next few years with or without major changes in public policy.

The patterns of business conduct that have resulted from and helped to shape the structure of this industry are discussed primarily in terms of past controversies about their consequences for the emergence and continuation of competition of degree and kind sufficient to protect the public interest.

The industry's performance is evaluated in terms of traditionally accepted standards of technological progressiveness, appropriateness of resource allocation, and equity in the distribution of income, wealth, and power. The concluding discussion of public policy alternatives centers around the basic questions of whether the computer industry should be (1) placed in the traditional, but evolving, category of "industries affected with a public interest," which require direct government regulation of business conduct; (2) left to its own devices without government interference in either conduct or structure, or (3) restructured so as to achieve conduct consistent with the public interest without the need for direct regulation of the public-utility type.

The computer industry's performance can be judged also in terms of its crucial role in recent years as a primary source of the information-processing systems used not only in business but throughout the society. Because of the pervasiveness of computerized information processing and the consequences for the institutional structure generally of technical changes in information systems, the structure of power to control the computer industry has special implications for the continuation of democracy not characteristic of most other industries. Computers are taking on not only the sort of indispensability attained earlier by automobiles and petroleum products but also some of the characteristics of printing and publishing. Centralized control of such an industry, unless made adequately responsive to public needs through democratic government regulatory mechanisms cannot for long be tolerated without sacrifice of freedom. Evaluation of performance from this standpoint, therefore, requires that the computer industry's structure be evaluated not only in terms of the structural attributes usually associated by economists with competitive business practices and technological efficiency, but also in terms of the effect of industry charac-

---

[3] In the spring of 1976 the government's case against IBM began its second year in the district court in New York. Almost a year had been devoted to the market definition issues, followed by the introduction of evidence relating to conduct. The case of *Telex* v. *IBM* was settled by the two parties just prior to Supreme Court review of the U.S. Circuit Court of Appeals decision reversing the district court award of damages to Telex. Several private suits are still pending. The most important is *Memorex* v. *IBM*, which has not yet gone to trial. Either the Justice Department's or Memorex's case could radically change the structure, conduct, and performance of this industry.

teristics on the nature of social change in information handling and its consequences for individual freedom.

II. MARKET STRUCTURE

Electronic data-processing equipment was first produced and used during World War II for military purposes, such as for the massive number of simple, but time-consuming, arithmetic calculations required in figuring artillery shell trajectories. In 1951, 6 years after the end of that war, the Bureau of the Census took delivery of Univac I, which was the first commercially built *electronic* data-processing system (EDP).[4]

International Business Machines first offered an EDP system for sale in April 1953. That IBM 701 was intended for use in nuclear research. The IBM 702 was that company's first computer intended for business use. The first installation was made early in 1955. From 1952–1973, IBM had four "generations" of computers. Each generation in the past lasted about 6 years and each new one embodied some technological advances over earlier generations. Each new generation has included to some degree changes in processors, storage devices, input-output devices, and software. Since it first began to market electronic data-processing equipment in 1952, IBM has introduced about 600 different electronic data-processing products.[5]

Although the electronic data-processing equipment industry began only in the 1950s, the functions performed by computing equipment, by and large, were not new. The new electronic technology had made possible new ways of satisfying the needs of business, government, and scientific researchers for systems for processing information. Thus, the computer industry supplemented, and to some extent replaced, earlier products used to satisfy a portion of the demand for equipment and services to make information processing more efficient. To some extent, of course, supply creates its own demand. Technological improve-

---

[4] Electronic equipment makes use of vacuum tubes or more recently developed substitutes for vacuum tubes, such as transistors, semiconductors, or integrated circuits. Electrical equipment makes use of electricity for heat or motive power but is not called electronic. One early large-scale computer used mechanical switches operated by electricity but no vacuum tubes. For more information about the history and technology of the industry see *Telex* v. *IBM*, "Stipulation of Background Facts Concerning Electronic Data Processing, the Products, the Industry, the Parties, and the Issues," *Appendices A and B to the Final Pretrial Order*, Apr. 12, 1973, U.S. District Court for Northern District of Oklahoma, no. 72-C-18; no. 72-C-89 (consolidated).

[5] Processors are electronic equipment in which the "number crunching" takes place. They are often known as CPUs, which is an abbreviation standing for central processing units. Storage devices are disk, tape, or other mechanical and electrical mechanisms for recording, storing, and playing back information, usually in the form of coded messages expressed in binary numbers. Input-output devices are analogous to the microphones, radio antennae, and speakers in a hi-fi system. They include IBM card processors, high-speed printers, and the televisionlike devices used by airline passenger reservation clerks. Software consists of messages used to instruct the processors on what is to be done with all information that is put in.

ments in information processing have tended to increase the amount of information that is processed. Therefore, many of the markets now served by the computer industry did not exist, or were very much smaller, before the electronic computer. Nevertheless, the structure of control of precomputer information-processing industries played a major role in determining the evolution of the industry after the technological advances of World War II made electronic data-processing possible.

Four of the eight present-day American manufacturers of complete electronic data-processing systems were well-established suppliers of one or another portion of the precomputer information-processing equipment market. These four include National Cash Register, Burroughs (adding machines), Sperry Rand (formerly Remington-Rand, office equipment including tabulating machines), and IBM (typewriters, punch cards, and tabulating machines). It was the tabulating machine, however, for which general-purpose electronic computers were the closest substitute product. Although electronic computers originally were used to replace desk calculators in scientific and military uses, and continue to be used extensively for such purposes, the primary submarket for EDP equipment has become the application of electronic computers to the routine filing and processing of business information both quantitative and verbal. In the early 1950s, when electronic computers became technically possible, every firm using punched-card tabulating-machine equipment as a major component of its information-processing system became automatically a potential customer for computer companies. Therefore, those firms then supplying punched-card tabulating-machine equipment were seriously threatened by competition from the products of the emerging computer technology. Similarly, those companies with established supplier-customer relationships with users of punched-card tabulating-machine data-processing systems had an advantage in marketing the new electronic substitute products.

In 1952, the United States Department of Justice sued IBM for allegedly monopolizing the tabulating-machine industry. At that time, IBM had approximately a 90 per cent share of the tabulating machine market; Remington Rand accounted for the remainder.[6]

Sperry Rand acquired Univac so the two firms that supplied tabulating machines became the early leaders in both the tabulating-machine and electronic computer markets. In 1956, IBM and Sperry Rand shared the electronic data-processing markets almost equally, as shown in Table 1. At that time, electronic computers were used relatively much more in scientific research "number crunching" applications than in business-information processing. In 1956, IBM accounted for about 85 per cent of the *new* installations, as the large tabulating-machine replacement market began to be tapped. The early IBM general-purpose computers were designed for data input from 80-column tabulating

[6] U.S. Congress, Senate, Committee on the Judiciary, Subcommittee on Antitrust and Monopoly, *The Computer Industry*, pt. 7, *Hearings on S.1167*, 93rd Cong., 2d sess., 1974, p. 5090. Statement of the Computer Industry Association submitted by A. G. W. Biddle, executive director.

TABLE 1
Shares of Total Revenues from EDP Markets for the World and the United States, 1956

COMPANY	U.S. AMOUNT ($ MILLIONS)	PER CENT	WORLD AMOUNT ($ MILLIONS)	PER CENT
IBM	42,174	42.9	39,276	47.5
Sperry Rand-Univac	50,329	51.2	37,590	45.5
All others	—	5.9	—	7.0

Source: "Findings of Fact," *Honeywell, Inc.* v. *Sperry Rand* (Civil Action 4-67 Civ. 138, U.S. Dist. Court, 4th Dist., Minn.) U.S., Congress, *Hearings on S.* 1167, p. 5090.

cards on which were stored the data files of most of the potential customers. Sperry Rand's tenth of the tabulating-machine market was based on 90-column cards and equipment. In competition with Sperry-Rand and the other entrants into the EDP market, IBM had the advantage of offering compatible EDP equipment and services to customers already relying on IBM for information processing.

Thus, the dominant position of IBM in the tabulating-machine market was transformed by successful defensive action into a dominant position in the EDP market. Judge Larson's "Findings of Fact" in the *Honeywell, Inc.* v. *Sperry Rand* case included market shares of nine computer-system companies from 1955–1967, based on retail sales value of the installed base of EDP equipment. These data are shown in Table 2. From 1957–1967 IBM's share, as measured by these data, varied between 65 and 80 per cent for both the world and the domestic markets.

In most industries, market shares can be measured either by share of sales revenues received by each firm selling the products of the industry, or by the share of the total value of shipments, including interplant transfers, accounted for by each firm, or by production data. In the computer industry, some of the revenue is received from the sale of equipment, but much of the revenue results from the leasing of equipment and software. Sales revenues and revenues from leases, of course, cannot be added together to measure a firm's share of the market unless all firms have the same proportions of each of the two types of revenue. Value of shipments or production data are not available, but estimates have been made regularly by the International Data Corporation of the stock of EDP equipment in use. By valuing the leased equipment at the price that would be charged if it were purchased rather than leased, estimates have been made of the value of the "installed base" and the share of that total value accounted for by each company that either sells or leases EDP equipment.

In a particular year, a company might put in place a smaller or larger share than it accounted for in the already installed base. For this reason, such installed

TABLE 2

Retail Sales Value of Installed Base of EDP Equipment and Relative Shares of Major Suppliers, United States and World, 1955–1967

	SR		IBM		HONEYWELL		RCA		NCR		BURR		GE		CDC		PHILCO	
	NUMBER	PER CENT	NUMBER	PER CENT	NUMBER	PER CENT	NUMBER	PER CENT	NUMBER	PER CENT	NUMBER	PER CENT	NUMBER	PER CENT	NUMBER	PER CENT	NUMBER	PER CENT
1955(W)	31,920	38.10	47,372	56.55	—	—	4,200	5.01	280	0.33	—	—	—	—	—	—	—	—
1955(D)	31,920	38.48	46,553	56.12	—	—	4,200	5.06	280	0.34	—	—	—	—	—	—	—	—
1956(W)	50,190	18.38	206,569	75.66	—	—	4,200	1.54	280	0.10	11,782	4.32	—	—	—	—	—	—
1956(D)	50,190	18.64	202,852	75.32	—	—	4,200	1.56	280	0.10	11,782	4.38	—	—	—	—	—	—
1957(W)	81,270	15.94	402,872	79.01	1,680	0.33	4,200	0.82	280	0.05	19,580	3.84	—	—	—	—	—	—
1957(D)	81,270	16.31	391,238	78.54	1,680	0.34	4,200	0.84	280	0.06	19,470	3.91	—	—	—	—	—	—
1958(W)	115,710	15.93	566,001	77.92	6,720	0.93	12,600	1.73	280	0.04	23,582	3.25	1,484	0.20	—	—	—	—
1958(D)	115,710	16.34	548,035	77.40	6,720	0.95	12,600	1.78	280	0.04	23,205	3.28	1,484	0.21	—	—	—	—
1959(W)	178,836	17.28	778,253	75.18	11,760	1.14	13,860	1.34	1,176	0.11	42,437	4.10	8,904	0.86	—	—	—	—
1959(D)	178,836	17.75	750,997	74.54	11,760	1.17	13,860	1.38	1,176	0.12	42,033	4.17	8,904	0.88	—	—	—	—
1960(W)	220,332	15.65	1,023,224	72.66	11,760	0.84	32,970	2.34	4,704	0.33	47,258	3.36	38,328	2.72	12,852	0.91	16,800	1.91
1960(D)	220,332	16.24	971,804	71.62	11,760	0.87	32,970	2.43	5,880	0.43	46,090	3.40	38,328	2.82	12,852	0.95	16,800	1.24
1961(W)	303,156	14.44	1,490,818	71.00	39,732	1.89	60,690	2.89	16,716	0.80	53,835	2.56	67,209	3.20	42,756	2.04	25,200	1.20
1961(D)	303,156	15.49	1,355,232	69.25	39,732	2.03	58,170	2.97	14,530	0.74	51,353	2.62	66,915	3.42	42,756	2.18	25,200	1.29
1962(W)	319,662	11.34	2,004,576	71.09	62,706	2.22	107,520	3.81	55,226	1.96	59,781	2.12	97,701	3.46	80,808	2.87	31,920	1.13
1962(D)	319,662	12.35	1,810,110	69.91	58,380	2.25	89,376	3.45	47,863	1.85	57,354	2.22	95,349	3.68	80,808	3.12	30,240	1.17
1963(W)	397,509	10.13	2,764,129	70.46	71,077	1.81	167,084	4.26	108,648	2.77	97,451	2.48	129,507	3.30	151,851	3.87	35,616	0.91
1963(D)	397,509	11.15	2,489,221	69.84	64,701	1.84	123,981	3.48	94,817	2.66	90,794	2.55	125,979	3.53	142,275	3.99	33,936	0.95
1964(W)	570,759	10.68	3,650,610	68.46	129,810	2.43	204,937	3.83	159,638	2.99	169,538	3.11	169,538	3.17	243,740	4.56	41,664	0.78
1964(D)	570,759	11.79	3,306,253	68.30	118,915	2.46	147,267	3.04	133,919	2.77	147,737	3.05	160,823	3.32	214,970	4.44	39,984	0.83
1965(W)	728,923	10.79	4,398,308	65.10	255,444	3.78	236,204	3.50	219,122	3.24	253,541	3.75	228,588	3.38	392,171	5.80	44,352	0.86
1965(D)	728,923	12.08	3,938,446	65.28	231,874	3.84	173,122	2.87	173,083	2.87	217,018	3.60	201,587	3.34	328,318	5.44	40,488	0.87
1966(W)	1,006,114	10.10	6,504,163	65.30	517,084	5.19	338,217	3.40	294,745	2.96	321,807	3.23	372,592	3.74	565,291	5.68	39,816	0.40
1966(D)	1,006,114	11.27	5,910,929	66.20	464,134	5.20	244,984	2.74	214,716	2.40	271,117	3.04	311,518	3.49	468,781	5.25	35,952	0.40
1967(W)	1,246,925	9.40	8,891,566	66.98	619,538	4.67	541,338	4.08	432,466	3.26	387,943	2.92	431,557	3.25	697,116	5.25	25,704	0.19
1967(D)	1,246,925	10.59	8,014,659	68.06	555,936	4.72	381,653	3.24	298,094	2.53	346,223	2.94	355,925	3.02	554,053	4.71	21,840	0.19

Source: "Opinion," *Honeywell, Inc. v. Sperry Rand* (Civil Action 4-67 Civ 138, U.S. Dist. Court, 4th Dist., Minn.), p. 157. U.S. Congress, *Hearing on S. 1167*, p. 5104.

base, market-share statistics give rise to much confusion unless interpreted very carefully. A firm that ceased to produce EDP equipment might continue to have a share of the installed base so long as the equipment previously produced and sold or leased continued to be used. Shares estimated with installed-base or rental-revenue data are good indicators of a firm's market share, if shares are stable for long time periods, but they cannot reflect recent changes in a firm's share of new business.

Table 3 shows the International Data Corporation's estimates of the value at the end of 1973 of the installed base of general-purpose EDP systems in the United States. The share of IBM was 63.8 per cent. Its next largest competitor—Honeywell—accounted for only 9.4 per cent. The third largest firm was Sperry Rand-Univac with 8.1 per cent. By 1975, two major corporations had withdrawn from the computer business—General Electric and Radio Corporation of America. The installed base of these two firms was taken over by Honeywell and Sperry Rand, respectively.

These data show why the structure of the American computer industry is sometimes described with the phrase "Snow White and the Seven Dwarfs." But such aggregates as "value of installed base" and "revenues from EPP products" cover up many of the important structural characterstics of the many submarkets within which a large variety of types of computer products and

TABLE 3

Value of Installed Base of General Purpose EDP Equipment Supplied by Systems Manufacturers and Plug-compatible Peripheral Companies, United States, 1973

	VALUE ($ MILLIONS)	TOTAL (PER CENT)
IBM	17,406	63.8
PCM	1,325	4.9
Honeywell	2,578	9.4
Univac	2,205	8.1
Burroughs	1,421	5.2
CDC	973	3.6
NCR	737	2.7
DEC	134	.5
Xerox	390	1.4
Others	132	.4
Total	27,301	100.0

Source: U.S. Congress, Senate, Subcommittee on Antitrust and Monopoly, *The Computer Industry, Hearings on S.1167,* 93d Cong., 2d sess., p. 7, p. 5095.

services are bought and sold. We must examine this variety of end products and also the intermediate products used as components in their production, or conjointly, in their use.

End-product Lines

In the *Telex* v. *IBM* antitrust case, a number of revealing confidential documents were put into evidence and thereby made public. One of these documents, reproduced in part as Table 4, gives a very convenient listing not only of IBM's

TABLE 4
IBM Product-line Assessment Summary

SYSTEM-PRODUCT	ASSESSMENT	COMPETITION
Large systems		
—	Deficient	CDC Star-100
Model 195	Deficient	CDC Cyber 70, mod 76
Model 165	Equal	Univac 1110
Model 155	Equal	Burroughs B6700, HIS H6080
Intermediate systems		
Model 145	Equal	RCA 6, HIS H6040
Model 135	Superior	RCA 2, NCR C-200
Model 30	Deficient	Univac 9300/9400, NCR C-200, Burroughs B2500, HIS H1015
Model 22	Deficient	NCR C-200
Model 25	Deficient	Univac 9200, NCR 3-100 and C-200, Burroughs B2500, HIS H115-2
System/370 advanced function		
Multiprocessing	Deficient	Univac 1100 series, Burroughs B6700/B7700
Relocate	Equal	RCA 3, RCA 7, Burroughs B6700/B7700
Sensor base	Deficient	Control data, digital equipment, Xerox data systems
Small commercial systems		
T-55	Superior	HIS H115/H115-2/H125, UN 9300/9400
T-54	Equal	NCR C-100, UN 9200, HIS H110
Model 20	Deficient	NCR C-50, UN 9200, HIS H115, H115-2
System/3	Equal	NCR C-50 and C-100, UN 9200, HIS H105 and H115
IBM 6400	Deficient	Burroughs L series, Mixdord 800, Philips 350

TABLE 4 (Continued)

SYSTEM-PRODUCT	ASSESSMENT	COMPETITION
Sensor-based and small scientific systems		
1800	Deficient	General automaton 18/30, alternative application approaches, minicomputers in general
1130	Deficient	General Automation 18/30, minicomputers in general
System/7	Deficient	Honeywell, DEC, Varian, Hewlett-Packard
Storage products		
Tape drives		
2401 series	Deficient	Ampex, Bucode, Texas Instruments, Potter, Telex
2420 series	Deficient	Potter, Telex, Bucode, S.T.C.
3420 series	Equal	Potter, Telex, Bucode, S.T.C.
Fir	Equal	Ampex, Potter
Birch	Superior[a] (not rated)	No competition
Drum and disk drives		
2310	Deficient	Memorex, Computer Hardware, Inc.
2311	Deficient	Memorex, Marshall, Telex, Greyhound, Talcott
2314A/2314B	Deficient	Telex, Memorex, Calcomp, Marshall, CDC, Ampex
2319/IFA	Superior	Telex, Memorex, Calcomp, Marshall, CDC, Ampex
3330	Superior	Century Data Systems
2395	Superior	Advanced Memory Systems (SSU)
Winchester	Equal[a] (deficient)	Telex, Memorex, CDC, Calcomp, Marshall
Disk packs	Deficient	Memorex, Caelus, BASF, CDC
Strip files	Equal	NCR
LCS (2361)	Deficient	Ampex, Lockheed, Fabri-Tek, Data Products
Main memory (S/360, S/370)	Deficient	Data Recall Corp., Fabri-Tek, Ampex, Cogar, Weismantel, Standard Computer
Card-paper tape-printer products		
Card I/O	Equal	No 80-column plug-to-plug competition
Paper tape I/O	Deficient	Honeywell, GE, Tally, Teletype
Printers		
1403N1	Deficient	Telex, Potter
3211	Superior	No comparable competitive product

293

TABLE 4 (Continued)

SYSTEM-PRODUCT	ASSESSMENT	COMPETITION
Canopus (MED.-500 LPM)	Equal	Data Products, Mohawk Data Sciences
5203-3	Equal	Potter, Data Products
OCR and MICR products		
OCR		
1287	Equal	NCR, Recognition Equipment, Inc., CDC 935, Univac, Honeywell
1288	Superior	COC 915, COC 955
Shark	Equal	Recognition Equipment, Inc. (input-3)
MICR		
MICR		
Inscriber	Deficient	NCR 482, Burroughs series 100 and 200
Sorter-reader	Deficient	Burroughs B9134-1 OCR/MICR
Data entry products		
029/059	Deficient	Univac 1701/1710 (buffered)
5496	Equal	DDC 9601 and 9610
129	Equal	Univac 1701/1710 (buffered)
IBM 50	Deficient	Mohawk Data Sciences, Honeywell, Viatron
Viking 1	Deficient[a] (superior)	Keypunch-Univac, Clustered Systems-Inforex, Computer Machinery Corp., price advantage as remote
Data collection products		
357/1030	Deficient	CDC, RCA
2790	Equal	Friden Mis, Data Pathing, Inc., Solar, Burroughs TU 100/900
Communications products		
Communications controllers		
2701	Deficient[a] (equal)	ITT, Memorex, Sanders
2702/2703	Deficient	Memorex 1270, Burroughs 1800
27RM	Equal[a] (deficient)	Comcet 20, 40, 60, Honeywell 16 series, Varian Mini's, Univac C/SP
27RL	Superior[a] (not rated)	Memorex 1270/1271, Interdata
Operator-oriented terminals:		
2740, 2741	Deficient	Teletype Corp., Dura, Datel, Anderson-Jacobson, Memorex 1240
Low/medium speed batch terminals		
1059, 2770	Deficient	TTY ASR, Datel 31, Univac DCT 500/1000, GE Terminet 300,

TABLE 4 (Continued)

SYSTEM-PRODUCT	ASSESSMENT	COMPETITION
3735	Equal	Memorex 1280 Burroughs TC series, Compat 88 23, Cogar System 4, Victor Nixdorf 820
27AX	Deficient	Memorex 180, GE Terminet 300, TTY KSR 4210
High-speed terminals: 2770, 2780	Deficient	Data 100, Remcom, Univac DCT 2000
Processor terminals System/6	Equal	Univac 9200
1130, S/360 20	Deficient	HIS model 5, Data 100 78 2
Remote display terminals 2260/2265	Deficient	Univac Uniscope 100, Datapoint 2200, Digivue 2000
3270	Equal	Univac Uniscope 100, Datapoint 2000

^a Change from previous assessment, which is in parentheses.
Source: The Computer Industry, Hearings on S. 1167, op. cit., pp. 5111–5112. *Telex* v. *IBM*, Plaintiff's Exhibit No. 128.

product line, but of the comparable products in each category offered by other companies in August 1971. The document also reveals an assessment of the quality of IBM's products—an assessment made by one IBM department for use in management decision making.

A perusal of Table 4 shows that IBM faced quite different sets of competing companies in the different segments of its 1971 product line. The first five categories are complete EDP systems that include input-output, storage, and processing equipment as well as software. Within each of the major categories the table shows several models that differ from each other in the quantity of data that can be processed and stored and perhaps also in the specific uses for which they were not appropriate or most efficient. Note that most of the competing products listed for these systems categories are products of the companies listed in Tables 1, 2, and 3. Not only did the "dwarfs" have relatively smaller shares than IBM of the installed base of EDP systems over the years, but also most of those smaller competitors had more limited computer product lines than IBM.

If data on each of the submarkets in which IBM participates were examined, they most likely would reveal variations in IBM's market shares among these submarkets. Table 4 itself enables us to conclude that concentration is greater in the particular submarkets than for EDP equipment considered generally because the firms other than IBM are more specialized suppliers—that is, they offer a more limited line of products.

The second five major product categories consist not of complete data-processing systems, but are, instead, categories of products used in conjunction with each other and with other products, such as CPUs, not separately listed. A large system, for example, model 195, would have included such storage products as drum and disk drives and main memories, as well as input-output products of some type. Such products are known as peripheral equipment.

Plug-compatible Peripheral Equipment

Table 4 shows that, in 1971, IBM faced competition in the peripheral-equipment product categories from firms whose names do not appear among its competitors in the first five "systems" categories. Until the late 1960s, such competition barely existed. A number of independent peripheral-equipment manufacturers had existed from the early years of the electronic computer era, but their role had been limited to supplying printers, tape or disk drives, and so on to computer systems manufacturers as original equipment in the same way that automobile tire manufacturers supply tires to auto companies for use on new cars. The smaller computer systems manufacturers were not sufficiently vertically integrated to make all of the components for the systems they put together and offered under their own brand names. Even IBM purchased some such peripheral equipment for use in its systems.

In 1966, du Pont requested bids on tape drivers to replace the tape drives it was then using on its IBM computer system. Just as one might shop around for a new set of tires for a General Motors automobile, du Pont sought and found a lower-priced product of comparable quality when Telex Corporation, an original-equipment tape-drive manufacturer, won the bid. Telex went on in the late 1960s to expand production and successfully enter the market for replacement tape drives used in IBM systems. Telex was followed by a number of other independent competitors in what came to be known as the plug-compatible peripheral-equipment market. These firms included Memorex, California Computer Products, Ampex, Potter Instruments, and a number of other small firms.[7]

Security analyst Eugene K. Collins gives seven factors that accounted for the successful entry of independent manufacturers directly into the end-user markets for peripherals attached to the IBM System/360 family of systems products that had been introduced as the third generation of IBM computers in the mid-1960s:

1. The potential market was large, particularly among IBM systems users, because standard peripherals and interfaces were used over virtually the entire IBM System 360 family;
2. The economies of scale of product development and manufacturing were not significant barriers to entry;
3. Technological progress in peripherals had been slow—perhaps because IBM never had to compete on a peripheral subsystem level (all previous

[7] See "Prepared Statement of Eugene K. Collins, director of research, Evans & Company, New York, N.Y.," in ibid., pp. 5380–5393.

end-user competition within the industry had been on a total bundled computer system level);

4. Profit margins were excellent, based on manufacturing costs and projected marketing and field service expenses;

5. Peripherals were an increasingly large portion of the dollar value of a total computer system (in 1960, peripherals were about 20 per cent of the total dollar value of a system and the central processing unit was 80 per cent; by 1970, the split was about 50–50; and, by 1980, peripheral subsystems are expected to represent about 80 per cent of the total value of a system);

6. One of the two major barriers to entry into the general-purpose computer industry, software compatability with IBM, was avoided by making the independent peripherals fully compatible with IBM software and systems, such that the peripherals were "transparent" to the main frame —they looked exactly like IBM peripherals to the central processing unit; and, finally,

7. The other major barrier to entry—capital—was reduced significantly, in part by investment enthusiasm for young technology companies in the late 1960s, but more importantly by the fact that an independent peripheral equipment manufacturer could address one market (for example, the digital tape-drive market) and was not forced to develop an entire computer systems family, including central processing units, an operating system, applications software, and all of the related peripheral subsystems—as a prerequisite to entry.[8]

Collins went on to say:

During 1970, shipments of independent peripheral subsystems manufacturers increased sharply. Telex alone shipped about $80 million in equipment and was budgeting shipment levels for 1971 that were approaching the levels of some of the surviving systems manufacturers that had been attempting to penetrate IBM's market for a considerably longer period of time.... Plug-compatible manufacturers were achieving what IBM's systems competition had failed to do—they were providing some real competition.[9]

The reaction of IBM to this competition is discussed subsequently in the section on business practices. Before turning attention to questions of conduct, let us look at other important aspects of industrial structure: vertical integration and channels of distribution.

Backward Vertical Integration: Semiconductors

Just as peripheral products are components of EDP systems, so are semiconductors components in main memories, central processing units, and in other parts of computer systems. The electronic computer industry began with the application of vacuum tube technology to data processing. The heart of the computer has been and continues to be the electronic circuitry built around the successors to vacuum tubes: transistors and other semiconductors.

When IBM introduced its first electronic computer in 1953, all the vacuum tubes were purchased from outside suppliers. The first successful transistor was

[8] Ibid., pp. 5387–5388.
[9] Ibid., p. 5388.

demonstrated at Bell Telephone Laboratories in 1947—an invention for which John Bardeen, Walter Brattain, and William Shockley later received a Nobel Prize.[10]

In 1955, Shockley established the Shockley Transistor Corporation in Santa Clara County, California, from which there sprang, directly or indirectly, nearly 25 semiconductor suppliers as skilled scientific personnel moved on to form semiconductor divisions in established companies, including Fairchild. Texas Instruments was among the original 12 licensees of Bell Labs in 1952. It became a major producer of germanium transistors and, in 1954, announced the first silicon transistor. In 1958, Jack Kilby at Texas Instruments invented the integrated circuit, which was to revolutionize computer technology after it became commercially available in 1964. By 1973, annual factory sales of semiconductors had surpassed $2 billion, 40 per cent of which were accounted for by business computer end uses, not counting IBM's production or use.[11]

The first vacuum-tube using the 701 computer of IBM was produced until 1959, when the IBM 1401 was introduced using germanium transistors. The more reliable, but more costly, silicon transistors were used at that time primarily in military applications. Also, IBM produced part of its requirements of germanium transistors for the 1401, but supplemented its supply with purchases from Texas Instruments and Fairchild. In 1964, the 1401 was phased out of production as IBM introduced its third generation of computer systems. These were a group of systems covering the size spectrum from the very largest down through intermediate sizes, all of which had a common architecture for which peripherals and software were compatible. The whole 360 line was designed around a hybrid circuit called Solid Logic Technology (SLT). Although integrated circuits had been invented several years earlier, the SLT was a less advanced component. It consisted of a 1-inch square of ceramic substrate to which was attached the necessary resistors, diodes, capacitors, and transistors. All SLTs were produced by IBM's own components division.

On the question of why IBM originally chose complete backward vertical integration to obtain the basic components of the System/360 line, Marilyn Walter-Carlson offers the following judgments:

> these packages were not available outside IBM and production was absolutely critical to the success of the 360 computer—it was a "you bet your company" product. IBM's organization charts show how critical these components were; the components division operated semiautonomously until mid-1963, when the entire division was suddenly pulled under the jurisdiction of Vincent Learson, where it remained until the end of 1966, when shipments of the 360s were back on schedule, presumably because SLT yields were finally satisfactory. IBM stayed with the SLT technology until the introduction of the 370s in 1970, although the independent semi-

---

[10] The history of this important industry is related in detail in "Prepared Statement of Marilyn Walter-Carlson, vice-president and associate director, Research Shareholders Management Co., Los Angeles, Calif.," *The Computer Industry*, op. cit., pp. 5412–5436. (Hereafter referred to as *The Computer Industry*.)

[11] Ibid., p. 5434.

conductor companies had by then introduced many other faster and denser devices. Was IBM cautious, or was it deliberately bringing the heart of its machines in-house? We think the evidence shows that the latter answer is correct. If IBM [were] being cautious, it could have selected several of the semiconductor houses which were proliferating in the early 1960s as suppliers, thereby guaranteeing itself at least one second source. But it was only in 1966–1967, when the components division was released from Learson's jurisdiction, that the decision was made to phase out the manufacture of all discretes and purchase these devices from outside suppliers. . . . We estimate that IBM purchases about $50 million of devices outside and produces about $600 million.[12]

After 1970, when IBM introduced the System/370 line of products, technical change was quite rapid both within IBM and in the remaining portion of the semiconductor industry as the integrated circuitry was further developed. Through photochemical etching processes, whole circuits are produced on very small chips, a number of which are produced simultaneously on a wafer. The newer technology may be making the design of the semiconductor components an integral part of the design of the computer products themselves. Thus, the continued production of standard integrated circuits for computer-industry use by an independent semiconductor industry may require more standardization in the computer industry than now exists.

Forward Vertical Stages

Electronic data-processing equipment is used to render services to end users. Use of the equipment requires a very high degree of skill, technical knowledge, and organizational capacity, as well as the investment of capital in the system. These ancillary services that accompany the use of the equipment can be divided conveniently into three categories: (1) the capital investment service, (2) technical maintenance of the equipment, and (3) software, or computer programming services.

From the end user's point of view, provision of all of these ancillary functions in-house would constitute vertical backward integration. Only main frame computer systems manufacturers are in a position to render all such services to themselves in their own information-processing systems. From the viewpoint of the equipment manufacturers, provision of all of these ancillary services to the end user of the equipment would constitute vertical forward integration. A third alternative structure entails the existence of firms independent of both the end user and the equipment manufacturer to render one or more of the ancillary services. The industry is characterized by a combination of all three types of vertical arrangements, but IBM's vertical forward integration into capital investment service, maintenance, and software is a most important structural characteristic.

The provision of the capital-investment service by the equipment manufacturer takes place in two important ways:

[12] Ibid., p. 5423.

1. The equipment, the software, and the maintenance are offered as a package on a monthly or yearly lease basis with equipment installed in the facilities of the end user.
2. The installation is made at a service bureau location operated by the equipment manufacturer and the end user purchases data-processing services.

At the year end, in 1973, the United States installed base of computers was valued at $30 billion by International Data Corporation. Of that total, 58.8 per cent was IBM equipment. Of the IBM portion, 41.5 per cent was rented from IBM directly. One third of the IBM portion was user owned. One fourth was leased to the user by a third-party leasing company that had purchased the equipment from IBM.[13]

The service bureau market is relatively decentralized. IDC estimated in its 1974 testimony that the top 10 firms accounted for only 29 per cent of the revenues, with Control Data the leader with 6.7 per cent after its acquisition of IBM's Service Bureau Corporation.[14]

The International Data Corporation estimated that as much as 90 per cent of the software actually in use in 1974 was *not* supplied to the user as a separately priced item by an outside firm.[15]

Prior to the 1956 consent decree in the 1952 case, IBM restricted its business to two vertical arrangements.[16] The end user had the choice of either leasing equipment from IBM or buying data-processing services from IBM's service bureau. Although economists often stress the causal role of industry structure in determining business conduct, the structural consequences of the practice of refusing to sell equipment are evident.[17] Not only is the used equipment market eliminated, but the entrance of competitors into any phase of the business requires entry into all phases, thus greatly raising the barriers to entry into the whole group of potential markets if the integrated firm has a dominant position. Such was alleged to be the case by the Department of Justice in its 1952 complaint against IBM. That complaint was directed at remedying IBM's dominance in the tabulating-machine business. However, by 1956, the computer era had arrived. The allegations and provisions of the settlement of that case are discussed subsequently, although court-ordered regulatory constraints on conduct might be considered to be part of the structural characteristics of an industry.

III. CONDUCT

Each firm operating in any industry conducts its affairs so as to achieve its own objectives subject to constraints imposed on it by itself and from outside forces,

---

[13] "Testimony of John P. Breyer, executive vice-president, International Data Corporation, Exhibit 1," ibid., pp. 4933–5023, at p. 4973.

[14] Ibid., p. 5009.

[15] Ibid., p. 5015.

[16] See *United States* v. *International Business Machines Corporation*, CCH 1956 Trade Cases para. 68, 245 (SDNY 1956), and "Prepared Statement of Ralph E. Miller, economist, Washington, D.C.," *The Computer Industry*, op. cit., pp. 5620–5636.

[17] See Carl Kaysen, *United States* v. *United Shoe Machinery Corporation* (Cambridge, Mass.: Harvard University Press, 1956), pp. 64–73.

including other firms and governments.[18] In the computer industry, the firms other than IBM have been constrained very much by IBM's actual and potential conduct. Although IBM also has been constrained by the conduct of other firms in the industry, the primary limitation on its freedom to do as it pleases has come from actual and potential government-imposed constraints. Having started the computer era as the dominant firm in the markets for business-information-processing machines and services, IBM has been forced either to defend its dominant position or to acquiesce in the withering away of its market power to avoid antitrust action by other firms and government. Undoubtedly it has done some of each. By 1974, its share of the market appears to have reached an all-time low, and 15 private and one government antitrust cases were pending against it.

Writing in 1968, just before the beginning of the wave of antitrust cases, economist William G. Shepherd concluded:

> All in all, IBM's position verges on monopoly in economic even if not in legal terms. . . . IBM appears to have gained and held its market share mainly via substantial and pervasive price discrimination of several sorts. This is possible because IBM probably has large amounts of overhead or floating costs in its development and sales-support activities. Accordingly, IBM is inherently able and induced by rational profit maximizing to engage in systematic price discrimination on a large scale. This has probably played a major role in forestalling new entry, except in isolated submarkets (such as large systems) where IBM's technical inferiority is so great that it cannot be offset.[19]

Shepherd attributed the relatively high overhead, or floating, costs to four sources: (1) production costs of hardware are small relative to costs of research and development, sales, and customer support for complete EDP systems; (2) product-development costs are mingled for the broad range of products in the IBM product line; (3) much software has been accumulated and is made available exclusively to its customers, but without explicit charges; and (4) IBM's resources devoted to customer-support activities are so large as to afford opportunities for discrimination. These conditions would allow models for which competition is keenest to be priced closer to the direct costs of production than other models. Entry would, thereby, be easiest for a competitor that also offered not only a complete system of equipment and support services, but also as broad a line as IBM. Such a competitor would still face the fact of a large installed base yielding a steady flow of revenue long after the costs of its production were incurred.

Such have been the obstacles to entry and successful competition with IBM from the beginning of the computer era. The question remains whether the cost

---

[18] For a systematic exposition of the economic theory of the firm in terms of constraints and constraint-changing actions by firms, see Irvin M. Grossack and David Dale Martin, *Managerial Economics, Microeconomic Theory, and the Firm's Decisions*, (Boston: Little, Brown, 1973).

[19] William G. Shepherd, *Market Power and Economic Welfare, An Introduction* (New York: Random House, 1970), pp. 227–228.

of power that Shepherd attributed to IBM can be used without violation of the antitrust laws. The legal issues are not clear-cut by any means because the concept of price discrimination that Shepherd used is not the definition used in the Robinson-Patman Act, which requires that the *same product* be sold to some users for less than the price to others. Thus, the issue is whether IBM has engaged in patterns of conduct that constitute monopolizing or attempts to monopolize as prohibited by the Sherman Act. Just that issue is now before the courts in a number of the antitrust suits.

This essay is not an appropriate place in which to attempt to render a judgment. Instead, a few of the allegations and facts will be related that have come to light and that may provide some basis on which the reader can form conclusions not only about the industry but also about the adequacy of the law. We will begin with the 1952 government complaint and the terms of the 1956 settlement; go on to look at some of the internal evidence from IBM documents divulged in the process of litigation; and then examine the findings of the district court in the *Telex* case.

The 1956 Consent Decree

The electronic computer industry was just emerging in 1956 when IBM consented to a court order that was a classic case of a "conduct remedy." A review of that decree not only shows much about the pattern of conduct prevalent in the early 1950s, but also shows the explicit regulatory constraints under which IBM has been operating. Economist Ralph Miller's statement to the Hart antitrust subcommittee summarized the decree and its consequences as follows:

> 1. IBM was required to offer for sale all equipment that was generally available on lease, and the purchase prices had to have "a commercially reasonable relationship" to the rental terms. Leases were limited to a term of one year. Except for maintenance and repair, all services offered to lessees had to be offered at reasonable charges.
> The importance of leasing as an exclusionary practice had recently become clear in the *American Can* and second *Shoe Machinery* cases. These provisions prevented the gross abuses that had been discovered there.
> 2. IBM could not prohibit the use of its equipment in a system with non-IBM components. IBM could not tie its maintenance to the purchase of its hardware; nor could it require the use of IBM tabulating cards by any owner or lessee of its equipment (not even as a condition relating to maintenance or warranty of the equipment).
> These provisions were attempts to split the integrated data-processing market into segments that could be entered by smaller, specialized firms.
> 3. IBM had to offer training to independent repairmen (including any users desiring such training), and it had to offer to sell parts and subassemblies to owners and to independent maintenance firms.
> This was apparently a special effort to break open the technology of the equipment. It is noted here because scale economies in maintenance have become important in the computer industry, and, so long as maintenance is provided by manufacturers, these scale economies are an advantage of large size in the computer industry. It is, therefore, worth noting that the

consent decree attempted to encourage independent maintenance and repair service.

4. IBM was required to grant nonexclusive licenses under any, some, or all of its patents, at reasonable royalties (royalty-free, for patents . . . on tabulating cards or tabulating-card equipment), to anyone applying for such licenses. This provision covered all present patents, plus any that might be obtained for 5 years.

5. IBM was required to place all of its service bureau activities in a separately organized, but wholly owned, subsidiary corporation (called the Service Bureau Corporation, or SBC). The SBC was not to use the IBM name or any IBM facilities or personnel. It was required to keep separate accounts and to cover its costs; and it was not to receive any favorable terms in dealings with IBM unless those terms were offered to all other service bureaus.

As a group, the remedies in the 1956 consent decree were conduct remedies applied to the conditions in the tabulating industry as that industry was understood at the time. There is only one comment that need be made about them: they did not succeed in reducing IBM's dominance of either the tabulating industry or of the computer industry that grew out of it.[20]

The Service Bureau Corporation created by the 1956 decree was transferred by IBM to Control Data Corporation (CDC) at the time of the settlement of the *CDC* v. *IBM* antitrust case in 1973. International Business Machines consented to stay out of the service bureau market for 6 years. If it should choose to reenter at the end of that period, it will remain subject to the 1956 consent decree. In February 1973, soon after the announcement of the terms of the settlement of the *Control Data* case, the Data Center segment of the Association of Data Processing Service Organizations (ADAPSO) called on the government to seek, in its case, to get a court order permanently excluding IBM from reentering the service bureau business.[21]

The 1956 consent decree undoubtedly affected the conduct of IBM as the computer era emerged, even if it failed to eliminate IBM's position of dominance. The decree's provisions became a constraint on conduct and, therefore, they have constituted an important part of the structure of the industry. Within that set of constraints there emerged a set of independent firms competing with IBM in leasing IBM equipment, in developing software for use with IBM's EDP systems, and to a lesser extent in rendering maintenance services. Such competitors, however, have operated under conditions in which their chief competition was a very powerful firm on which they were dependent and whose decisions on product design, price policies, and contractual terms served as constraints on their own decisions.

Pricing Discretion and Discrimination

The ability of IBM to adjust its prices to forestall competition was revealed in a cryptic memorandum written November 21, 1969, by IBM's director of

---

[20] *The Computer Industry*, op. cit., pp. 5630–5631.

[21] "ADAPSO/SIA Position Paper on IBM's Monopolization of the Software Products and Services Industry," *The Computer Industry*, op. cit., pp. 4858–4864.

business practices to the director of marketing.[22] The text of this memo follows:

Thoughts for Consideration

The viability of IBM's risk lease is dependent on price leadership and price control.

By means of price leadership, IBM has established the value of data-processing usage.

IBM then maintains or controls that value by various means: (timing of new technology insertion; functional pricing; coordinated management of delivery, support services and inventory; refusal to market surplus used equipment; refusal to discount for age or for quantity; strategic location of function in boxes; "solution selling" rather than hardware selling; refusal to support subsequent-used hardware, etc.

Unbundling has created a new threat to IBM's price control.

By eliminating fixed-price solution selling of hardware eventually leading to increased price competition.

Functional pricing already under pressure because of OEM activity. Unbundling will increase that pressure.

Equalization of subsequent use adds value to existing third-party inventories.

Seriously reduced capability to maintain—ahead of supply.

Legal problems are emerging as a result of certain practices which are key underpinnings to price control.

Refusal to market used machines and parts. Refusal to sell bills of material. Maintenance parts prices.

The key underpinnings to our control of price are interrelated and interdependent. One cannot be changed without impacting others.

These interrelationships are not well or widely understood by IBM management. Our price control has been sufficiently absolute to render unnecessary direct management involvement in the means, ...

The D.J. [Department of Justice] complaint specifically covers varying profit margins and an intensive investigation of this issue would reveal the extent of our price control and its supporting practices. Such a revelation would not be helpful to our monopoly defense.

If IBM's price control is seriously threatened, either from the market (because of unbundling) or from legal exposure (because of the supporting practices) or from the D.J. (because of demands for remedy), it is necessary that IBM management fully understand its import in order to decide:

Negotiations' strategy with D.J. good versus bad practices remedies good versus bad structural remedies (or) decision to litigate.

Pricing approach to new systems.

Reduction of legal risk relating to practices.

Recommendation

Assemble a small, knowledgeable, secure group to think through these issues, particularly in their interrelationship—define the emerging environment and the various new forces which indicate significant new change—

---

[22] This memorandum was among the many IBM company documents turned over to the court by the discovery procedures involed in the *Control Data* v. *IBM* case with which were combined the pretrial evidence gathering processes of several other private antitrust suits. The document was found by Burton R. Thorman, a lawyer on the staff of the Antitrust Division and introduced into evidence in the government case and also in the *Telex* case. See ibid., p. 5113.

and map the rudimentary elements of strategy or alternate strategies for consideration by management.[23]

This memorandum illustrates that a large market share alone is insufficient basis for a dominant firm to sustain unchallenged its power to prevent profits from being squeezed by entry of alternative sources of supply. It also shows the temptations to sustain power by engaging in conduct that might give evidence of the existence of illegal power. It is not surprising that this memorandum was among the 1200 documents from the settled *Control Data* case that IBM fought all the way to the Supreme Court to keep out of evidence in the government's case.[24]

Plug-compatible Peripherals Competition

The emergence of the plug-compatible peripheral-equipment submarket in the late 1960s was discussed in Section II. The change in conduct by IBM that resulted from the structural changes is considered here. The approximately 30,000 pages of the record of the *Telex* v. *IBM* case are concerned primarily with IBM's reaction to the Peripheral Computer Machinery (PCM) threat to its installed base and revenues.

In January 1970, the General Services Agency moved to encourage all Federal agencies to switch from IBM tape and disk memories to compatible equipment offered at less cost to the taxpapers by the "PCM" companies. At that time almost 18 per cent of one IBM tape-drive-model type in use were nonIBM substitutes, but the PCM companies' share was much smaller for most disk and tape-drive models. In February 1970, top management in IBM designated the peripheral problem a "key corporate strategic issue" and began planning conduct changes to meet the threat.[25]

The threat to IBM consisted of a very real possibility that customers unwilling to shift their whole system from IBM to one of the other "main-frame" systems companies would be willing to shop around for lower prices (monthly rental rates) on pieces of their IBM system. In the spring of 1970, IBM had announced, but not yet delivered, its new fourth-generation System/370 models designed to gradually replace the third-generation System/360 models. The PCM companies were taking a growing share of the System/360 installed base and threatened eventually to do the same with the System/370 line. If IBM had reacted simply with massive price cuts (monthly rentals) on each piece of equipment offered by a PCM company, not only would it have laid itself open to antitrust actions for predatory price cutting, but it also would have greatly reduced its own revenues on a number of high-profit-margin items in its product line. Therefore, IBM's top management vetoed direct price-cutting proposals and adopted more subtle strategies designed to limit its revenue-reducing moves to the specific

---

[23] Ibid.

[24] See Biddle testimony in ibid., p. 5073.

[25] See Gerald Brock, *The U.S. Computer Industry 1954–1973: A Study of Market Power* (Cambridge, Mass.: Ballinger, 1975), Chap. 8, and excerpts preprinted in ibid., pp. 5664–5681.

customers who were about to switch to PCM companies. The specific strategies adopted included the offering of new products at lower prices while counting on inertia to prevent massive shifts by its customers to the lower-priced alternatives. Also, IBM redesigned some products to make more difficult the competitors' task of achieving plug-to-plug compatibility, and offered new lease terms to lock in customers for longer periods.

Product design changes included, for example, a marketing strategy called the Mallard Program announced in September 1970. This program was designed to hold the company's market for the model 2314 disk drive. The 2314 was originally used in conjunction with the larger System/360 models. It was a direct-access storage device on which 29 million bytes of data could be stored and transferred in and out of the CPU at the rate of 312,000 bytes per second. The transfer of data between the disk and the CPU required a model 2314 controller. As many as eight disk drives could be handled by one controller.

International Business Machines could expect many users of large 360 systems to switch to large 370 systems. The large 370 systems would use new, technically more advanced, model 3330 disk drives. The large 360 system users that converted to the 370 would be turning in 2314 disk drives suitable for use on the smaller System/370 model 145. Thus, the ability of the PCM companies to offer disk drives to replace IBM model 2314 was a threat not only to the continuing installed base of System/360s, but also to the leasing of disk drives for the System 370/145.

The Mallard Program consisted initially of the offering of disk-drive model 2319A for use with the 370/145 and eventually included a 2319B for use with the large 360 systems as the PCM's cut into that 2314 market to a greater extent than expected. The 2319A consisted of a modified 2314 control unit located inside the CPU of the 370/145 and three 2314 disk drives in a single box. The price of the package was $1555 per month, compared with $2875 for a 2314 controller and three 2314 disk drives—a 46 per cent price reduction. Thus, IBM accomplished a price reduction for new 370/145 installations without losing any revenue from the existing installed base of 2314s on 360s and also made it very difficult technically for the PCM companies to design a plug-compatible competing product for adding onto the 370/145. Furthermore, it was possible to defend the company against an antitrust allegation of predatory price cutting by claiming the 2319A to be a new product.

In December 1970, IBM announced the 2319B for installation on System/360. A modified controller was offered at the old price, but the three-spindle disk-drive package was offered at a price 26 per cent below the price of three 2314s, even though the performance specifications were unchanged. To get the lower price, however, the user had to order the 2319B and have it physically installed in place of the 2314 equipment—a change that embodied some down time and was most likely to be made by users contemplating switching to a Telex product.

In May 1971, IBM adopted a Fixed-Term Lease Plan for most disk, tape, and printer products. Instead of a month-to-month lease, the user was offered the option of signing up for 1 or 2 years with a rental price reduction of 8 per cent or 16 per cent, respectively. The month-to-month lease had charged extra for use of the system more than 176 hours per month. The fixed-term lease eliminated the extra charges for the heavy users so that the price reduction could amount to as much as 35 per cent for the 2-year lease.

Other responses of IBM in the early 1970s to the PCM competition are documented in the record of the *Telex* v. *IBM* case and are reviewed by Gerald Brock.[26] The lower court found the evidence persuasive and awarded $259 million in damages to Telex, but the circuit court of appeals overruled and dismissed the case. The appeals court's grounds for overruling were primarily that the district court had incorrectly defined the market in which monopoliza- tion had occurred. Rather than treating IBM system-compatible peripheral equipment as a market, the Court of Appeals for the Tenth Circuit, in February 1975, ruled that IBM competed in the sale of its peripherals not only with the PCM companies, but also with all the other main-frame manufacturers. The court said that "IBM's share of the data-processing industry as a whole is insufficient to justify any inference of market power . . . ."[27]

The Supreme Court must ultimately rule on the legality of business practices with which the dominant firm in the computer industry responds to competition. The practices of IBM seem to have fostered rental over purchase, "bundling" of software with hardware, selling systems rather than equipment, and changing interface standards.

IV. PERFORMANCE

Performance in the computer industry can be evaluated in terms of the effects the industry has had in changing information processing over time. Performance can be judged also in terms of a comparison of what has happened with what might have happened if a more competitive structure of control had existed. Public policy must be made also with a view to the future and the course of events that are yet to come as a consequence of past conduct.

Technical progress over time in computerized information-processing systems has undoubtedly been very rapid compared with changes in other industries. Much of that progress resulted from changes made outside the computer in- dustry as such and in electronics generally. Much progress came from the competitive pressure from new entrants, whether or not they survived. Some has come from the dominant firm in the industry. If competition had not been as great as it was, it seems quite likely that the rate of innovation would have been less. Continued rapid technical progress will hinge on the degree to which a structure at least as competitive as that of the past is maintained. Pending court cases, however, may result in a radical change toward less competition or much more competition, as the issues of the lawfulness of IBM's conduct and power are adjudicated.

[26] Ibid.
[27] *IBM* v. *Telex*, 510 Fed. Rept. (2d) 894 (1975).

The appropriateness of resource allocation cannot be directly measured and judged. If one uses the allocation that would have resulted were all markets perfectly competitive as a standard, then one can draw inferences of malallocation from evidence of less than perfectly competitive structures. Barriers to entry are one such structural imperfection. Successful entry has obviously not been completely barred in the computer industry. No crucial mineral input has been pre-empted, as is the case in many mineral based industries, nor have patents presented insurmountable barriers. Capital requirements, however, have played a major role in inhibiting the expansion of capacity and increased market shares of entering companies. In this respect, success breeds success. IBM's large lease and high profits over the years since the tabulating-machine days have given it an advantage in an industry in which leasing practices required new suppliers to also be financiers of their customers' purchases.

Performance can also be judged in terms of an industry's effects on the distribution of income, wealth, and power in the society. In this respect, the computer industry has very special characteristics. Increased interdependence in economic activity in the last quarter century has left each individual dependent to an ever greater extent on the workings of "the system." The computerization of the information flows within the society has produced a particular dependence of each person on the computer. Centralization of control over the development, management, and maintenance of the nation's computers holds a threat of power over the individual that cannot be judged merely in terms of profits and efficiency in resource use.

V. PUBLIC POLICY

Pricing discrimination among product markets when practiced by a large, diversified corporation is a barrier to entry of specialized firms into specific markets. The power to engage in such pricing practices is also a barrier to entry if the threat is known to exist—known either to a potential specialized competitor or to those to which it must go for capital. Power to price lower, relative to costs, in some markets than in others is facilitated by possession of some monopoly power in some markets. However, such pricing can result from nothing more than the multimarket nature of the large firm and some time lags between attempts at entry into particular markets. Simultaneous entry by specialized firms in all the markets of the dominant firm would, of course, make discrimination impossible. Even then, however, a firm with substantial reserves of liquid assets could use its "deep pocket" to outlast the competitors, and, market-by-market, reestablish its monopoly power.

Therefore, even if bundling were effectively prohibited by a conduct remedy, a problem will remain. The regulation of pricing practices by court decree or by public-utility-type controls would require government oversight of accounting practices, the ascertainment of costs directly attributable to each product and market, and allocation of joint and common costs among products and markets.

Such regulation has proved to be sufficiently difficult and its effectiveness sufficiently questionable in other industries that a structural remedy has much to be said for it.

Dissolution of the dominant firm in the computer industry as so to have separate firms for each product and each market would assure that management itself would price each product with a view to maximizing profits separately in each market. The joint costs would no longer be joint. The essential question of policy in the computer industry has to do with the consequences of "jointness" of costs for the level of costs. There is no a priori reason for assuming that jointness—that is, the multiproduct character of large firms such as IBM— exists because lower levels of cost result from it. Indeed, if power results from the existence of such "multimarkets," then the fruits of that power could justify higher costs than with a more specialized and decentralized structure of control.

It should be technologically possible to achieve in the computer industry a decentralized product structure that "unbundled" not only the pricing, but also the production, of a reasonable number of related products and services that together constitute an EDP system. The requisites of such a policy include, however, not only a governmental mechanism for accomplishing the appropriate corporate reorganizations, but also the creation of a computer-industry standard-making mechanism to assure adequate compatibility among the components designed and manufactured by many separate firms. The National Bureau of Standards exists for precisely such purposes, and it should play a major role in the implementation of a policy of competition in the computer industry.

Another requisite of the decentralization of production of systems components is some new structure of control of the systems maintenance function. The traditionally predominant, but not universal, practice of bundling maintenance with the sale or lease of equipment might not be practical or efficient with the typical user's EDP system consisting of plug-compatible equipment from several manufacturers. The development of a competitive market in systems maintenance, however, would be greatly facilitated by the appropriate standardization of interfaces.

A crucial question remains: Would such a decentralized structure of control be conducive to continued rapid technological development and innovation? The innovativeness of the smaller, more specialized firms in the industry in the past suggests that a structural, competitive remedy of the sort suggested here would increase both the incentives and the capacities for innovation if, and only if, the standards-making mechanism is sufficiently flexible.

The risks to society of stifling technical progressiveness in the computer industry by this structural remedy must be judged against the alternatives. A policy of direct government regulation of business practices of one or a few dominant firms, whether attempted with court decree or regulatory commission, also has associated with it a risk of stifling technical progressiveness. The third alternative—a laissez faire policy—would leave the evolution of both structure and conduct to the market mechanism as now structured. No reason exists for confidence that the performance in the future would be as good as it has been in the past. Forces already in process could lead soon to the demise of competition from independent plug-compatible peripheral-equipment producers. As the industry matures, competition among a few integrated, multimarket, multinational EDP systems suppliers is quite likely to move toward the same sort of tacit collusion and government-assisted cartelization that exists in other industries characterized by tight oligopoly.

The growing significance of electronic, computerized information-processing systems in the economy, the government, and, indeed, in the whole structure of society also must be considered in formulating public policy with respect to industry structure. Decentralization of control of the nation's information-processing system was accomplished two centuries ago by the Bill of Rights, which assured freedom of the press, freedom of the pulpit through separation of church and state, and conflict resolution through due process of law implemented in open courts. Similarly, the right of the individual's privacy was protected by prohibition of unreasonable search and seizure. The purpose of such public policies on information are not obsolete; however, in the computer age, such constitutional rights may be insufficient.

As more and more information is processed electronically, both the free flow of information to each citizen and the privacy of each individual may be threatened by a structure of this industry that centralizes control of the installed base in a single or a few powerful, national corporate bureaucracies. Government regulation of a centralized corporate control structure does not offer much assurance of countervailing power against this kind of noneconomic threat to continued acceptable industry performance. The traditional Anglo-Saxon approach to centralized power is its dissolution. That policy goes back at least as far as 1215, when 25 barons forced King John to sign the Magna Charta and, thereby, began parliamentary government in an age of absolute monarchy. In the face of some uncertainty about the economic consequences of alternative policies for this industry, this writer would tilt toward structural remedies that are more consistent with the evolution of political democracy and individual freedom in our society than either private or public, centralized, bureaucratic control.

SUGGESTED READINGS

BOOKS

Brock, Gerald. *The U.S. Computer Industry 1954–1973: A Study of Market Power.* Cambridge, Mass.: Ballinger Publishing Company, 1975.

GOVERNMENT PUBLICATIONS

U.S. Congress, Senate, Committee on the Judiciary, Subcommittee on Antitrust and Monopoly, *Hearings on the Industrial Reorganization Act: The Computer Industry, Hearings on S. 1167,* 93d Cong., 2d sess., pt. 7, 1974.

JOURNAL AND MAGAZINE ARTICLES

Datamation, published monthly by Technical Publishing Company, 1301 South Grove Avenue, Barrington, Ill. 60010.

Computerworld, published weekly by International Data Corporation, 60 Austin Street, Newtonville, Mass. 02160.

CHAPTER 9

the telephone industry

MANLEY R. IRWIN

I. INTRODUCTION

Few products of contemporary civilization rival the ubiquitousness of the telephone instrument. It is pivotal to commerce, it is mandatory for government, it is essential to the home. For most of us the telephone is communication; and communication is the nervous system of a highly interdependent economy.

Despite such pervasiveness, the telephone industry resists easy analysis or ready identification. That evasion is somewhat surprising when one recognizes that we are dealing with a regulated industry subject to scrutiny by state and Federal commissions. The problem is that the telephone industry is dominated by companies that do not render telephone service as such, but, rather, control stock in companies that do render such service to the subscribing public. The telephone industry, in short, is run by holding companies.

The holding company owns both the buyer of telephone equipment and the seller of telephone equipment. The buyer of equipment is a legal monopoly franchised to provide service to the subscribing public. The seller of equipment is a manufacturer that fabricates, assembles, and installs communications equipment to the regulated carrier. The policies, practices, and customs of both are coordinated by the telephone holding company.

From the industry's point of view, the holding company is responsible for a system that has given this country a communication network unmatched in quality and reliability. From the critics' point of view, the holding company has extended a legal monopoly beyond the bounds of the public utility principle. Whatever the merit of each position, a public debate has erupted as to the optimum structure of the telephone industry. The outcome of that debate will determine the structure, conduct, and performance of this industry in the decades to come.

312

History

The telephone industry is synonymous with the evolution and growth of the Bell System. That evolution, in turn, rested on the patent grant. The original patent, filed by Alexander Graham Bell, was born in controversy. The patent was contested in the courts, and it was not until the Supreme Court ruled by a four-to-three vote, in 1876, that the validity of the Bell patent was upheld. This decision marked the beginning of what later became known as the Bell System.

The Bell interests established telephone companies, franchised rights to the telephone instrument, and extended telephone service to major metropolitan areas of the United States. Through the formation of a holding company, Bell embarked on a policy of horizontal integration by purchasing stock in licensee companies and subsequently acquiring competing companies. Through acquisition of the Western Electric Company, the Bell integrated into the equipment market. By the turn of the century, the Bell System had become the dominant force in the U.S. telephone service—due largely to the organizing genius of Theodore Vail, chairman of the American Telephone and Telegraph Company (AT&T).

That Bell's monopoly rested on its patent was not lost on AT&T. Patents expire and, with that expiration, entry into both telephone service and telephone manufacturing was all but inevitable. But Bell took countermeasures to protect itself. In the 1890s, AT&T established an engineering division to engage in research and development and to stymie competition when the basic patent expired. And Bell threw resources into the engineering group—with employment rising from 52 to 203 persons from 1894–1902.

At first, AT&T generated patents that acted to cement Bell's control over wire telephone technology. However, later, it was clear that wireless transmission (radio) threatened AT&T's control over telephony. Hence, R&D was broadened to include related and allied fields of telephone technology as well.

The strategy pursued by AT&T's engineering group was continued by the formation of Bell Telephone Laboratories in the mid-1920s. Whatever the organizational climate, Bell's patent portfolio grew—and with it virtual control over telephone technology—to include switching, transmission, and station apparatus.

Although Bell's patent position in long-distance telephone was virtually impregnable, the company pursued a market strategy that aided and abetted that control; namely, refusal to interconnect long-distance facilities with that of non-Bell rivals. The result found non-Bell subscribers forced to lease two phones: one for local calls and one for long-distance calls. Little wonder that the independent company found the opportunity to sell out to Bell attractive and irresistible.

Destructive competitive rate wars and an interconnection policy eventually led to industry "rationalization"—regulation. Regulation first evolved at the state level. In 1910, however, the Interstate Commerce Commission (ICC) extended jurisdiction over interstate telephone service. By World War I, the industry was well on its way to the status of a regulated monopoly. Indeed, Bell's Chairman Vail invited, embraced, and welcomed public regulation as an alternative to competition.

By 1914, Bell experienced its first skirmish with the Department of Justice. Bell had consolidated its control over the telephone industry, and Vail had acquired its old rival, the Western Union Telegraph Company. The Justice Department threatened antitrust action. As a tribute to Vail's foresight, he reached an accommodation by agreeing to the divestiture of Western Union, and the antitrust suit never materialized.

In the 1920s, the Bell System reached a partial standoff with the non-Bell independent companies. Bell agreed to interconnect some of its toll facilities with independents, and its acquisition policy was now sanctioned by the Interstate Commerce Commission (ICC). However, by the late 1920s, Congress began to examine the feasibility of establishing a separate commission devoted entirely to telephone service as well as radio communications. In 1934, Congress created the Federal Communications Commission (FCC).

Commissions have been known to experience life cycles, and the FCC proved no exception. In its youth, idealism plus a robust appropriation from Congress enabled the FCC to embark on an investigation of AT&T as a holding company, with particular emphasis on the financial transaction occurring among and between Bell's vertical and horizontal affiliates. The investigation concluded that the FCC possessed the necessary authority to regulate AT&T. With the exception of some cost-accounting recommendations, the FCC embarked on a program of informal monitoring of Bell's service, rates, profits, and construction program. Structural reform of holding company control was apparently not given serious consideration.[1]

World War II had a profound impact on the state of research and development in telecommunications. The nation's resources and talent were poured into radar, microwave transmission, rocketry, and solid-state electronics. Such R&D was to later sow the seeds for a technological upheaval in the communications industry, seeds that were not to sprout until the late 1950s but were to beset the industry to this day.

After the war, a second antitrust skirmish hit AT&T. In 1949, the Department of Justice filed a suit alleging that Western Electric had achieved monopoly control of the equipment market in violation of Section 2 of the Sherman Act.[2] The 1949 complaint sought to divest AT&T of Western Electric, to dissolve Western into three competing companies, and to require that the Bell operating companies purchase their equipment and supplies on a competitive bid basis.

In 1956, the antitrust suit was dropped; more accurately, the Justice Department entered into a consent decree with Bell.[3] The agreement required Bell to

---

[1] U.S. Congress, House, FCC, *Report on the Investigation of the Telephone Industry in the United States*, H. Rep. 340, 76th Cong., 1st sess., 1939.

[2] *United States* v. *Western Electric Co.*, Civil no. 17-49 (D.N.J. filed Feb. 14, 1949).

[3] *Consent Decree in United States* v. *Western Electric Co.*, Civil no. 17–49 (D.N.J., Jan. 23, 1956).

make available its portfolio of 8000 patents to all comers on a royalty-free basis. Presumably, such openness and availability would encourage and promote rivalry in the equipment market. The decree, however, sacrificed structural reform.[4] As a holding company, AT&T was permitted to retain control of the 23 Bell operating companies and ownership of Western Electric—its manufacturer. The Bell operating companies continued to buy the bulk of their equipment from Western Electric. To the extent that the premise of the consent decree was the extension of access to the equipment market, that premise proved invalid. Vertical integration was not only sanctioned, but the decree also conferred an air of legitimacy to AT&T's control of utility and manufacturer.

The 1956 consent decree did more. It held out the holding company as a structural model for the entire communication industry. The non-Bell carriers did not miss the message and the model's implications. Independent companies copied the organizational structure of AT&T and embarked on a similar program of both horizontal and vertical acquisition. The result saw a decline of independent telephone companies. All but a few of the remaining telephone equipment suppliers found a "home" as part of the holding company family. By the late 1960s, some 80 per cent of all non-Bell Telephone service was provided by affiliates of telephone holding companies.[5] In short, the consent decree cartelized the telephone equipment market.

By 1967, a presidential Task force was launched to assess domestic and overseas policy. The task force recommended the merger of overseas voice and record carriers and the introduction of satellite technology into the continental United States. But the study sidestepped the pervasiveness of the telephone holding companies and dismissed the vertical integration matter as essentially an antitrust issue.[6]

Ironically, antitrust action began in the late 1960s against a non-Bell holding company, the General Telephone System (GTE). Replicating AT&T, GTE has grown through horizontal and vertical mergers—the Hawaiian Telephone Company is an example of the former. International Telephone and Telegraph (ITT), an equipment supplier, complained that once joining the GTE system, Hawaiian Telephone would buy its equipment from GTE's captive suppliers, thus leaving ITT out in the cold.

A district court ruled that indeed GTE's integration of utility and manufacturer did constitute market foreclosure and ordered holding company divestiture of its manufacturing affiliates.[7] A circuit court of appeal agreed that GTE was guilty of equipment foreclosure, but held that a private party could not seek

---

[4] U.S. Congress, House, Committee on the Judiciary, *Consent Decree Program of the Department of Justice, Hearings Before the Antitrust Subcommittee*, 85th Cong., 2d sess., 1958.

[5] United States Independent Telephone Association, *Holding Company Report*, May 1973; see also *Telephone Engineer and Management* (Oct. 1, 1973), p. 132.

[6] President's Task Force on Communication Policy, *Final Report*, Dec. 7, 1968.

[7] Final Judgment, *International Telephone and Telegraph Corporation* v. *General Telephone & Electronics Corporation and Hawaiian Telephone Company*, U.S. Dist. Court for the Dist. of Hawaii, Civil no. 2754, Dec. 13, 1972.

relief in a private suit. The case has been remanded to the trial court and a decision is now pending.

In November 1974, another antitrust shoe dropped. This time the Justice Department filed a complaint against AT&T's control of Bell operating companies and Bell's control over Western Electric.[8] Not unlike the GTE suit, the government complaint sought to sever AT&T's control of Bell operating companies and to divest the Bell System of Western. The Bell System has affirmed its intention to contest the suit vigorously.

Finally, the FCC, in the early 1970s, embarked on an investigation of Bell's vertical market structure as that structure influences telephone rates and services. After 4 years of investigation, the FCC's trial staff recommended that the holding company had directed policies leading to the market foreclosure of telephone equipment.

> AT&T, the holding company, in orchestrating a series of policies and practices, employs the legitimate franchise telephone services to achieve illegitimate market exclusion in manufacturing. AT&T's orchestration of events is appropriately described by the Sherman Act as "monopolization."[9]

These challenges, whether private or public, obviously move the telephone holding company into the center of the policy arena. In a sense, the suits mark a dialogue over the virtues and/or infirmities of holding company control—a dialogue that swept the electric power industry in the late 1920s and 1930s, culminating in the Public Utility Holding Act of 1935. The final outcome of these current suits, is, of course, conjectural; however, the issues are so crucial that judicial review may well be superseded by legislative action.

II. MARKET STRUCTURE

The predominance of the holding company in controlling the bulk of our telephone service in the United States can be seen in Table 1. The American Telephone and Telegraph Company accounts for more than 80 per cent of all local, or exchange, service in the United States; and the Long Lines Division of AT&T accounts for more than 90 per cent of the long-distance, or toll service, in the country. Along with its Bell operating companies, AT&T accounts for nearly 100 million telephone sets in the United States.

The non-Bell market accounts for the remaining segment of telephone service and includes some 1400 independent telephone companies. Most companies are located in the rural areas in the United States, render exchange service to their subscribers, and interconnect their facilities with AT&T. The holding company control is central to the structure of the independent market.

---

[8] *United States* v. *American Telephone and Telegraph*, Civil Suit no. 17, filed Nov. 1974.

[9] FCC, in the matter of American Telephone and Telegraph Company and the Associated Bell System Companies, Docket no. 10.19129, phase 2, *Statement and Recommendations of the Common Carrier*, Bureau's Trial Staff, Feb. 2, 1976, p. 9.

TABLE 1
Telephone Holding Company

	NUMBER OF COMPANIES	NUMBER OF TELEPHONES	PER CENT
Bell System (AT&T)	23	99,902,000	83
GTE	29	9,513,200	7.8
United Utilities	21	2,358,500	.01
Continental Telephone	87	1,432,500	.01
Central Telephone Utilities	10	960,000	.007
Mid-Continent	43	535,400	.004

Source: R. J. Emerine, et al., *A Planning Study for an Investigation of Corporate Structures in the Telecommunications Common Carrier Industry* (Cambridge, Mass.: ABT Associates, 1974).

The Bell System

The American Telephone and Telegraph Company epitomizes holding company organization in the telephone industry; it controls stock and some 23 operating companies, as shown by Table 2.

In 1973, AT&T's assets approached $68 billion, operating revenues exceeded $23 billion, profits were $5 billion, and plant construction almost $10 billion annually. The company had more than three quarters of a million employees, and its stock was held by over 3 million shareholders. The size and magnitude of these assets reflect to some extent the capital intensity of the telephone industry.

In addition to owning some 23 Bell operating companies throughout the country, AT&T is vertically integrated through its ownership of Western Electric as a manufacturer. Western Electric is the tenth largest firm in the United States in sales; it enjoys assets of more than $3 billion and sales of some $6 billion.

Western Electric manufactures a variety of equipment, some 250,000 different products ranging from wire, cable, switching apparatus, and transmission gear to telephone handsets. Western Electric also installs equipment for the Bell operating companies, operates repair centers for such equipment, and acts as the supply agent for the Bell operating companies by purchasing equipment and hardware from outside vendors. The operating companies take most of their equipment requirements from Western Electric.[10] The result is that Western Electric accounts for the bulk of the telecommunication equipment manufactured in the United States. (Bell claims 65 per cent.)[11]

Bell Telephone Laboratory (BTL), the research and development arm of the

[10] FCC, Investigation into AT&T's Rates, phase 2. (Hereafter cited as Docket no. 19129.) Trial Staff Exhibit no. 127, Nov. 1974, Washington, D.C.

[11] U.S. Congress, Senate, Committee on the Judiciary, *Hearings before the Subcommittee on Antitrust and Monopoly: The Industrial Reorganization Act*, 93rd Cong., 1st sess., 1973. Testimony of S. Fletcher, Western Electric.

TABLE 2
AT&T's Ownership in Bell Operating Companies

ACCOUNT 101.1 INVESTMENTS IN AFFILIATED COMPANIES	TOTAL VOTING RIGHTS IN AFFILIATES (PER CENT)	TELEPHONES SERVED (000)
New England Telephone and Telegraph Company	85.42	5,705
New York Telephone Company	100.00	11,705
New Jersey Bell Telephone Company	100.00	5,301
Bell Telephone Company of Pennsylvania	100.00	6,793
Diamond State Telephone Company	100.00	432
Chesapeake and Potomac Telephone Company	100.00	971
Chesapeake and Potomac Telephone Company of Maryland	100.00	2,821
Chesapeake and Potomac Telephone Company of Virginia	100.00	2,331
Chesapeake and Potomac Telephone Company of W. Virginia	100.00	794
Southern Bell Telephone and Telegraph Company	100.00	9,038
South Central Bell Telephone Company	100.00	7,620
Ohio Bell Telephone Company	100.00	4,431
Michigan Bell Telephone Company	99.99	5,142
Indiana Bell Telephone Company Inc.	100.00	1,867
Wisconsin Telephone Company	100.00	1,949
Illinois Bell Telephone Company	99.33	6,719
Northwestern Bell Telephone Company	100.00	4,558
Southwestern Bell Telephone Company	99.99	12,175
Mountain States Telephone and Telegraph Company	87.76	5,196
Pacific Northwest Bell Telephone Company	89.29	2,822
Pacific Telephone and Telegraph Company	90.18 ⎫	12,012
Pacific Telephone and Telegraph Company– Preferred	78.17 ⎭	

Source: AT&T, *Annual Report*, 1972 (Account 101.1: Investments in Affiliated Companies).

Bell System, is co-owned by both AT&T and Western Electric. The laboratory, with a budget of some $600 million, performs R&D and fundamental research and development for AT&T and carries out specific design and development activities for Western Electric.

In the over-all sense, the components of AT&T—Bell Laboratory, the operating companies, and Western Electric—make up what is familiarly known as the Bell System. At the top of the system sits AT&T, controlling interest in the buying and selling of equipment—the buyer being a regulated utility, and the seller an unregulated manufacturer. In a real sense, AT&T straddles both a regulated and nonregulated telecommunication market.

A series of transactions occurs within and among the various components of the holding company system. A first transaction originates between AT&T's General Department and the various Bell operating companies. The General Department renders a management consulting service to the Bell companies, including advice on marketing, finance, engineering, tariffs, and regulatory developments. As part of this service, AT&T makes available the results of BTL's laboratory output to the operating companies.

If operating company revenues rise, the revenue flow to AT&T increases; if operating revenues fall, the revenue flow to AT&T declines. If AT&T decides its management advice has increased in value, it can bill the operating company at a higher percentage than the traditional 1 per cent. No operating company has refused to subscribe to AT&T management consulting service; nor has any operating company refused to pay for such service on the ground that its costs exceed the service value received. The operating companies are, after all, subsidiaries of the holding company.

A second line of transactions occurs between the operating company and Western Electric. These transactions are sanctioned under a Standard Supply Contract in which Western assumes the obligation of supplying equipment and hardware at the lowest possible cost to the various operating companies. The operating companies, on the other hand, are not obligated to buy from Western Electric; however, in practice, the operating companies take most of their equipment from Western.

The Non-Bell Companies

Non-Bell holding company control of buyer and seller is nowhere near as complete as AT&T's. The closest to it is the General Telephone System (GT&E) with 23 operating companies, manufacturing affiliates, and a research laboratory. The GT&E Service Corporation provides management consulting services to the GT&E operating companies and subsidiaries; Automatic Electric and Lenkurt sell the various operating companies equipment and supplies; and Automatic Electric acts as a procurement agent on behalf of the GT&E.

Holding company control of research, and manufacturing of telephone service and its related activities, is not without its proponents. The carriers insist that such integration promotes research and development, enhances product innovation, lowers equipment prices, reduces the telephone rates, insures quality service, and enables the operating companies to respond to the needs of the telephone subscriber. The holding company insists that telephone service mandates a systems approach, an approach that embraces not merely telephone service in one particular area, but in all related activities from R&D to marketing and from repair to installation. Any entity other than holding company control over the various aspects of the industry would, in the view of the carriers, compromise the quality of the service and render vulnerable the technological integrity of the entire system.

The systems concept is, of course, not without its compelling logic. If a single holding company is valid for 80 per cent of the industry, why should 10 per cent remain outside that holding company control? Should public policy not mandate holding company control over the *entire* telephone industry, consolidating both Bell and non-Bell into a system capable of enjoying allegedly vast economies of scale and economies of integration. To date, no one has put forth the last step of holding company control over the entire U.S. telephone system. Certainly, no industry as spokesman has recommended that a massive corporate consolidation is in the best interest of both the industry and the subscribing public.

Regulation

As noted, the holding company straddles both the regulated and nonregulated sectors of the telecommunication industry. The regulated side, the telephone operating company, rests on the assumption that competition, or market rivalry, is unworkable and inefficient owing to the "natural monopoly" conditions of telephone service. Natural monopoly usually assumes that the industry enjoys economies of scale over relevant demand, that capital costs preclude market entry; or that the service is uniquely tied to the public's convenience and necessity. If, for any of these reasons, competition is ruled out, then the imperatives of technological efficiency lead to the creation of a single entity endowed with the status of a public monopoly. Public policy, thus, creates a regulated utility and bars market entry, and the franchised firm submits its cost and investment to regulatory scrutiny and review.

Regulation becomes a surrogate for market competition and stands between the consumer and the utility. An administrative process endeavors to protect the subscribing public from extortionate rates, while affording the firm an opportunity to earn a reasonable return on its invested capital. The line between the interest of the consumer and the interest of the utility is neither clearly defined nor readily identifiable. Hence, regulation is an exercise in the adversary process.

Over time, regulation has reduced itself to a cost-plus scenario. A first component of a utility's cost is the combination of its operating expenses, outlays for wages, salaries, maintenance, depreciation, charity contributions, and the like. The utility is permitted to recover those costs on a dollar-for-dollar basis. A second cost is that of capital, or the rate of return that the utility is permitted to earn on its investment rate base. The investment would include wire, cable, telephone poles, handsets, switching gear, and so on—all used to render telephone service to the public (cost of capital is a composite of debt and equity.) The total revenue requirements to the regulated utility must first cover operating expenses and generate a return on invested capital. Both translate into the telephone user's bill.

The determination of revenue requirements underscores a key difference between a company rendering service in a competitive sector of the economy and a firm rendering service in the regulated sector. Ideally, a firm under competition achieves profits through cost reduction to the extent that market rivalry inhibits price increases.

The incentive for a regulated firm, however, is quite different. Here the firm's revenue requirement, a function of operating expense and net invested capital, often creates an incentive for the firm to seek higher rates in order to justify higher costs—rates are determined on the premise that consumer demand is relatively insensitive to price increases.

Nor are the incentives under regulation symmetrical. If the investment rate base or operating expense rises, presumably the firm's percentage of return remains the same; if operating expense or the rate base falls, the percentage of return again remains constant. Although these tendencies are oversimplified, the point remains that the firm is permitted to earn a fixed return on its net capital investment. Therein lies the burden and frustration of regulation. How can a regulatory agency reward or penalize a firm when its rate of return—profit—is impervious to market performance. Once a firm is endowed with public utility status, the carrot and stick of profits and losses becomes distorted and muted.

If regulation is beset by a system of disincentives when the carrier stands alone, public regulation is infinitely more complex when a holding company owns both buyer and seller of equipment. Now billions of dollars of hardware—absent the objective benchmark of competitive bids—is sold in-house among and between members of the same corporate family. Buyer and seller do not deal with each other at arms' length; and expenditures and prices become "intracorporate transactions." Little wonder that when regulatory agencies begin seriously to examine the reasonableness of equipment prices billed to the utility, they begin by pulling the yarn of the telephone carrier and wind up with the equipment sweater in their lap.[12] The agency must now cross the line into the nonregulated sector of manufacturing.

Intracorporate transactions within the telephone holding company also yield intriguing secondary effects. The carriers equipment market—given its captive manufacturer—tends to be insulated from penetration from independent or outside vendors. Thus denied access, the outside firm looks for a patron, a home, an assured market. What can be more attractive than affiliation with a telephone utility? The results finds holding companies spawning holding companies—each reaching for more horizontal and vertical integration. The equipment market, thus, becomes closed and impenetrable—all in the name of the "systems" approach.

III. MARKET CONDUCT

Despite the essentially closed environment of the telephone holding company, recently the telecommunications industry has experienced an eruption of

---

[12] California Utility Commission, Investigation on the Commissions' own matter on the rates, tolls, rules, charges, operations, practices of the Pacific Telephone and Telegraph Co., Decision no. 67369 (Case no. 7409), July 26, 1962.

competitive market pressures. These pressures have prompted the telephone holding company—specifically AT&T—to reassess its practices and policies and to adjust both price and nonprice policies in the face of a new market environment. To appreciate the intensification of market rivalry, it is useful to contrast the Bell System before and after the eruption of competition.

Before Competitive Pressures: The Bell Operating Companies

The tariffs, rates, or charges posted by Bell operating companies have in the past tended toward broad averages—averages that include a composite of old and new plant, of high- and low-cost traffic routes. Telephone companies, in short, engaged in postage-stamp pricing. Pricing resulted in flat rates and embraced a value-of-service concept (as much as the traffic will bear). Those who regarded telephones as absolutely essential paid higher rates; those subscribers who regarded telephones as less essential paid lower rates. Presumably, business subscribers paid more for service than residential customers.

Almost by definition, the telephone subscriber leased an end-to-end service from the local operating carrier. Prior to 1968, the subscriber was prohibited by filed tariffs to attach or hook up nontelephone handsets to the dial-up network. Bell's policy was backed up by state regulatory agencies, and a failure to adhere to such policies could result in forfeiture of telephone service. In some extreme cases, subscribers were prohibited from placing plastic covers on telephone directories on the grounds that the user trespassed telephone company property.

Telephone accounting methods paralleled the company's rate structure. Costs were broad, general, and amorphous, and a disaggregation of revenue and costs of a particular route or of a specific piece of equipment could be determined only after a special study—if then. True, the rate categories identified profits or losses, but cost and price averaging often masked the specific cost associated with rendering service to a customer class.

Not surprisingly, telephone company service was sold to a captive market. Subscribers tended to come to the utility, not the utility to the subscriber. Marketing efforts were largely passive, and telephone companies were organized around work skills—traffic, commercial, and plant—rather than marketing or sales research. All in all, the Bell System rendered an end-to-end service under the principles laid down by Theodore Vail of "one system, one policy, one company."[13]

Western Electric and the Bell Telephone Laboratory

Prior to the eruption of competitive pressures, BTL and Western Electric experienced minimal outside challenge in both R&D and equipment. Bell

---

[13] *The Use of the Carterphone Device in Message Toll Telephone Service*, Docket no. 16942, *Thomas F. Carter and Carter Electronics Corp., Dallas, Texas* v. *American Telephone and Telegraph Co., Associated Bell System Companies, el al.*, Docket no. 17073, 1968. See also H. M. Trebing, "Common Carrier Regulation—The Silent Crisis," *Law and Contemporary Problems*, **34**: 305, Spring 1969.

Telephone Laboratory developed equipment for Western Electric, which, in turn, manufactured hardware for the Bell operating companies. Traditionally, Bell Laboratory did not contact operating companies directly, but rather reported its R&D to AT&T, which, in turn, informed the companies of new products, new standards, and new Bell System practices. In fact, Bell operating companies were prohibited from engaging in R&D efforts.

Although Western Electric manufactured more than 250,000 separate products, Western grouped its products into 12 broad cost categories, among which are transmission, station apparatus, switching, and so on. Each category was assigned a standard cost that included materials, labor, and loading expenditure. Again, the concept of broad cost averaging dominated. The switching category, for example, included machines of different vintages, some ranging back to World War II and some including recent computerized hardware.

A similar situation occurred with Western Electric's prices. Western's price were determined by multiplying a standard cost against a predetermined price factor. The price contained a profit markup to achieve a desired target rate of return on Western Electric's investment. As in costs, prices were grouped under broad product classifications with an identical price factor applied irrespective of equipment vintage.

To the extent that the operating telephone company took the bulk of their equipment needs from Western Electric, Western regarded marketing as secondary in importance. Indeed, the company merely recorded orders from the 23 Bell operating companies, thus alleviating the necessity of marketing, advertising or touting its wares to its customers/

AT&T

As the parent holding company, AT&T promulgated, coordinated, and policed both price and nonprice policies of the Bell System through an organization known as the General Department. The organization served as a prototype for organizing the 23 Bell operating companies; in a sense, the operating companies tended to be mirror images of the General Department's table of organization. Such were the policies and practices of the Bell System before the eruption of market competition.

Competitive Access

The Bell System as a closed system has been compelled to reassess, re-evaluate, and recast its price and nonprice policies. That reassessment can be traced to three factors: changes in communication technology, modifications in FCC policy, and entry of new competitive firms into the service and equipment market.

First, technological change in telephony has quickened a pace that traces its source to World War II. Satellites, computers, microwave, fibreoptics, and micro processors all suggested that the base of the telecommunications art is no longer confined to the incumbent firm or its R&D laboratory, no matter how distinguished. Stated differently, the patent alone is no longer immunizing the telephone utility from technological change.

Second, the FCC, in the late 1960s, promulgated several decisions that broadened the opportunities for market access and communications service and equipment. The FCC's Carterphone decision attempted to sever the tie-in between telephone lines and telephone equipment—a decision that held important implications for the telephone user.[14] Now the subscriber could buy equipment from noncarrier vendors and attach that equipment to telephone lines as well as lease both lines and equipment from his local operating company. Consumer choice has broadened, and that choice was exercised with a vengeance.

In addition, the FCC approved the creation of specialized common carriers, firms who sought to develop communications submarkets supposedly overlooked by the service offering of the incumbent utilities.[15] And, finally, the commission authorized new entities to provide domestic satellite service within the United States, including, among other corporations, IBM.[16]

Taken as a whole, these developments created an environment for market access in the telecommunication industry and threatened the status quo of the holding company. Both telephone and, indeed, the Bell operating companies found themselves faced with new alternatives and choices in equipment, in service, and in supplies. Competition erupted and it was to have a far-reaching impact on the price and nonpricing responses of the telephone holding company.

Impact of Market Changes: The Operating Telephone Companies

The operating telephone companies were the first to experience the impact of competitive change. Telephone subscribers could no longer be regarded as captive. A subscriber could choose to buy equipment from a U.S., Canadian, German, or Japanese company, as well as lease equipment from the utility. Once selecting a non-Western Electric product, that option translated into a loss of the carrier's investment base, a base on which the carrier hoped to earn a profit. The outside manufacturer now posed a threat to the telephone utility.

The carriers reacted with dispatch. The Bell operating companies reduced tariffs on Private Business Exchanges (PBXs), data modems, and key telephone system equipment, equipment vulnerable to outside competition.[17] The operating companies re-evaluated their leasing policy to subscribers and introduced an array of flexible pricing options to the business user. In some cases, the competitive pressure was so intense that the Bell operating companies elected to purchase non-Western Electric equipment in order to retain the patronage of their

---

[14] Ibid., p. 1.

[15] FCC, Docket no. 18920, In the matter of establishment of policies and procedures for consideration of applications to provide specialized common carrier services in the domestic public point to point microwave radio service and proposed amendments to parts 21, 43, and 61 of the Commission's rules. July 17, 1970.

[16] FCC, In the matter of Changes in the Corporate Structure of CML Satellite Corporation, Jan. 1975.

[17] FCC Docket no. 19129, Jan. 1975. Testimony of M. R. Irwin.

telephone subscribers. Fissures, however slight, began to develop within the structure of the vertically integrated holding company.

A second reaction found the operating company moving away from flat rate, or value of service, pricing as a basis for its tariffs. Bell began to introduce tariff tied specifically to the cost of rendering service. Bell's Hi-Lo tariffs, for example, a reaction to the entrance of specialized carriers, repealed the averaging principle and dropped rates for low-cost routes and raised rates for thin traffic, or high-cost routes. Subsequently, such a tariff was overturned by the FCC.

The operating companies also embarked on a program of re-examining their costs, which, in turn, led to a consideration of new accounting practices, moving away from the traditional uniform systems of accounts. Refined accounting as a management tool was proposed to give the operating company greater precision in determining its revenues, its cost, and, hence, the profitability of a particular or specific service class.[18]

Finally, the operating companies embarked on a process of corporate reorganization. The traditional table of organization oriented around craft skills no longer appeared relevant or responsive to competition. Marketing became the key word and sales organizations were rejuvenated in the various Bell operating companies. By the late 1970s, only some 9 of the 23 Bell operating companies conformed to the table of organization recommended by AT&T.[19]

The Bell Telephone Laboratory and Western Electric

Nor was Bell or Western Electric insulated from the competitive and technological pressures. Bell Telephone Laboratory formed a new organization that interfaced with the operating companies directly so as to identify, assess, and solve carriers' technical problems. More unsettling, the Laboratory found itself thrust into the marketing arena and in an environment somewhat alien to a nonprofit organization.[20] A Bell Laboratory marketing organization was created to track product costs, evaluate telephone tariff offerings and to assess, aid, and abet the companies in their new competitive environment.

Western Electric's conduct also experienced a transformation as a result of competition. Western Electric's broad, aggressive classification of products was reorganized and refined. Products exposed to competitive pressures were placed in smaller categories to track costs and prices with precision and accuracy. Western Electric's pricing policies were subject to re-evaluation to the extent that Western began to unbundle its costs and prices, tying prices to specific costs and again moving away from the broad, aggregate averaging concept.

Finally, Western Electric established a formal marketing organization within corporate headquarters. The organization touted its particular products to the

---

[18] FCC, Docket no. 19129, Trial Staff Exhibit, McKinsey study of Business Terminal Market, Nov. 1973.

[19] FCC, Docket no. 19129, Trial Staff Exhibit, presentation by C. W. Owens, AT&T, "Reorganization Issue," AT&T President's Conference, Nov. 1973.

[20] BTL's new marketing organization is called the Customer Service Engineering Group.

operating companies and fed back to Western Electric the status of its equipment, its hardware, and its supplies.[21] Clearly, Western was experiencing a new ball game for many of its products.

American Telephone and Telegraph Company

The American Telephone and Telegraph Company, witnessing both its buyer and supplier affiliate moving away from the traditional and long-standing practices of the Bell system, issued a moratorium on corporate reorganization on the grounds that diversity tended to erode the traditional unity of the Bell System. But, after a corporate study, the holding company found itself reorganized and moving toward a new competitive structure, with special emphasis on the marketing operations.[22]

The American Telephone and Telegraph Company also established the Bell System Purchase Product Division to further centralize the procurement practices of the operating companies.[23] The purpose of the new organization was to assist the operating companies in equipment selection from outside vendors. Presumably, the large operating companies did not possess the in-house expertise or talent to assess and evaluate equipment made by non-Western Electric sources. To the FCC's trial staff, however, such centralization tended to reimpose a greater control by the holding company over the buying side of vertical integration and, thus, to remove what little discretion had been given to the Bell operating companies.

The competitive impact on Bell's price and nonprice policies was profound and far-reaching. Operating company tariffs dropped, the utilities introduced new rate options, the carriers developed new accounting procedures, the carriers augmented their marketing organization, Bell Laboratory was reorganized, Western's equipment costs were unbundled, Western established a formal sales organization, and corporate structure was realigned, both at the holding company as well as the operating company level. However fragile and tentative, the ripple effects of market competition penetrated throughout the Bell organization.

Yet, amidst these changes, the holding company called for a moratorium on further policy experiments in competition.[24] Bell insisted that competition and regulation did not mix and invited a greater regulatory scrutiny over its equipment affiliate. In the trade-off between competition and regulation, the holding company obviously preferred the quiet sanction of government regulation.

---

[21] Created in 1972, Western Electric's new marketing organization is entitled The Sales, Service Consulting Group. See FCC, Docket no. 19129, Trial Staff Exhibit, "Sales Support," by E. C. Deutschle.

[22] "New Muscle in Marketing," *The Bell Telephone Magazine*, July–Aug. 1974.

[23] FCC, Docket no. 19129, Trial Staff Exhibit 175, 1974.

[24] J. D. de Butts, chairman of AT&T, "An Unusual Obligation" (speech delivered to the NARUC, Seattle, Wash., Sept. 20, 1973).

IV. PERFORMANCE

In assessing the performance of the telephone holding company, a search for performance benchmarks has traditionally proved illusive. Consider the price performance of long distance telephone service. Toll rates have generally declined since World War II. Everyone is familiar with the 3-minute call for an after 9:00 P.M. call. But local rates have experienced an increase over time.[25] What is the net effect on the consumer? Do toll rate reductions wash out exchange rate increases so that the telephone user enjoys a net gain? Do exchange rate increases cancel out toll rate reductions so that the subscribers suffer a net loss? And what is a proper benchmark to monitor such price movements?

Or, consider the service rendered by the Bell operating companies. The carriers insist that the United States enjoys the highest-quality service in the world. Granting that assertion, what is the trade-off between service reliability and service cost? What is the definition of optimum quality, and is it possible to pay for too much quality? Clearly, the benchmark to evaluate such quality rests essentially within the prerogatives of the operating carrier.

Or, consider the R&D efforts of the industry. The Bell System prides itself on the research contributions of Bell Laboratory, and BTL's reputation is worldwide. But what is the optimum amount of resources allocated for R&D? What is the trade-off between R&D and cost? What should be the expected payoff for an annual budget of three quarters of a billion dollars? The FCC's trial staff insisted that BTL's budget was almost out of control. And, rather than impose some accountability on BTL, AT&T preferred to pass the cost to the operating companies and, hence, the consumer.

Finally, consider Western Electric's performance. Bell insists that vertical integration promotes efficiency and innovation. Western's cost-reduction program anually produces millions of dollars in savings. Western's prices enjoy a price of 30 per cent or more, versus similar products supplied by independent vendors.[26] But are the benchmarks employed to verify Western's performance valid and comparable? Do other suppliers enjoy a captive market for their products? Do independent vendors gain access to the construction forecast of their customers? Is it valid to compare costs among firms experiencing vast disparities in production volume? Historically, no ready response has addressed this question. But market conditions in telecommunications have changed. If nothing else, the intensification of competition has erected a market benchmark for the first time. That benchmark has put forth an interesting commentary on two areas of vertical integration: cost reduction and product innovation.

---

[25] Richard Gabel, *Development of Separation Principles in the Telephone Industry*, Institute of Public Utilities, Michigan State University, Division of Research (East Lansing: Michigan State University Press, 1967).

[26] James Billingsley, "Values of Vertical Integration in the Bell System" (Speech delivered to the Wisconsin Telephone Company, Sixth Annual Seminar on Economics of Public Utilities, Oshkosh, Wis., Mar. 8, 1973).

Cost Reduction

The market entry of firms offering products competitive with Western Electric has prompted Western to embark on a cost reduction of products exposed to an outside benchmark. Stated differently, Western's cost reduction was entrusted to, and impelled and spurred by, product competition. Table 3 illustrates this occurrence.

The vast preponderance of Western's product line is immune from direct competition. But, if market rivalry has promoted Western to reassess the cost of a few products in order to achieve lower prices, then one is left with an intriguing question: What if Western's *entire* product line were exposed to an outside market benchmark? Would Western's remaining products experience a similar intensified cost-reduction program?

Product Innovation

The intensification of market competition has provided additional insight into Bell's track record on innovation. Again, the experience of Western Electric is instructive. Prior to competitive pressures, BTL designed a product, Western manufactured, AT&T announced it, and the operating companies bought it. The innovation process was said to be optimized under vertical integration.

But market competition spurred Bell's innovative efforts. The very existence of a product demanded by either telephone subscribers or the telephone company implied a gap in BTL's R&D and a void in Western's product line.

The effects of external pressure were startling. Bell Telephone Laboratory reordered its R&D priorities and quickened its development effort; Western embarked on crash programs—in some cases by passing BTL by designing equipment unilaterally.[27] Western constructed a plant producing competitive

---

TABLE 3
Cost Reduction

NON-WESTERN ELECTRIC	WESTERN ELECTRIC
PBXs	
TE 400 (Japanese)	800 A PBX
NA 409 (Japanese)	101/810 PBX
Community Dial Offices	
SA-1 (Canadian)	5A CDO
Key Telephone Systems	
TIE-1030 (Japanese)	718/1434 Telephone Units
Transmission	
Lenkurt (American)	D-1 Channel Bank

Source: FCC, Docket no. H 19129, 1975. Testimony by M. R. Irwin.

[27] FCC, Docket no. 19129, Trial Staff Exhibit 146, Nov. 1974.

PBXs in some 14 months, in contrast to the 6-year cycle normally experienced.[28] As was observed in a recent Bell study:

> it cannot be denied that at the present time our "competitors" are not so much "out-selling" or "out-merchandising" the Bell System, they are "out-innovating" or "out-marketing" it.[29]

Clearly, market competition has not been without its impact. If nothing else, the nonintegrated firm has erected a performance benchmark—however tenuous. That benchmark has suggested that industry statements as to system efficiency and innovation may be essentially self-serving.

V. PUBLIC POLICY

Public policy possess at least three options in addressing the holding company concept of horizontal and vertical integration. The first would sustain the present structure of the industry and maintain the status quo. The second would extend regulation to all facets of holding company control—specifically, manufacturing affiliates. The third would decentralize or abolish holding company control, particularly with regard to vertical supply affiliates.

The Status Quo

The status quo argues that the holding company is the optimum market organization to render telephone service to the public. Such a policy would sanction Bell's ownership of Western Electric and AT&T's ownership of the operating companies. Such a policy argues that the holding company reduces equipment, cost and prices, fosters R&D, optimizes innovation, is responsive to the needs of the operating company, and creates a system that is largely internal and self-propelling in its incentives.[30]

The status quo position insists that the common ownership of R&D, of manufacturing, and of telephone service under holding company control leads to systemic integrity, coordination, and optimization redounding ultimately to the benefit of the subscriber.

The holding company is not without its economic costs, however, and raises a series of unresolved policy questions. What benchmark is to insure the least cost equipment? What incentive is to insure minimum prices on hardware? What incentive is to insure the optimum racking up for priorities? What is the incentive to spur market innovation and to drive a corporation toward market

---

[28] S. E. Bonsack, "A Discussion of Marketing Function in Telecommunications Under Conditions of Growing Competition," in *New Challenges to Public Utility Management*, Institute of Public Utilities, Michigan State University (East Lansing: Michigan State University Press, 1974).

[29] FCC, Docket no. 19129, *Policy Study Report*, Corporate Planning, AT&T (1972), Trial Staff Exhibit 147, 1974.

[30] FCC, Docket no. 19129, Testimony of Bill Witner, K. McKay, vice-president, Bell Telephone Laboratory, transcript Vol. 82, p. 12,687, 1974.

efficiency? What is to check Western Electric's responsiveness to the needs of the operating company?

The status quo policy falls short of addressing the technological changes now gaining momentum in the industry. To this extent, the status quo policy is a vote for the past rather than the future. It fails to consider the minimal impact on new products, new services, and new technical capabilities available to the operating companies and, ultimately, to the telephone subscriber. The status quo policy argues that end-to-end service gives adequate option and choice to the user, and that the outside vendors are content to remain in the position of a subcontractor to vertical affiliates.

Certainly, competition has rendered the status quo policy suspect. Competition has prompted the Bell System to reassess its prices, its policies, its costs, its marketing and, indeed, its organizational structure. Such an examination was not self-propelled, but was, rather, inspired—indeed, impelled by external market forces.

Regulation

A second policy option would argue that competition in the equipment segment of the market is unworkable and that equipment suppliers are natural monopolies manifesting the characteristics of economies of scale and prohibitive capital expenditures. The result would see a shift in the status of such supplier from unregulated manufacturer to regulated utility, entitled to earn a return commensurate with that of any other regulated entity.

Several advantages attend this approach. First, Western Electric, for all practical purposes, does possess market power over its prices and profits. Explicit regulation would merely formalize Western's monopoly status. Second, direct regulation would enable the FCC to disallow any excess return of Western at other costs that would be found to be unjustified and thus, through such disallowances, reduce the cost of the operating companies and, hopefully, the rates to the subscribing public. And, finally, direct regulation would enable the commission to examine, assess, and detail the cost accounting and the practices and the expenditures of equipment subsidiaries as they have a direct impact on on the costs of the operating companies.

Public utility regulation as an extension of holding company control carries with it several disadvantages. First of all, regulation cannot deal very effectively with the problem of corporate incentives. What impetus prompts the integrated manufacturer to reduce its costs, re-examine its prices, reassess its product line, and spur its responsiveness to the needs of its ultimate customers? Something more than regulatory lag must be called into place. And what is to provide an adequate benchmark to assess the priorities of research and development and assess the responsiveness of R&D to the needs of the operating companies?

Second, a policy based on regulating a manufacturer's rate of return may be appealing in the short term, but it may prove disappointing in the long term. Disallowances rest essentially on cost, and the real question is how to introduce an incentive system that will reward the corporation for cost reduction. Inserting a limitation on profits may actually result in higher costs, to the extent that the manufacturer pursues a cost-plus strategy not dissimilar to any public utility.

Third, a policy that extends regulation over equipment manufacturers rests on the assumption that capital requirements prohibit entry in telecommunications equipment and scale economies foreclose such entry on grounds of economy and efficiency. Our recent experience in equipment competition and market access contradicts that assumption. Even Western Electric grants the assumption of the concept of optimum-sized manufacturing plants.[31]

Finally, extending regulation over the equipment suppliers of telephone holding companies opens up a policy Pandora's box: If one manufacturer experiences economies of scale, would it not be appropriate for all manufacturers to be consolidated under the ownership of a sole holding company? And should not a giant merger occur? And who would qualify for such an acquisition: IBM, Texas Instruments, Stromberg-Carlson, Anaconda Wire and Cable? Where does one draw the line between computer manufacturing, telecommunications manufacturing, and solid-state device manufacturing? Clearly, the move for directly extending the regulation of all components of holding company control knows no limits..

Competition

A third policy alternative would move both the R&D and manufacturing sectors of the industry to one of entry, diversity, and competition. This policy would recommend a restructuring of the holding company. The holding company would no longer control buyer of equipment and seller of equipment. Telephone operating companies would be allowed to stand on their own corporate feet—buying equipment, supplies, services, and hardware in an open and competitive environment. This third option is currently under review, creating a rash of antitrust suits for the industry.

Conclusion

What is the response of the telephone holding company to these alternatives to public policy? Generally, the answer is unequivocal: preserve the status quo. The problem with such a policy prescription is that corporate accountability is proving to be frustratingly difficult, whether to the market place or to the regulatory agency. When, for example, GTE, the second-largest telephone holding company, found its horizontal mergers questioned by state commissions, the company insisted that such mergers resided beyond state jurisdiction.[32] When horizontal mergers were questioned by the FCC, GTE successfully pleaded that

---

[31] FCC, Docket no. 19129, testimony of M. Tannebaum, Western Electric, Transcript no. 15,059, 1974.

[32] *International Telephone and Telegraph* v. *Public Utilities Commission of Ohio, et al.*, 247 N.E. 2d 276 (1968).

as a holding company, it resided beyond the reach of the 1934 communication law.[33] Yet, when GTE found itself mired in a private antitrust suit, the company scrambled back to the FCC and entered the plea of a prodigal son.

When AT&T recently became disenchanted with some of the procompetitive pronouncements of the FCC, the holding company found itself asserting the virtues of state jurisdiction. When some states attempted to treat Western Electric's profits as equivalent to those of a telephone utility, AT&T insisted Western incurred the risks of a manufacturer. But, when the Department of Justice filed a suit ordering its divestitute of Western, AT&T insisted that the FCC's jurisdiction over the Bell System was total, complete, and overriding.[34]

Now the focus of public policy and the telephone holding company has shifted. Holding companies are pleading for congressional legislation that will immunize them from the twin assault of antitrust and competition.[35] Whatever the outcome of this legislative effort, the attempt to circumvent regulation and the market place is beset by two questions: (1) Can Congress, or, for that matter, anybody, successfully legislate a moratorium against technological change in the telephone industry? (2) Given the political coalescence of corporate and union power in this industry, what institution will protect the interest of the consuming public? Although these issues remain unanswered, it is clear that the telephone industry is now at a major fork in the policy road. It is also clear that the stakes are enormous.

SUPPLEMENTARY READING

BOOKS

Brooks, John. *The First Hundred Years.* New York: Harper & Row, Publishers, 1976

Irwin, Manley R. *Telecommunications Policy: Integration vs. Competition.* New York: Praeger Publishers, Inc., 1970.

Kahn, Alfred E. *Economics of Regulation.* Vols. 1 and 2. New York: John Wiley & Sons, Inc., 1970.

MSU Public Utilities Papers. *New Challenges in Public Utility Management.* East Lansing: Michigan State University Press, Institute of Public Utilities, Graduate School of Business Administration, 1974.

Trebing, Harry M., ed. *Essays on Public Utility Pricing and Regulation.* Graduate School of Business Administration, Institute of Public Utilities, Michigan State University. Lansing: Michigan State University Press, 1970.

———, and M. R. Irwin. "A Survey of Problems Confronting the Communications Industry in the United States." In *Telecommunications for Canada,* edited by H. Edward English. London: Methuen & Co., Ltd., 1973.

[33] Applications for Consent to Transfer Control of Hawaiian Telephone Company as holder of Radio Licenses and Cable Landing Licenses to General Telephone and Electronics, 4 FCC 2d 421 (1966), p. 186.

[34] *United States* v. *American Telephone and Telegraph, et. al.,* Civil Action no. 74-1968, U.S. District Court, District of Columbia. Defendants Answering Memorandum submitted pursuant to the court's order of Feb. 27, 1975.

[35] *Wall Street Journal,* Feb. 3, 1976, p. 10.

Weiss, Leonard, and Allyn Strickland. *Regulation: A Case Approach.* New York: McGraw-Hill Book Company, 1976.

Wilcox, Clair, and William G. Shepherd, *Public Policies Toward Business*, Homewood, Ill.: Richard D. Irwin, Inc., 1975.

GOVERNMENT PUBLICATIONS

FCC. *Investigation of the Telephone Industry in the United States* (Pursuant to Public Resolution no. 8, 74th Cong.). Washington, DC.: U.S. Government Printing Office, 1938.

Statement and Recommendation of the Common Carrier Bureau's Trial Staff, FCC, In the Matter of American Telephone and Telegraph Company and Associated Bell System Companies, Docket no. 19129 (phase 2) Feb. 2, 1976.

Final Report, President's Task Force on Communication Policy, Dec. 7, 1968.

U.S. Congress, House, Committee on the Judiciary, *Hearings on Consent Decree Program of the Department of Justice Before Subcommittee no. 5*, 75th Cong., 2d sess., 1956.

U.S. Senate, Congress, Committee on the Judiciary, *Hearings on the Industrial Reorganization Act, Before the Subcommittee on Antitrust and Monopoly*, 93rd Cong., 2d sess., 1974.

United States of America v. *American Telephone and Telegraph Company*, Western Electric Company Inc., Civil Action no. 74-1698, Nov. 1974.

JOURNAL AND MAGAZINE ARTICLES

Averich, H., and L. Johnson. "Behavior of the Firm Under Regulatory Restraint," *American Economic Review*, **52**:1052 (Dec. 1962).

Billingsley, J. R. "Values of Vertical Integration in the Bell System." Paper read at *Wisconsin Telephone Seminar*, Sixth Annual Seminar on Economics of Public Utilities, Oshkosh, Wis., 1973.

Irwin, Manley R. "The Computer Utility: Competition or Regulation." *Yale Law Journal*, **76**:1299 (June 1967).

———, and Kenneth Stanley. "Regulatory Circumvention and the Holding Company." *Journal of Economic Issues*, **8**:2 (June 1974).

Trebing, Harry, "Common Carrier Regulation: The Silent Crisis." *Law and Contemporary Problems*, **34**:299 (Spring 1969).

"Telephones at 100—Transformed by Technology." *Electronics*, **48**: 90 (Dec. 1, 1975.)

CHAPTER 10

the banking industry

WILLIAM G. SHEPHERD

I. INTRODUCTION

Banking is not a large industry.[1] It is only part of "the financial sector." Some of its main operations and effects are esoteric and little known. Yet, as the allocator of credit and control, banking is unique and important. Its influence extends through the rest of the economy.

Basic Concepts: A Summary

There are two kinds of structure to be analyzed. One is the banking market—ranging from local on up to international levels—in which banks compete and cooperate with each other. The second type of structure is the banking relationship, between a company and its primary (or only) banker.

The core functions of banking are simple: to handle deposits and payments, to extend credit, and to supervise the use of deposits and payments. Recently these have grown more complex, but the basic kind of business (sound operations and stable profits) remains the same, even for the more advanced, global bankers along Wall Street.

---

[1] Parts of this chapter are drawn from Chaps. 11 and 12 of Clair Wilcox and William G. Shepherd, *Public Policies Toward Business*, 5th ed. (Homewood, Ill.: Irwin, 1975); and W. G. Shepherd, *The Treatment of Market Power* (New York: Columbia University Press, 1975). Chaps. 2–6. For basic sources on banking in the U.S., see David Alhadeff, *Monopoly and Competition in Banking* (Berkeley: University of California Press, 1954); Gerald R. Fischer, *American Banking Structure* (New York: Columbia University Press, 1968); and J. M. Guttentag and E. S. Herman, *Banking Structure and Performance* (New York: New York University Press, 1967).

A lively, and often searching, appraisal of banking is given by Martin Mayer, *The Bankers* (New York: Weybright and Talley, 1974). Almarin Phillips lucidly puts the case for more competition in "A Competitive Policy for Depository Financial Institutions," a chapter in Almarin Phillips, ed., *Promoting Competition in Regulated Markets* (Washington, D.C.: Brookings, 1975).

In the larger view, American banking first grew slowly and locally, but changed rapidly after the Civil War. It matured during 1890–1930 in several directions, but the bankers' traumas of the Great Crash of 1929–1933 brought on an obsession—among bankers and public officials—with security, to be reinforced by rigid divisions and regulations. Since about 1960, banking has increasingly bent and flowed around these constraints, with rapid changes by the larger banks since 1965.

The 1970s appear to be a watershed for the banking sector and policies because technology, motivation, and policy constraints are changing. The choices are in two dimensions. One is the degree of competition. Will regulations and limits be relaxed? Can there be more flexibility while preserving enough security? The second direction of policy choice is the appropriate extent and forms of public enterprise in banking activities. Public units already cover many credit needs, mingle with private banking, and perform basic operations (for example, deposit insurance and reserve management). Are these units performing well? Are further activities appropriate?

The policy choices bridge the three main categories of public policies—antitrust, regulation, and public enterprise—and the sector is unusually sophisticated and transitional.[2] Therefore, this chapter can only skim the main issues and offer rough policy judgments as a focus for the reader's thinking. First we review the banking industry's scope and history: what it is and how it has evolved. Next comes structure, both in banking markets and bank-client relationships. Scale economies are also summed up in Section II. Then, Section III treats banking behavior, which mixes traditional restrictions with, in some directions, increasing competition. Section IV finds that although banking performance in the United States has been checkered, it has been, possibly, superior by international comparison. Section V suggests that further policy changes are in order, as judged by economic criteria. It also notes that, throughout the chapter, the reader should bear in mind that "public" policies often tend to reflect banking power (and even increase it) rather than to constrain it.

History

The Sector

Banking is what bankers do. The cashier's window handles only a small and peripheral part of the main business. As part of the financial sector, banking specializes in making loans, money transfers, and supervision—in a mnemonic phrase: *credit, clearing,* and *counseling.*[3] It coexists and partly overlaps with investment banking, insurance savings and loans, and other financial "industries," as shown in Figure 1. All provide capital in some form. Banking

[2] These basic policy types and choices are presented in Wilcox and Shepherd, op. cit.

[3] Mayer's description (op. cit.), is especially clear; see also the various studies in the Commission on Money and Credit's study, *Private Financial Institutions* (Englewood Cliffs, N.J.: Prentice-Hall, 1963).

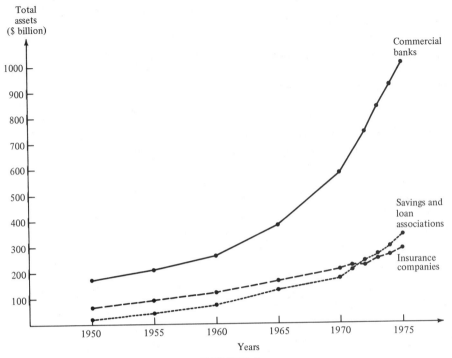

FIGURE 1
Parts of the financial sector.

specializes in business and consumer loans, under regulations that seek to assure "sound banking." But other kinds of units also provide credit, in large volume, as shown in Table 1.

The "banking system" is actually quite complex, as shown in Figure 2. In the textbook version, banks simply accept deposits, which permit them to expand loans by some multiple. Depositors use checks, which are then cleared under the Federal Reserve System (FRS). The Fed "manages" the money supply and interest rates by various tools.

Actual conditions are less precise and involve more economic power and complexity. The heart of banking is loans to business, and at the core of these are the "banking relationships." These relationships are stable and intimate: the bank comes to know all about any firm that relies on it for much capital.[4] Prudent bankers must know their risks, and so bank and company officials operate on long-standing terms of mutual trust and familiarity. In some cases, bankers are directors of their client firms, but that is only a surface sign of the real relationships behind the scenes.

[4] See Shepherd, op. cit., Chap. 2. See also L. L. Werboff and M. E. Rosen, "Market Shares and Competition Among Financial Institutions," in *Commission on Money and Credit*, op. cit., pp. 265–331. Mayer (op. cit.) tends to exaggerate the number of banks with which firms maintain primary relationships.

TABLE 1
Various Sources of Credit, 1970

PRIVATE (CLAIMS HELD BY PRIVATE FINANCIAL INSTITUTIONS)	VOLUME ($ BILLIONS)	
Commercial banks	435.2	
Savings institutions	251.2	
Insurance and pension funds	287.8	
Other finance	74.1	

PUBLIC (BANKING AND INSURANCE ENTITIES)	INDICATORS OF SIZE, 1973 ($ BILLIONS)	
Personal Security		
Old Age and Survivors Insurance (Social Security)	41.3	(benefits paid)
Federal Disability Insurance Trust Fund	4.5	(benefits paid)
Federal Unemployment Insurance	5.8	(benefits paid)
Federal Employees Life Insurance	39.9	(insurance in force)
Veterans Special Life Insurance Fund	5.3	(insurance in force)
Federal Hospital Trust Fund	7.0	(payments)
Federal Supplementary Medical Insurance Trust Fund	2.5	(payments)
Housing		
Federal National Mortgage Association	26.3	(loans insured)
Federal Home Loan Bank Board	13.8	(loans insured)
Federal Home Loan Mortgage Corporation	3.1	(loans insured)
Federal Housing Administration	78.2	(mortgages insured)
Veterans Administration	42.4	(mortgages insured)
Finance		
Federal Deposit Insurance Corporation	5.6	(funding)
Federal Savings and Loan Insurance Corporation	3.3	(funding)
Securities Investors Protection Corporation	1.0	(authorized capital)
Overseas Private Investment Corporation	11.0	(face amount of insurance)
Export-Import Bank	8.2	(loans insured)
Agriculture		
Banks for Cooperatives	2.3	(assets)
Federal Intermediate Credit Banks	8.2	(assets)
Federal Land Banks	9.3	(assets)
Federal Crop Insurance Corporation	1.0	(assets)
Other		
Student Loan Insurance Fund	4.0	(loans insured)
Federal Insurance Administration (urban, other)	0.1	(assets)

Source: *U.S. Statistical Abstract* and *U.S. Federal Budget*, various years.

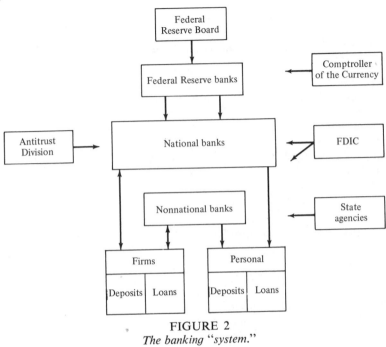

FIGURE 2
The banking "system."

Banks acquire funds from depositors of various kinds (checking deposits, savings, certificates of deposit, commercial accounts, and so on). See Table 2. They dispose of funds chiefly by loans and lines of credit, but also, increasingly, in a range of other debt forms. Before 1960, bank loans to companies were mainly short-term credit, to finance routine cash needs of firms (for example, seasonal inventory shifts and payrolls). Recently, there has been a strong shift into long-term loans, for nonrecurring basic corporate projects. Short-term loans are covered primarily by collateral. Long-term loans are "covered" by predicted cash flows, a much riskier matter; and large firms have become sharply more reliant on debt (that is, their capital structure has become more highly *leveraged*) since 1960. This has drawn banks ever deeper into the whole of corporate planning and risk sharing. The banks' own risks have risen dramatically.[5] The banking relationship now involves real—often great—mutual risk and dependence.

So private commercial banks nurse along their core of prime clients as their central concern. They also perform small-scale "retailing" functions, of the kinds that you can observe (checking, savings deposits, safety boxes, and mortgages). In seeking to maximize their profits, consistent with some degree of "prudence," they basically manage a set of assets and liabilities (recently "liability management" has become about as important as "asset management").

[5] Mayer, op. cit., rates this risk as very high. Events during 1973–1975—including the massive souring of some bank loans and investment accounts and the failure of several sizable banks—are confirming that the risk exposure of banks is well above 1940–1960 levels. The very largest banks are among the most highly exposed, as we will see subsequently in more detail.

TABLE 2
Assets and Liabilities of All U.S. Commercial Banks, 1950–1974

ACCOUNT	1950	1960	1970	1974
Assets[a]				
Cash, balances, items in process	40.4	52.2	94.0	126.5
Currency and coin	2.2	3.4	7.1	8.4
Balances with banks, including reserve	28.5	30.6	47.1	65.9
Cash items in process of collection	9.7	18.3	39.8	52.2
Securities (book value)	74.8	82.0	142.7	189.8
U.S. Treasury and other agencies	62.3	61.1	59.3	53.4
States and subdivisions	8.2	17.6	67.9	99.9
Federal funds sold and related	0.0	0.0	16.3	35.3
Other loans and discounts	53.2	120.5	300.4	494.1
Commercial and industrial	22.0	43.4	113.4	177.2
Real estate loans	13.7	28.8	73.3	126.2
Residential	10.4	20.4	45.6	78.8
Other	2.3	8.4	27.7	47.4
Other financial institutions	.2	7.1	15.9	33.6
Farmers	2.9	5.7	11.2	18.4
Individuals	10.2	26.5	66.3	102.6
Bank premises and real estate	1.3	3.2	9.6	14.2
Total assets	170.5	260.7	581.5	884.8
Liabilities				
Deposits	156.1	230.5	485.5	710.3
Demand	118.8	156.8	249.0	302.8
Time	37.3	73.7	236.5	274.4
Savings				
Business and personal	129.4	189.0	397.3	555.7
Government	12.6	22.6	49.7	65.5
Domestic interbank	12.3	15.8	29.2	42.0
Miscellaneous liabilities	2.1	6.8	46.5	104.7
Capital accounts	11.7	21.1	43.2	61.6
Equity	11.6	21.0	41.0	57.3
Stock	3.6	6.3	11.4	14.6
Surplus and reserves	8.0	14.7	29.6	42.7
Total liabilities, etc.	170.5	260.7	581.5	884.8

[a] Subcategories shown do not necessarily cover all items.
[b] Not available separately.
Source: FDIC *Accounts* and Federal Reserve *Bulletin*, issued periodically.

These private activities are touched at many points by public banking units. The Federal Reserve System manages clearing and reserves, and it guarantees the whole system's liquidity. The Federal Deposit and Investment Corp (FDIC insures the mass of deposits—and, indirectly, the security of the individual banks.

TABLE 3
Evolution of Commercial Banking: Selected Data, 1870–1974

	1870	1900	1920	1930	1935	1950	1960	1965	1970	1974
National banks										
Number	1,612	3,731	8,024	7,247	5,425	4,971	4,824	4,707	4,621	4,537
Assets ($ billions)	1.6	4.9	23.3	28.8	26.0	89.7	148.5	264.9	340.8	516.6
Non-national banks										
Number	325	9,322	22,885	17,026	10,622	9,705	9,525	9,298	9,065	8,742
Assets ($ billions)	.2	6.4	29.8	45.5	33.9	89.5	131.5	189.2	236.2	365.4
Branch banks and offices as a per cent of all bank offices	1.0	1.6	5.7	15.7	21.3	31.6	53.0	63.6	(72)[b]	(76)
New banks and de novo branches (previous 5 years)	—[a]	—	—	1,352	—	1,238	3,477	5,953	7,148	(8,500)
Bank suspensions	3	36	168	—	32	5	4	6	1	34
FDIC insured deposits, as a per cent of all deposits	—	—	—	—	37	47	56	58	60	62

[a] —indicates data not available.
[b] ( ) indicates estimate.
Source: U.S. Department of Commerce, *Historical Statistics* (Washington, D.C.: U.S. Government Printing Office, 1957), and *Statistical Abstract* (Washington, D.C.: U.S. Government Printing Office, annual).

Public units cover many special credit needs by direct loans or credit guarantees on private-bank loans (for example, on some mortgages and student loans).

Public regulation is also extensive, so much so that it virtually defines the industry. Thus, banking is what properly chartered and regulated banks do. The main banks are Federally chartered, but many are state chartered (see Table 3). Such banks are rigidly limited to banking, as distinct from such other financial activities as insuring and investing in stocks, as well as from all other commercial and industrial operations, such as making steel or growing tomatoes. In other countries, banking is not thus limited, often mingling all manner of commercial activities and industrial power.[6] Yet, even these restrictions are being modified in the United States. There is doubt, as we will see, that regulation actually applies the *public* interest and yields good effects in the United States.

Evolution

The main lines of evolution in banking in the United States are given in Table 4. The origins were local, in supplying credit and quasi-moneys to oil the wheels of nascent commerce.[7] The First and Second National banks (1787–1836) stirred a variety of local and political resistance, so that subsequent banking in the United States remained mainly a localized operation. By 1900, a range of (1) state and national, (2) branch and single-unit, and (3) grass-roots and Wall Street banks had evolved.

Charters were given liberally in most areas, to help foster development. Bankers' activities spread into many lines, just as they still do in most other industrial economies. Banks were variously engaged in investing, factoring, brokering, merger-promoting, underwriting, and other "financial" operations —and in directing many industrial companies—as well as in the traditional deposit banking. By 1900, unit banking prevailed, but branch banking then spread, and by 1935 held more than half of banking assets. Now it handles the great majority of all banking activities. Yet, antibranching restrictions have remained tight in many states, as local banks resisted the incursions—and new competition —of big-city money.[8]

Instability has been a chronic problem in a local banking system, for panic runs on banks could arise at any time, spread, and cause the widespread destruction of deposits as well as of the banks themselves. This occurred in the 1870s, 1890s, 1907–1908, and of course in 1929–1933 (see Figure 3). By 1930, the new

[6] On foreign patterns, see Wilcox and Shepherd, op. cit., Chap. 20; R. L. Sayers, ed., *Banking in Western Europe* (New York: Macmillan, 1962); David Alhadeff, *Competition and Controls in Banking: A Study of the Regulation of Bank Competition in Italy, France, and England* (Berkeley: University of California Press, 1968); and Eleanor Hadley, *Antitrust in Japan* (Princeton: Princeton University Press, 1971).

[7] See Fischer, op. cit. and, for more details, Davis R. Dewey, *Financial History of the United States* (New York: Longmans, 1911).

[8] Fisher, op. cit., covers the shifts in branching policy thoroughly. Unit banking is found mainly between the Mississippi and the Rockies, with widespread branching to the west. East of the Mississippi there is mainly limited branching.

TABLE 4
Milestones in Banking and Public Policy

1782–1840	Early banks form (Bank of North America, 1782; 28 state-chartered banks by 1800; Bank of United States, 1791–1811; Second Bank of United States, 1816–1832; 901 banks by 1840).
1864–1865	National Bank Act (amended) sets conditions for charters, favors unit banking, covers most state banks (1556 banks in existence).
1865–1900	Growth and turbulence. Unit banks become prevalent, policies shift to limit branching (4338 banks in 1886 to 29,151 in 1910).
1907	Panic threatens the entire banking system, once again.
1914	Federal Reserve System is created.
1920–1935	Turmoil, then collapse; 15,000 bank suspensions (9000 in 1930–1933 alone) and 7000 mergers. Federal Reserve fails to support the system during 1929–1933. Half the states prohibit branching by 1930, and most others limit it.
1933–1935	Bank Acts fix banking rules, define limits. Reconstruction Finance Corp. (RFC) created in 1932, continues until 1952. Federal Deposit Insurance Corp. (FDIC) created in 1933–1934.
1930s	Many Federal credit agencies are started (farming, housing, etc.).
1930s–1950s	Bank cooperation is approved and reinforced. Bank of America (San Francisco) leads in branching, becomes the largest bank.
1950s	Banking share in the financial sector begins to slip by 1950s.
1951–1963	Bank merger wave; many major horizontal mergers.
1956	Bank Holding Company Act legitimizes, but limits, bank holding companies.
1960	Bank Merger Act. Moderate; it tries to define criteria and assign agency jurisdiction.
1960s	Term loans assume greater importance. One-bank holding companies spread.
1961–1964	Several Antitrust Division cases attack bank cooperation. James Saxon, comptroller of the currency, opens up entry and chartering policies.
1963	*Philadelphia National Bank* case stops a major merger. Later cases further tighten limits on horizontal mergers.
1965–1974	"Performance banking" spreads, led by First National City Bank of New York.
1970	Bank Holding Company Act is amended to permit (and limit) holding companies.
1970–1975	Rise in holding companies, to include nearly all large banks. Bank failures increase to significant levels. FDIC and comptroller arduously arrange absorptions of several tottering banks.
1974	Federal Reserve intervenes to influence bank support on real estate and other loans.
1974–1976	The period of high-risk exposure passes, with only a few bank failures.

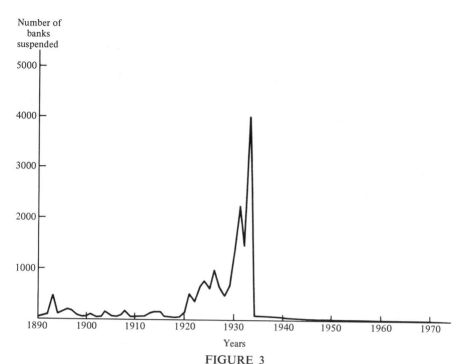

FIGURE 3

Bank suspensions since 1890. Source: Historical Statistics of the United States, 1957, and the Federal Deposit Insurance Corporation.

Federal Reserve Board had powers to avert most failures, but by a monumental error of omission they did not use these powers. The 1929–1932 trauma led to a six-part set of policies to assure "sound" banking:

1. The FIC guaranteed most deposits, by insurance and inspection.
2. Banks were sealed off from all other activities.
3. The Federal Reserve System stood ready to keep the whole system liquid enough so that failures could not spread.
4. New entry was tightly restricted, to avert the "unstable" effects of competition (branching was also more tightly limited).
5. Examiners of the FDIC, Federal Reserve, Comptroller of the Currency, and state agencies would scrutinize all operations, to prevent risky loans and other actions.
6. Price competition among banks (for example, by offering interest on deposits) was officially restricted in various ways.

Some of these new policies merely reflected the internecine struggles among banking interest groups. Others helped all banks at the expense of the rest of society. And some policies genuinely reflected "the public interest." Altogether, they doubled and tripled the policy safeguards that were needed in order to assure the optimum degree of stability.[9]

At any rate, banking became tightly restricted in the 1930s, and during 1930–1960 it was manned by traumatized managers with a passion for security. There were exceptions, as the Bank of America and others quickly sought ways around the limits.[10] By the 1950s, the pressures and experiments were rising, but only after 1965 did the main lines change appreciably. By 1975 the changes included:

1. A shift (perhaps to be reversed soon) from prudence to performance as the aim of the larger banks.
2. A shift from safe, secured short-term loans to riskier—even speculative—long-term loans and debt instruments.
3. Increased speed and flexibility in portfolio-type operations, including those in the Euro-dollar market, real estate, railroads, and so on.
4. A massive shift to bank holding companies during 1969–1974, which entered a growing range of financial markets (factoring, credit cards, and so on).[11]
5. Increased entry after 1960, both by new banks and by more branching.

Underlying these changes were technological gains in data processing, which were evolving toward giant capacities to hold deposits and clear transactions instantly. Most physical trappings of banking operations (checks, cashiers, bonds and the like) are now superfluous, for a unified giro type of clearing system can do virtually all of it by computer.[12] Much of the operations and technology of banking, therefore, continue as a form of cultural lag, which might be reduced by more competition, wise regulation or public banking units, or by some mixture of the three.

The basic "banking" function of evaluating risk and supplying credit remains at the core of bank activities, and much of it requires just that blend of local, thorough knowledge that bankers have come to have about their prime clients. No computer can replace that, and banking in the United States may well be, on the whole, a more efficient credit allocator than any other. Yet, two problems remain. First, bankers *make* security by the very act of granting credit (or standing ready to supply it). *They do not just find what a firm's degree of risk is.* Therefore, ties between the leading banks and firms can exclude credit for, and competition by, new and smaller firms (see Section III for more on this). Second, banks can err; during 1965–1974, the push for "performance" led many of the

---

[9] See Phillips, op. cit. and Alhadeff, op. cit. (1954) for clear discussions of these policy overlaps.

[10] Mayer, op. cit., vividly presents these conditions and changes.

[11] The Federal Reserve has limited these spreading activities to a narrow range, still closely related to banking operations (see Wilcox and Shepherd, op. cit., Chap. 12).

[12] Giro operations involve direct transfers among accounts, bypassing the check writing and clearing operations. Operations are fewer and more decentralized, and the paperwork and sorting (as made clear in Mayer, op. cit.), are much less necessary. Because clearing operations are enormous *and* rapidly growing, a giro system may become technically imperative, in any event.

largest banks into highly risky loans and portfolio choices (see section IV.3). This put the whole system's stability under severe stress during 1974–1975. Therefore, a marked improvement in the credit-allocating function may still be possible.

Altogether, the 1960–1975 changes may not be a "revolution," but they are strong and, in part, overdue as a correction of the hyperrestrictions of the 1930s. Yet, they have not sharply modified the basic patterns of banking concentration and the tightness of banking relationships. And they leave the performance of banking still an open question.

Note that the public role in banking has shifted. Public restrictions and supervision have marginally receded, whereas public banking and support activities have grown and affected areas more directly. Although public banking is less extensive than is common abroad, it is still much more important than the usual image—that private banking is the whole of the industry—allows.

The whole set of public regulations and agencies is a "crazy quilt," as the Federal Reserve noted as long ago as 1938.[13] The overlapping activities of Federal and state regulations are summarized in Table 5. These formal lines do not show the full range of activities and conflicts. Thus, the Federal Reserve was active during 1974–1975 in getting banks to renew support for real estate trusts and other shaky firms; that goes well beyond its traditional role of general support. The Antitrust Division has entered deeply into—even dominated—the screening of mergers since 1961, pushing aside the other agencies in many respects. The then controller of the currency, James J. Saxon, during 1961–1965 dropped most of the long-standing bars to new entry.

Still, Table 5 faithfully conveys the degree to which "regulation" is mixed and, therefore, *full responsibility is not borne by any single unit*. Note also that regulation touches only on security, market presence, and minimum prices. There is no economic regulation of the classic, complete sort: of maximum prices and permitted profits.[14] Therefore, banking regulation verges on self-regulation, which—when it reduces competition among oligopolists—is often the least satisfactory type of regulation.[15]

II. MARKET STRUCTURE

We shall consider banking markets and then banking relationships in this section. Then we shall evaluate the economies of scale that might justify tight structure.

[13] "The banking picture emerges as a crazy quilt of conflicting powers and jurisdictions, of overlapping authorities and gaps in authority, of restrictions making it difficult for banks to serve their communities and make a living, and of conditions making it next to impossible for public authorities to apply adequate restraints at a time and in conditions when this may be in the public interest." U.S. Department of the Treasury, Federal Reserve Board, *Annual Report* (Washington, D.C.: U.S. Government Printing Office, 1938).

[14] Compare this with regulation as described and analyzed in Wilcox and Shepherd, op. cit., Chaps. 13–18, and Shepherd, op. cit., Chaps. 5 and 9.

[15] Wilcox and Shepherd, op. cit., Chaps. 14, 18, and 24.

TABLE 5
Regulatory Coverage in Banking

1971 NUMBER	ASSETS ($ BILLIONS)		COMP-TROLLER OF THE CURRENCY	FEDERAL RESERVE	FDIC	STATE AGENCIES
4599	376	National Banks				
		Chartered by	*			
		Examined by	*	*	*	
		Reserves required by	*	*	*	
		Subject to regulations of	*	*	*	
		Mergers and branches limited by	*	*		
1128	136	State Member Banks				
		Chartered by				*
		Examined by		*	*	
		Reserves required by		*		
		Subject to regulations of	*	*	*	*
		Mergers and branches limited by		*		*
7875	124	Insured Non-member Banks				
		Chartered by				*
		Examined by			*	*
		Reserves required by				*
		Subject to regulations of		*	*	*
		Mergers and branches limited by			*	*

Banking and Trust Departments

First, *total concentration*. This is substantial and steady. The share of the largest 20 banks in all commercial bank assets has remained at about 29 per cent from 1960 to 1974. The share of the largest bank holding companies has risen.

There are several strong forces at work. Big-city and international operations have grown more rapidly. Branching and mergers have had marginal effects. The new holding companies, especially among the largest banks, have expanded assets in new lines. Generally, the push to grow and "perform" has been strongest in the larger banks. The large banks' position has been diluted, however, by their greater risk exposure in the 1970s.

Total banking concentration is high, and bank trust departments are even more highly concentrated.[16] The upper tier of the 15 largest bank trust departments holds a solid $120 billion or more of assets. Abroad, concentration tends to be even higher.

Concentration in Banking Markets

Because banking occurs at local, regional, national, and international levels, defining banking markets is endlessly debatable. Yet, it is widely agreed that much banking is genuinely local: it has to be, so that bankers can be aware of their clients' true conditions and risks.[17] Table 6 sums up local banking concentration. The large markets are moderate-to-tight oligopolies, whereas the smaller city markets tend to have tighter structure. Yet, many small cities have surprisingly low concentration.

On the whole, structure has been tight and stable for decades, although there have been some shifts and perhaps a very slow receding of the average degree of concentration.[18] In addition, the very largest banks may have faced increasing competition as they entered new activities and foreign markets. Yet, banking markets probably continue to have tighter structure than the average found in other markets.[19]

These levels and trends reflect the balance among (1) mergers, (2) internal growth, and (3) entry, including the chartering of new banks. Public policies influence all of these. Horizontal mergers were largely stopped by 1963, and new entry was liberalized during 1961–1965. The mergers strongly raised concentration: new entry, strong as it has seemed, has scarcely caused it to abate at all in the larger cities.[20]

---

[16] U.S. Congress, House, Committee on Banking and Currency, *Commercial Banks and Their Trust Activities, Hearings*, 2 vols., 90th Cong., 2d sess., 1968; Irwin Friend et al., *Investment Banking and the New Issues Market* (Cleveland: World, 1967); and Mayer, op. cit. Morgan Guaranty Trust, Chase Manhattan, Bankers Trust, and First National City Bank alone hold nearly $70 billion in assets.

[17] See Phillips, op. cit. and sources cited there, including especially Alhadeff, op. cit., and the series of bank merger decisions.

[18] This is the consensus from *Commission on Money and Credit*, op. cit.; Guttentag and Herman, op. cit.; Phillips, op. cit.; and others.

[19] On nonfinancial markets, see William G. Shepherd, *Market Power and Economic Welfare* (New York: Random House, 1970), Chaps. 7–10.

[20] David A. Alhadeff and Charlotte P. Alhadeff, "An Integrated Model for Commercial Banks," *Journal of Finance*, **12**: 24–43 (1957), and Shepherd, *The Treatment of Market Power*, op. cit.

TABLE 6
Banking Concentration in Selected U.S. Cities, 1970

METROPOLITAN AREA	TOTAL DEPOSITS ($ BILLIONS)	PER CENT HELD BY LARGEST 3 BANKS
Largest 7		
New York, N.Y.	69.6	48
Chicago, Ill.	23.7	43
Los Angeles, Calif.	15.4	70
San Francisco, Calif.	13.2	78
Detroit, Mich.	11.0	62
Philadelphia, Pa.	10.3	46
Boston, Mass.	7.1	61
Others		
Phoenix, Ariz.	2.0	90
Portland, Ore.	2.0	80
Columbus, Ohio	1.7	93
Hartford, Conn.	1.5	89
Nashville, Tenn.	1.4	90
Jacksonville, Fla.	1.1	77
Albany, Ga.	.1	100
Lowell, Mass.	.2	98
South Bend, Ind.	.6	56
Galveston, Tex.	.3	50
National total	433.4	

Source: FDIC, *Summary of Accounts and Deposits in All Commercial Banks*, 1970 (Washington, D.C.: U.S. Government Printing Office, 1973).

Banking Relationships

Bank-client relationships are hard to appraise because—to the banks and firms involved—they are highly sensitive. Data about them are not collected or published by any official agency. The relationships are also subtle and hard to quantify. Bank directorships have been researched, and their patterns reflect some of the underlying connections.[21] Together with other financial folklore, they indicate that there are strong and stable ties among leading banks and companies. Within the whole array, there are clusters around certain bank

[21] U.S. Congress, House, Subcommittee on Antitrust, *Interlocks in Corporate Management*, 89th Cong., 1st sess., 1965; U.S. Congress, House, Committee on Banking and Currency, 1967; and the same committee, *Commercial Banks and Their Trust Activities*, op. cit.

groups, especially the descendants of the original Rockefeller and Morgan interests.[22] The largest firms tend to have several relationships, partly for local contacts and also to play the banks off against each other. Yet, in the greater mass of firms each tends to have a single strong banking relationship that reflects—and influences—its status. The relationships are not permanent, but they change infrequently. Each embodies a large investment of time, disclosure, and mutual advantages; they cannot easily be offset by a competing bank's offer to lend at a lower interest rate.

Banking relationships, therefore, embed most leading firms and banks in a strong, informal structure that resists competitive changes. This structure tends to limit competition, both in banking and in other markets. It provides capital on favorable terms to the firms that are related to the leading banks, and so it tends to deter the entry and rise of small firms.

Trust departments could cement these patterns by steering trust holdings toward clients' stocks. Yet, this is not an extensive practice. Several banks do link their lending and trust policies appreciably, in some cases holding shares and directorates in two or more competing industrial firms. However, most trust holdings are managed separately, partly to avoid the awkward conflicts among the roles of shareholder, lender, counselor, and director that can arise.[23] The common complaint about trust holdings is more the reverse: that they have been shallowly managed, not that they have aggressively taken every chance to use inside information gained through dealings with their primary clients. As a result of herdlike swings and clustering among a few prominent stocks, trust departments may have impaired stability and a wider allocation of capital on the stock markets.[24] But they have not exerted much concerted power over other sectors.

Economies of Scale

Economies of scale in the narrow loan-making operation have been estimated many times over, although often with indirect data. The consensus appears to be that the minimum efficient scale (where the average cost curve more or less bottoms out) is rather small, in the range of $50 million in deposits.[25] Even if this is too low by a factor of 10, it still permits viable competition even in the smaller cities, and far less concentration than is found in the larger ones.

The retailing function now can be done in microscopically small units, including automatic sidewalk units, which handle most transactions. Therefore, technology permits almost limitless branching for many of these operations.

The more complex banking operations might, however, have major scale

---

[22] See James C. Knowles, "The Rockefeller Financial Group," in Ralph Andreano, ed., *Superconcentration/Supercorporation* (Andover, Mass.: Warner Modular Publications, 1973).

[23] Mayer, op. cit.

[24] See ibid. and "How the Terrible Two-tier Market Came to Wall Street," *Fortune*, **88**: 80 (1973).

[25] See Phillips, op. cit. and Guttentag and Herman, op. cit.

economies. Thus, a large bank with 500 loan officers can include highly specialized experts (for example, engineers and geologists) on the staff. They, in turn, may improve the depth of knowledge about clients' prospects. Portfolio management might also be done better by larger teams.

Yet, against this is the bureaucratic effect of size and hierarchy—committee nonthink—which can reduce efficiency.[26] Also, economies may be purely *pecuniary*—from monopoly advantages and inside information—rather than *technical.*

There has been little research on these complex functions, and no clear indication either way. Therefore, one can safely doubt that any important technical economies exist in the more complex activities of banks. This may seem to deny the skills of the larger, more sophisticated banks. However, these are simply unproved so far.

By contrast, the basic nationwide clearing function has become a natural monopoly, as computer technology has progressed. In practice, there is not yet a fully centralized operation, but conditions now do warrant a single system, more completely unified than at present. Much of it would need to be on a giro basis. Bankers and depositors dislike yielding the tangible forms of their participation, but these old ways have their economic costs.

Now consider scale economies in banking relationships. To a slight extent, large firms need bankers that are also large. Large accounts can be divided among several banks, and indeed many of the largest firms do just that. The older links in pre-1960 years were highly personal, one to one. The newer " performance" banking involves a higher degree of objective evaluation, which any good medium-sized bank can do well. And riskier strategies by large firms need to be pooled among several banks—with independent evaluation—rather than borne by just one. That, too, has become common in the financing of actual loans.

There may be pecuniary advantages in large-scale single-banking relationships. Access to insider information may favor the larger banks and make their support and advice appear more valuable to clients. Also, their size and traditional status may let them provide cheaper capital. But these gains maybe strictly pecuniary, not of social value. In short, technical economies of scale do not clearly explain the closeness and stability of banking relationships among leading banks and dominant firms.

Trust departments, too, offer little or no technical scale economies. The larger ones have not performed better in recent years, by innate quality of analysis or even by private portfolio results.[27] This is so, despite their ability to specialize more completely and to exploit inside information more fully.

A rounded evaluation is that banking structure in the United States—on every basis—is a good deal tighter than social economies would require. This

---

[26] This problem, of "X-inefficiency," is common in all large, secure organizations. See Shepherd, *Market Power and Economic Welfare*, op. cit.; and Harvey Leibenstein, "Allocative Efficiency v. 'X-efficiency,'" *American Economic Review*, **54**:392–415 (June 1966).

[27] Mayer, op. cit., sums up the expert opinion on this.

is likely to transmit the same condition to industrial markets via banking re-lationships (see Section III), with special force in the mass of medium-sized and local markets. In other countries, concentration may be even higher and more entangled with industrial interests (perhaps naturally, because the national economies are much smaller). Yet, banking concentration in the United States remains a serious problem, on both levels.

III. CONDUCT

Banking has long had a fraternal, "professional" code of ethics against price cutting and many other competitive causes of instability. Interest is not to be given on deposits; gentlemen's agreements keep banks from encroaching on each other's areas; and large accounts are not crassly competed for. These private restrictions have variously been reinforced by public agencies, often in great detail and force. Indeed, much banking regulation fits the hypothesis that it is invoked by the established banking interests to support their preferred cartel restrictions. In recent years, again, this has been modified toward freer competition. However, the main restrictive patterns remain.

Package Banking

Behavior also includes more neutral, or quite competitive, parts. The basic practice is to mingle services to the main clients, under package or full-service approaches. Many specific banking services are not costed out or priced separately. They are treated as part of an on-going, complex, mutual sharing of interests. This is partly inherent and unavoidable. It also permits much hidden price discrimination in the whole provision and pricing of bank services. There have been marginal shifts toward unbundling these services from time to time, but the traditional mingling remains. Indeed, banks themselves often do not know the true costs of many of the services they are providing for many of their clients.

Behavior also includes the setting of credit prices and amounts for borrowers. The shift into long-term loans has made many firms deeply dependent on their bankers for strategic funds and advice. A loan is defined mainly by its price (the interest rate); size; and rate of repayment. In theory, these vary smoothly by degrees, so that each bank has an upward sloping curve showing the supply of funds for each client (see Figure 4). Funds would always be available at some price.

In practice, there are deviations and gaps. Amounts and costs of loans are often set rigidly (for example, a fixed volume at a fixed interest rate). This often excludes some potential borrowers completely (funds are simply unavailable) and provides favored clients with more than they want (examples are in Figure 4). Although the result may approximate a smooth supply curve for the whole market in some respects, it can have deviant effects on the allocation of capital

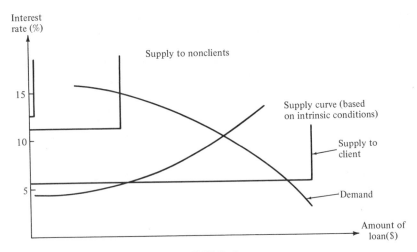

FIGURE 4
Banking supply to alternative borrowers.

within the array of borrowers. Thus, in tight-money periods, whole categories of borrowers often cannot borrow at *any* price.

Of course, the supply of funds should vary to fit the true risk of the loan. But this variation can be distorted, and it often is. Banks tied to dominant firms will be aware that loans to small competitors or entrants will reduce the return-risk value of their prior loans. Therefore, their loan-supply curves to these outside firms will be higher than true risk conditions would warrant. Conversely, their backing of the established firms will, in itself, reduce their risk, shifting their loan-supply curve down.[28] As Figure 5 shows, this will increase the disparity in interest rates and market shares between the leading and lesser firms.

Borrowing costs do differ markedly among size classes and market positions of firms. The share of excess disparity in these differences is not known, for the issue has not been well researched. The share may be large, where banking is concentrated and relationships between the leading banks and firms are stable. These conditions are met in many markets, both local and national.

Price Fixing

Banks have long cooperated among themselves on many matters, including their prices and terms of service. Much of this has been encouraged by public officials for over a century, in order to promote stability. Security-minded bankers since the 1930s have been especially willing to avoid unstable competition, so that no bank fails. Policies shifted moderately in the 1960s toward challenging some market-rigging actions. But the basic habits remain, often sanctioned or enforced by a public agency.[29]

---

[28] These patterns are discussed more fully in Shepherd, *The Treatment of Market Power*, op. cit., Chaps. 2–4.

[29] See Fischer, op. cit., and Alhadeff, op. cit., for compact reviews of these issues.

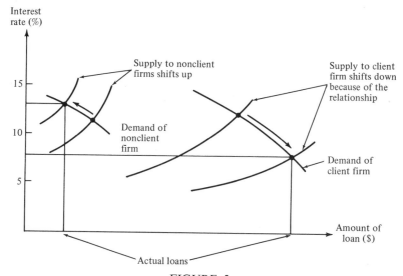

FIGURE 5
Effects of banking relationship on loan amounts and price.

The traditional aim has been to prevent the offering of interest payments on deposits. Banks early developed "clearinghouse agreements" limiting interest payments. These came to be reinforced by state regulations in the 1920s. The 1933 and 1935 banking acts prohibited interest on demand deposits and gave the Federal Reserve power (under "Regulation Q") to limit interest rates on time and savings deposits. Clearinghouse agreements continue to the present, and there is much informal cooperation on banking terms. State banking rules are, to a large extent, used as a vehicle for defining and enforcing the agreements. The American Banking Association has also played this role, although less explicitly.

The Antitrust Division challenged bank price fixing in several cities during 1961–1964, much to the bankers' surprise. The cases ended mainly in compromise, and so banking collusion is not illegal per se. It has only been abated, especially the more open forms.

Other terms of service (hours of opening and kinds of bank services) have also been subject to joint agreements of varying tightness. Moreover, gentlemen's agreements not to encroach into each others' area have been pervasive; they have long been extended in some states into antibranching laws that prohibit new entry and raise concentration.[30] These patterns have, like so much else, been modified by the 1960–1975 shifts toward performance banking and the rise in branching. Yet, much of their substance remains.

---

[30] Twelve states still prohibit all branch banking; 21 permit statewide branching; and others have partial limits on branching. Actual degrees of control are often extremely difficult to appraise.

Exclusion

Behavior also involves the exclusion of sizable groups of customers. Borrowers with small size and/or market shares are routinely avoided by many banks; often, during credit squeezes, by nearly all banks. Certificates of deposit (CD) and other high-interest forms have been provided only in large denominations thereby excluding small savers altogether. For example, CDs of $10,000 have provided interest 2 and 3 points higher than savings deposit interest. Many bank trust departments will handle large accounts only, in some cases $500,000 or more. This, too, excludes the small customer. Whole categories of loans—for example, farming and health—are often excluded.

Cost factors explain only a portion of these exclusions. Service could still be offered at higher, cost-covering prices, if cost were the only factor. The other reasons include the tendency toward joint agreement not to compete in certain areas and the willingness of bankers to forego marginal profit opportunities.

A Digression on Stock Brokerage[31]

Large-scale trading by the trust departments of bigger banks and other institutional investors has recently forced more competition on the stock brokerage industry. From 1792–1970, broker's fees were fixed by the stock exchanges in ways that made the larger trades extremely lucrative. To by-pass these fees, large traders evolved a "third market," which soon absorbed much of the market volume. By self-interest—and the Antitrust Division's pressure on the Securities and Exchange Commission (SEC)—fees on large trades were put on a competitive basis in 1970. This has worked well, and it also has encouraged better performance in the brokerage houses. In 1975, it was extended to all trades. Vertical pressure by bankers and others, thus, eroded brokerage fee fixing.

On the whole, banking retains much of its cooperative restraint, despite the shifts during 1960–1975. The resulting prices and allocations of credit reflect these special behavior patterns.

IV. PERFORMANCE

Banking performance has several quite particular components. We first will consider the prices, profits, efficiency, stability, innovation, and equity of private banking operations. Next we will evaluate regulation itself. Then we will appraise public banks and programs. Only a brief summary is possible, but the main lines are reasonably clear. Banking performance is generally good, but with clear defects. Much regulation is superfluous. Most public bank entities perform reasonably well.

---

[31] On this issue, see H. Michael Mann, in Phillips, op. cit.; and U.S. Congress, Senate, Subcommittee on Securities, *Securities Industry Study*, 92d Cong., 1st sess., 1971. (See, especially, the study by Irwin Friend and Marshall Blume.)

Bank Performance

Prices

The interest-rate spread between bank loans and borrowings has reflected a degree of monopoly. The spread has narrowed in recent years as performance banking has developed new sources of funds since 1960.

Perhaps more important, the structure of prices (that is, of interest rates) has discriminated in favor of larger, monopolistic client firms, for reasons noted in Section III. The observed differentials are often more than 5 percentage points (for example, between 8 and 13 per cent).[32] But this understates the true contrast, for many lesser firms are often unable to get credit at any price (that is, the price is infinite).

On personal loans and deposits, too, the price structure is highly differentiated. Part of this reflects the lower unit costs in handling large accounts. But much of it is price discrimination.

Profits

These price levels and structures are reflected in relatively high profit rates. The reported rates of return on equity are probably reduced by a degree of internal inefficiency. Yet, even so, these rates of return are well above the competitive range. They are more stable than any but the most monopolistic industries (for example, computers and utilities). Table 7 includes a selection from various cities.[33] There are, of course, many influences on profit rates, including managerial skill and growth rates in the region. Still, a degree of monopoly profits is common.

Efficiency

There are three levels of efficiency to consider. *Internal efficiency* has been mediocre, especially before 1965, according to the consensus among expert observers. The overriding concern for security induced a narrow, traditional range of activities. Liability management was largely by rote, foregoing excellent profit opportunities. Banks have clung to their old clients, neglecting good alternative prospects. And, to take the most obvious surface indications, bank premises have traditionally displayed a degree of gold-plating. Certain other inputs, including staff and managerial ranks, also have tended to be used beyond efficient levels, especially in the more sheltered banks.[34]

More recently, a number of excesses have probably occurred, this time toward dubious loans and investments. By 1970–1974, many of the largest banks—

---

[32] See periodic business loan studies by the Federal Reserve Board, and D. Jacobs, *Business Loan Costs and Bank Market Structure* (New York: National Bureau of Economic Research, 1971).

[33] These reported rates of return are often on preferred, as well as common, stock. Therefore, they may be biased downward by some degree, compared to industrial profit rates. Also, the 1971–1973 period has had temporary downward pressures on bank rates of return. The long-run averages are higher.

[34] See Alhadeff, op. cit.; Mayer, op. cit.; and "S and L's Break Out of Their Shell," *Fortune*, **86**: 152 (1972).

TABLE 7
Profitability in Selected Major U.S. Banks, 1971–1973

BANKS	ASSETS, 1973 ($ BILLIONS)	NET INCOME AFTER TAX AS A PER CENT OF EQUITY, 1971–1973
San Francisco		
Bank America Corp.	49.4	13.8
New York		
First National City Corp.	44.0	13.2
Chase Manhattan Corp.	36.8	12.0
J. P. Morgan & Co.	20.4	14.3
Chicago		
Continental Illinois Corp.	16.9	12.3
First Chicago Corp.	15.6	11.9
Los Angeles		
Western Bancorp.	17.9	11.1
Security Pacific Corp.	13.5	10.5
Other Banks		
Mellon National Corp.		
(Pittsburgh)	9.6	9.7
First National Boston Corp.	8.0	11.3
National Detroit Corp.	6.7	11.2
First Pennsylvania Corp.	6.2	16.2
First International Bancshares		
(Dallas)	5.1	14.8

Source: Fortune 500 *Directory*, 1974.

including the most aggressive and innovative ones, like First National City of New York—were deep into such questionable loans as Penn Central, REITs (real estate investment trusts), ill-fated office construction in New York City, and speculation in Euro-dollars. The bizarre, high-interest-rate conditions of 1973–1974 do not explain all, or even most, of the resulting poor results and high stress. Many of these loans reflected astonishingly thin analysis, especially by leading big-city banks that should have known better.[35]

[35] See Mayer, op. cit., "Are the Banks Wrecking the Economy?" *Fortune*, **91**: 111 (1975), and "How the Bankers Got Trapped in the REIT Disaster," *Fortune*, **91**: 112 (1975). These trenchant articles in *Fortune* concern bank policies and construction loans.

The *allocation of resources* in banking operations has also been restricted, again, especially before 1965. This was most apparent in retailing operations. The short opening hours (9:30 A.M. to 2:30 P.M., weekdays only, was common) and the fewness of neighborhood branches are only two common instances. By 1961, many cities were very clearly "underbanked," as the rapid new entry and branching since then have demonstrated. Improved services have coincided precisely with the rise in competition, and many are still to come in some areas.

The *allocation of capital* has been restricted and distorted, in various degrees. In total, and especially for certain regions and groups of firms, the volume of credit has been smaller and at higher prices. The innate tilt in capital supply toward established, secure firms, and away from small and new competitors has been increased. The post-1960 changes have not corrected this basic problem, for the underlying conditions remain.

The whole degree of inefficiency has been moderate rather than extreme especially by international comparison. And its severity is possibly receding, as the degree of competition and flexibility has risen. Yet these losses are serious and widespread, and they have altered the structure of many other markets toward a higher degree of monopoly.

Stability of Banks

The stability of banks has been high, much higher than the optimum degree of security. Bank failures largely ceased from 1935–1969, thanks to the layers of regulation, FDIC coverage, and cartel restrictions, combined with the extremely prudent behavior of the older bankers (recall Figure 3).[36] Entrepreneurship and risk taking were abnormally low.

Stability does provide some external benefits. But FDIC insurance and inspection have provided at least an optimal degree of security. The rest, including the marked conservatism, was excessive. The extra range of stability was achieved at the large cost of banking efficiency and innovation.

The modest post-1969 rise in bank stress and failures reflects both (1) a reversion toward normal degrees of risk taking, and also (2) the rush into certain dubious loans and investments after 1965. The next decade will determine whether banking (under public policy influences) approximates optimal risk taking or veers between the extremes. At present, the outcome is in doubt, and the system contains individual banks spread across the whole range between the extreme types.

Innovation

Innovation traditionally has been slow, again partly because of public policy resistance. New services have been introduced and diffused slowly. New technology has also tended to be absorbed at a moderate-to-slow pace by the mass of banks. Moreover, banks largely have been passive in developing and adopting the new techniques. Almost all the changes have been prepared externally and

---

[36] See Alhadeff, op. cit.; Mayer, op. cit.; and Phillips, op. cit.

injected by energetic outside firms, often against considerable bankers' reluctance. Thus, computer handling was prepackaged by computer firms. Sidewalk push-button transaction units are a rather belated innovation, started from outside. Efficient portfolio management was an innovation that spread slowly among the older bankers. On the whole, and continuing even now, banking innovation has been slow, in line with the surrounding inhibitions on entrepreneurship. This is clearest in the appraisals given by the *private* business press; it is not just an abstract judgment.

In a larger sense, the whole system has failed to innovate in certain directions. The clearest instance is the avoidance of the giro system, which is far simpler than the present check-clearing system. It has been fully tested in widespread use abroad, in many countries under varying conditions. By contrast, the moves toward "checkless" banking and fuller credit-card use follow inefficient lines. Yet, because a giro system by-passes some of the conventional banking processes, it is likely to be avoided, perhaps indefinitely, unless deliberate steps are taken to develop it.

Equity

In appraising the defects, one bears in mind that the system as a whole may be generally more efficient and fair than is found in most other countries. Still, the defects are serious.

Fairness is affected by several of the conditions just noted. Exclusion and price discrimination affect both business and personal clients. Generally, the interest differentials against smaller borrowers exceed the differences in costs and intrinsic risk. Many small borrowers are excluded outright. Interest rates paid to savers are also biased against small customers more than costs would justify. Again, many small customers are flatly excluded from the more lucrative offerings (for example, large certificates of deposit) and from many trust departments. Even such small aspects as banking hours, location, and services have tended to put poorer citizens at a disadvantage.

In the whole picture, banking has favored its established, richer customers. This is quite natural, because banking would naturally *reflect* the distribution of capital rather than equalize it. Natural or not, such defects suggest a need for better policy actions.

Evaluating Regulation

Some policy actions—especially regulation—have been extensive and, in part, probably *counter-productive*.[37] The regulatory patchwork is complex and costly, an industry by itself. It employs many thousands of professionals, with an aggregate expenditure running to at least $50 million. Regulators go deeply into banks' affairs, usually quietly but often spectacularly. The more thorough regulation is, the more it disrupts the banks' normal operations.[38] It has to make

[37] See especially Phillips, op. cit., and Alhadeff, op. cit.
[38] Mayer, op. cit., conveys vividly the practical impact of regulatory supervision on bank operations. The temporary disruption is often severe.

thousands of complex judgments about performance and new competition, in deciding applications for entry and merger. Some of the regulation is done superbly; other aspects, especially at the state level, are bureaucratic and passive (and most agencies are grossly understaffed).

Most regulation, perhaps all of it, is economically wasted, for its objective—optimum bank stability—is already assured by deposit insurance and Federal Reserve support for the whole system. Even—or especially—when it is done thoroughly, it is most wasteful. Not only are the direct resources used pointlessly, but also, the regulation itself operates to suppress competition and discourage entrepreneurship. This is clearest in the state antibranching regulations, but it pervades the whole system of restraints.

There are three possible benefits to offset these costs. (1) *Security* is increased. However, deposit insurance provides enough security already. (2) *Regulation* keeps banks more on an arm's length basis with industrial firms. The abuses and monopoly effects that mingling makes possible (abroad and, before 1933, in the United States) are avoided. Yet, much implicit mingling already occurs indirectly, in banking relationships and portfolio operations. And the separation is a simple matter of law; it does not require a small army of regulatory officials, bank examiners, and accountants to stay in force. (3) The *local character* of banking may be enhanced. But this, too, arises from rules (for example, against bank branching), rather than regulation of operations. And "localness" often has led to inefficiency and restrictive behavior.

Most banking regulation, therefore, wastes resources and induces further inefficiency in banking. It does not constrain the key economic variables—maximum prices, discrimination, and profit rates—in line with efficient and fair criteria. Rather, it maintains certain restrictive patterns, largely as if it consisted of self-regulation by the industry itself.

Public Banking Entities

These units primarily (1) maintain the basic integrity of the system (for example, FDIC and Federal Reserve), and (2) cover unmet credit needs of certain classes of borrowers, either by direct loans or guarantees. These utility and residual roles leave the lucrative operations to the private banks and, indeed, enhance their profitability. By contrast, there are mainstream public banks in most other industrial countries.[39] Some are on a very large scale, and all of them compete normally and successfully with private banks. During 1932–1952, the Reconstruction Finance Corporation in the United States rescued and supported private firms in a wide range of industry, banking, farming, and trade. These investment banking operations were very large scale and complex—indeed, RFC became the largest industrial lender in the United States—and all agree that its operations were well performed. But this was a residual, supportive role,

[39] See Sayers, op. cit.; Wilcox and Shepherd, op. cit., Chaps. 19 and 20; and Stuart Holland, ed., *The State as Entrepreneur* (White Plains, N.Y.: International Arts and Sciences Press, 1972).

strictly excluded from commercial banking, and it was closed out after 1952.[40]

Presently, public units are extensive and, on the whole, growing. Some are hybrids, and there is much variety of form. Their performance generally is regarded as good. The main ones—for example, Federal Reserve and FDIC— earn profits, perhaps even unnecessarily high profits. Their prices for service are generally low enough to accomplish their social purpose but also high enough to meet economic criteria (of cost covering, minimizing of unnecessary subsidy, and the like). Some are subsidized, but this is usually indirect, via the public absorption of private risks. Few, if any, of them exhibit the pathological behavior that direct subsidies often induce in other programs.

Most of them appear to be efficiently operated. Such evaluations have to be imprecise, for the forms, objectives, and budgetary criteria of the public banks are varied. The Federal Reserve, FDIC, Federal National Mortgage Association (the FNMA became quasi-public after 1971), and other older entities are, it is agreed by experts, well managed. The Federal Reserve does have a tendency to gold-plate, along the lines of many older private banks. And certain newer programs—such as the FHA support for renovation of private housing during 1969–1974—have developed corruption and waste. But these specific effects have been limited, and they arise in the nonbanking side of the programs (for example, in house inspection).

Banking security has been improved efficiently by the public banking operations of the FDIC and Federal Reserve, of course, and the whole range of units has been reasonably innovative. As for equity, the usual tendency for effects to grow less progressive as time passes has occurred. Most programs benefited the smaller depositors, borrowers, farmers, small businessmen, and home buyers more at their beginning than at present. Indeed, these programs indirectly benefit the private banks, construction, and other businesses handling the credit operations. Like other public programs, these units need skeptical reappraisals of their fairness.

Altogether, public banking in the United States has shown good economic and social performance. Although it is quite extensive, it has been confined to supportive and residual roles. It has performed reasonably well in these roles— along with the routine economic operations.

V. PUBLIC POLICY

We already have touched on most of the specific policy issues. Many of them are knit into one basic question: What role should competition play in banking? Some observers suggest competition should become universal, as in any "normal" industry. Others want public regulation and/or public banking to cover all essentials, in order to (1) assure stability and (2) meet large social needs. During 1960–1975, older limits were eaten away, and competition—or at least an over-

---

[40] There was a move to revive the RFC in 1974–1975 by a range of influential *private* bankers.

lapping of activities—increased in certain directions. Should this shift go farther? Should regulation be abolished or at least reduced? Should public banking be enlarged?

The 1970s are a watershed, and the policy choices are unusually wide and open. Because the issues are not being forced and distorted by a severe crisis, the policy choices may well be open to handling in a rational, unbiased process of adjustment.

The objectives include efficiency and equity, both in banking and in its effects throughout other markets. This calls for the following results: (1) less discrimination against small savers and borrowers, (2) stricter banking supervision of industrial management, (3) closer external constraints on bank managerial performance, and (4) innovation toward a more efficient clearing basis for the larger system.

A distinguished group of experts has urged greater competition as the means to these goals.[41] The 1960–1975 changes mostly fitted that direction, less by public choice than by private experimentation. And further innovation will probably continue that trend. Some public policies still tightly limit competition, and even the more open chartering basis since 1961 has scarcely affected the main banking markets. Some of the official support for price fixing and other cooperation has been withdrawn. Banks are mingling in some adjacent markets (although not very far afield).

Therefore, a degree of de facto deregulation has already occurred. Further formal deregulation might not achieve much further change. The shift has yielded some of the predictable tonic effects on performance (as well as some rash and dubious decisions). But it leaves certain problems untouched. There is still a degree of discrimination and exclusion against small customers. Banks are still often passive to a mediocre level of management in their client firms. Banks are still immune to take-over discipline.[42] And innovation toward a giro system is not occurring.

For these problems, more direct action appears to be appropriate.[43] There are several directions and combinations of policies to choose among: the following three appear to offer a reasonably good balance.

1. Regulation would be further reduced, selectively. Deposit insurance would continue, but chartering would be liberalized and most of the regulatory inspection of banks would cease. Takeovers of banks would be permitted, under certain conditions, although banking operations and accounts would be kept separate from nonbanking activities. The present involvement in salvaging failing banks could continue (as in First National Bank of San Diego and Franklin National

---

[41] These include, especially, Phillips and Alhadeff, among those authors cited here.

[42] Again, this is because the 1933 banking law prohibits combining bank and nonbank activities. The bank holding companies formed since 1960 further ward off any chance that banks will be disciplined—as are most other firms in the economy—by the threat of being wholly or partially taken over if their performance is inferior.

[43] See Shepherd, *The Treatment of Market Power*, op. cit., Chap. 6, for a fuller statement of the policy choices.

of New York in 1973-1974), but with no official commitment to avoid failure at any cost.

2. Several experimental public banking units would be created (or expanded from existing programs). They would have differing emphases. One would be to extend the more favorable terms, which large savers now get (as on certificates of deposits), to all savers large and small. A second emphasis would be to provide funds and management advice to worthy small firms and new competitors. This would greatly expand the existing small-business loan programs and enrich their support with crucial advisory services (which private banking clients already get as a matter of course). Present small-business loan programs are tiny and shallow, by comparison.

A third emphasis would be on investment banking.[44] This would provide equity capital for small and new competitors. It would also take holdings in firms with X-inefficiency, but which offer clear prospects for improvement. This partial take-over function would need to be adroitly and professionally handled. It would require little or no net public cost, while improving the quality of management in the target companies and reaping capital gains for the public purse. It offers an important supplement to antitrust policies in treating the older tight oligopolies. These industries—as is indicated in other parts of the book—appear to be largely immune to Section 2 of the Sherman Act. This activity could also include holdings in private banks that need better management. This sort of public investment bank—which has been thoroughly experimented with abroad—would be strictly professional, seeking to earn high profits and capital gains for the public and to improve economic performance in private firms. Perhaps for the public and to improve economic performance in private firms. Perhaps there would best be several such public banks, to provide competition and variety among them as well as with private banks.

3. The Federal Reserve, or some new related central-banking unit, would establish a giro system, as an alternative to the present clearing operations.

Conclusion

Within these three policy directions, there is much room for experimenting and learning, as technology matures and external conditions change. Together, they have a balance and depth that cover most of the apparent gaps in banking performance. More competition alone will not do, nor, assuredly, will a continuation of the present duplicative nonsystem of "regulation." All these standard policy tools—antitrust, regulation, and public enterprise—are appropriate, in varying degrees. All three are already present, but in a different form and balance from what optimal treatment would include. The need is to see them for what they are and then to adjust them, in order to help make a good banking system into an excellent one.

[44] For a discussion of these possibilities and of lessons from experience, see William G. Shepherd, ed., *Public Enterprise: Economic Analysis of Theory and Practice* (Lexington, Mass. Heath Lexington Books, 1976), Chap. 9.

SUGGESTED READINGS

BOOKS AND MONOGRAPHS

Alhadeff, David A. *Monopoly and Competition in Banking.* Berkeley: University of California Press, 1954.

————. *Competition and Controls in Banking: A Study of the Regulation of Bank Competition in Italy, France, and England.* Berkeley: University of California Press, 1968.

Commission on Money and Credit. *Private Financial Institutions.* Englewood Cliffs, N.J.: Prentice-Hall, Inc., 1963.

Dewey, Davis R. *Financial History of the United States.* New York: Longmans, Green & Company, 1911.

Fischer, Gerald R. *American Banking Structure.* New York: Columbia University Press, 1968.

Friend, Irwin, et al. *Investment Banking and the New Issues Market.* Cleveland: World Publishing Company, 1967.

Guttentag, J. M., and E. S. Herman, *Banking Structure and Performance.* New York: New York University Press, 1967.

Hadley, Eleanor. *Antitrust in Japan.* Princeton, N.J.: Princeton University Press, 1971.

Holland, Stuart. *The State as Entrepreneur.* White Plains, N.Y.: International Arts and Sciences Press, 1971.

Jacobs, Donald P. *Business Loan Costs and Bank Market Structure.* New York: National Bureau of Economic Research, 1971.

Mayer, Martin. *The Bankers.* New York: Weybright and Talley, 1974.

Phillips, Almarin, ed. *Promoting Competition in Regulated Markets.* Washington, D.C.: The Brookings Institution, 1975.

Sayers, R. L. ed. *Banking in Western Europe.* New York: Macmillan Publishing Co. Inc., 1962.

Shepherd, William G. *Market Power and Economic Welfare.* New York: Random House, Inc., 1970.

Shepherd, William G., ed. *Public Enterprise: Economic Analysis of Theory and Practice.* Lexington, Mass.: Heath Lexington Books, 1976.

Shepherd, William G. *The Treatment of Market Power.* New York: Columbia University Press, 1975.

Wilcox, Clair, and William G. Shepherd. *Public Policies Toward Business*, 5th ed. Homewood, Ill.: Richard D. Irwin, Inc., 1975.

GOVERNMENT PUBLICATIONS

U.S. Congress, House, Committee on Banking and Currency, *Commercial Banks and Their Trust Activities*, 2 vols. 90th Cong., 2d sess., 1968.

U.S. Congress, House, Committee on Banking and Currency, *Control of Commercial Banks and Interlocks Among Financial Institutions*, 90th Cong., 1st sess., 1967.

U.S. Congress, House, Subcommittee on Antitrust, *Interlocks in Corporate Management*, 89th Cong., 1st sess., 1965.

U.S. Congress, Senate, Subcommittee on Securities, *Securities Industry Study*, 92d Cong., 1st sess., 1971.

ARTICLES

Alhadeff, David A. and C. P. Alhadeff. "An Integrated Model for Commerialc Banks," *Journal of Finance*, **12**: 24–43 (1957).

Business Week. "The Great Banking Retreat," Apr. 21, 1975, pp. 45–102.

———. "The New Banking," Sept. 15, 1973, pp. 94–106.

Fortune "How the Terrible Two-tier Market Came to Wall Street," **88**: 80 (1973).

———. "The S. and L.'s Break Out of Their Shell," **86** 152 (1972).

Knowles, James C. "The Rockefeller Financial Group." In Ralph Andreano, ed., *Superconcentration/Supercorporation*. Andover, Mass.: Warner Modular Publications, 1973.

CHAPTER 11

major league team sports

ROGER G. NOLL

I. INTRODUCTION

The major league sports industry is an exceptionally interesting subject for economic study. Its allure for economists does not lie in its size, for by any reasonable measure the team sports industry is not big business. The total revenue of all teams in the four major team sports—baseball, basketball, football, and hockey—is less than half the revenue of such mundane endeavors as the manufacture of cardboard boxes or the canning of fruits and vegetables. Pro teams have revenues ranging approximately from those of a large gas station to those of a department store or large supermarket.

The team sports business is interesting to economists primarily because of the complex operating rules and special legal status of the industry. Nearly every phase of the operations of a team or a league is influenced by practices and rules that limit economic competition within the industry. In most cases, government has either sanctioned or failed to attack effectively these anticompetitive practices. Consequently, professional team sports provides economists with a unique opportunity to study the operation and performance of an effective, well-organized cartel.

II. MARKET STRUCTURE

As do most businesses, a sports team operates in several markets, some of which are local and some of which are national. The most important product markets are the sale of admissions and concessions at home contests and the sale of the right to broadcast play-by-play accounts of games. The most important input markets are the acquisition of skilled professional players and of a facility for staging contests. The characteristics of each of these four markets are somewhat

365

different, so that each must be examined separately. In general, although 119 professional sports teams operated in the major leagues in 1975, rarely would more than a few find themselves competing in a particular market.

The Player Market

Although a few especially gifted athletes can play at the highest professional level in more than one sport, such individuals are extremely rare. Consequently, each sport has essentially a separate player market through which teams acquire athletes with skills specific to that sport. All teams conduct international searches for players. Even the uniquely American game of football has engaged in an international search for talent since the 1960s when it found a productive use for European soccer players as place kickers.

Superficially, the structure of the player market appears competitive. In each sport, 25 to 40 firms all employ approximately equal numbers of athletes; concentration ratios on the demand side of these markets are, therefore, quite low. On the supply side, a tiny proportion of the population is skillful enough to play major league athletics, and only a handful have the ability to become stars. Still, in any year the number of, say, .300 hitters in baseball or 50-yard-per game running backs in football is sufficiently numerous that the market is likely to be reasonably competitive.

Despite these appearances, the player market is not competitive. Although the details differ from sport to sport, professional sports leagues all have some version of a player reservation system—a mechanism for reducing the competition for players among teams in the league.

Leagues have separate rules for regulating competition for three types of players: rookies, players about to begin a professional career; veterans whose present team desires to retain their services; and veterans who are no longer wanted by their current employer. The effect of all three systems is to divide the relevant pool of present and potential major league players into separate submarkets—one for each team—in which each team has an exclusive bargaining right with the players assigned to its submarket.

The method for allocating exclusive bargaining rights for rookies is the free agent draft. In every sport, at a specified time during the year—typically at the conclusion of the high school and college season in the same sport—teams in each league, normally in reverse order of finish during the previous season, select players from among eligible amateur athletes to be added to their reserve list. A player may then negotiate only with the team that selected him, and, in all sports except baseball, rights to negotiate with the player perpetually belong to the selecting team, unless it trades or sells those rights to another member of the league. In baseball, if a player does not sign a contract with the team that drafted him within 6 months, his name returns to the list of athletes eligible for the draft.

In all sports, a veteran player has some freedom to change teams, even if his current employer wants to retain the rights to his services. This is done by exercising the option to play out his contract. What this means is that a player can gain his freedom to negotiate with another team by playing an additional year in football and basketball or an additional 3 years in hockey under the terms of his last contract. (In football, he need be paid only 90 per cent of his previous salary during his option year.)

After playing out his option, the player is not completely unencumbered in his ability to negotiate a job with a different employer. The team that signs the player who has played out his option must indemnify the team that he left with some combination of players, draft choices, and cash to compensate his old team for its loss due to his departure. The compensation requirement—called the Rozelle rule, after its inventor, Commissioner Peter Rozelle of the National Football League (NFL)—reduces the amount a team is willing to pay a player who has played out his option, and, thereby, the wage that he will obtain in the competition for his services.

In baseball, the rights of a team to a player were unlimited, as long as the team kept the player on its active roster, until the 1976 season. Under the old system, once a player signed his first professional contract, the rights to negotiate with him were the exclusive property of one team, as long as his team satisfied the terms of the contract.[1]

In December 1975, baseball's system of perpetual rights was dealt a heavy blow. Two pitchers, Dave McNally and Andy Messersmith, allowed one full year to pass without signing contracts. They then asserted that they were free agents, arguing that the text of the baseball player contract did not specifically indicate that negotiating rights were permanent. A labor arbitrator ruled that the pitchers' interpretation of the contract was valid, and this ruling has thus far withstood several court appeals by team owners.

This ruling ends the reserve system for experienced veteran players, but not for players in the first few years of their careers. In July 1976, the players and owners agreed that a system much like the old one will be applied to younger players, but that players with several years of major league experience will be free to play out their option year and let at least some of the teams bid competitively for their service without having to compensate the player's old team.

In all sports, if a team no longer wants to retain the services of a player, several possibilities are available. First, the team may trade the player to another team for other players and/or draft choices. Second, the team may sell the rights to negotiate with the player to another team. In baseball, a player with 10 years' experience has the right to veto the assignment of his contract to any particular team, and, in other sports, some players have succeeded in including similar rights in their contracts. Nevertheless, even in these cases, the player cannot negotiate with several teams while a trade is pending and then veto all proposed trades except one to the team he favors. A player may never negotiate with any

---

[1] Twice, Charles O. Finley, owner of the Oakland Athletics, has, amazingly, relinquished his rights to bargain with a star player. Both—Ken "Hawk" Harrelson and Jim "Catfish" Hunter—subsequently signed lucrative contracts with other teams after spirited competition for their services.

team while under contract to another, and he must decide whether to veto a trade without discussing the matter with any team other than his current employer. And, for all but the handful of players with veto rights, a player has no alternatives other than playing for the team that acquires his contract or retiring from the league.

The third alternative for a team that wants to remove a player from its roster is to place him on waivers. The waiver list is a pool of players available for drafting by other teams, again in reverse order of finish. Each team in the same league then decides whether to claim the player on waivers at a price specified in league rules. The price varies from $100 in football to $20,000 in baseball. Only if all teams decide not to claim the player for this price does he then become a free agent, available to negotiate with any team he chooses. Of course, the amount of salary increase he can expect is, to say the least, limited once he has been released by his present team after all other teams have decided against obtaining him by trade, purchase, or waiver.

The sports with extensive minor leagues—baseball and hockey—have an additional set of rules for preventing competition for minor league professionals. These rules are similar to those regulating the acquisition of rookies and waivered veterans, with a player becoming eligible for a drafting procedure at certain stages of his career or when a major league club for whom he is under contract removes him from its roster of reserved players.

The effect of this labyrinth of rules is to grant each team a monopsony in an artificially created submarket of the market for players. This monopsony is broken only when a new league emerges. Although a new league nearly always adopts rules dividing the player market among its teams, interleague competition still emerges. A player will be drafted by one team in each league, and these two teams will then engage in duopsonistic competition for his services. Two competitors, of course, constitute a far cry from perfect competition. Even so, the effect of a new league on salaries is dramatic, usually leading to a doubling of salaries within the first year or two. For example, the following are the salary increments enjoyed by three players as a result of the emergence of the World Hockey Association (WHA) in 1972.

	SALARY ($)[a]		
PLAYER	1971–1972 NHL	1972–1973 WHA	1972–1973 NHL OFFER
Gerry Cheevers	57,000	200,000	70,000
John McKenzie	48,000	100,000	100,000
Derek Sanderson	50,000	300,000	80,000

[a] Taken from contracts submitted in evidence in *Philadelphia World Hockey Club, Inc.* v. *Philadelphia Hockey Club, Inc.*, U.S.D.C. Eastern Pennsylvania C.A. 72-1661 and *Boston Professional Hockey Association* v. *Derek Sanderson*, U.S.D.C. Massachusetts C.A. 72-2490c.

These figures illustrate the value of the player reservation system to teams. The system gives each team a property right in the players on its roster. The value of that property right is the discounted present value of the sum of difference in the player's competitive wage, and the wage is actually paid over his remaining career.[2] Trades of players, many of which involve cash payments, represent the purchase and sale of this "property."

The player reservation system as practiced by sports leagues is a classic case of a restraint of trade through the division of markets and agreements not to compete; as such, it is a textbook example of a violation of the antitrust statutes. Although leagues maintain that these restraints are reasonable—an issue we will explore when we consider the industry's behavior—all standing court precedents conclude that they are anticompetitive.

Only baseball has specifically had its player reservation system exempted from antitrust protection. This exemption dates from the days of the Federal League, which, just prior to the outbreak of World War I, attempted to become a third major league. The Federal League was frustrated in this effort by the reserve clause, which prevented its acquisition of established major league players. In an ensuring antitrust case the Federal League attempted to undo the reserve system.[3] The court ruled that baseball was exempt from antitrust prosecution because it was not engaged in interstate commerce and, therefore, was beyond the scope of Federal regulatory law. Interestingly, the district court judge in the case was Kenesaw Mountain Landis who, shortly thereafter, became commissioner of baseball.

The second attack on baseball's reserve clause was launched in the late 1940s when another league, this time in Mexico, tried to attain major league status. Major league baseball could not enforce its reserve clause in Mexico, but it did rule that players signing with the Mexican League would forever thereafter be barred from American organized baseball. Two cases emerged from this action, but one never came to trial as baseball lifted its suspension of the plaintiff player.[4] In the other case, the Supreme Court steadfastly stuck to the baseball exemption, although it disagreed with the earlier decision.[5] The Court found unacceptable the earlier ruling that baseball was not interstate commerce, but took Congress' subsequent failure to reverse the Court by specifically incorporating baseball into the coverage of the antitrust statutes as an implied congressional

---

[2] The discounted present value of a stream of revenues through time is the amount a prudent investor would pay today to earn those revenues, given the current rate of interest. For example, if someone will pay $10.00 per year forever and if the interest rate at which money can be borrowed or lent is 10 per cent, then a prudent investor should be willing to pay $100.00 for the right to receive $10.00 annually. The formula for calculating present value (PV) from a stream of revenues (R_i) in each of n years is

$$PV = \sum_{i=1}^{n} \frac{R_i}{(1 + r)^i}$$

where r is the rate of interest.

[3] *Federal Baseball Club* v. *National League* 259 U.S. 200 (1922).

[4] *Gardella* v. *Chandler*, 172 F.2d 402 (2d Cir. 1949).

[5] *Toolson* v. *New York Yankees*, 346 U.S. 356 (1953).

exemption of the sport. The Court also ruled that to reverse itself more than 30 years later would be unfair to investors who had entered the industry expecting the antitrust exemption to remain.

The third major challenge to the reserve clause was offered by Curt Flood, "a grand little center fielder"[6] for the St. Louis Cardinals who decided to retire to Majorca rather than play in Philadelphia, the city to which he was traded by the Cardinals. Once again, the Supreme Court upheld the exemption, although this time it removed yet another reason for its support: that investors deserved a consistent policy.[7] The Court recognized that having enjoyed monopoly rights in the past is no argument for continuing to enjoy them in the future; however, the Court continued to pass the buck by arguing that Congress had had more than 50 years to reverse the Court if it had seen fit to do so.

This last support upon which the baseball exemption is based is weak, indeed, and a good candidate for future reversal. (In fact, William O. Douglas, who voted with the majority in *Toolson*, switched sides in the 5-3 *Flood* decision.) The failure of Congress to act is not equivalent in content to the passage of a specific exemption because it could have numerous explanations. The failure to enact an exemption could stem from an implicit decision in Congress to concern itself with more important matters than overturning a bad court decision in an economically unimportant industry. Congress has exempted numerous business activities from antitrust liability, including agricultural marketing cooperatives and most regulated industries. Thus, the Court could just as easily conclude that the failure of Congress to act implies that it is less enthusiastic about a baseball exemption than about all the other exemptions that have been enacted. Finally, the Court itself does not follow this line of reasoning in other cases. Many major Supreme Court decisions—school desegregation; one man, one vote; and the rights of those arrested—are reversals of earlier Court decisions to which Congress made no response.

In other sports, the courts have been unwilling to exempt player reservation systems from antitrust liability. The NFL employed a baseball-like reserve system until it lost an antitrust case,[8] adopting the Rozelle rule thereafter as another mechanism to achieve the same economic effect. Recently, the NFL was challenged again, with the Rozelle rule the focus of the dispute.[9] In the *Kapp* case, the judge found the NFL's player reservation system in violation of the antitrust statutes. The *Mackey* case involved 32 players who have played out their options. The court ruled that the Rozelle rule was an illegal, collusive agreement to prevent competition for their services. In hockey, the baseball-like reserve system was found illegal in a 1973 decision;[10] hockey subsequently has

---

[6] According to columnist Red Smith, *New York Times*, June 21, 1972.

[7] *Flood* v. *Kuhn*, 407 U.S. 258 (1972).

[8] *Radovich* v. *National Football League*, 352 U.S. 445 (1957).

[9] *Kapp* v. *NFL*, U.S.D.C. Northern California, C-72-537 and *Mackey* v. *NFL*, U.S.D.C. Minnesota, C-4-72-277. Decisions about the legality of the Rozelle rule were handed down in 1975; however, the issue will not be resolved until the owners exhaust their opportunities for appeal.

[10] *Philadelphia World Hockey* v. *Philadelphia Hockey Club, Inc.*, U.S.D.C. Eastern Pennsylvania C.A. 72-1661.

instituted the option system. Finally, Oscar Robertson, acting in his capacity as president of the National Basketball Association Players Association (NBA), filed an antitrust suit that challenged the NBA's counterpart to the Rozelle rule.[11] Just before the case was to go to trial, it was settled out of court when the NBA agreed to abandon the compensation payment if a player signed with a new team.

One can only conclude that, in the mid-1970s, the player reservation system, although still partially in effect in all sports, is crumbling. Even baseball's cherished exemption may not withstand another legal challenge.

Player Unions

The recent wave of court cases attacking the player reservation system is due in large measure to yet another structural feature of the player market. In the mid-1960s, players in all sports began to build effective, militant players' associations. Although these organizations do not focus on the use of collective bargaining to establish individual salaries,[12] in every other respect they seek the same objectives as other labor unions. Generally, the unions have been active in seeking institutional changes within sports that improve the bargaining position of players in the salary negotiation process. Antitrust attacks on the player reservation system have been financed by player associations, notably the *Flood*, *Mackey*, and *Robertson* cases. In addition, player associations have sought, and in hockey and baseball have obtained, arbitration of salary disputes.

In salary arbitration, a player and his team each make "final" salary offers. An arbitration board, selected by labor and management, then picks one or the other figure (but no other—that is, they cannot set a salary other than one of the two proposed by the parties). The arbitration board is instructed to make its decision on the basis of the earnings of other players of comparable ability and experience in the sport; the board may not consider the particular financial condition of either the player or his team.

Salary arbitration does not eliminate monopsony in the player market, for as long as players, on average, are paid a monopsony wage, arbitration by a single player cannot lead to his procuring a competitive wage. But the structural impact of arbitration is still important, since it eliminates the possibility of a team's behaving as a discriminating monopolist. Each player can be said to have a reservation salary below which he will either retire from the sport or give his team less than his full playing effort. With a monopsonized player market, a team has the market power to pay the player only his reservation price in order to obtain his services. Consequently, two players of equal ability and experience but differing reservation prices could be paid different wages. An arbitration

---

[11] *Robertson, et al.* v. *NBA, et al.*, U.S.D.C. Southern Dist. of New York, 70 Civ. 1526.

[12] The only wage issues normally included in collective bargaining in sports are the salary minimum for a major league athlete, the proportionality factor between a player's option-year salary and his salary in the prior year, and the maximum percentage reduction in salary a team can offer.

procedure with results based on the average relation between pay and performance provides a salary boost to players whose reservation price is low.

National Broadcasting Rights

Rights to broadcast sports contests are sold in two markets. In one, leagues
sell to national networks the rights to national broadcasts, whereas in the other,
individual teams sell the rights to those games that are not broadcast nationally
to broadcasters in the area round the team's home city.

Two key institutional rules in professional sports govern the structure of the
broadcasting market. The first is the granting to a team of exclusive control
over broadcasts of any team in the same league within its home metropolitan
areas. This prevents a team in one city from broadcasting its games into the
home area of another team.

The second major institutional arrangement in broadcasting is the Sports
Broadcasting Act of 1961,[13] which exempts leagues from antitrust prosecution
if they choose to sell national broadcasting rights on a league, rather than team,
basis. The Sports Broadcasting Act was passed by Congress after a series of
court cases had made sports broadcasting competitive. These decisions held
illegal both leaguewide national broadcasting contracts and the league rules
prohibiting radio broadcasts into another team's territory and television broadcasts on days when the home team was not playing or was playing in another
city. All that the courts were willing to permit was blackouts of telecasts when
the home team was at home—a practice overturned by Congress in 1974 for
games that were sold out.

For a few years in the late 1950s, national broadcasting rights were sold
competitively. Four networks were formed to offer professional football, three
involving NFL teams and one involving the AFL. Two competitive national
broadcasts of major league baseball were offered twice weekly, one focusing
primarily on the Yankees during their heyday, but also involving four other
teams, and another involving most, but not all, of the remaining teams.

Within a few years after the passage of the Sports Broadcasting Act, all
national broadcasting contracts in sports were negotiated with leagues. In football, the national contract has come to dominate telecasts: all NFL regular
season and play-off game rights are now sold by the league to national networks.
Only radio broadcasts and preseason telecasts are controlled by individual teams.
In other sports, even though local rights are still important, fees from league
sales of national rights have grown in importance. In baseball, for example,
national rights constituted less than 20 per cent of total broadcast revenues in
1955. By 1970, 47 per cent of revenues from broadcasting came through national
contracts.[14]

---

[13] P.L. 87-331 (75 Stat. 732).
[14] Ira Horowitz, "Sports Broadcasting," in Roger G. Noll, ed., *Government and the Sports Business* (Washington, D.C.: Brookings, 1974), p. 287.

The switch from teams to leagues as the source of national contracts profoundly affected the structure of the national broadcasting rights market. Prior to that act, in each sport, between 6 (hockey) and 24 (football after the emergence of the AFL) teams were potential sellers of broadcasting rights. On the demand side, three large national networks plus a fourth loose federation of independent stations were potential buyers. After the act was passed, only one or two entities were selling rights in each sport, a potentially dominating position for the leagues when confronting even as tight an oligopoly as the national television networks.

The financial consequences of the law were predictable: much greater broadcasting revenue for sports enterprises. The first broadcasting package negotiated by major league basketball after the passage of the act, when all other national contracts had finally expired, went into effect in 1965; it approximately tripled the national broadcasting revenues of the sport over the previous few years, from $2 million to $6 million spread among 20 teams. In football, the first leaguewide contract negotiated by the NFL went into effect in 1964. It raised revenues per team from broadcasting from $383,000 to $1,061,000.[15] Obviously, the antitrust exemption of the leaguewide package conferred an important monopoly advantage on sports, for despite the fact that the new contracts called for the broadcast of fewer games than had been telecast in prior years, revenues jumped dramatically. Meanwhile, local broadcasting revenues in baseball continued their annual growth of about 8 per cent per year—even though the number of games available for local broadcast had increased with the reduction in national telecasts from four per week to one.

Another piece of evidence illustrating the monopoly power of sports leagues can be found in comparing the fees paid for the rights to broadcast sporting events with the fees paid to the suppliers of other types of television programming. Given its cost structure, the maximum a network can pay for a sports broadcast and still earn a normal profit (12 per cent after tax rate of return on investment) is about 45 per cent of the advertising revenue generated by the program; leagues actually average 38 per cent for national rights. For a regular series in prime time, the maximum the network could pay is 50 per cent of revenues; in fact, series average about 40 per cent.[16] Producers of series programming incur production costs for programs equal to about 32 per cent of broadcasting revenues. The cost to the sports enterprise of allowing its game to be telecast is effectively nothing—that is, the entire rights' fee is a net increment to revenue.[17] Thus, sports enterprises, by bargaining as a unit for national rights,

---

[15] Ibid., pp. 287–288.

[16] Roger G. Noll, Merton J. Peck, and John J. McGowan, *Economic Aspects of Television Regulation* (Washington, D.C.: Brookings, 1973), Chap. 3 and Appendix B.

[17] It often is alleged by sports entrepreneurs that the televising of games in the same area where that game or even another game is being played will hurt the gate at the latter. If so, broadcasts would have a cost to a team equal to the decline in net gate receipts that they caused. After analyzing the available data on this issue, Horowitz concludes: "On balance . . . it is by no means obvious that, over an extended period of time, telecasts—even of home games on a selective basis—have hurt, or would hurt, gate receipts." Horowitz, op. cit., p. 286.

essentially neutralize the tight television network oligopoly, capturing about 80 per cent of the economic rent gathered by the broadcast, compared to the capture of about half the rent by series producers.

It is difficult to find a more clear-cut example of monopolistic rent than the revenues sports leagues receive from national broadcasting rights. Furthermore, this monopoly rent owes its presence to explicit government action—the legalization through the Sports Broadcasting Act of a cartel arrangement to sell broadcasting rights.

Admissions, Concessions, and Local Broadcasts

The market for admissions to home games, including the concession sales that accompany admissions, is essentially a local one. The Baltimore Orioles once surveyed the fans attending their home games during a season and found that approximately 75 per cent lived within 45 minutes driving time of the stadium.[18] In an antitrust suit tried in 1975, the Oakland Raiders, San Francisco 49ers, and Washington Redskins revealed that between 80 and 90 per cent of their season tickets—which account for virtually all tickets sold for all three teams—were sold to residents of the metropolitan area in which the team played.[19] Even out-of-town ticket sales are not necessarily transacted in a national or regional market because visitors may be in a team's city for reasons other than the desire to attend a game, or distant firms may acquire tickets to entertain clients in the team's home city.

Although the admissions market is local, nevertheless teams in two sports have a substantial interest in the home attendance of other teams. In baseball and football, the visiting team receives part of the gate, receiving between 10 and 20 per cent in baseball and 40 per cent in football. In all sports, the costs of league operations are paid out of a fixed percentage assessment of gate receipts, so that the more successful teams pay a higher proportion of league costs than do the weak franchises. As a result, league members have some interest in investigating the market potential of proposed locations of new or relocated teams.

Part of the market for broadcasts of games is local or regional. Although national telecasts of selected games are offered in all four major sports, in all but football the sale of rights for local and regional broadcasts can be a more important source of revenue than the sale of national rights. In the early 1970s, in baseball, for example, teams received roughly $400,000 each as their share of national broadcasting revenues, but averaged nearly $1 million each from local broadcasts (leagues capture another $450,000 per team from special events such as the All-Star game and World Series, but much of this goes to the players and their pension fund). The Los Angeles Dodgers received $1.8 million for local broadcasting rights, more than four times their share of national revenues.[20]

[18] *Baltimore Baseball Club Survey: 1954*, Baltimore Orioles, 1955.
[19] *Hecht* v. *Pro-Football, Inc.*, U.S.D.C. for District of Columbia, C.A. 2815-66.
[20] Horowitz, op. cit., p. 291.

In the admissions and local broadcasting markets, a team faces only a few competitors, and these usually offer imperfect substitutes for the team's product. Three out of four major league teams enjoy a local monopoly in their sport. The remaining teams have only one competitor. Some competition comes from either professional teams in other sports or amateur teams—high school and college—in all sports. Of course, obvious differences in the quality of play and the focus of fan loyalties make amateur sports an imperfect competitor for the pros. In addition, the amateurs and the pros try to avoid temporal competition. Generally, the amateurs schedule most games on Fridays and Saturdays, whereas the pros concentrate more on Sunday and the middle of the week, a tactic intended primarily to avoid competition for broadcasting audiences and between attendance at amateur contests and broadcast audience for the pros.

Competition among pro teams in different sports is minimized by the seasonality of each. Although all sports overlap somewhat in their playing schedules,[21] only hockey and basketball are in direct competition during their entire seasons.

On the demand side, the market for attendance at games is, of course, competitive, but the number of participants is a relatively small fraction of the population. The Baltimore Orioles survey produced the surprising result that in a year in which the Orioles drew more than one million fans, fewer than 100,000 different people attended a game. In attendance at the typical game during the 80 home dates would be a few thousand season-ticket holders, a few thousand regular fans who attend several games a year, and only a few hundred individuals who attend a game once or twice a year. In football, where NFL teams draw about 400,000 fans during the regular season, nearly all seats are sold as season tickets, so that even taking account of the sharing of season tickets it is unlikely that more than 80,000 different individuals will attend a home game of most teams during a season. In hockey and basketball, the numbers are even smaller. These teams average 5,000 to 20,000 per game in attendance, with between half and all of the attendance accounted for by season tickets. Because most metropolitan areas that contain major league teams range in population from 2 to 6 million, it follows that for most teams only a few per cent of the residents of its home city ever attend a professional game.

Such is not the case when it comes to sports broadcasts. In most cities, a single radio or television broadcast of a game will reach more people than will attend the game in person in an entire season. And here audience shares, particularly of telecasts, are sufficiently large that simultaneous broadcasts by two teams in different sports would directly compete, in that each would have a significantly smaller audience than if the broadcasts were not simultaneous. Nevertheless, simultaneous broadcasts are rare. Scheduling differences and the

---

[21] At the league level, the decision to overlap seasons is conscious; presumably, major league baseball and the NFL each could reduce the duration of its season by two weeks and produce a monopoly for each for part of September. That they choose not to do so may reveal an inability to coordinate strategies, but more likely it reveals a relatively low degree of competition between the sports.

effects of the division of the nation into time zones mean that teams located in the same city, whether in the same or different sports, generally do not play at exactly the same time.

Structural Spillovers from Sports Broadcasting

The demand side of the market for broadcasting rights as seen by a team or league is not the broadcasting audience, but radio and television stations and advertisers. In most cities, numerous radio stations make the market for radio rights competitive; however, few cities have more than a handful of television stations, and no city has more than a few VHF stations, which for various technical reasons reach a much larger audience (usually nearly twice as large) as UHF stations offering the same programs. Because the advertising revenue captured by a broadcast is proportional to the size of its audience, a VHF station can always outbid a UHF station if it chooses to enter the competition for broadcasting rights.

Advertisers of both national and local sports broadcasts are usually large firms in oligopolistic industries in which nonprice competition can confer market advantages. The majority of major league games, national and local, are sponsored by a brewery, an oil company, a firm in banking and finance, and an automobile company. Prior to the ban on cigarette advertising, a majority of teams were sponsored by a tobacco manufacturer as well. Other industries with firms that sponsor broadcasts are soft drinks, insurance, airlines, tires, cosmetics, and shaving products.[22]

Two aspects of sports sponsorship are important. First, although sponsors tend to be large, oligopolistic firms, the number of industries from which they are drawn is sufficiently large that the demand side of the advertising market is competitive. Second, to the extent that sports advertising is a unique product, in a given sport the local monopoly enjoyed by a team and the national monopoly possessed by a league confer a competitive advantage on a single oligopolist. For example, when the New York Mets were organized, their broadcasting rights were sold to the brewers of Rheingold beer. In the next few years, sales of Rheingold in the New York market overtook and passed sales of Ballantine, the sponsors of the then-fading Yankees.[23]

The benefits of this kind of market boost are not necessary captured by the oligopolist, because he is one of several competitors for sponsorship of sports broadcasts. The team or league, being one of a few sources of sports broadcasts, is in a position to capture some of the benefits advertising confers on the sponsor, particularly radio broadcasts because radio, too, is competitive. A VHF television station or a national network, being one of a few possible outlets for televised sports, is also in a position to capture some of these benefits.

[22] Horowitz, op. cit., pp. 312 and 316.
[23] Horowitz, op. cit., p. 315.

Facilities

The market for facilities in which to stage contests is also local, although less so for a team than for the owner of a facility (usually a local government). Obviously, a stadium or arena cannot be moved to another city; a team, however, has some freedom to move to another city; hence, competition among facilities for a team is a possibility. Although facilities available for sports have other uses, few are fully utilized—especially the stadiums used for football and baseball. As a result, even if the local market for a facility is a bilateral monopoly, the balance of bargaining strength favors the team. On several occasions teams have used the threat of moving to another city as a device for obtaining better rental bargains. For instance, after losing the Braves to Atlanta, Milwaukee County Stadium attracted the then-Pilots, now-Brewers, from Seattle by offering to charge only $1 annual rent for the first million admissions sold. Similarly, RFK Stadium in Washington, D.C., tried to keep the Senators baseball team, and later to attract the San Diego Padres, by offering attractive rental agreements.

The consequence of intercity competition for baseball and football teams is that nearly all stadiums lose money. During the 1970–1971 season, 20 publicly owned baseball and football stadiums, for which financial information was publicly available, lost a total of more than $8 million, with most of the loss accounted for by the stadiums built in the 10 years immediately preceding the survey.[24] This is a predictable result, given the structure of costs of a sports facility. Most of the costs of the stadium, once it has been built, are fixed. Regardless of the extent of use of the facility, interest on bonds must be paid and maintenance of the field and seats must be continued at some minimum level. As long as there are more facilities than teams to play in them, competition among stadium authorities will force rents down to the point at which they cover only the costs of staging contests. Operators of facilities owned by local governments may be willing to accept even lower rents because they will consider the effect on tax revenues of keeping a team in the city in calculating the minimum rent they are willing to accept.

Barriers to Entry

In principle, two kinds of competitive entry into sports are possible. A local monopoly could be broken by the entry of new teams, and a national monopoly enjoyed by a league could be eroded by the formation of new leagues. The latter could lead to entry in local monopolies if new leagues choose to locate in the home towns of established teams.

In practice, with few exceptions, entry has taken place only in the form of competitive leagues, for league rules prevent most forms of competition among their members. With two major exceptions, expansion franchises in a major league have never constituted economically meaningful entry: they normally have

---

[24] Benjamin A. Okner, "Subsidies of Stadiums and Arenas," in Noll, op. cit., p. 341.

been located in cities previously lacking a member of the expanding league, and the teams have participated in the broadcasting and player policies that preclude interteam competition in those markets. To illustrate why entry must be through new leagues, we will begin by examining the barriers to entry in a particular locality.

The presence of local monopoly in admissions, local broadcasts, and facilities has two possible causes. First, the monopoly may be natural in that only one or two teams in a particular sport are economically viable, given the cost and demand conditions in the market. Second, institutional barriers may preclude entry.

The previous analysis of the various sports markets surely suggests that institutional barriers are important. Membership in a league confers "territorial rights" on a team. The details differ from sport to sport, but the effect of these rights in all cases is to protect a member against facing direct competition in its home city. No other team in the league is permitted to schedule games or broadcasts of games in another league member's home city without the approval of the home team.

These rules do not totally rule out the entry of a second team into a city. The Los Angeles Dodgers, for example, were paid an indemnity by the California Angels when the American League placed the Angels in the Dodger's home territory. And when the NFL and the AFL merged, the San Francisco 49ers and the New York Giants were indemnified for granting NFL membership to their competing AFL teams, the Oakfield Raiders and the New York Jets. Furthermore, new competitors can be introduced when a new league is formed without approval from or compensation to established teams in other leagues.

The territorial rights do, however, constitute a potential barrier to entry for several reasons. First, because a home team must give its approval if its market is to be shared, the costs of entry are increased by the requirement that the established team's acquiescence be purchased. Second, the territorial rights in broadcasting reduce the potential revenue of other teams by denying them the possibility of selling broadcasting rights in the territory of another team, such as selling rights to broadcast a home game in the visiting team's home town.

Entry into markets with no major league team can be forestalled by a monopolistic league. Each league has a set of formal procedures for deciding whether a new team will be admitted. One requirement is that a very large majority of existing league members (typically three quarters) agree to admit another team. Another is a similar vote among the membership to determine the price of entrance.

In all cases the price is expressed as a minimal franchise fee plus another price at which existing teams will sell the newcomer the rights to certain veteran players, usually the bottom half or third of players in terms of quality. The league also will require that the new entrant buy a certain number of players from each member. The reasons for this rather complicated mechanism for establishing new teams are, for the most part, derived from the tax laws. According to past Internal Revenue Service (IRS) practice, a team can deduct as a depreciation expense the amount spent on players, but not the amount paid for a franchise, during the few years after the team is purchased. These noncash depreciation expenses can be deducted from other income to determine income tax liability. The ultimate effect of this tax treatment is that the Federal government ends up paying for 50 to 70 per cent of the cost of a team through reductions in the tax liability of team owners.[25]

In addition, leagues are usually organized as nonprofit entities, which are not allowed to pay dividends to their owners, the teams. In order to maintain their nonprofit status, the expansion revenues must go directly to the teams in the league and not pass through the league. Even if leagues were for-profit corporations, payment directly to teams avoid the income taxation that would be levied on a league if it received expansion payments that were then divided among the members as dividends.

League rules for creating new teams guarantee that nearly all members must be satisfied with the terms on which an expansion franchise is granted and thereby enable the league to behave as a monopolist in selling membership. Without the near-unanimity requirement, in a year in which several teams faced severe economic hardship, a league might sacrifice long-term profit maximization and vote for the admission of several new teams in order to raise capital. The possibility of this happening, however, is lower, the greater the number of teams that must acquiesce to it.

Monopolization of expansion franchises, like any other monopoly, leads to a slower rate of expansion at a higher price per franchise than is warranted by market conditions. It also serves to maintain high prices for existing teams. Thus, some viable markets can be expected to be without franchises. Nevertheless, the extent to which leagues can husband franchises to maximize financial gain is limited by the threat that a competitive league can be formed.

The possibility of a new league being organized is not a tight check on the monopolistic position of teams and leagues. First, the formation of a successful new league is possible only if several cities possess an excess demand for a particular professional sport. If the number of such cities is too few to constitute an entire league, permanent monopoly rents can accrue to teams in markets big enough for a new entrant to succeed and to all members of a league from slow expansion at high franchise prices. Second, if a league can enforce its player reservation system against a new league, the entrant does not have access to established major league stars. As a result, the start-up costs associated with attaining major league status in the eyes of the sports fan are increased, for the league must develop its own stars from among the ranks of amateurs and minor league professionals.

Only baseball has succeeded in enforcing its reserve clause against new entrants. All other sports have succeeded in requiring new entrants to honor the clause in player contracts requiring an option year before the player can change

---

[25] For more details, see Benjamin A. Okner, "Taxation and Sports Enterprises," in Noll, op. cit., Chap. 6.

teams, although the new league need not compensate the old for signing players who have played out their option. For example, the Memphis team in the World Football League succeeded in signing three star players from the Miami NFL team, but obtained their service only one year later, after they had played out their options with Miami.

A final institutional mechanism that has been deployed to forestall entry is the exclusive rental agreement to obtain a stadium. One of the original owners of a World Football League franchise wanted to locate his franchise in Washington, D.C., where the NFL Redskins play to full capacity and have a waiting list several thousand long to obtain season tickets. This team eventually settled in Florida because it was unable to secure an adequate playing facility in the Washington area. Only two stadiums large enough to accommodate a major league football team are located in the Washington metropolitan area: RFK Stadium, the home of the Redskins, and the University of Maryland stadium. The latter is unavailable for professional contests, and the former, by agreement with the Redskins, is available for professional football only if the Redskins approve.

In 1966, an attempt was made to break the exclusive lease between the Redskins and the operators of the stadium.[26] Before the merger of the two professional football leagues, an attempt was made to obtain an AFL expansion franchise for Washington, but it was thwarted by the exclusive lease. This led to an antitrust suit against the Redskins, the NFL, and the D.C. Armory Board, the operator of RFK Stadium, by the promoters of the AFL franchise. The initial decision in the case, which is on appeal, ruled that the lease was not an antitrust violation. One basis for the appeal is that the judge instructed the jury that the plaintiff was required to show that Washington could support two football teams in order to have a valid antitrust claim. This instruction apparently ignored the importance of potential competition in holding down prices of established firms.

Because stadiums generally lose money, a new entrant faces a significant absolute cost barrier if it must construct its own playing facility. Only if a local government authority is willing to build a second money-losing facility—in the face of excess capacity in the first—can this barrier be eliminated when the incumbent team has an exclusive lease. Presumably, the political demand to obtain a second team in a sport—particularly in a new, untried league—is likely to be less than the desirability to voters of attracting the first major league team. To build a facility requires either the passage of a bond issue encumbering the voters or the election of politicians willing to commit taxes to guarantee that the expenses of constructing a stadium will be paid. Because only a small proportion of voters actually attend games, the source of majority-rule approval of financing these money-losing ventures must lie in the presumed benefits to a city of acquiring "major league" status.[27] Once this status has been attained, the per-

[26] *Hecht* v. *Pro-Football, Inc.*, loc. cit.
[27] For a discussion of these benefits, see Okner, op. cit., pp. 327 ff.

ceived benefits of acquiring another team are reduced, making it more difficult to obtain voter approval of additional facilities.

Is the Sports Monopoly Natural?

The preceding discussion leads to the conclusion that institutional impediments *could* foreclose economically warranted entry. Whether entry *is* foreclosed depends on an assessment of cost and demand conditions in sports, and, in particular, examination of the possibility that teams are natural monopolies.

The precise definition of natural monopoly is more complicated than is needed for the purposes of this chapter; let it be sufficient to say that a natural monopoly exists if indivisibilities in the production process cause the minimum feasible size of a firm to be roughly equal to the quantity of output demanded at the price that is just sufficient to generate revenues that exactly cover total costs.

In sports, the production function describing the "technology" of operating a sports franchise has definite indivisibilities. League rules, which no individual team can change, dictate the minimum number of players a team can field and the number of games per season a team must play. Furthermore, because a team must be reasonably competitive athletically to generate fan interest, the general playing quality of a league determines a minimum feasible quality for each team. Finally, a league member is committed to pay the costs associated with transporting team members to other cities to play away games. Failure to satisfy any of these minimum requirements for league membership—including the requirement to field a respectable team—will cause a team to be expelled from the league.

In the short run, the minimum expenditure commitment of a team is a very high percentage of its total costs. Table 1 shows approximate costs of teams in the major sports, broken down by expenditure categories. League rules require that a player receive his full contractual salary if he is not released from the team before a relatively early date in the playing season, so that in the short run player costs are fixed. During the course of a few years, salary costs can be reduced somewhat, but the requirement that a representative team be fielded places limits on this. Within a league, the teams with the biggest salary expenditures will spend between two and three times as much as the teams with the lowest salaries; hence, it is unlikely that any team could cut its salary budget below half of the leaguewide average.

Of the remaining costs, only rent on a stadium and payments to the league to defer common expenses, such as referees and umpires, are typically based on revenues and, therefore, not subject to minimum bounds. Rents vary from 5 to 20 per cent of revenues for all but a few teams, and league payments are another 5 to 10 per cent. Together these rarely total more than 25 per cent of costs. Consequently, on a year-to-year basis, 75 per cent, and in the long run more than half, of the expenditures of a team represent minimum, indivisible commitments required to continue in business.

TABLE 1
Income Statements of Average Teams by League

| | (IN THOUSANDS OF DOLLARS) | | | | | |
	ABA[a] 1971	NBA 1971	NFL 1970	MLB 1969	NHL 1973	WHA 1973
Operating Revenues	620	1760	4850	5225	4150	850
Games	500	1200	2700	3200	3450	700
Broadcasts	20	360	1850	1420	550	100
Other	100	200	300	605	150	50
Direct Costs	1120	1815	3350	4955	2750	1500
Player compensation	400	700	2000	1070	1000	600
Games	300	600	950	1190	1350	625
General administrative	300	340	350⎫	1375	225	175
Promotion	120	175	50⎭		75	100
Player development	0	0	0	1320	100	0
Operating Profit	−500	−55	1500	270	1400	−650
Other Income	70	55	200	n.a.[b]	100	0
Cash Flow	−430	0	1700	270	1500	−650
Indirect Costs	140	435	600	445	500	100
Player amortization	110	370	500	445	500	100
Interest	30	65	100	n.a.	n.a.	n.a.
Book Profit Before Taxes	−570	−435	1100	−175	1000	−750
Benefit of Ownership After Taxes	−155	217	1150	357	1000	−225

[a] ABA, American Basketball Association; NBA, National Basketball Association; NFL, National Football League; MLB, Major League Baseball; NHL, National Hockey League; WHA, World Hockey Association.
[b] n.a. = no basis for estimate.
Source: Summaries of tables in Roger G. Noll, "The U.S. Team Sports Industry: An Introduction," Government and the Sports Business, (Washington, D.C.: Brookings, 1974), pp. 12–26. Details of estimates and sources of information are presented in these tables.
Note: Except for the last line, figures are estimates of teams of average quality for each league. Each league has a few teams that do much better and a few that do much worse financially than these averages show. The "benefit of ownership" calculations assume that the owner of the team is in the 50 per cent marginal tax bracket for Federal income tax and that he has sufficient other income to take advantage of the tax write-off possibilities of any book loss the team might experience. Most owners are probably sufficiently wealthy that their marginal tax rate is at least 50 per cent.
Definitions: Player compensation includes wages, fringe benefits, and the present value of deferred salaries for players, coaches, and managers. Game costs include rents, maintenance of playing field, equipment, training camps, travel, and other expenses associated with staging contests. Player development refers to subsidies of amateur and minor professional leagues.

To determine whether cost indivisibilities in sports are sufficient to cause a natural monopoly requires two additional pieces of analysis. The first is to calculate the minimum profit a team must earn in order to stay in business in the long run. The second is to examine the demand conditions in each sport to determine how many teams are viable in each market.

Determining "normal profits" in sports is horrendously complicated because of the extremely labor-intensive production method in the industry. The typical balance sheet of a sports enterprise lists almost no tangible capital investments, nor are its net assets likely to be even close to a reasonable approximation of the sales value of the enterprise. Consider the financial statement of the Milwaukee Bucks basketball team for 1970 (see Table 2). The entire investment of the team in tangible, physical capital is $21,000 in furniture and fixtures, ignoring whatever may be the investment in the subsidiary (a summer camp). The items listed as "NBA contracts," on the asset side of the ledger, are payments due from expansion teams as part of the fee for joining the league; on the liability side are payments due other teams for the expansion that granted the Bucks a franchise.

TABLE 2
Milwaukee Bucks Balance Sheet

Current Assets		
Cash, investments, accounts receivable, and prepaid expenses		$2,389,356
Current maturities of NBA contracts receivable		117,857
Deferred costs of employment contracts		644,700
	Total current	$3,151,913
Long-term Assets		
NBA contracts receivable		$ 353,572
Deferred costs of employment contracts		1,216,667
Furniture and fixtures		21,014
Original player costs		885,124
Subsidiary assets		18,523
Certificates of deposit		750,000
	Total long term	$3,244,900
	Total assets	$6,396,813
Current Liabilities		
NBA contract payable		$ 250,000
Accounts payable, accrued liabilities, and advance revenues		1,069,938
Employment contracts payable		514,989
	Total current	$1,834,927
Long-term Liabilities		
NBA contract payable		$ 250,000
Employment contracts payable		1,345,833
Deferred taxes		137,000
	Total long term	$1,732,833
	Total liabilities	$3,567,760
Shareholder's Equity		$2,829,053
	Total liabilities and equity	$6,396,813

Source: Milwaukee Professional Sports and Services, Inc., 1970 *Annual Report*.

Entries relating to employment contracts represent a bookkeeping practice by the team to capture certain tax advantages. If a player is signed to a multiyear contract that, among other things, calls for part of his salary to be deferred, the team can deduct the deferred payment at the time the obligation is accrued if the team "funds" the deferred payment. What this means is that if a player, as part of his contract for this year, is to be paid $10,000 20 years from now, a team that invests the $10,000 in certain low-risk investments can deduct the deferred payment this year in computing its tax liabilities and, meanwhile, earn the interest payments on the investment.

Another major asset of the team is termed original player costs. This represents the current value of the player contracts purchased by the Bucks during the expansion in which they obtained their franchise. Once again, this reflects an accounting practice designed to take advantage of the tax ruling that enables a team to depreciate the cost of a player contract over the expected playing career of a player, which is normally taken to be 5 years. In 1970, the Bucks claimed about $270,000 in player depreciation, which, given corporate income taxes of about 50 per cent, reduced their income tax liability by about $135,000.

The original investment in player contracts is not really an investment in particular players; it is the purchase from the other teams of the right to have exclusive bargaining rights, through the player reservation system, with a proportionate share of the athletes in the sport. The particular athletes drafted by the team from other rosters as part of the league expansion are simply the first group whose athletic career is the exclusive property of the expansion team. In the future, they are replaced through trades and free agent drafts by other players. The asset that creates value in these contracts is not a contract itself, but the rules prohibiting competition among teams. These assets guarantee that competition for players, for broadcasting revenues, for home gate receipts, and for a place in which to play will not erode the profit earned from the player. And the assets that generate this profit—the restrictive rules in the league— have essentially a zero cost of production. These anticompetitive agreements among teams constitute essentially all of the assets of every team in professional sports except the few that own their own playing facilities.

The question thus arises: What, if anything, is the true investment of society's scarce resources in a sports franchise? For one thing, an owner commits himself to operating a team for a year, which means that some expenditures are made before any revenues accrue. The owner assumes the risk that revenues will be insufficient to cover these commitments; therefore, some profit must be expected by the owner to induce him to take this risk. In addition, a new team must undertake certain promotional expenditures to generate fan interest. These costs, plus minimal investments in physical capital, represent the team's only true investments in the sense of commitments of society's scarce resources. For most teams these costs will come to no more than a few hundred thousand dollars, which implies that "normal" profits—those necessary to induce teams into the industry if cartel rights did not have to be purchased—are probably substantially less than $100,000 annually. All of the profits in excess of a few tens of thousands of dollars represent earnings created by monopoly rights.

One task remains in determining whether these monopoly profits signal excess demand for sports: to examine the demand for sports to see whether entry would leave teams with sufficient revenues to cover costs.

The demand for sports in a particular city depends on normal economic factors—price and income—plus the quality of the team, the quality and ease of access of the facility in which it plays, and the alternatives available in the city for entertainment and recreation. Large cities have more people from which a team can generate an audience, but they are also more congested and have more entertainment alternatives. On balance, these factors produce a positive effect of population on attendance, holding other things constant, although a doubling of population will lead to less than a doubling of attendance.

Similarly, because of differences in teams and their playing schedules, the attendance generated by two teams will exceed the attendance either one would capture if it were a monopolist. Multiple teams increase the number of days on which a game is available and reduce the congestion at a given game by lowering average attendance. In addition, if teams play in different locations, they reduce the average distance of area residents to the nearest source of games. For these reasons, a second team will cause some net addition to total attendance in its sport.

Statistical analysis of attendance at sports contests provides a rough estimate of the minimum population in a metropolitan area that can sustain a major league team in each professional sport, assuming that a team is viable as long as it makes positive profits. These minimum populations are shown in Table 3. They represent the size of a city required for the break-even operation of a team, neglecting any tax benefits that might be captured from the depreciation of player contracts.

TABLE 3
Minimum Size of a Metropolitan Area for a Successful Team
(population in millions)

SPORT	YEARS	1 TEAM	2 TEAMS[a]	3 TEAMS[a]
Baseball	1970–1971	1.9	3.4	4.9
Basketball	1969–1971	4.0	7.6	10.7
Football	1968	1.0	3.1	5.4
Hockey	1972–1973	.9	2.6	5.6

[a] Assumes that half of the attendance of the second team and two thirds of the attendance of the third team are captured from competitors in the same sport, and that teams are of average quality, making play-offs in basketball and hockey about half the time.
Source: Calculated from statistical analysis of the demand for attendance at sports contests in Roger G. Noll, "Attendance and Price Setting," in Noll, ed., *Government and the Sports Business* (Washington, D.C.: Brookings, 1974), Chap. 4.

Because few teams compete against other teams in the same sport in the same city, direct statistical analysis of the effects of such competition on the minimum population required for multiple teams is not possible. Table 3 contains one rough approximation that is consistent with what is known about existing teams. For example, two financially successful professional football teams operate in the San Francisco-Oakland metropolitan area, which had a population of approximately 3.1 million in 1970. Two successful hockey franchises were located in the Boston metropolitan area in 1972–1973, although one had great difficulty scheduling games in the arenas owned by the other. The Boston metropolitan area had a population of 2.8 million in 1970. In New York, with a population of nearly 12 million, two extremely successful franchises operate in all four sports, with at least one in each sport earning profits as great as any team in its sport. In baseball, two teams operate in Chicago, one of which is very successful while the other is marginal. Two teams that apparently suffer losses operate in the San Francisco-Oakland area. According to Table 3, the Bay area is about 10 per cent too small to be able to support its baseball teams. This, coupled with its cold summer weather, probably makes it economically unviable as a location for two baseball teams.

The preceding leads to the conclusion that the territorial rights of teams do foreclose warranted entry in the largest cities, but that in the smallest cities in each league a team is a natural monopoly in that only one is viable. In baseball, for example, cities such as Atlanta, Kansas City, Milwaukee, and San Diego are probably not viable locations for one baseball team, let alone two, whereas cities such as Cincinnati, Houston, and Minneapolis probably can support one, but not two, teams. Nevertheless, the largest cities have too few teams. Chicago, Los Angeles, and New York appear to be large enough for a third baseball team, and Philadelphia and Detroit for a second. Similar findings apply to all the other sports: most current franchise cities are natural monopolies, but the largest could support more teams. And, in football and hockey, a few cities now lacking teams are apparently large enough to support one.

These findings are, of course, crucially dependent on the existence of the monopolistic market positions enjoyed by league members. Of the calculations shown in Table 3, only those for basketball were based on a situation in which two established leagues compete for players, and the minimum city sizes for viable operations are much larger for basketball than for the others. Had basketball salaries not accelerated due to competition between the ABA and NBA, each team would have paid, on average, about $400,000 less per year in salaries during the 1970s. This would reduce the minimum metropolitan area population for one viable team to under two million.

The results in Table 3 also depend on the gate sharing arrangement of the league. In baseball and football, the visiting team receives part of the gate. As a result, teams in smaller markets are more likely to be economically viable. Teams from small markets receive more from the games they play in the best markets than they pay from home game receipts to teams from those markets. Were baseball to raise the visiting team share from the current 10 per cent

(National League) or 20 per cent (American League) to the 40 per cent paid in football, the minimum population for a financially successful first team would fall to about 1.3 million, making all cities that now have teams viable locations.

The main conclusion to be drawn from the financial analysis of major league sports is that the market structure of the industry is highly dependent on the league rules that regulate the sharing of revenue, the business competition among members, and the expansion of the league. Although some teams are natural monopolies, others are not. Although all teams benefit from anticompetitive league rules, the biggest beneficiaries are the teams in the largest cities, which, because of the entry barriers created by league rules, earn monopoly profits.

III. CONDUCT

Economists have long debated the appropriateness of the conventional assumption that businessmen seek to maximize profits. In sports, the issue is of central importance because the effect and desirability of prohibitions against competition depend critically on the motivation of team owners. The major justification offered by sports entrepreneurs for the player reservation system is that it prevents a single team from so monopolizing playing talent that it destroys fan interest in the game and, thereby, causes massive financial failure in the league.

This argument is valid only if the primary motivation of team owners is the unconstrained maximization of games won. If so, the owner with the greatest financial strength—probably the owner in the best market—will continue to acquire players until his team is sure to win all of its games. The resulting lopsided contests will prove uninteresting to fans, especially in other cities, and every team—including the certain victor—will fail financially.

If owners seek only victory, the player reservation system does prevent the result described here, for it prevents the best-financed team from acquiring the players whose contracts are the exclusive property of other teams, at least unless it obtains their acquiescence.

If owners seek to make profits, the player reservation system has no effect on the distribution of playing strengths among teams. Without a player reservation system, the team for whom a player can generate the most revenues will offer him the highest salary, and all players will, in equilibrium, play for the team for which they have the greatest value. If any player is earning a wage from one team that falls short of his value to another, profit maximization by the latter will prompt it to offer him a higher salary if he will switch teams.

With a player reservation system, the player cannot accept the higher wage and move to the team that values him most highly. But the teams can engage in the sale and trade of player contracts. If a team is paying a player exactly what he is worth to that team, but his value to another team is greater, both teams can benefit from a sale of the player's contract. Through sale, the player's current team shares the player's greater value in another city with his new team. Thus, under both regimes the player ends up with the team for which he generates the greatest revenue. The only difference is that without a player reservation system, the player receives that greater value through a competitive labor market, whereas with a player reservation system, the player's original team receives it from the sale of his contract.

A third possible motivation of sports owners is that they maximize victories subject to a requirement that the team earn some minimum amount of profit (perhaps zero, or perhaps even negative). The predicted result of this motivational assumption is intermediate between those of the two other hypotheses. Each team would attempt to acquire a stronger team than would a profit maximizer, assuming that the most profitable strength earns profits in excess of the minimum satisfactory amount. Among the predictions of this hypothesis is that no profitable team would ever sell a player unless it was for the purpose of hiring a better one, and then it would only sell a player that was worse than the one that was acquired. Another prediction is that no team would earn more than minimum profits as long as any opportunity for making an expenditure to improve the team existed.

Ticket prices, too, should be affected by the motivation of the owner. The less important are profits to the sports entrepreneur, the more likely that teams will set prices on a cost-plus basis—that is, without profit motivation, a team that is highly successful on the field and also earns a large profit would be expected to cut prices.

Evidence on Motivation

From the preceeding, data on player sales, profits, and ticket prices should provide some clue as to the motivation of sports owners. In fact, these data all support the profit-maximization hypothesis.

The only definitive data on player transactions were collected by the Congress for a few selected years between 1929 and 1950 in connection with an investigation of professional baseball. During this period the worst team in the American League in terms of won-lost percentage was the St. Louis Browns. The Browns showed cumulative profits during this 30 year period of about $1.1 million and net sales of player contracts of approximately $2.3 million. From this one can conclude that, although the Browns' entire profit was accounted for by the sale of players, nevertheless the team could not have been an unabashed maximizer of victories. It sold more than $1 million more in players than was necessary for break-even operations, some of whom presumably could have added a few victories to the Browns' miserable record.

During the same period, the Brooklyn Dodgers were a better-than-average team, tying for the fifth-best won-lost percentage among the 16 teams then in major league baseball. They also had the fourth highest profits in baseball—and a net income from the sales of player contracts of more than $800,000. In fact, they were the second-leading team in the National League in terms of net player sales. Had they sought primarily victory on the field, they would not have sold so many players while earning profits but failing to win the most games.

Recent history in professional basketball also illustrates the tendency for players to move toward the cities that value them most highly. The Los Angeles Lakers have continually maintained their playing strength—and their status as one of the most profitable basketball franchises—by acquiring talent from other teams. Among the players of star or superstar status acquired by the Lakers from other teams through either cash purchases or, when economic aspects of the transaction are not considered, unequal trades are Wilt Chamberlin, Bill Bridges, Happy Hairston, Gail Goodrich, Connie Hawkins, and Kareem Abdul-Jabbar.

Another prime basketball market is New York City, and the Knickerbockers and Nets have also been active in the acquisition of players from other teams through transactions with strong economic overtones. Among the stars that the New York teams acquired from franchises in smaller markets are Jerry Lucas, Dave DeBuscherre, Earl Monroe, Julius Erving, and Rick Barry.

There is also no evidence that teams become so good that they actually begin to lose money. Table 4 shows the ranking of baseball teams by cumulative won-

TABLE 4
Ranking of Baseball Teams by League in Cumulative Profits and Cumulative Wins, 1929–1950

TEAM	WON-LOST RECORD		ESTIMATED PROFITS ($ MILLIONS)	RANK
	FRACTION WON	RANK		
American League				
New York	.617	1	8.5	1
Detroit	.537	2	4.7	2
Cleveland	.534	3	3.7	3
Boston	.508	4	−2.1	8
Washington	.481	5	2.7	4
Philadelphia	.451	6	1.091	6
Chicago	.449	7	1.3	5
St. Louis	.420	8	1.088	7
National League				
St. Louis	.587	1	6.0	1
Brooklyn	.529	2	3.9	2
Chicago	.529	3	2.92	4
New York	.524	4	2.89	5
Pittsburgh	.508	5	3.2	3
Boston	.463	6	− .3	8
Cincinnati	.463	7	1.6	6
Philadelphia	.394	8	0	7

Source: James P. Quirk and Mohamed El Hodiri, "The Economic Theory of a Sports League," in Roger G. Noll, *Government and the Sports Business* (Washington, D.C.: Brookings, 1974), Chap. 2.

lost record and estimated cumulative profits during the 1929–1950 period. In both leagues, artistic and financial success go hand in hand, with the best team also being the most profitable. There is no evidence that any team—even the dynastic Yankees—surpassed the profit-maximizing team strength.

The ticket prices charged by the most profitable teams show no evidence of the kind of cost-plus pricing that would be predicted by the models assuming the maximization of games won. In baseball, the eight teams that were most profitable during 1970 and 1971 earned about $1.8 million per team more in net revenue than the baseballwide average.[28] Their ticket prices were not statistically significantly different from other teams. Obviously, they did not cut ticket prices or purchase more player contracts to improve performance, in response to greater profits. In basketball, the New York Knickerbockers are, by far, the most profitable franchise. They also charge, by more than $2.00 per ticket, the highest prices in basketball. Clearly, they are quite profit-oriented, but this is to be expected because they are a subsidiary of a publicly held corporation. The Lakers are more typical of sports in their ownership, being a privately held corporation that is controlled by a wealthy individual who also is an owner of franchises in hockey and football. They are the second most profitable basketball team and charge the second-highest prices.

The final evidence that sports enterprises are generally profit-oriented is the contrast between average behavior in sports and the behavior of the very few teams that are not totally profit-oriented. In baseball, Phil Wrigley of the Chicago Cubs and the late Tom Yawkey of the Boston Red Sox have long been regarded as "sportsmen" owners. These teams charge, by far, the lowest prices in baseball. They also have atypically low local broadcasting revenues. The Cubs refuse to schedule night games at home, even though all other teams have found that night games are more profitable. The Red Sox were the only team to lose a significant amount of money during the 1929–1950 period. During this same period, the Red Sox and Cubs ranked second and third in purchases of player contracts. Still, they were unable to achieve dominance in their leagues, finishing fourth and tied for second, respectively, in cumulative won-lost percentage.

The histories of the Cubs and Red Sox illustrate two important phenomena. First, these teams behave so differently from others that it is reasonable to conclude that the others are motivated mainly by profit. Second, their inability to dominate play—or even to win their share of pennants (since 1940, the Cubs captured one pennant, the Red Sox three)—indicates that a few sportsmen owners do not succeed in unbalancing competition on the field by acquiring most of the good players.

The performance of sports enterprises supports the conclusion that neither the purpose nor the effect of the player reservation system is to prevent economically irrational owners from destroying the balance of strength among teams in a sport. Instead, as economics predicts, its effects are to lower player salaries to the benefit of owners and, through sales from weak to strong teams, to increase

---

[28] Noll, "Attendance and Price Setting," op. cit., pp. 125–126.

the revenues of the former. Although this can make more teams in a league viable—for example, by converting the disastrous Browns to a profitable venture in the 1929–1950 period—it is not any more effective than more direct revenue-sharing arrangements, such as splitting gate receipts and broadcasting revenues among participating teams.

Cartel Cheating

A sports league is, in economic terms, an organization of competing firms that designs and enforces rules to limit competition. The monopoly rights enjoyed by teams are created by the league cartel, for, in the absence of league rules, teams could be expected to compete in the broadcasting and player markets, and in the larger cities some competition in the admissions and stadium markets would also ensue.

In a competitive market, equilibrium price and output are economically efficient in that price is equated to marginal cost. Should a situation arise in which firms are earning profits in excess of the amount necessary to keep them economically viable, the expansion of existing firms and the entry of new firms will increase output, force down prices, and return profits to the competitive equilibrium. The process by which competition lowers prices and profits operates because each firm perceives an incentive either to expand output or to enter the market in response to excess demand, even though its behavior, and that of its competitors, eventually leads to lower profits for all.

In a cartel, firms perceive the same incentive to engage in behavior that, were it followed by all, would destroy the monopoly profits generated by the cartel's anticompetitive arrangements. Consequently, the cartel is inherently unstable. Its members will perceive an incentive to respond to new opportunities to gain a competitive advantage, either by violating the rules (especially if the violation is likely to go undetected) or by behaving competitively should a situation arise that is not covered by league rules.

To combat this behavior, all cartels—including those in sports—must devise penalties for violating the rules, information systems for detecting violations, and procedures for revising rules in response to new economic conditions. Each league in professional sports has a published, continuously updated list of operating rules (in addition to playing rules) that serves these functions. And, judging from the frequency with which rules are changed and penalties invoked, sports leagues are continually beset by the problem of cheating—that is, behavior by one or more members that erodes the monopoly profits of all. Of course, in the sense used here, cheating is not a pejorative term. In an industry that is not cartelized, behavior that is cheating in a cartel is called innovative and competitive.

Cheating by violation of league rules is not common in professional sports, but it is by no means unknown. Violation of most of the monopolistic rules practiced by a league is extremely obvious when it takes place. A team cannot play or broadcast a game in another team's home territory without easily being detected, nor would it be able to sign a player from another team's roster without instant recognition. Enforcement of these rules involves granting the commissioner of a sport the power to impose stiff penalties on violators. Commissioners have the power to impose heavy fines—in the form of money, players, or even expulsion from the league. Because detection is virtually certain, gain virtually impossible, and significant loss amost inevitable, the most obvious forms of cheating almost never occur.

Two recent cases illustrate the mechanics by which leagues enforce these rules in the rare instances in which they are broken. George McGinnis and Julius Erving, two exceptionally talented basketball forwards, played the first few years of their careers for teams in the ABA. Nevertheless, the NBA draft rights to each were still valid, the Philadelphia 76ers having rights to McGinnis and the Milwaukee Bucks to Erving. Both players were signed by another NBA team, with the New York Knickerbockers signing McGinnis and the Atlanta Hawks coming to terms with Erving. The league then severely fined both teams and declared each contract invalid. The exact amount of the fines is not precisely known, but the fines involved both cash and the loss of negotiating rights with other players.

Violations of a few rules are extremely difficult to detect. One is the roster limit. Every sport sets a limit on the number of players that can be under contract to any one team. Even though teams cannot easily field more than the legal number of players without detection, they can rather easily sign contracts with a number that exceeds the roster limit. In case of injury or an unexpectedly bad performance, a legal roster player can then be replaced by an alleged "free agent" who "just happened" to be ready to play. Although he is not being used, the illegally signed player can be playing minor league ball, sometimes under an assumed name, or simply attending secret, separate practice sessions held by the team somewhere other than the team's normal practice area.

In 1974, the Houston Oilers were accused of stashing players—of having 58 players under contract despite the 47-man roster limit of the NFL. An official of the team was reportedly fined $5000 by the league office for this practice, a trivial sum in comparison with the salaries these 11 players were likely to have been paid. Similar stashing episodes have taken place in baseball, but they have become rarer with the demise of the minor league system. In the days when scores of independent minor leagues were operating, a team had a good chance of keeping the talents of an illegally signed, talented young prospect unnoticed on some obscure minor league team. (If the player were noticed, another team might try to buy his contract from the minor league club and discover that he was already under major league contract.)

To keep the player from being noticed while developing his skill, the team would impose strange requirements on the minor league team to keep his record from appearing too good, such as playing him part of the time in the wrong position so that he would have a poor fielding record, or leaving him out of the lineup against weak pitchers to depress his batting average. These tactics, of course, could not work for long, but they gave the team a little extra time to decide whether to place a player on the roster and, thereby, to protect him from acquisition by a competitor.

Interfering with the mechanism by which free agents are drafted is also a relatively easy way to cheat. For example, a few years ago several football teams received a letter from a top college prospect warning them against "wasting a draft choice" on the player because he had decided to play baseball instead of football. Upon contacting the player, one owner discovered that the player was unaware of the letters and, in fact, was leaning toward football. Apparently another team in the league, desirous of his services, had tried to dissuade others from drafting the player so that he would still be available by the time the draft had proceeded to the team's turn. (The identity of the culprit was never publicly disclosed.)

The most common form of cheating is violation of the spirit, but not the letter, of league rules, in response to a new competitive opportunity. In so doing, a team usually can expect the advantage it gains to be temporary. Either league rules will be changed to make the team's action illegal, or other teams will all adopt the same practice, often to the detriment of all.

Currently, the possibility of subscription television (pay TV) on cable television systems has led to this kind of cheating. League rules prohibit broadcasting into another team's territory; however, cable pay TV is not, technically, broadcasting. In 1973, the New York Knickerbockers sold rights to their home games to a pay-TV firm who then proceeded to offer them on a cable system in the home territory of the Philadelphia 76ers. This prompted the league to employ economists at the Rand Corporation to help it devise rules for dealing with cable television; meanwhile the Knicks and/or their licensee derived some temporary advantage.

Perhaps the most important example of innovative behavior that gets around league rules was the development of baseball's minor league farm system by Branch Rickey. During the 1920s, several minor leagues refused to allow their players to be drafted by major league teams. Instead, they sold player contracts to the highest bidder, thereby extracting some of the gains of the major's reserve system. Rickey's innovation was simple but devastating: his team, the St. Louis Cardinals, acquired or established exclusive agreements with minor league teams. They could sign players to minor league contracts, without exceeding the Cardinal's roster limit, and then refuse to sell the contracts to any team except themselves.

Rickey soon realized that his innovation had even better possibilities. He rapidly developed a larger minor league farm system than was required to develope players only for the Cardinals, and the Cardinals became the biggest net seller of player contracts in baseball. Rickey had discovered an intricate mechanism to monopolize playing talent without paying for it (players were signed as youngsters to become minor league players) and without violating the roster limit. As a result, the Cardinals became the best team in the National League, despite being located in a relatively small market that was, nonetheless, shared with another major league team. They also became the league's most profitable team, earning well over half of their profits from the sale of player contracts.

By the time the other teams realized what had taken place, the Cardinals were entrenched in the minor leagues. Formation of an equal number of competing teams was impossible unless economically unviable teams were to be created. And prohibition of the farm system meant returning to a situation in which independent minor league teams sold players competitively to the majors. The only remaining step—a limitation on the number of teams that a major league franchise could own—was of dubious legality should Rickey challenge it and, was, in any event, a confiscation of property that the owners were unlikely to find agreeable. Commissioner Landis, who opposed the farm system on the grounds that it would prove too expensive and destabilizing of competitive balance, brought the issue to a head by declaring several farm system players available to other teams on the ground that their major league teams were violating the roster limit. The owners overrode him and he did not choose to invoke his ultimate power: to declare a practice illegal because it threatened the "integrity of the game." Not until the economic collapse of the minor leagues in the 1950s did the leagues succeed in achieving a relatively even distribution of minor league farm teams.

The demise of the minors provides another example of innovative competition in baseball. The minors were killed by television. National and regional telecasts destroyed attendance at minor league games on Saturdays and Sundays, and, as a result, teams began to lose money. Major league teams responded by subsidizing the farm system. By 1970, major league teams were receiving about $1.4 million each in broadcasting revenue, but each was subsidizing the minor leagues to the tune of $1.3 million.

The rules of baseball governing territorial rights were written when radio, not television, was the broadcasting vehicle of principal interest to the owners. These rules permitted broadcasts of major league teams into the home territories of lower-status leagues, even when the minor league team was playing at home. This was, of course, a benign provision; radio was hardly a threat to minor league attendance.

With the advent of television, opportunities for lucrative broadcasting contracts increased, and teams began televising games regionally and nationally. Television did erode minor league attendance, by direct competition and by the invidious comparisons of the skill with which the game was played. The latter point was emphasized by a Los Angeles sports writer who reported the following conversation after the first televised World Series: "I'll wager that the Series telecast killed baseball on the Coast. By your standards, Bobby Brown is just an average third baseman. By our standards, he pulled fielding plays such as we on the Pacific Coast had never seen before." The response: "Wait until you see a miracle worker like Billy Cox. He'll finish off the Pacific Coast League all by himself."[29]

[29] *New York Times*, Dec. 9, 1952, p. 46.

In the late 1940s, baseball could have devised a policy toward broadcasting that took account of the effect of broadcasts on the minor leagues. But, once extensive telecasting had begun, politically and legally there was no return—and the minor leagues were essentially dead. As the figures on revenues, costs, and minor league survival rates attest, it is by no means obvious that baseball has benefited from television, despite its ability to establish monopoly prices in both the local and national broadcasting markets. The natural tendency of businessmen to respond competitively, rather than collusively, to the opportunity for short-run gain outside the reach of cartel rules undermined the ability of baseball to take full advantage of its legalized monopoly in television rights.

Cartel Innovation

In some instances, innovations that benefit all teams, or at least that hurt no one, require league approval if they are to be tried. Examples include changes in playing rules (the American League's designated hitter, the old AFL's 2-point conversion), increases in league membership through expansion or merger, and relocation of franchises.

These changes normally require consent by a large majority of league members —usually three quarters. Two features of cartels make this a difficult obstacle to surmount. First, the entrepreneurial skills and foresight of cartel members are certain to differ. In a competitive enrivonment, only one skilled entrepreneur need perceive an innovation. He will pursue it first, and his competitors will be forced to follow or face permanent competitive disadvantage, even demise. But to achieve a three-quarters majority, each innovative idea must appeal to some entrepreneurs of below-average vision and ability.

A second feature that retards innovation is the incentive facing each member to fake injury in the hopes of receiving compensation. For example, when the American League decided to become a truly American league by placing the California Angels in Los Angeles, the Angels had to pay damages to the Dodgers —in retrospect, a wholly unnecessary ransom to one of the nation's most successful franchises. More generally, an owner, if his vote is critical, may collect some bribe from the proponents of change by holding out at the beginning.

As a result of these features, cartels can be expected to be exceptionally conservative. Although this retards the adoption of bad ideas, it also weeds out much that is worthwhile. If good business ideas outnumber the bad—and continued technical progress indicates that they do—the result is inefficiently slow progress.

In most instances, the introduction of a competitive league is a response to failure to change on the part of the established league. For a new league to survive, it must be able to acquire viable franchise sites and quality players. Its success depends, therefore, on a failure by an established league to expand as fast as it should. Furthermore, new leagues or financially troubled older ones often adopt playing and institutional innovations many of which eventually are adopted by more successful—and more conservative—competitors. Thus, the

ABA added the 3-point long-shot basket, the World Football League used a limitation on total salary payments by a team rather than a player reservation system, and, in response to financial difficulties, the American League inserted the Designated Hitter into the lineup to add offense to a game many regard as too dull for contemporary tastes. Meanwhile, innovative owners—from Bill Veeck (who once pinch-hit a midget to draw a certain walk) to Charles Finley (who favors orange balls and two-platoon baseball)—are not only criticized by their peers, but pressured to leave the sport.

Conclusion

The actions of sports entrepreneurs indicate that the appropriate model for analyzing the industry is the familiar theory of a profit-maximizing, competitive firm that belongs to a cartel. The cartel has stability problems, owing to the fact that owners take advantage of opportunities to violate rules when they think they can get away with it and to respond competitively, rather than collusively, to situations not fully covered by league rules—often in so doing preventing the adoption of new rules to restore the cartel's ability to create protected monopolies. The cartel also tends to be lethargic, finding the adoption of mutually beneficial changes difficult.

Because a few cartel rights are difficult to breach—territorial rights and league membership, for example—the cartel can generate monopoly rents despite its weaknesses. And, because it can create barriers to entry, the introduction of competitive leagues is only a loose check on its operations. The result is economic inefficiencies of the following types:

1. Too few cities have teams, and too few teams are located in the largest markets.
2. Too few players are induced to play.
3. The operating and playing rules change too slowly.
4. Too few games are telecast, especially simultaneously.
5. Prices in the product market are too high for both tickets and broadcasting rights, although broadcasting is itself a source of inefficiency owing to its imperfectly competitive market structure.

IV. PUBLIC POLICY

The business of professional sports has been successful in the past in obtaining governmental sanction of its anticompetitive practices. The long-standing antitrust exemption of baseball's reserve clause, recently upheld in *Flood* v. *Kuhn*, is only one example. Legislative action has explicitly exempted cartel relations for selling broadcasting rights, and, in football, legislation passed in 1966 exempted the merger of the NFL and AFL from antitrust actions. Finally, local governments have raised barriers to the entry of new leagues by granting exclusive leases to publicly owned facilities and, in many cases, by renting these facilities at rates below cost.

Until the 1970s, the only major setback suffered by professional sports was the decision in *Radovich* v. *NFL*, which declared illegal football's counterpart to the baseball reserve clause. Although Congress did not override this decision with exempting legislation, as it later overrode judicial decisions that found leaguewide broadcasting packages illegal, the effect of *Radovich* is impossible to discern. By 1963, football had replaced the reserve system with the equally effective option-compensation system. The so-called Rozelle rule went without legal challenge until a spate of antitrust cases was launched by players in the mid-1970s.[30]

Since 1970, government has become less willing to sanction anticompetitive practices in sports. In 1971, the ABA and NBA requested congressional approval of a merger of the leagues. After protracted hearings, the Senate Subcommittee on Antitrust and Monopoly drew up a bill granting permission to merge—but only on the conditions that (1) the option-compensation system be eliminated, (2) the leagues adopt a revenue-sharing system in which the ABA received a proportionate share of broadcasting rights and the visiting team received 30 per cent of the gate, and (3) the free agent draft be changed so that a rookie would be bound to the team that drafted him for only 2 years. Because the NBA did not approve the terms of the bill, it died in committee and the leagues were not merged until 1976, when the settlement of the Robertson case forced the NBA to adopt conditions (1) and (3).

The record of pro sports has also not been good of late in winning court tests of its anticompetitive practices. In *Philadelphia World Hockey Club, Inc.*, Judge Higgenbotham ruled hockey's player reservation system unenforcible because it violated antitrust laws. His ruling permitted the WHA to retain the National Hockey League players it had signed, amounting to about 25 per cent of the previous season's NHL rosters. In *Kapp* v. *NFL* and in *Mackey et al.* v. *NFL*, the Rozelle rule was held to be a per se antitrust violation, although this will be appealed. In *Laird* v. *U.S.*,[31] the proportion of the original cost of a football team that can be allocated to player contracts and depreciated was reduced from 99 to 43 per cent in a decision still on appeal. If this decision holds, it will reduce the potential after-tax income to the owners of the Tampa and Seattle NFL expansion franchise by more than $1 million per year for the first 5 years they own the teams. The franchises originally sold for $16 million; depending on the tax status of the owners and how long each owner expected to retain the

---

[30] *Kapp* v. *NFL* and *Mackey, et al.* v. *NFL* have been discussed here; in addition, in *Smith* v. *NFL*, former Washington Redskins defensive back Yazoo Smith sued to recover the amount by which his first-year salary was depressed because of lack of competition for his services.

[31] Civ. 17892, U.S.D.C., Northern Georgia.

team, the ruling if it stands, will diminish the value of each team by $4 million to $7 million.[32]

Despite the gains in the last few years in undoing some of the special privileges enjoyed by sports, the long-run significance of the favorable judicial attitude is open to serious question. Even if the player reservation system is struck down, product market competition will still come only from new leagues, and historically competitive leagues always have either failed or merged. Although only football currently enjoys legislative permission for mergers, congressional permission appears necessary only if someone is likely to contest the merger as an antitrust violation. Usually, only players have done so in the past and, as the Robertson case settlement illustrates, they will permit mergers as long as competition for veteran players is protected. In any event, the other sports may well succeed in convincing Congress that legislative protection should be extended to them. Judging from the report of the Senate Subcommittee on Antitrust and Monopoly on the proposed merger of the two professional basketball leagues, Congress apparently was willing to permit merger if the leagues would guarantee that merger would not cause a reduction in the number of franchises and a restoration of the option-compensation system for controlling players.[33] Congress has shown no evidence to date of undoing most of the anticompetitive practices pertaining to the product market for sports, such as collective bargaining in the sale of broadcast rights, exclusive territorial franchises, and the tight controls leagues place on expansion.

Even if the opposition of players to mergers is overcome through liberalizing the contractual relationships of players and teams, the practices that most affect sports fans are unlikely to be affected. Only when an entire league can be formed does competition work in favor of the fan by increasing his access to sporting events. As already argued here, this is a weak control on the anticompetitive practices of established leagues.

The present antitrust environment is unlikely to deal with the issues affecting fans in large part because none of the major participants in the business of sports has an incentive to make the industry competitive. Clearly, both existing and potential owners regard the various restrictions against competition as desirable because they are the source of the profitability of ownership. A new league that gained entrance to the industry only by destroying these product market protec-

---

[32] If the team is sold each time the player depreciation is exhausted, the sales price will almost all be taxed as capital gains. For a wealthy individual, the capital gains tax rate is about half the rate on earned income. The ruling prevents the team from claiming about $8 million in depreciation over 5 years, which would reduce taxes by about $5.5 million could it be claimed. When the team is sold, capital gains taxes would claim $2.8 million more than if depreciation had not been taken. This cycle could be repeated every 5 years by different owners. The present value of an indefinite stream of revenues of plus $1.1 million every year and minus $2.8 million every 5 years is, at a 10 per cent discount rate, about $6.5 million. If the team is never sold, the 5 years of depreciation are worth, in present value terms, about $4 million.

[33] S. 2372, reported Sept. 18, 1972. The bill eventually died in committee when the leagues could not agree to merge under the terms of the bill. For further discussion, see Noll, op. cit., pp. 426–428.

tions would severely reduce its own future profits by so doing. Furthermore, players have no interest in increasing product market competition. The additional profitability of sports that results from these anticompetitive practices increases the market value of established players and generates a source of additional revenues that, through collective bargaining, can be shifted, at least in part, from owners to players.

In order to make sports more competitive in the economic sense, direct government intervention is probably necessary. Basically, this can take one of three forms: legislation can be written setting down the terms under which leagues can gain certain antitrust exemptions; a government agency could be established to deal with sports as a regulated industry, controlling some or all aspects of its behavior in both product and labor markets; or the Department of Justice could attack the structure of sports as anticompetitive on grounds other than those normally raised when players or competitive leagues seek antitrust relief.

Needless to say, the pros and cons of these alternative mechanisms are complicated, and a definitive review of them is not within the bounds of this chapter.[34] A summary judgment is that the performance of regulatory institutions in other industries is not particularly good, especially when the purchasers of the regulated industry's products are not particularly well represented by armies of lawyers and experts in the proceedings of the agency, so that enactment of a law establishing a Federal commission on sports would probably be unwise, and perhaps disastrous. Similarly, the demands on the Antitrust Division of the Department of Justice are so great compared to its resources that litigating suits against professional sports probably should not have a high priority in that agency especially because the actual outcome in terms of the institutional arrangements that the judicial system might favor is so much in doubt.

This leaves legislative remedy. The performance of the Senate Subcommittee on Antitrust and Monopoly in response to the requests for a basketball merger gives some hope for this alternative. Although the subcommittee did not directly attack many of the league practices that most affect fans, it did go a long way toward hammering out a workable set of rules for league operations. A significant achievement was its recognition of the importance of league rules regarding the sharing of revenues as a more important factor in determining the size and stability of leagues than the rules regarding competition for players. Because the issue at hand before Congress involved the sport for which consumer demand is weakest, compared to the three other major sports, it is not particularly surprising that the proposed legislation did not deal with the rules governing expansion, territorial rights, and exclusive stadium leases. Judging from the relatively sophisticated approach of the subcommittee to the problems of professional basketball, it is at least conceivable that a more sweeping examination of all sports might produce sensible legislative decisions on these issues as well.

---

[34] A more complete discussion can be found in Noll, *Government and the Sports Business*, op. cit., especially Steven R. Rivkin, "Sports Leagues and the Federal Antitrust Laws," and Roger G. Noll, "Alternatives in Sports Policy," pp. 387–428.

SUGGESTED READINGS

NONTECHNICAL

Andreano, Ralph. *No Joy in Mudville: The Dilemma of Major League Baseball.* Cambridge: Schenkman, 1965.

Durso, Joseph. *The All-American Dollar: The Big Business of Sports.* Boston: Houghton-Mifflin Company, 1971.

Koppett, Leonard. *A Thinking Man's Guide to Baseball.* New York: E. P. Dutton & Co., Inc., 1967.

Peterson, Robert. *Only the Ball Was White.* Englewood Cliffs, N.J.: Prentice-Hall, Inc., 1970.

Seymour, Harold. *Baseball: The Early Years.* New York: Oxford University Press, Inc., 1960.

———. *Baseball: The Golden Age.* New York: Oxford University Press, Inc., 1970.

Veeck, Bill, with Ed Linn. *Veeck—As in Wreck.* New York: G. P. Putnam's Sons, 1962.

TECHNICAL

El Hodiri, Mohamed, and James Quirk. "An Economic Model of a Professional Sports League." *Journal of Political Economy,* **70** (Nov.–Dec. 1971), pp. 1302–1319.

Jones, J. C. H. "The Economics of the National Hockey League." *Canadian Journal of Economics,* **2** (Feb. 1969), pp. 1–20.

Neale, Walter C. "The Peculiar Economics of Professional Sports." *Quarterly Journal of Economics,* **78** (Feb. 1964), pp. 1–14.

Noll, Roger G., ed. *Government and the Sports Business.* Washington, D.C.: The Brookings Institution, 1974.

Quirk, James. "An Economic Analysis of Team Movements in Professional Sports." *Law and Contemporary Problems,* **38** (Winter–Spring 1973), pp. 42–66.

Rottenberg, Simon. "The Baseball Players Labor Markets." *Journal of Political Economy,* **64** (June 1956), pp. 242–258.

Scully, Gerald W. "Economic Discrimination in Professional Sports." *Law and Contemporary Problems,* **38** (Winter–Spring 1973), pp. 67–84.

———. "Pay and Performance in Major League Baseball." *American Economic Review,* **64** (Dec. 1974), pp. 915–930.

Sloane, Peter J. "The Economics of Professional Football: The Football Club as a Utility Maximizer." *Scottish Journal of Political Economy,* **18** (June 1971), pp. 121–146. *Note:* Football here means soccer.

Topkis, Jay H. "Monopoly in Professional Sports." *Yale Law Journal,* **58** (Apr. 1949), pp. 691–712.

CHAPTER 12
the physicians' service industry
ELTON RAYACK

I. INTRODUCTION

"From a 'blessed benevolence' or a 'private luxury' medical care has gradually assumed the status of a necessity and a 'civic right.'"[1] The changed attitude toward medical care, the increase in population, and rapidly rising personal incomes have generated a pronounced growth in the demand for medical services. In 1929, private and public expenditures for medical care amounted to $3.6 billion, or 3.6 per cent of the gross national product (GNP); by 1973, they exceeded $94 billion and their share of the GNP, 7.7 per cent, had more than doubled.

Although private expenditures on medical care have increased more than fifteenfold since 1929, a growing share of the costs of medical care is being borne by the public sector. Public care as a per cent of total medical care expenditures doubled—from 13 to 26 per cent—from 1929–1966. The role of the public sector increased at an even more rapid rate with the start of the Federal Medicare program in July 1966, so that, in 1973, government expenditures accounted for almost 40 per cent of the nation's medical costs. The major share of public funds for medical care comes from the Federal government—about two thirds in 1973. Since 1960, Federal expenditures have increased 744 per cent, compared with a 272 per cent increase in state and local funds. Given Medicare and its probable extension the Federal government is destined to play an even larger role in the medical market in future years.

Medical care services and products are provided for by four major interrelated, yet quite distinct, industries—physicians, hospital, drug, and dental services—and a number of subsidiary industries. This chapter will concern itself

---

[1] Herman M. Somers and Anne R. Somers, *Doctors, Patients, and Health Insurance* (Washington, D.C.: Brookings, 1961), p. 133.

TABLE 1

Private Consumer Expenditures for Health Services
and Supplies, by Type of Expenditure,
1950 and 1972 (in millions of dollars)

	1950	1972
Total	8,501	46,170
Hospital care	1,965	14,840
Physicians' services	2,597	12,419
Dentists' services	961	4,771
Other professional services	370	1,395
Drugs	1,716	7,340
Eyeglasses and appliances	482	1,960
Nursing-home care	110	1,345
Expense for prepayment	300	2,000

Source: U.S. Department of Health, Education, and Welfare, *Social Security Bulletin*, **31**:18 (Apr. 1968) and **36**:1 (Jan. 1973).

primarily with the physicians' service industry, which, in 1972, attracted 27 per cent of the private consumers' medical dollar (see Table 1).

The $14.8 billion spent by consumers on the services of physicians, as large as the number is, greatly understates the economic significance of the doctor's role. For not only is the physician a supplier of services, but he also determines, in great part, the extent to which hospitals are utilized as well as the type and quantity of drugs consumed.

The idea of medical care as a basic necessity is of relatively recent origin. Only 75 years ago, poor patients were sent to hospitals to die. Nor could the patient at the turn of the century find much solace in the fact that he would receive the services of a physician, for, as a distinguished medical authority has stated: "I think it was about the year 1910 or 1912 when it became possible to say of the United States that a random patient with a random disease consulting a doctor chosen at random stood better than a fifty-fifty chance of benefiting from the encounter."[2] Under those conditions, the absence of any great public outcry for medical care is readily understandable.

During the last 50 years, the science and technology of modern medicine have created an incredible array of new tools and methods for controlling the forces of nature related to health—new and complex laboratory tests for accurate diagnoses, electronic and radar devices for pinpointing organic processes, heart-lung machines, the artificial kidney, organ transplantation, the electron microscope, and, perhaps the most revolutionary event in the history of medicine, the discovery of antibiotics. All these developments, and hundreds more, along with

[2] L. J. Henderson, as quoted in Alan Gregg, *Challenge in Contemporary Medicine* (New York: Columbia University Press, 1956), p. 13.

the general rise in the standard of living, have produced dramatic decreases in death rates and increases in life expectancy. Crude death rates fell from 17.2 per cent per 1000 population in 1900 to 9.3 in 1971. In 1900, an infant had a life expectancy of 47 years; by 1971, he could look forward to 71 years of life, an increase of almost 50 per cent.

Yet, despite these advances, the available data suggest that *morbidity rates have actually risen*! The paradox of longer life and more illness may in great part be explained by the increased significance of the aged in our population. The increased life span has led to a higher incidence of the chronic degenerative diseases associated primarily with the aged and to a decline in acute infectious diseases, which primarily attack the young. Influenza and pneumonia, tuberculosis and enteritis—all acute infectious diseases that primarily attack the young —were the "killers" at the beginning of the century. Recently, the leading causes of death have been diseases of the heart, cancer, and vascular lesions of the central nervous system—chronic diseases associated primarily with older age groups. Because the chronic diseases are frequently of long duration, they add significance to the demand for medical care.

Despite the enormous benefits reaped from the medical revolution, and paradoxically in part because of it, for more than two decades there has been considerable controversy concerning the adequacy of the operation of the market for medical services. The debate has focused on several major interrelated problems:

1. The sharp growth in demand for physician's services has not been matched by a sufficient increase in supply. The resulting shortage is reflected in enormous increases in the incomes of doctors and heavy reliance on the use of foreign-trained physicians. Because the latter are often less adequately trained than graduates of American medical schools, there is serious concern about a possible deterioration in the quality of medical care.

2. The medical care component of the Bureau of Labor Statistics (BLS) Consumer Price Index (CPI) has, since the end of World War II, risen more rapidly than any other item priced. The increases in hospital daily service charges have been particularly sharp, but physicians' fees, the item of primary concern in this chapter, also have bolted upward. While the CPI increased 165 per cent between 1945 and 1974, physicians' fees rose by 215 per cent.

3. There is a real need to develop new techniques in the methods of producing and financing medical care. Discussion of alternatives has focused on several key questions: Does group practice offer opportunities for reducing costs and improving the quality and the quantity of medical services? Has the profession gone too far in the direction of specialization? Would it be desirable to develop health practitioners less highly trained than the medical doctor to take over some of the tasks of the expensively produced physician? Are there insurance techniques or methods of reimbursing the physician that might place a check on rising medical costs?

4. Serious doubts have been raised concerning the quality of American medical care. Major studies have been conducted indicating physicians engage in

substantial amounts of unnecessary surgery and that the quality of care provided by many general practitioners leaves much to be desired. Data on infant mortality, life expectancy, and death rates suggest that there are serious deficiencies in American medical care. In 1972, the United States had higher infant mortality rates than 11 other countries. Life expectancy for American males ranges from about 1.2 to 5 years behind that of males in Norway, Sweden, Denmark, the Netherlands, France, England, and Canada. It is of particular economic significance that the United States has significantly higher death rates for males between the ages of forty and fifty-five—the most productive years—than did 14 other well-developed nations.[3]

II. MARKET STRUCTURE

In 1971, there were 322,288 physicians in active practice in the United States. Of these 194,922 (61 per cent) were in office-based practices; 68,798 (21 per cent) in hospital-based practices as full-time staff or in training as interns or residents; and 58,498 (18 per cent) in other types of practice such as Federal service, full-time medical school faculty, administrative medicine, laboratory medicine, preventative medicine, or research.[4]

Despite enormous technological changes in the industry, the most common type of firm remains that of the solo practitioner, the man with a solely owned private practice. Sixty per cent of the private practitioners are in solo practice, about 19 per cent are in two-man partnerships or in some type of informal relationship with one or more physicians, another 19 per cent are working under some formal relationship with three or more physicians, and the remaining 2 per cent are physicians employed by other physicians or by organizations other than hospitals.[5]

Although solo practice continues as the dominant form of business organization, the scientific and technological revolutions in medicine have forced sweeping changes in other characteristics of medical practice. Perhaps no other development so dramatically reflects the twentieth-century revolution in medical practice as the growth of specialization. No longer is it possible for the general practitioner to effectively meet the medical needs of the public with his accumulated knowledge and the few tools carried in his proverbial "little black bag." So vast is the amount of medical knowledge amassed during this century that it is virtually impossible for any single physician to master all but a small portion of the science and art of modern medicine. As recently as 1931, about 80 per cent of all physicians were in general practice or part-time specialities; by 1971, only 17 per cent were in general practice.

---

[3] The United Nations, *Demographic Yearbook, 1972* (New York: The United Nations, 1973).

[4] U.S. Department of Health, Education, and Welfare, *Health Resource Statistics, 1972–1973* (Washington, D.C.: U.S. Government Printing Office, 1973), pp. 187 and 488. Also, Christ N. Theodore and Gerald E. Sutter, "A Report on the First Periodic Survey of Physicians," *Journal of the American Medical Association*, 202:520 (Nov. 6, 1967).

[5] Theodore and Sutter, op. cit., p. 520.

An inevitable concomitant of specialization is mutual dependence. Interdependence is not limited to physicians organized in groups. Even the solo practitioner must depend on other physicians in various specialties to whom he can refer patients with ailments beyond his knowledge or ability to treat successfully. Nor is the specialist independent, for almost his entire practice flows from the referral of general practitioners and physicians in other specialties.

Another major development increasing the dependence of physicians on others has been the phenomenal growth in number of other health personnel. In 1900, for every physician in practice, there was one other health practitioner. Today, the ratio of professional and technical workers in the health field to physicians is almost four and one-half to one.

The dependence of the physician on others also has increased because it is no longer financially possible for him to acquire more than an infinitesimal fraction of the costly tools so essential for modern medical care; laboratory, diagnostic medical, and surgical equipment are so expensive that they impose heavy burdens even on the resources of entire communities. As a result, the hospital, to a substantial extent, has become the workshop of the doctor. Doctors now earn nearly half their income from hospital-connected work.[6]

The large number of firms in the physicians' service industry and the small size of each might suggest that we are dealing with an industry closely approximating perfectly competitive conditions. However, there are other elements in the market structure—the nature of the product, consumer ignorance, and the various powers vested in the industry's key professional organization, the American Medical Association (AMA)—that combine to make the industry one of the most highly monopolistic in the country. Let us turn to an examination of these factors.

Consumer Ignorance and Professional Power

A prerequisite for the effective operation of any market is that the consumer have considerable knowledge concerning the nature of the product so that he can make a rational choice in attempting to maximize his satisfaction. A fundamental characteristic of the medical services' market, however, is the relative lack of knowledge on the part of the consumer. Medical knowledge is extraordinarily complex, so complex that the knowledge possessed by the physician concerning the necessity for, or consequences of, treatment is tremendously greater than that possessed by the consumer.

It is the physician who decides whether or not drugs are required, whether or not hospitalization is desirable, whether or not surgery is necessary, and by his recommendation he can create a demand for his own product. The consumer has no way of knowing which alternative is best for him—he must rely on his

---

[6] George Bugbee, "Administration and the Professional in the Hospital," Address for the Upper Midwest Hospital Conference, Health Information Foundation (mimeo), May 1960, p. 2. Cited by Somers and Somers, op. cit., pp. 68–69.

faith in the integrity and competence of the physician. Moreover, the consequences of a wrong choice on the part of the consumer can be disastrous.

In recognition of the inevitable baneful consequences of permitting *caveat emptor* to prevail in the medical market place, society has granted considerable power to organized medicine to maintain quality standards and to police the profession.[7] And it is precisely this delegation of authority that is the seminal source of the AMA's power.

Membership and Formal Structure of the AMA

Approximately 219,000, or 78 per cent, of America's physicians are in the ranks of organized medicine. Aside from southern Negro physicians barred because of color, nonmembers are primarily physicians outside private practice—in the armed services, medical school professors, physicians engaged in research, doctors-in-training, and public health officers. A 1960 study indicated that only 35 per cent of the physicians not in private practice were AMA members. Of physicians engaged in private practice, however, probably about 80 per cent are members of the AMA.

The formal structure of the AMA is patterned roughly after the American Federal system, with governing bodies at the Federal, state, and county levels At the base of organized medicine's political pyramid are 1966 county medical societies. The county societies are "component" bodies of the 55 autonomous state and territorial associations, and the latter are, in turn, "constituent" associations of the summit federation, the AMA. Except in rare instances, it is not possible for a physician to join the AMA directly; he must first be admitted to the county of state medical society. The county societies select delegates to the governing body of their state societies and the latter—not the membership—choose representatives to the AMA policy-making House of Delegates.

Although the AMA constitution designates the 238-member House of Delegates as its legislative and policy-making body, much, if not most, of the effective power at the national level rests with the House-elected board of trustees. Because the House meets for a few days semiannually, many of the basic policy and administrative decisions are of necessity left to the board. Although technically responsible to the House of Delegates, the board functions with practically no supervision when the House is not in session, and the AMA constitution gives the board a blank check on organized medicine's treasury. The members of the board, in effect, "perform the typical role of corporate directors."[8]

---

[7] For a brilliant analysis of the significance and implications of consumer ignorance and uncertainty in the purchase of medical care, see Kenneth J. Arrow, "Uncertainty and the Welfare Economics of Medical Care," *American Economic Review*, **53**:941 (Dec. 1963).

[8] David R. Hyde, Payson Wolff, Anne Gross, and Elliott Lee Hoffman, "The American Medical Association: Power, Purpose, and Politics in Organized Medicine," *Yale Law Journal*, **43**:943 (May 1954). This article is a classic in the field and a basic source of primary data on organized medicine.

Medical Licensure, Medical Schools, and Hospitals

The laudable goal of medical licensure is to ensure practioners competence through tests, minimum education requirements, or some other demonstration of ability. In order to practice in a particular state or territory a physician must meet the requirements of that political unit's medical examining board. The policies of the various state boards of medical examiners are virtually identical with those of the AMA. This is an inevitable product of the fact that, in about half the states, the medical society recommends appointees to the state board; in others, the society nominates candidates for the office; and in one, the State Medical Society Board of Censors itself constitutes the State Board of Medical Examiners.

In granting sole authority to the boards to issue licenses, society has, in effect, given considerable power to organized medicine to restrict the supply of physicians and to influence the patterns of medical care for the benefit of the profession. As Milton Friedman has argued, licensure is the "key to the control" that the AMA exercises over the number of physicians trained. Its essential control is at the stage of admission to medical school. Medical schools are approved by the AMA Council on Medical Education; to stay on the approved list, a school must meet the standards set up by the council. The council's approval is crucial to the existence of a medical school, because, in almost every state in the United States, a person must be licensed to practice medicine, and to get the license he must be a graduate of an approved school. Generally, the list of approved schools is identical with the list of schools approved by the council. Loss of approval would make it extremely difficult for a school's graduates to obtain licenses. That is why the licensure procedure is the key to the effective control of admission.[9] By directly exerting pressure on schools to restrict admissions, or by requiring very high-quality standards, the AMA can restrict the supply of physicians.

State licensure laws together with the activities of the AMA Council on Medical Education and Hospitals also make it possible for organized medicine to exercise control over admission to practice in hospitals. The council approves hospitals as well as medical schools. Of crucial significance is the fact that the council has "final responsibility for approval of internship programs."[10] State licensure generally requires a candidate to complete an internship in an "approved" hospital before being admitted to practice, and the licensing boards' lists of approved schools are generaly identical to the AMA council list. Loss of council approval would be a deadly blow to a hospital because it would then be virtually impossible for it to obtain the staff of interns so vital for the operation of a hospital today. The threat of council disapproval has been an effective weapon to exert pressure on hospitals to follow the AMA line in organized medicine's many battles against the development of group practice.

[9] Milton Friedman, *Capitalism and Freedom* (Chicago: University of Chicago Press, 1962), pp. 150–155.

[10] AMA, *Directory of Approved Internships and Residencies* (Chicago: AMA, 1964), p. 1.

In addition to being regulated by the medical practices acts of the various states, the physician is governed by the AMA *Principles of Medical Ethics.* Frequently, "unethical" practices have been interpreted by AMA leadership to include such acts as participation in local insurance schemes not approved by organized medicine, association with health practitioners the AMA refers to as "cultists" (for example, osteopaths, chiropractors, and optometrists), and acceptance of salaried arrangements that are not in accord with the AMA sacrosanct fee-for-service principle.

Organized medicine's power over the physician to make him conform to its standards exists for the most part at the county society level. Not only does the county society have the sole authority to admit a physician to membership, "there is no right to a hearing and no appeal from the society's verdict" to deny membership.[11] In addition, most discipline cases have been handled at the county level with not even so much as a report being made to the state society.

Ethical standards of the AMA can often be enforced against an offending physician at the county society level without any formal action. As Oliver Garceau pointed out 35 years ago in discussing the sanctions available to organized medicine:

> First, of course, and never out of use, is social pressure in a small group. The social life of the county society is important to some doctors. Few can wholly disregard it, simply because a doctor can ill afford more than a few enemies, certainly not the hostility of an organized group in positions of local prominence. His reputation is a fragile thing, and his income and practice depend upon being called in consultation, though perhaps more vitally on being able to call his colleagues in emergencies. Ostracism becomes a terrible weapon in such a business.[12]

What Garceau wrote in 1940 has even greater validity today due to the fantastic growth in medical specialization. Under present conditions, denial of patient referrals and consultation can drastically reduce a specialist's income.

Should informal pressures prove inadequate to compel a recalcitrant physician to mend his ways, formal sanctions can be invoked by the county society's board of censors. Formal action could result in denial of membership application or expulsion from the county medical society, actions that can have dire consequences for the offending physician. Nonmembership may prevent an applicant from taking advantage of reciprocal licensing provisions to practice in other states. In Delaware, a physician moving from Chester, Pennsylvania, was recently denied licensure "because he was not affiliated with any of the hospitals in Chester and he did not belong to the Medical Society in the county in which he practiced."[13]

A nonmember may also find it very costly, or impossible, to purchase malpractice insurance. Insurance rates are sometimes 20 to 100 per cent higher for

[11] Hyde et al., op. cit., p. 950.

[12] Oliver Garceau, *The Political Life of the American Medical Association* (Cambridge, Mass.: Harvard University Press, 1941), p. 103.

[13] *Federation Bulletin,* June 1965, p. 205.

nonmembers, and some insurance companies refuse to issue them policies. According to 1958 AMA data, one in seven living physicians had been the target of a malpractice suit or claim. The annual cost of damages, settlements, and legal fees in 1970 exceeded $90 million! Because such claims are so frequent and costly, adequate insurance is a necessity for the physician.[14]

Nonmembership has its greatest impact in the severe limits it places on the opportunity to practice. A nonmember may be blocked from specialty certification and, hence, barred from the more lucrative specialty practice. Most damaging of all, he will be denied the use of most hospital facilities. Because perhaps about half the average doctor's income is derived from hospital-connected work, being barred from the use of hospitals can be a devastating blow.

The Medical Lobby

In addition to the economic power the AMA derives from its position as a professional association, it has substantial financial resources that enable it to engage in costly propaganda campaigns, extensive political activity, and vigorous lobbying. During the last 20 years, the AMA has spent millions— more than any other single pressure group—to maintain a highly effective Washington lobby. In 1949 and 1950, AMA lobbying expenditures were almost double those of the second-ranked lobbyist and greater than those of such big spenders as the National Association of Manufacturers, the AFL-CIO, and the various veterans' organizations. In 1951 and 1952, the AMA finished a strong third and second, respectively,[15] as it successfully fought President Truman's national health insurance proposals and legislation that would have provided much-needed Federal aid for medical schools.

The AMA's 1965 campaign against Medicare broke all recent records for expenditures by lobbyists. In the *first quarter* of 1965, the AMA spent more than $950,000. Since reports of spending by lobbyists were first required by Federal legislation in 1947, there have been only 4 years when spending by any organization reached or exceeded $900,000—and in three of those occasions the AMA was the group involved. None of this, it should be noted, includes the spending of state and county medical societies affiliated with the AMA.

Moreover, the AMA budget does not include all the expenditures by organized medicine in fighting legislation it considers inimical to its interests. In September 1961, the AMA created the American Medical Political Action Committee (AMPAC) as an independent operation for the purpose of organizing doctors into an effective political action group. AMPAC was formed by the AMA because the latter, as a corporation, is forbidden to make direct campaign contributions for political candidates. The board of directors of AMPAC was

[14] Hyde et al., op. cit., p. 951, and U.S., Department of Health, Education, and Welfare, *Report of the Secretary's Commission on Medical Malpractice*, Appendix (Washington, D.C.: U.S. Government Printing Office, 1973), p. 1.

[15] *Legislators and Lobbyists* (Washington, D.C.: Congressional Quarterly Service, 1965), pp. 33, 34, and 37.

appointed by the AMA Board of Trustees,[16] and, in 1962, the AMA supported AMPAC with a $50,000 contribution. By mid-1963, AMPAC had helped establish political action committees in all states but Mississippi and Ohio. In the 1962 elections it distributed to congressional candidates about $250,000, a figure that does not include the expenditures of committees at the state and local level.[17] The funds in 1962 were devoted to four key Senate races and 75 to 80 House races, with most of the money going to support members of the House Ways and Means Committee who were opposed to the King–Anderson bill.[18] In the 1964 political campaign, AMPAC spent $402,000 and was seventeenth in a list of 164 organizations filing reports with the U.S. House of Representatives. According to a tabulation by the *Washington Post*, AMPAC and its 38 state and local committees donated a total of $1.5 million to more than 300 congressional candidates in the 2 years since the 1972 elections, years when health insurance legislation was a major issue before Congress.[19]

III. CONDUCT

Analysis of the behavior of physicians and their professional organizations reveals a long history of price discrimination, severe restrictions on entry into the field, widespread opposition to marketing innovations, particularly with respect to the development of voluntary health insurance, restrictive practice by specialists vis-à-vis general practitioners and among specialists, and restrictions imposed on the activities of health practitioners who are not medical doctors.

Price Discrimination

Price discrimination by physicians—that is, varying fees with the income of patients—has become the classic textbook illustration of the discriminating monopolist. By charging higher prices for the rich and lower prices for the poor, the physician is increasing his income by taking advantage of the smaller elasticity of demand for medical services on the part of the wealthy.

Price discrimination by physicians is not, as doctors argue, merely a charitable activity to aid the poor. A Health Information Foundation—National Opinion Research Center survey of family doctors, in 1955, revealed that 63 per cent take "ability to pay" into account when setting fees. The survey also found that such price discrimination is more common among members of specialized societies, big-city practitioners, and those in the Far West than among general practitioners in small communities where doctors are likely to be in the best position to evaluate the patient's income and wealth. In commenting on this survey, the Somers have concluded that "apparently [sliding fees] are now used

---

[16] *New York Times*, Mar. 18, 1962, p. 70.
[17] *Wall Street Journal*, July 2, 1963, p. 12.
[18] *Medical Economics*, Nov. 6, 1962, p. 267.
[19] *Congressional Quarterly Weekly Report*, Jan. 21, 1966, pt. 1, p. 72; *Providence Evening Bulletin*, Oct. 29, 1974, p. A–16.

primarily as a device for raising fees above the standard, as increasingly established by health insurance practices, rather than for lowering them for the poor, their major historical justification."[20] Furthermore, as Reuben A. Kessel points out:

> Existing evidence indicates that if income and wealth differences are held constant, people who have medical insurance pay more for the same service than people who do not have such insurance. Union leaders have found that the fees charged have risen as a result of the acquisition of medical insurance by their members. . . . Members of the insurance industry have found that "the greater the benefit provided the higher the surgical bill." This suggests that the principle used for the determination of fees is . . . what the traffic will bear.[21]

Restrictions on Entry

In 1925, the Association of American Medical Colleges (AAMC) organized the Commission on Medical Education to make a study of the education principles involved in medical education and licensure. The work of the commission was in great part financed by the AMA. The commission's *Final Report*, released in 1932, stated:

> It is clear that in the immediate past there has been a larger production [of physicians] than necessary and that at the present time we have an oversupply . . . of at least 25,000 physicians in this country. . . . An oversupply is likely to introduce excessive economic competition, the performance of unnecessary services, an elevated total cost of medical care, and conditions in the profession which will not encourage students of superior ability and character to enter the profession.[22]

The concern of the commission over "excessive economic competition" was undoubtedly a product of sharply falling medical income. Between 1929–1932, the incomes of physicians fell almost 40 per cent.

In a not too veiled recommendation for a restrictionist policy, the report concluded: "Those responsible for medical education and for the licensure of physicians, particularly for graduates from foreign medical schools, should have the situation clearly before them."[23] The commission's *Final Report* laid the groundwork for organized medicine's drive to restrict the production of physicians during the 1930s.

In an editorial in August 1932, the *Journal of the American Medical Association* (JAMA) stated that "the United States already has more doctors in proportion to its population than any other country in the world," and that "if this ratio is still further increased it is evident that an oversupply of doctors threatens with an inevitable lowering of the standards of the profession." The editorial concluded prophetically that "perhaps there is need for professional birth control."[24]

[20] Somers and Somers, op. cit., pp. 53–54.

[21] Reuben A. Kessel, "Price Discrimination in Medicine," eds., William Breit and Harold M. Hochman, *Readings in Microeconomics* (New York: Holt, 1968), pp. 320–321.

[22] *Final Report of the Commission on Medical Education* (New York, 1932), pp. 89, 93, and 100.

[23] Ibid., p. 100.

[24] *JAMA*, **99**:765 (Aug. 27, 1932).

In his presidential address before the AMA convention in mid-1933, Dr. Dean D. Lewis asserted: "There apparently is an overproduction of doctors. How such an overproduction can be controlled is a problem for the Council on Medical Education and Hospitals."[25] A year later there was no question in the mind of the new president of the AMA, Dr. Walter L. Bierring, concerning both the overproduction of doctors and what to do about it:

> one is forced to the conviction that more doctors are being turned out than society needs and can comfortably reward. . . . The time has arrived for the American Medical Association to take the initiative and point the way. During the coming year the association, through the Council on Medical Education and Hospitals, will institute a resurvey of the medical schools of the country . . . it will require real courage and tenacity to bend the educational processes to the urgent social and economic needs of the changing order. A fine piece of educational work could well be done if we were to use only half of the seventy-odd medical schools in the United States.[26]

The mechanism for exerting pressure on the medical colleges with respect to admission policy was the survey of medical schools conducted by the AMA Council on Medical Education in cooperation with the Federation of State Medical Boards and the AAMC. During the years 1934–1936, the council visited and evaluated 89 schools in the United States and Canada. In reporting on its survey to the Annual Congress on Medical Education, Medical Licensure, and Hospitals in 1936, the council was able to state: "Most of the schools . . . which . . . allowed themselves to yield to the demands of this increasing number of applicants and to take in larger numbers of students than they have been able to care for properly . . . have expressed their readiness to cooperate with us by reducing the size of their student body."[27] In 1937, the chairman of the council reported: "A reduction in the quota of students received for admission is now being made by a number of our medical schools."[28]

The AMA pressure on medical schools had a substantial impact. Despite the fact that there was virtually no change in the number of applicants between the academic years 1933–1934 and 1938–1939, the number of acceptances fell by 1355, a decline of 17.9 per cent, and the percentage of applicants accepted fell by 17.8 per cent. Fully 74 per cent of the decline in the number of applicants accepted occurred within 2 years of the AMA's Council on Medical Education's 1935 warning to medical schools against the admission of larger classes.[29] The success of organized medicine's restrictionist activities during the 1930s con-

[25] *JAMA*, **100**:1908 (June 17, 1933).

[26] Walter L. Bierring, "The Family Doctor and the Changing Order," *JAMA*, **102**:1997 (June 16, 1934).

[27] *JAMA*, **106**:1393 (Apr. 18, 1936); *JAMA*, **108**:771 (Mar. 6, 1937).

[28] *Journal of Medical Education*, **35**:224 (Mar. 1960).

[29] It is of more than passing interest that the AMA's own detailed 1200-page official history, published in 1947, contains not a single word of reference to its restrictionist objectives of the 1930s! See Morris Fishbein, *A History of the American Medical Association, 1847–1947* (Philadelphia: Saunders, 1947).

tributed to the shortage of physicians that has persisted since the end of World War II.

In the post-World War II years, the demand for medical services continued to grow, and there was a pronounced rise in the number of applicants to medical schools. Pressure for medical education grew tremendously, but the inadequacy of existing facilities set an upper limit to the number of students who could be enrolled. Although the annual number of applicants for the years 1947–1950 was about double the pre-World War II annual rate, the increase in the number accepted was relatively small; whereas in the pre-World War II years more than 50 per cent of the applicants were accepted annually, in the post-World War II years, acceptance dropped to about the 30 per cent level.

In the face of rising demand for medical education and the resultant stresses and strains imposed on existing medical school facilities, the AMA again turned toward restrictionism. However, instead of exerting direct pressure on medical schools to curtail enrollment as it did in the 1930s—this was not necessary because a ceiling on admission was already effectively established by the limited facilities—the AMA in the post-World War II years turned toward slowing down the growth in the number of doctors by vigorously opposing the provision of much-needed Federal aid to medical education.

1. From 1946 to 1950, the AMA vigorously and vehemently opposed all forms of Federal aid to medical education that would tend to increase the supply of physicians, arguing not only that there was no danger of a shortage of physicians, but that there was even the possibility of a surplus by 1960.

2. As the pressures for Federal aid grew, organized medicine retreated somewhat and, in the years 1951–1958, reluctantly accepted the principle of such aid for one-time construction grants when there was a "demonstrated emergency." However, it continued to deny there was any danger of a physician shortage and maintained its strong opposition to Federal aid for the operational expenses of medical schools. To still demands for Federal aid, the AMA pressed its program of seeking funds for medical schools from private sources.

3. After 1958, the AMA finally conceded that there was a real danger of a serious physician shortage, that medical schools were in dire financial need, and, therefore, Federal assistance for construction purposes was necessary. It was, nevertheless, still opposed to Federal aid for scholarships and for operational expenses. However, so successful in preventing an adequate growth of medical schools was organized medicine's 20-year campaign against Federal aid that even the AMA finally admitted that it would take prompt and massive aid to prevent a serious shortage of physicians.[30]

Restrictive Practices and Voluntary Insurance

Despite the recent denials of organized medicine, there is abundant evidence to demonstrate that the AMA was a vigorous opponent of private health

[30] A detailed discussion of the AMA opposition to Federal aid to medical schools is presented in this writer's *Professional Power and American Medicine* (New York: World, 1967), pp. 81–101.

insurance in the early 1930s. The AMA then argued that "all such schemes are contrary to sound public policy and that the shortest road to the commercialization of the practice of medicine is through the supposed rosy path of insurance."[31] By 1949, private health insurance—"the voluntary way"—had become to the AMA "the American way." The metamorphosis from passionate enemy to reluctant lover had been completed with the threat of compulsory insurance as the catalytic agent. The purpose of this section is to examine the practices of organized medicine as it responded to the development of voluntary health insurance.

Farmers Union Hospital Association

In 1929, Dr. Michael Shadid contributed $20,000 to the Farmers Union Hospital Association, enabling it to establish the Community Hospital Clinic of Elk City, Oklahoma, perhaps the first consumer cooperative in the field of medical care. The members of the cooperative own the hospital, pay the staff doctors fixed salaries, and receive medical care on a prepaid basis. From its inception and for more than two decades, the cooperative was harassed by the local county medical society. Dr. Shadid, the hospital's first medical director, was the medical society's prime target. Despite the fact that he had been a respected member of the medical society for 20 years, organized medicine tried to destroy him and his hospital. Because the society's members had no legitimate reason for expelling Dr. Shadid, they resorted to the incredibly ludicrous procedure of dissolving the society for 6 months and then reorganizing without him! The county society also tried to get legislation passed that would have had the effect of outlawing the Community Hospital Clinic. For more than 20 years, other members of the hospital's staff were barred from the local medical society. Finally, in 1950, the Farmers Union Hospital Association brought suit against the county society and its members. Charging its opponents with being involved in a conspiracy in restraint of trade, the union sued for $300,000 in damages and threatened to carry the case to the Supreme Court. Although the county society employed delaying tactics, it finally agreed to settle out of court. The damage suit was dropped as the medical society agreed to admit the cooperative's doctors to membership.[32]

The Group Health Association

In 1937, employees of the Federal Home Owners' Loan Corporation in Washington, D.C., formed a nonprofit cooperative—the Group Health Association (GHA). Aided by a $40,000 grant from the loan corporation, they equipped a clinic, engaged doctors, and assessed themselves monthly prepayments to

---

[31] *JAMA*, **99**: 1951 (Dec. 3, 1932).

[32] James Howard Means, *Doctors, People, and Government* (Boston: Little Brown, 1953), pp. 175–176; U.S. Congress, Senate Subcommittee on Health of the Committee on Labor and Public Welfare, *Hearings on S.1805, Cooperative Health Act*, 81st Cong., 2d sess., 1950, pp. 213–217; U.S. Congress, House Committee on Interstate and Foreign Commerce, *Hearings on Health Inquiry*, 83rd Cong., 2d sess., 1954, pt. 6, p. 1787.

finance medical care and hospitalization for themselves and their families and sought members in other Federal agencies. Almost immediately, GHA was attacked on legal grounds by the District of Columbia Medical Society as being improperly engaged in the insurance business and in the "corporate practice of medicine."[33]

Two basic characteristics of the GHA plan aroused (and still arouse) the ire of organized medicine: (1) "Closed panel" practice—that is, subscribers to the insurance plan, if they are to receive its benefits, must use doctors associated with the plan—and (2) the use of a "prepayment" rather than fee-for-service system. Under prepayment, the subscriber, for a fixed premium paid in advance, is guaranteed certain specific services. Organized medicine much prefers the fee-for-service system because it gives the physician considerably more control over the price—he can charge what the market will bear.

When the attempt to destroy the GHA by legal action in the courts failed, the medical society resorted to direct action. The district society ruled that GHA doctors were "unethical" for participating in closed-panel practice and refused them admission to the medical society or, if they were already in it, expelled them. Doctors who consulted with GHA physicians were threatened with expulsion from the medical society. Pressure was brought to bear on local hospitals to close their doors to GHA physicians, and, as a result, the doctors were unable to treat the GHA patients in those hospitals. The press reported stories of sick people denied treatment, consultation, or operations. Some of the doctors resigned under the pressure, but most stood by the GHA. The AMA national office condemned the GHA plan as unethical, sent staff members to advise the District of Columbia Medical Society, and instructed the *JAMA* editor to bring the situation to the attention of the entire medical profession.[34]

The actions of organized medicine made it very difficult for the GHA to recruit physicians and to assure its subscribers the quality care for which they had paid. Only July 31, 1938, Assistant Attorney General Thurman Arnold announced that the Department of Justice proposed to prosecute the district society and the AMA under the Federal antitrust laws if a grand jury investigation resulted in an indictment. In less than 3 months a special grand jury returned indictments. In a subsequent hearing before Justice James M. Proctor in the U.S. District Court for the District of Columbia, the indictment was quashed on the ground that medical practice was not a "trade" and, hence, not subject to the antitrust laws. In March 1940, the court of appeals reversed the decision by Justice Proctor, a trial was hed, and, in April 1941, the jury found the medical associations guilty as charged. Organized medicine than carried the case to the court of appeals, which, by a unanimous vote, upheld the jury's decision. In a ringing indictment, Associate Justice Justin Miller, who delivered the opinion, blasted organized medicine in words that went to the heart of the problem:

[33] Committee on Research in Medical Economics, *Restrictions on Free Enterprise in Medicine* (New York, 1949), p. 12.

[34] Morris Fishbein, *A History of the American Medical Association* (Philadelphia: Saunders, 1947), p. 545.

Professions exist because the people believe they will be better served by licensing especially prepared experts to minister their needs. The licensed monopolies which professions enjoy constitute in themselves severe restraints upon competition. But they are restraints which depend upon capacity and training, not special privilege.

Neither do they justify concentrated criminal action to prevent the people from developing new methods of serving their needs. There is sufficient historical evidence of professional inadequacy to justify occasional popular protest.

The better educated laity of today questions the adequacy of present-day medicine. Their challenge finds support from substantial portions of the medical profession itself. The people give the privilege of professional monopoly and the people may take it away.[35]

The decision, upheld by a unanimous Supreme Court opinion on January 18, 1943, pointed out that the medical societies had combined and conspired to prevent the successful operation of the GHA by taking the following steps: "(1) to impose restraints on physicians affiliated with Group Health by threat of expulsion or actual expulsion from the societies; (2) to deny them the essential professional contacts with other physicians; and (3) to use coercive power of the societies to deprive them of hospital facilities for patients."[36] The loss of the case was a serious blow to the prestige and power of organized medicine and a crucial victory for the "independent" insurance plans.

Health Insurance Plan of Greater New York (HIP)

The Health Insurance Plan of Greater New York was the product of several years of planning aimed at providing prepaid comprehensive medical service of high quality for persons of moderate means in the New York metropolitan area. The initial impetus for the plan came from New York's Mayor LaGuardia, when, in 1944, he announced that the city would pay half the premiums of group health insurance for municipal employees if the coverage could be truly comprehensive. With the help of $855,000 in loans (subsequently repaid in full) supplied by several philanthropic foundations, HIP began to operate in March 1947. The services are currently provided by 31 medical groups scattered throughout New York City and Nassau City. The plan does not cover hospital expenses, only doctor's bills, but the plan requires its members to join Blue Cross or some other hospitalization plan.

From its inception, HIP ran into difficulties with organized medicine, which again raised the cry that the free choice of physician was being denied. The local medical societies subjected HIP to the same kind of pressure exerted against prepaid group-practice plans in other parts of the country. The situation came to a head in 1960 and exploded in the press when a hospital-accredited obstetrician in Staten Island died of an ulcer worsened by what his colleagues said was

---

[35] Committee on Research in Medical Economics, op. cit. pp. 13 and 14; and *New York Times*, June 16, 1942, p. 1.

[36] *AMA* v. *United States*, 317 U.S. 519(1943), as quoted in Franz Goldmann, *Voluntary Medical Care Plans in the United States* (New York: Columbia University Press, 1948), pp. 55–61.

cruel overwork. A staff position for a badly needed assistant for the doctor had been refused. About 30 months prior to his death, Staten Island's three large hospitals suddenly closed their doors and, until the controversy flared up in the press, did not permit a single additional HIP physician to have staff privileges. This despite the fact that 24,000 of HIP subscribers lived on Staten Island.

Aroused by these developments, the New York State Legislative Committee on Health Insurance Plans held public hearings. As the *New York Times* stated in reviewing the hearings:

> There is no doubt that, for the past 30 months, no HIP physician has been given the privilege of admitting patients to any of the three nonprofit Staten Island hospitals. This has been a formidable handicap for HIP in giving its subscribers the best and promptest hospital care. It is clear also, from the testimony of the hospital representatives themselves, that this has come about primarily because of their dislike of, and opposition to, the group practice, prepayment types of medical service—"a repugnant ideology" as one of them called it. As usual, ideological differences bred personal antagonism that led to ostracism. No evidence was given that the denial of hospital privileges in any case is based on a lack of professional skill.[37]

Under public pressure, the hospitals on the island agreed to appoint to their staffs five physicians associated with HIP.[38]

The fight over hospital appointments for HIP physicians however, was not over. Two years later, the presiding supervisor of the town of Hempstead asserted that it is an "irrefutable fact that there is serious discrimination and it must be ended."[39] In response, Nassau County, with 60,000 HIP subscribers, on October 29, 1962, became the first county in the nation to prohibit discrimination against physicians associated with group medical plans.[40] About a year later the New York state legislature took similar action.[41]

The Russellton Medical Group

The Russellton Medical Group is a comprehensive prepaid direct-service organization that operates clinics in several towns in Western Pennsylvania. After long and persistent efforts to obtain courtesy staff privileges for its physicians at a New Kensington hospital, the group filed suit on March 29, 1967 in the U.S. District Court of Pittsburgh. The suit asked for $2.4 million in damages, charging that the hospital violated the Fifth and Fourteenth amendments to the Constitution as well as other Federal statutes in denying staff privileges to its physicians. The complaint asked that the hospitals be permanently enjoined from denying the plaintiffs admission to its medical staff, and charged that the executive committee of the hospital medical staff adopted a secret resolution stating: "No member of the medical staff shall endorse any application, vote

---

[37] *New York Times*, June 17, 1960, as quoted in *Public Health Economics and Medical Care Abstracts*, University of Michigan School of Public Health, Aug. 1960, p. 396.
[38] *Public Health Economics*, Sept. 1960, p. 6.
[39] *Public Health Economics*, July 1963, p. 6.
[40] Ibid.
[41] *New York Times*, Nov. 11, 1964, p. 45.

for or otherwise directly or indirectly assist any physician associated with the Russellton Medical Group in obtaining any medical staff privileges at the hospital."[42]

Aided in its legal battle by the Group Health Association of America, the Russellton group, late in 1967, won an agreement admitting seven additional Russellton physicians to the staff of the hospital. The settlement also stated: "No such physician shall be discriminated against or denied appointments to or membership on the medical staff, because of his association with or participation in any medical group practice or health insurance plan, program or fund." The group expressed satisfaction that the case was settled without litigation and the district court dismissed the suit.[43]

Numerous other cases could be discussed that demonstrate the aggressive tactics of the AMA in opposing various kinds of insurance: the Kaiser Permanente Hospital Plan in California, the Civic Medical Center in Chicago, Blue Cross in Wisconsin, the Complete Service Bureau in San Diego, the United Mine Workers Welfare and Retirement Fund in several states, the Union Medical Fund of the hotel industry in New York City, and many more. However, presentation of these cases would add nothing new to our discussion[44] because the fundamental reason for organized medicine's opposition (protection of its vested economic interest through control of the medical market) and the tactics employed (threats of coercion, expulsion from the membership in the medical society, and denial of consultation and hospital privileges) follow a pattern similar to those in the cases already discussed.

There is, however, another tactic of considerable effectiveness that organized medicine has used in its war on prepaid medical service plans. After initial reluctance, the AMA encouraged growth of the doctor-dominated Blue Shield plans to maintain organized medicine's control over the medical market. In 26 states, the medical societies induced state legislatures to pass restrictive legislation that made it extremely difficult for plans other than Blue Shield to operate. In 15 of these states, the restrictive legislation actually granted professional-controlled plans a virtual monopoly in the prepayment medical care field.[45] Organized medicine's control is ensured through various means by these states. In some, the directors of the plan must be doctors, or approved by the medical society. In others, the incorporators must be doctors, thus blocking lay formation of medical-service plans.

There are important indications that the legislative barriers erected against lay-sponsored plans are beginning to crumble. In 1959, the Ohio legislature passed a new enabling act authorizing lay-sponsored plans to provide subscribers with medical, hospital, and dental services.[46] The previous enabling act,

---

[42] *Group Health and Welfare News*, Apr. 2, 1967.

[43] *Group Health and Welfare News*, Nov. 1, 1967.

[44] U.S. Congress, *Hearings on National Health Program*, 1946, pt. 5, pp. 2630 and 2646; U.S. *Congressional Record*, 81st Cong., 2d sess., Nov. 27, 1950–Jan. 2, 1951, Vol. 94, pt. 12, pp. 16,862–16,863; Carter, op. cit., pp. 170–183; and *Medical World News*, June 7, 1963.

[45] U.S. Congress, *Hearings on Health Inquiry*, op. cit., p. 1779.

[46] Somers and Somers, op. cit., p. 357.

in existence since 1941, was among the most restrictive in the country as far as the non-Blue Shield plans were concerned.

Organized medicine received an even more severe blow in New Jersey, where the state law had given the state medical society complete control over medical-service plans. The Group Health Insurance Plan of New Jersey had sought a license in 1961 and was turned down because it did not have the approval of the state medical society. Group Health initiated a test case and, in 1961, the state supreme court ruled that the section of the law that gave the state medical society the authority to approve medical-surgical plans was unconstitutional. The law also required that an approved medical-surgical plan must have 51 per cent of the doctors in a county as member physicians. The court, in 1961, did not rule on the 51 per cent requirement.

In what may well be a major decision, setting a precedent for other states, the court, on July 16, 1964, found the 51 per cent rule also unconstitutional. On the basis of this opinion, the court ordered the state to reconsider the Group Health Insurance Plan's application. A quote from the New Jersey Supreme Court opinion succinctly brings into focus the fundamental theme of this section:

> We think that such a power to restrict, or indeed, to prohibit competition in a field so vitally connected with the public welfare may not constitutionally be placed in the hands of a private organization such as the medical society, which has an interest in promoting the welfare of the only existing medical service corporation [Blue Shield] in the state.[47]

But the AMA is not giving up on its attempt to control health insurance. Late in 1967, the National Association of Blue Shield Plans (NAMSP) took an action permitting the operation of a plan without approval by the medical society. The AMA House of Delegates requested the NABSP to rescind the action and asked quite bluntly that all plans " continue to serve as an economic arm of the medical profession in offering sound alternatives to the public in the voluntary financing of health care."[48]

Jurisdiction Disputes Among the Health Professions

Despite its demonstrated unity against outside pressures, the AMA is far from a monolithic organization. Internally it is a house divided; general practitioners battle specialists and various types of specialists battle one another as each group is engaged in a struggle to protect or expand its domain over segment of the human anatomy. The conflict is an ancient one, almost as old as the practice of medicine itself.

Scientific, technical, and demographic changes during the last several decades have fragmented the profession into a number of competing specialties. The general practitioner (GP), who formerly claimed as his jurisdiction the treatment of all health problems of the individual—medical, surgical, psychiatric, diagnos-

[47] University of Michigan School of Public Health, *Public Health and Economics and Medical Care Abstracts*, Aug. 1963, pp. 378–379; Sept. 1963, p. 477.
[48] *The AMA News*, Dec. 11, 1967, p. 5.

tic, and therapeutic—has seen his job territory steadily whittled down by the emergent specialists. Yet, according to the AMA, the general practitioner engages in "treatment of the whole body, largely through nonsurgical means."[49]

Therein lies the heart of the conflict. Because the whole body is the sum of its parts, the GP frequently finds himself in conflict with the various "parts" specialists over the right to practice. Furthermore, because the parts are highly interrelated—and in rather close proximity to each other—specialists frequently transgress each others' anatomical or therapeutic jurisdictions. The boundary lines between one specialty and another are often indistinct. The difficulty of defining jurisdiction is reflected in a survey of 1084 specialists conducted by, *Medical Economics.*[50] Ninety-one per cent conceded they were "uncertain" about fringe areas of their field where the issue is which of two specialists is better able to handle a given procedure. At what age level should the pediatrician's "right" to treat the patient end and the internist's begin? When does the general surgeon invade the rightful territory of the thorasic, orthopedic, or gynecological surgeon? Because definitive answers to these questions cannot be given, the present organization of medicine, largely on a fee-for-service basis makes conflict among practitioners inevitable.

Internally, as the GP's battle the specialists and the specialists battle each other, organized medicine is faced with a dilemma similar to that bedeviling society in its relationship with organized medicine as a whole: When does the power to set quality standards—a power considered socially desirable to delegate to professionals—become a device for restricting practice with socially undesirable results?

Conflicts Within the Profession

In June 1964, the physicians at Mary's Help Hospital in Dale City, California, adopted the following bylaw:

> From the date of the opening of the new Mary's Help Hospital in Dale City, California, an applicant may be considered for surgical and obstetrical privileges only if he meets one of the following qualifications:
>
> a. Is a fellow of his respective American college, or
> b. Is a diplomate of his respective American board, or
> c. Has the requisite training necessary to become a diplomate of his respective American board and can present a letter from such specialty board stating that he is qualified for examination on that board.
>
> The qualifications in (a), (b), and (c) above shall not be required in order that an applicant may be considered for privileges as a surgical assistant.

"To put it another way," commented *Medical Economics*, "No GPs need apply."[51]

The GPs in the dispute proposed a bylaw amendment that provided for accept-

[49] *Today's Health Guide* (AMA, 1965), pp. 312–314.
[50] *Medical Economics.* Feb. 15, 1960, p. 88.
[51] *Medical Economics.* May 31, 1965, pp. 60–65.

ance of an applicant who "has been individualy evaluated and upon the basis of his training and experience and demonstrated ability is deemed competent to be granted the privileges sought." Despite a year of GP lobbying, the amendment was rejected.

Such restrictions on the right to practice are common throughout much of our hospital system. Many hospitals function under a "closed staff" arrangement whereby a list of physicians is maintained and only those on the list are authorized to admit patients; all other physicians are automatically barred. Generally, university, teaching, and government operated hospitals invite physicians to join the staff; physicians themselves do not initiate applications. Community and church related hospitals are more open in that any physician may apply for admitting privileges. However, the license to practice does not carry with it automatic admitting privileges.

The widespread existence of restrictions on hospital staff privileges is reflected in a survey of staffing patterns of hospitals in eight communities located in various sections of the United States, with populations ranging from 62,000 to more than 2.5 million. The survey revealed that most of the hospitals imposed various kinds of restrictions on privileges. Personal interviews with physicians in the communities brought to the surface deeply held feelings of "bitterness, resentment, and jealousy" on the part of those against whom barriers had been erected.[52] The prevalence of restrictive staff arrangements is also borne out by the hundreds of articles on the problem that have appeared in medical journals since the end of World War II and the numerous professional society committees that have been established periodically to find a "solution." The GP, it must be emphasized, is not the only physician against whom barriers are erected; similar restrictions are imposed against specialists who have not been "certified" by one of the 19 American specialty boards.

The bitterness among GP and noncertified specialists is readily understandable. Barred completely from some of the better teaching hospitals, or restricted to minor ones, they are also locked out from many voluntary hospitals and severely limited in their staff privileges in others. Without staff privileges, or with privileges severely limited, the practitioner must relinquish a patient requiring hospitalization to a specialist having access to a hospital. At best, the noncertified doctor, in a case involving his hospitalized patient, may be given the opportunity to act as an assistant to a certified specialist who then takes on the major responsibility in the care of the patient. Because nearly half of medical incomes are earned in hospitals, the threat posed by staff restrictions to the earnings and status of a physician could be substantial.

The Question of Quality

Are restrictions on staff privileges an attempt to raise standards in hospitals, as the specialists with privileges hold? Or, as many hospital-barred physicians argue, are they monopolistic devices for limiting competition?

[52] Patricia L. Kendall, "The Relationship Between Medical Educators and Medical Practitioners," *Journal of Medical Education*, pt. 2, **40**:187 (Jan. 1965).

There is some strong evidence that the quality of much general practice is in fact inadequate. In a careful in-depth interview survey of general practice in North Carolina, a medical team from the University of North Carolina, found numerous serious deficiencies. This report and others[53] indicate that the conditions found in North Carolina are also common far beyond that state's border.

Reports of inferior practice, however, are not limited to general practitioners. Specialists also have come in for considerable criticism. Three major studies in recent years demonstrated the existence of a substantial amount of unnecessary surgery and inferior surgical treatment, particularly with respect to appendectomies and hysterectomies.[54]

It is clear from such studies of both general practitioners *and* specialists that some kind of quality control is necessary to protect the patient. The studies are equally clear in indicating that specialty-board certification for hospital privileges is no guarantee of adequate quality.

Specialty-Board Certification as a Restrictive Device

That board-certified specialists have used high-quality standards as a device to maintain or increase their incomes through restriction of competition is indicated by two kinds of evidence: (1) particular specialty-board rules for certification that are clearly aimed at restriction of competition and have no bearing on quality, and (2) specific cases in which certification requirements have been used to suppress competition.[55]

Several specialty boards required *applicants* for certification to be American citizens, a requirement that bars foreign doctors from even applying for certification for at least 5 years (the residence requirement for United States citizenship). The burden on the foreign doctor is especially great because, even after the application for certification is filed, the other requirements are such that it may take several more years before he is actually certified. With the recent influx of foreign physicians into the United States, the citizenship-requirement barrier takes on added significance. That a number of specialty boards do not have citizenship requirements suggests that those that do are not simply concerned with quality. Whatever else citizenship may confer on an individual, it does not improve his ability as a physician.

The provisions of certification of foreign doctors by the American Board of Dermatology are particularly revealing: "Graduates of Foreign Medical Schools, not citizens of the United States of Canada, who will return to their homeland

---

[53] Oscar L. Peterson et al., "An Analytical Study of North Carolina General Practice 1953–1954," *Journal of Medical Education*, pt. 2, **31**:22 (Dec. 1956); Kendall, op. cit., pp. 181–186; Oscar L. Peterson, "Medical Care Research," ed., in John H. Knowles, *Hospitals, Doctors, and the Public Interest* (Cambridge, Mass.: Harvard University Press, 1965). Peterson cites Canadian and Australian studies that came up with similar findings.

[54] Ray E. Trussell, *The Quantity, Quality, and Costs of Medical and Hospital Care Secured by a Sample of Teamster Families in the New York Area* (New York: Columbia University School of Public Health and Administrative Medicine, 1962), p. 3; *JAMA*, **151**:360 (Jan. 1953); J. Frederick Sparling, "Measuring Medical Care Quality," *Hospitals*, **36**:62 (Mar. 16, 1962).

[55] The specialty board requirements discussed in this section are in *Directory of Medical Specialists*, Vol. 12 (Chicago: Marquis–Who's Who, Inc., 1965–1966).

after completion of approved residency training in dermatology are eligible for nonresident certification." However, to get such certification, the foreign doctor must present "A notarized statement that the applicant is (a) returning to his homeland to remain and to practice there; (b) that he will surrender his special certification should he ever return to practice in the United States or Canada." The specialty boards for internal medicine and orthopedic surgery have similar provisions for foreign physicians. The neurological surgery board grants to foreign doctors special "foreign certification" that are issued only *after* the doctor has returned to his home country.

A number of boards want the applicant for certification to submit letters of reference, and some require that the letters be from board-certified specialists in the applicant's community. This makes it possible for a certified specialist to block a potential competitor. In *Medical Economics'* survey of 1084 board-certified specialists, one of the most frequently cited "arbitrary" requirements was the letter of reference from a certified man in the community.[56]

There are other arbitrary rules of the various boards that indicate more of a concern for competition than for quality. Both the boards of anesthesiology and of ophthalmology reserve "the right to reject any applicant for any reason deemed advisable and without stating the same." The otalaryngology board has a similar provision. Because this board also requires that an applicant present letters of reference from certified specialists in his community, the arbitrary power to deny certification is particularly suspect. The board of dermatology states that its "records are confidential throughout," that "examination marks will not be divulged to the applicant," and that "the findings of the board are subject to its discretion and are final." Clearly, none of these provisions can be defended on grounds that they maintain quality.

Most of the specialty boards, in their descriptions of certification requirements, include a passage similar to the following found in the American Board of Surgery statement:

> The American Board of Surgery has never been concerned with measures that might gain special privileges or recognition for its diplomates in the practice of surgery. *It is neither the intent nor has it been the purpose of the board to define requirements for membership on the staffs of hospitals.* The prime object of the board is to pass judgment on the education and training of broadly competent and responsible surgeons, not who shall or shall not perform surgical operations. The board specifically disclaims interest in or recognition of differential emoluments that may be based on certification.[57]

Because specialty-board certification is so widely used throughout the United States as a criterion for hospital staff privileges, how can we explain these emphatic disclaimers? In part, the disclaimers may be an attempt to forestall an attack on the specialty boards from breaking out among GP and uncertified specialists within the ranks of organized medicine. Perhaps even more important is a desire to avoid becoming embroiled in the large number of court battles

[56] *Medical Economics*, May 23, 1960, p. 278.
[57] *JAMA*, **15**:414 (Sept. 29, 1952).

between hospitals and barred physicians. Furthermore, the explicit restriction disclaimer may be a useful device for preventing the boards from being subjected to prosecution under the antitrust laws as conspiracies in restraint of trade.

The most significant characteristic of the disclaimer, however, is that *it does not say that the boards will oppose the use of specialty-board certification as a requirement for staff privileges.* A hospital medical staff, using maintenance of standards as a justification, can, with impunity, bar noncertified physicians from hospital privileges, and the specialty board can then hide behind the ploy that these are "local" matters over which it has no rightful control.

A recent court case illustrates the nature of the problem. A physician's application for staff privileges was rejected by the governing board of a non-profit hospital upon recommendation of the medical staff. The doctor was able to convince the local judge to order the hospital to admit him. On appeal, the Kansas Supreme Court reversed the trial judge and restated the basic rule of law applicable to the situation:

> It seems to be practically the unanimous opinion that private hospitals have the right to exclude licensed physicians from the use of the hospital, and that such exclusion rests within the sound discretion of the managing authorities.[58]

In a recent issue of *Hospitals*, Attorney James E. Ludlam reported: "Either by circumstances or default, the ultimate control of medical standards has become the function of the medical staff. It is in this setting that the quality of the individual physician's practice can be subject to continuous audit. More important, the continuation of his medical staff privileges usually has important economic meaning to the individual doctor." How widespread are the conflicts over staff privileges is also indicated by Mr. Ludlam: "A reported legal case involving medical staff privileges was a rarity 20 to 30 years ago, but now the number of cases in the books is increasing at a geometric rate. . . . Even more serious, these reported cases are only the exposed part of the iceberg."[59]

The desire to restrict competition is reflected in a revealing roundtable discussion conducted by the journal *Medical Economics*. One of its editors asked the panelists whether they had ever run into situations in which "a horde of staff doctors, such as GPs, have suddenly had their privileges withdrawn." Dr. Charles E. Letourneau, president of the American College of Legal Medicine, replied, "Yes, typically this happens when a horde of surgical specialists moves into an area only to discover there's not enough surgery around. I've seen it affect four or five hospitals in the same community. Board-certified men tried to freeze out the competition completely, although local GPs have been there for 30 years doing good work."[60]

---

[58] *Foote* v. *Community Hospital of Beloit, Kansas* (Sept. 9, 1965), as reported in *Hospitals*, **39**:96 (Nov. 1, 1965).
[59] James E. Ludlam, "Legal Shares for the Hospital," *Hospitals*, **38**:38 (Aug. 1, 1964).
[60] *Medical Economics*, Apr. 5, 1965, p. 90.

Nor are the conflicts limited to specialists versus GPs. When Dr. Letourneau, who has been called in to resolve hundreds of staff conflicts, was asked how they arise, he commented as follows:

Many of them have to do with privileges—the question of who should be allowed to do what. Wherever specialties overlap there's likely to be contention. General surgeons clash with gynecologists. Plastic surgeons clash with nose and throat men.

Take two board certified men, one in surgery and one in OBG [obstetrics and gynecology]. The general surgeon says he can do a procedure as well as the next fellow. Not in his special field, says the gynecologist.

I remember one case where we decided to give all the fractures to the orthopods [orthopedic surgeons]. No go. The general surgeons decided they just weren't going to hand over all those cases. Eventually there may be enough orthopods to change the ground rules and make them stick. Meanwhile both factions have access to the disputed area of fractures.[61]

Clearly, the physician's income was at issue and not the quality of medical care.

Even certification, however, is no guarantee of hospital staff privileges, particularly if a physician takes a position opposed to the wishes of organized medicine. A 13-year physician-hospital dispute that received some national notoriety was finally settled out of court in Bellaire, Ohio, in 1965. The fight began in 1952 with the establishment of the Bellaire Clinic and the Bellaire Medical Group, a prepaid group insurance plan of the United Mine Worker's Welfare and Retirement Fund. The clinic's doctors are members of the medical group. Because of organized medicine's long-standing opposition to prepaid group practice plans, clinic doctors had difficulty becoming admitted to staff privileges in the Bellaire Hospital and were barred from medical society membership. One of the clinic doctors was Dr. James E. Sams. His application for membership in the local medical society was rejected, even though he was certified by the American Board of Obstetrics and Gynecology and the county had no other specialists in obstetrics and gynecology. As a direct consequence of the rejection of his membership application by the medical society, he was denied hospital privileges. In March 1963, the clinic and its physicians accused the society and the hospital of "a 10-year history of harassment, discrimination, and obstruction,"[62] and filed two suits—one for $2.5 million in damages for conspiracy and restraint of trade and another seeking to end the discrimination. After a 2-year struggle, the case was settled out of court: Dr. Sams won courtesy staff privileges in the hospital and the local medical society agreed to amend its bylaws to allow any physician whose membership is rejected to request binding arbitration to determine whether the rejection was justified.[63]

---

[61] Ibid., p. 103.
[62] *Hospitals*, **39**:116 (June 16, 1965).
[63] *Group Health and Welfare News*, **6**:7 (Mar. 1965); **6**:1 (May 1965).

Organized Medicine and Other Health Professions

This brief section merely summarizes points that are developed fully else-where.[64]

Osteopathy

In its harassment of America's 12,000 osteopathic physicians, organized medicine has employed all of its traditional weapons. The AMA has branded osteopaths as "cultists," fought against their receiving recognition through licensure, barred them from membership in local medical societies, denied them the right to practice in AMA dominated hospitals, and prevented physicians from associating with them professionally, from lecturing in their medical schools, and from participating in their professional meetings. Not until the latter part of the 1960s did the AMA begin to accept osteopathic physicians as full members of the medical profession.

Chiropractic

For about five decades the AMA and its state and county societies have pressed a relentless war against chiropractors. It has attacked them publicly as "frauds" and "quacks" and fought vigorously against giving them recognition through state licensure. When unsuccessful in preventing licensure, organized medicine has pursued a program of containment through securing statutory limits on the ailments chiropractors could treat and on the techniques they could employ. The AMA has lobbied against Federal payment of tuition for veterans seeking chiropractic training under the GI Bill, against approval of chiropractic schools by the Department of Labor, against Veterans Administration (VA) recognition of—and reimbursement for—chiropractic care, against deferment of chiropractic students under the Selective Service System, and against the appointment of doctors of chiropractic in the Department of Medicine and Surgery of the VA. Although the AMA has made considerable concessions to the osteopathic profession in recent years, there does not seem to be any prospect for a similar modification in its attitude toward chiropractic as a "dangerous cult."

Optometry

Optometrists and physicians, particularly opthalmologists, have been en-gaged in bitter jurisdictional disputes for decades. Despite the fact that optome-trists have long been generally recognized as legitimate health practitioners—the optometry act of the District of Columbia in 1924 completed optometric licensing coverage for the entire nation—their right to practice has for decades been challenged by the AMA and they have been subjected to the same kind of harassment tactics employed by organized medicine against osteopaths and chiropractors.

[64] Elton Rayack, *Professional Power and American Medicine* (New York: World, 1967), Chap. 6.

IV. PERFORMANCE

As we have shown, organized medicine—the AMA and the various specialty boards—plays a fundamental role in the production and distribution of medical care. By its restrictions on entry into medicine it has inflicted heavy social costs both on individuals who were prevented from practicing medicine and on the general public, which was unable to buy all the medical services it wanted. The success of those restrictionist policies has, during the last couple of decades, contributed to a serious shortage of physicians' services and to an extraordinarily sharp rise in the incomes of doctors. Furthermore, AMA opposition to certain technological and organizational changes in the production and distribution of medical care has had an adverse effect on the quality of medical care and made it more difficult to reduce its cost. Let us turn to an examination of these points.

The Shortage of Physicians' Services, Physicians' Incomes, and the Search for Substitutes

For analysis of physicians' services, a useful definition of shortage—that is, one that makes it possible to test for its presence—is that a shortage exists when the quantity physicians' services supplied increases less rapidly than the quantity demanded at incomes received by physicians in the recent past. Under such conditions, the income of physicians relative to the incomes of others will tend to rise. As the relative income of physicians rises, there will be attempts to substitute less costly services for the services of physicians. The following discussion indicates that there has been a persistent and marked rise in the relative income of physicians and that the pressure of unsatisfied demand has been channeled into a search for less costly substitutes—that is, the analysis shows that a shortage does currently exist.

Table 2 indicates clearly the pronounced rise in the relative income of physicians since 1939. From 1939 to 1951, the mean income of physicians (column 1) increased 218 per cent. This increase exceeded the percentage increase for other occupational classes by the following percentages: nonsalaried dentists, 42 per cent; nonsalaried lawyers, 113 per cent; professional technical and kindred workers, 74 per cent; managers, officials, and proprietors, 132 per cent; full-time employees, all industries, 40 per cent (percentage calculated from data in Table 2, columns 1, 3, 4, 5, 6, and 7).

The analysis can be further extended to 1971 using median rather than mean income data: Between 1947—the first year for which median income data are available—and 1971, physicians' incomes rose 388 per cent. During those years, the percentage rise in doctors' incomes was 43 p er cent greater than the percentage rise for managers, o fficials, and proprietors and 84 per cent greater than the percentage rise in th e average annual earnings for full-time employees in all industries.

The earnings data in Table 2 take no account of the increased specialization

TABLE 2

Income of Physicians and Selected Occupational Classes, for Selected Years, 1939–1971

	(1)	(2)	(3)	(4)	(5)	(6)	(7)
					MEDIAN WAGE OR SALARY INCOME OF		
	MEAN NET INCOME OF NONSALARIED PHYSICIANS	MEDIAN NET INCOME OF NONSALARIED PHYSICIANS	MEAN NET INCOME OF NONSALARIED DENTISTS	MEAN NET INCOME OF NONSALARIED LAWYERS	PROFESSIONAL, TECHNICAL, AND KINDRED WORKERS	MANAGERS, OFFICIALS, AND PROPRIETORS (NONFARM)	AVERAGE ANNUAL EARNINGS PER FULL-TIME EMPLOYEES, ALL INDUSTRIES
1939	4,229	—	3,096	4,301	1,809	2,136	1,264
1943	8,370	—	5,715	5,945	—	—	1,951
1947	10,726	8,744	6,610	7,437	—	3,345	2,589
1951	13,432	13,150	7,820	8,855	4,071	4,134	3,231
1955	—	16,107	—	—	5,055	5,290	3,847
1959	—	22,100	—	—	6,287	6,670	4,557
1963	—	25,050	—	—	7,182	7,411	5,190
1964	—	28,380	—	—	7,460	7,560	5,503
1965	—	28,960	—	—	7,572	8,175	5,710
1966	—	32,170	—	—	8,204	8,730	5,959
1967	—	34,730	—	—	—	—	—
1968	—	37,620	—	—	9,960	9,765	—
1969	—	40,550	—	—	11,062	10,822	—
1970	—	41,500	—	—	11,577	11,292	7,551
1971	—	42,700	—	—	11,853	12,412	8,059

Source: For columns 1, 3, and 4: U.S. Department of Commerce, Survey of Current Business, 29:18 (Aug. 1949), Tables 1 and 2; 30:9 (Jan. 1950), Table 2; 31:11 (July 1951), Table 1; 32:6 (July 1952), Table 3; and for column 2; Medical Economics, pp. 112, 128, 129 (Oct. 1946) and Physicians' Earnings and Expenses (reprint of articles based on Medical Economics continuing survey), 1960, p. 8; for columns 5 and 6: U.S. Bureau of the Census, Current Population Reports Series, no. P-60, various issues; for column 7, U.S. Department of Commerce, Survey of Current Business, 39:37 (July 1959); 44:30 (July 1964); and 54:7 (July 1974). The 1963 median net incomes in column 2 are from Medical Economics, p. 64 (Nov. 2, 1964); the 1965 and 1966 figures are from Medical Economics, p. [...] are from U.S. Department of Commerce, Statistical Abstract, 1973. (Washington, D.C.: U.S. Government Printing

and training physicians. Because specialists earn higher incomes than general practitioners, the rise in the relative incomes of physicians as a whole could be, it might be argued, a product of the trend toward specialization rather than of shortages. In addition, part of the rise in medical incomes may be explained by the necessity for paying physicians additional compensation for the income loss during the greater training period characteristic of recent years.

The effects of specialization on the income data cannot be separated from the effect of the longer training period because the latter is primarily a result of increased specialization. The average length of training for doctors after completion of medical school has increased from about 2 years in 1940 to about $3\frac{1}{2}$ years in 1959. Specialty-board certification of specialists requires from 2 to 6 years, depending on the specialty, of residency training beyond the internship. Because the number of specialists as a percentage of private practitioners has risen from 24 to 71 per cent since 1940, the increase in the average period of training for physicians as a whole is essentially a product of the trend toward specialization. Hence, if an examination of the relevant data can eliminate greater specialization as the explanation of the rise in the relative incomes of physicians as a whole, such an examination would at the same time rule out the longer training period as a basic cause of the rise.

The relative incomes of both specialists and GPs have increased markedly (see Tables 3 and 4). However, in 1939–1959, the percentage increase in the mean income of the GP was 37 per cent greater than the percentage increase for specialists. Since 1959, the median incomes of specialists and the GP have increased at about the same rate. These facts suggest a shortage of *both* the specialist and the GP and, furthermore, that the rise in the relative incomes of

---

TABLE 3

Mean Net Income of Full Specialists and General Practitioners, 1939–1959

PHYSICIANS	INCOME ($)						INCREASE (PER CENT)
	1939	1943	1947	1951	1955	1959	
Full specialists	6,184	11,808	14,442	17,112	20,010	26,800	333
General practitioners[a]	3,940	7,511	10,254	14,467	16,317	21,500	446

[a] For 1939–1951, the incomes of the GP and partial specialists have been combined by weighing each in accordance with its respective number in the 1939 *Medical Economics* survey. For 1955 and 1959, *Medical Economics* presented median net incomes for partial specialists and the GP combined and for full specialists. Those median net income figures have been adjusted upward by $2000 for specialists and $1500 for the GP by this writer to arrive at the estimated mean net incomes for 1955 and 1959. The upward adjustment was based on the average difference between median and mean net incomes of $1892 in 1955 and 1959 for doctors as a whole (see Table 5, columns 2 and 4). The resulting mean net incomes of full specialists and the GP, when averaged for 1955 and 1959 to arrive at the mean net income for doctors as a whole, differ by 0.2- and 1 per cent, respectively, from the mean net income for doctors as a whole, indicating an insignificant error in the estimate.
Source: *Medical Economics*, quadrennial surveys.

TABLE 4

Median Net Income of Specialists and General Practitioners, 1959–1966

| | INCOME ($) | | INCREASE |
	1959	1966	(PER CENT)
General practitioners	20,000	27,720	39
Specialists	24,800	34,325	38

Source: *Medical Economics*, "Quadrennial Surveys" (Oct. 21, 1960), pp. 69 ff. (Dec. 11, 1967).

physicians as a whole did not result from the trend toward specialization and increased training.

The shortage in the supply of physicians' services, reflected in their rapidly rising relative incomes, has led to a pronounced movement in the direction of substituting for the services of doctors the cheaper services of personnel with less training and experience. The attempt at substitution has been particularly marked in the use of foreign-trained personnel. With the passage of the Information and Education Exchange Act of 1947 (effective July 1949), there began a steadily rising influx of foreign-trained physicians. From 1950–1973 the number of interns and residents rose from about 21,500 to 56,244. During the same period the percentage of intern and resident positions filled by foreign personnel rose almost threefold, from 9.6 to 32.7 per cent.

The high failure rate of 50 to 70 per cent on tests given to foreign trainees by the Educational Council for Foreign Medical Graduates (ECFMG) compared dismally with a failure rate on licensure exams of about 3 per cent for graduates of approved schools in the United States. That the high failure rate of foreign-trained personnel is largely a reflection of their relatively inadequate training and skill is borne out by the evidence and testimony of many who have studied the problem. When hospitals, staffed by foreign medical graduates who had not passed the ECFMG examinations were threatened with loss of approval of their internship and residency programs, it was reported that: "Many hospitals, believing that the situation is hopeless without uncertified foreign graduates, will defy the ban and risk losing accreditation."[65] As the department director of the Office of Cultural Exchange has observed: "Some [hospitals] see the foreign physicians as a source of cheap labor" and "turn to the Exchange Visitor Program . . . to meet staffing problems."[66]

The impact of immigration is also shown in medical licensure data. From 1959 to 1966, more than 17 per cent of the physicians licensed and representing additions to the profession were foreign graduates. In 1967, almost 46 per cent of the newly licensed physicians were foreign graduates.

[65] *House Physician Reporter*, Jan. 1962, p. 2.
[66] *JAMA*, **179**:44 (Feb. 24, 1962).

Approximately 75 per cent of the foreign medical graduates now serving in internship and residency programs and most of the newly licensed foreign physicians are from developing countries.[67] Thus, ironically, the world's richest country finds itself heavily dependent on the poorest nations of the world to provide a substantial amount of its medical care.

The shortage of physicians' services has led to a search for substitutes in unusual directions. Hospitals in increasing numbers are relying on third- and fourth-year medical school students to take histories and do physicals under supervision. Lacking an adequate house staff, hospitals are letting registered nurses perform many services once performed only by doctors, despite the fact that this is a practice barred by a number of state laws. A number of hospitals are welcoming graduates of osteopathic schools to house-staff positions formerly barred to them by long standing and rigid AMA policy. Despite the vigorous opposition of organized medicine, the number of chiropractors increased 127 per cent from 1940 to 1960, more than three times the percentage increase in the number of doctors.

The Rising Cost of Medical Care

Perhaps no other development has contributed more to the controversy over the provision of medical services during the last couple of decades than the spiraling prices of medical care.

From 1947 to 1965, while the "all-items" index rose 41 per cent, the all-medical-care figure, physicians' fees, and hospital daily service charges rose 86, 72, and 248 per cent, respectively (see Table 5). During the 5-year period following the passage of Medicare-Medicaid legislation in 1965, all medical care, physicians' fees, and hospital charges climbed 35, 37, and 88 per cent, respectively, as the all-items index rose 23 per cent. In the 1970–1973 period, the all-items index,

---

TABLE 5
Percentage Increases in Prices of Selected Items in the Consumer Price Index, Selected Periods, 1947–1973

EXPENDITURES	1947–1973	1947–1965	1965–1970	1970–1973
All items	99	41	23	14
All medical care items	186	86	35	14
Physicians' fees	169	72	37	14
Hospital daily service charges	631[a]	248	88	14[a]

[a] The hospital daily service charges index is for the 1947–1971 period. The Bureau of Labor Statistics ceased publication of that item in 1971.
Source: U.S. Bureau of Labor Statistics, Consumer Price Index (Washington, D.C.: U.S. Government Printing Office, various years).

[67] Harold Margulies, Lucille S. Block, and Francis K. Cholko, "Random Survey of U.S. Hospitals with Approved Internship and Residencies," Journal of Medical Education, 43:713 (June 1968).

all medical care, and physicians' fees each increased 14 per cent. Over the entire period 1947–1973, the percentage increases for the all-medical-care index, physicians' fees, and hospital daily service charges were enormously greater than the percentage increase for "all items"—88, 71, and 537 per cent, respectively.

Resistance to Innovation

For about half a century, organized medicine has resisted the development of "group practice," particularly when the practice has been tied to a prepayment insurance scheme. Group practice has been defined by the Public Health Service as "a formal association of three or more physicians providing services in more than one field or specialty, with income from medical practice pooled and redistributed to the members according to some prearranged plan."[68] There are a number of possible advantages to group practice: (1) the pooling of skills of a number of specialists to serve the needs of the patient; (2) salutary effects of the doctor being subject to observation by his peers; (3) easy access to the services of specialists at little or no additional costs; (4) lower costs through economies of scale resulting from the pooling of capital investment; and (5) further use of ancillary personnel and equipment.

Despite the possible advantages of group practice, it has shown no significant growth. In 1965, only 6.6 per cent of American physicians were practicing in multispecialty groups, 3.5 per cent in single-specialty groups, and 0.9 per cent in general practice groups. Furthermore, only about 2 per cent of all the groups used the prepayment mechanism.[69] A major reason for this slow growth, as already discussed in this chapter, has been the opposition of the AMA.

Thus, in addition to restricting the supply of physicians' services, organized medicine has attempted to control the medical market structure in order to maintain the fee-for-service system, a system under which the price-discriminating solo practitioner can exercise monopolistic power. In pursuit of this goal, the AMA opposed the development of voluntary insurance and came reluctantly to its support only when confronted with the threat of compulsory health insurance. The AMA was particularly adamant in its opposition to voluntary insurance that took the form of prepaid group practice, a method of medical cost financing that lessens the control the individual physician has over fees. In discussing the AMA opposition to experimentation in the organization and financing of medical care, Professor Milton Friedman has commented sharply: "These methods of practice may have good features and bad features, but they are technological innovations that people ought to be free to try out if they wish. There is no basis for saying conclusively that the optimal technical method is practice by an independent physician. Maybe it is group practice, maybe it is by corporations. One ought to have a system under which all varieties can be tried."[70]

[68] G. H. Hunt, M.D., and M. S. Goldstein, *Medical Group Practice in the United States*, Public Health Service Publication No. 77, 1951, p. 1.

[69] *Survey of Medical Groups in U.S., 1965* (Chicago: AMA, 1968), p. 11.

[70] Friedman, op. cit., p. 154.

Specialty restrictionism has been a factor contributing to a decline in the number of GPs. Authorities who have studied the causes of the decline invariably point to restrictions on hospital privileges as one of the key factors discouraging students from pursuing a career in general practice. Recent studies also indicate that specialists are increasingly taking over the functions of general practitioners because families are turning toward specialists for *basic* medical care as well as specialized services.

But is not this development socially desirable? Is it not *always* better for the patient to use a specialist rather than a general practitioner? The answer is no! To the extent that specialty restrictionism has led to the use of the higher-priced services of the specialist as a substitute for the general practitioners' services, *on the assumption that the GP could have provided services of equal quality*, there is definitely a malallocation of resources. The loss is not simply in terms of the higher prices paid by the consumers for medical services; even more significant is the waste of resources involved in training specialists when the smaller amount of resources devoted to the training of the GP would have been adequate. If a patient has a brain tumor, it is obvious that it would be more desirable for him to be operated on by a neurosurgeon than by a GP. However, most common ailments, normal deliveries of babies, minor surgery, and even much uncomplicated major surgery surely can be handled by the GP; in these cases, to compel the use of the costly services of specialists is to waste resources. Furthermore, if there is to be efficient use of our medical resources, *specialists should specialize*, because, as Dr. Ratner notes, "if a specialist doesn't see special cases, he's not going to remain a specialist since he will lack experience. We see this in pediatrics, where, as we all know, the pediatrician who was trained extensively to take care of these very serious illnesses ends up spending most of his time parading a series of well babies through an assembly line setup."[71]

Another effect of the vacuum created by the decline of the GP is that the patient often "becomes his own diagnostician and decides which kind of specialist he should approach."[72] The kind of treatment he gets may be less of a function of what his medical condition requires than of the particular specialist he chooses. Suppose, for example, a patient has an ulcer. A surgeon may properly recommend surgery, a psychiatrist analysis, and an internist treatment by medicine. What is appropriate from the viewpoint of the patient depends on the nature of his medical condition. But whether he receives surgery, analysis, or medication—given the consumer's lack of knowledge in medical matters—may depend on whether he goes to the surgeon, the psychiatrist, or the internist. The specialist, because of consumer ignorance, has considerable power to create a demand for his services. The GP, acting as a family physician in such situations, can, because he has vastly greater medical knowledge than the consumer, help him make a rational choice among competing specialists. There is enough evidence of unnecessary surgery to indicate that this is, in fact, a serious problem.

[71] Herbert Ratner, "Deficiencies in Present Day Medical Education," *General Practitioner*, **32**:187 (July 1965).
[72] "The Graduate Education of Physicians," p. 34.

Another undesirable effect of hospital medical staff restrictionism is that the noncertified physician and GP tend to be barred from the better teaching hospitals. As a result, they are channeled into proprietary hospitals and, increasingly, in recent years, have turned toward building hospitals of their own where they are able to treat their patients. Cut off from better teaching hospitals, the noncertified physician or GP loses out on the intellectual stimulation and educational opportunities such an institution can provide. Such isolation can only produce a deterioration in the quality of medical care.

V. PUBLIC POLICY

To deal with the problems related to the cost, distribution, and quality of medical care, two major proposals—the adoption of some form of national health insurance and the development of health maintenance organizations (HMOs)—have been the subject of legislation, considerable congressional debate, and widespread discussion in the popular press. These are complex issues over which there is considerable controversy. The following section can do no more than comment on some of the more important elements of the debate.

National Health Insurance

In 1945, less than 25 per cent of the population had any kind of health insurance. Since then, private health insurance has grown so phenomenally that, by 1973, about 80 per cent of the population under sixty-five years of age had private health insurance covering hospitalization and surgery while more than half had partial coverage for physicians' home or office visits. In addition, most of the population over sixty-five is covered by Medicare and a significant portion of the poor benefit from Medicaid.

Despite the enormous growth in both private and public insurance programs, there are several serious defects in the existing public-private mix of medical care. Most important of all, the poor are still inadequately covered. In 1970, only 39 per cent of persons in families with incomes of less than $3000 had hospital insurance coverage, compared with 90 per cent of those in the $10,000 or higher groups. A similar pattern exists for surgical insurance.[73] Furthermore, while Medicaid has helped families on welfare and others with low incomes, because state-determined benefits and eligibility rules vary enormously—Medicaid and a number of other public programs are Federal-state matching programs—millions of low-income individuals receive no coverage at all and for millions more the benefits are extremely low. Government outlays for personal health care expenditures in 1969 varied from a per capita high of $161 in New York to a low of $48 in Mississippi. While public outlays per person averaged $91

---

[73] U.S. Department of Health, Education, and Welfare, Social Security Administration, *Medical Care Expenditures, Prices, and Costs: Background Book* (Washington, D.C.: U.S. Government Printing Office, 1973), p. 83.

nationally, only 13 states registered outlays of $90 or more per person, while in another 12 states the amount was less than $70.[74] Moreover, although Medicare has assisted the aged poor, it does not provide for long-term institutional treatment such as nursing-home care.

A second major weakness of our health insurance coverage is its inadequacy in providing protection against the catastrophic costs associated with prolonged illness or disease. Insurance plans generally set an upper limit on benefits so that even affluent families could be wiped out financially by prolonged illness or the extremely high costs of some modern medical procedures.

A third weakness of the system is that it is inefficient, encourages high cost care, and does little to encourage preventative medicine. Many insurance plans pay benefits only if the patient is hospitalized. To cut the costs to the patient, physicians will frequently recommend hospitalization even though treatment in the doctor's office, in the patient's home, or in an out-patient clinic may be socially less costly and just as effective for the patient. Preventative medicine is often not covered. Hence, checkups, which might prevent, or at least mitigate, the occurrence of costly or long-term illness are neglected. This is aggravated by the prevalence of a fee-for-service payment system under which physicians are reimbursed for treating the sick rather than for care aimed at preventing illness.

So serious are these defects that the debate is no longer over *whether* there should be national health insurance legislation but rather over *what kind* should be adopted. A plethora of bills are being considered by congressional committees, ranging from the AMA supported "Medicredit" plan (Health Care Insurance Act S444, H.R. 2222) to the labor-backed comprehensive health insurance bill introduced by Senator Edward Kennedy and Representative Griffiths (S3, H.R. 22).

In essence, the AMA's Medicredit plan would provide a substantial subsidy for, but not alter, the existing system. Participation in the plan would be completely voluntary. The poor would receive vouchers from the Federal government to cover insurance premiums while all others would have from 10 to 99 per cent of their premiums paid through income tax credits on a sliding scale based on income. The bill would provide 60 days of hospital care with a $50 deductible (paid by the insured) per hospital stay. It would also cover the first $500 spent for outpatient care, the first $500 for physician care, and the first $500 for dental care—all subject to a deductible equal to 10 per cent of a family's combined taxable income minus the amount of out-of-pocket payments for basic benefits. Based on taxable income, the income tax credit would cover a percentage of the premium paid for basic benefits and the entire premium for catastrophic benefits.

The AMA's Medicredit proposal is the most conservative of the plans being offered in that, aside from the subsidy and certain minimum standards for insuring benefits, it relies completely on the existing medical care market structure.

[74] Ibid., pp. 13 and 14.

It includes no quality or utilization controls and provides no incentives to augment or improve the resources for the delivery of medical care. While increasing the demand for medical care, the Medicredit plan would rely on the existing market structure to allocate resources and control costs. Hospitals would continue to be paid on the basis of realized costs and physicians on the basis of "reasonable and customary fees," with no incentives to keep down costs or fees. Given the increased demand resulting from the subsidy and the noncompetitive nature of the medical care industry, the Medicredit plan will surely lead to an acceleration of the increase in medical care prices—higher incomes for physicians, hospitals, and private insurance companies—and no improvement in allocative efficiency. In sum, as the Somers have stated, "Medicredit provides no administrative mechanism for government responsibility to protect its open-ended financial commitment or for controlling the program in any other way than to assure that qualifying policies meet minimum benefit standards." Perhaps the most socially significant aspect of Medicredit is that it reflects the AMA's acceptance of "the unavoidable necessity for a degree of Federal regulation of health insurance, at least to the extent of setting national minimum benefits standards. This would have been inconceivable only a few years ago."[75]

At the other extreme of recent national health insurance proposals is the Kennedy–Griffiths Health Security Act. It would repeal Medicare and provide a program of compulsory insurance covering almost all medical expenses, without limitations or deductibles, for all Americans. It would be financed out of payroll taxes and general revenues and administered by the Federal government. Physicians could choose to be paid on a capitation, salary, or fee-for-service basis. Initially, fees would be established by a fee schedule, but, if total bills for fee-for-service exceeded a predetermined amount, the individual fees would be reduced proportionately. The intent of this provision is to encourage physicians to join comprehensive health service plans by reducing the income they are likely to earn in solo practice on a fee-for-service basis and by guaranteeing their incomes if they are compensated by salaries or capitation payments. Cost control would be maintained primarily by budget ceilings and allocations, with a national health budget prepared each year by a five-member full-time Health Security Board. Ten regional offices and about 100 suboffices would carry out the actual administration of the plan. A national Health Resource Development Fund would be used for the support of innovative health programs in education, manpower, and group practice. The proposal does not assign any role to private insurance carriers.

The major advantage of the Kennedy–Griffiths bill is that it recognizes that access to medical care is a necessity and avoids the use of a means test for eligibility, an approach that usually leads to "a double standard and a 'two-class' quality of care. One of the objectives of a national system must be to end

---

[75] Herman M. Somers and Anne R. Somers, *Milbank Memorial Fund Quarterly*, **50**:190 (Apr. 1972).

such discrimination."[76] In addition, the legislation calls for quality controls requiring referrals to specialists from primary physicians, continuing education for medical personnel, and utilization reviews. Restrictive state laws as to licensure and interstate mobility and the development and operation of group-practice plans would be inoperative under the program.

A major problem that is likely to arise under a plan of the Kennedy-Griffiths type is that of underfinancing. As noted here, the primary mechanism for controlling costs would be the budget ceilings set by a national health budget prepared by a health board each year. If unit costs rose much more than anticipated —not an unlikely development with increased demand in the presence of a noncompetitive market—the program funds would be inadequate to meet necessary program expenditures. This probably would lead to an attempt to control costs by government edict and a bitter conflict between the providers (physicians and hospitals) and the administrators of the program.

Health Maintenance Organizations

Health maintenance organizations (HMOs) are insurance schemes that offer comprehensive health services at a prepaid annual fee. They provide a mix of outpatient and hospital services through a single organization and a single payment mechanism. More than seven million Americans now receive comprehensive health care from organizations of this type such as the Kaiser Permanente program in California and the HIP of New York City.

Legislation aimed at stimulating the growth of HMOs—the Health Maintenance Organization Act—was adopted by Congress in December 1973. The act authorizes Federal expenditures of $375 million during a 5-year period to aid in the development of HMOs. Assistance would fall into four categories: (1) aid for feasibility studies, (2) planning, (3) initial development, and (4) initial operation. To receive assistance, HMOs would have to meet certain minimum standards specified in the act, with priority given to rural or medically underserved areas. The greatest stimulus to the growth of HMOs may come from the acts requirement that employers of at least 25 persons who offer them health insurance must give them the option of HMO coverage if there is an HMO in the community that meets Federal standards.

Health maintenance organizations are commonly defended as an effective mechanism for controlling costs. Basically, there are three ways in which HMOs can control costs. First, the revenues of HMOs are a fixed amount not based on the kind or amount of service rendered to a patient. Consequently, they have a financial incentive to provide care in the most economical way possible—that is, through the use of the least costly service consistent with maintaining quality. By contrast, in a fee-for-service system, the physician has an incentive to provide the most expensive treatment—the more care provided, the greater the income of the physician. Furthermore, because HMOs are faced with fixed revenues, they are encouraged to prevent illness in order to hold down costs.

[76] Ibid., p. 181.

Second, by providing comprehensive health care, HMOs will tend to lower hospital utilization rates and emphasize reliance on less costly outpatient services. Blue Cross and Blue Shield plans, on the other hand, have tended to stimulate excessive hospital use by making benefits contingent on hospitalization, whereas out-patient service costs must be paid for by the individual; as a result, if the alternatives present themselves, the physician will recommend hospitalization to cut the patient costs.

Third, by providing an alternative to existing plans, HMOs may increase the competitive pressure on those plans to control costs.

Although a number of studies indicate that HMOs do reduce costs,[77] those incentives that reduced costs may also provide an incentive to reduce quality. As Sylvia A. Law has written, "There is no economic incentive for an HMO to provide a prolonged and intensive course of life-saving treatment. Incentives for economy can also be incentives for no care or inferior care. For example, if a hearing defect can be ignored, compensated for with a hearing aid, or permanently corrected with expensive surgery, an HMO will have an economic motive to do nothing or to prescribe a hearing aid. The danger that HMOs will provide inferior care is particularly acute when the organization is a profit-making one, when the physician's compensation is based on a percentage of profit rather than a fixed salary, when physicians work only part-time for the HMO and also have a private fee-for-service practice, when HMO enrollees have no alternative means of obtaining medical care, and when the HMO population is exclusively poor or aged." Law suggests that "The dangers inherent in HMO development could be alleviated by extensive government regulations of the quality of care provided, by a requirement of direct and effective consumer control of the HMO, or by the effective introduction of competition and informed consumer choice into the health care market."[78]

Society has delegated considerable power to the AMA and its constituent societies and, as we have seen, they have all too frequently used that power in a socially undesirable manner. Organized medicine has restricted entry into the medical profession, thereby imposing heavy costs both on individuals barred from practicing medicine and on society, which is getting less medical care than it needs. It has often, and with considerable success, opposed technological changes in the organization and distribution of medical services, innovations that could have raised the quality and reduced the costs of medical care. Furthermore, through its aggressive political lobbying, the AMA has been enormously successful in resisting legislation it did not want passed or, when that was not possible, molding the legislation so that it was in a form more acceptable to organized medicine.

Many proposals for improving the quality and reducing the cost of American medical care are currently being discussed: group-practice techniques for re-

---

[77] U.S. Department of Health, Education, and Welfare, *Towards a Comprehensive Health Policy for the 1970s* (Washington, D.C.: U.S. Government Printing Office, 1971.

[78] Sylvia A. Law, *Blue Cross, What Went Wrong?* (New Haven: Yale University Press, 1974), p. 108.

ducing the unnecessary utilization of hospitals; expanding the opportunities for increasing the efficiency of medical education; the use of "new types of personnel to relieve the physician of those tasks not requiring the long (and extremely costly) period of education and training that characterizes medicine in the United States";[79] and comprehensive systems of financing medical care with universal compulsory coverage—employer-employee plans financed with Federal subsidies to cover low-income groups, or some variant of a national health insurance scheme paid by general taxation. But no matter what proposals are made for technological innovation or the financing of medical care, no matter how desirable these changes might be, whether they are tried, or how successful they will be if tried, they will, to a significant extent, depend on the response of organized medicine. Unfortunately, the way the AMA has used its market power in the past leaves little reason for society to be sanguine about the cooperativeness of organized medicine in the future.

What, then, can be done to curb the power of organized medicine? A basic requirement is the elimination of its control over licensing. As Milton Friedman has argued, and as we have discussed, licensure is the key to AMA power. After surveying the effects of organized medicine's activities, Friedman concluded:

> When these effects are taken into account, I am myself persuaded that licensure has reduced both the quantity and quality of medical practice; that it has reduced the opportunities available to people who would like to be physicians, forcing them to pursue occupations they regard as less attractive; that it has forced the public to pay more for less satisfactory medical services; and that it has retarded technological development both in medicine itself and in the organization of medical practice. I conclude that licensure should be eliminated as a requirement for the practice of medicine.[80]

Few would be prepared to go as far as Friedman's vigorous laissez faire position. The social acceptance of licensing in medicine indicates general belief in the desirability of providing protection for the consumer through the maintenance of standards. Fortunately, however, it is not necessary to go as far as Friedman suggests. A more moderate approach is possible whereby AMA power can be curbed and at the same time socially acceptable medical standards maintained.

"In occupational licensing," as Walter Gellhorn has stated, "the choice is not between some regulation and none. The choice is between licensing for the sake of the occupations and, on the other hand, licensing for the sake of the public at large."[81] The argument generally made in support of having licensing boards controlled by professionals drawn from the regulated occupation is that only those professionals can have the technical competence required for the evaluation of license applicants. Gellhorn points the way out of this dilemma: "The solution of this difficulty . . . lies in creating a responsible administrative

[79] Rashi Fein, *The Doctor Shortage* (Washington, D.C.: Brookings, 1967), p. 11.
[80] Friedman, op. cit., p. 158.
[81] Walter Gellhorn, *Individual Freedom and Governmental Restraints* (Baton Rouge, La.: State University Press, 1956), p. 143. (Italics supplied.)

body that, if need be, may employ vocationally experienced staff members and *that should in all instances recruit suitable advisory groups from within the affected occupations.*[82] The italicized words hold the key to curbing the power of organized medicine. The physician's role on a medical licensing board should be in an *advisory* capacity; his control over licensing *policy* should be eliminated.

The principle of using physicians only in an advisory capacity has general applicability. The principle is applicable to the machinery for accrediting medical schools, to the determination of staff privileges in hospitals, to the limitations imposed on nonmedical health practitioners, to the operation of utilization review procedures, and to the determination of "reasonable charges" under the Medicare programs. Only if this principle is vigorously and generally applied can the social problems created by the contradictions in the concept of professionalism be resolved in society's interest. *Wherever there is a need to set standards in the medical market and the possibility of a conflict of interest exists, physicians should not be in policy-making positions.*

[82] Ibid., p. 151.

SUGGESTED READINGS

BOOKS AND PAMPHLETS

Fein, R. *The Doctor Shortage.* Washington, D.C.: The Brookings Institution, 1967.

Friedman, Milton. *Capitalism and Freedom.* Chicago: University of Chicago Press, 1962.

Garceau, Oliver. *The Political Life of the American Medical Association.* Cambridge, Mass.: Harvard University Press, 1941.

Klarman, H. *The Economics of Health.* New York: Columbia University Press, 1965.

Law, Sylvia A. *Blue Cross, What Went Wrong?* New Haven: Yale University Press, 1974.

Rayack, Elton. *Professional Power and American Medicine.* Cleveland, Ohio: World Publishing Company, 1967.

Somers, Herman M., and Anne R. Somers. *Doctors, Patients, and Health Insurance.* Washington, D.C.: The Brookings Institution, 1961.

Stevens, Rosemary. *American Medicine and the Public Interest.* New Haven: Yale University Press, 1971.

GOVERNMENT PUBLICATIONS

U.S. Department of Health, Education, and Welfare. *Physicians for a Growing America.* Report of the Surgeon General's Consultant Group on Medical Education, Washington, D.C., 1959.

———. *Report of the National Conference on Medical Costs.* Washington, D.C., 1967.

———. *Health Manpower Perspective: 1967*, Public Health Service Publication, no. 1667.

JOURNAL AND MAGAZINE ARTICLES

Arrow, K. J. "Uncertainty and the Welfare Economics of Medical Care." *American Economic Review*, **53**: 941 (Dec. 1963).

Hyde, D. R., P. Wolff, A. Gross, and E. L. Hoffman. "The American Medical Association: Power, Purpose, and Politics in Organized Medicine." *Yale Law Journal*, **43** : 938 (May 1954).

Kessel, R. "Price Discrimination in Medicine." *Journal of Law and Economics*, **1** : 20 (Oct. 1958).

Muller, C. "Economic Analysis of Medical Care in the United States," *American Journal of Public Health*, **51**:33 (Jan. 1961).

CHAPTER 13

conglomerates: a "nonindustry"

WILLARD F. MUELLER

The large modern corporation typically is not confined to a single industry but embraces many lines of business and its operations extend into the far corners of the earth. We shall call such a firm a conglomerate enterprise.

Such business organizations are not new. Sixty years ago, before they were stopped by the Department of Justice, the major meat packets of the nation were assembling large commercial empires that spanned many industries and many countries.[1] What is new is that, in much of the economy, conglomerate enterprise is no longer the exception, but the rule.

This transformation of the corporation is no less significant than the replacement of many highly fragmented industries by oligopolistic ones by the great merger movement in around 1900. Economists responded to the new industrial structure of that era by developing the theory of oligopoly. This theory, which explains market power created by the structure of a particular industry, is not adequate to explain many features of an economy increasingly dominated by conglomerate firms.

The growth of conglomerate enterprise threatens to make obsolete much traditional industrial organization theory that has held favor in the economics profession since the 1930s. Theories of oligopoly, for example, that were framed to explain market conduct and performance in terms of the market structure of an industry, are no longer adequate tools of analysis in an age in which conglomerate firms are enjoying greater and greater dominance. For the power that such firms can bring to bear within a particular industry—and, hence, the influence they can exert over prices, output, new entry, and innovation—depends on their market position not just in that one industry but also in all their many lines of business at home and abroad. When the same huge firms are among the

[1] See the report to President Wilson by the newly created Federal Trade Commission, FTC, *Report on the Meat-packing Industry* (Washington D.C.: U.S. Government Printing Office, June 24, 1919.)

leading producers in separate industries—for example, coal and petroleum—the industry lines themselves may become blurred. This is not to argue that traditional industrial organization theory and research are meaningless, but rather to emphasize a need for including conglomeration as an additional structural variable in explaining behavior in many contemporary industries.

Because all huge firms are conglomerates to varying degrees, Corwin Edwards coined the term, *conglomerate bigness*.[2] Because bigness and conglomerates are correlated, increasing centralization of the economy in a relatively few vast corporations is one index of the growing importance of conglomerate bigness in the economy.[3] We, therefore, begin our discussion of conglomerate bigness by examining the growing centralization of the economy, and especially the unique role conglomerate mergers have played in the process in recent years.

I. INDUSTRIAL CENTRALIZATION AND CONGLOMERATE BIGNESS

Although the great merger movement around 1900 centralized control over much of manufacturing, at the time, manufacturing represented a relatively small part of the economy. Whereas in around 1900 income originating in agriculture almost equalled income originating in manufacturing, today income originating in manufacturing is 10 times greater than that in agriculture.

Moreover, compared with today's industrial elite, the early twentieth-century business monarchs ruled very modest domains. Today's two largest manufacturing corporations, alone, have greater sales (even after adjusting for inflation) than did all manufacturing companies combined in 1900.

But the leading corporations have not only grown larger in an absolute sense, but in a relative sense as well. Since the mid-1920s, the leading corporations have expanded substantially their share of the total assets held by corporations engaged primarily in manufacturing. The top corporations' share rose primarily during periods of rapid growth by mergers: first during the frenzied—although relatively brief—movement of 1926–1931, and, again, during the accelerating merger activity since 1950.

The sharpest increase in the postwar years occurred from 1966 to 1968, when the share held by the top 200 industrials jumped from 57 per cent to 61 per cent.[4] Indeed, by 1968, the top 100 held a larger share than had been held by the top 200 in 1950, an increase attributable primarily to mergers. Following the sharp

[2] Corwin Edwards, "Conglomerate Bigness as a Source of Power," in *Business Concentration Price Policy* (Princeton, N.J.: Princeton University Press, Conference of National Bureau of Economic Research, 1955), pp. 346–347.

[3] In 1968, 181 of the 200 largest industrials manufactured ten or more products; in 1960, only 149 of the 200 largest made ten or more products. FTC, Staff Report, *Economic Report on Corporate Mergers* (Washington, D.C.: U.S. Government Printing Office, 1969), p. 224. Hereafter referred to as FTC, *Merger Report*.

[4] Ibid., p. 173.

drop in merger activity after 1969, the top 200 corporations' share of industrial assets has remained at the new merger-achieved highs.[5]

Some economists seem to infer that there exists no problem of industrial centralization and conglomeration unless the share of assets held by the top 100 or 200 firms does not increase continually. But this misses a crucial point. The most relevant measure of conglomerate bigness is the share held by *all* very large corporations. One such index is the share held by industrial corporations with assets of $1 billion or more. Whereas in 1929 there were only three corporations of this size, by 1973 there were 136. These large corporations' share of manufacturing assets grew from 8 per cent in 1939 to 53 per cent in 1973.[6] Although inflation of asset values explains part of the upward trend,[7] the crucial fact is that, in 1973, so few corporations controlled more than one half of all manufacturing assets. Moreover, another 24 per cent of the assets were held by corporations with assets between $100 million and $1 billion; many of these corporations are also quite conglomerated.

The trend toward growing centralization and conglomerate bigness is even greater than shown here because corporate decision making is, in many instances, further centralized by numerous corporate joint ventures among the large corporations. For example, leading petroleum companies operate hundreds of joint ventures, both with other large corporations and numerous smaller ones. Such joint ventures involve the partial merging of the parties involved. By forming new communities of interest or by strengthening existing ones, joint ventures create the capacity to reduce both actual and potential competition among their large corporate parents.

The enormous merger movement in manufacturing during the 1960s was part of a broader picture of centralization and conglomeration in the American economy. Increasingly, manufacturing corporations acquired many large non-manufacturing concerns. Firms engaged in retail distribution, insurance, broad-

---

[5] The top 200 corporations' share of total industrial assets is even larger than the preceding estimates suggest. Many corporations hold large investment interests in other domestic and foreign corporations. Were these unconsolidated assets included in the calculations, the top 200 corporations may hold as much as two thirds of all assets of United States corporations engaged primarily in manufacturing. See U.S. Congress, Senate, Subcommittee on Antitrust and Monopoly, Committee on the Judiciary, *Economic Concentration, Hearings*, 91st Cong., 1st sess., pt. 8, 1969, p. 4550. (Testimony of Willard F. Mueller.) Additionally, large corporations operate numerous facilities that actually are owned by the Federal government. Although data are incomplete, in 1967, government-owned property operated by private corporations had assets of $14.7 billion. See U.S. Congress, Joint Economic Committee, Subcommittee on Economy in Government, *Economy in Government Procurement and Property Management*, 90th Cong., 2d sess., Apr. 1968, p. 7. Because most of these facilities were operated by the largest corporations they contribute to a further concentration of control over productive resources in the United States.

[6] 1929 estimates based on Norman Collins and Lee Preston, "The Size Structure of the Largest Industrial Firms, 1909–1958," *American Economic Review*, **51**:1005–1011 (Dec. 1961); 1973 estimates from FTC, *Quarterly Financial Report for Manufacturing Corporations*, Fourth Quarter (Washington, D.C.: U.S. Government Printing Office, 1973), p. 61.

[7] After adjusting for changes in the wholesale price level for 1929–1973, 15 corporations would have had assets exceeding $1 billion in 1929 and would have controlled 18 per cent of manufacturing assets.

casting, newspapers, and the utilities also were caught up in the movement. Even the holding company returned to prominence as a vehicle by which non-industrial corporations, especially railroads and banks, extended their control and influence over major industrial activities.[8]

II. MERGERS AND INDUSTRIAL CONGLOMERATION

One of the most important characteristics of recent merger activity is that as it intensified, the share of horizontal and vertical mergers declined sharply, as more and more mergers were of the conglomerate type. Horizontal mergers are those among companies producing identical or very closely interchangeable products—for example, two manufacturers of steel products. Vertical mergers are those between companies in a buyer-seller relationship—for example, a shoe manufacturer and a shoe retailer. Conglomerate mergers are those between companies that are neither direct competitors nor in a buyer-seller relationships with one another. Such mergers may be subdivided into three claasses: (1) Geographic market extension mergers, which involve mergers among companies producing identical products but selling in separate geographic (economic) markets—for example, a fluid milk processor in Chicago merging with a fluid milk processor in New York; (2) *product extension* mergers, which involve mergers between companies that are functionally related in production and/or distribution but sell products not in direct competition with each other—for example, a fluid milk company merging with an ice cream company; and (3) *pure* conglomerate mergers, which involve mergers between companies that fall in none of these categories—for example, a railroad and a tire manufacturer.

In the period 1948/1955, most mergers were horizontal or vertical in nature. As rules of law relative to such mergers became increasingly stringent and as merger activity accelerated, a growing share of mergers were of the conglomerate variety. The result was to enhance further the absolute and relative size of many already large corporations, as well as to create many new ones. Twenty-five large corporations whose growth was accelerated sharply by mergers, primarily conglomerate mergers, are shown on Table 1.[9] This list is restricted to corporations already ranking among the 100 largest industrials in 1974. Many of these already were substantial firms in 1960, when ten ranked among the top 100 industrials and 22 ranked among the top 500. Whereas sales of all corporations engaged primarily in manufacturing grew by 135 per cent from 1960–1974, these corporations grew by 772 per cent. All but two of these 25 corporations grew by more than 500 per cent and 11 grew by more than 1000 per cent during the period. All had annual sales of more than $2 billion in 1974, and all but one increased its rank among the top industrial corporations.

---

[8] FTC, *Merger Report*, op. cit., pp. 65–67.
[9] Eighteen of these firms were included in the FTC list of the 25 most active acquiring manufacturing corporations for the period 1961–1968. Ibid., pp. 260–261. All others were also substantial acquirers.

TABLE 1

Twenty-five Large Corporations Making Extensive Acquisitions, 1961–1974

| | SALES[a] | | GROWTH, | RANK AMONG INDUSTRIALS | |
| | 1974 | 1960 | 1960–1974 | | |
CORPORATION	($)	($)	(PER CENT)	1974	1960
ITT	11,154	811	1,375	10	51
Continental Oil	7,041	694	1,015	17	64
Atlantic-Richfield	6,740	561	1,201	18	77
Occidental Oil	5,719	3	—	20	—[b]
Tenneco	5,001	535	935	25	85
Phillips Petroleum	4,981	1,200	415	25	31
LTV	4,768	148	3,222	29	285
RCA	4,594	1,486	209	31	25
Union Oil	4,419	427	1,035	34	107
Rockwell Industries	4,408	116	3,800	35	353
Sun Oil	3,800	750	507	37	59
Beatrice Foods	3,541	443	799	42	105
W. R. Grace	3,472	553	629	44	80
Greyhound	3,458	287	1,205	45	—[c]
Litton Industries	3,082	188	1,639	53	249
McDonald-Douglas	3,075	437	604	54	110
Ralston Purina	3,073	510	603	55	92
Philip Morris	3,042	330	922	57	140
Singer	2,661	526	506	66	86
CPC International	2,570	276	831	71	171
TRW	2,486	420	592	76	113
Georgia Pacific	2,432	222	1,095	79	213
Gulf & Western	2,296	24	—	83	—[b]
Textron	2,114	383	552	89	124
FMC	2,074	364	570	91	129
Total 25 corporations	102,001	11,694	772		
All manufactures	1,010,000	431,329	134		

[a] Sales for consolidated subsidiaries.
[b] Not among the 1000 largest industrials in 1960.
[c] Rank based on predecessor corporation.
[d] Not primarily an industrial corporation in 1960.

But these mergers did much more than increase the absolute size of the acquiring corporations. Today, all of these corporations operate in many geographic and product markets, and most have extensive foreign as well as domestic holdings. In a word, they are huge *conglomerate* enterprises.

Because the boundaries of such an enterprise extend far beyond particular industries and even nations, its economic significance cannot be comprehended by traditional analyses that focus on individual industries. To capture the unique and multifaceted dimensions of corporate conglomeration requires an in-depth examination of individual enterprises. We shall therefore examine in some detail the growth and current scope of International Telephone and Telegraph Corporation (ITT), the most pervasive conglomerate acquirer during the 1960s.

III. ITT: THE ANATOMY OF A CONGLOMERATE

In 1960, International Telephone and Telegraph Corporation embarked on an ambitious diversification-through-merger program to transform itself from what its chairman, Harold S. Geneen, characterized as "primarily a one-product company."[10] Although it had not yet become a household word, ITT already was a substantial enterprise in 1960; it had sales of $811 million and ranked fifty-first among the nation's largest industrials. In the four decades following its founding in 1920, it had become a large international manufacturer of telecommunication equipment and an operator of telephone communication systems.

From 1960 to 1974, its sales grew by 1375 per cent, making it tenth among the nation's industrials. Even this understates ITT's actual size. Its total 1974 consolidated assets of $11 billion did not include the Hartford Fire Insurance Company and other unconsolidated corporations with combined assets exceeding $7 billion; nor did they include the many government-owned facilities that it operated. In 1970, it operated 13 NASA and Department of Defense installations and manufacturing plants with combined assets of $527 million.[11]

Like many other new conglomerates, ITT is a leading defense-space company. But unlike most others, it also has a vast international organization that, according to an ITT annual report, "is constantly at work around the clock—in 67 nations on six continents," in activities extending "from the Arctic to the Antarctic and quite literally from the bottom of the sea to the moon. . . ."[12]

During 1961–1968, ITT acquired 52 domestic and 55 foreign corporations, with the acquired domestic companies alone holding combined assets of about $1.5 billion. During 1969, alone, ITT's board of directors approved 22 domestic and 11 foreign acquisitions. The three largest—Hartford Fire Insurance Company, Grinnell Corporation, and Canteen Corporation—added more than $2 billion, which brought its acquisitions total for the decade to near $4 billion, far ahead of any other company. Since 1969, it has acquired more than 50 domestic and foreign firms for which it paid about $350 million.[13]

As a result of its acquisition effort, by 1974, its traditional line of telecommunications and electronics manufacturing accounted for only one fifth of its total

[10] ITT, Annual Report, 1967, p. 3.
[11] Prepared testimony of Willard F. Mueller, in United States v. ITT and Grinnell Corporation, Civil no. 13319, Appendix 5.
[12] ITT, Annual Report, 1968.
[13] Williard F. Mueller, "The ITT Settlement: A Deal with Justice?" Industrial Organization Review, 1:80 (1973).

revenues. Much of the rest was derived from the operations of leading firms acquired in such diverse businesses as electronics, life insurance, consumer finance, car rentals, hotels, banking, chemical cellulose and lumber, residential construction, and silica for the glass, chemical metallurgical, ceramic, and building industries.

If another merger of major dimensions with American Broadcasting Company (ABC) had not been abandoned in January 1968, after a challenge by the Department of Justice, ITT would have been established also as a leader in radio and television broadcasting in the United States. It also would have been engaged in the operation of motion picture theaters and amusement centers, the manufacture and sale of phonograph records, and publishing.

Significantly, most of ITT's acquired assets came not from small, ailing companies, but from profitable corporations that were already leaders in their field: Rayonier Corporation had assets of $292 million and was the world's leading producer of chemical cellulose; Continental Baking Company had assets of $186 million and was the world's largest baking and cake company; Avis, Inc. had assets of $49 million and was the world's second-largest car rental system; Sheraton Corporation of America, with assets of $286 million, was the world's largest hotel and motel system; Levitt & Sons, Inc., with assets of $91 million, was the leading builder of single-family dwellings; Grinnell Corporation, with assets of $184 million, was the largest producer of automatic fire protection systems; Canteen Corporation had assets of $140 million and operated one of the largest vending machine systems; and Hartford Fire Insurance Corporation was one of the oldest and largest property and casualty insurance writers, with assets in 1974 of $3.5 billion.

Although ITT is primarily a manufacturing corporation, selling to and buying from thousands of other businesses, it also touches directly the lives of millions. As a consumer, you can buy furnishings for your home with personal loans from one of ITT's finance subsidiaries; you can buy radios, phonographs, tape recorders, and TV sets made by ITT in Germany and England; insure your home at ITT-Hartford Fire Insurance; buy your life insurance from one of ITT's life insurance subsidiaries; invest your savings in ITT-Hamilton Management mutual funds; munch on ITT-Continental Hostess bakery products; savor an ITT-Smithfield ham; buy cigarettes and coffee from ITT-Canteen vending machines; stay at hotels or motels owned by ITT-Sheraton; buy books from ITT's Bobbs-Merrill publishing division; or attend one of ITT's technical and business schools. Finally, had the ABC-ITT merger not been blocked by the Justice Department, you could have been ITT's guest for an evening of TV viewing.

Moreover, part of each American's tax dollars spent on defense and space programs goes to ITT, which is one of the nation's prime defense contractors. International Telephone and Telegraph maintains Washington's "hot lines" to Moscow, mans the Air Force Distant Early Warning System (DEW) and the giant Ballistic Missile Early Warning System (BMEWS) sites in Greenland and Alaska.

With its numerous foreign operations, ITT is an important force in international economic affairs. Since 1960, ITT has acquired more than 80 foreign companies and now controls about one third of Europe's telecommunications business.

Some ITT officials are better known in circles of national and international diplomacy than in business. They have included such notables as former U.N. Secretary-General Trygve Lie, as director of ITT Norway; one-time Belgium Premier Paul-Henri Spaak, as a director of ITT Belgium; two members of the British House of Lords; a member of the French National Assembly; and, at home, John A. McCone, former director of the CIA, and Eugene R. Black, who is widely known in international economic and political circles where he has held such important posts as the special financial advisor to the Secretary-General of the United Nations, and financial advisor to the Sheik of Kuwait, as well as board member of dozens of large corporations. It is not unfair to ask, are such men on ITT's board because of their business acumen or their power and prestige in domestic and international politics? This raises a corollary question of who is more powerful in international diplomacy, the U.S. State Department or huge international conglomerates like ITT?

Nor is concern with these matters based on mere speculation or conjecture. Recent public exposés document widespread corporate misconduct in foreign affairs. The Senate Foreign Relations Subcommittee on Multinational Corporations documented ITT's efforts to overthrow the Allende government in Chile, including efforts to fund subversion by the CIA.[14] Nor is this intervention in the affairs of other nations unique.[15] Most recently, in a "sensational Belgium trial," the managing director of Belgium-ITT was found guilty of bribing a high official of the Belgian state telephone service.[16]

The growing multinational character of huge conglomerates raises important issues concerning their national allegiances. Their multinational make-up inevitably creates dual loyalties that make it difficult to perceive the American national interest in their dealings at home and abroad.

Quite clearly, massive conglomerate corporations like ITT have dimensions of economic and political power extending beyond that held by the traditional large corporations that, while large in absolute terms, are more narrowly specialized in relatively few lines of industry. We shall not here fully analyze the competitive ramifications of this colossal conglomerate enterprise. (Subsequently, we shall explore ways in which ITT and other conglomerates have deployed their resources to injure competition.) But we shall examine briefly a generally neglected dimension of conglomerate power, the potential to shift the balance of bargaining power between corporations and labor unions.

[14] U.S. Congress, Senate, Committee on Foreign Relations, Subcommittee on Multinational Corporations, *International Telephone and Telegraph Company and Chile, 1970–1971, Report*, 93d Cong., 1st sess., June 21, 1973, pp. 4–6.
[15] See Morton Mintz and Jerry Cohen, *America, Inc.* (New York: The Dial, 1971), pp. 330–337, who document ITT's political power in Great Britain, Canada, Denmark, Iceland, and the United States.
[16] *New York Times*, July 27, 1975, Sec. 3, p.1.

One characteristic of the conglomerate is its special capacity to practice cross subsidization, the practice of using profits from one line of business to support another line. Because the conglomerate operates in many fields, in some of which it earns large profits, it may use its "excess" profits to subsidize losses in some of its lines of business. If the subsidized market is small compared to the corporation's overall operations, subsidization may have little impact on over-all profitability.

Discussion of cross subsidization is usually restricted to its impact on the competitive process. Here we shall examine its potential for enhancing a corporation's power vis-à-vis the labor unions with which it bargains.

Traditionally, even America's largest corporations—General Motors, Standard Oil (N.J.), and U.S. Steel—operated in relatively few industries. Even today, a single union represents the bulk of the steelworkers in the United States. In such cases, the collective bargaining process involves a rather direct confrontation between the labor union and the corporation with which it bargains. But, as corporations operate across a growing spectrum of industries and own plants in many nations, they achieve great flexibility and discretion at the bargaining table.

This characteristic of the conglomerate creates a new environment for the collective bargaining process. Industrial conglomeration may dissipate the bargaining power of an individual trade union if its members are in an industry that represents a small part of the total business of a huge conglomerate. As one union leader put it, "If the outfit we bargain with provides only 20 per cent of the conglomerate's profit, our strike doesn't hurt them that much." In practice, a struck plant may represent far less than 20 per cent of a conglomerate's total business.

International Telephone and Telegraph Corporation provides an instructive example. Although ITT was already a large corporation on the eve of its transformation into a huge multinational conglomerate, its operations then were centered largely on telecommunications. But, in less than a decade, the picture changed sharply, as its operations became so widely dispersed that it was no longer heavily dependent on any one operation for its income.

Today, individual products may be made in ITT companies in many countries, to an extent that almost defies grouping. It is no longer dependent on any one line of business, and this has important implications for collective bargaining. First, many ITT employees are located outside the United States, and much of ITT's income originates abroad. Second, many of its domestic employees are not affiliated with any union. This is particularly true of employees in the service fields, such as insurance companies, mutual funds, and vending machine operations. Third, even ITT's organized employees are members of many different unions in different industries.

Even a partial listing of the unions that bargain with ITT is long. It includes, IUE, IBEW, Communications Workers, Auto Workers, Machinists, Steelworkers, Molders and Allied Workers, Plumbers, Teamsters, Bakery and

Confectionary Workers, Hotel and Restaurant Employees, Pulp and Sulphite Workers, Chemical Workers, and Papermakers and Paperworkers.

Its growing conglomeration gives ITT the potential for shifting the balance of economic power between it and the individual labor unions representing its workers. Consider, for example, ITT Continental Baking. As the nation's alrgest baking corporation, Continental already was a formidable bargainer prior to merging with ITT. But now that it is a part of ITT, it accounts for less than 4 per cent of ITT's net income. Thus, should the Bakery and Confectionary Workers go on strike for a full year and completely shut down the domestic portion of ITT's baking operations, ITT's over-all profit margins would not be affected critically. Strikes by other individual unions in many other fields would have an even smaller impact on ITT's over-all operation.

Conceivably, multinational conglomerates could become essentially strike-proof in dealing with unions in individual nations. Some unions have responded to the conglomerate corporation with coordinated bargaining, which is designed to bring together all the major international unions dealing with a conglomerate. European labor unions are currently exploring the feasibility of coordinated bargaining with such huge multinational corporations as British Petroleum, Unilever, and BASF.

Labor's response to growing conglomerate power demonstrates again that centralization of economic power causes and invites responses that reach beyond product markets to affect more general and far-reaching economic relationships. With prophetic insight, the late Senator Estes Kefauver, in urging strengthening of the antimerger law, observed,

> The concentration of great economic power in a few corporations necessarily leads to the formation of large nationwide unions. The development of the two necessarily leads to big bureaus in government to deal with them.[17]

IV. CONGLOMERATE MERGERS: MOTIVES

Just what do these developments augur for the future of our economic and political institutions? It is well to begin by appreciating what they do not promise: They do not promise to usher in a new era of productive efficiency or technological advance. Although our knowledge is far from complete, it is clear that recent merger activity was not propelled primarily by the technological imperatives of large scale. Rather, most *large* mergers were motivated by special factors that, while conferring advantage and privilege on the private parties involved, promised no corresponding social benefit. Space permits only a brief review of the evidence.

Perhaps no concept so rapidly captured the imagination of so many as that conglomerate merger managers were able to reap the benefits of synergism—

---

[17] U.S. Congress, House, *Report No. 1191 on H.R. 2734*, 81st Cong., 1st sess. Aug, 4, 1949, p. 13.

that is, where combining separate substances produces an effect greater than that resulting from the substances used separately. In the popular trade parlance, synergism results in two plus two equaling five.[18] This thesis held that the explanation for the conglomerate merger wave was to be found in the new management techniques of the merger makers. The Jimmy Lings (LTV) and Tex Thortons (Litton Industries) were viewed as a new breed of business manager, omniscient men who could make dynamic firms out of lethargic ones,[19] who could make two blades of grass grow where others struggled to grow one.

For a time there was superficial evidence that the new conglomerates could, indeed, outperform other corporations relying primarily on internal growth. A number showed spectacular increases in their profit performance. This apparent superior profit performance became reflected in seemingly ever-rising stock prices. Few of the new conglomerates were praised more highly than Litton Industries, whose top management team, headed by Tex Thorton, had been schooled in the system analysis approach so popular at the Pentagon. During 1958–1969, Litton acquired at least 97 relatively small companies in such diverse fields as military and commercial ships, medical X-ray equipment, frozen foods, textbooks, store fixtures and refrigeration equipment, office calculators, typewriters, power transmission equipment, microwave ovens, and education systems.

In what seemed indisputable evidence of synergism, Litton management had a magical record of earnings growth. Earnings per share of common stock doubled from 1960–1962, more than doubled again from 1962–1965, and very nearly doubled from 1965–1967. This profit performance became reflected in the astronomical rise in the value of its common stock, which rose from a low of $6 per share in 1960 to $104\frac{3}{4}$ in early 1968. Then a precipitous decline set in.

[18] See "Wall Street: The Lure of $2 + 2 = 5$," *Newsweek*, May 8, 1967, p. 82. This theme echoed the contemporary explanations given for the great merger wave peaking in 1929, when journalists also "discovered" that merger makers of that day were making "business history by adding two and two to make five." *Business Week*, Nov. 27, 1929, p. 27.

[19] Among the proponents of this belief are W. Fred Weston, "The Nature and Significance of Conglomerate Firms," *St. Johns Law Review*, Spring 1970, pp. 66–80; and Neil H. Jacoby, "The Conglomerate Corporation," *The Center Magazine*, July 1969, p. 41. In 1970, J. Fred Weston presented research findings analyzing the performance of 60 conglomerates in U.S. Congress, Senate, Committee on the Judiciary, *Hearings on Economic Concentration before the Subcommittee on Antitrust and Monopoly*, 91st Cong., 2d sess., pt. 8, 1969, pp. 4735–4751. J. Fred Weston, "Conglomerate Firms and Economic Efficiency," in pt. 8, *The Conglomerate Merger Problem*. His analysis of various dimensions of their financial performance led Weston to conclude, "Given the unfavorable earnings potentials in the industries from which many of the 'conglomerates' started as a base, their performance suggests that economies have been achieved." p. 4740. Examination of Weston's conglomerates for the period since 1967 reveals a decidedly different picture than he observed. From 1958–1967, the earnings of these conglomerates per share rose at an annual rate twice that of firms composing the Dow Jones Industrial Average (DJIA). From 1967–1974, the earnings per share of firms in the DJIA grew 5.5 times more rapidly than Weston's conglomerates (five were acquired after 1967 and, therefore, were excluded in the latter comparison). Similarly, whereas in 1967 the price-earnings ratio of Weston's conglomerates was 13 per cent above that of the DJIA, in 1974, the DJIA was 27 per cent above the conglomerates. Finally, whereas in 1967 the conglomerates' earnings on net worth were 8 per cent higher than the average of all manufacturing corporations, in 1974, such earnings were 28 per cent below this average.

The first blow to the synergism mystique surrounding Litton came when its profits declined in 1968, the first annual decline in its history. The initial reaction was one of guarded disbelief. As one financial analyst put it, "So hallowed had Litton's name become that, presumably, it was unthinkable among its disciples that the company could ever have anything but one banner year after another ad infinitum."[20] In the face of a generally ebullient stock market Litton's common stock tumbled to a low of $68 in 1968. But the unthinkable happened: 1968 did not prove to be an exception. Instead, it was the beginning of a long downward slide in Litton's fortunes, as its common stock fell to a low of $2\frac{7}{8} in 1974 when it incurred losses of $1.29 per share.

Nor was Litton an exception among leading conglomerates. LTV's common stock rose from an average price of $21 in 1960 to $108 in 1968; it then plummeted to $9.5 in 1974. In contrast, the *Moody's Industrial* average of stocks rose by more than 50 per cent from 1960–1974.

How, then, were some conglomerates able for so long to conceal from stockholders the truth about their corporation's true financial health? The answers lie in management's ability to "manage" profit performance by exploiting a host of accounting and tax gimmicks open to firms growing by mergers. The new conglomerate managers did not discover new management techniques, but rather a seemingly endless number of tax, accounting, and financial gimmicks that favored merger over internal growth. Events in the coal industry show how the discovery of a tax gimmick by one firm triggered other mergers and drastically restructured an industry almost overnight. In 1966, Continental Oil Company acquired Consolidation Coal Company, the country's largest coal producer. According to a Treasury Department report, the merger involved a complicated transaction that permitted Continental to save more than $175 million taxes.[21] Shortly thereafter, Kennecott Copper Company, using the same tax gimmick, acquired Peabody Coal Company, the nation's second-largest coal company. In 1968, the third-largest coal producer was purchased by Occidental Petroleum. Thus, in just 3 years, the three largest coal companies merged into other large corporations, resulting in private gains of hundreds of millions of dollars at the taxpayer's expense.

This is only one of many examples. Consider the effects of the tax loss carry forward provisions of the internal revenue code. After the merger creating the Penn Central railroad, it was able to establish a tax loss carry forward of between $500 million and $600 million. The *Wall Street Journal* reported that "Working under [its] tax shelter . . . the new company could acquire many profitable ventures and still pay no taxes for 5 or 6 years."[22] Not too surprisingly, Penn Central subsequently became an active acquirer of profitable companies. Its holdings included two big real estate developers, Buckeye Pipeline Company,

---

[20] *Financial World*, **129**:12 (Feb. 14, 1968).

[21] U.S. Treasury Department, *Tax Reform Studies and Proposals*, Joint Publication of the House Committee on Ways and Means and the Senate Committee on Finance (Washington, D.C.: U.S. Government Printing Office, Feb. 5, 1969), pt. 2, pp. 268–269.

[22] *Wall Street Journal*, Apr. 17, 1968, p. 25.

Southwestern Oil & Gas Company, Royal Petroleum Company, and a large interest in the Madison Square Gardens Corporation. The last acquisition gave Penn Central an interest in New York's professional basketball and hockey teams, the Knickerbockers and the Rangers. Such helter-skelter growth certainly did not contribute to economic efficiency. Indeed, Penn Central's purchases of nontransportation businesses helped exhaust its working capital, which created the liquidity crises that forced the company into bankruptcy proceedings in June 1970. This experience illustrates that the economy would have been better off had Penn Central management devoted more time to running the trains on time than on making mergers that reduced its tax obligations.

Perhaps the most notorious device used by a merger-active company to accelerate its earnings per share of common stock without increasing real earnings is pooling-of-interest accounting. Under pooling-of-interest accounting the book values of merging companies are combined. This permits an acquiring company to list the value of assets at less than their real costs. Abraham J. Briloff demonstrated how Gulf & Western was able to increase greatly its reported earnings following its 1967 acquisition of Paramount Pictures.

> In its 1967 statements, Gulf & Western asserted that its earnings had more than doubled—from $22 million the previous year to $46 million. While this was certainly dramatic, supplemental data furnished by the report were even more euphoric. They revealed that companies acquired during 1967 contributed a whopping $22 million to the conglomerate's 1967 income, although these companies had earned only $2.6 million during 1966.
> Whether this extraordinary increase in earnings was attributable to the special brilliance and genius of Gulf & Western's management depends on how one defines brilliance and ingenuity. The enormous profit inflation was triggered by Gulf & Western's wholesale disposition of television rights to the Paramount Pictures library. Gulf & Western simply disposed of properties which they had acquired in the acquisition of Paramount.
> By using the pooling-of-interest method of accounting, the conglomerate was able to pay out over $184 million for its 1967 acquisitions, while reflecting only a cost of less than $100 million on its books. It accomplished this by equating the cost of the 1967 acquisitions with the written down (or written off) amounts shown on the books of Paramount and the other acquired companies—that is, $100 million. The other $84 million was free to be used to bolster reported earnings and, as asserted above, a good part of it was so used.[23]

The numerous mergers of ITT offered it a seemingly limitless variety of ways of increasing *reported* earnings per share without any real improvement in operating efficiency. Most important has been its exploitation of the opportunities of accounting rules that permit merging companies to pool their interests. As noted here, the accounting procedure permits companies to pay well above the market price of a company and yet show only the book value of the acquired company. A little-publicized Staff Report of the House Antitrust Subcommittee shows how ITT's use of pooling-of-interest accounting permitted ITT to greatly over-

---

[23] Abraham J. Briloff, "Financial Motives for Conglomerate Growth," *St. John's Law Review*, Spring 1970, p. 877.

state earnings from 1964 to 1968. During that period, it paid $1278 million in stock for companies with a net worth of $534 million. If this excess payment for "goodwill" had been amortized during a 10-year period, ITT's actual reported net income for 1968 would be overstated by 70.4 per cent.[24] This is only one of several methods used by ITT to increase its profits on common stock. It also increased the company's leverage by increasing the ratio of debt capital and preferred stock to common stock.[25] After acquisition, it frequently changed its depreciation policy. Changes in accounting procedures by ITT-Sheraton, Continental Baking, and Rayonier increased ITT's profits by $7.2 million in 1968; this accounting change alone accounted for 11.8 per cent of the increase in ITT's earnings from 1967 to 1968.[26] None of these changes was reported in the notes to ITT's financial statements in 1968.[27]

The failure of ITT to disclose the true source of its ever-growing earnings per share came under increasing fire from financial analysts. For example, Mr. David Norr, partner of First Manhattan Company and a member of the Accounting Principles Board, severely criticized ITT's 1970 annual report for not reflecting retroactively the results of the many companies it had acquired. Norr thought this omission was sufficient grounds for the New York Stock Exchange to halt trading in ITT securities.[28] The exchange did not see fit to discipline one of its leading members.

Other financial analysts have reported their frustrations in seeking to learn the true source of ITT's rising earnings. In an "Alert for Portfolio Managers," investment analysts Scheinman, Hochstin, and Trotta warned, "ITT continues its financial advertising blitz in the financial media with the eye-catching caption, "Here's the story again—in case you missed it in the press."[29] But after careful study of ITT's financial statements—and with no help from ITT—these analysts found that, in 1968 and 1969, 34 per cent of ITT's increased earnings per share were due to such nonrecurring sources of income as sale of securities and plants.[30] The report added that it had "good reason to believe that similar or analogous transactions of even greater magnitude took place in 1970."[31] It concluded that "the key to ITT's 'growth' in 1970 share earnings (ex. Hartford Fire) lies in the undisclosed elements which were responsible for the 1970 increase in deferred taxes—equivalent to 40 cents a share of ITT earnings in 1970."[32]

[24] U.S. Congress, House, Antitrust Subcommittee of the Committee on the Judiciary, *Investigation of Conglomerate Mergers, Staff Report*, 92d Cong., 1st sess., June 1, 1971, p. 414.
[25] Ibid., p. 140.
[26] Ibid., p. 139.
[27] Ibid.
[28] "Accountant Urges Better Reporting Practices," *New York Times*, July 24, 1971. A recent *Fortune* article states that ITT "almost automatically switches the companies it acquires over to its own accounting policies . . . ," which tends to increase current reported earnings. "Harold Geneen's Moneymaking Machine Is Still Humming," *Fortune*, Sept. 1972, p. 90.
[29] Scheinman, Hochstin, and Trotta, "Alert for Portfolio Managers," Supplement P, July 1971, p. 1.
[30] Ibid., p. 1.
[31] Ibid., p. 3.
[32] Ibid.

Fortune magazine reported that, in 1971, ITT again reaped large capital gains from its Hartford Fire Insurance Company acquisition, and that it was likely to continue to do so for many years to come:

> Last year Hartford netted a total of $105 million. The fact that $36 million of this amount came from capital gains was not recorded. Hartford's unrealized capital gains amounted to about $270 million at the end of last year and, barring a major stock market crash, should for years be available to supplement the steadily growing stream of interest and dividend income that rolls out of the company's portfolio.[33]

Hartford is a deep well from which ITT apparently can pump increased reported earnings for years to come. Little wonder an ITT executive described it, "a gold mine."[34]

Banks and investment companies, as in past merger movements, were leading promoters of mergers in the 1960s. One Wall Street investment banker was quoted as follows concerning the shenanigans involved in many merger deals: "I suppose you could call some of it dirty. But it's so much fun. How can anything that much fun be dirty?" However, even some conservative financiers became increasingly concerned lest these questionable tactics ultimately backfire on the business community. Listen to this warning of Paul Costman Cabot, the dean of the Boston financial community, long-time director of J. P. Morgan & Company and one-time treasurer of Harvard University.

> It shocks me that so many investment companies are playing the game too. It works like this: A take-over guy comes to them and says, "I'm going to take over such-and-such at such a price 50 per cent over the current market price. Why don't you buy 5 per cent of the stock and tender it to me when my offer comes out?" So the take-over guy gets a block of stock in friendly hands and the investment company gets an assured, easy profit. Even if the take-over fails, the raped company marries someone else and the investment company still makes out. This is a game that's going to give the whole investment company business a bad name.[35]

Cabot observes, "It seems that each generation is cursed with problems all born of greed and a lust for power." After recounting various adverse effects flowing from these developments, Mr. Cabot concludes, "Possibly the most objectionable feature is the concentration of control and power in so few hands."[36]

These are only among the most obvious gimmicks and motivations that often make mergers a preferred method of growth. Several studies document how various tax and accounting rules and practice encouraged mergers for reasons unrelated to economic efficiency.[37] An FTC report concluded, "The balance of

---

[33] *Fortune*, op. cit., p. 216.

[34] Ibid., p. 212.

[35] Prepared statement of P. C. Cabot before the U.S. Congress, House, Committee on Ways and Means, *Hearings on Tax Reform*, 91st Cong., 1st sess., Mar. 12, 1969.

[36] Ibid.

[37] FTC, Staff Report, op. cit., pp. 69–160. Briloff, op. cit., pp. 872–879; and Henry B. Reiling, "EPS Growth from Financial Packaging: An Accounting Incentive in Acquisitions," *St. Johns Law Review*, Spring 1970, pp. 880–894. Roger Sherman, "How Tax Policy Induces Conglomerate Mergers," *National Tax Journal*, Dec. 1972, pp. 521–529.

evidence so far available lends little support to the view that the current merger movement reflects, in substantial measure, efforts to exploit opportunities to improve efficiency in resource allocation. On the contrary, there are abundant indications that certain institutional arrangements involving tax and accounting methods, aided by speculative developments in the stock market, have played a major role in fueling the current merger movement."[38]

The accounting and tax gimmickry pursued by some conglomerates ultimately caught up with them, and their stock fell from the dizzy heights of the late 1960s. But it would be a mistake to conclude from this that market forces may ultimately punish some conglomerates (or, more correctly, their stockholders) for their financial manipulations, thereby somehow dissipating any undesirable effects growing from industrializing conglomeration and centralization. Students of industrial history are familiar with many cases where firms with merger-achieved market power performed inefficiently after they became very large; yet they continued to present a serious public policy problem. U.S. Steel is a classic example of this. It was created in 1901 by "a combination of combinations" and on a foundation of watered stock. Shielded from competition by its tremendous market power, U.S. Steel nevertheless was very inefficient and had a lackluster research and development program.[39] It has presented one of America's most intractable public policy problems for more than half a century. The lesson to be learned from this is that once huge corporations are formed they do wither away.

It should not be inferred that the recent merger movement was primarily the product of "new conglomerates" challenging the industrial establishment of big business. Although the new conglomerates caught most of the headlines, old-line big companies and some not so new conglomerates actually made most of the large mergers. For example, seven big petroleum companies ranked among the top 25 acquirers during the 1960s. Other long-established companies ranking among the top 25 acquirers during the 1960s were ITT, U.S. Plywood, McDonnell Aircraft, North American Rockwell, and RCA. Many of these established firms, including ITT, also used tax and accounting gimmicks.

None of the preceding is to imply that all mergers are promoted to exploit accounting and tax gimmicks or are for purposes of greed or personal aggrandizement. Many, doubtless, promote efficiency and many others have little impact one way or the other. The literally thousands of the small mergers that have occurred in recent decades fall in these classes. In the preceding, and in what follows, we are concerned primarily with mergers by and among *large* corporations, where the merger for efficiency hypothesis finds little support.

[38] FTC, *Merger Report*, op. cit., p. 159; cf. Samuel R. Reid, *Mergers and the Economy* (New York: McGraw-Hill, 1968).

[39] George W. Stocking, *Basing Point Pricing and Regional Development* (Chapel Hill, N.C.: University of North Carolina Press, 1954), p. 140; Edwin Mansfield, "Size of Firm, Market Structure, and Innovation," *Journal of Political Economy*, **71**:556–576 (Dec. 1963); Walter Adams and Joel Dirlam, "Big Steel, Invention and Innovation," *Quarterly Journal of Economics*, **80**:169 (May 1966).

V. CONGLOMERATE BIGNESS AND THE POLITICAL PROCESS

We have seen that the recent wave of very large mergers has not been motivated primarily by a quest for economic efficiency. This fact alone would not necessarily cause a serious public policy problem were not our economic system becoming centralized in ways that may transform adversely both our political and economic institutions. Corwin Edwards in his seminal article on the conglomerate enterprise, spelled out how such firms are able to extend their economic power into political power:

> The political strength of the great concern is an aspect of its ability to spend. . . . The campaign contributions of large companies and the occasional case of direct or indirect bribery are probably the least significant source of the large company's political power. More important, the large company spends whatever money is needed to argue effectively on behalf of its interest where a particular issue affects it. . . . The work of many people may be required in assembling facts and preparing persuasive arguments relevant to thse decisions. . . . Large concerns are increasingly skilled in these processes, primarily because they take such work seriously and do it on a large scale.[40]

Edwards made these observations just before merger activity began accelerating in 1954–1955. Since then mergers have increasingly centralized the economy in a relatively few vast conglomerate enterprises, thereby further transforming our economic-political order. Simply put, this centralization process is destroying our traditional pluralistic political processes, which rest on a diffused, dispersed, heterogeneous pattern of industrial ownership. Justice William O. Douglas articulated well the American tradition toward centralized economic power when he observed, "Power that controls the economy should be in the hands of elected representatives of the people, not in the hands of an industrial oligarchy. Industrial power should be decentralized. It should be scattered into many hands so that the fortunes of the people will not be dependent on the whim or caprice, the political prejudices, the emotional stability of a few self-appointed men. The fact that they are not vicious men but reasonable and social-minded is irrelevant."[41]

Historians may well record the 1970s as the period when the political power of large corporations was unmasked, making it an issue of great political debate. First came revelations of improper domestic political conduct. International Telephone and Telegraph employed its considerable power in a well-orchestrated drive to receive a favorable antitrust consent decree.[42] The Watergate investigations uncovered numerous illegal political contributions by large corporations. In April 1974, Mr. George M. Steinbrenner, chairman of the board of American Shipbuilding Corporation and owner of the New York Yankees, became the first corporate executive ever indicted on felony charges in connection with illegal

---

[40] Edwards, op. cit.
[41] *United States* v. *Columbia Steel Company et al.*, 334 U.S. 495 (1948).
[42] Mueller, "The ITT Settlement: A Deal with Justice?" op. cit., pp. 67–86.

corporate political contributions.[43] The numerous disclosures of domestic corporate misconduct in political affairs soon were overshadowed by evidence of massive corporate bribery and political interventions in the affairs of other nations. The ITT efforts to overthrow the Allende government in Chile have been documented by the Senate Foreign Relations Committee.[44] United Brands admitted it made a $1.3 million payment to an official of the Honduras government to reduce that country's banana tax; it subsequently admitted making payments of $750,000 to officials of the Italian government.[45]

Northrop Corporation paid $30 million in agents' fees to influence sales of its aircraft to foreign countries. Of this, $450,000 was paid to two Saudi Arabian generals. It subsequently told the Securities Exchange Commission (SEC) it made improper commission payments to five countries.[46] Gulf Oil disbursed $4 million to the ruling political party in South Korea; $110,000 to the President of Bolivia; and $350,000 to his political party. The SEC has charged Gulf with falsifying financial reports to conceal $10.3 million in contributions to politicians at home and abroad from 1960–1972.[47] Tenneco, Inc., the huge conglomerate, admitted it made payments to state and local officials in the United States as well as payments to foreign "consultants" to acquire "properties or materials from foreign governments."[48]

Lockheed Aircraft Corporation paid huge amounts to foreign officials and political organizations to influence aircraft sales to foreign governments. In Saudi Arabia, alone, it has paid or committed $106 million in "commissions" since 1970, millions of which were funneled to Saudi officials through numbered accounts in Liechtenstein and Geneva. It subsequently disclosed making large bribes to government officials in Japan and Italy. It admitted making a $1.1 million payment to a "high Dutch official" whom the Dutch government identified as Prince Bernhard, husband of Queen Juliana.[49] Lockheed's political clout in America had previously been demonstrated by its success in getting the Congress to guarantee a $195 million loan to Lockheed.

Perhaps no observer of the large modern corporation was surprised that America's largest industrial corporation apparently is also one of the top corporate contributors to foreign elections. During the last 10 years, Exxon Corp.

[43] "Before and After the Felony," *New York Times*, Sept. 7, 1975, sect. 3, p. 1. Steinbrenner and the corporation subsequently pleaded guilty to reduce charges and were fined $15,000 and $20,000, respectively.

[44] *The International Telephone and Telegraph Company and Chile, 1970–1971*, op. cit., passim.

[45] *Wall Street Journal*, Aug. 19, 1975, p. 7.

[46] "U.S. Company Payoffs Way of Life Overseas," *New York Times*, May 5, 1975, p. 1. "Northrop Uncovers $861,000 That Unit Paid in 5 Countries," *Wall Street Journal*, Feb. 23, 1976, p. 2.

[47] "Gulf's Accounts of Political Gifts Abroad Stir Anger Overseas, Questions at Home," *Wall Street Journal*, May 19, 1975, p. 2.

[48] "Tenneco, Inc. Discloses to SEC Payments to Public Officials in U.S. and Overseas," *Wall Street Journal*, Feb. 17, 1976, p. 2.

[49] "Lockheed Data Payoffs in L-1011 Sales Overseas Is Sent to Senate Unit by Mistake," *Wall Street Journal*, Sept. 15, 1975, p. 3. "Lockheed Payoffs Prompt Fugitive Hunt in Italy, Raids in Japan, and Suit in U.S.," *Wall Street Journal*, Feb. 25, 1976, p. 30. "The Big Payoff," *Time*, **107**:28 (Feb. 23, 1976).

has contributed more than $59 million to various political parties in Italy, alone.[50] Inexplicably, Exxon even contributed $86,000 to the Italian Communist party. It also has admitted making political contributions in Canada and one other country, as well as payments in three unnamed countries to government officials and officials of government-owned companies.

America's second-largest industrial, General Motors (GM), also joined the ranks of large corporations making political contributions abroad, although the contributions disclosed to date have been modest when compared to Exxon's. General Motors officers admitted giving contributions in the "five-figure" bracket to each of Canada's two major political parties in that country's latest elections.[51] General Motors also made $250,000 in political contributions in Korea as well as $225,000 to the South Korean National Defense Fund, a quasi-government group that raises funds for national defense from "voluntary contributions."[52] A stockholder proposal calling on GM to "affirm the non-partisanship of the corporation" was defeated, with 95.8 per cent of the votes cast against the motion.

Nor are these isolated cases of corporate bribery and illegal political activities at home and abroad. At least six drug companies have disclosed making bribes abroad. By early 1976, the SEC had received about 30 "corporate confessions" of wrongdoing and, according to one SEC official, "the number is climbing so rapidly no one has time to count."[53]

Many businessmen evidently condone such practices. A study by the Conference Board, a big-business-supported research institution, found that half of the executives it surveyed defended foreign payments as a normal way of doing business.[54] However, one top executive of a large multinational firm took a dim view of the practice. "The disclosures," he said, "have further eroded public confidence in United States corporations, here and abroad."[55]

Until recently, the evidence of the relationship between corporate economic and political power consisted of a rich body of case studies, such as recent revelations have touched on, and other detailed examinations of individual instances of the connection between economic and political power.[56] These case studies often were challenged as being unrepresentative of big corporations in general and, therefore, were not considered proof that there existed any general relationship between large corporate size and political power. Recently,

[50] "Exxon Concedes That Donations in Italy Were for Promoting 'Business Objectives,'" *Wall Street Journal*, July 17, 1975, p. 2. "Exxon Says Donations in Italy Exceed $46 million; Communists Got $86,000," *Wall Street Journal*, July 14, 1975, p. 10. "Exxon Discloses More Foreign Payments in Filing, Says SEC May Demand Details," *Wall Street Journal*, Sept. 26, 1975, p. 6.
[51] "GM Disclaims Political Gift to S. Koreans," *Washington Post*, Aug. 5, 1975, p. D7.
[52] Ibid.
[53] "The Corporate Rush to Confess All," *Business Week*, 2420:22 (Feb. 23, 1976).
[54] "Strange Developments," *New York Times*, Feb. 15, 1976, p. F11.
[55] Ibid.
[56] See the discussion by Samuel J. Elderoveld, "American Interest Groups: A Survey of Research and Some Implications for Theory and Method," in Henry Ehrmann, ed., *Interest Groups in Four Continents* (Pittsburgh, Pa.: Pittsburgh University Press, 1960).

the case study evidence has been re-enforced by a cross-industry analysis by John Siegfried, who has quantified statistically the relationship between absolute firm size and political power. Specifically, Siegfried finds a statistically significant negative correlation between absolute firm size and the "effective" rax rate paid by corporations—that is, holding other things the same, the larger the corporation the lower its effective tax rate.[57] Although this is only one measure of the effective use of corporate power, it is appropriate to infer that if corporations are able to use their political power to influence their effective tax rates, they can use it effectively in other ways as well. Indeed, in a subsequent study of the petroleum industry, Lester M. Salamon and Siegfried found evidence of large corporations' "success at utilizing public authority" to advance their corporate interests. They concluded:

> Particularly striking was (1) the discovery of a negative relationship between firm size and effective corporate income tax rates; (2) empirical evidence systematically linking the relative dominance of large firms in the refining industry in each state to the level of state motor vehicle fuel excise tax rates; and (3) a pattern of regulatory policies with substantial economic payoffs for the industry.[58]

There is, thus, persuasive evidence that conglomerate bigness may have adverse political consequences. The question remains, however, whether such merger-induced centralization of corporate resources has any impact on the effectiveness of competition.

VI. CONGLOMERATE MERGERS AND THE COMPETITIVE PROCESS

Economists have identified a variety of ways in which mergers may injure competition. The most obvious injury occurs when merging companies are direct competitors: For example, there was the attempted merger of Bethlehem Steel with Youngstown Steel in 1956. Such horizontal mergers injure competition by eliminating a significant direct competitors. After the court decision prohibiting the Bethlehem-Youngstown merger,[59] as well as a number of subsequent Supreme Court decisions, horizontal mergers among large companies declined sharply.

Although during the 1950s many economists would have taken a tolerant attitude toward a horizontal merger of this magnitude,[60] today nearly all applaud the Bethlehem-Youngstown decision, and many embrace the even

[57] John J. Siegfried, "Market Structure and the Effect of Political Influence," *Industrial Organization Review*, 3:1–17 (1975).

[58] Lester M. Salamon and John J. Siegfried, "The Relationship Between Economic Structures and Political Power: The Energy Industry," in Thomas D. Duchesneau, ed., *Competition in the U.S. Energy Industry* (New York: Ballinger, 1975), p. 381.

[59] *United States* v. *Bethlehem Steel Corporation*, 168 F. Supp. 576 (1958).

[60] Several prominent economists testified in behalf of Bethlehem, arguing that the merger would actually enhance competition because Bethlehem would not otherwise enter the Midwest market, a prediction subsequently proved false.

stricter rules of law spelled out in subsequent cases. Merger-enforcement policy toward horizontal mergers represents a great victory for antitrust policy.[61] Had it been otherwise—had public policy permitted mergers of the Bethlehem-Youngstown variety—concentration levels in many industries would have increased greatly in the postwar years.

Similarly, mergers among companies in buyer-seller relationships also have some readily discernible anticompetitive effects. For example, such vertical mergers may *foreclose* part of the market to competitors, perhaps triggering a series of defensive mergers by other companies that fear the loss of their markets.[62]

But the economic effects are less self-evident in the case of so-called conglomerate mergers—that is, mergers between companies that are neither horizontally nor vertically related. Since 1960, most larger mergers have been conglomerate in nature. The case study of ITT, the most active acquirer since 1960, illustrates how conglomerates can acquire companies in diverse fields. Some economists reason that competition is not injured so long as the merging companies are not direct competitors. In other words, they reason that there is no link between growing, over-all industrial concentration and conglomeration and the quality of competition in particular markets. As Professor M. A. Adelman is fond of reciting whenever growing conglomeration is discussed, "absolute size is absolutely irrelevant." Indeed, Adelman argues that "a truly conglomerate merger cannot be attacked in order to maintain competition, because it has no effect on any market structure."[63]

This view is based on the overly simplistic assumption that competition is determined solely by the structure of a particular market. As such, it overlooks the fact that the multimarket nature of many large industrial corporations enables them to engage in practices that are peculiarly characteristic of conglomerate firms. As a result, they often enjoy economic power that differs from the traditional concept of market power—which results from the characteristics of a particular market: the extent of seller concentration, the degree of product differentiation, and the conditions of entry. Traditional market power manifests itself in group behavior that enhances the group's profits for the benefit of its members at the expense of its customers or suppliers.

Although the long-run profit performance of a conglomerate is largely a function of the structure of its various markets, the organizational characteristics of the large conglomerate give it a unique capacity to alter the structures of the

---

[61] U.S. Congress, House, Antitrust Subcommittee, *The Celler-Kefauver Act: Sixteen Years of Enforcement*, 90th Cong., 1st sess., Staff Report, 1967. Since 1950, the antitrust agencies have challenged more than 1000 mergers, practically all of which involved horizontal and vertical mergers.

[62] See Willard F. Mueller, "Public Policy Toward Vertical Mergers," in J. Fred Weston and Sam Peltzman, eds., *Public Policy Towards Mergers* (Goodyear Publishing Co.: Pacific Palisades, Calif., 1969), pp. 150–166.

[63] M. A. Adelman, "The Antimerger Act, 1950–1960," *American Economic Review*, **51**:243 (May 1961).

markets in which it operates.[64] Hence, the conglomerate may not only possess traditional market power—that is, power vis-à-vis customers or suppliers—but power vis-à-vis actual or potential rivals. The nature and extent of such power depends on the relationship between the conglomerate firm's structure—its relative size, diversification, and profit capabilities in its individual markets—and that of rivals, customers, and suppliers.[65]

Specifically, business conglomeration enlarges two lines of conduct unavailable to single-market firms: the practices of cross subsidization and of reciprocity. It also widens the scope of mutual interdependence among large firms and leads to greater competitive forebearance among them. Conglomeration by merger accelerates the development of conglomerate options and mutual interdependence and allows such conduct characteristics to become significantly more pervasive than they would be if conglomeration could be achieved by internal growth alone.

This is not to imply, of course, that conglomerate power always has anticompetitive consequences. Indeed, there are special market settings in which conglomerate power is used to inject new competition into the market. Specifically, in industries where market concentration is high and new entry difficult, a conglomerate firm may increase competition by entering the industry by internal growth or by acquiring a small factor in such a market and subsequently expanding it.[66]

Cross Subsidization

The first thing to note about large conglomerate corporations is that the great majority operate across many industries and hold prominent positions in the most concentrated manufacturing industries.[67] In addition to being especially prominent occupants of concentrated industries, the largest corporations hold leading positions in many industries. For example, by 1963, 70 of the 100 largest manufacturers were the leading producers in four or more industries. This was up sharply from 1958, when there were only 43 companies in this class.[68] Moreover, the heavy merger activity of the largest companies since 1963 has further increased their leadership positions by today.

Because the large conglomerate generally enjoys abnormally high profits in at least some of its markets, it may expand its power by coupling such noncompetitive profits with an ability to "shift marketing emphasis and resources

---

[64] FTC, *Merger Report*, op. cit., pp. 225–230. The following discussion of the sources of conglomerate power draws heavily from the FTC report, which was prepared under the author's directions. I wish particularly to acknowledge Professor Robert E. Smith, now of the University of Oregon, for helping to develop the ideas presented in this section of the report.

[65] For a discussion of other ways in which business conglomeration may enlarge the conduct options of firms, see Edwards, op. cit., pp. 334–352.

[66] Howard H. Hines, "Effectiveness of 'Entry' by Already Established Firms," *Quarterly Journal of Economics*, **71**:132–150 (Feb. 1957).

[67] FTC, *Merger Report*, op. cit., pp. 214–215.

[68] Ibid., p. 216.

among its various markets."[69] If a conglomerate firm earned a competitive rate of return in each of its product markets, it would have no "excess" profits with which to subsidize particular product lines. But, as we have seen, when a firm operates in many markets, it generally possesses market power in one or more of its important markets and, hence, secures noncompetitive long-run profits. The amount of such profits depends, of course, not only on the degree of market power that the conglomerate firm has in its various markets, but also on its total sales in markets where it has market power.

When a firm enjoys large noncompetitive profits, it possesses the *option* of engaging in special competitive tactics not open to the firm earning only a competitive return. Conglomeration is an instrument through which these options can be exercised. By operating in many markets, the conglomerate can use excess profits in some markets to subsidize losses in other markets, either by price cuts or by incurring a substantial increase in costs—for example, abnormally large advertising outlays. If the subsidized markets are small when compared to the over-all operations of the firm, subsidization may have very little impact on over-all profitability. When a firm undertakes this policy after a rational investment decision, it expects to enhance its long-run profits by virtue of the effects of subsidization on the structure of the subsidized markets and the firm's relative position in these markets.

Not only may such practices have a direct impact on industrial concentration, but one conglomerate merger may beget others, as nonconglomerate firms within an industry respond defensively to the entrance by a conglomerate with the capacity to employ cross-subsidization tactics. The reaction of an official of the Sunshine Biscuit Company, itself a sizable firm (1965 sales of $201 million), to a proposed merger between its leading competitor, National Biscuit Company (NBC), and Coca Cola, illustrates that even substantial enterprises may respond defensively to mergers that promise to increase the market power of their rivals. One of Sunshine's directors stated:

> While there has been a tendency toward lack of interest in proposals of consolidation in the past, the recent reports of NBC and Coca Cola, although now called off, would in my opinion justify our careful consideration of this offer [from American Tobacco]. . . .
>
> It seems definitely certain that if our competitor with an already larger advertising fund than ours should join with someone with similar advantages—*that we could be snowed under in this field, much to the detriment of our future sales and profits.*[70]

This illustrates the essentially contagious nature of conglomerate mergers, as less powerful firms feel obliged to merge with others lest they "be snowed under" by the superior power of their conglomerate rivals. Corwin Edwards summarizes aptly the advantages conferred by this dimension of conglomerate power:

[69] John Narver, *Conglomerate Mergers and Market Competition* (Berkeley: University of California Press, 1967), p. 105. See Chap. 5 in Narver for a discussion of other sources of economic power possessed by a conglomerate enterprise.

[70] FTC, *Merger Report*, op. cit., pp. 6–124. (Italics supplied.)

It can absorb losses that would consume the entire capital of a smaller rival . . . . Moment by moment the big company can outbid, outspend, or outlose the small one; and from a series of such momentary advantages it derives an advantage in attaining its large aggregate results.[71]

Many case studies have demonstrated how large corporations have used their conglomerate-derived power to engage in cross-subsidization.[72] Although the effects are not always anticompetitive, the evidence demonstrates unmistakably that conglomeration confers conduct options not open to specialized firms.

Reciprocal Selling

We turn now to another competitive strategy open to conglomerate firms reciprocal selling. Simply defined, this practice involves taking your business to those who bring their business to you. It becomes important as a potentially harmful competitive strategy under two conditions: (1) When the market structure creates special *incentives* in the promotion of a firm's sales; and (2) when the product and organizational characteristics of a business will create extensive *opportunities* for engaging in the practice. In short, both the incentive and the opportunity are prerequisites to its successful use.[73]

A firm has an incentive to engage in reciprocity when doing so promises to increase its profits. In purely competitive markets there would be no incentive. In the absence of product differentiation, price alone would govern sales and purchases. But, in markets of relatively few firms, sellers recognize their interdependence. Each, knowing that it may influence the price level by its decisions, avoids price competition. Firms in these markets, therefore, have an incentive to engage in various nonprice strategies to promote sales—for example, advertising, innovation, promotion, and tying arrangements. Reciprocal selling is another such nonprice strategy.

In markets where firms sell a specialized product to firms similarly organized, there generally are few opportunities to practice reciprocity. It arises only when each firm produces something required in the operations of the other. An enterprise must purchase goods or services from companies that are also potential customers for its products to make possible the arrangement, "You buy from me and I'll buy from you."[74]

The volume of sales that may be influenced by reciprocal trading depends on the number, volume, and type of products bought and sold. A single-line producer will have relatively few opportunities, whereas a firm that buys and sells

---

[71] Edwards, op. cit., pp. 334–335.

[72] FTC, *Merger Report*, op. cit., pp. 406–457; John Blair, *Economic Concentration* (New York: Harcourt, 1972), pp. 43, 51, 363–367, and 594.

[73] For further elaboration of the conditions necessary to practice reciprocity, see George W. Stocking and Willard F. Mueller, "Business Reciprocity and the Size of Firms," *Journal of Business of the University of Chicago* (Apr. 1957), and FTC, *Merger Report*, op. cit., pp. 323–332.

[74] It is not necessary that a firm buy directly from its potential customer if it can work out multilateral reciprocity arrangements through third parties. See Stocking and Mueller, op. cit., p. 84.

a large variety and volume of products has the best opportunity to engage in reciprocal dealing. It is in the large conglomerate enterprise that reciprocal dealing develops into a major strategy for expanding sales.

Some economists have dismissed reciprocity as a significant anticompetitive problem by resorting to a simple theoretical model. This dismissal is most categorical among economists of the Chicago School, who reason (1) that in perfectly competitive markets reciprocity can have no adverse effects, (2) that firms with monopsony power can exploit their power without resorting to reciprocity, and (3) that reciprocity is prompted primarily by a desire to increase efficiency by eliminating selling costs. After dismissing reciprocity on these theoretical grounds, members of the Chicago School usually close their argument on the subject by echoing Professor George Stigler's observation that, in any event, "reciprocity is probably much more talked about than practiced and is important chiefly where prices are fixed by the state or a cartel."[75]

This problem is too complex to dispose of with such simple logic. Analysis of reciprocity must begin with the recognition that most contemporary markets, although falling short of monopoly, are sufficiently concentrated so that price competition already is somewhat muted. As noted here, in such markets, oligopolists have an incentive to resort to a variety of nonprice strategies to promote sales. Reciprocity is such a strategy. But, unlike most others, the capacity to practice it depends on the over-all size and conglomeration of the firm, not its position in an individual market.

In the real world, reciprocity is found in the broad spectrum of markets falling between the polar extremes of perfect compeition and monopoly. Stigler et al. fail to explain adequately the competitive process in such markets and, therefore, minimize the potential market power that reciprocity may confer on its users. They find some "frictions" in imperfectly competitive markets, but conclude that, "A plausible explanation for reciprocity under effectively competitive conditions is the desire to minimize costs of searching and selling."[76] Thus, they believe it is "plausible" that most reciprocity is merely a means of cutting the costs of locating and persuading customers, something to be applauded, not condemned. The only exceptions they find to reciprocity motivated by the quest to minimize selling cost are in markets in which firms have monopoly power or in markets subject to regulation. But here, again, they see reciprocity mainly as having a beneficial influence, either by reducing producers' surplus to the monopsonistic buyer or by enabling the market to approach a more optimal allocation of resources in regulated markets.

This analysis is wrong because of the unrealistic assumptions concerning the structural environment in which reciprocity is practiced. It greatly underrates the capacity and propensity of large conglomerate firms to practice reciprocity.

[75] See George Stigler, "Reciprocity," and Roland Coase, "The Conglomerate Merger," working papers for the Nixon Task Force on Productivity and Competition, Feb. 18, 1969. These arguments are also made by James M. Ferguson, "Tying Arrangements and Reciprocity: An Economic Analysis," *Law and Contemporary Problems*, Summer 1965, **30**: 552–580.

[76] J. H. Lorie and P. Halpern, "Conglomerates: The Rhetoric and the Evidence," *Journal of Law and Economics*, **13**:149–166 (Apr. 1970).

These authors apparently have not looked at, or have ignored, the considerable evidence showing that in imperfectly competitive industrial markets—covering a wide range of competitive structures—reciprocity is a pervasive, and often decisive, factor in determining the allocation of sales.[77] It can restructure markets by increasing concentration and by raising entry barriers to new competitors, and it can make prices more rigid.

Significantly, the firm engaging in reciprocity to expand its market share need not have a monopoly or monopsony in the conventional sense. Indeed, it may have relatively modest market shares as a buyer, certainly falling far short of monopsonistic dominance. The classical *Waugh Equipment* case, frequently cited by the Chicago School, illustrates this point.[78] *Waugh* was the first reciprocity case brought by the antitrust authorities.[79] Briefly, the facts are these. In 1924, three officials of Armour & Company became affiliated with the Waugh Equipment Company. Because one of these was an Armour vice-president in charge of traffic, he was in a position to work out reciprocity arrangements with the railroads by promising to route Armour business on railroads that agreed to buy draft gears from Waugh. As a result, Waugh increased its share of the draft gear market from about 1.5 per cent in 1924 to nearly 50 per cent by early 1930. During that period, Waugh sold to nearly every railroad in the country.[80]

Importantly, Armour did not have monopsony power in the traditional sense —that is, a dominant share of the market. It did not hold a commanding position as a purchaser of freight cars; it accounted for less than 2 per cent of all railroad freight shipments in 1929. Armour derived its bargaining advantage because, through Waugh Equipment Company, it was the *only* meat packer tied in with a draft gear supplier to railroads. This enabled it to exchange favors with the railroads.[81]

---

[77] For an extensive discussion of the scope and practice of reciprocity see FTC, *Merger Report*, op. cit., pp. 332–397.

[78] See Ferguson, op. cit. and Lorie and Halpern, op. cit.

[79] *Waugh Equipment Company*, 15 FTC 232 (1931).

[80] FTC, *Merger Report*, op. cit., pp. 338–340.

[81] Similarly, the facts disclosed in the *Consolidated Foods* case, *FTC v. Consolidated Foods, Inc.*, 380 U.S. 592 (1965), demonstrate that, although the Consolidated Foods Corporation was a large (measured in absolute terms) grocery wholesaler and retailer, it made a very small share of total grocery product purchases, in the order of 1 per cent. Nor is market concentration high in the purchase of food products by food retailers; the top 20 chains control about 31 per cent of food store sales. Moreover, grocery product manufacturing firms with which Consolidated Foods practiced reciprocity covered a broad spectrum of industrial structures, ranging from low to highly concentrated. Yet the record in the *Consolidated Foods* case demonstrates that firms in these various industries had an incentive and, indeed, did engage in reciprocity with Consolidated Foods. The 1963 four-firm concentration ratios for industries with which Consolidated was proven to have practiced reciprocity varied considerably: meat packing 27 per cent; pickles and other pickled products, 29 per cent; canned vegetables, 38 per cent; canned baby foods, 93 per cent; canned soups, 83 per cent. U.S. Department of Commerce, *Concentration Ratios in Manufacturing* (Washington, D.C.: U.S. Government Printing Office, 1967).

These examples, plus other evidence, demonstrate that firms have both the incentive and capacity to practice reciprocity in imperfectly competitive markets covering a wide range of structural settings. As shown in the FTC, *Merger Report*, op. cit., pp. 332–386, reciprocity has been practiced in a broad spectrum of industrial settings, even including the service industries, although there are fewer opportunities to practice it there than in industrial settings.

Nor is it correct to infer that none of this would have happened had railroad rates not been regulated. For had the railroads simply behaved like other oligopolists, each still would have had an incentive to gain or retain business by nonprice compeition—in this case reciprocity—thereby not disturbing the price structure, and the ultimate result would have been the same. Moreover, the effects of the practice are no less objectionable merely because a regulated industry is involved. For had Armour-Waugh achieved monopoly power in draft gears, or perhaps shared such power with another firm or two, the railroads almost certainly would have ended up paying higher prices for draft gears.

Nor is it an answer to say that competition was not injured because the draft gear industry was quite oligopolistic prior to these developments. For whereas before the injection of reciprocity into the picture the draft gear industry was quite easy to enter, thereafter, new entrants faced much more formidable entry barriers because they would have to be conglomerates capable of practicing reciprocity to compete on an equal footing with Armour-Waugh.

It is a mistake to assume reciprocity can only foreclose entry by very small firms. As documented by the FTC Merger Report, entry into an industry by even a billion-dollar corporation can be prevented by reciprocity-created entry barriers when the market has become tied up by larger rivals.[82] For example, in 1962, the Cities Service Corporation found its entry into the rubber-oil market blocked because the major tire companies had developed extensive reciprocity arrangements with other large petroleum companies.

Nor is there legitimate basis in fact for the argument expressed by Stigler that reciprocity generally "restores flexibility of prices" in oligopolistic markets.[83] This is patent nonsense. Logic and industrial experience argue that the reverse is more likely to be the case. When firms become associated as reciprocity partners, "outsiders" soon learn that it is futile to compete for such accounts, for doing so promises to "spoil" the open portion of the market (that not covered by reciprocity agreements) while failing to dislodge business from reciprocity partners, who, at most, simply renegotiate transaction prices. Indeed, once reciprocity becomes pervasive in an industry, reciprocity partners tend to minimize price as a factor in their transactions.

This is not idle speculation. The available evidence demonstrates that reciprocity creates tight trading bonds among practitioners. And while reciprocity partners often claim that they only deal with one another on an "all-or-other-things-being-equal" basis (and, indeed, this is often the case), reciprocity partners often so completely short-circuit the market that they do not adequately test it to discover their lowest price alternatives. In fact, it is not uncommon to pay prices above the going market price, although not for the reasons Stigler assumes—namely, to grant secret price concessions to customers; rather, they do so in order not to rock the boat in an otherwise stable market. This is illustrated by an Atlantic-Richfield Trade Relations manual, dated July 1, 1966,

[82] Ibid., pp. 383–384.
[83] Stigler, op. cit., p. 3.

outlining buyers' procedures for selecting vendors. It directed buyers to place business with bidders offering the lowest cost, "unless other factors, *including trade relations*, make it advisable to pay a higher price."[84] This is not an isolated incident. Not only do firms frequently pay higher prices to their reciprocity partners, they, at times, even accept lower-quality products in their drive to maintain an equitable balance of payments.[85] Such facts cannot be reconciled with the Chicago School's predictions that, in oligopolistic markets, reciprocity (1) is practiced mainly as a device to discover new customers, (2) erodes price rigidity, and (3) generally improves the allocation of resources.[86]

The manner in which conglomerate mergers enhance the reciprocity opportunities of already huge corporations was documented in the case of several of ITT's major acquisitions. For example, when ITT was considering its acquisition of Avis, Inc., the second-largest car rental company, the ITT board was informed by its staff of the reciprocity opportunities created by the merger: "As one of the largest purchasers and renters of automobiles from two of the major manufacturers, the Avis relationship can possibly develop additional markets for our manufacturing operations that would otherwise not be available to us, especially for our components business."[87] In 1967, ITT-Avis purchases from Chrysler totaled $28 million and from General Motors $23 million.[88] It is hardly surprising, therefore, that ITT anticipated that Avis' purchasing power might "develop additional markets [with GM and Chrysler] that would not otherwise be available to us . . . ."[89] A merger of ITT and Avis promised not only to increase ITT's sales but Avis' as well. Robert Townsend, Avis president at the time it was acquired by ITT, immediately recognized the great reciprocity potential inherent in a merger with ITT. Even before the merger was consummated, Townsend asked ITT to use its business with ITT suppliers to increase Avis' business.[90]

The record in the *ITT-Grinnell* case shows many instances of reciprocal dealing by ITT. For example, ITT-Sheraton purchased Philco-Ford TV sets in return for Ford's use of Sheraton hotel rooms and services.[91] ITT-Lamp Division explored ways of increasing its sales potential by virtue of ITT-Continental Baking Company's purchases of equipment.[92] The record further demonstrated that Grinnell Corporation already practiced reciprocity prior to its merger with ITT and that the merger greatly increased its potential use of the practice.[93]

[84] FTC, *Merger Report*, op. cit., p. 387.
[85] Ibid., pp. 392–393.
[86] See footnote 75.
[87] U.S. Congress, House, Antitrust Subcommittee, House Committee on the Judiciary. *Investigation of Conglomerate Corporations: Hearing on*, 91st Cong., 1st sess., pt. 3, 1969, p. 371.
[88] Ibid., p. 601.
[89] Ibid.
[90] *United States* v. *International Telephone & Telegraph Corporation*, Civil Action no. 13319, PX 125 and PX 126. Hereafter cited as *ITT-Grinnell* case.
[91] Ibid., PX 136–137, Tr. 1877–1879.
[92] Ibid., PX 180.
[93] Ibid., Government's "Proposed Findings and Conclusions of Law" cites many examples, pp. 53–59.

The record of the *ITT-Canteen* case documented how ITT promoted reciprocity with banks. The Justice Department discovered more than 30 identical letters written to banks stating, in part, "It is a pleasure being a customer of your bank and perhaps a member of our corporate family can likewise do business with you."[94] In this case, ITT was using reciprocity to sell insurance to banks. Similarly, although the government never completed its discovery efforts in the *ITT-Hartford Fire Insurance* case—the case was settled before the final trial— substantial evidence of actual reciprocity and reciprocity opportunities was developed in the preliminary injunction proceedings.[95]

Chairman Harold Geneen testified in the ITT-Hartford preliminary injunction that ITT had a long, well-established antireciprocity policy. Yet the record in the *ITT-Grinnell* case demonstrates that Geneen himself had engaged in reciprocity arrangements.[96] In view of the evidence, it is obvious that Chairman Geneen's strict antireciprocity policy was honored in the breach. Indeed, Geneen admitted that the only ITT personnel ever reprimanded for violating this policy were those whose reciprocity activities were uncovered in the antitrust suits.[97]

As the House antitrust staff study of ITT concluded:

A major consideration in ITT's merger program was the acquisition of companies that would reinforce marketing efforts of other ITT subsidiaries. This crossfertilization of total system effort was expected to confer desirable heft in particular markets and to increase the competitive strength of the individual subsidiaries in their business activities with outsiders.[98]

Although the ITT case ultimately was settled by a controversial consent decree,[99] Richard McLaren, head of the Antitrust Division, maintained even after he had settled the cases that the challenged acquisitions involved "systematic reciprocity and the power to develop further reciprocity arrangements through interrelationships of the different companies. . . . I think a strong economic case can be made against those mergers."[100]

Continued conglomerate expansion—both by merger and internal growth— promises to increase reciprocity opportunities, threatening thereby to result in closed-ciruit markets from which medium or small businesses are excluded. Thus, oligopoly in individual markets would be magnified in circular integration, by which purchases of the leading firms would be tied to sales, foreclosing

[94] U.S. Congress, Senate, Committee on the Judiciary, *Hearings on the Nomination of Richard G. Kleindienst*, 92d Cong., 2d sess., Mar. and Apr. 1972, p. 1252. (Hereafter cited as *Kleindienst Hearings*.)

[95] See "Memorandum in Support of Government's Motion for Preliminary Injunctions," *United States* v. *International Telephone & Telegraph Corporation and the Hartford Fire Insurance Company*, undated.

[96] *ITT-Grinnell* case, op. cit., PX 123–126.

[97] Ibid., Tr. 1651–1655; Geneen deposition, p. 48.

[98] U.S. Congress, House, Antitrust Subcommittee of the Committee on the Judiciary, *Investigation of Conglomerate Mergers*, 91st Cong., 1st sess., June 1, 1971, p. 125.

[99] Mueller, op. cit.

[100] *Kleindienst Hearings*, op. cit., pp. 121–122.

the opportunities of firms without substantial reciprocity opportunities to gain access to the inner circle of firms. As stated in *Fortune*:

> trade relations between the giant conglomerates tend to close a business circle. Left out are the firms with narrow product lines; as patterns of trade and trading partners emerge between particular groups of companies, entry by newcomers becomes more difficult.[101]

Indeed, *Fortune* concludes that "the United States economy might end up completely dominated by conglomerates happily trading with each other in a new kind of cartel system."[102]

VII. CONGLOMERATE INTERDEPENDENCE AND COMPETITIVE FORBEARANCE

We have seen how the current merger movement is contributing to the creation of a dual economy in which a few hundred enormous corporations are expanding their control over the bulk of industrial activity and the literally thousands of smaller businesses share the remainder. We also have seen how conglomerate mergers propelling this centralization have greatly increased the reciprocity opportunities of large corporations as they expand their product lines, thereby increasing the potential buyer-seller linkages with other corporations.

But growing reciprocity opportunities are only the most obvious manifestation of the changed competitive environment flowing from growing conglomeration. Reciprocity is but a sympton of the larger problem of *conglomerate interdependence and competitive forbearance* that is the inevitable concomitant of an economy in which most commerce is controlled by a relatively few huge corporations.

It is now well recognized in economic theory and industrial experience that, in a market of few sellers, firms tend to behave interdependently. That is, each seller takes into account the direct and indirect consequences of its price, output, and other market decisions. This is called oligopolistic interdependence.

The theory of oligopoly explains the behavior of firms operating in a single market where their discretion in pricing is constrained by certain structural characteristics of the market. Those especially relevant are market concentration, product differentiation, and barriers facing would-be entrants.

The competitive conduct characteristics of particular markets may be influenced not only by these three traditional structural characteristics, but also by the conglomerate character of some of the firms operating in the market. We have just seen that a conglomerate enterprise possesses a unique capacity to practice reciprocal selling. In addition, however, the multimarket characteristics of firms may result in what we will call *conglomerate mutual interdependence and competitive forbearance*[103] among actual and potential competitors—an inter-

---

[101] *Fortune*, **71**:194 (June 1965).
[102] Ibid.
[103] Edwards first identified this problem in op. cit., pp. 346 ff.

firm relationship that differs from *oligopolistic interdependence* as traditionally viewed.

Conglomerate interdependence and forbearance can arise because (1) the same or related decision makers have simultaneous access to both firms or (2) the firms share contact points in input output markets that create a mutual awareness of common interests. Interlocking directorates, intercorporate stockholdings, and joint ventures represent the first set of factors facilitating coordinated relationships among firms. A *firm's* structure—that is, its size and conglomerateness—constitutes the second set of factors creating a commonness of interest. These determine the number and nature of the contact points that the firms will share. By increasing both size and diversification, the conglomerate merger increases the number of contacts shared with competitors, suppliers, and customers, thereby increasing the mutual awareness of common interests among firms. Simply put, growing conglomeration and over-all industrial concentration greatly broaden and extend traditional "communities of interests" among key industrial decision makers.

The current merger movement has greatly increased the "contact points" among large corporations and, therefore, the likelihood that conglomerates will exercise forbearance in their competitive confrontations.[104]

Table 2 shows how mergers increased the number of actual or potential con-

---

TABLE 2
Number of Horizonal and Vertical Contact Points
Among 113 Large Manufacturing Corporations and
Between ITT and 112 Other Firms, 1965 and 1968

TYPE OF CONTACTS	NUMBER OF INSTANCES		CHANGE 1965–1968 (PER CENT)
	1965	1968	
Horizontal	12,552	15,579	+24.1
Vertical	59,044	72,579	22.9
Total	71,596	88,158	

CONTACTS BETWEEN ITT AND 112 OTHER CORPORATIONS

Horizontal	369	499	35.2
Vertical	2,113	2,816	33.3
Total	2,482	3,315	33.6

Source: The sample consisted of all corporations among the 100 largest manufacturing corporations in 1965 or 1968. The analysis was made by Leonard Weiss and I. Curtis Jernigen, Jr., "Changes in Corporate Interdependencies Between 1965 and 1968," Appendix 7 of the prepared testimony of Willard F. Mueller in *U.S. v. ITT and Grinnell Corporation*, Civil No. 13319.

---

[104] FTC, *Merger Report*, op. cit., pp. 198–224.

tact points among 113 of the largest corporations during 3 years of extensive merger activity—1966–1968.[105] It shows that, in 1968, these firms had 15,579 horizontal contact points, or an average of 111 each. This means that, on the average, each corporation met firms from among the 112 others as actual competitors 111 times. The potential vertical contact points were much more numerous, as each of these firms had an average of 642 potential buyer-seller relationships. From 1965–1968, the number of horizontal contact points among these corporations increased by 24.1 per cent, and the potential vertical relationship rose by 22.9 per cent. The increase of such linkages involving ITT, the leading acquirer during the period, rose more rapidly than for all companies. By 1968, ITT had 499 horizontal and 2816 potential vertical contact points with the other 112 firms. Practically all of this increase was due to ITT's numerous large mergers during this brief 3-year period.

Perhaps the simplest form of conglomerate interdependence involves price decisions. Firms meeting as competitors in many markets are likely to regard each other with greater deference than if their decisions were constrained solely by structural conditions in particular markets.

But conglomerate interdependence may take more subtle firms, as conglomerates accommodate and harmonize their behavior. Although generally ignored or overlooked by economists, antitrust proceedings provide rich evidence of such behavior going back more than half a century. This evidence demonstrates the inherent logic of conglomerate power: to possess it inevitably invites its use.

For example, after du Pont became a large diversified corporation in the early 1920s, it developed a community of interests with other leading national and international corporations. The evidence demonstrates that when these corporations met as actual or potential competitors, they often exercised mutual forbearance. As early as 1923, a du Pont vice-president explained his company's policy toward Imperial Chemical Industries of Great Britain (ICI), the world's second-largest chemical firm, which it met in many international markets:

> It is not good business sense to attempt an expansion in certain directions if such an act is bound to result as a boomerang of retaliation. It has been the du Pont Company's policy to follow such lines of common sense procedure . . .[106]

Du Pont's philosophy of self-restraint in dealing with ICI was summed up succinctly as follows:

> This was done on the broad theory that cooperation is wiser than antagonism and that in the matter of detail the chances in the long run were that the boot was just as likely to be on one leg as on the other.[107]

---

[105] A horizontal contact point is assumed to exist where each of a pair of firms produced the same four-digit product. A vertical contact point is assumed to exist where a pair of firms manufactured a product required as a significant input by the other firm.

[106] Cited in Willard F. Mueller, *Du Pont: A Case Study of Firm Growth* (Ph.D. diss., Vanderbilt University, 1955), p. 393.

[107] Ibid.

Irénée du Pont pointed out, in 1927, that it was his company's policy to encourage the establishment of an esprit de corps among the country's "great corporations." As he put it, the du Pont company felt "that the great corporations of the country, especially those that are leaders in business ethics and in service to the economic structure, should stand together without fear of veiled threats from companies which are more predatory."[108]

Standing together may prove to be a euphemism for avoiding actual or potential competition with one another. For example, Union Carbide and Carbon, in 1931, purchased rights to a process for manufacturing a transparent wrapping material it thought might be competitive with du Pont's cellophane. Lammot du Pont reported that in a conversation on this topic with Union Carbide officials:

> They assured me repeatedly they did not wish to rush into anything; most of all a competitive situation with du Pont. Their whole tone was most agreeable .... In the course of the conversations, various efforts at cooperation between Carbide and du Pont were referred to and in every case assurances of their desire to work together.[109]

There also is evidence that, in recent times, du Pont has continued the "common sense procedures" it discovered earlier in its history as a conglomerate enterprise.[110]

A recent, well-documented example of conglomerate confrontation and swift accommodation involved a large conglomerate food manufacturer and food retailer, Consolidated Foods Corporation, and a large multimarket food retailer, National Tea Corporation.[111] As a manufacturer of many food products as well as a food retailer, Consolidated met National on two fronts, as a supplier and a competitor in food retailing. In early 1965, Consolidated attempted to expand its supermarket sales in Chicago by initiating an aggressive "miracle prices" campaign, claiming, "price levels slashed on over 5000 items." Because National had annual supermarket sales of around $250 million in Chicago, its profit margins were threatened by Consolidated's move. National responded quickly by having its president warn that the next day there would be fewer Consolidated lines on National shelves. Consolidated got the word. It not only stopped its price campaign immediately, but it further accommodated National by selling its Chicago stores.

The lesson to be learned from this confrontation is clear. Conglomerate interdependence and forbearance eliminated Consolidated as an aggressive rival in food retailing. Because Consolidated was a food manufacturer as well as a food retailer, the competitive strategies it followed in one market boomeranged by inviting retaliation in another. Had National not been one of its customers, Consolidated could have behaved independently of National in expanding food

---

[108] Ibid.
[109] Ibid., p. 202.
[110] FTC, *Merger Report*, op. cit., pp. 463–467.
[111] Ibid., pp. 468–470.

retailing operations in Chicago and consumers would have benefited from its aggressive price campaign.

This and other evidence[112] demonstrate how shared contact points can induce forbearance and interdependence. The exchange of reciprocal favors among conglomerate corporations involves shared contact points, but the contemplated consequences of such sharing need not be limited to reciprocal buying. The interfirm structural framework characterized by the shared contact points leads to the consideration, proposal, and possible realization of acts of conglomerate interdependence and forbearance that can affect market shares, entry, and pricing practices. Reciprocal buying is symptomatic, a manifestation of the more general problem of conglomerate interdependence and forbearance. Conglomerate interdependence and forbearance may well represent the most serious threat to competition resulting from the growing merger-achieved centralization of economic resources among a relatively few conglomerates that meet as actual or potential competitors or customers in many markets. Its ultimate result is a closed economic system in which price and other business decisions by vast conglomerates become largely immune from the disciplining influence of the market. Such a system smacks of the Zaibatsu system in Japan, in which a handful of huge financial-industrial conglomerates working in concert with the state exercise great control over many key economic and political decisions. Although such a system may be acceptable to the Japanese, it clearly runs counter to the basic assumptions of a free competitive enterprise system relying on the market to discipline the use of private economic power.[113]

Conglomeration by merger accelerates the development of such a system, and, when it involves large firms, widens the market power differential between the largest firms and other firms in the economy. There, thus, exists a causal relationship between the growing merger-achieved centralization of control over American industry and the competitive structure and behavior found in particular markets occupied by giant conglomerate enterprises. It is extremely difficult to quantify how growing aggregate concentration and conglomeration changes the structure and behavior of particular markets. However, the available case studies of cross subsidization, reciprocity, and conglomerate interdependence provide important evidence of the effects. This case study evidence is re-enforced by a statistical analysis that finds a significant positive relationship between the share of an industry held by the nation's 200 largest industrial corporations and increases in concentration within the industry. This finding supports the hypothesis that the more extensive the presence of very large corpora-

---

[112] Ibid., pp. 458–471.

[113] Interestingly, an editorial in the *Wall Street Journal*, Mar. 26, 1969, p. 20, also emphasized this danger of growing centralization and conglomeration: "More important, unchecked expansion of conglomerates would eventually reduce competition and impair the efficiency of our approximation of a free-market economy. When ties among large corporations get too widespread and too involved, it seems to us they will impede the free movement of prices and capital even if the merged corporations are not in the same fields. Certainly, the consolidation of various corporations into conglomerates could invite a vastly increased concentration of economic power, which gives us pause on both economic and social grounds."

tions in an industry, the greater is the likelihood that market concentration will rise.[114]

This causal link has rich implications for public policy toward conglomerate mergers. It may provide an important bridge between the concern with over-all centralization of economic power expressed by the Congress in enacting the Celler-Kefauver Act, and the language of the act that focuses on competition in specific markets. We turn now to the questions of whether existing legislation and its enforcement are adequate to cope with the problems created by the increasing conglomeration of American industry.

VIII. PUBLIC POLICY

Public policy must begin with the premise that large conglomerate enterprises will not wither away. Even very inefficient large corporations do not fail in contemporary America. Because of anticipated catastrophic consequences to stockholders, employees, and entire communities, when a large corporation's survival is threatened, either the government bails it out—for example, Lockheed Aircraft[115]—or permits it to merge with another large corporation, even a direct competitor—for example, Douglas Aicraft.[116]

This does not mean the economy must become ever more centralized in a few vast conglomerates, or that nothing can be done to reduce the existing level of centralization. The following steps would result in an erosion of existing centralization as well as insure greater public responsibility in the use of con-glomerate power.

Adequate Antitrust Funding

The antitrust agencies have always been seriously underfunded. If cost-benefit analysis were used to determine appropriate funding levels, a sound case could be made for enormous increases in funds for the agencies. For example, the plaintiffs bringing treble damage cases against General Electric and other members of the "great electrical conspiracy" of the 1950s received awards exceeding $500 million. This is greater than the combined antitrust budgets for the FTC and the Antitrust Division since 1890. In addition, prices of electrical equipment subject to the conspiracy fell 10 per cent or more following the government's case.

---

[114] FTC, *Merger Report*, op. cit., pp. 230–234. For an analysis of this study see Leonard Weiss, "Quantitative Studies of Industrial Organization," in M. D. Intriligator, ed., *Frontiers of Quantitative Economics* (Amsterdam: North-Holland, 1971), pp. 378–379. An unpublished study by A. A. Heggestad and S. A. Rhodes finds that conglomerate interdependence reduces competitive rivalry in banking: "Multi-market Interdependence and Local Market Competition" (Aug. 1976).

[115] When Lockheed faced bankruptcy, the Federal government guaranteed $195 million of its debt.

[116] When Douglas Aircraft encountered serious financial difficulties, the Antitrust Division approved its acquisition, in 1967, by one of its leading competitors, McDonnell Company.

Without adequate funding, the antitrust agencies are hopelessly undermanned and outgunned in most litigation with large corporations. An order of magnitude of this mismatch is that ATT reportedly has budgeted at least $50 million to "defend" itself in the recent suit brought by the Antitrust Division. This is about three times greater than the *total* annual budget of the Antitrust Division.

Quite clearly, unless antitrust is to remain a paper tiger, appropriations must be increased significantly in the next few years.

Strengthening the Merger Law

More vigorous antitrust enforcement, alone, will not deal effectively with conglomerate mergers and problems resulting from existing levels of conglomeration. New legislation is required to overcome these problems.

Following the traditional case-by-case antitrust approach, it could take a decade or more to explore the outer boundaries of the existing law. Indeed, since the ITT case was settled in 1971, no big conglomerate cases have been brought. A more direct approach will be required if conglomerate merger activity accelerates once again as general economic conditions improve. Specifically, legislation needs to be enacted that applies special legal standards to very large mergers. This legislation would recognize explicitly that such mergers pose serious economic and political dangers that transcend the economist's narrow preoccupation with a merger's competitive impact on an isolated market,

Briefly, the law would require that before a "very large" merger could occur the FTC must make an explicit finding: first, that the merger did not have the effect of substantially lessening competition under the existing law; *and,* second, that the merger was in the public interest because it promised to increase competition, efficiency, or provide other economic benefits in which the public would share. For this purpose, a very large merger might be defined as one resulting in a corporation with sales or assets in excess of $500 million and in which each company has sales or assets in excess of $50 million. Evidence concerning the issues involved would be developed before the FTC in a public hearing to which the Antitrust Division of the Department of Justice could be a party. Interested members of the public should be permitted and encouraged to participate in such hearings.

Such strict restraints on large conglomerate mergers would both prevent most merger-induced conglomeration and contribute to the erosion of existing market concentration. By preventing large corporations from entering new industries by acquiring large corporations, such firms would be encouraged to enter other industries by building new capacity or by acquiring small concerns. Then, instead of merely substituting themselves for an already large competitor in an industry, it would increase the number of significant competitors, thereby eroding the market position of entrenched firms.[117]

---

[117] William G. Shepherd, "Leading-firm Conglomerate Mergers," *Antitrust Bulletin,* Winter 1968, pp. 1361–1382.

Legislation Requiring Divestitures

Vigorous enforcement of existing and new-merger legislation may effectively prevent further conglomerate centralization, but it will do little to erode existing centralization. History suggests that widespread and expeditious divestiture in an industry requires direct legislation. Perhaps the most familiar such legislation was the Public Utilities Holding Company Act of 1935, which specified massive divestiture. However, there are other instructive examples. The direct legislative approach also has been taken to divest conglomeratelike centralizations of power. The Banking Act of 1933, which divorced investment banking from commercial banking, restructured numerous large and medium-sized banks. The result was the spin-off of such large investment bankers as First Boston Corporation and Morgan Stanley & Company. Many of today's leading regional brokerage firms also had their genesis in the massive divestiture required by the 1933 act. As a result, our banking structure is much less centralized than it would be otherwise. Similarly, the McKellar-Black Air Mail Act of 1934 forced General Motors to relinquish its interests in various air carriers and airline manufacturers. These various acts accomplished more industrial decentralization than the total achieved under the Sherman Act since its enactment in 1890.

These experiences teach that the direct legislative route would be far preferable to antitrust action in divesting existing conglomerations of power in areas that the Congress views as being particularly troublesome. A likely target is the energy industry, where vast multinational petroleum corporations have come to control large shares of alternative energy sources, especially crude oil and natural gas coal, uranium, oil shale, and tar sands.[118] It would consume for decades all the resources of the antitrust agencies to achieve an even modest degree of deconglomeration in these areas. The Congress could spell out guidelines that would restructure the energy industry in a relatively few years. Although the legislative approach probably should be used sparingly, there doubtless are other areas in which legislative action would be infinitely more effective and less time-consuming than conventional antitrust enforcement. Unless the legislative approach is used, the antitrust agencies will remain hopelessly mired down in a few big cases and have no real impact on existing levels of industrial conglomeration.

Eliminating Corporate Secrecy Via Federal Chartering

Even at best, the preceding measures will not bring about sufficient industrial restructuring to insure that conglomerate power will be disciplined by the market place. Because of the enormous economic and political power of modern conglomerate corporations, explicit recognition should be made that they are not

---

[118] Willard F. Mueller and Roy A. Prewitt, "Structure of the Petroleum Industry and Its Relation to Oil Shale and Other Energy Sources," in FTC, *Economic Papers, 1966–1969* (Washington, D.C.: Government Printing Office, 1970), pp. 184–200.

purely *private* institutions. There is a need for an explicit public policy declaration that the large conglomerate corporation's business is very much the *public's* business. Simply put, the huge conglomerate enterprises that control most industrial resources are quasi-public institutions that have been granted the privilege—although not the explicit responsibility—of running the American economy. The ITT chairman, Harold Geneen, acknowledged this when he said, "Increasingly, the larger corporations have become the primary custodians of making our entire system work."[119] This quite naturally raises questions of legitimacy, of whether these powerful corporations are running the economy in the public interest.

Justice William O. Douglas identified the problem more than three decades ago when he observed: "Enterprises . . . which command tremendous resources . . . tip the scales on the side of prosperity or on the side of depression, depending on the decisions of the men at the top. This is tremendous power, tremendous responsibility. Such men become virtual governments in the power at their disposal. In fact, if not in law, they become affected with a public interest."[120]

An appropriate first step in recognizing that the large corporation is not a purely private enterprise is to require that all very large corporations receive a corporate charter from the Federal government rather than from individual states.[121] In the nearly 100 years since New Jersey amended its constitution, in 1875, to liberalize greatly the incorporation process, state chartering statutes have become increasingly framed to suit the interests of corporate enterprises. The whole thrust of this development has been to confer on the corporation the rights and privileges of private citizens. Yet, during that period, as more and more of the economy became the domain of enormous corporate enterprises, they increasingly have taken on the characteristics of public enterprises as they influence directly and indirectly the livelihood of all Americans.

A Federal chartering statute would spell out a set of corporate *responsibilities* as well as *rights*. A major purpose of such a charter should be to remove the veil of secrecy covering much corporate decision making vital to the public interest. It need be restricted to only the very largest corporations, perhaps those controlling assets of $250 million or more. (The 379 industrial corporations of this size controlled 67 per cent of all manufacturing assets in 1974.) Among the provisions of such a charter are the following:

---

[119] Quoted in Anthony Sampson, *The Sovereign State of ITT* (New York: Stein & Day, 1973), p. 125.

[120] William O. Douglas, *Democracy and Finance* (New Haven, Conn.: Yale University Press, 1940), p. 15.

[121] For a more detailed discussion of this writer's views on Federal chartering see *Testimony of W. F. Mueller Before the Monopoly Subcommittee of the Select Committee on Small Business*, U.S. Congress, Senate, 90th Cong., 1st sess., Nov. 1971, and W. F. Mueller, "Corporate Disclosure: The Public's Right to Know," in A. Rappaport and L. Revsine, eds., *Corporate Financial Reporting* (Evanston, Ill.: Northwestern University Press, 1972), pp. 67–94. For a recent legislative proposal seeking Federal chartering, see "The Corporate Citizenship and Competition Act," introduced by Congressman James V. Stanton of Ohio, *Congressional Record*, May 22, 1975.

Extensive visitation privileges for the chartering agency to insure it ready access to relevant corporate information.

Much more extensive public reporting of the sources of investment, revenues, and profits than is now required by the SEC.

Extensive public disclosure of the volumes of all products manufactured and sold, including such information corporations currently supply the Bureau of the Census under strict rules of confidentiality.

Public disclosure of corporate Federal income tax returns.

Disclosure of certain social costs.

Disclosure of intercorporate financial ties.

Disclosure of publicly owned facilities operated or leased by private corporations.

Disclosure of various details of the corporation's foreign operations, and prohibitions against political intervention in the affairs of other nations.

Public representation on the board of directors where necessary to obtain information on corporate affairs.

This, then, in skeletal form, is a program for providing greater public disclosure of corporate affairs. It clearly is not an attack on our market economy but an effort to perfect it. Although Federal chartering is not a panacea, it is an essential first step in recognizing the large modern corporation for what it is—an essentially public institution.

Nor is this proposal a substitute for a vigorous program to make competition more effective wherever possible or for the other reforms mentioned here. On the contrary, it complements efforts to improve competition by opening new opportunities for the operation of "natural" market forces. However, even though the program recognizes that competition is not dead as an important disciplining influence in most American industries, it also recognizes that giant conglomerate corporations enjoy great discretion in making numerous decisions that affect our social, cultural, political, and economic welfare. More complete disclosure by large corporations, therefore, serves the dual objective of aiding natural market forces and of providing the broader benefits to society that flow from more complete information of corporate affairs. The elimination of unnecessary corporate secrecy is based on what Justice Louis Brandeis emphasized as "the essential difference between corporations and natural persons."

SUGGESTED READINGS

BOOKS

Mintz, Morton, and Jerry Cohen. *America, Inc.* New York: The Dial Press, 1971.
Nader, Ralph and Mark J. Green, eds. *Corporate Power in America.* New York: Grossman Publishers, 1973.

Narver, John. *Conglomerate Mergers and Market Competition.* Berkeley: University of California Press, 1967.

Reid, Samuel Richardson. *Mergers, Managers, and the Economy.* New York: McGraw-Hill Book Company, 1968.

Winslow, John F. *Conglomerates Unlimited.* Bloomington: Indiana University Press, 1973.

JOURNAL ARTICLES

Briloff, Abraham J. "Financial Motives for Conglomerate Growth." *St. John's Law Review,* **44**: 872–879 (Spring 1970).

Edwards, Corwin. "Conglomerate Bigness as a Source of Power," in *Business Concentration and Price Policy.* Conference of National Bureau of Economic Research (Princeton, N.J.: Princeton University Press, 1955), pp. 346–347.

Geneen, Harold S. "Conglomerates: A Businessman's View." *St. John's Law Review,* **44**: 723–742 (Spring 1970).

Mueller, Willard F. "The ITT Settlement: A Deal with Justice?" *Industrial Organization Review,* **1**: 80 (1973).

Shepherd, William G. "Leading-firm Conglomerate Mergers." *Antitrust Bulletin,* **13**: 1361–1382 (Winter 1968).

Siegfried, John J. "Market Structure and the Effect of Political Influence." *Industrial Organization Review,* **3**: 1–17 (1975).

Weston, J. Fred. "The Nature and Significance of Conglomerate Firms." *St. John's Law Review,* **44**: 66–80 (Spring 1970).

GOVERNMENT PUBLICATIONS

FTC, Staff Report, *Economic Report on Corporate Mergers,* (Washington, D.C.: U.S. Government Printing Office, 1969).

U.S. Congress, House, Antitrust Subcommittee, Committee on the Judiciary, *Investigation on Conglomerate Mergers,* 92d Cong., 1st sess., June 1, 1971.

U.S. Congress, Senate, Subcommittee on Multinational Corporations, *The International Telephone and Telegraph Company and Chile, 1970–1971,* 93d Cong., 1st sess., June 21, 1973.

U.S. Congress, Senate, Committee on the Judiciary, *Hearings on the Conglomerate Merger Problem Before the Subcommittee on Antitrust and Monopoly,* 91st Cong., 2d sess. (1969 and 1970).

CHAPTER 14

public policy in a
free enterprise economy

WALTER ADAMS

When Congress passed the Sherman Act of 1890, it created what was then—and what has remained—a uniquely American institution. Heralded as a magna carta of economic freedom, the Sherman Act sought to preserve competitive free enterprise by imposing legal prohibitions on monopoly and restraint of trade. The objective of the act, according to Judge Learned Hand, was not to condone *good* trusts or condemn *bad* trusts, but to forbid *all* trusts. Its basic philosophy and principal purpose was "to perpetuate and preserve, for its own sake and in spite of possible cost, an organization of industry in small units which can effectively compete with each other."[1]

THE ANTIMONOPOLY LAWS

Specifically, the Sherman Act outlawed two major types of interference with free enterprise: collusion and monopolization. Section 1 of the act, dealing with collusion, stated: "Every contract, combination . . . or conspiracy, in restraint

[1] *United States* v. *Aluminum Company of America*, 148 F.2d 416 (C.C.A. 2d, 1945). In elaborating on the goals of the Sherman Act, Judge Hand stated: "Many people believe that possession of unchallenged economic power deadens initiative, discourages thrift, and depresses energy; that immunity from competition is a narcotic, and rivalry is a stimulant, to industrial progress; that the spur of constant stress is necessary to counteract an inevitable disposition to let well enough alone. Such people believe that competitors, versed in the craft as no consumer can be, will be quick to detect opportunities for saving and new shifts in production, and be eager to profit by them. . . . True, it might have been thought adequate to condemn only those monopolies which could not show that they had exercised the highest possible ingenuity, had adopted every possible economy, had anticipated every conceivable improvement, stimulated every possible demand. . . . Be that as it may, that was not the way that Congress chose; it did not condone 'good' trusts and condemn 'bad' ones; it forbade all. Moreover, in so doing it was not necessarily actuated by economic motives alone. It is possible, because of its indirect social or moral effect, to prefer a system of small producers, each dependent for his success upon his own skill and character, to one in which the great mass of those engaged must accept the direction of a few. These considerations, which we have suggested only as possible purposes of the Act, we think the decisions prove to have been in fact its purposes."

of trade or commerce among the several States, or with foreign nations, is hereby declared illegal." As interpreted by the courts, this made it unlawful for businessmen to engage in such collusive action as agreements to fix prices; agreements to restrict output or productive capacity; agreements to divide markets or allocate customers; agreements to exclude competitors by systematic resort to oppressive tactics and discriminatory policies—in short, any joint action by competitors to influence the market. Thus, Section 1 was, in a sense, a response to Adam Smith's warning that "people of the same trade seldom meet together even for merriment and diversion, but the conversation ends in a conspiracy against the public, or in some contrivance to raise prises."[2]

Section 2 of the Sherman Act, which deals with monopolization, provided that: "Every person who shall monopolize or attempt to monopolize, or combine or conspire with any other person or persons to monopolize any part of the trade or commerce among the several States, or with foreign nations, shall be deemed guilty of a misdemeanor, and . . . punished." This meant that businessmen were deprived of an important freedom, the freedom to monopolize. Section 2 made it unlawful for anyone to obtain a stranglehold on the market either by forcing rivals out of business or by absorbing them. It forbade a single firm (or a group of firms acting jointly) to gain a substantially exclusive domination of an industry or a market area. Positively stated, Section 2 attempted to encourage an industry structure in which there are enough independent competitors to assure bona fide and effective market rivalry.

As is obvious from even a cursory examination of the Sherman Act, its provisions were general, perhaps even vague, and essentially negative. Directed primarily against *existing* monopolies and *existing* trade restraints, the Sherman Act could not cope with specific practices that were, and could be, used to effectuate the unlawful results. Armed with the power to dissolve existing monopolies, the enforcement authorities could not, under the Sherman Act, attack the *growth* of monopoly. They could not nip it in the bud. For this reason Congress passed, in 1914, supplementary legislation "to arrest the creation of trusts, conspiracies and monopolies *in their incipiency and before consummation.*"[3] In the Federal Trade Commission Act of 1914, Congress set up an

[2] *The Wealth of Nations*, Book 1, Chap. 10. Here it should be pointed out that businessmen engage in trade restraints and organize monopolies not because of any vicious and antisocial motives, but rather because of a desire to increase personal profits. As George Comer, former chief economist of the Antitrust Division, once observed, monopolies are formed "not because businessmen are criminals, but because the reports from the bookkeeping department indicate, in the short run at least, that monopoly and restraints of trade will pay if you can get away with [them]. It will pay a large corporation to agree with its competitors on price fixing. It pays to operate a basing point or zone price system. If patent pools can be organized, especially with hundreds or thousands of patents covering a whole industry, the profits will be enormous. If an international cartel can be formed which really works, the very peak of stabilization and rationalism is reached. If the management of all the large units in an industry can get together with the labor unions in the industry, a number of birds can be killed with one stone. And, finally, if the government can be persuaded to legalize the restrictive practices, the theory of 'enlightened competition' is complete." "The Outlook for Effective Competition," *American Economic Review, Papers and Proceedings*, 36:154 (May 1946).

[3] U.S. Congress, Senate, Committee on the Judiciary, S. Rep. 695, 63rd Cong., 2d sess., 1914, p. 1. (Italics supplied.)

independent regulatory commission to police the industrial field against "all unfair methods of competition." In the Clayton Act of the same year Congress singled out four specific practices that past experience had shown to be favorite weapons of the would-be monopolist: (1) price discrimination—that is, local price cutting and cut-throat competition; (2) tying contracts and exclusive dealer arrangements; (3) the acquisition of stock in competing companies; and (4) the formation of interlocking directorates between competing corporations. These practices were to be unlawful whenever their effect was to substantially lessen competition or to create tendencies toward monopoly. Thus, price discrimination, for example, was not made illegal per se; it was to be illegal only if used as a systematic device for destroying competition—in a manner typical of the old Standard Oil and American Tobacco trusts.[4] The emphasis throughout was to be on prevention rather than cure. The hope was that—given the provisions of the 1914 laws to supplement the provisions of the Sherman Act—the antitrust authorities could effectively eliminate the economic evils against which the antitrust laws were directed. The thrust of the Celler-Kefauver Anti-Merger Act of 1950 was aimed at the same objectives.

THE CHARGES AGAINST MONOPOLY

What those evils were never has been clearly stated, and perhaps, never has been clearly conceived, by the sponsors of antitrust legislation. In general, however, the objections to monopoly and trade restraints—found in literally tons of antitrust literature—can be summarized as follows:[5]

1. *Monopoly affords the consumer little protection against exorbitant prices.* As Adam Smith put it, "the price of monopoly is, upon every occasion, the

---

[4] A congressional committee explained the background of the price discrimination provision of the Clayton Act as follows:

"In the past it has been a most common practice of great and powerful combinations engaged in commerce—notably the Standard Oil Company and the American Tobacco Company, and others of less notoriety, but of great influence—to lower prices of their commodities, oftentimes below the cost of production in certain communities and sections where they had competition, with the intent to destroy and make unprofitable the business of their competitors, and with the ultimate purpose in view of thereby acquiring a monopoly in the particular locality or section in which the discriminating price is made.

"Every concern that engages in this evil practice must of necessity recoup its losses in the particular communities or sections where their commodities are sold below cost or without a fair profit by raising the price of this same class of commodities above their fair market value in other sections or communities.

"Such a system or practice is so manifestly unfair and unjust, not only to competitors who are directly injured thereby but to the general public, that your committee is strongly of the opinion that the present antitrust laws ought to be supplemented by making this particular form of discrimination a specific offense under the law when practiced by those engaged in commerce."

U.S. Congress, House, Committee on the Judiciary, H. Rep. 627, 63rd Cong., 2d sess., 1914, pp. 8–9.

[5] For a good summary of the charges against monopoly as well as the claims made in support of monopoly, see Clair Wilcox, *Competition and Monopoly in the American Economy*, Temporary National Economic Committee Monograph, no. 21 (Washington, D.C.: U.S. Government Printing Office, 1941), pp. 15–18. (Hereafter referred to as TNEC Monograph.)

highest which can be got. The natural price, or the price of free competition, on the contrary is the lowest which can be taken, not upon every occasion indeed, but for any considerable time taken together. The one is upon every occasion the highest which can be squeezed out of the buyers, of which, it is supposed, they will consent to give; the other is the lowest which the sellers can commonly afford to take, and at the same time continue their business."[6] The consumer is, under these conditions, open to prey to extortion and exploitation—protected only by such tenuous self-restraint as the monopolist may choose to exercise because of benevolence, irrationality, concern over government reprisals, or fear of potential competition.

The monopolist generally can charge all the traffic will bear, simply because the consumer has no alternative sources of supply. The consumer is forced to pay the monopolist's price, turn to a less desirable substitute, or go without. His freedom is impaired, because his range of choice is artificially limited.

An example, while admittedly extreme, serves to illustrate this point. It involves tungsten carbide, a hard-metal composition of considerable importance in such industrial uses as cutting tools, dies, and so on. In 1927, tungsten carbide sold in the United States at $50 per pound; but after a world monopoly was established by General Electric (GE) and Friedrich Krupp A.G. of Germany, under which GE was granted the right to set prices in the American market, the price promptly rose to a maximum of $453 per pound. During most of the 1930s the price fluctuated between $225 and $453 per pound, and not until 1942—when an indictment was issued under the antitrust laws—did the price come down. Thereafter, it fluctuated between $27 and $45 per pound.[7]

2. *Monopoly causes a restriction of economic opportunity and a misallocation of productive resources.* Under free competition, it is the consumer who, through his dollar votes in the market place, decides how society's land, labor, and capital are to be used. Consumer tastes generally determine whether more cotton and less wool, more cigarettes and less pipe tobacco, and more aluminum and less steel shall be produced. Under free competition the consumer is in this strategic position because businessmen must, if they want to make profits, do as the consumer demands. Because a businessman, under competition, is free to enter any field and to produce any type and quantity of goods he desires, the tendency will be for him to do those things that the consuming public (in its wisdom or ignorance) deems most valuable. In short, under a truly competitive system, the businessman can improve himself only by serving others. He can earn profits only by obeying the wishes of the community as expressed in the market.

Under monopoly, by contrast, the individual businessman finds his freedom of enterprise limited. He cannot do as he pleases, because the monopolist has the power of excluding newcomers or stipulating the terms under which new-

[6] Smith, op. cit., Book 1, Chap. 7.

[7] See C. D. Edwards, *Economic and Political Aspects of International Cartels*, Senate Committee on Military Affairs, Monograph, no. 1 (Washington, D.C.: U.S. Government Printing Office, 1946), pp. 12–13.

FIGURE 1

Free competition versus price fixing. Source: Thurman W. Arnold, *Cartels of Free Enterprise?* Public Affairs Pamphlet No. 103, 1945; reproduced by courtesy of Public Affairs Commission, Inc.

comers are permitted to survive in an industry. The monopolist can interfere with a consumer-oriented allocation of resources. He, instead of the market, can determine the type and quantity of goods that shall be produced. He, and not the forces of supply and demand, can decree who shall produce what, for whom, and at what price. In the absence of competition, it is the monopolist who decides what *other* businessmen shall be allowed to do and what benefits the consuming public shall be allowed to receive.

A good illustration of this is the Hartford-Empire Company, which once was an undisputed monopolist in the glass bottle industry. Through its patent control over glass bottling machinery, Hartford-Empire held life-and-death power both over the producers already in the industry and those attempting to enter it. As one observer described the situation,[8] Hartford had become benevolent despot to the glass container. Only by its leave could a firm come into the industry; the ticket of admission was to be had only upon its terms; and from its studied decision there was no appeal. The candidate had to subscribe to Hartford's articles of faith; he could not be a price cutter or a trouble maker. He could not venture beyond his assigned bailiwick or undermine the market of his partners in the conspiracy. Each concern had to accept the restrictions and limitations imposed by Hartford. Thus, the Buck Glass Company was authorized to manufacture wine bottles for sacramental purposes only. The Sayre Glass Works was

[8] See W. H. Hamilton, *Patents and Free Enterprise*, TNEC Monograph, no. 31 (Washington, D.C.: U.S. Government Printing Office, 1941), pp. 109–115.

restricted to producing "such bottles, jugs, and demijohns as are used for vinegar, ciders, sirups, bleaching fluids, hair tonics, barber supplies, and fluid extracts." Knox Glass Bottle Company was allowed to make only amber-colored ginger ale bottles. Mary Card Glass Company could not make products weighing more than 82 ounces. Baurens Glass Works Inc. was licensed to provide bottles for castor oil and turpentine, but none to exceed 4 ounces in capacity. Here, indeed, was a shackling of free enterprise and a usurpation of the market—a private government more powerful than that of many states. Here, indeed, was a tight little island, where the law of the monopolist was supreme and unchallenged. Only through antitrust prosecution were the channels of trade reopened and the Hartford dictatorship dissipated.[9]

3. *Monopoly often restrains technological advances and, thus, impedes economic progress.* As Clair Wilcox points out, "the monopolist may engage in research and invent new materials, methods, and machines, but he will be reluctant to make use or these inventions if they would compel him to scrap existing equipment of if he believes that their ultimate profitability is in doubt. He may introduce innovations and cut costs, but instead of moving goods by price reduction he is prone to spend large sums on alternative methods of promoting sales; his refusal to cut prices deprives the community of any gain. The monopolist may voluntarily improve the quality of his product and reduce its price, but no threat of competition compels him to do so."[10]

Our experience with the hydrogenation and synthetic rubber processes is a case in point. This, one of the less illustrious chapters in our industrial history, dates back to 1926, when I. G. Farben of Germany developed the hydrogenation process for making oil out of coal—a development that obviously threatened the entrenched position of the major international oil companies. Soon after this process was patented, Standard Oil Company of New Jersey concluded an agreement with I. G. Farben, under which Farben promised to stay out of the world's oil business (except inside Germany) and Standard agreed to stay out of the world's chemical business. "By this agreement, control of the hydrogenation process for making oil outside Germany was transferred to the Standard Oil Company in order that Standard's petroleum investment might be fully protected. In the United States, Standard licensed only the large oil companies which had no interest in exploiting hydrogenation. Outside the United States, Standard . . . proceeded to limit use of the process so far as the threat of competing processes and governmental interest [of foreign countries] permitted."[11] As a result, this revolutionary process was almost completely suppressed, except in Germany where it became an effective tool for promoting the military ambitions of the Nazi government.

The development of synthetic rubber production in the United States was

[9] See *United States* v. *Hartford-Empire Co. et al.*, 323 U.S. 386 (1945).

[10] Wilcox, op. cit., pp. 16–17.

[11] Edwards, op. cit., p. 36. For a popular discussion of the I.G.-Standard marriage, see also G. W. Stocking and M. W. Watkins, *Cartels in Action* (New York: Twentieth Century Fund, 1946), Chap. 11, especially pp. 491–505.

similarly retarded by the I.G.-Standard marriage of 1928. Because Buna rubber, under the agreement of 1928, was considered a chemical process, it came under the exclusive control of I. G. Farben—both in and outside Germany. Farben, however, was not interested in promoting the manufacture of synthetic rubber anywhere except in Germany, and proceeded, therefore—both for commercial (that is, monopolistic) and nationalistic reasons—to forestall its development in the United States. Farben had, at least, the tacit support of its American partner. As a result, the outbreak of World War II found the United States without production experience or know-how in the vital synthetic rubber field. In fact, when the Goodrich and Goodyear tire companies attempted to embark on synthetic rubber production, the former was sued for patent infringement and the latter formally threatened with such a suit by Standard Oil Comaany (acting under the authority of the Farben patents). This happened in November 1941, one month before Pearl Harbor. Not until after our formal entry into World War II was the Farben-Standard alliance broken under the impact of antitrust prosecution and the production of vital synthetic rubber started in the United States. Here, as in the case of hydrogenation, monopolistic control over technology had serious implications not only for the nation's economic progress but also its military security.[12]

4. *Monopoly tends to impede the effectiveness of general stabilization measures and to distort their structural impact on the economy.* Monopolistic and oligopolistic firms, as John Kenneth Galbraith suggests, may insulate themselves against credit restrictions designed to curb investment and check inflation. They may do so by raising prices to offset higher interest costs, by raising prices to finance investment out of increased profits, or by resorting to the capital market rather than to banks for their supply of loanable funds. Competitive firms, by contrast, cannot raise prices to compensate for higher interest charges. They cannot raise prices to finance investment out of higher profits. They cannot readily turn to the capital market for funds. Their lack of market control makes them the weakest borrowers and poorest credit risks, and they must, therefore, bear the brunt of any "tight money" policy. In short, monopolistic and oligopolistic firms not only can undermine the effectiveness of monetary control in their sector of the economy, but also shift the burden of credit restrictions to the competitive sector and, thus, stifle its growth. The implications for concentration need not be belabored.[13]

---

[12] See W. Berge, *Cartels: Challenge to a Free World* (Washington, D.C.: Public Affairs Press, 1944), pp. 210–214; G. W. Stocking and M. W. Watkins, *Cartels or Competition* (New York: Twentieth Century Fund, 1948), pp. 114–117; J. Borkin and C. A. Welsh, *Germany's Master Plan* (New York: Duell, Sloan, 1943). For a contrary view, see F. A. Howard, *Buna Rubber* (New York: Van Nostrand, 1947).

[13] "Market Structure and Stabilization Policy," *The Review of Economics and Statistics*, **39**:131, 133 (May 1957). For further discussion of sellers' inflation, administered price inflation, and inflation in the midst of recession—in short, the relation between market structure and general price stability—see also U.S. Congress, Senate, Judiciary Committee, *Hearings on Administered Prices Before the Subcommittee on Antitrust and Monopoly*, pt. 1, 1957, and pts. 9 and 10, 1959; and U.S. Congress, Joint Economic Committee, *The Relationship of Prices to Economic Stability and Growth*, 85th Cong., 2d sess., 1958.

5. *Monopoly threatens not only the existence of a free economy, but also the survival chances of free political institutions.* Enterprise that is not competitive cannot for long remain free, and a community that refuses to accept the discipline of competition inevitably exposes itself to the discipline of absolute authority. As Mutual Security Administrator Harold Stassen once observed, "world economic history has shown that nationalization and socialization have come when there has been complete consolidation and combination of industry, not when enterprise is manifold and small in its units. . . . We must not permit major political power to be added to the other great powers that are accumulated by big business units. Excessive concentration of power is a threat to the individual freedoms and liberties of men, whether that excessive power is in the hands of government or of capital or of labor."[14] The enemy of democracy is monopoly in all its forms, and political liberty can survive only within an effective competitive system. If concentrated power is tolerated, giant pressure groups will ultimately gain control of the government or the government will institute direct regulation of organized pressure groups. In either event, free enterprise will then have to make way for collectivism, and democracy will be superseded by some form of authoritarianism.

This objection to monopoly, this fear of concentrated economic power, is deeply rooted in American traditions—the tradition of federalism, the separation of church and state, and the tripartite organization of our governmental machinery. It is the expression of a sociopolitical philosophy of the decentralization of power, a broad base for the class structure of society, and the economic freedom and opportunity for new men, new ideas, and new organizations to spearhead the forces of progress. It stands in stark contrast to the older European varieties of free enterprise, which merely involve curbs on governmental powers without similar checks on excessive private power.[15]

---

[14] Address reprinted in *Congressional Record*, Feb. 12, 1947, p. A545. See also H. C. Simons, *Economic Policy for a Free Society* (Chicago: University of Chicago Press, 1948); F. A. Hayek, *The Road to Serfdom* (Chicago: University of Chicago Press, 1945); R. A. Brady, *Business as a System of Power* (New York: Columbia University Press, 1943); G. W. Stocking, "Saving Free Enterprise from Its Friends," *Southern Economic Journal*, **19**:431 (Apr. 1953). Also relevant in this connection are the repeated warnings by the FTC to the effect that "the capitalist system of free initiative is not immortal, but is capable of dying and dragging down with it the system of democratic government. Monopoly constitutes the death of capitalism and the genesis of authoritarian government." *The Basing Point Problem*, TNEC Monograph, no. 42 (Washington, D.C.: U.S. Government Printing Office, 1941), p. 9.

[15] This point was well made by Senator Cummins, in 1914, when he pressed for adoption of the Federal Trade Commission Act and the Clayton Act:

"We have adopted in this country the policy of competition. We are trying to preserve competition as a living, real force in our industrial life; that is to say, we are endeavoring to maintain among our business people that honorable rivalry which will prevent one from exacting undue profits from those who may deal with him. . . . We are practically alone, however, in this policy. . . . England long ago became indifferent to it; and while that great country has not specifically adjusted her laws so as to permit monopoly they are so administered as to practically eliminate competition when the trade affected so desires. France has pursued a like course.

"Austria, Italy, Spain, Norway, Sweden, as well as Belgium, have all pursued the course of permitting combinations and relations which practically annihilate competition, and Germany,

By way of illustrating this charge against monopoly, some students contend that the rise of Hitler in Germany was facilitated by the pervasive cartelization of the German economy—by the absence of competitive freedom in German business and the lack of democratic freedom in German government. Similarly, they point our that unregulated private monopoly was the breeding ground for Italian facism and Japanese totalitarianism. Whether or not these correlations are scientifically valid is difficult to determine. Certainly, the seriousness of a danger is not easy to evaluate. "Who can say whether any particular warning is due to overcautioness, timidity, or even superstition or, on the other hand, to prudence and foresight? . . . It is, of course, possible that 'monopoly' is merely a bugbear frightening the believers in free enterprise and free society; but it is equally possible that we have underestimated the danger and have allowed the situation to deteriorate to such a degree that only a very radical effort can still save our social and political system."[16]

---

our most formidable rival, so far as commerce is concerned, not only authorizes by her law the formation of monopolies, the creation of combinations which restrain trade and which destroy competition, but oftentimes compels her people to enter into combinations which are in effect monopolies. We are, therefore, pursuing a course which rather distinguishes us from the remainder of the commercial world.

"I pause here to say, and I say it emphatically and earnestly, that I believe in our course; I believe in the preservation of competition, I believe in the maintenance of the rule that opens the channels of trade fairly and fully to all comers. I believe it because it seems to me obvious that any other course must inevitably lead us into complete State socialism. The only monopoly which civilized mankind will ever permanently endure is the monopoly of all the people represented in the Government itself." *Congressional Record*, June 30, 1914, p. 11,379.

Since World War II, the contrast between the American and European approaches to the monopoly problem has been considerably reduced. Several nations in Western Europe have enacted restrictive practices legislation that, although not as far-reaching as the American prototype, nevertheless reflects a growing awareness of the problem. See European Productivity Agency, *Guide to Legislation on Restrictive Business Practices*, 2 vols. (Paris: Organization for Economic Cooperation and Development, 1960).

[16] F. Machlup, *The Political Economy of Monopoly* (Baltimore: The Johns Hopkins Press, 1952), pp. 77–78. Many students of the concentration movement, including the distinguished historian Charles A. Beard, feel that monopoly is to a considerable extent the creature of government action and inaction. Professor Beard explained his position to a congressional committee as follows:

"I should like to emphasize the fact that our state and national governments have a responsibility for the corporate abuses and economic distress in which we now flounder. It is a matter of common knowledge that corporations are not natural persons. They are artificial persons. They are the creatures of government. Only with the sanction of government can they perform any acts, good or bad. The corporate abuses which have occurred, the concentration of wealth which has come about under their operations, all can be laid directly and immediately at the door of government. The states of the American Union and the Congress of the United States, by their actions and their inaction, have made possible the situation and the calamities in which we now find ourselves." U.S. Congress, *Subcommittee on the Judiciary*, Hearings, 75th Cong., 1st sess., 1937, pt. 1, p. 72.

See also W. Adams and H. M. Gray, *Monopoly in America: The Government as Promoter* (New York: Macmillan, 1955).

THE EXTENT OF CONCENTRATION

In discussing the concentration of economic power, it is important to distinguish between *market* concentration[17] and *aggregate* concentration.

Market concentration indicates the share of business held by the leading firms in an industry—usually the top four or eight firms. Although concentration ratios cannot fully describe the number and size distribution of companies in an industry, they do serve as a convenient index or proxy of the degree of market power held by the largest firms. Like any other single statistic, of course, they are not the last word on the subject.

Concentration ratios are usually computed with reference to the SIC classification system, which ranges from 2-digit major industry groups to seven-digit product categories. Table 1 illustrates the point:

TABLE 1

SIC CODE	DESIGNATION	NAME
20	Major industry group	Food and kindred products
208	Industry group	Beverages
2085	Industry	Distilled liquors
20853	Product class	Bottled liquors
20853–51	Product	Whiskey
–55	Product	Gin
–57	Product	Vodka

The most readily available and widely used concentration ratios are those computed for four-digit industries. These ratios show a pattern of the richest variation, ranging from extremely high to relatively low concentration. Among the extremely concentrated industries, in 1970, in which the four largest producers accounted for 75 per cent or more of total industry shipments, were telephone apparatus (94 per cent), electric lamps (93 per cent), flat glass (92 per cent), motor vehicles (91 per cent), cereal preparations (90 per cent), chewing gum (85 per cent), cigarettes (84 per cent), steam engines and turbines (77 per cent), and photoequipment and industrial gases (75 per cent).

Highly concentrated industries, in which the four largest producers accounted for 50 to 74 per cent of total industry shipments, included organic fibers (73 per cent), explosives (72 per cent), metal cans (72 per cent), tires and inner tubes (72 per cent), soaps and detergents (70 per cent), beet sugar (65 per cent), synthetic rubber (64 per cent), transformers (59 per cent), biscuits and crackers

[17] For conflicting views on the extent of concentration in the American economy, see M. A. Adelman, "The Measurement of Industrial Concentration," *Review of Economics and Statistics*, 33:269 (Nov. 1951); and J. M. Blair, "The Measurement of Industrial Concentration: A Reply," *Review of Economics and Statistics*, **34**:343 (Nov. 1952).

(59 per cent), automatic vending machines (57 per cent), and storage batteries (56 per cent).

Moderately concentrated industries, in which the four largest producers accounted for 25 to 49 per cent of total industry shipments, included semiconductors (49 per cent), distilled liquor (47 per cent), construction machinery (42 per cent), petroleum refining (33 per cent), dehydrated food products (33 per cent), envelopes (31 per cent), fertilizers (30 per cent), periodicals (28 per cent), and costume jewelry (26 per cent).

Industries with relatively low concentration, in which the four largest firms accounted for less than 25 per cent of total industry shipments, were represented by fluid milk (20 per cent), lighting fixtures (18 per cent), knit fabric mills (17 per cent), newspapers (16 per cent), dresses (10 per cent), special dies and tools (7 per cent), ready-mix concrete (6 per cent), and fur goods (6 per cent).

The frequency distribution of manufacturing industries according to the foregoing concentration categories is summarized in Chart 1. It is clear that a significant number of industries are highly concentrated, but market concentration is, nevertheless, moderate or relatively low in the greater part of manufacturing.

Certain caveats are recommended to guard against unwarranted conclusions based on these figures. First, it is difficult to define an "industry," and high concentration in one industry may not be very significant if its product competes actively with that of another industry—that is, where the cross-elasticity of demand is high. For example, concentration in the field of textile fibers, taken as a whole, may, for public policy purposes, be more relevant than concentration in silk, wool, cotton, rayon, nylon, Orlon, Acrilan, Dynel, Dacron, and so on taken separately. Second, some giant firms are listed as members of one industry, although their capital assets are spread over a number of other industries. General Motors, for example, is listed as an automobile producer, although some of its capital investment lies in such fields as Diesel engines, electric appliances, refrigerators, and so on—a fact that results in partial overstatement of the degree of concentration in the automobile industry. Third, imports are not reflected in the concentration ratios, although their significance may be substantial in some industries, such as chemicals, cameras, typewriters, clocks and watches, toilet preparations, and so on. Fourth, the ratios apply to concentration in national markets, but fail to reflect concentration in regional or local markets. Thus, the top four producers in the bread industry account for only 29 per cent of the national market, although their sales in some 23 states exceed 50 per cent and run still higher in individual cities. Finally, concentration must not be confused with monopoly. The mere fact that an industry is highly concentrated is not positive proof that the industry is monopolized or that its firms are in active collusion. Under extreme circumstances, it is even conceivable that as few as two companies are enough to provide effective competition in an industry. As Dexter Keezer, former vice-president of the McGraw-Hill Book Company, points out: "If the heads of the two surviving firms were the hard-driving, fiercely independent type of businessman who has played such a large part in the industrial development of the USA, two of them would be enough to

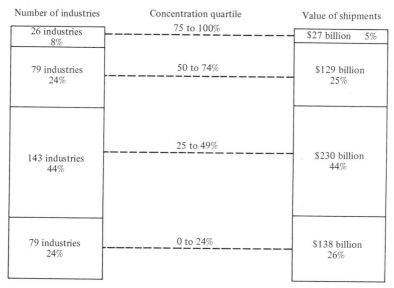

Number of industries	Concentration quartile	Value of shipments
26 industries 8%	75 to 100%	$27 billion 5%
79 industries 24%	50 to 74%	$129 billion 25%
143 industries 44%	25 to 49%	$230 billion 44%
79 industries 24%	0 to 24%	$138 billion 26%

CHART 1

Distribution of manufacturing industries by four-firm concentration-ratio quartiles, 1970. Of the 413 industry categories in the manufacturing sector, only 327 are included in the above calculations. Excluded were 18 local or small regional market industries, 15 industry categories composed of products " not elsewhere classified" within major industry groups, and 53 industry categories for which the census did not publish 1970 concentration ratios. Source: U.S. Bureau of the Census, Annual Survey of Manufacturers, 1970, "Value-of-Shipment Concentration Ratios by Industry," Chart provided by Willard F. Mueller and Larry G. Hamm, University of Wisconsin.

create a ruggedly competitive situation. But," Dr. Keezer adds, "if the two were of the genteel, clubby, and take-it-easy type, which is also known in the high reaches of American business, two companies might get together and tend to sleep together indefinitely. When the number of firms involved is small, the chances of having the industry animated by vigorously competitive leadership also seem to me to be small."[18]

As for trends since World War II, it is clear that average market concentration in manufacturing industries has shown no marked tendency to increase or decrease. This was the finding of Willard F. Mueller and Larry Hamm in an exhaustive analysis of 166 essentially comparable industries from 1947 to 1970.[19] As Table 2 shows, from 1947 to 1970, only slightly more industries experienced increases (86) than decreases (74) in concentration. Furthermore, for this 23-year period, average concentration only increased 1.8 per cent.

Nevertheless, Table 2 does indicate an interesting divergence in the trend of

---

[18] "Antitrust Symposium," *American Economic Review,* **39**:718 (June 1949).

[19] "Trends in Industrial Concentration, 1947–1970," *The Review of Economics and Statistics,* **56**:513 ff. (Nov. 1974).

TABLE 2
Change in Concentration from 1947 to 1970 in 166 Manufacturing Industries[a]

A. NUMBERS OF INDUSTRIES EXPERIENCING INCREASING AND DECREASING CONCENTRATION, 1947–1970[b]

CHANGE IN FOUR-FIRM CONCENTRATION 1947–1970 (IN PER CENT)	T66 IN-DUSTRIES	PRODUCER GOODS $N = 97$	CONSUMER GOODS: DEGREE OF DIFFERENTIATION			
			ALL $N = 69$	LOW $N = 20$	MODERATE $N = 33$	HIGH $N = 16$
21 or more	7	1	6	—	3	3
16–20	8	3	5	—	2	3
11–15	27	9	18	3	9	6
6–10	22	9	13	6	7	—
1–5	22	16	6	3	2	1
Number of industries with increased concentration	86	38	48	12	23	13
0	6	3	3	—	3	—
−1–5	31	26	5	2	2	1
−6–10	21	17	4	2	1	1
−11–15	9	8	1	1	—	—
−16–20	8	3	5	2	3	—
−21 or less	5	2	3	1	1	1
Number of industries with decreased concentration	74	56	18	8	7	3

B. AVERAGE UNWEIGHTED FOUR-FIRM CONCENTRATION[c]

1970	42.7	42.8	42.4	28.2	41.4	62.3
1967	41.4	41.9	40.8	26.0	39.7	61.6
1963	41.3	42.4	39.9	25.8	38.8	59.8
1958	40.3	42.4	37.4	23.8	36.7	55 9
1954	40.6	43.3	37.1	25.3	35.8	54.6
1947	40.9	44.1	36.3	27.8	35.0	49.6
Change 1947–1970	+1.8	−1.3	+6.1	+0.4	+6.4	+12.7

market concentration in producer goods and consumer goods industries. More producer goods industries experienced decreases (56) than increases (38). The contrast was more pronounced within the consumer goods industries when they are broken down according to the degree of product differentiation. In low product differentiation industries, increases outnumbered decreases by only three to two. By contrast, in moderately differentiated product industries, the increases exceeded the decreases by three to one and by four to one in the highly differentiated product industries. The average four-firm concentration ratios declined 1.3 per cent for producer goods industries, while they increased 6.1 per cent for consumer goods industries. Sharply divergent trends exist within the consumer goods subsample. The average concentration for products with a low degree of product differentiation declined from 1947 to 1958, but has risen persistently since then. Industries with a moderate and a high degree of product differentiation increased persistently in that period, with the increase in concentration in the highly differentiated products being more than twice as great as that for all consumer goods. Mueller and Hamm conclude that "product differentiation . . . appears to have exerted a powerful influence over the period, particularly since 1958. The recent increases in industries classified as low product differentiation may reflect the fact that some consumer goods industries that were still essentially undifferentiated in 1958 have become increasingly differentiated in recent years, due largely to extensive network TV advertising."[20] On the basis of these statistics, one might well argue that product differentiation (in consumer goods industries) proved to be a more formidable "entry" barrier than the alleged economies-of-scale imperatives in the producer goods sector.

Aggregate concentration, as distinct from market concentration, measures the centralized control that a group of firms exercises over more than one industry, product, or market. It measures the relative control that giant firms have over an entire sector of economic activity, such as manufacturing and mining, or trade and commerce, or transportation and public utilities, and so on. It is an index of the conglomerate concentration of power, and it is a first approximation of the discretionary power that may accompany such forms of structural organization.

The level of aggregate concentration is high. Table 3 shows the proportion of total manufacturing assets controlled by the largest companies in that sector.

[20] Ibid., p. 519.

---

[a] For the 413 manufacturing industries, data for the entire 1947–1970 period were available for only 166 of these industries. This sample represents about 44 per cent of total value added by manufacturers in 1970. CRs were estimated for 14 industries.
[b] Provided by Willard F. Mueller and Larry G. Hamm.
[c] Willard F. Mueller and Larry G. Hamm, "Trends in Industrial Market Concentrations, 1947–1970," *The Review of Economics and Statistics*, **56**:513 (Nov. 1974).
Source: U.S. Department of Commerce, Bureau of the Census, *Annual Survey of Manufacturers: 1970 Value-of-shipments Concentration Ratios.* (Washington, D.C.: U.S. Government Printing Office, 1972); and R. C. Parker, FTC, Bureau of Economics, *Comparable Concentration Ratios for 213 Manufacturing Industries Classified by Producer and Consumer Goods and Degree of Product Differentiation* (Washington, D.C.: U.S. Government Printing Office, Mar. 1967).

TABLE 3

Aggregate Concentration

	CORPORATE MANUFACTURING ASSETS (PER CENT)							
	1948	1958	1968	1969	1970	1971	1972	1973[a]
Top 100	40.2	47.0	49.2	48.2	48.5	48.9	47.6	44.7 (47.6)
Top 200	48.2	56.5	60.8	60.1	60.4	61.0	60.0	56.9 (60.3)

[a] From 1969 to 1973, the FTC changed the reporting rules for what firms should include as assets. The 1973 percentages excluded foreign assets that had been included in previous years. The numbers in parentheses represent the percentages that would have been published if no changes in the aggregate concentration series had occurred after 1968.
Source: Table provided by David W. Penn, Bureau of Economics, FTC.

From 1948 to 1968, the assets controlled by the top 100 and top 200 firms increased by 9 per cent and 12.6 per cent, respectively. Aggregate concentration has declined somewhat since 1968, but remains fairly constant and high. Viewed differently, the 100 largest controlled nearly the same share of assets (47.6 per cent) in 1973 as did the 200 largest (48.2 per cent) in 1948.

This trend is directly, and almost entirely, attributable to the magnitude velocity, and character of the post-World War II merger movement, especially in the 1960s. Table 4 shows the growing volume of "large" mergers since 1948 —that is, mergers where the acquired assets exceeded $10 million—and the proportion of such mergers consummated by the 200 largest companies. In nearly every year since 1948, the 200 largest were responsible for well over one half of the assets of the "large" manufacturing and mining companies acquired. During the entire period covered in Table 4, the top 200 acquired 57.6 per cent of the assets involved in these mergers. When acquisitions are ranked by the size of the acquiring company, it is again clear that the very largest firms negotiated the lion's share of these mergers—both by number and by assets acquired (see Chart 2).

Some of the companies acquired were large indeed. Of the $72.9 billion of assets acquired in 1492 acquisitions from 1948 to 1973, $36 billion were accounted for by 149 acquisitions where the acquired company had assets of $100 million or more. These largest acquisitions amounted to only 10 per cent of the number of acquisitions, but 49 per cent of the total assets acquired.

The extent to which mergers have contributed to aggregate concentration can also be seen in Chart 3, which isolates the merger component in the growth of the 200 largest manufacturing corporations. Over the 1947–1968 period, these corporations increased their share of assets held by 11.7 percentage points, of which 5.6 points were attributable to mergers. The change between 1960 and

TABLE 4

Large Acquisitions in Manufacturing and Mining by Firms Ranked Among
the 200 Largest Manufacturing Firms in 1972 (by year, 1948–1973)

YEAR	NO.	TOTAL LARGE ACQUISITIONS[a] ASSETS ($ MILLIONS)	NO.	LARGE ACQUISITIONS BY 200 LARGEST FIRMS[b] ASSETS ($ MILLIONS)	TOTAL LARGE ACQUISITIONS BY 200 LARGEST FIRMS (PER CENT) NUMBER	ASSETS
1948	4	63.2	4	63.2	100.0	100.0
1949	6	89.0	4	45.3	66.7	50.9
1950	5	186.3	1	20.0	20.0	10.7
1951	9	201.5	4	114.4	44.4	56.8
1952	16	373.8	7	195.0	43.8	52.2
1953	23	779.1	11	369.9	47.8	47.5
1954	37	1,444.5	15	930.2	40.5	64.4
1955	67	2,168.9	33	1,209.8	49.3	55.8
1956	53	1,882.0	27	1,244.3	50.9	66.1
1957	47	1,202.3	20	703.7	42.6	58.5
1958	42	1,070.6	19	699.6	45.2	65.3
1959	49	1,432.0	19	766.3	38.8	53.5
1960	51	1,535.1	22	841.9	43.1	54.8
1961	46	2,003.0	23	1,514.5	50.0	75.6
1962	65	2,241.9	25	1,052.5	38.5	46.9
1963	54	2.535.8	33	1,867.3	61.1	73.6
1964	73	2,302.9	31	1,055.7	42.5	45.8
1965	62	3,232.3	25	1,979.1	40.3	61.2
1966	75	3,310.7	25	1,803.1	33.3	54.5
1967	138	8,258.5	57	5,651.4	41.3	68.4
1968	173	12,554.2	79	8,550.2	45.7	68.1
1969	136	10,966.2	49	5,963.8	36.0	54.4
1970	90	5,876.0	29	2,670.0	32.2	45.4
1971	58	2,443.4	17	960.6	29.3	39.3
1972	58	1,860.3	17	553.8	29.3	29.8
1973[c]	55	2,896.4	19	1,175.6	34.5	40.6
Total	1,492	72,909.9	615	42,001.2	41.2	57.6

[a] Acquired firms with assets of $10 million or more.
[b] Ranked by 1972 total assets.
[c] Figures for 1973 are preliminary.
Note: Not included in this tabulation are companies for which data were not publicly available.
There were 327 such companies with assets of $7488.6 million for the period, of which 112 companies
with assets of $2708.9 million were acquisitions by the 200 largest firms.
Source: Bureau of Economics, FTC.

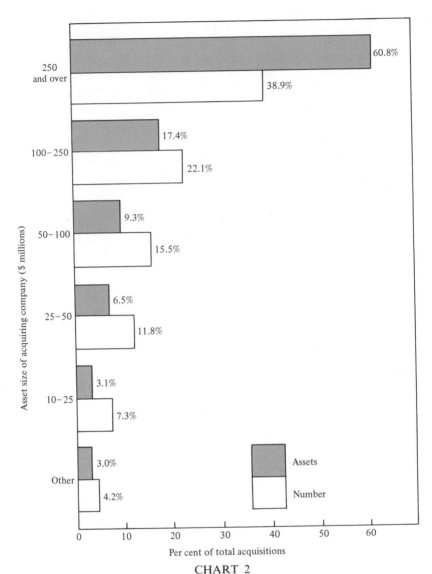

CHART 2

*Acquisitions by the size of the acquiring company, 1948–1972. This includes all manu-
facturing and mining acquisitions of $10 million or more. The per cent of total acquisitions
does not add up to 100 per cent because of rounding error. Source: FTC, Bureau of
Economics.*

1968 is even more dramatic. In 1968, the acquired assets of the large manufacturing and mining companies amounted to 44.9 per cent of all new investment.
Since 1968, however, this percentage has declined substantially to 19.1 per cent
in 1970, and to 7.7 per cent in 1973.

The character of the merger movement from 1948 to 1973 also explains an

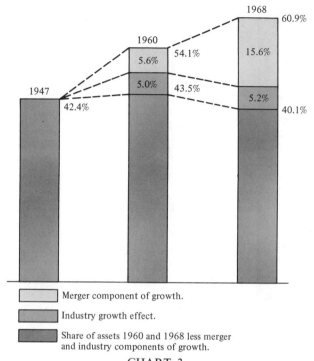

Merger component of growth.

Industry growth effect.

Share of assets 1960 and 1968 less merger and industry components of growth.

CHART 3

Share of assets of the 200 largest manufacturing corporations of 1968 and accumulative components of growth in 1947, 1960, and 1968. Source: FTC, Bureau of Economics.

apparent paradox: namely, that, despite the movement's magnitude, average market concentration remained relatively stable, although aggregate concentration rose appreciably. Chart 4, which shows a breakdown by types of merger during this period, illustrates this point. It highlights the relative decline of horizontal mergers—the only ones that register an effect on market concentration ratios—in the face of a startling rise in the relative importance of all types of conglomerate mergers.[21]

Spearheading this most recent phase of the merger movement have been the so-called new conglomerates. Five of these acquired more than $1 billion each by merger between 1961 and 1968, and in many cases bought out companies with leading positions in their industries. ITT, for example, acquired 47 com-

[21] Conglomerate mergers of the geographic market-extension type involve companies manufacturing the same product but selling it in different geographic markets: for example bakeries in New York and Chicago. (Such mergers are sometimes called chain horizontals because of their close resemblance to horizontal mergers.) Conglomerate mergers of the product-extension variety involve companies that functionally are related in production and/or distribution but do not sell products in direct competition with each other: for example, the union of soap and bleach manufacturers. Other conglomerate mergers involve companies having neither a buyer-seller relationship nor a functional connection in manufacturing or distribution, such as a shipbuilder and an ice cream manufacturer.

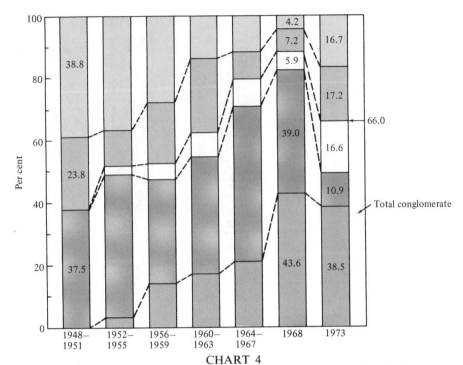

CHART 4

Distribution of total acquired assets in large mergers, by type, 1948–1973, for firms with assets of $10 million or more. Source: FTC, Bureau of Economics.

panies with combined assets of $1,487 million, including Continental Baking Company, the nation's largest baking firm; Sheraton Corporation of America, the largest owner-operator of guest rooms in the U.S.; Levitt & Sons, the largest home builder in the United States; and Avis, the second-largest car rental firm. Ling-Temco-Vought acquired 23 companies with combined assets of $1,901 million, including Wilson & Company, a major meat packer as well as a leader in sporting goods, drugs, and pharmaceuticals; Jones & Laughlin, a major steel company; and Braniff, a leading airline (which, of course, is not listed as a manufacturing corporation. Gulf & Western acquired 67 companies with combined assets of $2,882 million, including leading companies in the zinc, motion picture, sugar, cigar, rolling mill machinery, and other industries. Tenneco acquired 31 companies with assets of $1,196 million, and Teledyne Inc. acquired 125 companies with $1,026 million. Such mergers tend not only to increase aggregate concentration, but to give the 100 or 200 largest a leading market position in diverse industries.

The conglomerate merger movement has retreated somewhat from the heights it reached in 1968. By 1973, conglomerate mergers accounted for two thirds of all mergers, as compared to nearly 90 per cent of all mergers in 1968. Many of the conglomerate mergers were predicated on special conditions in the corporate financial markets caused by prosperous economic growth in the general economy. As these conditions changed in the early 1970s, the conglomerate merger movement lost some of its steam. In addition, the financial collapse of Ling-Temco-Vought and the Justice Department's antitrust suit against ITT further clouded the long-term viability of the "new conglomerates."

One final observation must be made. The foregoing data understate the degree of aggregate concentration because many of the largest manufacturing corporations are not fully independent business units. Firms can become interdependent via joint ventures and interlocking directorships. Between 1969 and 1973, there were an average of 239 new joint ventures in American industry recorded each year. Many of these were among the largest manufacturing and mining companies. Finally, of course, companies are often interlocked through common directors or managers with their suppliers, customers, potential competitors, and the financial institutions from which they borrow funds. In 1968, the FTC found that 50 top companies, for example, had 520 interlocks with companies ranking among the 1,000 largest manufacturing corporations; of these, 134 were interlocks with companies producing in the same five-digit product class.[22] In summary, then, joint ventures and interlocking ties further escalate the degree of aggregate concentration.

The significance of all this is still the subject of violent controversy, and all we can say—as Fritz Machlup suggests—is that economists regard the current degree of concentration either as (1) desirable and avoidable, (2) desirable and unavoidable, (3) undesirable and avoidable, or (4) undesirable and unavoidable.

PUBLIC POLICY ALTERNATIVES

Depending on which of these views is accepted, economists will then recommend one of the following policy alternatives with respect to concentrated industries: (1) maintenance of the status quo, which, by and large, is regarded as satisfactory; (2) imposition of public regulation or public ownership; or (3) rejection of both private and public monopoly and the promotion of vigorous competition under the antitrust laws. It is these policy alternatives that now will be examined in greater detail.

The Status Quo

The defenders of the status quo generally advocate a policy of noninterference with respect to our concentrated industries. They seem satisfied with the prevailing industrial structure, either because they believe that bigness and concentration are now controlled by the "right" people or because they refuse to regard concentration as indicative of pervasive monopolization.

[22] FTC, *Economic Report on Corporate Mergers* (Washington, D.C.: U.S. Government Printing Office, 1969).

Three distinct, although related, facets of this position are discernible. One is the belief that the business leader of today is a far cry from the robber baron of yesterday; the belief that industrial statesmanship, social responsibility, enlightened self-restraint, and progressive labor, customer, and supplier relations have replaced the exploitative behavior, the sharpshooting competitive practice, and the "public-be-damned" attitude of a bygone age—in short, the belief that the present managers of giant corporate enterprise have demonstrated their capacity for exercising industrial stewardship.[23]

The second facet of the status quo position is the "workable competition" thesis.[24] Its supporters hold that bigness and concentration are no cause for alarm, because competition is present and *working* in an economy such as ours where constant technological progress is reflected in ever-increasing output, lower prices, and new and improved products. They urge that the effectiveness of competition be judged not in terms of market structure—that is, the degree of concentration in particular industries—but rather by market results—that is, performance in the public interest. They suggest that an industry is "workably competitive"—regardless of the fewness of sellers in it—if it shows, among other things, "a progressive technology, the passing on to consumers of the results of this progressiveness in the form of lower prices, larger output, improved products, etc."[25] The emphasis here is on performance and results rather than on the structural organization that *compels* such performance and results.

The believers in workable competition usually buttress their position with the suggestion that "old-fashioned" competition—that is, competition among sellers and among buyers *within* an industry—be replaced with a more dynamic concept of interindustry or technological competition. Their argument is this: classical, intraindustry competition tends to promote maximum output, minimum prices, and optimum utilization of capacity; in short, it stimulates efficiency. But this efficiency is static and unprogressive in character. It makes no allowance for the research, development, and innovation required for economic

---

[23] David E. Lilienthal, *Big Business: A New Era* (New York: Harper, 1953), argues that the antitrust philosophy is no longer applicable and that the antitrust laws are, in fact, crippling America. He feels that the newer type of American big businessman is in little need of the restraints imposed by the antitrust laws. In contrast to Mr. Lilienthal's position, it is interesting to note that a distinguished Wall Street attorney, General William J. Donovan, disagrees. Mr. Donovan's warning, sounded in 1936, is still relevant today:

"Those who would remove the inhibitions of existing law must recognize that the alternative is not between the Sherman Act on the one hand and the regulation of industry by industry on the other. The alternative is between the continuance of the competitive system as a proper safeguard to the public, and the closest supervision and control of industry by the government. The self-interest of business in such matters would often be antagonistic to the interest of the public as a whole. The recent experience under the NRA shows the abuses that may arise by vesting in business the power of self-regulation without at the same time providing for adequate and capable supervision and control by a government agency." Address before the American Bar Association, 1936, quoted in V. A. Mund, *Government and Business* (New York: Harper, 1950), pp. 628–629.

[24] See, primarily, J. M. Clark, "Toward a Concept of Workable Competition," *American Economic Review*, **30**:241 (June 1940).

[25] E. S. Mason, "Antitrust Symposium," op. cit., p. 713. See also C. E. Griffin, *An Economic Approach to Antitrust Problems* (New York: American Enterprise Association, 1951).

growth. Even though it prevents concentration, it stifles progress. To have progress we need more, not less, concentration. Only bigness can provide the sizable funds necessary for technological experimentation and innovation in the industrial milieu of the twentieth century. Only monopoly earnings can provide the bait that lures capital to untried trails. Although progress may, thus, require high-power concentrations in many industries, this need not be a source of concern to society at large. Technological development will serve as an offset against any short-run position of entrenchment that may be established. The monopoly of glass bottles will be subverted by the introduction of the tin can; and the dominance of the latter will, in turn, be undermined by the introduction of the paper container. The consumer need not rely, therefore, on the static competition between large numbers of small firms as protection against exploitation. In the long run, he can find greater safety—and better things for better living to boot—in the technological competition of a small number of large firms that, through research and innovation, eventually destroy any position of market control that may be established.[26]

The third facet of the status quo position is the rather ingenious "countervailing power" thesis, which concedes the pervasiveness of concentration and monopoly, but maintains that the dangers of exploitation are minimized by certain built-in safeguards in our economy.[27] According to this thesis, the actual or real restraints on a firm's market power are vested not in its competitors, but in its customers and suppliers. These restraints are imposed not from the same side of the market (as under classical competition), but from the opposite side. Thus "private economic power is held in check by the countervailing power of those subject to it. The first begets the second."[28] A monopoly on one side of the market offers an inducement to both suppliers and customers to develop the power with which they can defend themselves against exploitation. For example, concentration in the steel industry will stimulate concentration among the industry's customers (automobile manufacturers) as well as among its suppliers (steelworkers). The result will be, so the argument runs, a balance of power within the economy—the creation of almost automatic checks and balances requiring a minimum of interference or "tampering."

The foregoing arguments in defense of the status quo are subject to a number of criticisms. As to the beneficence of industrial stewardship and workable competition, we should note that "results alone throw no light on the really significant question: have these results been *compelled* by the system—by competition—or do they represent simply the dispensations of managements which, with a wide latitude of policy choices at their disposal, happened for the moment to be benevolent or smart?"[29] In other words, what assurance do we have that

[26] See J. A. Schumpeter, *Capitalism, Socialism, and Democracy* (New York: Harper, 1943), p. 79 ff.

[27] See J. K. Galbraith, *American Capitalism: The Concept of Countervailing Power* (Boston: Houghton, 1952).

[28] Ibid., p. 118.

[29] Ben W. Lewis, "Antitrust Symposium," op. cit., p. 707.

the workable competition of today will not be transformed into the abusive monopoly or oppressive conspiracy of tomorrow? How, in the absence of competition or constant and detailed supervision, can we ever determine whether the performance of industrial giants does, in fact, serve the public interest and will continue to do so in the future? By what concrete yardsticks do we measure the workability of competition?

Second, with regard to the countervailing power thesis, it can be argued (1) that countervailing power often is undermined by vertical integration and top-level financial control, which blend the opposing sides of the market into one; (2) that the bilateral monopolies created through the countervailance process often conclude bargains prejudicial to the consumer interest (witness, for example, wage increases for the CIO steelworkers followed by price increases for the steel industry); (3) that the countervailing influence of technological or interindustry competition often is subverted by a combination of the potential competitors (witness, for example, the merger between motion picture houses and television networks); (4) that any countervailance through government action often is undermined by unduly intimate affiliation between regulator and regulatee (witness, for example, the ICC, which seems to have degenerated into a lobby on behalf of transporation interests); and, finally, (5) that the whole thesis rests on the dubious assumption that industrial giantism is inevitable under modern technological conditions—an assumption that still awaits scientific validation.[30]

Public Regulation or Public Ownership

The advocates of public regulation or public ownership hope simultaneously to ensure industrial efficiency and to avoid the abuses of private monopoly—not by the dissolution of monopoly but by its social control. Their argument runs along these lines: Competition in many basic industries is a thing of the past and has been replaced by trade agreements and price fixing, cartels, and monopolies. Although legislation to eliminate specific abuses of monopoly power can do some good, it cannot compel a return to competition in industries where it would be wasteful and undesirable. The facts of life are that efficient organization in mass production and mass distribution fields requires unification, coordination, and rationalization. Only monopoly can bring this about. But private monopoly is no guarantee of efficiency. By fixing prices, allocating production, and imposing levies on the efficient to keep the inefficient in production, the general level of prices is kept high, and incentives to modernization may be lacking. Hence, if monopoly is inevitable, it is preferable that such monopoly be publicly supervised or publicly owned.[31]

---

[30] For a more comprehensive critique of the countervailing power thesis, see W. Adams, "Competition, Monopoly, and Countervailing Power," *Quarterly Journal of Economics*, 67:469 (Nov. 1953).

[31] For this formulation of the argument, see the work of the British socialist, E. Davies, *National Enterprise* (London: Gollancz, 1946), p. 16.

Basic to this argument is the assumption that monopoly, or at least cooperation on a comprehensive scale, is necessary in many industries—the assumption that monopoly is inevitable under modern industrial conditions. It is this belief in the inevitability of monopoly that led men of such distinguished position, unimpeachable integrity, and obvious sincerity as Judge Gary (former president of the U.S. Steel) to advocate a public-utility-type regulation for concentrated industries. Thus, Judge Gary, as long ago as 1911, offered the following testimony to a congressional committee investigating the steel industry:

> I realize as fully, I think, as this committee that it is very important to consider how the people shall be protected against imposition or oppression as the possible result of great aggregations of capital, whether in the possession of corporations or individuals. I believe that is a very important question, and personally I believe that the Sherman Act does not meet and will never fully prevent that. I believe we must come to enforced publicity and governmental control, even as to prices, and, so far as I am concerned, speaking for our company, so far as I have the right, I would be very glad if we had some place where we could go, to a responsible governmental authority, and say to them, "Here are our facts and figures, here is our property, here our cost of production; now you tell us what we have the right to do and what prices we have the right to charge." I know this is a very extreme view, and I know that the railroads objected to it for a long time; but whether the standpoint of making the most money is concerned or not, whether it is the wise thing, I believe it is the necessary thing, and it seems to me corporations have no right to disregard these public questions and these public interests.
>
> "Your idea then," said Congressman Littleton of the committee, "is that cooperation is bound to take the place of competition and that cooperation requires strict governmental supervision?"
>
> "That is a very good statement," replied the Judge.[32]

Unfortunately, Judge Gary's faith in independent regulatory commissions has, in the light of American experience, not proved justified. These commissions— the ICC,[33] the Civil Aeronautics Board,[34] the Federal Power Commission (FPC),[35] the FCC[36]—have at times failed to regulate their respective industries in the public interest. Often these commissions adopted regulatory techniques that did little to promote operational efficiency and innovative progress; that were ineffective, costly, and debilitating; and that suffered from administrative

[32] Special Committee to Investigate the United States Steel Corporation, 62d Cong., 2d sess., 1911, H. Rept. 1127, quoted in W. Adams and L. E. Traywick, *Readings in Economics* (New York: Macmillan, 1948), p. 223.

[33] See, for example, S. P. Huntington, "The Marasmus of the ICC," *Yale Law Journal*, **61**: 467 (Apr. 1952); and, Senate Small Business Committee, *Competition, Regulation, and the Public Interest in the Motor Carrier Industry*, 84th Cong., 2d sess., 1956, S. Rept. 1693.

[34] See, for example, U.S. Congress, Senate, Small Business Committee, *Report on Role of Irregular Airlines in United States Air Transportation Industry*, 82d Cong., 1st sess., 1951, S. Rept. 540.

[35] See, for example, FPC, *In the Matter of the Phillips Petroleum Company*, Opinion no. 217, Docket no. G-1148, Aug. 16, 1951.

[36] See, for example, FCC, *In the Matter of American Broadcasting Company Inc. and United Paramount Theatres, Inc.*, Docket no. 10046, 1953; also B. Schwartz, *The Professor and the Commissions* (New York: Knopf, 1959).

incompetence, unimaginativeness, and dishonesty. Moreover, no satisfactory solution seems yet to have been found for the vexing problem of watching the watchers. (*Quis ipsos custodes custodiet?*) As ex-Senator Wheeler once sadly observed, "It seems to invariably happen, that when Congress attempts to regulate some group, the intended regulatees wind up doing the regulating."[37]

Dissatisfied with the past record of regulatory commissions, some groups have gone further and advocated the nationalization—that is, outright government ownership, of concentrated industries. Typical of these groups is the British Labour party, which, in 1948, demanded nationalization of the steel industry on the grounds that the public supervision of private monopoly is unworkable. Said the Labour party:

> A board controlling a private monopoly must, in the long run, be ineffective. Its activities must be negative. It can, for example, refuse to recommend a price increase, but it cannot force the industry to take steps to cheapen production. It has no power to make the monopoly spend money on new plant or scrap old plant. A supervised private monopoly can be prevented from doing the wrong things, but it cannot be forced to do the right things. In the future, the control of steel must be dynamic and purposeful, not negative and preventive. . . . There is no hope, then, in a supervised monopoly. The only answer is that steel must be made a public enterprise.[38]

According to the socialist, then, nationalization is preferable both to public regulation and to private monopoly. It is better than public regulation, because the latter has proved generally ineffective. It is better than private monopoly, because the power to control basic industries, and, hence, the economy, must be "democratized."[39] Such power must, according to the socialist, be held by the many and not as hitherto concentrated—without corresponding responsibility— in the hands of a few. There must be assurance that monopoly—a system that can be used for good or evil—will be used in the public interest. According to the socialist, a nationalized industry affords such assurance, simply because its management will be motivated by considerations of public service and not private profit.

The disadvantages of public ownership are fairly obvious: Administrators in nationalized industries may easily succumb to the disease of security, conservatism, procrastination, and bureaucracy. Their enterprises, as a result of super-centralization and lack of competitive incentives, may come to suffer from inflexibility and inelasticity. Moreover, the public enterprise may develop a tendency to use its monopoly power as a cloak for inefficient operation by resorting to the ready device of raising prices to meet increased costs and, thus, avoid showing a deficit. Finally, there is the distinct possibility that the very people in whose interest a particular industry may originally have been nationalized will

---

[37] Quoted in B. Bolles, *How to Get Rich in Washington* (New York: Dell, 1952), p. 23.

[38] *British Steel at Britain's Service*, quoted in Vernon A. Mund, *Government and Business* (New York: Harper, 1960), p. 548.

[39] See Ben W. Lewis, *British Planning and Nationalization* (New York: Twentieth Century Fund, 1952), pp. 43–45.

eventually lose control of it. This result is probable for two reasons: (1) General elections are no substitute for the market as an agency of social control (because people cannot indicate their dissatisfaction with a *particular* public enterprise by means of the ballot); and (2) the public enterprise, if it is to operate efficiently, must be "taken out of politics" and put in the hands of an autonomous body—again with the result of removing such enterprise from the direct control of the electorate.[40]

In summary, public regulation and public ownership suffer from the same basic drawback as private monopoly—namely, the concentration of power in the hands of a few. Such power may be used benignly or dangerously, depending on the men who possess and control it. They may be good men, benevolent men, and socially minded men; but society still confronts the danger of which Lord Acton so eloquently warned: Power corrupts, and absolute power corrupts absolutely.

The Promotion of Effective Competition

The advocates of greater competition through vigorous antitrust enforcement reject both the Scylla of private monopoly and the Charybdis of public ownership. Believing that the preservation of competitive free enterprise is both desirable and possible, they point out that this does not mean a return to the horse-and-buggy age, nor a strict adherence to the textbook theories of "perfect" or "pure" competition. What they advocate is a structural arrangement in private industry characterized by decentralized decision making and "effective" competition.

[40] See Hayek, op. cit.; L. Von Mises, *Planned Chaos* (New York: Foundation for Economic Education, 1947); C. E. Griffin, *Britain: A Case Study for Americans* (Ann Arbor: University of Michigan Press, 1950). These criticisms of public ownership are confirmed by the distinguished British scholar W. Arthur Lewis. In his "Recent British Experience of Nationalization as an Alternative to Monopoly Control" (a paper presented to the International Economic Association in 1951), Professor Lewis makes the following comments on Britain's experiment in socialism:

"The appointment of public directors to manage an undertaking is not sufficient public control. . . . Parliament is handicapped in controlling corporations by its lack of time. . . . Neither have Members of Parliament the competence to supervise these great industries. . . . Parliament is further handicapped . . . by paucity of information . . . for example, less information is now published about the railways than was available before they were nationalized. . . . Except in the case of transport, the British government has resisted proposals that public corporations should be treated in the same way [as private monopolies], with the result that the consumer is formally less well protected vis-a-vis public corporations than he was vis-a-vis private firms operating public utilities. . . . The [public] corporation's board, though publicly appointed, has many loyalties in addition to its loyalty to the public. It has also a loyalty to itself, and to its own staff, which may well conflict with the interests of the consumer. . . . Public corporations have not found it easy to dismiss redundant workers, or even to close down inefficient units or to expand more efficient units in some other place (for example, railways, mines). It may well turn out that public corporations are less able to promote this kind of efficiency than are private corporations, in the British atmosphere of tenderness toward established sources of income." (Quoted in Machlup, op. cit., p. 50.)

For more recent appraisal, see W. G. Shepherd and Associates, *Public Enterprise: Economic Analysis of Theory and Practice* (Lexington, Mass.: Heath, 1976).

Among the ingredients necessary for effective competition, the following are considered of primary importance:[41] (1) an appreciable number of sellers and buyers for substantially the same product, so that both sellers and buyers have meaningful alternatives of choice; (2) the economic, as well as legal, freedom to enter the market and gain access to essential raw materials; (3) the absence of tacit or open collusion between rivals in the market; (4) the absence of explicit or implicit coercion of rivals by a dominant firm or a group of dominant firms; (5) the absence of "substantial preferential status within the market for any important trader or group of traders on the basis of law, politics, or commercial alliances";[42] (6) the absence of diversification, subsidization, and political motivation to an extent where giant firms may escape the commercial discipline of a *particular* market or a *particular* operation.

Some economists feel that the maintenance of this type of competition may, under modern conditions, be difficult, if not impossible. They contend that anti-trusters are faced with the dilemma of choosing between "(1) firms of the most efficient size but operating under conditions where there is inadequate pressure to compel firms to continue to be efficient and pass on to the consumer the benefits of efficiency, and (2) a system in which the firms are numerous enough to be competitive but too small to be efficient."[43] According to this view our choice is between monopoly and efficiency, on the one hand, and competition and relative inefficiency, on the other.

The supporters of vigorous antitrust enforcement deny that such a choice is necessary, at least in many of our highly concentrated industries. The following reasons are usually given for rejecting the ostensible conflict between competition and efficiency. First, large firms, although technologically imperative in many industries, need not assume the Brobdingnagian proportions of some present-day giants. The unit of technological efficiency is the plant and not the firm. This means that, although there are undisputed advantages in the large-scale integrated steel operations at Gary, or Pittsburgh, or Birmingham, there seems little technological justification for combining these functionally separate plant units into a single administrative giant.[44]

Second, it seems significant that many of our colossal firms were not formed to gain the technical advantages of scale, but organized instead to achieve monopolistic control over the market and to reap profits from the sale of inflated

---

[41] See C. D. Edwards, *Maintaining Competition* (New York: McGraw-Hill, 1949), pp. 9–10.

[42] Ibid., p. 10.

[43] A. R. Burns, "Antitrust Symposium," op. cit., p. 603.

[44] In his definitive study of 20 representative industries, Joe S. Bain found that, in 11 out of 20 cases, the lowest-cost (most efficient) plant would account for less than $2\frac{1}{2}$ per cent of the industry's national sales; in 15 out of 20 cases, for less than $7\frac{1}{2}$ per cent; and in only one case, for more than 15 per cent. Moreover, in estimating multiplant economies, Bain concluded that in 6 out of 20 industries, the cost advantages of multiplant firms were "either negligible or totally absent"; in another 6 industries, the advantages were "perceptible" but "fairly small"; and in the remaining 8 industries, no estimates could be obtained. [*Barriers to New Competition* (Cambridge: Harvard University Press, 1956), pp. 73 and 85–88 ff.] These findings hardly support the contention that existing concentration in American industry can be explained in terms of technological imperatives.

securities. Giantism in industry today is not unrelated to the investment banker's inclination of yesteryear to merge and combine competing companies for the sake of promoter's profits.

Third, there is mounting evidence that industrial concentration is not necessarily the result of spontaneous generation or natural selection, but often is the end product of unwise, man-made, discriminatory, and privilege-creating governmental action. In an era of "big government," when the structural impact of Federal activity is no longer neutral, the government's spending, taxing, proprietary, legislative, and regulatory powers have often been used—unintentionally, in some instances—to throttle competition and restrict opportunity. Especially in the regulated industries, government has become an instrument for promoting concentration far beyond the imperatives of technology and economics.[45]

Finally, to the extent that profit figures are valid as measures of comparative efficiency, it seems that in a number of cases medium-sized and small firms outperform their giant rivals. Moreover, a breaking down of huge firms does not necessarily have fatal effects on efficiency *or* profitability. In the public utility field, for example, the comprehensive dissolution program carried out under the Public Utility Holding Company Act of 1935 has resulted in increased efficiency and profitability among the successor companies. This was demonstrated in the above-average appreciation in the security values of the successor companies that occurred despite declining utility rates, higher costs, and the inevitably higher taxes.[46] On the basis of experience, therefore, it may not be unreasonable to suggest, as *Fortune* does, that there are areas in American industry where an unmerging process among the giants can contribute both to increased efficiency and more vigorous competition.[47]

If such an unmerging process were to be accomplished through antitrust action, three types of market structure would have to be identified and dealt with: namely, horizontal, vertical, and conglomerate integration.

1. The horizontal size of *some* firms would have to be reduced, if competition is to be promoted, because an oligopolistic industry structure often results in conscious or unconscious parallelism among the giant firms. Price leadership, live-and-let-live policies, nonprice competition, and so on—in short, the type of gentlemanly behavior that imposes higher and more inflexible prices on the consumer—are common among firms of oligopolistic size, because each fears retaliation by its large rivals as punishment for independence and nonconformity.

2. Vertically integrated size would, in some cases, have to be reduced because the large integrated concern can apply the squeeze—both on prices and supplies —to its smaller rivals who are both its customers and competitors.[48] A case in

---

[45] See Adams and Gray, op. cit., especially Chap. 3.

[46] See W. Adams, "The Dilemma of Antitrust Aims: A Reply," *American Economic Review,* **42**:895 (Dec. 1952).

[47] See editorials in *Fortune* (Mar. and Apr. 1938).

[48] U.S. Congress, Senate, Small Business Committee, *Monopolistic Practices and Small Business,* 82d Cong., 2d sess., 1952, pp. 21–55; also, *The Distribution of Steel Consumption, 1949–1950,* 82d Cong., 2d sess., 1952.

point here would be a fully integrated aluminum firm that simultaneously supplies independent fabricators with aluminum ingot and then competes with them in the market for fabricated products.[49]

3. Conglomerate integration would pose a problem, because the widely diversified giant can exercise undue power as a buyer of materials, energy, transportation, credit, and labor; and also because such a concern often enjoys special advantages in litigation, politics, public relations, and finance.[50]

In launching a comprehensive program against these forms of integration a case-by-case approach seems preferable to any absolute prohibition on size per se. Moreover, to avoid any major conflicts with vested interests, enforcement might at first be confined to new industries where the problem of concentration is not yet extreme and where structural arrangements have not yet been solidified. This may have significant results because ours is a dynamic economy in which new industries—if they remain competitive—can substantially curb the power of older and more entrenched interests. Finally, to forestall any possible interference with industrial efficiency, antitrust prosecution might be confined to cases where the goals of competition and efficiency are not in conflict. Toward that end, the antitrust laws can be amended to provide that "any corporation whose size and power are such as to substantially lessen competition and tend to create a monopoly in any line of commerce shall be dissolved into its component parts, *unless* such corporation can demonstrate that its present size is necessary for the maintenance of efficiency."[51] Given a provision of this sort, the dilemma of antitrust may be resolved and our twin goals of competition and efficiency actively promoted.

Antitrust enforcement along these lines, however, is not enough if competitive free enterprise is to be maintained. Competition must become the core of an

---

[49] See *United States* v. *Aluminum Company of America*, 148 F.2d 416 (C.C.A. 2d, 1945).

[50] See Edwards, *Maintaining Competition*, op. cit., pp. 99–108. It has been said, for example, that General Motors has so much conglomerate power that it could successfully enter the ice cream industry and capture a predetermined share of the business. "It would matter little whether General Motors is an efficient ice cream manufacturer or whether its ice cream is indeed tastier than more established brands. By discrete price concessions, by saturation advertising, by attractive promotional deals, it could commit its gargantuan financial power to the battle until only so much competition as General Motors is prepared to tolerate would be left in the industry. . . . Put differently, in a poker game with unlimited stakes, the player who commands disproportionately large funds is likely to emerge victorious." Testimony of Walter Adams. U.S. Congress, Senate, *Subcommittee on Antitrust and Monopoly, Judiciary Committee, Hearings*, 86th Cong., 1st sess., 1959, p. 4780.

[51] Cf. U.S. Congress, House, Monopoly Subcommittee, Judiciary Committee, *Hearings*, 81st Cong., 1st sess., 1949, pt. 2-B, pp. 1311–1339 and 1600–1625. For an endorsement of this general position, see C. Kaysen and D. F. Turner, *Antitrust Policy* (Cambridge, Mass.: Harvard University Press, 1959). Recently, Senator Philip A. Hart introduced a bill, reminiscent of the Public Utility Holding Company Act, which provides for deconcentration in certain basic industries by legislative action rather than by lengthy court proceedings under the antitrust laws. (U.S. Congress, Senate, Subcommittee on Antitrust and Monopoly, *The Industrial Reorganization Act, Hearings on S.1167*, 93d–94th Cong., 1973–1975, pts. 1–9.)

integrated national economic policy.[52] It must be positively promoted, rather than negatively preserved.[53] It must have an environment that provides opportunity for new men and is receptive to new ideas. To create such an environment, a number of recommendations merit consideration:

1. Defense contracts, accelerated amortization privileges, and other wartime bonanzas coming down the government pike should not be restricted to a favored few, but distributed to many firms so as to assure the nation of a broad industrial base for future defense efforts.[54]

2. In the disposal of government property—whether war surplus, synthetic rubber plants, or atomic energy installations—to private industry, sales should be made in a manner calculated to encourage competitive newcomers rather than to rigidify existing patterns of industrial control.

3. The corporate tax structure should be overhauled so as to remove present penalties on the growth and expansion of small business.[55]

4. Government financing of small business should be more than polite encouragement for prospective hot-dog stands and gasoline stations.

5. The patent laws should be revised so as to prevent monopolistic abuse of the patent grant without destroying the incentives for invention. This may entail compulsory licensing of patents on a royalty-free basis in cases involving violations of the antitrust laws; compulsory licensing of patents on a reasonable royalty basis in cases of patent suppression and nonuse; and outright prohibition of restrictive and exclusive licensing provisions in private patent agreements. In any event, an invention made as a result of government financing or subsidy should become part of the public domain

[52] See U.S. Congress, House, Small Business Committee, *United States* v. *Economic Concentration and Monopoly*, 79th Cong., 2d sess., 1947.

[53] As Vernon Mund observes, "a policy of individual enterprise and price competition is a highly elaborate and complex plan for organizing the conduct of economic activity. It is a plan, however, which is not self-enforcing. When the policy of competition is accepted, it must be implemented by positive measures to provide for its creation, maintenance, and preservation. Competition is a form of human behavior; and like other behavior it should be conducted according to good manners and morals. The big mistake which government has made with respect to economic regulations is in thinking that in the absence of direct price control (as in the case of public utilities) government intervention is not necessary. The lessons of history clearly show that we cannot have fair competition unless positive measures are taken to create and maintain it." (Mund, op. cit., p. 642.)

[54] See, for example, U.S. Congress, Senate, Small Business Committee, *Concentration of Defense Contracts*, 82d Cong., 1st sess., 1951, Rept. 551; U.S. Congress, House, Committee on Expenditures in the Executive Departments, *Inquiry into the Procurement of Automotive Spare Parts by the United States Government*, 82d Cong., 2d sess., H. Rept. 1811, 1952; Attorney General, *Report Prepared Pursuant to Section 708(e) of the Defense Production Act of 1950*, 1950; Joint Committee on Defense Production, *Hearings on Tax Amortization*, 82d Cong., 1st sess., 1951.

[55] See U.S. Congress, Senate, Small Business Committee, *Tax Problems of Small Business*, 83rd Cong., 1st sess., 1953, S. Rept. 442; J. K. Butters and J. Lintner, *Effect of Federal Taxes on Growing Enterprises* (Boston: Harvard Business School, 1945); J. K. Butters, J. Lintner, and W. Carey, *Effects of Taxation: Corporate Mergers* (Boston: Harvard Business School, 1951).

and not allowed to accrue as private property to the corporation doing the contract research.[56]

6. Any further exemptions from the antitrust laws should be discouraged, and some existing exemptions re-examined.[57] We must stop what Leverett S. Lyon has called the "growing tendency in the United States for special groups to identify their limited good with the national good and to ask government for subsidy, support, or special protection rather than for laws which increase competitive opportunity."[58] Such laws as the Webb-Pomerene Act, for example, which exempts foreign trade associations from the Sherman Act, should be drastically revised or altogether repealed.[59]

7. Protective tariffs, quotas, and similar restrictions that serve to shield highly concentrated industries from the potential inroads of foreign competition should be reduced or repealed.

8. Incorporation and licensing laws should not be made a front for monopolistic privilege and restrictive practices.

9. The advisability of a progressive tax on advertising—with a generous

---

[56] In this connection the attorney general has recommended that "where patentable inventions are made in the course of performing a government-financed contract for research and development, the public interest requires that all rights to such inventions be assigned to the Government and not left to the private ownership of the contractor. Public control will assure free and equal availability of the inventions to American industry and science; will eliminate any competitive advantage to the contractor chosen to perform the research work; will avoid undue concentration of economic power in the hands of a few large corporations; will tend to increase and diversify available research facilities within the United States to the advantage of the government and of the national economy; and will thus strengthen our American system of free, competitive enterprise." *Investigation of Government Patent Practices and Policies,* Vol. 1 (Washington, D.C.: U.S. Government Printing Office, 1947), p. 4. Obviously, it makes little sense to permit—as in the past—"publicly financed technology to be suppressed, used restrictively, or made the basis of an exaction from the public to serve private interests." Ibid., p. 2.

[57] The problem of exceptions from the antitrust laws is well illustrated in the following story about a Polish ghetto, told by Congressman Celler:

"The rabbi of the synagogue said: 'There is a very poor family on the other end of the ghetto. They have not raiment, they have not food, and they have not shelter. You are too poor yourselves'—he said to his congregation—'to help them, but I have an idea. . . . On the Sabbath eve when you praise the Lord for the fruitage of the earth and you praise him by drinking a glass of wine, do not drink the full glass of wine. Drink a half a glass of wine, and the next morning when you come to the temple, I will have a barrel, and as you all come in, you will pour the half glass of wine that you left from the night before in the barrel. The Lord will not mind being blessed by the drinking of half a glass of wine, and at a given time the barrel will be filled. I will sell the barrel of wine and give the proceeds to this poor family. You will not be hurt; nobody will be harmed, and even the good Lord will bless you for it.' At a given time the barrel was opened and lo and behold, it was all water, and the rabbi reprimanded every member in the congregation, and they all had this answer: 'We figured what difference would a half glass of water make in a full barrel of wine.' . . . That is what is happening here. If we keep whittling away, and whittling away, and everybody asks to be exempted, everybody asks to put the half a glass of water in the full barrel of wine, we will have a barrel of water, and we will have no antitrust laws left." U.S. Congress, House, Subcommittee on the Study of Monopoly Power, *Hearings on S.14,* 81st Cong., 1st sess., pt. 1, 1949, pp. 267–268.

[58] "Government and American Economic Life," *Journal of Business,* **22**:89 (Apr. 1949).

[59] Committee on the Webb-Pomerene Act, American Economic Association, "The Webb-Pomerene Law: A Consensus Report," *American Economic Review,* **37**:848 (Dec. 1947).

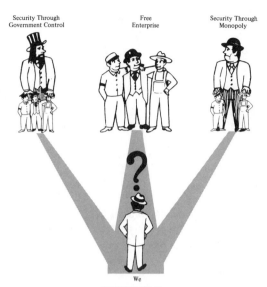

FIGURE 2

Public policy alternatives: the road ahead. Source: Thurman W. Arnold, *Cartels of Free Enterprise?* Public Affairs Pamphlet No. 103, 1945; reproduced by courtesy of the Public Affairs Commission, Inc.

exemption—should be examined, in an effort to prevent excessive advertising expenditures from acting as an obstacle to free entry in some concentrated industries.[60]

Such steps as these—and the list is by no means complete—may serve to stimulate an environment favorable to genuine free enterprise. The task is not easy, for we must strike a delicate balance between the businessman's search for profit and economic security, and society's insistence on freedom and opportunity for the newcomer. Although the task is difficult, it is not insuperable. Given a comprehensive and imaginative economic policy, it is likely that competition can be maintained (or revived), for the record shows that free enterprise in our generation has not failed; it has never been tried.

A hard look at the choice before us is indicated because, in the absence of positive action, we can expect little but aimless drifting and a gradual erosion of our traditional values. As Stocking and Watkins point out, "either the people must call a halt to the concentration—whether in governmental or private hands —of economic power, or they must be prepared to give up a competitive economy, bit by bit, year by year, until it is beyond recall. They will then be obliged to accept some collectivistic alternative that may give more short-run basic

[60] See W. H. Nicholls, *Pricing Policies in the Cigarette Industry* (Nashville, Tenn.: Vanderbilt University Press, 1951), pp. 412–415.

security but in the long run will almost certainly provide less freedom, less opportunity for experiment, less variety, less economic progress, and less total abundance."[61]

SUGGESTED READINGS

BOOKS AND PAMPHLETS

Adams, W., and H. M. Gray. *Monopoly in America: The Government as Promoter.* New York: Macmillan Publishing Co., Inc., 1955.

American Economic Association. *Readings in the Social Control of Industry.* New York: McGraw-Hill Book Company, 1942.

Bain, J. S. *Barriers to New Competition.* Cambridge, Mass.: Harvard University Press, 1956.

Blair, J. M. *Economic Concentration.* New York: Harcourt Brace Jovanovich, 1972.

Caves, R. *American Industry: Structure, Conduct, Performance,* 2d ed. Englewood Cliffs, N.J.: Prentice-Hall, Inc., 1967.

Dirlam, J. B., and A. E. Kahn. *The Law and Economics of Fair Competition: An Appraisal of Antitrust Policy.* Ithaca, N.Y.: Cornell University Press, 1954.

Drucker, P. F. *The Unseen Revolution.* New York: Harper & Row, Publishers, 1976.

Edwards, C. D. *Maintaining Competition.* New York: McGraw-Hill Book Company, 1949.

Fellner, W. *Competition Among the Few.* New York: Alfred A. Knopf, Inc., 1949.

Galbraith, J. K. *American Capitalism: The Concept of Countervailing Power.* Boston: Houghton Mifflin Company, 1952.

――――. *The New Industrial State.* Boston: Houghton Mifflin Company, 1967.

Hamberg, D. *R & D: Essays on the Economics of Research and Development.* New York: Random House, Inc., 1966.

Heflebower, R. B., and G. W. Stocking. *Readings in Industrial Organization and Public Policy.* Homewood, Ill.: Richard D. Irwin, Inc., 1958.

Kaysen, C., and D. F. Turner. *Antitrust Policy.* Cambridge, Mass.: Harvard University Press, 1959.

Lilienthal, D. E. *Big Business: A New Era.* New York: Harper & Row, Publishers, 1952.

Machlup, F. *The Political Economy of Monopoly.* Baltimore: The Johns Hopkins Press, 1952.

Mason, E. S. *Economic Concentration and the Monopoly Problem.* Cambridge: Harvard University Press, 1957.

---

[61] G. W. Stocking and M. W. Watkins, *Monopoly and Free Enterprise* (New York: Twentieth Century Fund, 1952), p. 526. We might profit from British experience, which the conservative London *Economist* has summarized as follows: "The fact is that British industrialists, under the deliberate leadership of the Tory Party in its Baldwin–Chamberlain era, have become distinguishable from British Socialists only by the fact that they still believe in private profits. Both believe in 'organizing' industry; both believe in protecting it, when organized, against any competition, either from foreigners or from native newcomers; both believe in standard prices for what they sell; both unite in condemning competition, the one as 'wasteful,' the other as 'destructive.' If free, competitive, private-enterprise capitalism is to continue to exist, not throughout the national economy, but in any part of it, then it needs rescuing from the capitalists fully as much as from the Socialists." *The Economist,* **139**:22 (June 29, 1946). Copyright *The Economist.* Reprinted by permission of the publishers.

Nelson, R. C. *Merger Movements in American Industry, 1896–1956*. Princeton, N.J.: Princeton University Press, 1959.

Phillips, A. (ed.), *Promoting Competition in Regulated Markets*. Washington, D.C.: Brookings Institution, 1975.

Reid, S. R. *The New Industrial Order*. New York: McGraw-Hill Book Company, 1976.

Scherer, F. M. *Industrial Market Structure and Economic Performance*. Chicago: Rand McNally & Co., 1970

Scherer, F. M., A. Beckenstein, E. Kaufer and R. D. Murphy. *The Economics of Multi-plant Operation: An International Comparisons Study*, Cambridge, Mass.: Harvard University Press, 1975.

Schumpeter, J. A. *Capitalism, Socialism and Democracy*. New York: Harper & Row, Publishers, 1942.

Shepherd, W. G. *Market Power and Economic Welfare*. New York: Random House, Inc., 1970.

Shepherd, W. G., *The Treatment of Market Power*. New York: Columbia University Press, 1975.

Shepherd, W. G. and Associates. *Public Enterprise: Economic Analysis of Theory and Practice*. Lexington, Mass.: Heath-Lexington Books, 1976.

Simons, H. C. *Economic Policy for a Free Society*. Chicago: University of Chicago Press, 1948.

Singer, E. M. *Antitrust Economics: Selected Legal Cases and Economic Models*. Englewood Cliffs, N.J.: Prentice-Hall, Inc., 1968.

Stigler, G. J. *The Organization of Industry*. Homewood, Ill.: Richard D. Irwin, Inc., 1968.

Stocking, G. W., and M. W. Watkins. *Cartels in Action*. New York: Twentieth Century Fund, 1946.

———. *Cartels or Competition?* New York: Twentieth Century Fund, 1947.

———. *Monopoly and Free Enterprise*. New York: Twentieth Century Fund, 1951.

Whitney, S. N. *Antitrust Policies*. New York: Twentieth Century Fund, 1958.

Wilcox, C., and W. G. Shepherd. *Public Policies Toward Business*. Homewood, Ill. Richard D. Irwin, Inc., 1975.

Williamson, O. E. *Markets and Hierarchies*. New York: Free Press, 1975.

GOVERNMENT PUBLICATIONS

FTC. *Economic Report on Corporate Mergers*. Washington, D.C.: U.S. Government Printing Office, 1969.

Hamilton, W. H. *Antitrust in Action*, Temporary National Economic Committee Monograph no. 16. Washington, D.C.: U.S. Government Printing Office, 1940.

Nelson, S., and W. Keim. *Price Behavior and Business Policy*. Temporary National Economic Committee Monograph, no. 1. Washington, D.C.: U.S. Government Printing Office, 1940.

U.S. Congress, House, Subcommittee on the Study of Monopoly Power, Judiciary Committee, *Study of Monopoly Power: Hearing on. S. 14*, pts. 1, 2-A, 2-B, 81st Cong., 1st sess., 1949.

U.S. Congress, Senate, Subcommittee on Antitrust and Monopoly, Judiciary Committee, *Hearings*, pts. 1–10, 85th and 86th Cong., 1957–1960.

U.S. Congress, Senate, Subcommittee on Antitrust and Monopoly, Judiciary Committee, *Economic Concentration*, pts. 1–8A, 88th–91st Cong., 1964–1970.

U.S. Congress, Senate, Subcommittee on Antitrust and Monopoly, Judiciary Committee, *The Industrial Reorganization Act, Hearings on S.1167*, 93d–94th Cong., pts. 1–9, 1973–1975.

U.S. Congress, Senate, Subcommittee on Multinational Corporations, Foreign Relations Committee, *Multinational Corporations and U.S. Foreign Policy, Hearings*, 93d–94th Cong., pts. 1–11, 1973–1975.

Wilcox, C. *Competition and Monopoly in American Industry*. Temporary National Economic Committee, Monograph, no. 21. Washington, D.C.: U.S. Government Printing Office, 1940.

JOURNAL AND MAGAZINE ARTICLES

Adams, W. "Dissolution, Divorcement, Divestiture: The Pyrrhic Victories of Antitrust." *Indiana Law Journal*, **27** (Fall 1951).

Adams, W. "The Military-Industrial Complex and the New Industrial State," *American Economic Review*, **58** (May 1968).

Adams, W. J. "Firm Size and Research Activity: France and the United States," *Quarterly Journal of Economics*, **84** (Aug. 1970).

Adelman, M. A. "Integration and Antitrust Policy." *Harvard Law Review*, **63** (Nov. 1949).

Comanor, W. S., and T. A. Wilson. "Advertising and the Advantages of Size," *American Economic Review*, **59** (May 1969).

Heflebower, R. "Economics of Size." *Journal of Business of the University of Chicago*, **24** (Apr. 1951).

Keezer, D. (ed.). "The Antitrust Laws: A Symposium." *American Economic Review*, **39** (June 1949).

Mason, E. S. "Current Status of the Monopoly Problem." *Harvard Law Review*, **62** (June 1949).

Scherer, F. M. "Firm Size, Market Structure, Opportunity, and the Output of Patented Inventions," *American Economic Review*, **55** (Dec. 1965).

Stigler, G. J. "The Case Against Big Business." *Fortune*, **45** (May 1952).

Stocking, G. W. "Saving Free Enterprise from Its Friends." *Southern Economic Journal*, **29** (Apr. 1953).

Wilcox, C. "On the Alleged Ubiquity of Monopoly." *American Economic, Review*, **40** (May 1950).

author index

517

subject index